CW01084845

Introduction to Machine Learning

Third Edition

Introduction to Machine Learning

Third Edition

Ethem Alpaydin

PHI Learning Private Limited
Delhi-110092
2019

This Indian Reprint—₹ 695.00
(Original U.S. Edition—₹ 3816.00)

INTRODUCTION TO MACHINE LEARNING, 3rd ed.
by Ethem Alpaydin

ISBN-978-81-203-5078-6

Original edition published by the MIT Press, Cambridge, MA, U.S.A.

Published by Asoke K. Ghosh, PHI Learning Private Limited, Rimjhim House, 111, Patparganj Industrial Estate, Delhi-110092 and Printed by Mudrak, D-61, Sector 63, Noida, U.P.-201301.

Brief Contents

Contents

Preface

Machine learning must be one of the fastest growing fields in computer science. It is not only that the data is continuously getting "bigger," but also the theory to process it and turn it into knowledge. In various fields of science, from astronomy to biology, but also in everyday life, as digital technology increasingly infiltrates our daily existence, as our digital footprint deepens, more data is continuously generated and collected. Whether scientific or personal, data that just lies dormant passively is not of any use, and smart people have been finding ever new ways to make use of that data and turn it into a useful product or service. In this transformation, machine learning plays a larger and larger role.

This data evolution has been continuing even stronger since the second edition appeared in 2010. Every year, datasets are getting larger. Not only has the number of observations grown, but the number of observed attributes has also increased significantly. There is more structure to the data: It is not just numbers and character strings any more but images, video, audio, documents, web pages, click logs, graphs, and so on. More and more, the data moves away from the parametric assumptions we used to make—for example, normality. Frequently, the data is dynamic and so there is a time dimension. Sometimes, our observations are multi-view—for the same object or event, we have multiple sources of information from different sensors and modalities.

Our belief is that behind all this seemingly complex and voluminous data, there lies a simple explanation. That although the data is big, it can be explained in terms of a relatively simple model with a small number of hidden factors and their interaction. Think about millions of customers who each day buy thousands of products online or from their local supermarket. This implies a very large database of transactions, but there is a pattern to this data. People do not shop at random. A person throwing a party buys a certain subset of products, and a person who has a baby at home buys a different subset; there are hidden factors that explain customer behavior.

This is one of the areas where significant research has been done in recent years—namely, to infer this hidden model from observed data. Most of the revisions in this new edition are related to these advances. Chapter 6 contains new sections on feature embedding, singular value decomposition and matrix factorization, canonical correlation analysis, and Laplacian eigenmaps.

There are new sections on distance estimation in chapter 8 and on kernel machines in chapter 13: Dimensionality reduction, feature extraction, and distance estimation are three names for the same devil—the ideal distance measure is defined in the space of the ideal hidden features, and they are fewer in number than the values we observe.

Chapter 16 is rewritten and significantly extended to cover such generative models. We discuss the Bayesian approach for all major machine learning models, namely, classification, regression, mixture models, and dimensionality reduction. Nonparametric Bayesian modeling, which has become increasingly popular during these last few years, is especially interesting because it allows us to adjust the complexity of the model to the complexity of data.

New sections have been added here and there, mostly to highlight different recent applications of the same or very similar methods. There is a new section on outlier detection in chapter 8. Two new sections in chapters 10 and 13 discuss ranking for linear models and kernel machines, respectively. Having added Laplacian eigenmaps to chapter 6, I also include a new section on spectral clustering in chapter 7. Given the recent resurgence of deep neural networks, it became necessary to include a new section on deep learning in chapter 11. Chapter 19 contains a new section on multivariate tests for comparison of methods.

Since the first edition, I have received many requests for the solutions to exercises from readers who use the book for self-study. In this new edition, I have included the solutions to some of the more didactic exercises. Sometimes they are complete solutions, and sometimes they give just a hint or offer only one of several possible solutions.

I would like to thank all the instructors and students who have used the previous two editions, as well as their translations into German, Chinese, and Turkish, and their reprints in India. I am always grateful to those who send me words of appreciation, criticism, or errata, or who provide feedback in any other way. Please keep them coming. My email address is `alpaydin@boun.edu.tr`. The book's web site is `http://www.cmpe.boun.edu.tr/~ethem/i2ml3e`.

It has been a pleasure to work with the MIT Press again on this third edition, and I thank Marie Lufkin Lee, Marc Lowenthal, and Kathleen Caruso for all their help and support.

Notations

x	Scalar value
$\boldsymbol{x}$	Vector
$\mathbf{X}$	Matrix
$\boldsymbol{x}^T$	Transpose
$\mathbf{X}^{-1}$	Inverse
X	Random variable
$P(X)$	Probability mass function when X is discrete
$p(X)$	Probability density function when X is continuous
$P(X\|Y)$	Conditional probability of X given Y
$E[X]$	Expected value of the random variable X
$\text{Var}(X)$	Variance of X
$\text{Cov}(X, Y)$	Covariance of X and Y
$\text{Corr}(X, Y)$	Correlation of X and Y
μ	Mean
σ^2	Variance
Σ	Covariance matrix
m	Estimator to the mean
s^2	Estimator to the variance
$\mathbf{S}$	Estimator to the covariance matrix

$\mathcal{N}(\mu, \sigma^2)$	Univariate normal distribution with mean μ and variance σ^2
$\mathcal{Z}$	Unit normal distribution: $\mathcal{N}(0, 1)$
$\mathcal{N}_d(\boldsymbol{\mu}, \boldsymbol{\Sigma})$	d-variate normal distribution with mean vector $\boldsymbol{\mu}$ and covariance matrix $\boldsymbol{\Sigma}$
x	Input
d	Number of inputs (input dimensionality)
y	Output
r	Required output
K	Number of outputs (classes)
N	Number of training instances
z	Hidden value, intrinsic dimension, latent factor
k	Number of hidden dimensions, latent factors
C_i	Class i
$\mathcal{X}$	Training sample
$\{x^t\}_{t=1}^N$	Set of x with index t ranging from 1 to N
$\{x^t, r^t\}_t$	Set of ordered pairs of input and desired output with index t
$g(x\|\theta)$	Function of x defined up to a set of parameters θ
$\arg\max_\theta g(x\|\theta)$	The argument θ for which g has its maximum value
$\arg\min_\theta g(x\|\theta)$	The argument θ for which g has its minimum value
$E(\theta\|\mathcal{X})$	Error function with parameters θ on the sample $\mathcal{X}$
$l(\theta\|\mathcal{X})$	Likelihood of parameters θ on the sample $\mathcal{X}$
$\mathcal{L}(\theta\|\mathcal{X})$	Log likelihood of parameters θ on the sample $\mathcal{X}$
$1(c)$	1 if c is true, 0 otherwise
$\#\{c\}$	Number of elements for which c is true
δ_{ij}	Kronecker delta: 1 if $i = j$, 0 otherwise

1 *Introduction*

1.1 What Is Machine Learning?

THIS IS the age of "big data." Once upon a time, only companies had data. There used to be computer centers where that data was stored and processed. First with the arrival of personal computers and later with the widespread use of wireless communications, we all became producers of data. Every time we buy a product, every time we rent a movie, visit a web page, write a blog, or post on the social media, even when we just walk or drive around, we are generating data.

Each of us is not only a generator but also a consumer of data. We want to have products and services specialized for us. We want our needs to be understood and interests to be predicted.

Think, for example, of a supermarket chain that is selling thousands of goods to millions of customers either at hundreds of brick-and-mortar stores all over a country or through a virtual store over the web. The details of each transaction are stored: date, customer id, goods bought and their amount, total money spent, and so forth. This typically amounts to a lot of data every day. What the supermarket chain wants is to be able to predict which customer is likely to buy which product, to maximize sales and profit. Similarly each customer wants to find the set of products best matching his/her needs.

This task is not evident. We do not know exactly which people are likely to buy this ice cream flavor or the next book of this author, see this new movie, visit this city, or click this link. Customer behavior changes in time and by geographic location. But we know that it is not completely random. People do not go to supermarkets and buy things at random. When they buy beer, they buy chips; they buy ice cream in summer and spices for Glühwein in winter. There are certain patterns in the data.

To solve a problem on a computer, we need an algorithm. An algorithm is a sequence of instructions that should be carried out to transform the input to output. For example, one can devise an algorithm for sorting. The input is a set of numbers and the output is their ordered list. For the same task, there may be various algorithms and we may be interested in finding the most efficient one, requiring the least number of instructions or memory or both.

For some tasks, however, we do not have an algorithm. Predicting customer behavior is one; another is to tell spam emails from legitimate ones. We know what the input is: an email document that in the simplest case is a file of characters. We know what the output should be: a yes/no output indicating whether the message is spam or not. But we do not know how to transform the input to the output. What is considered spam changes in time and from individual to individual.

What we lack in knowledge, we make up for in data. We can easily compile thousands of example messages, some of which we know to be spam and some of which are not, and what we want is to "learn" what constitutes spam from them. In other words, we would like the computer (machine) to extract automatically the algorithm for this task. There is no need to learn to sort numbers since we already have algorithms for that, but there are many applications for which we do not have an algorithm but have lots of data.

We may not be able to identify the process completely, but we believe we can construct *a good and useful approximation.* That approximation may not explain everything, but may still be able to account for some part of the data. We believe that though identifying the complete process may not be possible, we can still detect certain patterns or regularities. This is the niche of machine learning. Such patterns may help us understand the process, or we can use those patterns to make predictions: Assuming that the future, at least the near future, will not be much different from the past when the sample data was collected, the future predictions can also be expected to be right.

Application of machine learning methods to large databases is called *data mining.* The analogy is that a large volume of earth and raw material is extracted from a mine, which when processed leads to a small amount of very precious material; similarly, in data mining, a large volume of data is processed to construct a simple model with valuable use, for example, having high predictive accuracy. Its application areas are abundant: In addition to retail, in finance banks analyze their past data to build models to use in credit applications, fraud detection, and the stock market. In manufacturing, learning models are used for optimization, control, and troubleshooting. In medicine, learning programs are used for medical diagnosis. In telecommunications, call patterns are analyzed for network optimization and maximizing the quality of service. In science, large amounts of data in physics, astronomy, and biology can only be analyzed fast enough by computers. The World Wide Web is huge; it is constantly growing, and searching for relevant information cannot be done manually.

But machine learning is not just a database problem; it is also a part of artificial intelligence. To be intelligent, a system that is in a changing environment should have the ability to learn. If the system can learn and adapt to such changes, the system designer need not foresee and provide solutions for all possible situations.

Machine learning also helps us find solutions to many problems in vision, speech recognition, and robotics. Let us take the example of recognizing faces: This is a task we do effortlessly; every day we recognize family members and friends by looking at their faces or from their photographs, despite differences in pose, lighting, hair style, and so forth. But we do it unconsciously and are unable to explain how we do it. Because we are not able to explain our expertise, we cannot write the computer program. At the same time, we know that a face image is not just a random collection of pixels; a face has structure. It is symmetric. There are the eyes, the nose, the mouth, located in certain places on the face. Each person's face is a pattern composed of a particular combination of these. By analyzing sample face images of a person, a learning program captures the pattern specific to that person and then recognizes by checking for this pattern in a given image. This is one example of *pattern recognition.*

Machine learning is programming computers to optimize a performance criterion using example data or past experience. We have a model defined up to some parameters, and learning is the execution of a computer program to optimize the parameters of the model using the training data or past experience. The model may be *predictive* to make predictions in the future, or *descriptive* to gain knowledge from data, or both.

Machine learning uses the theory of statistics in building mathematical models, because the core task is making inference from a sample. The role of computer science is twofold: First, in training, we need efficient algorithms to solve the optimization problem, as well as to store and process the massive amount of data we generally have. Second, once a model is learned, its representation and algorithmic solution for inference needs to be efficient as well. In certain applications, the efficiency of the learning or inference algorithm, namely, its space and time complexity, may be as important as its predictive accuracy.

Let us now discuss some example applications in more detail to gain more insight into the types and uses of machine learning.

1.2 Examples of Machine Learning Applications

1.2.1 Learning Associations

In the case of retail—for example, a supermarket chain—one application of machine learning is *basket analysis*, which is finding associations between products bought by customers: If people who buy X typically also buy Y, and if there is a customer who buys X and does not buy Y, he or she is a potential Y customer. Once we find such customers, we can target them for cross-selling.

ASSOCIATION RULE

In finding an *association rule*, we are interested in learning a conditional probability of the form $P(Y|X)$ where Y is the product we would like to condition on X, which is the product or the set of products which we know that the customer has already purchased.

Let us say, going over our data, we calculate that $P(\text{chips}|\text{beer}) = 0.7$. Then, we can define the rule:

70 percent of customers who buy beer also buy chips.

We may want to make a distinction among customers and toward this, estimate $P(Y|X, D)$ where D is the set of customer attributes, for example, gender, age, marital status, and so on, assuming that we have access to this information. If this is a bookseller instead of a supermarket, products can be books or authors. In the case of a web portal, items correspond to links to web pages, and we can estimate the links a user is likely to click and use this information to download such pages in advance for faster access.

1.2.2 Classification

A credit is an amount of money loaned by a financial institution, for example, a bank, to be paid back with interest, generally in installments. It is important for the bank to be able to predict in advance the risk associated with a loan, which is the probability that the customer will default and not pay the whole amount back. This is both to make sure that the bank will make a profit and also to not inconvenience a customer with a loan over his or her financial capacity.

In *credit scoring* (Hand 1998), the bank calculates the risk given the amount of credit and the information about the customer. The information about the customer includes data we have access to and is relevant in calculating his or her financial capacity—namely, income, savings, collaterals, profession, age, past financial history, and so forth. The bank has a record of past loans containing such customer data and whether the loan was paid back or not. From this data of particular applications, the aim is to infer a general rule coding the association between a customer's attributes and his risk. That is, the machine learning system fits a model to the past data to be able to calculate the risk for a new application and then decides to accept or refuse it accordingly.

CLASSIFICATION

This is an example of a *classification* problem where there are two classes: low-risk and high-risk customers. The information about a customer makes up the *input* to the classifier whose task is to assign the input to one of the two classes.

After training with the past data, a classification rule learned may be of the form

IF income> θ_1 AND savings> θ_2 THEN low-risk ELSE high-risk

DISCRIMINANT

for suitable values of θ_1 and θ_2 (see figure 1.1). This is an example of a *discriminant*; it is a function that separates the examples of different classes.

PREDICTION

Having a rule like this, the main application is *prediction*: Once we have a rule that fits the past data, if the future is similar to the past, then we can make correct predictions for novel instances. Given a new application with a certain income and savings, we can easily decide whether it is low-risk or high-risk.

In some cases, instead of making a 0/1 (low-risk/high-risk) type decision, we may want to calculate a probability, namely, $P(Y|X)$, where X are the customer attributes and Y is 0 or 1 respectively for low-risk

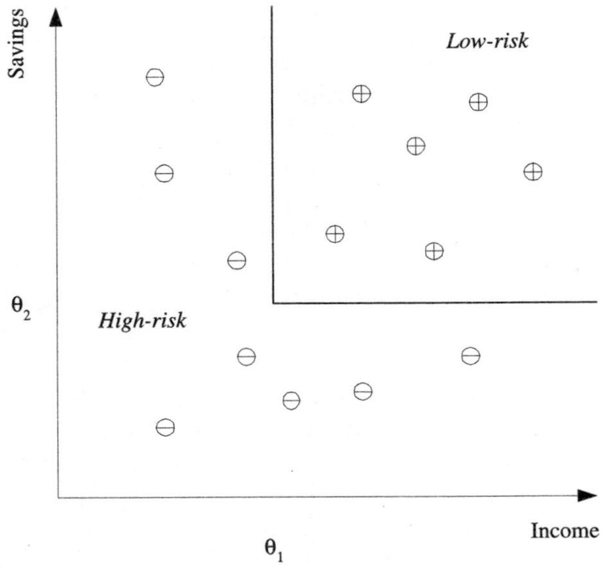

Figure 1.1 Example of a training dataset where each circle corresponds to one data instance with input values in the corresponding axes and its sign indicates the class. For simplicity, only two customer attributes, income and savings, are taken as input and the two classes are low-risk ('+') and high-risk ('−'). An example discriminant that separates the two types of examples is also shown.

and high-risk. From this perspective, we can see classification as learning an association from X to Y. Then for a given $X = x$, if we have $P(Y = 1|X = x) = 0.8$, we say that the customer has an 80 percent probability of being high-risk, or equivalently a 20 percent probability of being low-risk. We then decide whether to accept or refuse the loan depending on the possible gain and loss.

PATTERN RECOGNITION

There are many applications of machine learning in *pattern recognition*. One is *optical character recognition*, which is recognizing character codes from their images. This is an example where there are multiple classes, as many as there are characters we would like to recognize. Especially interesting is the case when the characters are handwritten—for example, to read zip codes on envelopes or amounts on checks. People have different handwriting styles; characters may be written small or large, slanted, with a pen or pencil, and there are many possible images corresponding to the same character. Though writing is a human invention, we do not have any system that is as accurate as a human reader. We do not have a formal description of 'A' that covers all 'A's and none of the non-'A's. Not having it, we take samples from writers and learn a definition of A-ness from these examples. But though we do not know what it is that makes an image an 'A', we are certain that all those distinct 'A's have something in common, which is what we want to extract from the examples. We know that a character image is not just a collection of random dots; it is a collection of strokes and has a regularity that we can capture by a learning program.

If we are reading a text, one factor we can make use of is the redundancy in human languages. A word is a *sequence* of characters and successive characters are not independent but are constrained by the words of the language. This has the advantage that even if we cannot recognize a character, we can still read t?e word. Such contextual dependencies may also occur in higher levels, between words and sentences, through the syntax and semantics of the language. There are machine learning algorithms to learn sequences and model such dependencies.

In the case of *face recognition*, the input is an image, the classes are people to be recognized, and the learning program should learn to associate the face images to identities. This problem is more difficult than optical character recognition because there are more classes, input image is larger, and a face is three-dimensional and differences in pose and lighting cause significant changes in the image. There may also be occlusion of certain inputs; for example, glasses may hide the eyes and eyebrows, and a beard may hide the chin.

In *medical diagnosis*, the inputs are the relevant information we have about the patient and the classes are the illnesses. The inputs contain the patient's age, gender, past medical history, and current symptoms. Some tests may not have been applied to the patient, and thus these inputs would be missing. Tests take time, may be costly, and may inconvenience the patient so we do not want to apply them unless we believe that they will give us valuable information. In the case of a medical diagnosis, a wrong decision may lead to a wrong or no treatment, and in cases of doubt it is preferable that the classifier reject and defer decision to a human expert.

In *speech recognition*, the input is acoustic and the classes are words that can be uttered. This time the association to be learned is from an acoustic signal to a word of some language. Different people, because of differences in age, gender, or accent, pronounce the same word differently, which makes this task rather difficult. Another difference of speech is that the input is *temporal*; words are uttered in time as a sequence of speech phonemes and some words are longer than others.

Acoustic information only helps up to a certain point, and as in optical character recognition, the integration of a "language model" is critical in speech recognition, and the best way to come up with a language model is again by learning it from some large corpus of example data. The applications of machine learning to *natural language processing* is constantly increasing. Spam filtering is one where spam generators on one side and filters on the other side keep finding more and more ingenious ways to outdo each other. Summarizing large documents is another interesting example, yet another is analyzing blogs or posts on social networking sites to extract "trending" topics or to determine what to advertise. Perhaps the most impressive would be *machine translation*. After decades of research on hand-coded translation rules, it has become apparent that the most promising way is to provide a very large number of example pairs of texts in both languages and have a program figure out automatically the rules to map one to the other.

Biometrics is recognition or authentication of people using their physiological and/or behavioral characteristics that requires an integration of inputs from different modalities. Examples of physiological characteristics are images of the face, fingerprint, iris, and palm; examples of behavioral characteristics are dynamics of signature, voice, gait, and key stroke. As opposed to the usual identification procedures—photo, printed signature, or password—when there are many different (uncorrelated) inputs, forgeries (spoofing) would be more difficult and the system would be more accurate, hopefully without too much inconvenience to the users. Machine learning is used both in the separate recognizers for these different modalities and in the combination of their decisions to get an overall accept/reject decision, taking into account how reliable these different sources are.

KNOWLEDGE EXTRACTION

Learning a rule from data also allows *knowledge extraction*. The rule is a simple model that explains the data, and looking at this model we have an explanation about the process underlying the data. For example, once we learn the discriminant separating low-risk and high-risk customers, we have the knowledge of the properties of low-risk customers. We can then use this information to target potential low-risk customers more efficiently, for example, through advertising. Learning also performs *com-*

COMPRESSION

pression in that by fitting a rule to the data, we get an explanation that is simpler than the data, requiring less memory to store and less computation to process. Once we have the rules of addition, we do not need to remember the sum of every possible pair of numbers.

OUTLIER DETECTION

Another use of machine learning is *outlier detection*, which is finding instances that do not obey the general rule and are exceptions. The idea is that typical instances share characteristics that can be simply stated and instances that do not have those characteristics are atypical. In such a case, we are interested in finding a rule that is as simple as possible and covers as large a proportion of our typical instances as possible. Any instance that falls outside is an exception, which may be an anomaly requiring attention such as fraud; or it may be a novel, previously unseen but valid case, and hence the other name *novelty detection*.

NOVELTY DETECTION

1.2.3 Regression

Let us say we want to have a system that can predict the price of a used car. Inputs are the car attributes—brand, year, engine capacity, mileage, and other information—that we believe affect a car's worth. The output is the price of the car. Such problems where the output is a number are *regression* problems.

REGRESSION

Let X denote the car attributes and Y be the price of the car. Again surveying the past transactions, we can collect a training data and the machine learning program fits a function to this data to learn Y as a function of X. An example is given in figure 1.2 where the fitted function is of the form

$$y = wx + w_0$$

for suitable values of w and w_0.

SUPERVISED LEARNING

Both regression and classification are *supervised learning* problems where there is an input, X, an output, Y, and the task is to learn the mapping from the input to the output. The approach in machine learning is that we assume a model defined up to a set of parameters:

$$y = g(x|\theta)$$

where $g(\cdot)$ is the model and θ are its parameters. Y is a number in regression and is a class code (e.g., 0/1) in the case of classification. $g(\cdot)$ is the regression function or in classification, it is the discriminant function separating the instances of different classes. The machine learning

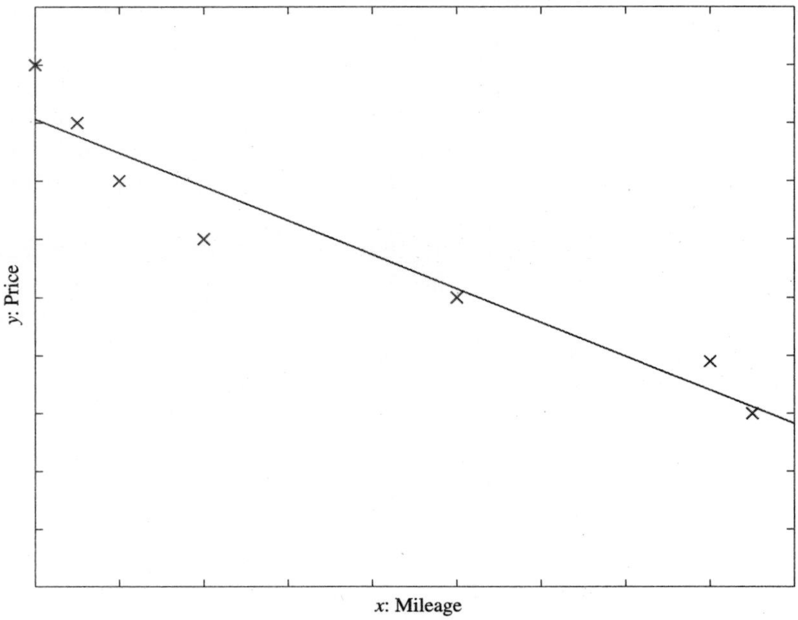

Figure 1.2 A training dataset of used cars and the function fitted. For simplicity, mileage is taken as the only input attribute and a linear model is used.

program optimizes the parameters, θ, such that the approximation error is minimized, that is, our estimates are as close as possible to the correct values given in the training set. For example in figure 1.2, the model is linear, and w and w_0 are the parameters optimized for best fit to the training data. In cases where the linear model is too restrictive, we can use, for example, a quadratic

$$y = w_2x^2 + w_1x + w_0$$

or a higher-order polynomial, or any other nonlinear function of the input, this time optimizing its parameters for best fit.

Another example of regression is navigation of a mobile robot, for example, an autonomous car, where the output is the angle by which the steering wheel should be turned at each time, to advance without hitting obstacles and deviating from the route. Inputs in such a case are provided by sensors on the car—for example, a video camera, GPS, and so forth. Training data can be collected by monitoring and recording the actions of a human driver.

We can envisage other applications of regression where we are trying to optimize a function.[1] Let us say we want to build a machine that roasts coffee. The machine has many inputs that affect the quality: various settings of temperatures, times, coffee bean type, and so forth. We make a number of experiments and for different settings of these inputs, we measure the quality of the coffee, for example, as consumer satisfaction. To find the optimal setting, we fit a regression model linking these inputs to coffee quality and choose new points to sample near the optimum of the current model to look for a better configuration. We sample these points, check quality, and add these to the data and fit a new model. This is generally called *response surface design.*

Sometimes instead of estimating an absolute numeric value, we want to be able to learn relative positions. For example, in a *recommendation system* for movies, we want to generate a list ordered by how much we believe the user is likely to enjoy each. Depending on the movie attributes such as genre, actors, and so on, and using the ratings of the user he/she has already seen, we would like to be able to learn a *ranking* function that we can then use to choose among new movies.

RANKING

1.2.4 Unsupervised Learning

In supervised learning, the aim is to learn a mapping from the input to an output whose correct values are provided by a supervisor. In unsupervised learning, there is no such supervisor and we only have input data. The aim is to find the regularities in the input. There is a structure to the input space such that certain patterns occur more often than others, and we want to see what generally happens and what does not. In statistics, this is called *density estimation.*

DENSITY ESTIMATION

CLUSTERING

One method for density estimation is *clustering* where the aim is to find clusters or groupings of input. In the case of a company with a data of past customers, the customer data contains the demographic information as well as the past transactions with the company, and the company may want to see the distribution of the profile of its customers, to see what type of customers frequently occur. In such a case, a clustering model allocates customers similar in their attributes to the same group,

1. I would like to thank Michael Jordan for this example.

providing the company with natural groupings of its customers; this is called *customer segmentation.* Once such groups are found, the company may decide strategies, for example, services and products, specific to different groups; this is known as *customer relationship management.* Such a grouping also allows identifying those who are outliers, namely, those who are different from other customers, which may imply a niche in the market that can be further exploited by the company.

An interesting application of clustering is in *image compression.* In this case, the input instances are image pixels represented as RGB values. A clustering program groups pixels with similar colors in the same group, and such groups correspond to the colors occurring frequently in the image. If in an image, there are only shades of a small number of colors, and if we code those belonging to the same group with one color, for example, their average, then the image is quantized. Let us say the pixels are 24 bits to represent 16 million colors, but if there are shades of only 64 main colors, for each pixel we need 6 bits instead of 24. For example, if the scene has various shades of blue in different parts of the image, and if we use the same average blue for all of them, we lose the details in the image but gain space in storage and transmission. Ideally, we would like to identify higher-level regularities by analyzing repeated image patterns, for example, texture, objects, and so forth. This allows a higher-level, simpler, and more useful description of the scene, and for example, achieves better compression than compressing at the pixel level. If we have scanned document pages, we do not have random on/off pixels but bitmap images of characters. There is structure in the data, and we make use of this redundancy by finding a shorter description of the data: 16×16 bitmap of 'A' takes 32 bytes; its ASCII code is only 1 byte.

In *document clustering,* the aim is to group similar documents. For example, news reports can be subdivided as those related to politics, sports, fashion, arts, and so on. Commonly, a document is represented as a *bag of words*—that is, we predefine a lexicon of N words, and each document is an N-dimensional binary vector whose element i is 1 if word i appears in the document; suffixes "-s" and "-ing" are removed to avoid duplicates and words such as "of," "and," and so forth, which are not informative, are not used. Documents are then grouped depending on the number of shared words. It is of course critical how the lexicon is chosen.

Machine learning methods are also used in *bioinformatics.* DNA in our genome is the "blueprint of life" and is a sequence of bases, namely, A, G,

C, and T. RNA is transcribed from DNA, and proteins are translated from the RNA. Proteins are what the living body is and does. Just as a DNA is a sequence of bases, a protein is a sequence of amino acids (as defined by bases). One application area of computer science in molecular biology is *alignment*, which is matching one sequence to another. This is a difficult string matching problem because strings may be quite long, there are many template strings to match against, and there may be deletions, insertions, and substitutions. Clustering is used in learning *motifs*, which are sequences of amino acids that occur repeatedly in proteins. Motifs are of interest because they may correspond to structural or functional elements within the sequences they characterize. The analogy is that if the amino acids are letters and proteins are sentences, motifs are like words, namely, a string of letters with a particular meaning occurring frequently in different sentences.

1.2.5 Reinforcement Learning

In some applications, the output of the system is a sequence of *actions*. In such a case, a single action is not important; what is important is the *policy* that is the sequence of correct actions to reach the goal. There is no such thing as the best action in any intermediate state; an action is good if it is part of a good policy. In such a case, the machine learning program should be able to assess the goodness of policies and learn from past good action sequences to be able to generate a policy. Such learning methods are called *reinforcement learning* algorithms.

REINFORCEMENT LEARNING

A good example is *game playing* where a single move by itself is not that important; it is the sequence of right moves that is good. A move is good if it is part of a good game playing policy. Game playing is an important research area in both artificial intelligence and machine learning. This is because games are easy to describe and at the same time, they are quite difficult to play well. A game like chess has a small number of rules but it is very complex because of the large number of possible moves at each state and the large number of moves that a game contains. Once we have good algorithms that can learn to play games well, we can also apply them to applications with more evident economic utility.

A robot navigating in an environment in search of a goal location is another application area of reinforcement learning. At any time, the robot can move in one of a number of directions. After a number of trial runs, it should learn the correct sequence of actions to reach to the goal state from an initial state, doing this as quickly as possible and without hitting any of the obstacles.

One factor that makes reinforcement learning harder is when the system has unreliable and partial sensory information. For example, a robot equipped with a video camera has incomplete information and thus at any time is in a *partially observable state* and should decide on its action taking into account this uncertainty; for example, it may not know its exact location in a room but only that there is a wall to its left. A task may also require a concurrent operation of *multiple agents* that should interact and cooperate to accomplish a common goal. An example is a team of robots playing soccer.

1.3 Notes

Evolution is the major force that defines our bodily shape as well as our built-in instincts and reflexes. We also learn to change our behavior during our lifetime. This helps us cope with changes in the environment that cannot be predicted by evolution. Organisms that have a short life in a well-defined environment may have all their behavior built-in, but instead of hardwiring into us all sorts of behavior for any circumstance that we could encounter in our life, evolution gave us a large brain and a mechanism to learn, such that we could update ourselves with experience and adapt to different environments. When we learn the best strategy in a certain situation, that knowledge is stored in our brain, and when the situation arises again, when we re-cognize ("cognize" means to know) the situation, we can recall the suitable strategy and act accordingly.

Learning has its limits though; there may be things that we can never learn with the limited capacity of our brains, just like we can never "learn" to grow a third arm, or an eye on the back of our head, even if either would be useful. Note that unlike in psychology, cognitive science, or neuroscience, our aim in machine learning is not to understand the processes underlying learning in humans and animals, but to build useful systems, as in any domain of engineering.

Almost all of science is fitting models to data. Scientists design experiments and make observations and collect data. They then try to extract knowledge by finding out simple models that explain the data they observed. This is called *induction* and is the process of extracting general rules from a set of particular cases.

We are now at a point that such analysis of data can no longer be done by people, both because the amount of data is huge and because people who can do such analysis are rare and manual analysis is costly. There is thus a growing interest in computer models that can analyze data and extract information automatically from them, that is, learn.

The methods we discuss in the coming chapters have their origins in different scientific domains. Sometimes the same algorithm was independently invented in more than one field, following a different historical path.

In statistics, going from particular observations to general descriptions is called *inference* and learning is called *estimation*. Classification is called *discriminant analysis* in statistics (McLachlan 1992; Hastie, Tibshirani, and Friedman 2011). Before computers were cheap and abundant, statisticians could only work with small samples. Statisticians, being mathematicians, worked mostly with simple parametric models that could be analyzed mathematically. In engineering, classification is called *pattern recognition* and the approach is nonparametric and much more empirical (Duda, Hart, and Stork 2001; Webb and Copey 2011).

Machine learning is also related to *artificial intelligence* (Russell and Norvig 2009) because an intelligent system should be able to adapt to changes in its environment. Application areas like vision, speech, and robotics are also tasks that are best learned from sample data. In electrical engineering, research in *signal processing* resulted in adaptive computer vision and speech programs. Among these, the development of *hidden Markov models* for speech recognition is especially important.

In the late 1980s with advances in VLSI technology and the possibility of building parallel hardware containing thousands of processors, the field of *artificial neural networks* was reinvented as a possible theory to distribute computation over a large number of processing units (Bishop 1995). Over time, it has been realized in the neural network community that most neural network learning algorithms have their basis in statistics—for example, the multilayer perceptron is another class of nonparametric estimator—and claims of brain-like computation have started to fade.

In recent years, kernel-based algorithms, such as support vector machines, have become popular, which, through the use of kernel functions, can be adapted to various applications, especially in bioinformatics and language processing. It is common knowledge nowadays that a good representation of data is critical for learning and kernel functions turn out to be a very good way to introduce such expert knowledge.

Another recent approach is the use of *generative models* that explain the observed data through the interaction of a set of hidden factors. Generally, *graphical models* are used to visualize the interaction of the factors and the data, and *Bayesian formalism* allows us to define our prior information on the hidden factors and the model, as well as to infer the model parameters.

Recently, with the reduced cost of storage and connectivity, it has become possible to have very large datasets available over the Internet, and this, coupled with cheaper computation, have made it possible to run learning algorithms on a lot of data. In the past few decades, it was generally believed that for artificial intelligence to be possible, we needed a new paradigm, a new type of thinking, a new model of computation, or a whole new set of algorithms.

Taking into account the recent successes in machine learning in various domains, it may be claimed that what we needed was not new algorithms but a lot of example data and sufficient computing power to run the algorithms on that much data. For example, the roots of support vector machines go to potential functions, linear classifiers, and neighbor-based methods, proposed in the 1950s or the 1960s; it is just that we did not have fast computers or large storage then for these algorithms to show their full potential. It may be conjectured that tasks such as machine translation, and even planning, can be solved with such relatively simple learning algorithms but trained on large amounts of example data, or through long runs of trial and error. Recent successes with "deep learning" algorithm supports this claim. Intelligence seems not to originate from some outlandish formula, but rather from the patient, almost brute-force use of a simple, straightforward algorithm.

Data mining is the name coined in the business world for the application of machine learning algorithms to large amounts of data (Witten and Frank 2011; Han and Kamber 2011). In computer science, it used to be called *knowledge discovery in databases.*

Research in these different communities (statistics, pattern recognition, neural networks, signal processing, control, artificial intelligence, and data mining) followed different paths in the past with different emphases. In this book, the aim is to incorporate these emphases together to give a unified treatment of the problems and the proposed solutions.

1.4 Relevant Resources

The latest research on machine learning is distributed over journals and conferences from different fields. Dedicated journals are *Machine Learning* and the *Journal of Machine Learning Research.* Journals such as *Neural Computation, Neural Networks,* and *IEEE Transactions on Neural Networks and Learning Systems* publish also heavily machine learning papers. Statistics journals like *Annals of Statistics* and the *Journal of the American Statistical Association* publish papers interesting from the point of view of machine learning, and many of the *IEEE Transactions* such as *Pattern Analysis and Machine Intelligence, Systems, Man, and Cybernetics, Image Processing,* and *Signal Processing* contain interesting papers related to either the theory of machine learning or one of its numerous applications.

Journals on artificial intelligence, pattern recognition, and signal processing also contain machine learning papers. Journals with an emphasis on data mining are *Data Mining and Knowledge Discovery, IEEE Transactions on Knowledge and Data Engineering,* and *ACM Special Interest Group on Knowledge Discovery and Data Mining Explorations Journal.*

The major conferences on machine learning are *Neural Information Processing Systems* (NIPS), *Uncertainty in Artificial Intelligence* (UAI), *International Conference on Machine Learning* (ICML), *European Conference on Machine Learning* (ECML), *Artificial Intelligence and Statistics* (AISTATS), and *Computational Learning Theory* (COLT). Conferences on pattern recognition, neural networks, artificial intelligence, fuzzy logic, and genetic algorithms, along with conferences on application areas like computer vision, speech technology, robotics, and data mining, have sessions on machine learning.

UCI Repository, at http://archive.ics.uci.edu/ml, contains a large number of datasets frequently used by machine learning researchers for benchmarking purposes. Another resource is the *Statlib Repository*, which is at http://lib.stat.cmu.edu. In addition to these, there are also repositories for particular applications, for example, computational biology, face recognition, speech recognition, and so forth.

New and larger datasets are constantly being added to these repositories. Still, some researchers believe that such repositories do not reflect the full characteristics of real data and are of limited scope, and therefore accuracies on datasets from such repositories are not indicative of anything. When some datasets from a fixed repository are used repeatedly while tailoring a new algorithm, we are generating a new set of "UCI algorithms" specialized for those datasets. It is like students who are studying for a course by solving a set of example questions only. As we see in later chapters, different algorithms are better on different tasks anyway, and therefore it is best to keep one application in mind, to have one or a number of large datasets drawn for that and compare algorithms on those, for that specific task.

Most recent papers by machine learning researchers are accessible over the Internet. Most authors also make their codes and data available over the web. Videos of tutorial lectures of machine learning conferences and summer schools are mostly available too. There are also free software toolboxes and packages implementing various machine learning algorithms, and among these, Weka at http://www.cs.waikato.ac.nz/ml/weka/, is especially noteworthy.

1.5 Exercises

1. Imagine we have two possibilities: We can scan and email the image, or we can use an optical character reader (OCR) and send the text file. Discuss the advantage and disadvantages of the two approaches in a comparative manner. When would one be preferable over the other?
2. Let us say we are building an OCR and for each character, we store the bitmap of that character as a template that we match with the read character pixel by pixel. Explain when such a system would fail. Why are barcode readers still used?

   SOLUTION: Such a system allows only one template per character and cannot distinguish characters from multiple fonts, for example. There are standardized fonts such as OCR-A and OCR-B—the fonts we typically see on the packaging of stuff we buy—which are used with OCR software (the characters in these fonts have been slightly changed to minimize the similarities between them). Barcode readers are still used because reading barcodes is still a better (cheaper, more reliable, more available) technology than reading characters in arbitrary font, size, and styles.
3. Assume we are given the task of building a system to distinguish junk email. What is in a junk email that lets us know that it is junk? How can the computer detect junk through a syntactic analysis? What would we like the computer to do if it detects a junk email—delete it automatically, move it to a different file, or just highlight it on the screen?

   SOLUTION: Typically, text-based spam filters check for the existence/absence of words and symbols. Words such as "opportunity," "viagra," "dollars," and characters such as '\$' and '!' increase the probability that the email is spam. These probabilities are learned from a training set of example past emails that the user has previously marked as spam. We see many algorithms for this in later chapters.

The spam filters do not work with 100 percent reliability and may make errors in classification. If a junk mail is not filtered, this is not good, but it is not as bad as filtering a good mail as spam. We discuss how we can take into account the relative costs of such false positives and false negatives later on. Therefore, mail messages that the system considers as spam should not be automatically deleted but kept aside so that the user can see them if he/she wants to, especially in the early stages of using the spam filter when the system has not yet been trained sufficiently. Spam filtering is probably one of the best application areas of machine learning where learning systems can adapt to changes in the ways spam messages are generated.

4. Let us say we are given the task of building an automated taxi. Define the constraints. What are the inputs? What is the output? How can we communicate with the passenger? Do we need to communicate with the other automated taxis, that is, do we need a "language"?
5. In basket analysis, we want to find the dependence between two items X and Y. Given a database of customer transactions, how can we find these dependencies? How would we generalize this to more than two items?
6. In a daily newspaper, find five sample news reports for each category of politics, sports, and the arts. Go over these reports and find words that are used frequently for each category, which may help you discriminate between different categories. For example, a news report on politics is likely to include words such as "government," "recession," "congress," and so forth, whereas a news report on the arts may include "album," "canvas," or "theater." There are also words such as "goal" that are ambiguous.
7. If a face image is a 100×100 image, written in row-major, this is a 10,000-dimensional vector. If we shift the image one pixel to the right, this will be a very different vector in the 10,000-dimensional space. How can we build face recognizers robust to such distortions?

   SOLUTION: Face recognition systems typically have a preprocessing stage for normalization where the input is centered and possibly resized before recognition. This is generally done by first finding the eyes and then translating the image accordingly. There are also recognizers that do not use the face image as pixels but rather extract structural features from the image, for example, the ratio of the distance between the two eyes to the size of the whole face. Such features would be invariant to translations and size changes.
8. Take, for example, the word "machine." Write it ten times. Also ask a friend to write it ten times. Analyzing these twenty images, try to find features,

types of strokes, curvatures, loops, how you make the dots, and so on, that discriminate your handwriting from that of your friend's.

9. In estimating the price of a used car, it makes more sense to estimate the percent depreciation over the original price than to estimate the absolute price. Why?

1.6 References

Bishop, C. M. 1995. *Neural Networks for Pattern Recognition.* Oxford: Oxford University Press.

Duda, R. O., P. E. Hart, and D. G. Stork. 2001. *Pattern Classification,* 2nd ed. New York: Wiley.

Han, J., and M. Kamber. 2011. *Data Mining: Concepts and Techniques,* 3rd ed. San Francisco: Morgan Kaufmann.

Hand, D. J. 1998. "Consumer Credit and Statistics." In *Statistics in Finance,* ed. D. J. Hand and S. D. Jacka, 69–81. London: Arnold.

Hastie, T., R. Tibshirani, and J. Friedman. 2011. *The Elements of Statistical Learning: Data Mining, Inference, and Prediction,* 2nd ed. New York: Springer.

McLachlan, G. J. 1992. *Discriminant Analysis and Statistical Pattern Recognition.* New York: Wiley.

Russell, S., and P. Norvig. 2009. *Artificial Intelligence: A Modern Approach,* 3rd ed. New York: Prentice Hall.

Webb, A., and K. D. Copsey. 2011. *Statistical Pattern Recognition,* 3rd ed. New York: Wiley.

Witten, I. H., and E. Frank. 2005. *Data Mining: Practical Machine Learning Tools and Techniques,* 2nd ed. San Francisco: Morgan Kaufmann.

2 *Supervised Learning*

We discuss supervised learning starting from the simplest case, which is learning a class from its positive and negative examples. We generalize and discuss the case of multiple classes, then regression, where the outputs are continuous.

2.1 Learning a Class from Examples

LET US say we want to learn the *class*, C, of a "family car." We have a set of examples of cars, and we have a group of people that we survey to whom we show these cars. The people look at the cars and label them; the cars that they believe are family cars are *positive examples*, and the other cars are *negative examples*. Class learning is finding a description that is shared by all the positive examples and none of the negative examples. Doing this, we can make a prediction: Given a car that we have not seen before, by checking with the description learned, we will be able to say whether it is a family car or not. Or we can do knowledge extraction: This study may be sponsored by a car company, and the aim may be to understand what people expect from a family car.

POSITIVE EXAMPLES

NEGATIVE EXAMPLES

After some discussions with experts in the field, let us say that we reach the conclusion that among all features a car may have, the features that separate a family car from other type of cars are the price and engine power. These two attributes are the *inputs* to the class recognizer. Note that when we decide on this particular *input representation*, we are ignoring various other attributes as irrelevant. Though one may think of other attributes such as seating capacity and color that might be important for distinguishing among car types, we will consider only price and engine power to keep this example simple.

INPUT REPRESENTATION

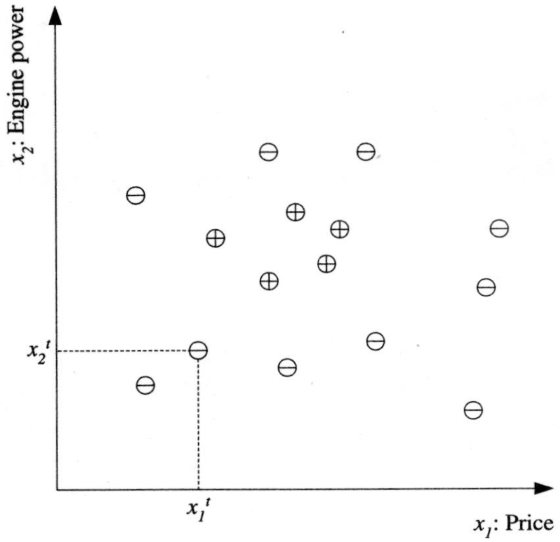

Figure 2.1 Training set for the class of a "family car." Each data point corresponds to one example car, and the coordinates of the point indicate the price and engine power of that car. '+' denotes a positive example of the class (a family car), and '−' denotes a negative example (not a family car); it is another type of car.

Let us denote price as the first input attribute x_1 (e.g., in U.S. dollars) and engine power as the second attribute x_2 (e.g., engine volume in cubic centimeters). Thus we represent each car using two numeric values

$$\mathbf{x} = \begin{bmatrix} x_1 \\ x_2 \end{bmatrix} \tag{2.1}$$

and its label denotes its type

$$r = \begin{cases} 1 & \text{if } \mathbf{x} \text{ is a positive example} \\ 0 & \text{if } \mathbf{x} \text{ is a negative example} \end{cases} \tag{2.2}$$

Each car is represented by such an ordered pair $(\mathbf{x}, r)$ and the training set contains N such examples

$$\mathcal{X} = \{\mathbf{x}^t, r^t\}_{t=1}^N \tag{2.3}$$

where t indexes different examples in the set; it does not represent time or any such order.

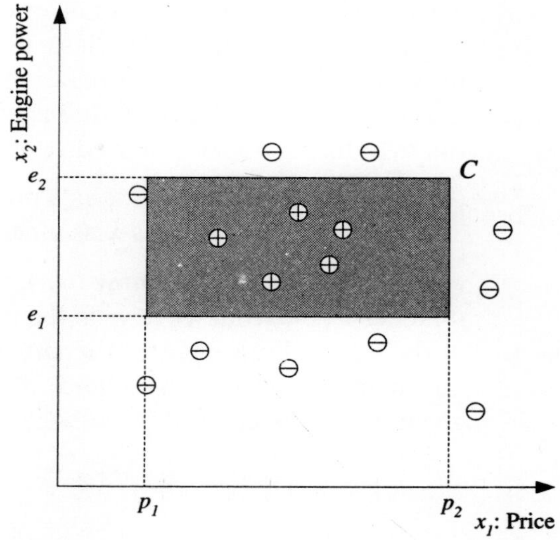

Figure 2.2 Example of a hypothesis class. The class of family car is a rectangle in the price-engine power space.

Our training data can now be plotted in the two-dimensional (x_1, x_2) space where each instance t is a data point at coordinates (x_1^t, x_2^t) and its type, namely, positive versus negative, is given by r^t (see figure 2.1).

After further discussions with the expert and the analysis of the data, we may have reason to believe that for a car to be a family car, its price and engine power should be in a certain range

$$(p_1 \leq \text{price} \leq p_2) \text{ AND } (e_1 \leq \text{engine power} \leq e_2) \tag{2.4}$$

for suitable values of p_1, p_2, e_1, and e_2. Equation 2.4 thus assumes C to be a rectangle in the price-engine power space (see figure 2.2).

HYPOTHESIS CLASS

Equation 2.4 fixes $\mathcal{H}$, the *hypothesis class* from which we believe C is drawn, namely, the set of rectangles. The learning algorithm then finds the particular *hypothesis*, $h \in \mathcal{H}$, specified by a particular quadruple of $(p_1^h, p_2^h, e_1^h, e_2^h)$, to approximate C as closely as possible.

HYPOTHESIS

Though the expert defines this hypothesis class, the values of the parameters are not known; that is, though we choose $\mathcal{H}$, we do not know which particular $h \in \mathcal{H}$ is equal, or closest, to C. But once we restrict our attention to this hypothesis class, learning the class reduces to the easier problem of finding the four parameters that define h.

The aim is to find $h \in \mathcal{H}$ that is as similar as possible to C. Let us say the hypothesis h makes a prediction for an instance $\mathbf{x}$ such that

$$h(\mathbf{x}) = \begin{cases} 1 & \text{if } h \text{ classifies } \mathbf{x} \text{ as a positive example} \\ 0 & \text{if } h \text{ classifies } \mathbf{x} \text{ as a negative example} \end{cases} \tag{2.5}$$

In real life we do not know $C(\mathbf{x})$, so we cannot evaluate how well $h(\mathbf{x})$ matches $C(\mathbf{x})$. What we have is the training set $\mathcal{X}$, which is a small subset of the set of all possible $\mathbf{x}$. The *empirical error* is the proportion of training instances where *predictions* of h do not match the *required values* given in $\mathcal{X}$. The error of hypothesis h given the training set $\mathcal{X}$ is

EMPIRICAL ERROR

$$E(h|\mathcal{X}) = \sum_{t=1}^{N} 1(h(\mathbf{x}^t) \neq r^t) \tag{2.6}$$

where $1(a \neq b)$ is 1 if $a \neq b$ and is 0 if $a = b$ (see figure 2.3).

In our example, the hypothesis class $\mathcal{H}$ is the set of all possible rectangles. Each quadruple $(p_1^h, p_2^h, e_1^h, e_2^h)$ defines one hypothesis, h, from $\mathcal{H}$, and we need to choose the best one, or in other words, we need to find the values of these four parameters given the training set, to include all the positive examples and none of the negative examples. Note that if x_1 and x_2 are real-valued, there are infinitely many such h for which this is satisfied, namely, for which the error, E, is 0, but given a future example somewhere close to the boundary between positive and negative examples, different candidate hypotheses may make different predictions. This is the problem of *generalization*—that is, how well our hypothesis will correctly classify future examples that are not part of the training set.

GENERALIZATION

MOST SPECIFIC HYPOTHESIS

One possibility is to find the *most specific hypothesis*, S, that is the tightest rectangle that includes all the positive examples and none of the negative examples (see figure 2.4). This gives us one hypothesis, $h = S$, as our induced class. Note that the actual class C may be larger than S but is never smaller. The *most general hypothesis*, G, is the largest rectangle we can draw that includes all the positive examples and none of the negative examples (figure 2.4). Any $h \in \mathcal{H}$ between S and G is a valid hypothesis with no error, said to be *consistent* with the training set, and such h make up the *version space*. Given another training set, S, G, version space, the parameters and thus the learned hypothesis, h, can be different.

MOST GENERAL HYPOTHESIS

VERSION SPACE

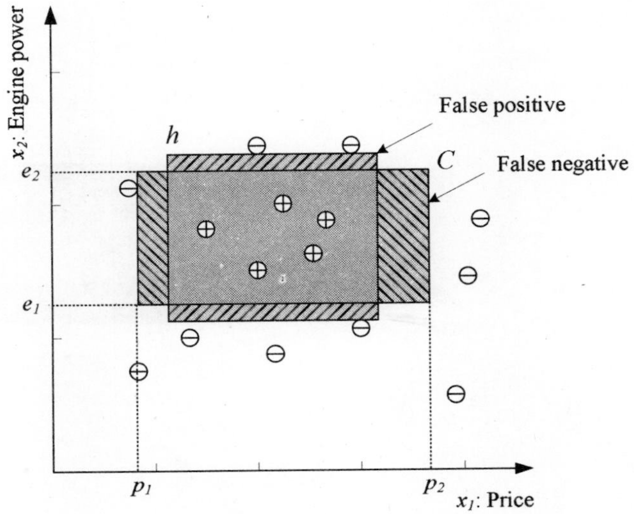

Figure 2.3 C is the actual class and h is our induced hypothesis. The point where C is 1 but h is 0 is a false negative, and the point where C is 0 but h is 1 is a false positive. Other points—namely, true positives and true negatives—are correctly classified.

Actually, depending on $\mathcal{X}$ and $\mathcal{H}$, there may be several S_i and G_j which respectively make up the S-set and the G-set. Every member of the S-set is consistent with all the instances, and there are no consistent hypotheses that are more specific. Similarly, every member of the G-set is consistent with all the instances, and there are no consistent hypotheses that are more general. These two make up the boundary sets and any hypothesis between them is consistent and is part of the version space. There is an algorithm called candidate elimination that incrementally updates the S- and G-sets as it sees training instances one by one; see Mitchell 1997. We assume $\mathcal{X}$ is large enough that there is a unique S and G.

Given $\mathcal{X}$, we can find S, or G, or any h from the version space and use it as our hypothesis, h. It seems intuitive to choose h halfway between S and G; this is to increase the *margin*, which is the distance between the boundary and the instances closest to it (see figure 2.5). For our error function to have a minimum at h with the maximum margin, we should

MARGIN

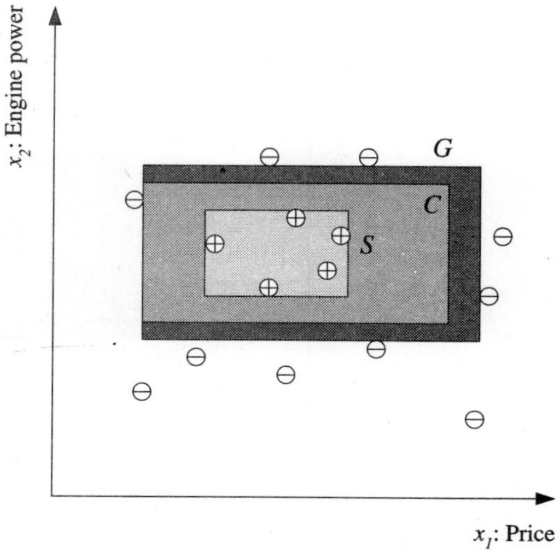

Figure 2.4 S is the most specific and G is the most general hypothesis.

use an error (loss) function which not only checks whether an instance is on the correct side of the boundary but also how far away it is. That is, instead of $h(\boldsymbol{x})$ that returns 0/1, we need to have a hypothesis that returns a value which carries a measure of the distance to the boundary and we need to have a loss function which uses it, different from $1(\cdot)$ that checks for equality.

In some applications, a wrong decision may be very costly and in such a case, we can say that any instance that falls in between S and G is a case of *doubt*, which we cannot label with certainty due to lack of data. In such a case, the system *rejects* the instance and defers the decision to a human expert.

DOUBT

Here, we assume that $\mathcal{H}$ includes C; that is, there exists $h \in \mathcal{H}$, such that $E(h|\mathcal{X})$ is 0. Given a hypothesis class $\mathcal{H}$, it may be the case that we cannot learn C; that is, there exists no $h \in \mathcal{H}$ for which the error is 0. Thus, in any application, we need to make sure that $\mathcal{H}$ is flexible enough, or has enough "capacity," to learn C.

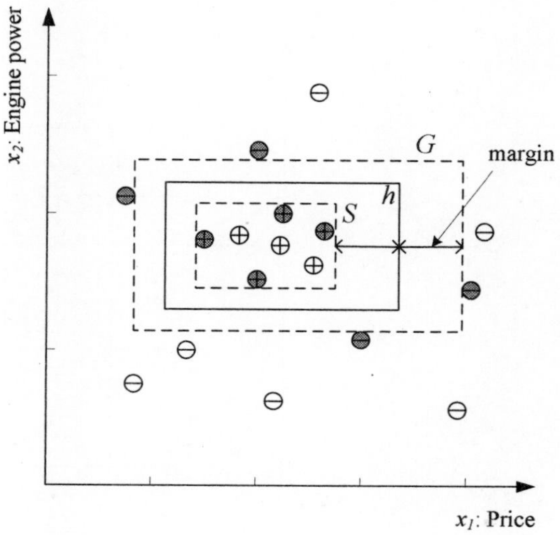

Figure 2.5 We choose the hypothesis with the largest margin, for best separation. The shaded instances are those that define (or support) the margin; other instances can be removed without affecting h.

2.2 Vapnik-Chervonenkis Dimension

Let us say we have a dataset containing N points. These N points can be labeled in 2^N ways as positive and negative. Therefore, 2^N different learning problems can be defined by N data points. If for any of these problems, we can find a hypothesis $h \in \mathcal{H}$ that separates the positive examples from the negative, then we say $\mathcal{H}$ *shatters* N points. That is, any learning problem definable by N examples can be learned with no error by a hypothesis drawn from $\mathcal{H}$. The maximum number of points that can be shattered by $\mathcal{H}$ is called the *Vapnik-Chervonenkis* (VC) *dimension* of $\mathcal{H}$, is denoted as $VC(\mathcal{H})$, and measures the *capacity* of $\mathcal{H}$.

VC DIMENSION

In figure 2.6, we see that an axis-aligned rectangle can shatter four points in two dimensions. Then $VC(\mathcal{H})$, when $\mathcal{H}$ is the hypothesis class of axis-aligned rectangles in two dimensions, is four. In calculating the VC dimension, it is enough that we find four points that can be shattered; it is not necessary that we be able to shatter *any* four points in two di-

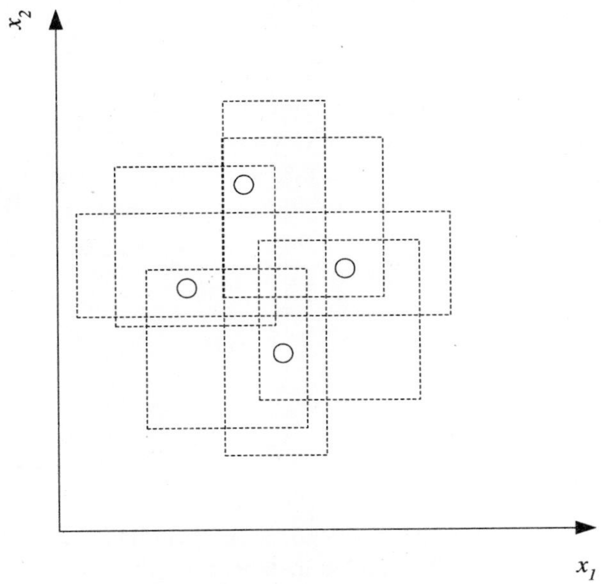

Figure 2.6 An axis-aligned rectangle can shatter four points. Only rectangles covering two points are shown.

mensions. For example, four points placed on a line cannot be shattered by rectangles. However, we cannot place five points in two dimensions *anywhere* such that a rectangle can separate the positive and negative examples for all possible labelings.

VC dimension may seem pessimistic. It tells us that using a rectangle as our hypothesis class, we can learn only datasets containing four points and not more. A learning algorithm that can learn datasets of four points is not very useful. However, this is because the VC dimension is independent of the probability distribution from which instances are drawn. In real life, the world is smoothly changing, instances close by most of the time have the same labels, and we need not worry about *all possible labelings.* There are a lot of datasets containing many more data points than four that are learnable by our hypothesis class (figure 2.1). So even hypothesis classes with small VC dimensions are applicable and are preferred over those with large VC dimensions, for example, a lookup table that has infinite VC dimension.

2.3 Probably Approximately Correct Learning

Using the tightest rectangle, S, as our hypothesis, we would like to find how many examples we need. We would like our hypothesis to be approximately correct, namely, that the error probability be bounded by some value. We also would like to be confident in our hypothesis in that we want to know that our hypothesis will be correct most of the time (if not always); so we want to be probably correct as well (by a probability we can specify).

PAC LEARNING

In *probably approximately correct* (PAC) *learning*, given a class, C, and examples drawn from some unknown but fixed probability distribution, $p(x)$, we want to find the number of examples, N, such that with probability at least $1 - \delta$, the hypothesis h has error at most ϵ, for arbitrary $\delta \leq 1/2$ and $\epsilon > 0$

$$P\{C\Delta h \leq \epsilon\} \geq 1 - \delta$$

where $C\Delta h$ is the region of difference between C and h.

In our case, because S is the tightest possible rectangle, the error region between C and $h = S$ is the sum of four rectangular strips (see figure 2.7). We would like to make sure that the probability of a positive example falling in here (and causing an error) is at most ϵ. For any of these strips, if we can guarantee that the probability is upper bounded by $\epsilon/4$, the error is at most $4(\epsilon/4) = \epsilon$. Note that we count the overlaps in the corners twice, and the total actual error in this case is less than $4(\epsilon/4)$. The probability that a randomly drawn example misses this strip is $1 - \epsilon/4$. The probability that all N independent draws miss the strip is $(1 - \epsilon/4)^N$, and the probability that all N independent draws miss any of the four strips is at most $4(1 - \epsilon/4)^N$, which we would like to be at most δ. We have the inequality

$$(1 - x) \leq \exp[-x]$$

So if we choose N and δ such that we have

$$4\exp[-\epsilon N/4] \leq \delta$$

we can also write $4(1 - \epsilon/4)^N \leq \delta$. Dividing both sides by 4, taking (natural) log and rearranging terms, we have

(2.7) $$N \geq (4/\epsilon)\log(4/\delta)$$

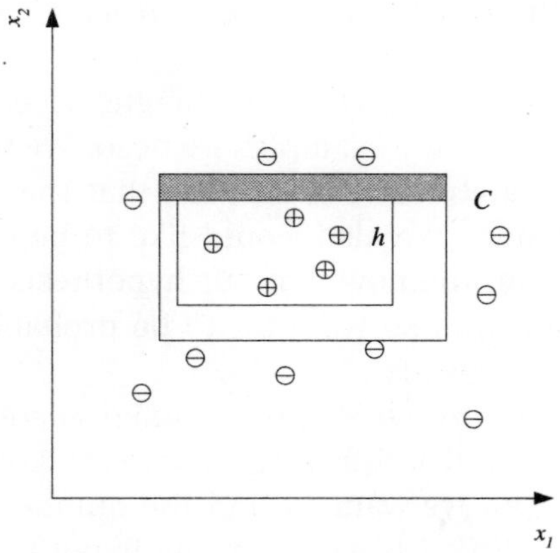

Figure 2.7 The difference between h and C is the sum of four rectangular strips, one of which is shaded.

Therefore, provided that we take at least $(4/\epsilon)\log(4/\delta)$ independent examples from C and use the tightest rectangle as our hypothesis h, with *confidence probability* at least $1 - \delta$, a given point will be misclassified with *error probability* at most ϵ. We can have arbitrary large confidence by decreasing δ and arbitrary small error by decreasing ϵ, and we see in equation 2.7 that the number of examples is a slowly growing function of $1/\epsilon$ and $1/\delta$, linear and logarithmic, respectively.

2.4 Noise

NOISE *Noise* is any unwanted anomaly in the data and due to noise, the class may be more difficult to learn and zero error may be infeasible with a simple hypothesis class (see figure 2.8). There are several interpretations of noise:

- There may be imprecision in recording the input attributes, which may shift the data points in the input space.

- There may be errors in labeling the data points, which may relabel

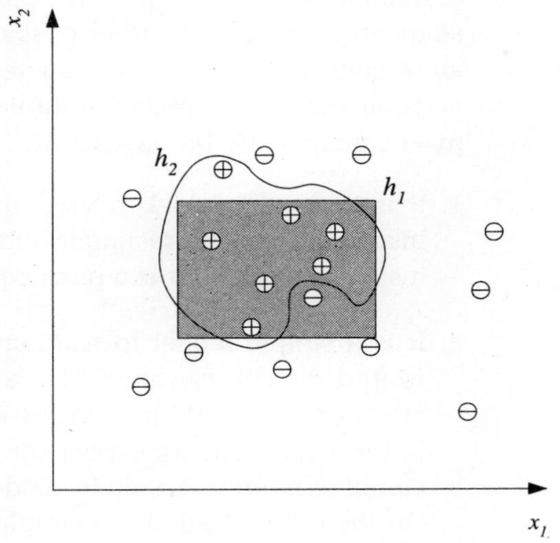

Figure 2.8 When there is noise, there is not a simple boundary between the positive and negative instances, and zero misclassification error may not be possible with a simple hypothesis. A rectangle is a simple hypothesis with four parameters defining the corners. An arbitrary closed form can be drawn by piecewise functions with a larger number of control points.

positive instances as negative and vice versa. This is sometimes called *teacher noise.*

- There may be additional attributes, which we have not taken into account, that affect the label of an instance. Such attributes may be *hidden* or *latent* in that they may be unobservable. The effect of these neglected attributes is thus modeled as a random component and is included in "noise."

As can be seen in figure 2.8, when there is noise, there is not a simple boundary between the positive and negative instances and to separate them, one needs a complicated hypothesis that corresponds to a hypothesis class with larger capacity. A rectangle can be defined by four numbers, but to define a more complicated shape one needs a more complex model with a much larger number of parameters. With a complex model, one can make a perfect fit to the data and attain zero error; see the wiggly shape in figure 2.8. Another possibility is to keep the model simple and allow some error; see the rectangle in figure 2.8.

Using the simple rectangle (unless its training error is much bigger) makes more sense because of the following:

1. It is a simple model to use. It is easy to check whether a point is inside or outside a rectangle and we can easily check, for a future data instance, whether it is a positive or a negative instance.

2. It is a simple model to train and has fewer parameters. It is easier to find the corner values of a rectangle than the control points of an arbitrary shape. With a small training set when the training instances differ a little bit, we expect the simpler model to change less than a complex model: A simple model is thus said to have less *variance*. On the other hand, a too simple model assumes more, is more rigid, and may fail if indeed the underlying class is not that simple: A simpler model has more *bias*. Finding the optimal model corresponds to minimizing both the bias and the variance.

3. It is a simple model to explain. A rectangle simply corresponds to defining intervals on the two attributes. By learning a simple model, we can extract information from the raw data given in the training set.

4. If indeed there is mislabeling or noise in input and the actual class is really a simple model like the rectangle, then the simple rectangle, because it has less variance and is less affected by single instances, will be a better discriminator than the wiggly shape, although the simple one may make slightly more errors on the training set. Given comparable empirical error, we say that a simple (but not too simple) model would generalize better than a complex model. This principle is known as *Occam's razor*, which states that *simpler explanations are more plausible* and any unnecessary complexity should be shaved off.

OCCAM'S RAZOR

2.5 Learning Multiple Classes

In our example of learning a family car, we have positive examples belonging to the class family car and the negative examples belonging to all other cars. This is a *two-class* problem. In the general case, we have K

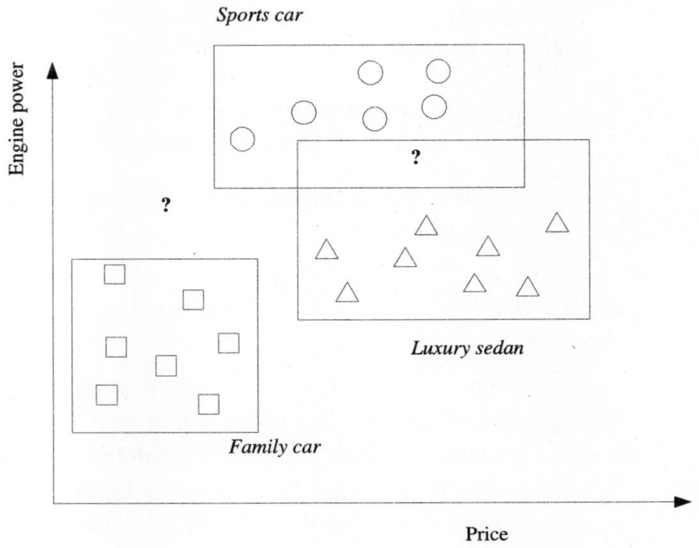

Figure 2.9 There are three classes: family car, sports car, and luxury sedan. There are three hypotheses induced, each one covering the instances of one class and leaving outside the instances of the other two classes. '?' are reject regions where no, or more than one, class is chosen.

classes denoted as $C_i, i = 1, \ldots, K$, and an input instance belongs to one and exactly one of them. The training set is now of the form

$$\mathcal{X} = \{\boldsymbol{x}^t, \boldsymbol{r}^t\}_{t=1}^N$$

where $\boldsymbol{r}$ has K dimensions and

$$r_i^t = \begin{cases} 1 & \text{if } \boldsymbol{x}^t \in C_i \\ 0 & \text{if } \boldsymbol{x}^t \in C_j, j \neq i \end{cases} \tag{2.8}$$

An example is given in figure 2.9 with instances from three classes: family car, sports car, and luxury sedan.

In machine learning for classification, we would like to learn the boundary separating the instances of one class from the instances of all other classes. Thus we view a K-class classification problem as K two-class problems. The training examples belonging to C_i are the positive instances of hypothesis h_i and the examples of all other classes are the negative instances of h_i. Thus in a K-class problem, we have K hypotheses to learn such that

$$h_i(\mathbf{x}^t) = \begin{cases} 1 & \text{if } \mathbf{x}^t \in C_i \\ 0 & \text{if } \mathbf{x}^t \in C_j, j \neq i \end{cases} \tag{2.9}$$

The total empirical error takes a sum over the predictions for all classes over all instances:

$$E(\{h_i\}_{i=1}^K|\mathcal{X}) = \sum_{t=1}^{N}\sum_{i=1}^{K} 1(h_i(\mathbf{x}^t) \neq r_i^t) \tag{2.10}$$

For a given $\mathbf{x}$, ideally only one of $h_i(\mathbf{x}), i = 1, \ldots, K$ is 1 and we can choose a class. But when no, or two or more, $h_i(\mathbf{x})$ is 1, we cannot choose a class, and this is the case of *doubt* and the classifier *rejects* such cases.

REJECT

In our example of learning a family car, we used only one hypothesis and only modeled the positive examples. Any negative example outside is not a family car. Alternatively, sometimes we may prefer to build two hypotheses, one for the positive and the other for the negative instances. This assumes a structure also for the negative instances that can be covered by another hypothesis. Separating family cars from sports cars is such a problem; each class has a structure of its own. The advantage is that if the input is a luxury sedan, we can have both hypotheses decide negative and reject the input.

If in a dataset, we expect to have all classes with similar distribution—shapes in the input space—then the same hypothesis class can be used for all classes. For example, in a handwritten digit recognition dataset, we would expect all digits to have similar distributions. But in a medical diagnosis dataset, for example, where we have two classes for sick and healthy people, we may have completely different distributions for the two classes; there may be multiple ways for a person to be sick, reflected differently in the inputs: All healthy people are alike; each sick person is sick in his or her own way.

2.6 Regression

In classification, given an input, the output that is generated is Boolean; it is a yes/no answer. When the output is a numeric value, what we would like to learn is not a class, $C(\mathbf{x}) \in \{0, 1\}$, but is a numeric function. In machine learning, the function is not known but we have a training set of examples drawn from it

$$\mathcal{X} = \{\mathbf{x}^t, r^t\}_{t=1}^N$$

INTERPOLATION

where $r^t \in \Re$. If there is no noise, the task is *interpolation*. We would like to find the function $f(x)$ that passes through these points such that we have

$$r^t = f(\mathbf{x}^t)$$

EXTRAPOLATION

REGRESSION

In *polynomial interpolation*, given N points, we find the $(N-1)$st degree polynomial that we can use to predict the output for any $\mathbf{x}$. This is called *extrapolation* if $\mathbf{x}$ is outside of the range of $\mathbf{x}^t$ in the training set. In time-series prediction, for example, we have data up to the present and we want to predict the value for the future. In *regression*, there is noise added to the output of the unknown function

$$r^t = f(\mathbf{x}^t) + \epsilon \tag{2.11}$$

where $f(\mathbf{x}) \in \Re$ is the unknown function and ϵ is random noise. The explanation for noise is that there are extra *hidden* variables that we cannot observe

$$r^t = f^*(\mathbf{x}^t, \mathbf{z}^t) \tag{2.12}$$

where $\mathbf{z}^t$ denote those hidden variables. We would like to approximate the output by our model $g(\mathbf{x})$. The empirical error on the training set $\mathcal{X}$ is

$$E(g|\mathcal{X}) = \frac{1}{N}\sum_{t=1}^{N}[r^t - g(\mathbf{x}^t)]^2 \tag{2.13}$$

Because r and $g(\mathbf{x})$ are numeric quantities, for example, $\in \Re$, there is an ordering defined on their values and we can define a *distance* between values, as the square of the difference, which gives us more information than equal/not equal, as used in classification. The square of the difference is one error (loss) function that can be used; another is the absolute value of the difference. We will see other examples in the coming chapters.

Our aim is to find $g(\cdot)$ that minimizes the empirical error. Again our approach is the same; we assume a hypothesis class for $g(\cdot)$ with a small set of parameters. If we assume that $g(\mathbf{x})$ is linear, we have

$$g(\mathbf{x}) = w_1x_1 + \cdots + w_dx_d + w_0 = \sum_{j=1}^{d} w_jx_j + w_0 \tag{2.14}$$

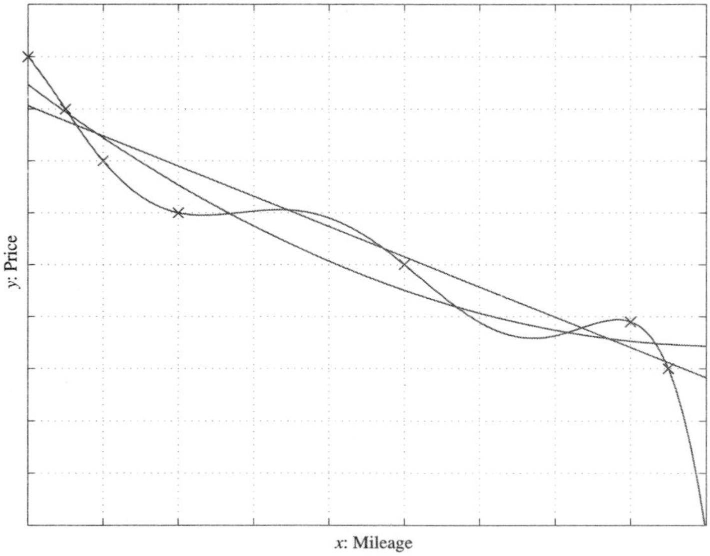

Figure 2.10 Linear, second-order, and sixth-order polynomials are fitted to the same set of points. The highest order gives a perfect fit, but given this much data it is very unlikely that the real curve is so shaped. The second order seems better than the linear fit in capturing the trend in the training data.

Let us now go back to our example in section 1.2.3 where we estimated the price of a used car. There we used a single input linear model

$$g(x) = w_1 x + w_0 \tag{2.15}$$

where w_1 and w_0 are the parameters to learn from data. The w_1 and w_0 values should minimize

$$E(w_1, w_0|\mathcal{X}) = \frac{1}{N}\sum_{t=1}^{N}[r^t - (w_1 x^t + w_0)]^2 \tag{2.16}$$

Its minimum point can be calculated by taking the partial derivatives of E with respect to w_1 and w_0, setting them equal to 0, and solving for the two unknowns:

$$\begin{aligned} w_1 &= \frac{\sum_t x^t r^t - \overline{x}\overline{r}N}{\sum_t (x^t)^2 - N\overline{x}^2} \\ w_0 &= \overline{r} - w_1\overline{x} \end{aligned} \tag{2.17}$$

Table 2.1 With two inputs, there are four possible cases and sixteen possible Boolean functions.

x_1	x_2	h_1	h_2	h_3	h_4	h_5	h_6	h_7	h_8	h_9	h_{10}	h_{11}	h_{12}	h_{13}	h_{14}	h_{15}	h_{16}
0	0	0	0	0	0	0	0	0	0	1	1	1	1	1	1	1	1
0	1	0	0	0	0	1	1	1	1	0	0	0	0	1	1	1	1
1	0	0	0	1	1	0	0	1	1	0	0	1	1	0	0	1	1
1	1	0	1	0	1	0	1	0	1	0	1	0	1	0	1	0	1

where $\overline{x} = \sum_t x^t/N$ and $\overline{r} = \sum_t r^t/N$. The line found is shown in figure 1.2.

If the linear model is too simple, it is too constrained and incurs a large approximation error, and in such a case, the output may be taken as a higher-order function of the input—for example, quadratic

$$g(x) = w_2x^2 + w_1x + w_0 \tag{2.18}$$

where similarly we have an analytical solution for the parameters. When the order of the polynomial is increased, the error on the training data decreases. But a high-order polynomial follows individual examples closely, instead of capturing the general trend; see the sixth-order polynomial in figure 2.10. This implies that Occam's razor also applies in the case of regression and we should be careful when fine-tuning the model complexity to match it with the complexity of the function underlying the data.

2.7 Model Selection and Generalization

Let us start with the case of learning a Boolean function from examples. In a Boolean function, all inputs and the output are binary. There are 2^d possible ways to write d binary values and therefore, with d inputs, the training set has at most 2^d examples. As shown in table 2.1, each of these can be labeled as 0 or 1, and therefore, there are 2^{2^d} possible Boolean functions of d inputs.

Each distinct training example removes half the hypotheses, namely, those whose guesses are wrong. For example, let us say we have $x_1 = 0$, $x_2 = 1$ and the output is 0; this removes $h_5, h_6, h_7, h_8, h_{13}, h_{14}, h_{15}, h_{16}$. This is one way to interpret learning: We start with all possible hypotheses and as we see more training examples, we remove those hypotheses that are not consistent with the training data. In the case of a Boolean function, to end up with a single hypothesis we need to see *all* 2^d training examples. If the training set we are given contains only a small subset of all possible instances, as it generally does—that is, if we know what the output should be for only a small percentage of the cases—the solution is not unique. After seeing N example cases, there remain 2^{2^d-N} possible functions. This is an example of an *ill-posed problem* where the data by itself is not sufficient to find a unique solution.

ILL-POSED PROBLEM

The same problem also exists in other learning applications, in classification, and in regression. As we see more training examples, we know more about the underlying function, and we carve out more hypotheses that are inconsistent from the hypothesis class, but we still are left with many consistent hypotheses.

So because learning is ill-posed, and data by itself is not sufficient to find the solution, we should make some extra assumptions to have a unique solution with the data we have. The set of assumptions we make to have learning possible is called the *inductive bias* of the learning algorithm. One way we introduce inductive bias is when we assume a hypothesis class $\mathcal{H}$. In learning the class of family cars, there are infinitely many ways of separating the positive examples from the negative examples. Assuming the shape of a rectangle is one inductive bias, and then the rectangle with the largest margin for example, is another inductive bias. In linear regression, assuming a linear function is an inductive bias, and among all lines, choosing the one that minimizes squared error is another inductive bias.

INDUCTIVE BIAS

But we know that each hypothesis class has a certain capacity and can learn only certain functions. The class of functions that can be learned can be extended by using a hypothesis class with larger capacity, containing more complex hypotheses. For example, the hypothesis class that is a union of two rectangles has higher capacity, but its hypotheses are more complex. Similarly in regression, as we increase the order of the polynomial, the capacity and complexity increase. The question now is to decide where to stop.

Thus learning is not possible without inductive bias, and now the question is how to choose the right bias. This is called *model selection*, which is choosing between possible $\mathcal{H}$. In answering this question, we should remember that the aim of machine learning is rarely to replicate the training data but the prediction for new cases. That is we would like to be able to generate the right output for an input instance outside the training set,

MODEL SELECTION

one for which the correct output is not given in the training set. How well a model trained on the training set predicts the right output for new instances is called *generalization*.

GENERALIZATION

For best generalization, we should match the complexity of the hypothesis class $\mathcal{H}$ with the complexity of the function underlying the data. If $\mathcal{H}$ is less complex than the function, we have *underfitting*, for example, when trying to fit a line to data sampled from a third-order polynomial. In such a case, as we increase the complexity, the training error decreases. But if we have $\mathcal{H}$ that is too complex, the data is not enough to constrain it and we may end up with a bad hypothesis, $h \in \mathcal{H}$, for example, when fitting two rectangles to data sampled from one rectangle. Or if there is noise, an overcomplex hypothesis may learn not only the underlying function but also the noise in the data and may make a bad fit, for example, when fitting a sixth-order polynomial to noisy data sampled from a third-order polynomial. This is called *overfitting*. In such a case, having more training data helps but only up to a certain point. Given a training set and $\mathcal{H}$, we can find $h \in \mathcal{H}$ that has the minimum training error but if $\mathcal{H}$ is not chosen well, no matter which $h \in \mathcal{H}$ we pick, we will not have good generalization.

UNDERFITTING

OVERFITTING

TRIPLE TRADE-OFF

We can summarize our discussion citing the *triple trade-off* (Dietterich 2003). In all learning algorithms that are trained from example data, there is a trade-off between three factors:

- the complexity of the hypothesis we fit to data, namely, the capacity of the hypothesis class,
- the amount of training data, and
- the generalization error on new examples.

As the amount of training data increases, the generalization error decreases. As the complexity of the model class $\mathcal{H}$ increases, the generalization error decreases first and then starts to increase. The generalization error of an overcomplex $\mathcal{H}$ can be kept in check by increasing the amount of training data but only up to a point. If the data is sampled from a line and if we are fitting a higher-order polynomial, the fit will be constrained to lie close to the line if there is training data in the vicinity; where it has not been trained, a high-order polynomial may behave erratically.

We can measure the generalization ability of a hypothesis, namely, the quality of its inductive bias, if we have access to data outside the training set. We simulate this by dividing the dataset we have into two parts. We use one part for training (i.e., to fit a hypothesis), and the remaining part is called the *validation set* and is used to test the generalization ability. That is, given a set of possible hypothesis classes $\mathcal{H}_i$, for each we fit the best $h_i \in \mathcal{H}_i$ on the training set. Then, assuming large enough training and validation sets, the hypothesis that is the most accurate on the validation set is the best one (the one that has the best inductive bias). This process is called *cross-validation*. So, for example, to find the right order in polynomial regression, given a number of candidate polynomials of different orders where polynomials of different orders correspond to $\mathcal{H}_i$, for each order, we find the coefficients on the training set, calculate their errors on the validation set, and take the one that has the least validation error as the best polynomial.

VALIDATION SET

CROSS-VALIDATION

Note that if we then need to report the error to give an idea about the expected error of our best model, we should not use the validation error. We have used the validation set to choose the best model, and it has effectively become a part of the training set. We need a third set, a *test set*, sometimes also called the *publication set*, containing examples not used in training or validation. An analogy from our lives is when we are taking a course: the example problems that the instructor solves in class while teaching a subject form the training set; exam questions are the validation set; and the problems we solve in our later, professional life are the test set.

TEST SET

We cannot keep on using the same training/validation split either, because after having been used once, the validation set effectively becomes part of training data. This will be like an instructor who uses the same exam questions every year; a smart student will figure out not to bother with the lectures and will only memorize the answers to those questions.

We should always remember that the training data we use is a random sample, that is, for the same application, if we collect data once more, we will get a slightly different dataset, the fitted h will be slightly different and will have a slightly different validation error. Or if we have a fixed set which we divide for training, validation, and test, we will have different errors depending on how we do the division. These slight differences in error will allow us to estimate how large differences should be to be considered *significant* and not due to chance. That is, in choosing between two hypothesis classes $\mathcal{H}_i$ and $\mathcal{H}_j$, we will use them both multiple times on a number of training and validation sets and check if the difference between average errors of h_i and h_j is larger than the average difference between multiple h_i. In chapter 19, we discuss how to design machine learning experiments using limited data to best answer our questions—for example, which is the best hypothesis class?—and how to analyze the results of these experiments so that we can achieve statistically significant conclusions minimally affected by random chance.

2.8 Dimensions of a Supervised Machine Learning Algorithm

Let us now recapitulate and generalize. We have a sample

$$\mathcal{X} = \{x^t, r^t\}_{t=1}^N \tag{2.19}$$

INDEPENDENT AND IDENTICALLY DISTRIBUTED (IID)

The sample is *independent and identically distributed* (*iid*); the ordering is not important and all instances are drawn from the same joint distribution $p(x, r)$. t indexes one of the N instances, x^t is the arbitrary dimensional input, and r^t is the associated desired output. r^t is 0/1 for two-class learning, is a K-dimensional binary vector (where exactly one of the dimensions is 1 and all others 0) for $(K > 2)$-class classification, and is a real value in regression.

The aim is to build a good and useful approximation to r^t using the model $g(x^t|\theta)$. In doing this, there are three decisions we must make:

1. *Model* we use in learning, denoted as

   $$g(x|\theta)$$

   where $g(\cdot)$ is the model, x is the input, and θ are the parameters.

   $g(\cdot)$ defines the hypothesis class $\mathcal{H}$, and a particular value of θ instantiates one hypothesis $h \in \mathcal{H}$. For example, in class learning, we have taken a rectangle as our model whose four coordinates make up θ; in linear regression, the model is the linear function of the input whose slope and intercept are the parameters learned from the data. The model (inductive bias), or $\mathcal{H}$, is fixed by the machine learning system designer based on his or her knowledge of the application and the hypothesis h is chosen (parameters are tuned) by a learning algorithm using the training set, sampled from $p(x, r)$.

2. *Loss function*, $L(\cdot)$, to compute the difference between the desired output, r^t, and our approximation to it, $g(x^t|\theta)$, given the current value

of the parameters, θ. The *approximation error*, or *loss*, is the sum of losses over the individual instances

$$E(\theta|\mathcal{X}) = \sum_t L(r^t, g(x^t|\theta)) \tag{2.20}$$

In class learning where outputs are 0/1, $L(\cdot)$ checks for equality or not; in regression, because the output is a numeric value, we have ordering information for distance and one possibility is to use the square of the difference.

3. *Optimization procedure* to find θ^* that minimizes the total error

$$\theta^* = \arg\min_\theta E(\theta|\mathcal{X}) \tag{2.21}$$

where arg min returns the argument that minimizes. In polynomial regression, we can solve analytically for the optimum, but this is not always the case. With other models and error functions, the complexity of the optimization problem becomes important. We are especially interested in whether it has a single minimum corresponding to a globally optimal solution, or whether there are multiple minima corresponding to locally optimal solutions.

For this setting to work well, the following conditions should be satisfied: First, the hypothesis class of $g(\cdot)$ should be large enough, that is, have enough capacity, to include the unknown function that generated the data that is represented in $\mathcal{X}$ in a noisy form. Second, there should be enough training data to allow us to pinpoint the correct (or a good enough) hypothesis from the hypothesis class. Third, we should have a good optimization method that finds the correct hypothesis given the training data.

Different machine learning algorithms differ either in the models they assume (their hypothesis class/inductive bias), the loss measures they employ, or the optimization procedure they use. We will see many examples in the coming chapters.

2.9 Notes

Mitchell proposed version spaces and the candidate elimination algorithm to incrementally build S and G as instances are given one by one;

see Mitchell 1997 for a recent review. The rectangle-learning is from exercise 2.4 of Mitchell 1997. Hirsh (1990) discusses how version spaces can handle the case when instances are perturbed by small amount of noise.

In one of the earliest works on machine learning, Winston (1975) proposed the idea of a "near miss." A near miss is a negative example that is very much like a positive example. In our terminology, we see that a near miss would be an instance that falls in the gray area between S and G, an instance which would affect the margin, and would hence be more useful for learning, than an ordinary positive or negative example. The instances that are close to the boundary are the ones that define it (or support it); those which are inside and are surrounded by many instances with the same label can be removed without affecting the boundary.

Related to this idea is *active learning* where the learning algorithm can generate instances itself and ask for them to be labeled, instead of passively being given them (Angluin 1988) (see exercise 5).

VC dimension was proposed by Vapnik and Chervonenkis in the early 1970s. A recent source is Vapnik 1995 where he writes, "Nothing is more practical than a good theory" (p. x), which is as true in machine learning as in any other branch of science. You should not rush to the computer; you can save yourself from hours of useless programming by some thinking, a notebook, and a pencil—you may also need an eraser.

The PAC model was proposed by Valiant (1984). The PAC analysis of learning a rectangle is from Blumer et al. 1989. A good textbook on computational learning theory covering PAC learning and VC dimension is Kearns and Vazirani 1994.

The definition of the optimization problem solved for model fitting has been getting very important in recent years. Once quite content with local descent methods that converge to the nearest good solution starting from some random initial state, nowadays we are, for example, interested in showing that the problem is convex—there is a single, global solution (Boyd and Vandenberghe 2004). As dataset sizes grow and models get more complex, we are also, for example, interested in how fast the optimization procedure converges to a solution.

2.10 Exercises

1. Let us say our hypothesis class is a circle instead of a rectangle. What are the parameters? How can the parameters of a circle hypothesis be calculated in

such a case? What if it is an ellipse? Why does it make more sense to use an ellipse instead of a circle?

SOLUTION: In the case of a circle, the parameters are the center and the radius (see figure 2.11). We then need to find S and G where S is the tightest circle that includes all the positive examples and G is the largest circle that includes all the positive examples and no negative example; any circle between them is a consistent hypothesis.

It makes more sense to use an ellipse because the two axes need not have the same scale and an ellipse has two separate parameters for the widths in the two axes rather than a single radius. Actually, price and engine power are positively correlated; the price of a car tends to increase as its engine power increases, and hence it makes more sense to use an oblique ellipse—we will see such models in chapter 5.

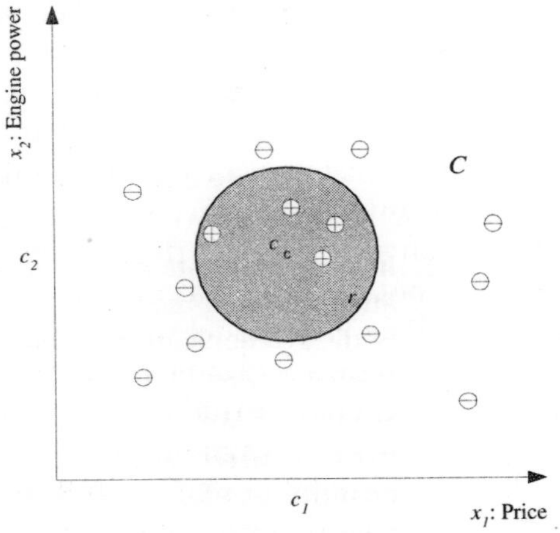

Figure 2.11 Hypothesis class is a circle with two parameters, the coordinates of its center and its radius.

2. Imagine our hypothesis is not one rectangle but a union of two (or $m > 1$) rectangles. What is the advantage of such a hypothesis class? Show that any class can be represented by such a hypothesis class with large enough m.

   SOLUTION: In the case when there is a single rectangle, all the positive instances should form one single group; with two rectangles, for example (see figure 2.12), the positive instances can form two, possibly disjoint clusters in the input space. Note that each rectangle corresponds to a conjunction on the two input attributes, and having multiple rectangles corresponds to a disjunction. Any logical formula can be written as a disjunction of conjunctions.

In the worst case ($m = N$), we have a separate rectangle for each positive instance.

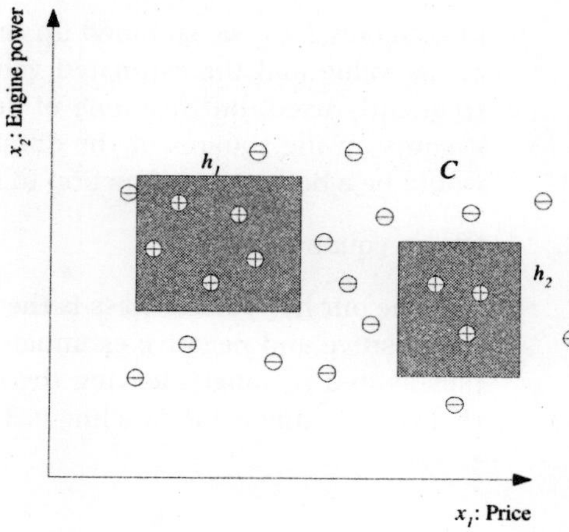

Figure 2.12 Hypothesis class is a union of two rectangles.

3. In many applications, wrong decisions—namely, false positives and false negatives—have a monetary cost, and these two costs may be different. What is the relationship between the positioning of h between S and G and the relative costs of these?

   SOLUTION: We can see that S makes no false positives, but only false negatives; similarly, G makes no false negatives, only false positives. So if false positives and false negatives are equally bad, we want our h to be halfway; if false positives are costlier, we want h to be closer to S; if false negatives are costlier, h should be closer to G.

4. The complexity of most learning algorithms is a function of the training set. Can you propose a filtering algorithm that finds redundant instances?

   SOLUTION: The instances that affect the hypothesis are those that are in the vicinity of instances with a different label. A positive instance that is surrounded on all sides by many positive instances is not needed, nor is a negative instance surrounded by many negative instances. We discuss such *neighbor-based* methods in chapter 8.

5. If we have a supervisor who can provide us with the label for any $\mathbf{x}$, where should we choose $\mathbf{x}$ to learn with fewer queries?

   SOLUTION: The region of ambiguity is between S and G. It would be best to be given queries there, so that we can make this region of doubt smaller. If a given instance there turns out to be positive, this means we can make S larger up to that instance; if it is negative, this means we can shrink G down until there.

6. In equation 2.13, we summed up the squares of the differences between the actual value and the estimated value. This error function is the one most frequently used, but it is one of several possible error functions. Because it sums up the squares of the differences, it is not robust to outliers. What would be a better error function to implement *robust regression*?

7. Derive equation 2.17.

8. Assume our hypothesis class is the set of lines, and we use a line to separate the positive and negative examples, instead of bounding the positive examples as in a rectangle, leaving the negatives outside (see figure 2.13). Show that the VC dimension of a line is 3.

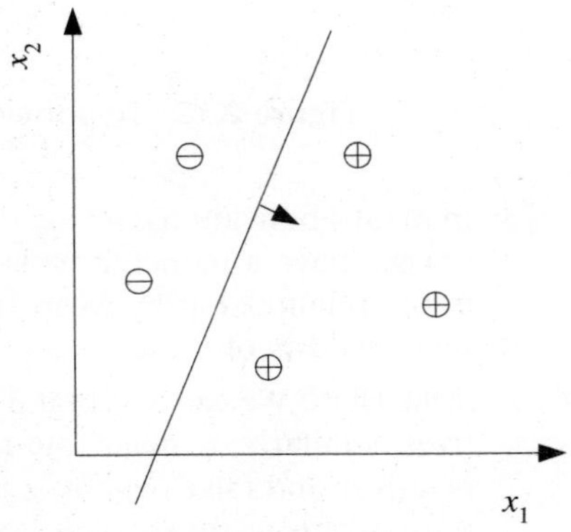

Figure 2.13 A line separating positive and negative instances.

9. Show that the VC dimension of the triangle hypothesis class is 7 in two dimensions. (Hint: For best separation, it is best to place the seven points equidistant on a circle.)

10. Assume as in exercise 8 that our hypothesis class is the set of lines. Write down an error function that not only minimizes the number of misclassifications but also maximizes the margin.

11. One source of noise is error in the labels. Can you propose a method to find data points that are highly likely to be mislabeled?

2.11 References

Angluin, D. 1988. "Queries and Concept Learning." *Machine Learning* 2:319–342.

Blumer, A., A. Ehrenfeucht, D. Haussler, and M. K. Warmuth. 1989. "Learnability and the Vapnik-Chervonenkis Dimension." *Journal of the ACM* 36:929–965.

Boyd, S., and L. Vandenberge. 2004. *Convex Optimization.* Cambridge, UK: Cambridge University Press.

Dietterich, T. G. 2003. "Machine Learning." In *Nature Encyclopedia of Cognitive Science.* London: Macmillan.

Hirsh, H. 1990. *Incremental Version Space Merging: A General Framework for Concept Learning.* Boston: Kluwer.

Kearns, M. J., and U. V. Vazirani. 1994. *An Introduction to Computational Learning Theory.* Cambridge, MA: MIT Press.

Mitchell, T. 1997. *Machine Learning.* New York: McGraw-Hill.

Valiant, L. 1984. "A Theory of the Learnable." *Communications of the ACM* 27:1134–1142.

Vapnik, V. N. 1995. *The Nature of Statistical Learning Theory.* New York: Springer.

Winston, P. H. 1975. "Learning Structural Descriptions from Examples." In *The Psychology of Computer Vision*, ed. P. H. Winston, 157–209. New York: McGraw-Hill.

3 Bayesian Decision Theory

We discuss probability theory as the framework for making decisions under uncertainty. In classification, Bayes' rule is used to calculate the probabilities of the classes. We generalize to discuss how we can make rational decisions among multiple actions to minimize expected risk. We also discuss learning association rules from data.

3.1 Introduction

PROGRAMMING COMPUTERS to make inference from data is a cross between statistics and computer science, where statisticians provide the mathematical framework of making inference from data and computer scientists work on the efficient implementation of the inference methods.

Data comes from a process that is not completely known. This lack of knowledge is indicated by modeling the process as a random process. Maybe the process is actually deterministic, but because we do not have access to complete knowledge about it, we model it as random and use probability theory to analyze it. At this point, it may be a good idea to jump to the appendix and review basic probability theory before continuing with this chapter.

Tossing a coin is a random process because we cannot predict at any toss whether the outcome will be heads or tails—that is why we toss coins, or buy lottery tickets, or get insurance. We can only talk about the probability that the outcome of the next toss will be heads or tails. It may be argued that if we have access to extra knowledge such as the exact composition of the coin, its initial position, the force and its direction that is applied to the coin when tossing it, where and how it is caught, and so forth, the exact outcome of the toss can be predicted.

UNOBSERVABLE VARIABLES
OBSERVABLE VARIABLE

The extra pieces of knowledge that we do not have access to are named the *unobservable variables.* In the coin tossing example, the only *observable variable* is the outcome of the toss. Denoting the unobservables by $\mathbf{z}$ and the observable as x, in reality we have

$$x = f(\mathbf{z})$$

where $f(\cdot)$ is the deterministic function that defines the outcome from the unobservable pieces of knowledge. Because we cannot model the process this way, we define the outcome X as a random variable drawn from a probability distribution $P(X = x)$ that specifies the process.

The outcome of tossing a coin is heads or tails, and we define a random variable that takes one of two values. Let us say $X = 1$ denotes that the outcome of a toss is heads and $X = 0$ denotes tails. Such X are Bernoulli-distributed where the parameter of the distribution p_o is the probability that the outcome is heads:

$$P(X = 1) = p_o \text{ and } P(X = 0) = 1 - P(X = 1) = 1 - p_o$$

Assume that we are asked to predict the outcome of the next toss. If we know p_o, our prediction will be heads if $p_o > 0.5$ and tails otherwise. This is because if we choose the more probable case, the probability of error, which is 1 minus the probability of our choice, will be minimum. If this is a fair coin with $p_o = 0.5$, we have no better means of prediction than choosing heads all the time or tossing a fair coin ourselves!

SAMPLE

If we do not know $P(X)$ and want to estimate this from a given sample, then we are in the realm of statistics. We have a *sample*, $\mathcal{X}$, containing examples drawn from the probability distribution of the observables x^t, denoted as $p(x)$. The aim is to build an approximator to it, $\hat{p}(x)$, using the sample $\mathcal{X}$.

In the coin tossing example, the sample contains the outcomes of the past N tosses. Then using $\mathcal{X}$, we can estimate p_o, which is the parameter that uniquely specifies the distribution. Our estimate of p_o is

$$\hat{p}_o = \frac{\#\{\text{tosses with outcome heads}\}}{\#\{\text{tosses}\}}$$

Numerically using the random variables, x^t is 1 if the outcome of toss t is heads and 0 otherwise. Given the sample {heads, heads, heads, tails, heads, tails, tails, heads, heads}, we have $\mathcal{X} = \{1, 1, 1, 0, 1, 0, 0, 1, 1\}$ and the estimate is

$$\hat{p}_o = \frac{\sum_{t=1}^{N} x^t}{N} = \frac{6}{9}$$

3.2 Classification

We discussed credit scoring in section 1.2.2, where we saw that in a bank, according to their past transactions, some customers are low-risk in that they paid back their loans and the bank profited from them and other customers are high-risk in that they defaulted. Analyzing this data, we would like to learn the class "high-risk customer" so that in the future, when there is a new application for a loan, we can check whether that person obeys the class description or not and thus accept or reject the application. Using our knowledge of the application, let us say that we decide that there are two pieces of information that are observable. We observe them because we have reason to believe that they give us an idea about the credibility of a customer. Let us say, for example, we observe customer's yearly income and savings, which we represent by two random variables X_1 and X_2.

It may again be claimed that if we had access to other pieces of knowledge such as the state of economy in full detail and full knowledge about the customer, his or her intention, moral codes, and so forth, whether someone is a low-risk or high-risk customer could have been deterministically calculated. But these are nonobservables and with what we can observe, the credibility of a customer is denoted by a Bernoulli random variable C conditioned on the observables $\boldsymbol{X} = [X_1, X_2]^T$ where $C = 1$ indicates a high-risk customer and $C = 0$ indicates a low-risk customer. Thus if we know $P(C|X_1, X_2)$, when a new application arrives with $X_1 = x_1$ and $X_2 = x_2$, we can

$$\text{choose} \begin{cases} C = 1 & \text{if } P(C = 1|x_1, x_2) > 0.5 \\ C = 0 & \text{otherwise} \end{cases}$$

or equivalently

(3.1) $$\text{choose} \begin{cases} C = 1 & \text{if } P(C = 1|x_1, x_2) > P(C = 0|x_1, x_2) \\ C = 0 & \text{otherwise} \end{cases}$$

The probability of error is $1 - \max(P(C = 1|x_1, x_2), P(C = 0|x_1, x_2))$. This example is similar to the coin tossing example except that here, the Bernoulli random variable C is conditioned on two other observable variables. Let us denote by $\boldsymbol{x}$ the vector of observed variables, $\boldsymbol{x} = [x_1, x_2]^T$. The problem then is to be able to calculate $P(C|\boldsymbol{x})$. Using *Bayes' rule*, it can be written as

BAYES' RULE

(3.2) $$P(C|\boldsymbol{x}) = \frac{P(C)p(\boldsymbol{x}|C)}{p(\boldsymbol{x})}$$

PRIOR PROBABILITY

$P(C = 1)$ is called the *prior probability* that C takes the value 1, which in our example corresponds to the probability that a customer is high-risk, regardless of the $\mathbf{x}$ value—It is the proportion of high-risk customers in our customer base. It is called the prior probability because it is the knowledge we have as to the value of C *before* looking at the observables $\mathbf{x}$, satisfying

$$P(C = 0) + P(C = 1) = 1$$

CLASS LIKELIHOOD

$p(\mathbf{x}|C)$ is called the *class likelihood* and is the conditional probability that an event belonging to C has the associated observation value $\mathbf{x}$. In our case, $p(x_1, x_2|C = 1)$ is the probability that a high-risk customer has his or her $X_1 = x_1$ and $X_2 = x_2$. It is what the data tells us regarding the class.

EVIDENCE

$p(\mathbf{x})$, the *evidence*, is the marginal probability that an observation $\mathbf{x}$ is seen, regardless of whether it is a positive or negative example.

$$p(\mathbf{x}) = \sum_C p(\mathbf{x}, C) = p(\mathbf{x}|C = 1)P(C = 1) + p(\mathbf{x}|C = 0)P(C = 0) \tag{3.3}$$

POSTERIOR PROBABILITY

Combining the prior and what the data tells us using Bayes' rule, we calculate the *posterior probability* of the concept, $P(C|\mathbf{x})$, *after* having seen the observation, $\mathbf{x}$.

$$\text{posterior} = \frac{\text{prior} \times \text{likelihood}}{\text{evidence}}$$

Because of normalization by the evidence, the posteriors sum up to 1:

$$P(C = 0|\mathbf{x}) + P(C = 1|\mathbf{x}) = 1$$

Once we have the posteriors, we decide by using equation 3.1. For now, we assume that we know the prior and likelihoods; in later chapters, we discuss how to estimate $P(C)$ and $p(\mathbf{x}|C)$ from a given training sample.

In the general case, we have K mutually exclusive and exhaustive classes; $C_i, i = 1, \ldots, K$; for example, in optical digit recognition, the input is a bitmap image and there are ten classes. We have the prior probabilities satisfying

$$P(C_i) \geq 0 \text{ and } \sum_{i=1}^{K} P(C_i) = 1 \tag{3.4}$$

$p(\mathbf{x}|C_i)$ is the probability of seeing $\mathbf{x}$ as the input when it is known to belong to class C_i. The posterior probability of class C_i can be calculated as

(3.5) $$P(C_i|\mathbf{x}) = \frac{p(\mathbf{x}|C_i)P(C_i)}{p(\mathbf{x})} = \frac{p(\mathbf{x}|C_i)P(C_i)}{\sum_{k=1}^{K} p(\mathbf{x}|C_k)P(C_k)}$$

BAYES' CLASSIFIER

and for minimum error, the *Bayes' classifier* chooses the class with the highest posterior probability; that is, we

(3.6) $$\text{choose } C_i \text{ if } P(C_i|\mathbf{x}) = \max_k P(C_k|\mathbf{x})$$

3.3 Losses and Risks

It may be the case that decisions are not equally good or costly. A financial institution when making a decision for a loan applicant should take into account the potential gain and loss as well. An accepted low-risk applicant increases profit, while a rejected high-risk applicant decreases loss. The loss for a high-risk applicant erroneously accepted may be different from the potential gain for an erroneously rejected low-risk applicant. The situation is much more critical and far from symmetry in other domains like medical diagnosis or earthquake prediction.

LOSS FUNCTION

EXPECTED RISK

Let us define action α_i as the decision to assign the input to class C_i and λ_{ik} as the *loss* incurred for taking action α_i when the input actually belongs to C_k. Then the *expected risk* for taking action α_i is

(3.7) $$R(\alpha_i|\mathbf{x}) = \sum_{k=1}^{K} \lambda_{ik} P(C_k|\mathbf{x})$$

and we choose the action with minimum risk:

(3.8) $$\text{Choose } \alpha_i \text{ if } R(\alpha_i|\mathbf{x}) = \min_k R(\alpha_k|\mathbf{x})$$

0/1 LOSS

Let us define K actions $\alpha_i, i = 1, \ldots, K$, where α_i is the action of assigning $\mathbf{x}$ to C_i. In the special case of the *0/1 loss* where

(3.9) $$\lambda_{ik} = \begin{cases} 0 & \text{if } i = k \\ 1 & \text{if } i \neq k \end{cases}$$

all correct decisions have no loss and all errors are equally costly. The risk of taking action α_i is

$$R(\alpha_i|\mathbf{x}) = \sum_{k=1}^{K} \lambda_{ik} P(C_k|\mathbf{x})$$

$$= \sum_{k \neq i} P(C_k|\mathbf{x})$$
$$= 1 - P(C_i|\mathbf{x})$$

because $\sum_k P(C_k|\mathbf{x}) = 1$. Thus to minimize risk, we choose the most probable class. In later chapters, for simplicity, we will always assume this case and choose the class with the highest posterior, but note that this is indeed a special case and rarely do applications have a symmetric, 0/1 loss. In the general case, it is a simple postprocessing to go from posteriors to risks and to take the action to minimize the risk.

In some applications, wrong decisions—namely, misclassifications—may have very high cost, and it is generally required that a more complex—for example, manual—decision is made if the automatic system has low certainty of its decision. For example, if we are using an optical digit recognizer to read postal codes on envelopes, wrongly recognizing the code causes the envelope to be sent to a wrong destination.

REJECT

In such a case, we define an additional action of *reject* or *doubt*, α_{K+1}, with $\alpha_i, i = 1, \ldots, K$, being the usual actions of deciding on classes $C_i, i = 1, \ldots, K$ (Duda, Hart, and Stork 2001).

A possible loss function is

$$\lambda_{ik} = \begin{cases} 0 & \text{if } i = k \\ \lambda & \text{if } i = K+1 \\ 1 & \text{otherwise} \end{cases} \tag{3.10}$$

where $0 < \lambda < 1$ is the loss incurred for choosing the $(K + 1)$st action of reject. Then the risk of reject is

$$R(\alpha_{K+1}|\mathbf{x}) = \sum_{k=1}^{K} \lambda P(C_k|\mathbf{x}) = \lambda \tag{3.11}$$

and the risk of choosing class C_i is

$$R(\alpha_i|\mathbf{x}) = \sum_{k \neq i} P(C_k|\mathbf{x}) = 1 - P(C_i|\mathbf{x}) \tag{3.12}$$

The optimal decision rule is to

$$\begin{array}{lll} & \text{choose } C_i & \text{if } R(\alpha_i|\mathbf{x}) < R(\alpha_k|\mathbf{x}) \text{ for all } k \neq i \text{ and} \\ & & R(\alpha_i|\mathbf{x}) < R(\alpha_{K+1}|\mathbf{x}) \\ (3.13) & \text{reject} & \text{if } R(\alpha_{K+1}|\mathbf{x}) < R(\alpha_i|\mathbf{x}), i = 1, \ldots, K \end{array}$$

Given the loss function of equation 3.10, this simplifies to

$$\text{choose } C_i \quad \text{if } P(C_i|\mathbf{x}) > P(C_k|\mathbf{x}) \text{ for all } k \neq i \text{ and } P(C_i|\mathbf{x}) > 1 - \lambda$$

(3.14) $$\text{reject} \quad \text{otherwise}$$

This whole approach is meaningful if $0 < \lambda < 1$: If $\lambda = 0$, we always reject; a reject is as good as a correct classification. If $\lambda \geq 1$, we never reject; a reject is as costly as, or costlier than, an error.

In the case of reject, we are choosing between the automatic decision made by the computer program and human decision that is costlier but assumed to have a higher probability of being correct. Similarly, we can imagine a cascade of multiple automatic decision makers, which as we proceed are costlier but have a higher chance of being correct; we discuss such cascades in chapter 17 where we talk about combining multiple learners.

3.4 Discriminant Functions

DISCRIMINANT FUNCTIONS

Classification can also be seen as implementing a set of *discriminant functions*, $g_i(\mathbf{x}), i = 1, \ldots, K$, such that we

(3.15) $$\text{choose } C_i \text{ if } g_i(\mathbf{x}) = \max_k g_k(\mathbf{x})$$

We can represent the Bayes' classifier in this way by setting

$$g_i(\mathbf{x}) = -R(\alpha_i|\mathbf{x})$$

and the maximum discriminant function corresponds to minimum conditional risk. When we use the 0/1 loss function, we have

$$g_i(\mathbf{x}) = P(C_i|\mathbf{x})$$

or ignoring the common normalizing term, $p(\mathbf{x})$, we can write

$$g_i(\mathbf{x}) = p(\mathbf{x}|C_i)P(C_i)$$

DECISION REGIONS

This divides the feature space into K *decision regions* $\mathcal{R}_1, \ldots, \mathcal{R}_K$, where $\mathcal{R}_i = \{\mathbf{x}|g_i(\mathbf{x}) = \max_k g_k(\mathbf{x})\}$. The regions are separated by *decision boundaries*, surfaces in feature space where ties occur among the largest discriminant functions (see figure 3.1).

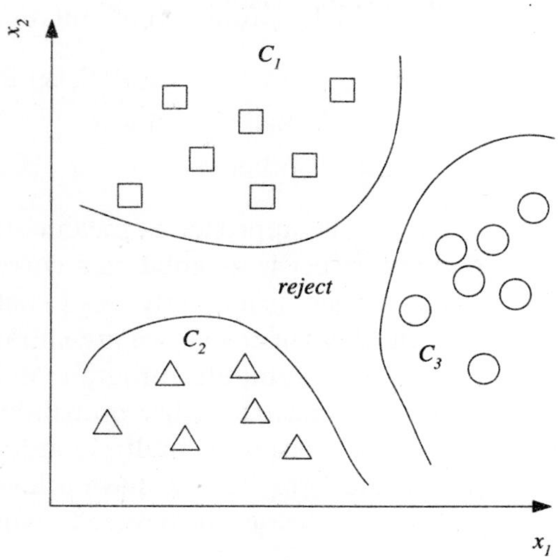

Figure 3.1 Example of decision regions and decision boundaries.

When there are two classes, we can define a single discriminant

$$g(\mathbf{x}) = g_1(\mathbf{x}) - g_2(\mathbf{x})$$

and we

$$\text{choose} \begin{cases} C_1 & \text{if } g(\mathbf{x}) > 0 \\ C_2 & \text{otherwise} \end{cases}$$

An example is a two-class learning problem where the positive examples can be taken as C_1 and the negative examples as C_2. When $K = 2$, the classification system is a *dichotomizer* and for $K \geq 3$, it is a *polychotomizer.*

DICHOTOMIZER
POLYCHOTOMIZER

3.5 Association Rules

ASSOCIATION RULE
BASKET ANALYSIS

An *association rule* is an implication of the form $X \rightarrow Y$ where X is the *antecedent* and Y is the *consequent* of the rule. One example of association rules is in *basket analysis* where we want to find the dependency between two items X and Y. The typical application is in retail where X and Y are items sold, as we discussed in section 1.2.1.

In learning association rules, there are three measures that are frequently calculated:

SUPPORT

- *Support* of the association rule $X \rightarrow Y$:

(3.16)
$$\text{Support}(X, Y) \equiv P(X, Y) = \frac{\#\{\text{customers who bought } X \text{ and } Y\}}{\#\{\text{customers}\}}$$

CONFIDENCE

- *Confidence* of the association rule $X \rightarrow Y$:

(3.17)
$$\begin{aligned} \text{Confidence}(X \rightarrow Y) \equiv P(Y|X) &= \frac{P(X, Y)}{P(X)} \\ &= \frac{\#\{\text{customers who bought } X \text{ and } Y\}}{\#\{\text{customers who bought } X\}} \end{aligned}$$

LIFT
INTEREST

- *Lift*, also known as *interest* of the association rule $X \rightarrow Y$:

(3.18)
$$\text{Lift}(X \rightarrow Y) = \frac{P(X, Y)}{P(X)P(Y)} = \frac{P(Y|X)}{P(Y)}$$

There are other measures as well (Omiecinski 2003), but these three, especially the first two, are the most widely known and used. *Confidence* is the conditional probability, $P(Y|X)$, which is what we normally calculate. To be able to say that the rule holds with enough confidence, this value should be close to 1 and significantly larger than $P(Y)$, the overall probability of people buying Y. We are also interested in maximizing the *support* of the rule, because even if there is a dependency with a strong confidence value, if the number of such customers is small, the rule is worthless. Support shows the statistical significance of the rule, whereas confidence shows the strength of the rule. The minimum support and confidence values are set by the company, and all rules with higher support and confidence are searched for in the database.

If X and Y are independent, then we expect lift to be close to 1; if the ratio differs—if $P(Y|X)$ and $P(Y)$ are different—we expect there to be a dependency between the two items: If the lift is more than 1, we can say that X makes Y more likely, and if the lift is less than 1, having X makes Y less likely.

These formulas can easily be generalized to more than two items. For example, $\{X, Y, Z\}$ is a three-item set, and we may look for a rule, such as $X, Z \rightarrow Y$, that is, $P(Y|X, Z)$. We are interested in finding all such rules having high enough support and confidence and because a sales database

APRIORI ALGORITHM

is generally very large, we want to find them by doing a small number of passes over the database. There is an efficient algorithm, called *Apriori* (Agrawal et al. 1996) that does this, which has two steps: (1) finding frequent itemsets, that is, those which have enough support, and (2) converting them to rules with enough confidence, by splitting the items into two, as items in the antecedent and items in the consequent:

1. To find frequent itemsets quickly (without complete enumeration of all subsets of items), the Apriori algorithm uses the fact that for $\{X, Y, Z\}$ to be frequent (have enough support), all its subsets $\{X, Y\}$, $\{X, Z\}$, and $\{Y, Z\}$ should be frequent as well—adding another item can never increase support. That is, we only need to check for three-item sets all of whose two-item subsets are frequent; or, in other words, if a two-item set is known not to be frequent, all its supersets can be pruned and need not be checked.

   We start by finding the frequent one-item sets and at each step, inductively, from frequent k-item sets, we generate candidate $k+1$-item sets and then do a pass over the data to check if they have enough support. The Apriori algorithm stores the frequent itemsets in a hash table for easy access. Note that the number of candidate itemsets will decrease very rapidly as k increases. If the largest itemset has n items, we need a total of $n + 1$ passes over the data.

2. Once we find the frequent k-item sets, we need to convert them to rules by splitting the k items into two as antecedent and consequent. Just like we do for generating the itemsets, we start by putting a single consequent and $k - 1$ items in the antecedent. Then, for all possible single consequents, we check if the rule has enough confidence and remove it if it does not.

   Note that for the same itemset, there may be multiple rules with different subsets as antecedent and consequent. Then, inductively, we check whether we can move another item from the antecedent to the consequent. Rules with more items in the consequent are more specific and more useful. Here, as in itemset generation, we use the fact that to be able to have rules with two items in the consequent with enough confidence, each of the two rules with single consequent by itself should have enough confidence; that is, we go from one consequent rules to two consequent rules and need not check for all possible two-term consequents (exercise 9).

Keep in mind that a rule $X \rightarrow Y$ need not imply causality but just an association. In a problem, there may also be *hidden variables* whose values are never known through evidence. The advantage of using hidden variables is that the dependency structure can be more easily defined. For example, in basket analysis when we want to find the dependencies among items sold, let us say we know that there is a dependency among "baby food," "diapers," and "milk" in that a customer buying one of these is very much likely to buy the other two. Instead of representing dependencies among these three, we may designate a hidden node, "baby at home," as the hidden cause of the consumption of these three items. Graphical models that we discuss in chapter 14 allow us to represent such hidden variables. When there are hidden nodes, their values are estimated given the values of observed nodes and filled in.

HIDDEN VARIABLES

3.6 Notes

Making decisions under uncertainty has a long history, and over time humanity has looked at all sorts of strange places for evidence to remove the uncertainty: stars, crystal balls, and coffee cups. Reasoning from meaningful evidence using probability theory is only a few hundred years old; see Newman 1988 for the history of probability and statistics and some very early articles by Laplace, Bernoulli, and others who have founded the theory.

Russell and Norvig (2009) give an excellent discussion of utility theory and the value of information, also discussing the assignment of utilities in monetary terms. Shafer and Pearl 1990 is an early collection of articles on reasoning under uncertainty.

Association rules are successfully used in many data mining applications, and we see such rules on many web sites that recommend books, movies, music, and so on. The algorithm is very simple and its efficient implementation on very large databases is critical (Zhang and Zhang 2002; Li 2006). Later, we see in chapter 14 how to generalize from association rules to concepts that need not be binary and where associations can be of different types, also allowing hidden variables.

RECOMMENDATION SYSTEMS

Recommendation systems are fast becoming one of the major application areas of machine learning. Many retail industries are interested in predicting future customer behavior using past sales data. We can visualize the data as a matrix where rows are the customers, columns are the items, and entries are the amounts purchased or maybe customer ratings; typically this matrix is very big and also very sparse—most customers have purchased only a very small percentage of the possible items. Though this matrix is very large, it has small rank. This is because there is lot of dependency in the data. People do not shop randomly. People with babies, for example, buy similar things. Certain products are always bought together, or never at the same time. It is these types of regularities, a small number of hidden factors, that makes the matrix low rank. When we talk about dimensionality reduction in chapter 6, we see how we can extract such hidden factors, or dependencies, from data.

3.7 Exercises

1. Assume a disease so rare that it is seen in only one person out of every million. Assume also that we have a test that is effective in that if a person has the disease, there is a 99 percent chance that the test result will be positive; however, the test is not perfect, and there is a one in a thousand chance that the test result will be positive on a healthy person. Assume that a new patient arrives and the test result is positive. What is the probability that the patient has the disease ?

   SOLUTION: Let us represent disease by d and test result by t. We are given the following: $P(d=1)=10^{-6}, P(t=1|d=1)=0.99, P(t=1|d=0)=10^{-3}$. We are asked $P(d=1|t=1)$.

   We use Bayes' rule:

$$
\begin{aligned}
P(d=1|t=1) &= \frac{P(t=1|d=1)P(d=1)}{P(t=1)} \\
&= \frac{P(t=1|d=1)P(d=1)}{P(t=1|d=1)P(d=1)+P(t=1|d=0)P(d=0)} \\
&= \frac{0.99\cdot 10^{-6}}{0.99\cdot 10^{-6}+10^{-3}\cdot(1-10^{-6})} = 0.00098902
\end{aligned}
$$

   That is, knowing that the test result is positive increased the probability of disease from one in a million to one in a thousand.

LIKELIHOOD RATIO

2. In a two-class problem, the *likelihood ratio* is

$$\frac{p(\mathbf{x}|C_1)}{p(\mathbf{x}|C_2)}$$

   Write the discriminant function in terms of the likelihood ratio.

   SOLUTION: We can define a discriminant function as

$$g(x)=\frac{P(C_1|x)}{P(C_2|x)} \text{ and choose } \begin{cases} C_1 & \text{if } g(x)>1 \\ C_2 & \text{otherwise} \end{cases}$$

We can write the discriminant as the product of the likelihood ratio and the ratio of priors:

$$g(x) = \frac{p(x|C_1)\,P(C_1)}{p(x|C_2)\,P(C_2)}$$

If the priors are equal, the discriminant is the likelihood ratio.

LOG ODDS

3. In a two-class problem, the *log odds* is defined as

$$\log \frac{P(C_1|\mathbf{x})}{P(C_2|\mathbf{x})}$$

Write the discriminant function in terms of the log odds.

SOLUTION: We define a discriminant function as

$$g(x) = \log \frac{P(C_1|x)}{P(C_2|x)} \text{ and choose } \begin{cases} C_1 & \text{if } g(x) > 0 \\ C_2 & \text{otherwise} \end{cases}$$

Log odds is the sum of log likelihood ratio and log of prior ratio:

$$g(x) = \log \frac{p(x|C_1)}{p(x|C_2)} + \log \frac{P(C_1)}{P(C_2)}$$

If the priors are equal, the discriminant is the log likelihood ratio.

4. In a two-class, two-action problem, if the loss function is $\lambda_{11} = \lambda_{22} = 0$, $\lambda_{12} = 10$, and $\lambda_{21} = 5$, write the optimal decision rule. How does the rule change if we add a third action of reject with $\lambda = 1$?

SOLUTION: The loss table is as follows:

	Truth	
Action	C_1	C_2
α_1: Choose C_1	0	10
α_2: Choose C_2	5	0

Let us calculate the expected risks of the two actions:

$$\begin{aligned} R(\alpha_1|x) &= 0 \cdot P(C_1|x) + 10 \cdot P(C_2|x) = 10 \cdot (1 - P(C_1|x)) \\ R(\alpha_2|x) &= 5 \cdot P(C_1|x) + 0 \cdot P(C_2|x) = 5 \cdot P(C_1|x) \end{aligned}$$

We choose α_1 if

$$\begin{aligned} R(\alpha_1|x) &< R(\alpha_2|x) \\ 10 \cdot (1 - P(C_1|x)) &< 5 \cdot P(C_1|x) \\ P(C_1|x) &> 2/3 \end{aligned}$$

If the two misclassifications were equally costly, the decision threshold would be at 1/2 but because the cost of wrongly choosing C_1 is higher, we want to choose C_1 only when we are really certain; see figure 3.2a and b.

If we add a reject option with a cost of 1, the loss table now becomes

	Truth	
Action	C_1	C_2
α_1: Choose C_1	0	10
α_2: Choose C_2	5	0
α_r: Reject	1	1

Let us calculate the expected risks of the three actions:

$$R(\alpha_1|x) = 0 \cdot P(C_1|x) + 10 \cdot P(C_2|x) = 10 \cdot (1 - P(C_1|x))$$
$$R(\alpha_2|x) = 5 \cdot P(C_1|x) + 0 \cdot P(C_2|x) = 5 \cdot P(C_1|x)$$
$$R(\alpha_r|x) = 1$$

We choose α_1 if

$R(\alpha_1|x) < 1 \Rightarrow P(C_1|x) > 9/10$

We choose α_2 if

$R(\alpha_2|x) < 1 \Rightarrow P(C_1|x) < 1/5$, or equivalently if $P(C_1|x) > 4/5$

We reject otherwise, that is, if $1/5 < P(C_1|x) < 9/10$; see figure 3.2c.

5. Propose a three-level cascade where when one level rejects, the next one is used as in equation 3.10. How can we fix the λ on different levels?
6. Somebody tosses a fair coin and if the result is heads, you get nothing; otherwise, you get \$5. How much would you pay to play this game? What if the win is \$500 instead of \$5?
7. Given the following data of transactions at a shop, calculate the support and confidence values of milk → bananas, bananas → milk, milk → chocolate, and chocolate → milk.

Transaction	Items in basket
1	milk, bananas, chocolate
2	milk, chocolate
3	milk, bananas
4	chocolate
5	chocolate
6	milk, chocolate

SOLUTION:

milk → bananas : Support = 2/6, Confidence = 2/4
bananas → milk : Support = 2/6, Confidence = 2/2
milk → chocolate : Support = 3/6, Confidence = 3/4
chocolate → milk : Support = 3/6, Confidence = 3/5

Though only half of the people who buy milk buy bananas too, anyone who buys bananas also buys milk.

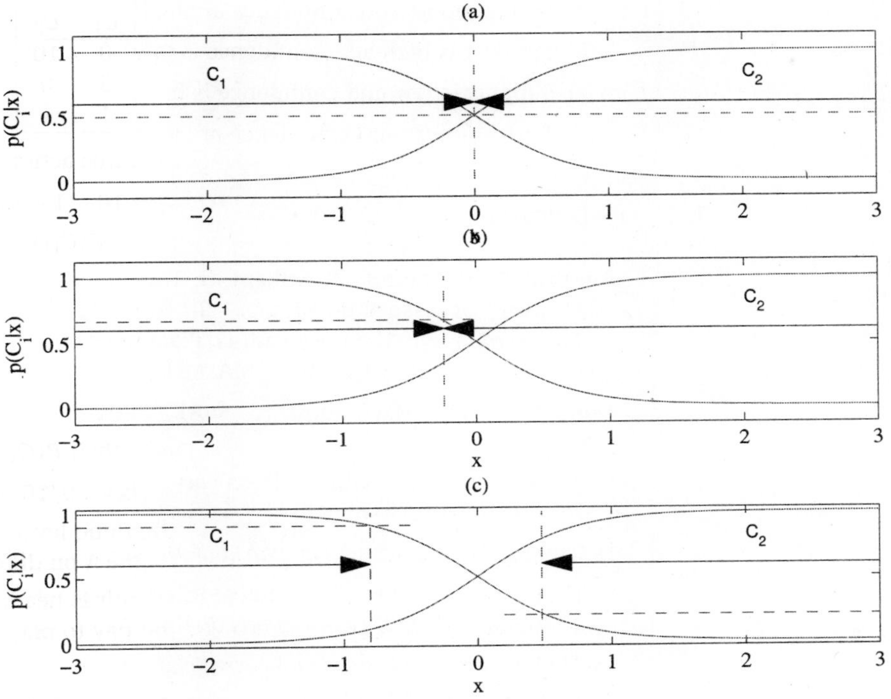

Figure 3.2 The boundary changes as the misclassification losses change. (a) The boundary is where the two posteriors are equal when both misclassifications are equally costly. (b) When the losses are not symmetric, the boundary shifts toward the class that incurs higher risk when misclassified. (c) When there is the option of reject, a region around the boundary is the region of reject.

8. Generalize the confidence and support formulas for basket analysis to calculate k-dependencies, namely, $P(Y|X_1, \ldots, X_k)$.
9. Show that as we move an item from the consequent to the antecedent, confidence can never increase: confidence$(ABC \rightarrow D) \geq$ confidence$(AB \rightarrow CD)$.
10. Associated with each item sold in basket analysis, if we also have a number indicating how much the customer enjoyed the product, for example, on a scale of 0 to 10, how can you use this extra information to calculate which item to propose to a customer?
11. Show example transaction data where for the rule $X \rightarrow Y$:

(a) Both support and confidence are high.

(b) Support is high and confidence is low.

(c) Support is low and confidence is high.

(d) Both support and confidence are low.

3.8 References

Agrawal, R., H. Mannila, R. Srikant, H. Toivonen, and A. Verkamo. 1996. "Fast Discovery of Association Rules." In *Advances in Knowledge Discovery and Data Mining*, ed. U. M. Fayyad, G. Piatetsky-Shapiro, P. Smyth, and R. Uthurusamy, 307–328. Cambridge, MA: MIT Press.

Duda, R. O., P. E. Hart, and D. G. Stork. 2001. *Pattern Classification*, 2nd ed. New York: Wiley.

Li, J. 2006. "On Optimal Rule Discovery." *IEEE Transactions on Knowledge and Data Discovery* 18:460–471.

Newman, J. R., ed. 1988. *The World of Mathematics*. Redmond, WA: Tempus.

Omiecinski, E. R. 2003. "Alternative Interest Measures for Mining Associations in Databases." *IEEE Transactions on Knowledge and Data Discovery* 15:57–69.

Russell, S., and P. Norvig. 2009. *Artificial Intelligence: A Modern Approach*, 3rd ed. New York: Prentice Hall.

Shafer, G., and J. Pearl, eds. 1990. *Readings in Uncertain Reasoning*. San Mateo, CA: Morgan Kaufmann.

Zhang, C., and S. Zhang. 2002. *Association Rule Mining: Models and Algorithms*. New York: Springer.

4 *Parametric Methods*

Having discussed how to make optimal decisions when the uncertainty is modeled using probabilities, we now see how we can estimate these probabilities from a given training set. We start with the parametric approach for classification and regression; we discuss the semiparametric and nonparametric approaches in later chapters. We introduce bias/variance dilemma and model selection methods for trading off model complexity and empirical error.

4.1 Introduction

A STATISTIC is any value that is calculated from a given sample. In statistical inference, we make a decision using the information provided by a sample. Our first approach is parametric where we assume that the sample is drawn from some distribution that obeys a known model, for example, Gaussian. The advantage of the parametric approach is that the model is defined up to a small number of parameters—for example, mean, variance—the *sufficient statistics* of the distribution. Once those parameters are estimated from the sample, the whole distribution is known. We estimate the parameters of the distribution from the given sample, plug in these estimates to the assumed model, and get an estimated distribution, which we then use to make a decision. The method we use to estimate the parameters of a distribution is maximum likelihood estimation. We also introduce Bayesian estimation, which we continue to discuss in chapter 16.

We start with *density estimation*, which is the general case of estimating $p(x)$. We use this for *classification* where the estimated densities are the class densities, $p(x|C_i)$, and priors, $P(C_i)$, to be able to calculate the posteriors, $P(C_i|x)$, and make our decision. We then discuss *regression* where the estimated density is $p(y|x)$. In this chapter, x is one-dimensional and thus the densities are univariate. We generalize to the multivariate case in chapter 5.

4.2 Maximum Likelihood Estimation

Let us say we have an independent and identically distributed (iid) sample $\mathcal{X} = \{x^t\}_{t=1}^N$. We assume that x^t are instances drawn from some known probability density family, $p(x|\theta)$, defined up to parameters, θ:

$$x^t \sim p(x|\theta)$$

LIKELIHOOD

We want to find θ that makes sampling x^t from $p(x|\theta)$ as likely as possible. Because x^t are independent, the *likelihood* of parameter θ given sample $\mathcal{X}$ is the product of the likelihoods of the individual points:

$$l(\theta|\mathcal{X}) \equiv p(\mathcal{X}|\theta) = \prod_{t=1}^{N} p(x^t|\theta) \tag{4.1}$$

MAXIMUM LIKELIHOOD ESTIMATION

In *maximum likelihood estimation*, we are interested in finding θ that makes $\mathcal{X}$ the most likely to be drawn. We thus search for θ that maximizes the likelihood, which we denote by $l(\theta|\mathcal{X})$. We can maximize the log of the likelihood without changing the value where it takes its maximum. $\log(\cdot)$ converts the product into a sum and leads to further computational simplification when certain densities are assumed, for example, containing exponents. The *log likelihood* is defined as

LOG LIKELIHOOD

$$\mathcal{L}(\theta|\mathcal{X}) \equiv \log l(\theta|\mathcal{X}) = \sum_{t=1}^{N} \log p(x^t|\theta) \tag{4.2}$$

Let us now see some distributions that arise in the applications we are interested in. If we have a two-class problem, the distribution we use is *Bernoulli*. When there are $K > 2$ classes, its generalization is the *multinomial*. *Gaussian* (*normal*) density is the one most frequently used for modeling class-conditional input densities with numeric input. For these three distributions, we discuss the maximum likelihood estimators (MLE) of their parameters.

4.2.1 Bernoulli Density

In a Bernoulli distribution, there are two outcomes: An event occurs or it does not; for example, an instance is a positive example of the class, or it is not. The event occurs and the Bernoulli random variable X takes the value 1 with probability p, and the nonoccurrence of the event has probability $1 - p$ and this is denoted by X taking the value 0. This is written as

$$P(x) = p^x(1-p)^{1-x}, x \in \{0, 1\} \tag{4.3}$$

The expected value and variance can be calculated as

$$\begin{aligned} E[X] &= \sum_x x p(x) = 1 \cdot p + 0 \cdot (1-p) = p \\ \text{Var}(X) &= \sum_x (x - E[X])^2 p(x) = p(1-p) \end{aligned}$$

p is the only parameter and given an iid sample $\mathcal{X} = \{x^t\}_{t=1}^N$, where $x^t \in \{0, 1\}$, we want to calculate its estimator, $\hat{p}$. The log likelihood is

$$\begin{aligned} \mathcal{L}(p|\mathcal{X}) &= \log \prod_{t=1}^{N} p^{(x^t)}(1-p)^{(1-x^t)} \\ &= \sum_t x^t \log p + \left(N - \sum_t x^t\right) \log(1-p) \end{aligned}$$

$\hat{p}$ that maximizes the log likelihood can be found by solving for $d\mathcal{L}/dp = 0$. The hat (circumflex) denotes that it is an estimate.

$$\hat{p} = \frac{\sum_t x^t}{N} \tag{4.4}$$

The estimate for p is the ratio of the number of occurrences of the event to the number of experiments. Remembering that if X is Bernoulli with p, $E[X] = p$, and, as expected, the maximum likelihood estimator of the mean is the sample average.

Note that the estimate is a function of the sample and is another random variable; we can talk about the distribution of $\hat{p}_i$ given different $\mathcal{X}_i$ sampled from the same $p(x)$. For example, the variance of the distribution of $\hat{p}_i$ is expected to decrease as N increases; as the samples get bigger, they (and hence their averages) get more similar.

4.2.2 Multinomial Density

Consider the generalization of Bernoulli where instead of two states, the outcome of a random event is one of K mutually exclusive and exhaustive states, for example, classes, each of which has a probability of occurring p_i with $\sum_{i=1}^{K} p_i = 1$. Let $x_1, x_2, \ldots, x_K$ are the indicator variables where x_i is 1 if the outcome is state i and 0 otherwise.

(4.5) $$P(x_1, x_2, \ldots, x_K) = \prod_{i=1}^{K} p_i^{x_i}$$

Let us say we do N such independent experiments with outcomes $\mathcal{X} = \{\boldsymbol{x}^t\}_{t=1}^N$ where

$$x_i^t = \begin{cases} 1 & \text{if experiment } t \text{ chooses state } i \\ 0 & \text{otherwise} \end{cases}$$

with $\sum_i x_i^t = 1$. The MLE of p_i is

(4.6) $$\hat{p}_i = \frac{\sum_t x_i^t}{N}$$

The estimate for the probability of state i is the ratio of experiments with outcome of state i to the total number of experiments. There are two ways one can get this: If x_i are 0/1, then they can be thought of as K separate Bernoulli experiments. Or, one can explicitly write the log likelihood and find p_i that maximize it (subject to the condition that $\sum_i p_i = 1$).

4.2.3 Gaussian (Normal) Density

X is Gaussian (normal) distributed with mean $E[X] \equiv \mu$ and variance $\text{Var}(X) \equiv \sigma^2$, denoted as $\mathcal{N}(\mu, \sigma^2)$, if its density function is

(4.7) $$p(x) = \frac{1}{\sqrt{2\pi}\sigma} \exp\left[-\frac{(x-\mu)^2}{2\sigma^2}\right], -\infty < x < \infty$$

Given a sample $\mathcal{X} = \{x^t\}_{t=1}^N$ with $x^t \sim \mathcal{N}(\mu, \sigma^2)$, the log likelihood is

$$\mathcal{L}(\mu, \sigma | \mathcal{X}) = -\frac{N}{2}\log(2\pi) - N\log\sigma - \frac{\sum_t (x^t - \mu)^2}{2\sigma^2}$$

The MLE that we find by taking the partial derivatives of the log likelihood and setting them equal to 0 are

(4.8) $$m = \frac{\sum_t x^t}{N}$$

$$s^2 = \frac{\sum_t (x^t - m)^2}{N}$$

We follow the usual convention and use Greek letters for the population parameters and Roman letters for their estimates from the sample. Sometimes, the hat is also used to denote the estimator, for example, $\hat{\mu}$.

4.3 Evaluating an Estimator: Bias and Variance

Let $\mathcal{X}$ be a sample from a population specified up to a parameter θ, and let $d = d(\mathcal{X})$ be an estimator of θ. To evaluate the quality of this estimator, we can measure how much it is different from θ, that is, $(d(\mathcal{X}) - \theta)^2$. But since it is a random variable (it depends on the sample), we need to average this over possible $\mathcal{X}$ and consider $r(d, \theta)$, the *mean square error* of the estimator d defined as

MEAN SQUARE ERROR

$$r(d, \theta) = E[(d(\mathcal{X}) - \theta)^2] \tag{4.9}$$

BIAS

The *bias* of an estimator is given as

$$b_\theta(d) = E[d(\mathcal{X})] - \theta \tag{4.10}$$

UNBIASED ESTIMATOR

If $b_\theta(d) = 0$ for all θ values, then we say that d is an *unbiased estimator* of θ. For example, with x^t drawn from some density with mean μ, the sample average, m, is an unbiased estimator of the mean, μ, because

$$E[m] = E\left[\frac{\sum_t x^t}{N}\right] = \frac{1}{N}\sum_t E[x^t] = \frac{N\mu}{N} = \mu$$

This means that though on a particular sample, m may be different from μ, if we take many such samples, $\mathcal{X}_i$, and estimate many $m_i = m(\mathcal{X}_i)$, *their* average will get close to μ as the number of such samples increases. m is also a *consistent* estimator, that is, $\text{Var}(m) \to 0$ as $N \to \infty$.

$$\text{Var}(m) = \text{Var}\left(\frac{\sum_t x^t}{N}\right) = \frac{1}{N^2}\sum_t \text{Var}(x^t) = \frac{N\sigma^2}{N^2} = \frac{\sigma^2}{N}$$

As N, the number of points in the sample, gets larger, m deviates less from μ. Let us now check, s^2, the MLE of σ^2:

$$\begin{aligned} s^2 &= \frac{\sum_t (x^t - m)^2}{N} = \frac{\sum_t (x^t)^2 - Nm^2}{N} \\ E[s^2] &= \frac{\sum_t E[(x^t)^2] - N \cdot E[m^2]}{N} \end{aligned}$$

Given that $\text{Var}(X) = E[X^2] - E[X]^2$, we get $E[X^2] = \text{Var}(X) + E[X]^2$, and we can write

$$E[(x^t)^2] = \sigma^2 + \mu^2 \text{ and } E[m^2] = \sigma^2/N + \mu^2$$

Then, plugging these in, we get

$$E[s^2] = \frac{N(\sigma^2 + \mu^2) - N(\sigma^2/N + \mu^2)}{N} = \left(\frac{N-1}{N}\right)\sigma^2 \neq \sigma^2$$

which shows that s^2 is a biased estimator of σ^2. $(N/(N-1))s^2$ is an unbiased estimator. However when N is large, the difference is negligible. This is an example of an *asymptotically unbiased estimator* whose bias goes to 0 as N goes to infinity.

The mean square error can be rewritten as follows—d is short for $d(\mathcal{X})$:

$$\begin{aligned}
r(d,\theta) &= E\left[(d-\theta)^2\right] \\
&= E\left[(d-E[d]+E[d]-\theta)^2\right] \\
&= E\left[(d-E[d])^2 + (E[d]-\theta)^2 + 2(E[d]-\theta)(d-E[d])\right] \\
&= E\left[(d-E[d])^2\right] + E\left[(E[d]-\theta)^2\right] + 2E\left[(E[d]-\theta)(d-E[d])\right] \\
&= E\left[(d-E[d])^2\right] + (E[d]-\theta)^2 + 2(E[d]-\theta)E[d-E[d]] \\
&= \underbrace{E\left[(d-E[d])^2\right]}_{variance} + \underbrace{(E[d]-\theta)^2}_{bias^2} \qquad (4.11)
\end{aligned}$$

The two equalities follow because $E[d]$ is a constant and therefore $E[d]-\theta$ also is a constant, and because $E[d-E[d]] = E[d]-E[d] = 0$. In equation 4.11, the first term is the *variance* that measures how much, on average, d_i vary around the expected value (going from one dataset to another), and the second term is the *bias* that measures how much the expected value varies from the correct value θ (figure 4.1). We then write error as the sum of these two terms, the variance and the square of the bias:

VARIANCE

$$r(d,\theta) = \text{Var}(d) + (b_\theta(d))^2 \qquad (4.12)$$

4.4 The Bayes' Estimator

Sometimes, before looking at a sample, we (or experts of the application) may have some *prior* information on the possible value range that a parameter, θ, may take. This information is quite useful and should be used, especially when the sample is small. The prior information does not tell us exactly what the parameter value is (otherwise we would not

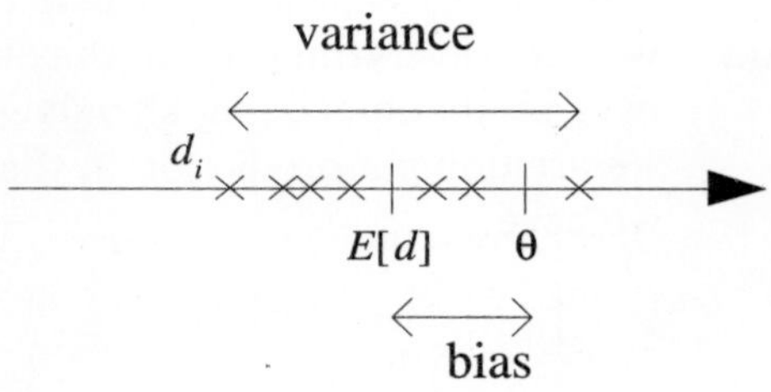

Figure 4.1 θ is the parameter to be estimated. d_i are several estimates (denoted by '×') over different samples $\mathcal{X}_i$. Bias is the difference between the expected value of d and θ. Variance is how much d_i are scattered around the expected value. We would like both to be small.

need the sample), and we model this uncertainty by viewing θ as a random variable and by defining a prior density for it, $p(\theta)$. For example, let us say we are told that θ is approximately normal and with 90 percent confidence, θ lies between 5 and 9, symmetrically around 7. Then we can write $p(\theta)$ to be normal with mean 7 and because

$$\begin{aligned} P\{-1.64 < \frac{\theta - \mu}{\sigma} < 1.64\} &= 0.9 \\ P\{\mu - 1.64\sigma < \theta < \mu + 1.64\sigma\} &= 0.9 \end{aligned}$$

we take $1.64\sigma = 2$ and use $\sigma = 2/1.64$. We can thus assume $p(\theta) \sim \mathcal{N}(7, (2/1.64)^2)$.

PRIOR DENSITY

The *prior density*, $p(\theta)$, tells us the likely values that θ may take *before* looking at the sample. We combine this with what the sample data tells us, namely, the likelihood density, $p(\mathcal{X}|\theta)$, using Bayes' rule, and get the

POSTERIOR DENSITY

posterior density of θ, which tells us the likely θ values *after* looking at the sample:

$$p(\theta|\mathcal{X}) = \frac{p(\mathcal{X}|\theta)p(\theta)}{p(\mathcal{X})} = \frac{p(\mathcal{X}|\theta)p(\theta)}{\int p(\mathcal{X}|\theta')p(\theta')d\theta'} \tag{4.13}$$

For estimating the density at x, we have

$$\begin{aligned} p(x|\mathcal{X}) &= \int p(x, \theta|\mathcal{X})d\theta \\ &= \int p(x|\theta, \mathcal{X})p(\theta|\mathcal{X})d\theta \\ &= \int p(x|\theta)p(\theta|\mathcal{X})d\theta \end{aligned}$$

$p(x|\theta, \mathcal{X}) = p(x|\theta)$ because once we know θ, the sufficient statistics, we know everything about the distribution. Thus we are taking an average over predictions using all values of θ, weighted by their probabilities. If we are doing a prediction in the form, $y = g(x|\theta)$, as in regression, then we have

$$y = \int g(x|\theta)p(\theta|\mathcal{X})d\theta$$

Evaluating the integrals may be quite difficult, except in cases where the posterior has a nice form. When the full integration is not feasible, we reduce it to a single point. If we can assume that $p(\theta|\mathcal{X})$ has a narrow peak around its mode, then using the *maximum a posteriori* (MAP) *estimate* will make the calculation easier:

MAXIMUM A POSTERIORI ESTIMATE

$$\theta_{MAP} = \arg\max_{\theta} p(\theta|\mathcal{X}) \tag{4.14}$$

thus replacing a whole density with a single point, getting rid of the integral and using as

$$\begin{aligned} p(x|\mathcal{X}) &= p(x|\theta_{MAP}) \\ y_{MAP} &= g(x|\theta_{MAP}) \end{aligned}$$

If we have no prior reason to favor some values of θ, then the prior density is flat and the posterior will have the same form as the likelihood, $p(\mathcal{X}|\theta)$, and the MAP estimate will be equivalent to the maximum likelihood estimate (section 4.2) where we have

$$\theta_{ML} = \arg\max_{\theta} p(\mathcal{X}|\theta) \tag{4.15}$$

BAYES' ESTIMATOR

Another possibility is the *Bayes' estimator*, which is defined as the expected value of the posterior density

$$\theta_{Bayes} = E[\theta|\mathcal{X}] = \int \theta p(\theta|\mathcal{X})d\theta \tag{4.16}$$

The reason for taking the expected value is that the best estimate of a random variable is its mean. Let us say θ is the variable we want to predict with $E[\theta] = \mu$. It can be shown that if c, a constant value, is our estimate of θ, then

$$\begin{aligned} E[(\theta - c)^2] &= E[(\theta - \mu + \mu - c)^2] \\ &= E[(\theta - \mu)^2] + (\mu - c)^2 \end{aligned} \tag{4.17}$$

which is minimum if c is taken as μ. In the case of a normal density, the mode is the expected value and if $p(\theta|\mathcal{X})$ is normal, then $\theta_{Bayes} = \theta_{MAP}$.

As an example, let us suppose $x^t \sim \mathcal{N}(\theta, \sigma^2)$ and $\theta \sim \mathcal{N}(\mu_0, \sigma_0^2)$, where μ_0, σ_0^2, and σ^2 are known:

$$\begin{aligned} p(\mathcal{X}|\theta) &= \frac{1}{(2\pi)^{N/2}\sigma^N} \exp\left[-\frac{\sum_t (x^t - \theta)^2}{2\sigma^2}\right] \\ p(\theta) &= \frac{1}{\sqrt{2\pi}\sigma_0} \exp\left[-\frac{(\theta - \mu_0)^2}{2\sigma_0^2}\right] \end{aligned}$$

It can be shown that $p(\theta|\mathcal{X})$ is normal with

(4.18) $$E[\theta|\mathcal{X}] = \frac{N/\sigma^2}{N/\sigma^2 + 1/\sigma_0^2} m + \frac{1/\sigma_0^2}{N/\sigma^2 + 1/\sigma_0^2} \mu_0$$

Thus the Bayes' estimator is a weighted average of the prior mean μ_0 and the sample mean m, with weights being inversely proportional to their variances. As the sample size N increases, the Bayes' estimator gets closer to the sample average, using more the information provided by the sample. When σ_0^2 is small, that is, when we have little prior uncertainty regarding the correct value of θ, or when N is small, our prior guess μ_0 has a higher effect.

Note that both MAP and Bayes' estimators reduce the whole posterior density to a single point and lose information unless the posterior is unimodal and makes a narrow peak around these points. With computation getting cheaper, we can use a Monte Carlo approach that generates samples from the posterior density (Andrieu et al. 2003). There also are approximation methods one can use to evaluate the full integral. We are going to discuss Bayesian estimation in more detail in chapter 16.

4.5 Parametric Classification

We saw in chapter 3 that using the Bayes' rule, we can write the posterior probability of class C_i as

(4.19) $$P(C_i|x) = \frac{p(x|C_i)P(C_i)}{p(x)} = \frac{p(x|C_i)P(C_i)}{\sum_{k=1}^{K} p(x|C_k)P(C_k)}$$

and use the discriminant function

$$g_i(x) = p(x|C_i)P(C_i)$$

or equivalently

$$g_i(x) = \log p(x|C_i) + \log P(C_i) \tag{4.20}$$

If we can assume that $p(x|C_i)$ are Gaussian

$$p(x|C_i) = \frac{1}{\sqrt{2\pi}\sigma_i} \exp\left[-\frac{(x-\mu_i)^2}{2\sigma_i^2}\right] \tag{4.21}$$

equation 4.20 becomes

$$g_i(x) = -\frac{1}{2}\log 2\pi - \log \sigma_i - \frac{(x-\mu_i)^2}{2\sigma_i^2} + \log P(C_i) \tag{4.22}$$

Let us see an example: Assume we are a car company selling K different cars, and for simplicity, let us say that the sole factor that affects a customer's choice is his or her yearly income, which we denote by x. Then $P(C_i)$ is the proportion of customers who buy car type i. If the yearly income distributions of such customers can be approximated with a Gaussian, then $p(x|C_i)$, the probability that a customer who bought car type i has income x, can be taken $\mathcal{N}(\mu_i, \sigma_i^2)$, where μ_i is the mean income of such customers and σ_i^2 is their income variance.

When we do not know $P(C_i)$ and $p(x|C_i)$, we estimate them from a sample and plug in their estimates to get the estimate for the discriminant function. We are given a sample

$$\mathcal{X} = \{x^t, \boldsymbol{r}^t\}_{t=1}^N \tag{4.23}$$

where $x \in \Re$ is one-dimensional and $\boldsymbol{r} \in \{0,1\}^K$ such that

$$r_i^t = \begin{cases} 1 & \text{if } \boldsymbol{x}^t \in C_i \\ 0 & \text{if } \boldsymbol{x}^t \in C_k, k \neq i \end{cases} \tag{4.24}$$

For each class separately, the estimates for the means and variances are (relying on equation 4.8)

$$m_i = \frac{\sum_t x^t r_i^t}{\sum_t r_i^t} \tag{4.25}$$

$$s_i^2 = \frac{\sum_t (x^t - m_i)^2 r_i^t}{\sum_t r_i^t} \tag{4.26}$$

and the estimates for the priors are (relying on equation 4.6)

$$\hat{P}(C_i) = \frac{\sum_t r_i^t}{N} \tag{4.27}$$

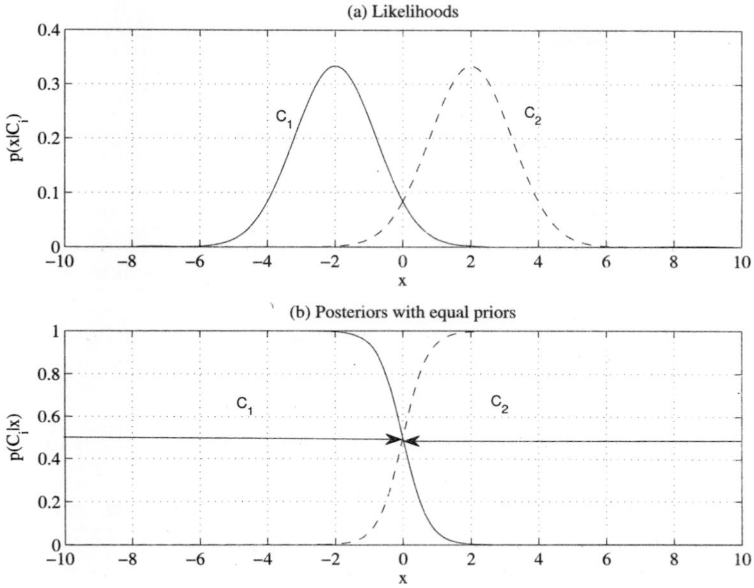

Figure 4.2 (a) Likelihood functions and (b) posteriors with equal priors for two classes when the input is one-dimensional. Variances are equal and the posteriors intersect at one point, which is the threshold of decision.

Plugging these estimates into equation 4.22, we get

(4.28) $$g_i(x) = -\frac{1}{2}\log 2\pi - \log s_i - \frac{(x-m_i)^2}{2s_i^2} + \log \hat{P}(C_i)$$

The first term is a constant and can be dropped because it is common in all $g_i(x)$. If the priors are equal, the last term can also be dropped. If we can further assume that variances are equal, we can write

(4.29) $$g_i(x) = -(x-m_i)^2$$

and thus we assign x to the class with the nearest mean:

$$\text{Choose } C_i \text{ if } |x-m_i| = \min_k |x-m_k|$$

With two adjacent classes, the midpoint between the two means is the threshold of decision (see figure 4.2).

$$g_1(x) = g_2(x)$$

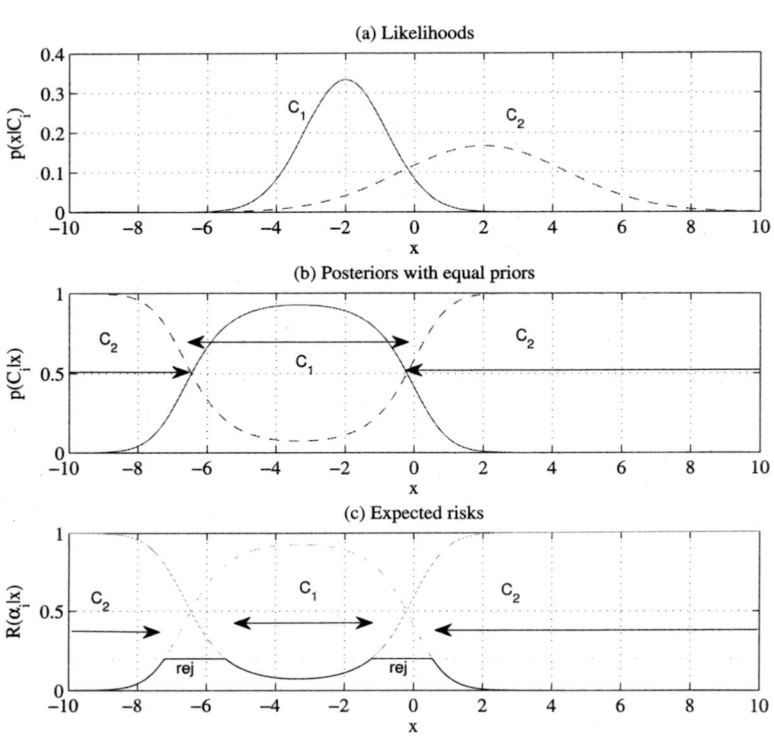

Figure 4.3 (a) Likelihood functions and (b) posteriors with equal priors for two classes when the input is one-dimensional. Variances are unequal and the posteriors intersect at two points. In (c), the expected risks are shown for the two classes and for reject with $\lambda = 0.2$ (section 3.3).

$$
\begin{aligned}
(x - m_1)^2 &= (x - m_2)^2 \\
x &= \frac{m_1 + m_2}{2}
\end{aligned}
$$

When the variances are different, there are two thresholds (see figure 4.3), which can be calculated easily (exercise 4). If the priors are different, this has the effect of moving the threshold of decision toward the mean of the less likely class.

Here we use the maximum likelihood estimators for the parameters but if we have some prior information about them, for example, for the means, we can use a Bayesian estimate of $p(x|C_i)$ with prior on μ_i.

One note of caution is necessary here: When x is continuous, we should not immediately rush to use Gaussian densities for $p(x|C_i)$. The classification algorithm—that is, the threshold points—will be wrong if the densities are not Gaussian. In statistical literature, tests exist to check for normality, and such a test should be used before assuming normality. In the case of one-dimensional data, the easiest test is to plot the histogram and to check visually whether the density is bell-shaped, namely, unimodal and symmetric around the center.

This is the *likelihood-based approach* to classification where we use data to estimate the densities separately, calculate posterior densities using Bayes' rule, and then get the discriminant. In later chapters, we discuss the *discriminant-based approach* where we bypass the estimation of densities and directly estimate the discriminants.

4.6 Regression

In regression, we would like to write the numeric output, called the *dependent variable*, as a function of the input, called the *independent variable*. We assume that the numeric output is the sum of a deterministic function of the input and random noise:

$$r = f(x) + \epsilon$$

where $f(x)$ is the unknown function, which we would like to approximate by our estimator, $g(x|\theta)$, defined up to a set of parameters θ. If we assume that ϵ is zero mean Gaussian with constant variance σ^2, namely, $\epsilon \sim \mathcal{N}(0, \sigma^2)$, and placing our estimator $g(\cdot)$ in place of the unknown function $f(\cdot)$, we have (figure 4.4)

$$p(r|x) \sim \mathcal{N}(g(x|\theta), \sigma^2) \quad (4.30)$$

We again use maximum likelihood to learn the parameters θ. The pairs (x^t, r^t) in the training set are drawn from an unknown joint probability density $p(x, r)$, which we can write as

$$p(x, r) = p(r|x)p(x)$$

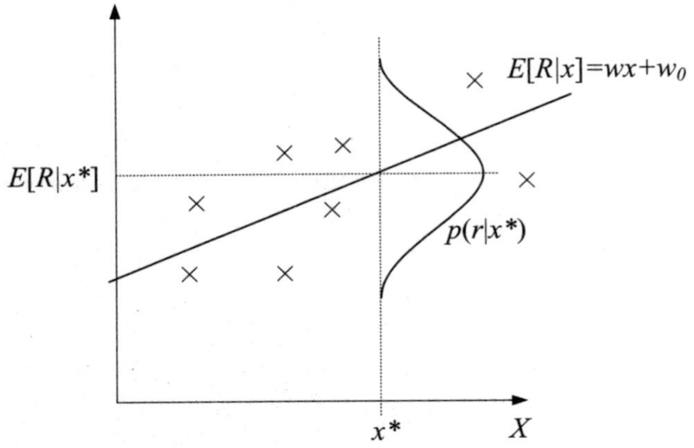

Figure 4.4 Regression assumes 0 mean Gaussian noise added to the model; here, the model is linear.

$p(r|x)$ is the probability of the output given the input, and $p(x)$ is the input density. Given an iid sample $\mathcal{X} = \{x^t, r^t\}_{t=1}^N$, the log likelihood is

$$\begin{aligned}\mathcal{L}(\theta|\mathcal{X}) &= \log \prod_{t=1}^{N} p(x^t, r^t) \\ &= \log \prod_{t=1}^{N} p(r^t|x^t) + \log \prod_{t=1}^{N} p(x^t)\end{aligned}$$

We can ignore the second term since it does not depend on our estimator, and we have

$$\begin{aligned}\mathcal{L}(\theta|\mathcal{X}) &= \log \prod_{t=1}^{N} \frac{1}{\sqrt{2\pi}\sigma} \exp\left[-\frac{[r^t - g(x^t|\theta)]^2}{2\sigma^2}\right] \\ &= \log\left(\frac{1}{\sqrt{2\pi}\sigma}\right)^N \exp\left[-\frac{1}{2\sigma^2}\sum_{t=1}^{N}[r^t - g(x^t|\theta)]^2\right] \\ &= -N\log(\sqrt{2\pi}\sigma) - \frac{1}{2\sigma^2}\sum_{t=1}^{N}[r^t - g(x^t|\theta)]^2\end{aligned} \tag{4.31}$$

The first term is independent of the parameters θ and can be dropped, as can the factor $1/\sigma^2$. Maximizing this is equivalent to minimizing

$$E(\theta|\mathcal{X}) = \frac{1}{2}\sum_{t=1}^{N}[r^t - g(x^t|\theta)]^2 \tag{4.32}$$

which is the most frequently used error function, and θ that minimize it are called the *least squares estimates*. This is a transformation frequently done in statistics: When the likelihood l contains exponents, instead of maximizing l, we define an *error function*, $E = -\log l$, and minimize it.

LEAST SQUARES ESTIMATE

LINEAR REGRESSION

In *linear regression*, we have a linear model

$$g(x^t|w_1, w_0) = w_1 x^t + w_0$$

and taking the derivative of the sum of squared errors (equation 4.32) with respect to w_1 and w_0, we have two equations in two unknowns

$$\begin{aligned}\sum_t r^t &= N w_0 + w_1 \sum_t x^t \\ \sum_t r^t x^t &= w_0 \sum_t x_t + w_1 \sum_t (x^t)^2\end{aligned}$$

which can be written in vector-matrix form as $\mathbf{A}\boldsymbol{w} = \boldsymbol{y}$ where

$$\mathbf{A} = \begin{bmatrix} N & \sum_t x^t \\ \sum_t x^t & \sum_t (x^t)^2 \end{bmatrix}, \ \boldsymbol{w} = \begin{bmatrix} w_0 \\ w_1 \end{bmatrix}, \ \boldsymbol{y} = \begin{bmatrix} \sum_t r^t \\ \sum_t r^t x^t \end{bmatrix}$$

and can be solved as $\boldsymbol{w} = \mathbf{A}^{-1}\boldsymbol{y}$.

POLYNOMIAL REGRESSION

In the general case of *polynomial regression*, the model is a polynomial in x of order k

$$g(x^t|w_k, \ldots, w_2, w_1, w_0) = w_k (x^t)^k + \cdots + w_2 (x^t)^2 + w_1 x^t + w_0$$

The model is still linear with respect to the parameters and taking the derivatives, we get $k+1$ equations in $k+1$ unknowns, which can be written in vector matrix form $\mathbf{A}\boldsymbol{w} = \boldsymbol{y}$ where we have

$$\mathbf{A} = \begin{bmatrix} N & \sum_t x^t & \sum_t (x^t)^2 & \cdots & \sum_t (x^t)^k \\ \sum_t x^t & \sum_t (x^t)^2 & \sum_t (x^t)^3 & \cdots & \sum_t (x^t)^{k+1} \\ \vdots & & & & \\ \sum_t (x^t)^k & \sum_t (x^t)^{k+1} & \sum_t (x^t)^{k+2} & \cdots & \sum_t (x^t)^{2k} \end{bmatrix}$$

$$\boldsymbol{w} = \begin{bmatrix} w_0 \\ w_1 \\ w_2 \\ \vdots \\ w_k \end{bmatrix}, \ \boldsymbol{y} = \begin{bmatrix} \sum_t r^t \\ \sum_t r^t x^t \\ \sum_t r^t (x^t)^2 \\ \vdots \\ \sum_t r^t (x^t)^k \end{bmatrix}$$

We can write $\mathbf{A} = \mathbf{D}^T\mathbf{D}$ and $\boldsymbol{y} = \mathbf{D}^T\boldsymbol{r}$ where

$$\mathbf{D} = \begin{bmatrix} 1 & x^1 & (x^1)^2 & \cdots & (x^1)^k \\ 1 & x^2 & (x^2)^2 & \cdots & (x^2)^k \\ \vdots & & & & \\ 1 & x^N & (x^N)^2 & \cdots & (x^N)^k \end{bmatrix}, \boldsymbol{r} = \begin{bmatrix} r^1 \\ r^2 \\ \vdots \\ r^N \end{bmatrix}$$

and we can then solve for the parameters as

$$\boldsymbol{w} = (\mathbf{D}^T\mathbf{D})^{-1}\mathbf{D}^T\boldsymbol{r} \quad (4.33)$$

Assuming Gaussian distributed error and maximizing likelihood corresponds to minimizing the sum of squared errors. Another measure is the *relative square error* (RSE):

RELATIVE SQUARE ERROR

$$E_{RSE} = \frac{\sum_t [r^t - g(x^t|\theta)]^2}{\sum_t (r^t - \overline{r})^2} \quad (4.34)$$

If E_{RSE} is close to 1, then our prediction is as good as predicting by the average; as it gets closer to 0, we have better fit. If E_{RSE} is close to 1, this means that using a model based on input x does not work better than using the average which would be our estimator if there were no x; if E_{RSE} is close to 0, input x helps.

COEFFICIENT OF DETERMINATION

A measure to check the goodness of fit by regression is the *coefficient of determination* that is

$$R^2 = 1 - E_{RSE}$$

and for regression to be considered useful, we require R^2 to be close to 1.

Remember that for best generalization, we should adjust the complexity of our learner model to the complexity of the data. In polynomial regression, the complexity parameter is the order of the fitted polynomial, and therefore we need to find a way to choose the best order that minimizes the generalization error, that is, tune the complexity of the model to best fit the complexity of the function inherent in the data.

4.7 Tuning Model Complexity: Bias/Variance Dilemma

Let us say that a sample $\mathcal{X} = \{x^t, r^t\}$ is drawn from some unknown joint probability density $p(x, r)$. Using this sample, we construct our estimate

$g(\cdot)$. The expected square error (over the joint density) at x can be written as (using equation 4.17)

$$E[(r-g(x))^2|x] = \underbrace{E[(r-E[r|x])^2|x]}_{noise} + \underbrace{(E[r|x]-g(x))^2}_{squared\ error} \tag{4.35}$$

The first term on the right is the variance of r given x; it does not depend on $g(\cdot)$ or $\mathcal{X}$. It is the variance of noise added, σ^2. This is the part of error that can never be removed, no matter what estimator we use. The second term quantifies how much $g(x)$ deviates from the regression function, $E[r|x]$. This does depend on the estimator and the training set. It may be the case that for one sample, $g(x)$ may be a very good fit; and for some other sample, it may make a bad fit. To quantify how well an estimator $g(\cdot)$ is, we average over possible datasets.

The expected value (average over samples $\mathcal{X}$, all of size N and drawn from the same joint density $p(r,x)$) is (using equation 4.11)

$$E_{\mathcal{X}}[(E[r|x]-g(x))^2|x] = \underbrace{(E[r|x]-E_{\mathcal{X}}[g(x)])^2}_{bias} + \underbrace{E_{\mathcal{X}}[(g(x)-E_{\mathcal{X}}[g(x)])^2]}_{variance} \tag{4.36}$$

As we discussed earlier, bias measures how much $g(x)$ is wrong disregarding the effect of varying samples, and variance measures how much $g(x)$ fluctuate around the expected value, $E[g(x)]$, as the sample varies. We want both to be small.

Let us see a didactic example: To estimate the bias and the variance, we generate a number of datasets $\mathcal{X}_i = \{x_i^t, r_i^t\}, i = 1, \ldots, M$, from some known $f(\cdot)$ with added noise, use each dataset to form an estimator $g_i(\cdot)$, and calculate bias and variance. Note that in real life, we cannot do this because we do not know $f(\cdot)$ or the parameters of the added noise. Then $E[g(x)]$ is estimated by the average over $g_i(\cdot)$:

$$\overline{g}(x) = \frac{1}{M}\sum_{i=1}^{M} g_i(x)$$

Estimated bias and variance are

$$\begin{aligned} \text{bias}^2(g) &= \frac{1}{N}\sum_t [\overline{g}(x^t) - f(x^t)]^2 \\ \text{variance}(g) &= \frac{1}{NM}\sum_t \sum_i [g_i(x^t) - \overline{g}(x^t)]^2 \end{aligned}$$

Let us see some models of different complexity: The simplest is a constant fit

$$g_i(x) = 2$$

This has no variance because we do not use the data and all $g_i(x)$ are the same. But the bias is high, unless of course $f(x)$ is close to 2 for all x. If we take the average of r^t in the sample

$$g_i(x) = \sum_t r_i^t / N$$

instead of the constant 2, this decreases the bias because we would expect the average in general to be a better estimate. But this increases the variance because the different samples $\mathcal{X}_i$ would have different average values. Normally in this case the decrease in bias would be larger than the increase in variance, and error would decrease.

In the context of polynomial regression, an example is given in figure 4.5. As the order of the polynomial increases, small changes in the dataset cause a greater change in the fitted polynomials; thus variance increases. But a complex model on the average allows a better fit to the underlying function; thus bias decreases (see figure 4.6). This is called the *bias/variance dilemma* and is true for any machine learning system and not only for polynomial regression (Geman, Bienenstock, and Doursat 1992). To decrease bias, the model should be flexible, at the risk of having high variance. If the variance is kept low, we may not be able to make a good fit to data and have high bias. The optimal model is the one that has the best trade-off between the bias and the variance.

BIAS/VARIANCE DILEMMA

If there is bias, this indicates that our model class does not contain the solution; this is *underfitting*. If there is variance, the model class is too general and also learns the noise; this is *overfitting*. If $g(\cdot)$ is of the same hypothesis class with $f(\cdot)$, for example, a polynomial of the same order, we have an unbiased estimator, and estimated bias decreases as the number of models increases. This shows the error-reducing effect of choosing the right model (which we called *inductive bias* in chapter 2—the two uses of "bias" are different but not unrelated). As for variance, it also depends on the size of the training set; the variability due to sample decreases as the sample size increases. To sum up, to get a small value of error, we should have the proper inductive bias (to get small bias in the statistical sense) and have a large enough dataset so that the variability of the model can be constrained with the data.

UNDERFITTING

OVERFITTING

Note that when the variance is large, bias is low: This indicates that $\overline{g}(x)$ is a good estimator. So to get a small value of error, we can take a large number of high-variance models and use their average as our estimator. We discuss such approaches for model combination in chapter 17.

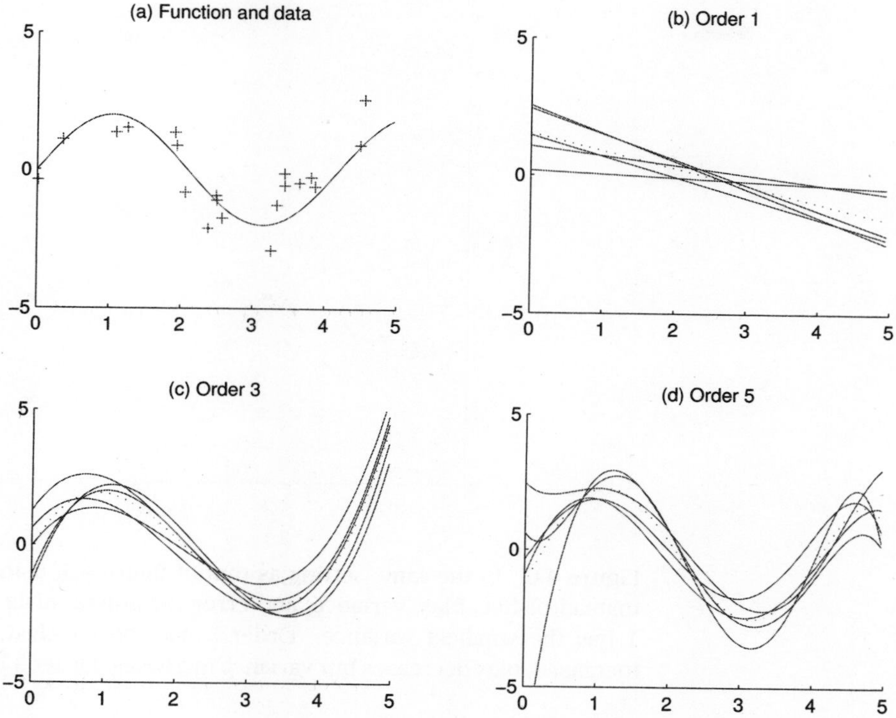

Figure 4.5 (a) Function, $f(x) = 2\sin(1.5x)$, and one noisy ($\mathcal{N}(0,1)$) dataset sampled from the function. Five samples are taken, each containing twenty instances. (b), (c), (d) are five polynomial fits, namely, $g_i(\cdot)$, of order 1, 3, and 5. For each case, dotted line is the average of the five fits, namely, $\overline{g}(\cdot)$.

4.8 Model Selection Procedures

There are a number of procedures we can use to fine-tune model complexity.

CROSS-VALIDATION

In practice, the method we use to find the optimal complexity is *cross-validation*. We cannot calculate the bias and variance for a model, but we can calculate the total error. Given a dataset, we divide it into two parts as training and validation sets, train candidate models of different complexities on the training set and test their error on the validation set left out during training. As the model complexity increases, training error keeps decreasing. The error on the validation set however decreases up to

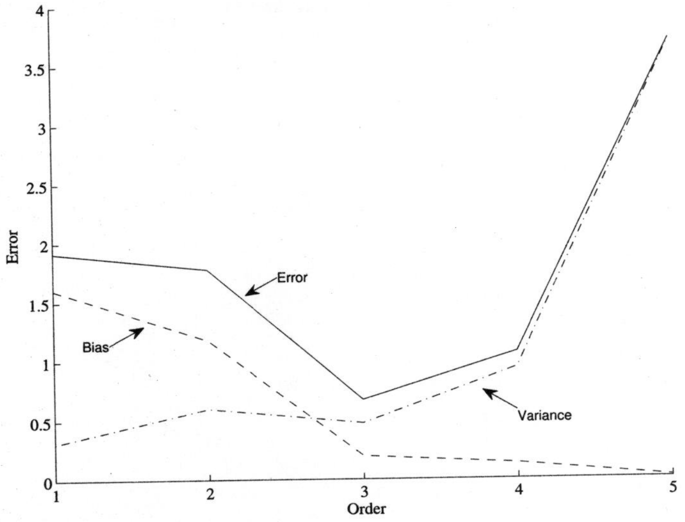

Figure 4.6 In the same setting as that of figure 4.5, using one hundred models instead of five, bias, variance, and error for polynomials of order 1 to 5. Order 1 has the smallest variance. Order 5 has the smallest bias. As the order is increased, bias decreases but variance increases. Order 3 has the minimum error.

a certain level of complexity, then stops decreasing or does not decrease further significantly, or even increases if there is noise in the data. This "elbow" corresponds to the optimal complexity level (see figure 4.7).

In real life, we cannot calculate the bias and hence the error as we do in figure 4.6; the validation error in figure 4.7 is an estimate of that except that it also contains the variance of the noise: Even if we have the right model where there is no bias and large enough data that variance is negligible, there may still be nonzero validation error. Note that the validation error of figure 4.7 is not as V-shaped as the error of figure 4.6 because the former uses more training data and we know that we can constrain variance with more data. Indeed we see in figure 4.5d that even the fifth-order polynomial behaves like a third-order where there is data—note that at the two extremes where there are fewer data points, it is not as accurate.

REGULARIZATION

Another approach that is used frequently is *regularization* (Breiman

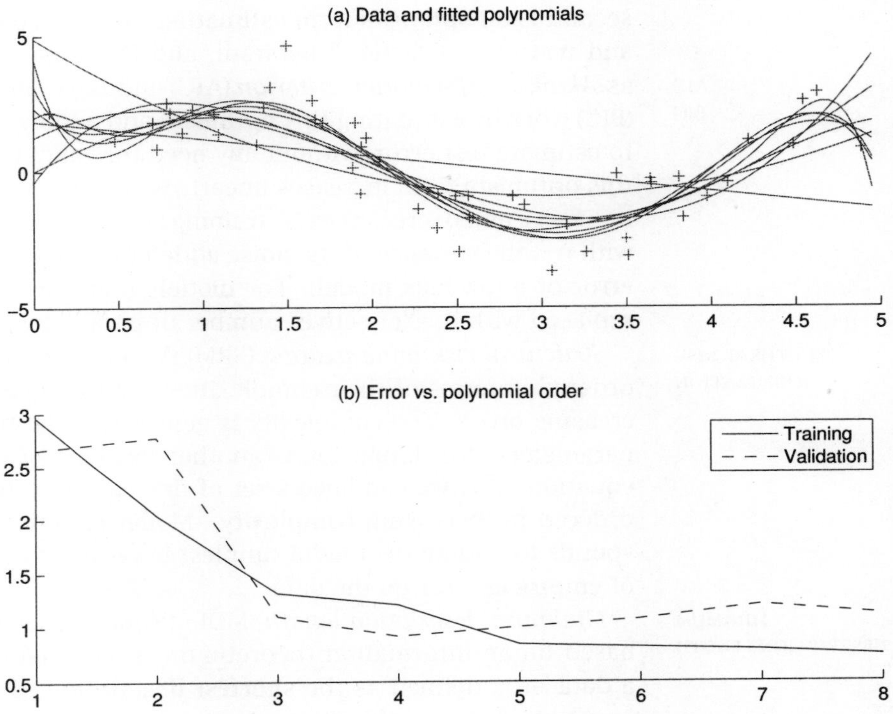

Figure 4.7 In the same setting as that of figure 4.5, training and validation sets (each containing 50 instances) are generated. (a) Training data and fitted polynomials of order from 1 to 8. (b) Training and validation errors as a function of the polynomial order. The "elbow" is at 3.

1998). In this approach, we write an *augmented error function*

(4.37) $E' = \text{error on data} + \lambda \cdot \text{model complexity}$

This has a second term that penalizes complex models with large variance, where λ gives the weight of this penalty. When we minimize the augmented error function instead of the error on data only, we penalize complex models and thus decrease variance. If λ is taken too large, only very simple models are allowed and we risk introducing bias. λ is optimized using cross-validation.

Another way we can view equation 4.37 is by regarding E' as the error on new test data. The first term on the right is the training error and the second is an *optimism* term estimating the discrepancy between training and test error (Hastie, Tibshirani, and Friedman 2011). Methods such as *Akaike's information criterion* (AIC) and *Bayesian information criterion* (BIC) work by estimating this optimism and adding it to the training error to estimate test error, without any need for validation. The magnitude of this optimism term increases linearly with d, the number of inputs (here, it is $k+1$), and decreases as N, training set size, increases; it also increases with σ^2, the variance of the noise added (which we can estimate from the error of a low-bias model). For models that are not linear, d should be replaced with the "effective" number of parameters.

AIC
BIC

STRUCTURAL RISK MINIMIZATION

Structural risk minimization (SRM) (Vapnik 1995) uses a set of models ordered in terms of their complexities. An example is polynomials of increasing order. The complexity is generally given by the number of free parameters. VC dimension is another measure of model complexity. In equation 4.37, we can have a set of decreasing λ_i to get a set of models ordered in increasing complexity. Model selection by SRM then corresponds to finding the model simplest in terms of order and best in terms of empirical error on the data.

MINIMUM DESCRIPTION LENGTH

Minimum description length (MDL) (Rissanen 1978; Grünwald 2007) is based on an information theoretic measure. *Kolmogorov complexity* of a dataset is defined as the shortest description of the data. If the data is simple, it has a short complexity; for example, if it is a sequence of '0's, we can just write '0' and the length of the sequence. If the data is completely random, we cannot have any description of the data shorter than the data itself. If a model is appropriate for the data, then it has a good fit to the data, and instead of the data, we can send/store the model description. Out of all the models that describe the data, we want to have the simplest model so that it lends itself to the shortest description. So we again have a trade-off between how simple the model is and how well it explains the data.

BAYESIAN MODEL SELECTION

Bayesian model selection is used when we have some prior knowledge about the appropriate class of approximating functions. This prior knowledge is defined as a prior distribution over models, $p(\text{model})$. Given the data and assuming a model, we can calculate $p(\text{model}|\text{data})$ using Bayes' rule:

$$p(\text{model}|\text{data}) = \frac{p(\text{data}|\text{model})p(\text{model})}{p(\text{data})} \tag{4.38}$$

$p(\text{model}|\text{data})$ is the posterior probability of the model given our prior subjective knowledge about models, namely, $p(\text{model})$, and the objective support provided by the data, namely, $p(\text{data}|\text{model})$. We can then choose the model with the highest posterior probability, or take an average over all models weighted by their posterior probabilities. We will talk about the Bayesian approach in detail in chapter 16.

If we take the log of equation 4.38, we get

$$\log p(\text{model}|\text{data}) = \log p(\text{data}|\text{model}) + \log p(\text{model}) - c \tag{4.39}$$

which has the form of equation 4.37; the log likelihood of the data is the training error and the log of the prior is the penalty term. For example, if we have a regression model and use the prior $p(\boldsymbol{w}) \sim \mathcal{N}(0, 1/\lambda)$, we minimize

$$E = \sum_t [r^t - g(x^t|\boldsymbol{w})]^2 + \lambda \sum_i w_i^2 \tag{4.40}$$

That is, we look for w_i that both decrease error and are also as close as possible to 0, and the reason we want them close to 0 is because the fitted polynomial will be smoother. As the polynomial order increases, to get a better fit to the data, the function will go up and down, which will mean coefficients moving away from 0 (see figure 4.8); when we add this penalty, we force a flatter, smoother fit. How much we penalize depends on λ, which is the inverse of the variance of the prior—that is, how much we expect the weights a priori to be away from 0. In other words, having such a prior is equivalent to forcing parameters to be close to 0. We discuss this in greater detail in chapter 16.

That is, when the prior is chosen such that we give higher probabilities to simpler models (following Occam's razor), the Bayesian approach, regularization, SRM, and MDL are equivalent. Cross-validation is different from all other methods for model selection in that it makes no prior assumption about the model or parameters. If there is a large enough validation dataset, it is the best approach. The other models become useful when the data sample is small.

4.9 Notes

A good source on the basics of maximum likelihood and Bayesian estimation is Ross 1987. Many pattern recognition textbooks discuss classification with parametric models (e.g., MacLachlan 1992; Devroye, Györfi, and

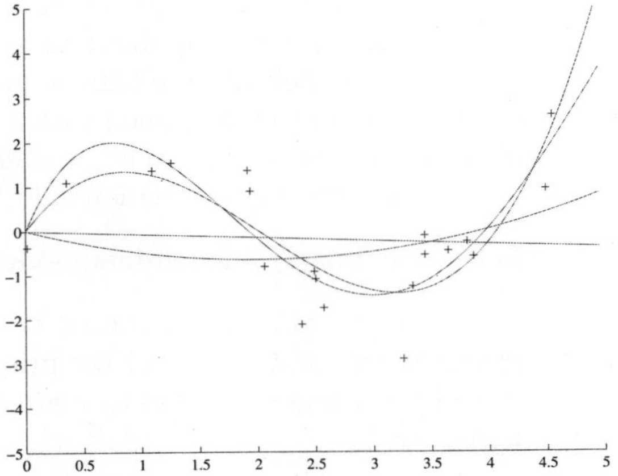

Figure 4.8 In the same setting as that of figure 4.5, polynomials of order 1 to 4 are fitted. The magnitude of coefficients increase as the order of the polynomial increases. They are as follows: 1 : $[-0.0769, 0.0016]^T$, 2 : $[0.1682, -0.6657, 0.0080]^T$, 3 : $[0.4238, -2.5778, 3.4675, -0.0002]^T$, 4 : $[-0.1093, 1.4356, -5.5007, 6.0454, -0.0019]^T$.

Lugosı 1996; Webb and Copsey 2011; Duda, Hart, and Stork 2001). Tests for checking univariate normality can be found in Rencher 1995.

Geman, Bienenstock, and Doursat (1992) discuss bias and variance decomposition for several learning models, which we discuss in later chapters. Bias/variance decomposition is for sum of squared loss and is for regression; such a nice additive splitting of error into bias, variance and noise is not possible for 0/1 loss, because in classification, there is error only if we accidentally move to the other side of the boundary. For a two-class problem, if the correct posterior is 0.7 and if our estimate is 0.8, there is no error; we have error only if our estimate is less than 0.5. Various researchers proposed different definitions of bias and variance for classification; see Friedman 1997 for a review.

4.10 Exercises

1. Write the code that generates a Bernoulli sample with given parameter p, and the code that calculates $\hat{p}$ from the sample.
2. Write the log likelihood for a multinomial sample and show equation 4.6.

3. Write the code that generates a normal sample with given μ and σ, and the code that calculates m and s from the sample. Do the same using the Bayes' estimator assuming a prior distribution for μ.

4. Given two normal distributions $p(x|C_1) \sim \mathcal{N}(\mu_1, \sigma_1^2)$ and $p(x|C_2) \sim \mathcal{N}(\mu_2, \sigma_2^2)$ and $P(C_1)$ and $P(C_2)$, calculate the Bayes' discriminant points analytically.

SOLUTION: Given that

$$\begin{aligned} p(x|C_1) &\sim \mathcal{N}(\mu_1, \sigma_1^2) = \frac{1}{\sqrt{2\pi}\sigma_1} \exp\left[-\frac{(x-\mu_1)^2}{2\sigma_1^2}\right] \\ p(x|C_2) &\sim \mathcal{N}(\mu_2, \sigma_2^2) \end{aligned}$$

we would like to find x that satisfy $P(C_1|x) = P(C_2|x)$, or

$$\begin{aligned} p(x|C_1)P(C_1) &= p(x|C_2)P(C_2) \\ \log p(x|C_1) + \log P(C_1) &= \log p(x|C_2) + \log P(C_2) \\ -\frac{1}{2}\log 2\pi - \log\sigma_1 - \frac{(x-\mu_1)^2}{2\sigma_1^2} + \log P(C_1) &= \cdots \\ -\log\sigma_1 - \frac{1}{2\sigma_1^2}\left(x^2 - 2x\mu_1 + \mu_1^2\right) + \log P(C_1) &= \cdots \end{aligned}$$

$$\left(\frac{1}{2\sigma_2^2} - \frac{1}{2\sigma_1^2}\right)x^2 + \left(\frac{\mu_1}{\sigma_1^2} - \frac{\mu_2}{\sigma_2^2}\right)x + \left(\frac{\mu_2^2}{2\sigma_2^2} - \frac{\mu_1^2}{2\sigma_1^2}\right) + \log\frac{\sigma_2}{\sigma_1} + \log\frac{P(C_1)}{P(C_2)} = 0$$

This is of the form $ax^2 + bx + c = 0$ and the two roots are

$$x_1, x_2 = \frac{-b \pm \sqrt{b^2 - 4ac}}{2a}$$

Note that if the variances are equal, the quadratic terms vanishes and there is one root, that is, the two posteriors intersect at a single x value.

5. What is the likelihood ratio

$$\frac{p(x|C_1)}{p(x|C_2)}$$

in the case of Gaussian densities?

SOLUTION:

$$\frac{p(x|C_1)}{p(x|C_2)} = \frac{\frac{1}{\sqrt{2\pi}\sigma_1}\exp\left[-\frac{(x-\mu_1)^2}{2\sigma_1^2}\right]}{\frac{1}{\sqrt{2\pi}\sigma_2}\exp\left[-\frac{(x-\mu_2)^2}{2\sigma_2^2}\right]}$$

If we have $\sigma_1^2 = \sigma_2^2 = \sigma^2$, we can simplify

$$\frac{p(x|C_1)}{p(x|C_2)} = \exp\left[-\frac{(x-\mu_1)^2}{2\sigma^2} + \frac{(x-\mu_2)^2}{2\sigma^2}\right]$$

$$= \exp\left[\frac{(\mu_1-\mu_2)}{\sigma^2}x + \frac{(\mu_2^2-\mu_1^2)}{2\sigma^2}\right]$$
$$= \exp(wx + w_0)$$

for $w = (\mu_1 - \mu_2)/\sigma^2$ and $w_0 = (\mu_2^2 - \mu_1^2)/2\sigma^2$.

6. For a two-class problem, generate normal samples for two classes with different variances, then use parametric classification to estimate the discriminant points. Compare these with the theoretical values.
7. Assume a linear model and then add 0-mean Gaussian noise to generate a sample. Divide your sample into two as training and validation sets. Use linear regression using the training half. Compute error on the validation set. Do the same for polynomials of degrees 2 and 3 as well.
8. When the training set is small, the contribution of variance to error may be more than that of bias and in such a case, we may prefer a simple model even though we know that it is too simple for the task. Can you give an example?
9. Let us say, given the samples $\mathcal{X}_i = \{x_i^t, r_i^t\}$, we define $g_i(x) = r_i^1$, namely, our estimate for any x is the r value of the first instance in the (unordered) dataset $\mathcal{X}_i$. What can you say about its bias and variance, as compared with $g_i(x) = 2$ and $g_i(x) = \sum_t r_i^t/N$? What if the sample is ordered, so that $g_i(x) = \min_t r_i^t$?
10. In equation 4.40, what is the effect of changing λ on bias and variance?

    SOLUTION: λ controls smoothness: If it is large, we may smooth too much and decrease variance at the expense of an increase in bias; if it is small, bias may be small but variance will be high.

4.11 References

Andrieu, C., N. de Freitas, A. Doucet, and M. I. Jordan. 2003. "An Introduction to MCMC for Machine Learning." *Machine Learning* 50:5–43.

Breiman, L. 1998. "Bias-Variance, Regularization, Instability and Stabilization." In *Neural Networks and Machine Learning*, ed. C. M. Bishop, 27–56. Berlin: Springer.

Devroye, L., L. Györfi, and G. Lugosi. 1996. *A Probabilistic Theory of Pattern Recognition.* New York: Springer.

Duda, R. O., P. E. Hart, and D. G. Stork. 2001. *Pattern Classification*, 2nd ed. New York: Wiley.

Friedman, J. H. 1997. "On Bias, Variance, 0/1-Loss and the Curse of Dimensionality." *Data Mining and Knowledge Discovery* 1:55–77.

Geman, S., E. Bienenstock, and R. Doursat. 1992. "Neural Networks and the Bias/Variance Dilemma." *Neural Computation* 4:1–58.

Grünwald, P. D. 2007. *The Minimum Description Length Principle.* Cambridge, MA: MIT Press.

Hastie, T., R. Tibshirani, and J. Friedman. 2011. *The Elements of Statistical Learning: Data Mining, Inference, and Prediction,* 2nd ed. New York: Springer.

McLachlan, G. J. 1992. *Discriminant Analysis and Statistical Pattern Recognition.* New York: Wiley.

Rencher, A. C. 1995. *Methods of Multivariate Analysis.* New York: Wiley.

Rissanen, J. 1978. "Modeling by Shortest Data Description." *Automatica* 14:465–471.

Ross, S. M. 1987. *Introduction to Probability and Statistics for Engineers and Scientists.* New York: Wiley.

Vapnik, V. 1995. *The Nature of Statistical Learning Theory.* New York: Springer.

Webb, A., and K. D. Copsey. 2011. *Statistical Pattern Recognition,* 3rd ed. New York: Wiley.

5 *Multivariate Methods*

In chapter 4, we discussed the parametric approach to classification and regression. Now, we generalize this to the multivariate case where we have multiple inputs and where the output, which is class code or continuous output, is a function of these multiple inputs. These inputs may be discrete or numeric. We will see how such functions can be learned from a labeled multivariate sample and also how the complexity of the learner can be fine-tuned to the data at hand.

5.1 Multivariate Data

IN MANY APPLICATIONS, several measurements are made on each individual or event generating an observation vector. The sample may be viewed as a *data matrix*

$$\mathbf{X} = \begin{bmatrix} X_1^1 & X_2^1 & \cdots & X_d^1 \\ X_1^2 & X_2^2 & \cdots & X_d^2 \\ \vdots & & & \\ X_1^N & X_2^N & \cdots & X_d^N \end{bmatrix}$$

where the d columns correspond to d *variables* denoting the result of measurements made on an individual or event. These are also called *inputs*, *features*, or *attributes*. The N rows correspond to independent and identically distributed *observations*, *examples*, or *instances* on N individuals or events.

INPUT
FEATURE
ATTRIBUTE
OBSERVATION
EXAMPLE
INSTANCE

For example, in deciding on a loan application, an observation vector is the information associated with a customer and is composed of age, marital status, yearly income, and so forth, and we have N such past customers. These measurements may be of different scales, for example, age in years and yearly income in monetary units. Some like age may be numeric, and some like marital status may be discrete.

Typically these variables are correlated. If they are not, there is no need for a multivariate analysis. Our aim may be *simplification*, that is, summarizing this large body of data by means of relatively few parameters. Or our aim may be *exploratory*, and we may be interested in generating hypotheses about data. In some applications, we are interested in predicting the value of one variable from the values of other variables. If the predicted variable is discrete, this is multivariate classification, and if it is numeric, this is a multivariate regression problem.

5.2 Parameter Estimation

MEAN VECTOR

The *mean vector* $\boldsymbol{\mu}$ is defined such that each of its elements is the mean of one column of $\mathbf{X}$:

$$E[\boldsymbol{x}] = \boldsymbol{\mu} = [\mu_1, \ldots, \mu_d]^T \quad (5.1)$$

The variance of X_i is denoted as σ_i^2, and the covariance of two variables X_i and X_j is defined as

$$\sigma_{ij} \equiv \text{Cov}(X_i, X_j) = E[(X_i - \mu_i)(X_j - \mu_j)] = E[X_i X_j] - \mu_i \mu_j \quad (5.2)$$

with $\sigma_{ij} = \sigma_{ji}$, and when $i = j$, $\sigma_{ii} = \sigma_i^2$. With d variables, there are d variances and $d(d-1)/2$ covariances, which are generally represented as a $d \times d$ matrix, named the *covariance matrix*, denoted as Σ, whose (i, j)th element is σ_{ij}:

COVARIANCE MATRIX

$$\Sigma = \begin{bmatrix} \sigma_1^2 & \sigma_{12} & \cdots & \sigma_{1d} \\ \sigma_{21} & \sigma_2^2 & \cdots & \sigma_{2d} \\ \vdots & & & \\ \sigma_{d1} & \sigma_{d2} & \cdots & \sigma_d^2 \end{bmatrix}$$

The diagonal terms are the variances, the off-diagonal terms are the covariances, and the matrix is symmetric. In vector-matrix notation

$$\Sigma \equiv \text{Cov}(\boldsymbol{X}) = E[(\boldsymbol{X} - \boldsymbol{\mu})(\boldsymbol{X} - \boldsymbol{\mu})^T] = E[\boldsymbol{X}\boldsymbol{X}^T] - \boldsymbol{\mu}\boldsymbol{\mu}^T \quad (5.3)$$

If two variables are related in a linear way, then the covariance will be positive or negative depending on whether the relationship has a positive or negative slope. But the size of the relationship is difficult to interpret because it depends on the units in which the two variables are measured.

CORRELATION

The *correlation* between variables X_i and X_j is a statistic normalized between -1 and $+1$, defined as

(5.4) $$\text{Corr}(X_i, X_j) \equiv \rho_{ij} = \frac{\sigma_{ij}}{\sigma_i \sigma_j}$$

If two variables are independent, then their covariance, and hence their correlation, is 0. However, the converse is not true: The variables may be dependent (in a nonlinear way), and their correlation may be 0.

SAMPLE MEAN

Given a multivariate sample, estimates for these parameters can be calculated: The maximum likelihood estimator for the mean is the *sample mean*, $\boldsymbol{m}$. Its ith dimension is the average of the ith column of $\mathbf{X}$:

(5.5) $$\boldsymbol{m} = \frac{\sum_{t=1}^{N} \boldsymbol{x}^t}{N} \text{ with } m_i = \frac{\sum_{t=1}^{N} x_i^t}{N}, i = 1, \ldots, d$$

SAMPLE COVARIANCE

The estimator of $\mathbf{\Sigma}$ is $\mathbf{S}$, the *sample covariance* matrix, with entries

(5.6) $$s_i^2 = \frac{\sum_{t=1}^{N} (x_i^t - m_i)^2}{N}$$

(5.7) $$s_{ij} = \frac{\sum_{t=1}^{N} (x_i^t - m_i)(x_j^t - m_j)}{N}$$

These are biased estimates, but if in an application the estimates vary significantly depending on whether we divide by N or $N-1$, we are in serious trouble anyway.

SAMPLE CORRELATION

The *sample correlation* coefficients are

(5.8) $$r_{ij} = \frac{s_{ij}}{s_i s_j}$$

and the sample correlation matrix $\mathbf{R}$ contains r_{ij}.

5.3 Estimation of Missing Values

Frequently, values of certain variables may be missing in observations. The best strategy is to discard those observations all together, but generally we do not have large enough samples to be able to afford this and we do not want to lose data as the non-missing entries do contain information. We try to fill in the missing entries by estimating them. This is called *imputation*.

IMPUTATION

In *mean imputation*, for a numeric variable, we substitute the mean (average) of the available data for that variable in the sample. For a discrete variable, we fill in with the most likely value, that is, the value most often seen in the data.

In *imputation by regression*, we try to predict the value of a missing variable from other variables whose values are known for that case. Depending on the type of the missing variable, we define a separate regression or classification problem that we train by the data points for which such values are known. If many different variables are missing, we take the means as the initial estimates and the procedure is iterated until predicted values stabilize. If the variables are not highly correlated, the regression approach is equivalent to mean imputation.

Depending on the context, however, sometimes the fact that a certain attribute value is missing may be important. For example, in a credit card application, if the applicant does not declare his or her telephone number, that may be a critical piece of information. In such cases, this is represented as a separate value to indicate that the value is missing and is used as such.

5.4 Multivariate Normal Distribution

In the multivariate case where $\boldsymbol{x}$ is d-dimensional and normal distributed, we have

(5.9) $$p(\boldsymbol{x}) = \frac{1}{(2\pi)^{d/2}|\boldsymbol{\Sigma}|^{1/2}} \exp\left[-\frac{1}{2}(\boldsymbol{x}-\boldsymbol{\mu})^T\boldsymbol{\Sigma}^{-1}(\boldsymbol{x}-\boldsymbol{\mu})\right]$$

and we write $\boldsymbol{x} \sim \mathcal{N}_d(\boldsymbol{\mu}, \boldsymbol{\Sigma})$ where $\boldsymbol{\mu}$ is the mean vector and $\boldsymbol{\Sigma}$ is the covariance matrix (see figure 5.1). Just as

$$\frac{(x-\mu)^2}{\sigma^2} = (x-\mu)(\sigma^2)^{-1}(x-\mu)$$

is the squared distance from x to μ in standard deviation units, normalizing for different variances, in the multivariate case the *Mahalanobis distance* is used:

MAHALANOBIS DISTANCE

(5.10) $$(\boldsymbol{x}-\boldsymbol{\mu})^T\boldsymbol{\Sigma}^{-1}(\boldsymbol{x}-\boldsymbol{\mu})$$

$(\boldsymbol{x}-\boldsymbol{\mu})^T\boldsymbol{\Sigma}^{-1}(\boldsymbol{x}-\boldsymbol{\mu}) = c^2$ is the d-dimensional hyperellipsoid centered at $\boldsymbol{\mu}$, and its shape and orientation are defined by $\boldsymbol{\Sigma}$. Because of the use of the inverse of $\boldsymbol{\Sigma}$, if a variable has a larger variance than another, it receives

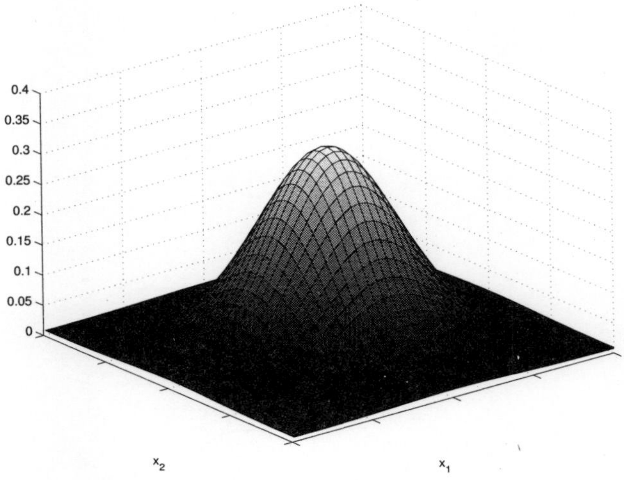

Figure 5.1 Bivariate normal distribution.

less weight in the Mahalanobis distance. Similarly, two highly correlated variables do not contribute as much as two less correlated variables. The use of the inverse of the covariance matrix thus has the effect of standardizing all variables to unit variance and eliminating correlations.

Let us consider the bivariate case where $d = 2$ for visualization purposes (see figure 5.2). When the variables are independent, the major axes of the density are parallel to the input axes. The density becomes an ellipse if the variances are different. The density rotates depending on the sign of the covariance (correlation). The mean vector is $\boldsymbol{\mu}^T = [\mu_1, \mu_2]$, and the covariance matrix is usually expressed as

$$\boldsymbol{\Sigma} = \begin{bmatrix} \sigma_1^2 & \rho\sigma_1\sigma_2 \\ \rho\sigma_1\sigma_2 & \sigma_2^2 \end{bmatrix}$$

The joint bivariate density can be expressed in the form (see exercise 1)

$$p(x_1, x_2) = \frac{1}{2\pi\sigma_1\sigma_2\sqrt{1-\rho^2}} \exp\left[-\frac{1}{2(1-\rho^2)}\left(z_1^2 - 2\rho z_1 z_2 + z_2^2\right)\right] \quad (5.11)$$

where $z_i = (x_i - \mu_i)/\sigma_i, i = 1, 2$, are standardized variables; this is called *z-normalization*. Remember that

Z-NORMALIZATION

$$z_1^2 + 2\rho z_1 z_2 + z_2^2 = \text{constant}$$

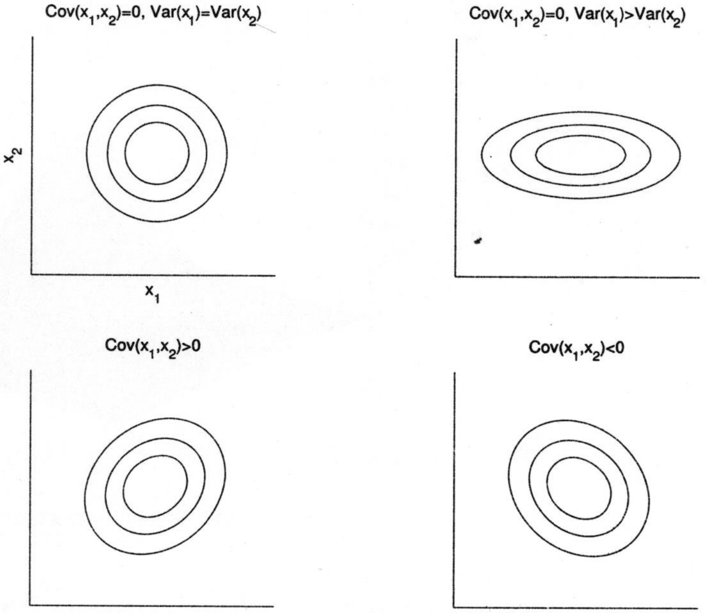

Figure 5.2 Isoprobability contour plot of the bivariate normal distribution. Its center is given by the mean, and its shape and orientation depend on the covariance matrix.

for $|\rho| < 1$, is the equation of an ellipse. When $\rho > 0$, the major axis of the ellipse has a positive slope and if $\rho < 0$, the major axis has a negative slope.

In the expanded Mahalanobis distance of equation 5.11, each variable is normalized to have unit variance, and there is the cross-term that corrects for the correlation between the two variables.

The density depends on five parameters: the two means, the two variances, and the correlation. $\boldsymbol{\Sigma}$ is nonsingular, and hence positive definite, provided that variances are nonzero and $|\rho| < 1$. If ρ is $+1$ or -1, the two variables are linearly related, the observations are effectively one-dimensional, and one of the two variables can be disposed of. If $\rho = 0$, then the two variables are independent, the cross-term disappears, and we get a product of two univariate densities.

In the multivariate case, a small value of $|\boldsymbol{\Sigma}|$ indicates samples are close to $\boldsymbol{\mu}$, just as in the univariate case where a small value of σ^2 indicates samples are close to μ. Small $|\Sigma|$ may also indicate that there is high correlation between variables. Σ is a symmetric positive definite matrix; this is the multivariate way of saying that $\text{Var}(X) > 0$. If not so, Σ is singular and its determinant is 0. This is either due to linear dependence between the dimensions or because one of the dimensions has variance 0. In such a case, dimensionality should be reduced to a get a positive definite matrix; we discuss methods for this in chapter 6.

If $\boldsymbol{x} \sim \mathcal{N}_d(\boldsymbol{\mu}, \Sigma)$, then each dimension of $\boldsymbol{x}$ is univariate normal. (The converse is not true: Each X_i may be univariate normal and $\boldsymbol{X}$ may not be multivariate normal.) Actually any $k < d$ subset of the variables is k-variate normal.

A special, *naive* case is where the components of $\boldsymbol{x}$ are independent and $\text{Cov}(X_i, X_j) = 0$, for $i \neq j$, and $\text{Var}(X_i) = \sigma_i^2, \forall i$. Then the covariance matrix is diagonal and the joint density is the product of the individual univariate densities:

$$p(\boldsymbol{x}) = \prod_{i=1}^{d} p_i(x_i) = \frac{1}{(2\pi)^{d/2} \prod_{i=1}^{d} \sigma_i} \exp\left[-\frac{1}{2}\sum_{i=1}^{d}\left(\frac{x_i - \mu_i}{\sigma_i}\right)^2\right] \tag{5.12}$$

Now let us see another property we make use of in later chapters. Let us say $\boldsymbol{x} \sim \mathcal{N}_d(\boldsymbol{\mu}, \Sigma)$ and $\boldsymbol{w} \in \Re^d$, then

$$\boldsymbol{w}^T\boldsymbol{x} = w_1x_1 + w_2x_2 + \cdots + w_dx_d \sim \mathcal{N}(\boldsymbol{w}^T\boldsymbol{\mu}, \boldsymbol{w}^T\Sigma\boldsymbol{w})$$

given that

$$E[\boldsymbol{w}^T\boldsymbol{x}] = \boldsymbol{w}^T E[\boldsymbol{x}] = \boldsymbol{w}^T\boldsymbol{\mu} \tag{5.13}$$

$$\begin{aligned}
\text{Var}(\boldsymbol{w}^T\boldsymbol{x}) &= E[(\boldsymbol{w}^T\boldsymbol{x} - \boldsymbol{w}^T\boldsymbol{\mu})^2] = E[(\boldsymbol{w}^T\boldsymbol{x} - \boldsymbol{w}^T\boldsymbol{\mu})(\boldsymbol{w}^T\boldsymbol{x} - \boldsymbol{w}^T\boldsymbol{\mu})] \\
&= E[\boldsymbol{w}^T(\boldsymbol{x} - \boldsymbol{\mu})(\boldsymbol{x} - \boldsymbol{\mu})^T\boldsymbol{w}] = \boldsymbol{w}^T E[(\boldsymbol{x} - \boldsymbol{\mu})(\boldsymbol{x} - \boldsymbol{\mu})^T]\boldsymbol{w} \\
&= \boldsymbol{w}^T\Sigma\boldsymbol{w}
\end{aligned} \tag{5.14}$$

That is, the projection of a d-dimensional normal on the vector $\boldsymbol{w}$ is univariate normal. In the general case, if $\mathbf{W}$ is a $d \times k$ matrix with rank $k < d$, then the k-dimensional $\mathbf{W}^T\boldsymbol{x}$ is k-variate normal:

$$\mathbf{W}^T\boldsymbol{x} \sim \mathcal{N}_k(\mathbf{W}^T\boldsymbol{\mu}, \mathbf{W}^T\Sigma\mathbf{W}) \tag{5.15}$$

That is, if we project a d-dimensional normal distribution to a space that is k-dimensional, then it projects to a k-dimensional normal.

5.5 Multivariate Classification

When $\boldsymbol{x} \in \Re^d$, if the class-conditional densities, $p(\boldsymbol{x}|C_i)$, are taken as normal density, $\mathcal{N}_d(\boldsymbol{\mu}_i, \boldsymbol{\Sigma}_i)$, we have

$$p(\boldsymbol{x}|C_i) = \frac{1}{(2\pi)^{d/2}|\boldsymbol{\Sigma}_i|^{1/2}} \exp\left[-\frac{1}{2}(\boldsymbol{x}-\boldsymbol{\mu}_i)^T\boldsymbol{\Sigma}_i^{-1}(\boldsymbol{x}-\boldsymbol{\mu}_i)\right] \tag{5.16}$$

The main reason for this is its analytical simplicity (Duda, Hart, and Stork 2001). Besides, the normal density is a model for many naturally occurring phenomena in that examples of most classes can be seen as mildly changed versions of a single prototype, $\boldsymbol{\mu}_i$, and the covariance matrix, $\boldsymbol{\Sigma}_i$, denotes the amount of noise in each variable and the correlations of these noise sources. While real data may not often be exactly multivariate normal, it is a useful approximation. In addition to its mathematical tractability, the model is robust to departures from normality as is shown in many works (e.g., McLachlan 1992). However, one clear requirement is that the sample of a class should form a single group; if there are multiple groups, one should use a mixture model (chapter 7).

Let us say we want to predict the type of a car that a customer would be interested in. Different cars are the classes and $\boldsymbol{x}$ are observable data of customers, for example, age and income. $\boldsymbol{\mu}_i$ is the vector of mean age and income of customers who buy car type i and $\boldsymbol{\Sigma}_i$ is their covariance matrix: σ_{i1}^2 and σ_{i2}^2 are the age and income variances, and σ_{i12} is the covariance of age and income in the group of customers who buy car type i.

When we define the discriminant function as

$$g_i(\boldsymbol{x}) = \log p(\boldsymbol{x}|C_i) + \log P(C_i)$$

and assuming $p(\boldsymbol{x}|C_i) \sim \mathcal{N}_d(\boldsymbol{\mu}_i, \boldsymbol{\Sigma}_i)$, we have

$$g_i(\boldsymbol{x}) = -\frac{d}{2}\log 2\pi - \frac{1}{2}\log|\boldsymbol{\Sigma}_i| - \frac{1}{2}(\boldsymbol{x}-\boldsymbol{\mu}_i)^T\boldsymbol{\Sigma}_i^{-1}(\boldsymbol{x}-\boldsymbol{\mu}_i) + \log P(C_i) \tag{5.17}$$

Given a training sample for $K \geq 2$ classes, $\mathcal{X} = \{\boldsymbol{x}^t, \boldsymbol{r}^t\}$, where $r_i^t = 1$ if $\boldsymbol{x}^t \in C_i$ and 0 otherwise, estimates for the means and covariances are found using maximum likelihood separately for each class:

$$\begin{aligned} \hat{P}(C_i) &= \frac{\sum_t r_i^t}{N} \\ \boldsymbol{m}_i &= \frac{\sum_t r_i^t \boldsymbol{x}^t}{\sum_t r_i^t} \\ \mathbf{S}_i &= \frac{\sum_t r_i^t(\boldsymbol{x}^t - \boldsymbol{m}_i)(\boldsymbol{x}^t - \boldsymbol{m}_i)^T}{\sum_t r_i^t} \end{aligned} \tag{5.18}$$

These are then plugged into the discriminant function to get the estimates for the discriminants. Ignoring the first constant term, we have

$$g_i(\boldsymbol{x}) = -\frac{1}{2}\log|\mathbf{S}_i| - \frac{1}{2}(\boldsymbol{x}-\boldsymbol{m}_i)^T\mathbf{S}_i^{-1}(\boldsymbol{x}-\boldsymbol{m}_i) + \log\hat{P}(C_i) \tag{5.19}$$

Expanding this, we get

$$g_i(\boldsymbol{x}) = -\frac{1}{2}\log|\mathbf{S}_i| - \frac{1}{2}\left(\boldsymbol{x}^T\mathbf{S}_i^{-1}\boldsymbol{x} - 2\boldsymbol{x}^T\mathbf{S}_i^{-1}\boldsymbol{m}_i + \boldsymbol{m}_i^T\mathbf{S}_i^{-1}\boldsymbol{m}_i\right) + \log\hat{P}(C_i)$$

QUADRATIC DISCRIMINANT

which defines a *quadratic discriminant* (see figure 5.3) that can also be written as

$$g_i(\boldsymbol{x}) = \boldsymbol{x}^T\mathbf{W}_i\boldsymbol{x} + \boldsymbol{w}_i^T\boldsymbol{x} + w_{i0} \tag{5.20}$$

where

$$\begin{aligned}
\mathbf{W}_i &= -\frac{1}{2}\mathbf{S}_i^{-1}\\
\boldsymbol{w}_i &= \mathbf{S}_i^{-1}\boldsymbol{m}_i\\
w_{i0} &= -\frac{1}{2}\boldsymbol{m}_i^T\mathbf{S}_i^{-1}\boldsymbol{m}_i - \frac{1}{2}\log|\mathbf{S}_i| + \log\hat{P}(C_i)
\end{aligned}$$

The number of parameters to be estimated are $K \cdot d$ for the means and $K \cdot d(d+1)/2$ for the covariance matrices. When d is large and samples are small, $\mathbf{S}_i$ may be singular and inverses may not exist. Or, $|\mathbf{S}_i|$ may be nonzero but too small, in which case it will be unstable; small changes in $\mathbf{S}_i$ will cause large changes in $\mathbf{S}_i^{-1}$. For the estimates to be reliable on small samples, one may want to decrease dimensionality, d, by redesigning the feature extractor and select a subset of the features or somehow combine existing features. We discuss such methods in chapter 6.

Another possibility is to pool the data and estimate a common covariance matrix for all classes:

$$\mathbf{S} = \sum_i \hat{P}(C_i)\mathbf{S}_i \tag{5.21}$$

In this case of equal covariance matrices, equation 5.19 reduces to

$$g_i(\boldsymbol{x}) = -\frac{1}{2}(\boldsymbol{x}-\boldsymbol{m}_i)^T\mathbf{S}^{-1}(\boldsymbol{x}-\boldsymbol{m}_i) + \log\hat{P}(C_i) \tag{5.22}$$

The number of parameters is $K \cdot d$ for the means and $d(d+1)/2$ for the shared covariance matrix. If the priors are equal, the optimal decision rule is to assign input to the class whose mean's Mahalanobis distance to the input is the smallest. As before, unequal priors shift the boundary

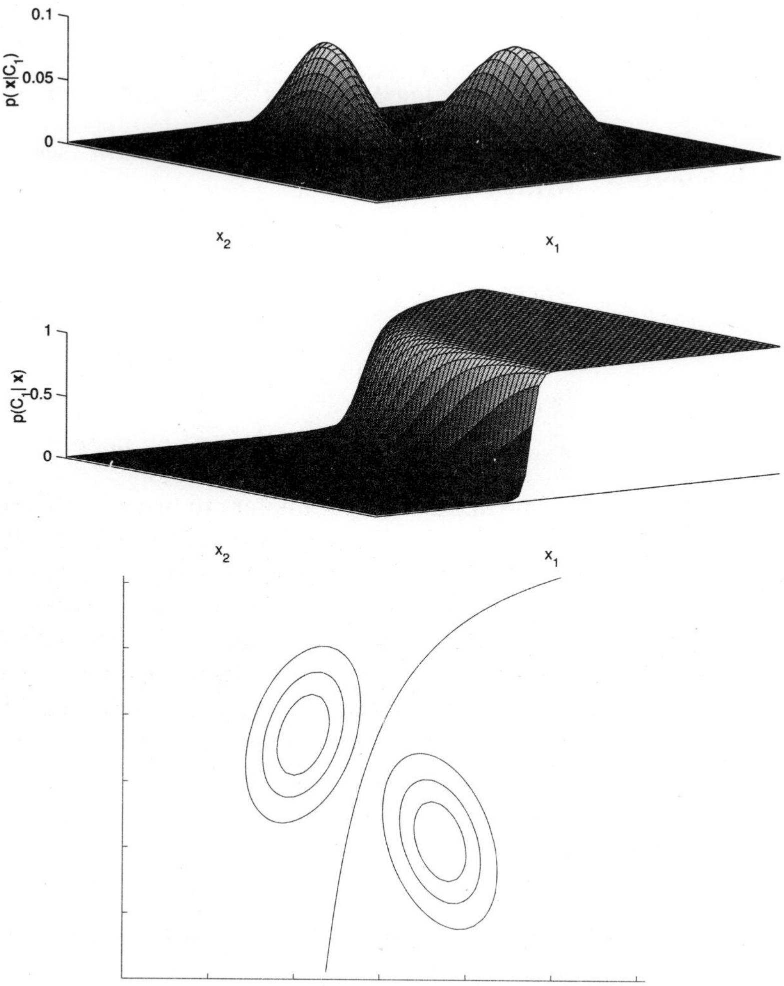

Figure 5.3 Classes have different covariance matrices. Likelihood densities and the posterior probability for one of the classes (top). Class distributions are indicated by isoprobability contours and the discriminant is drawn (bottom).

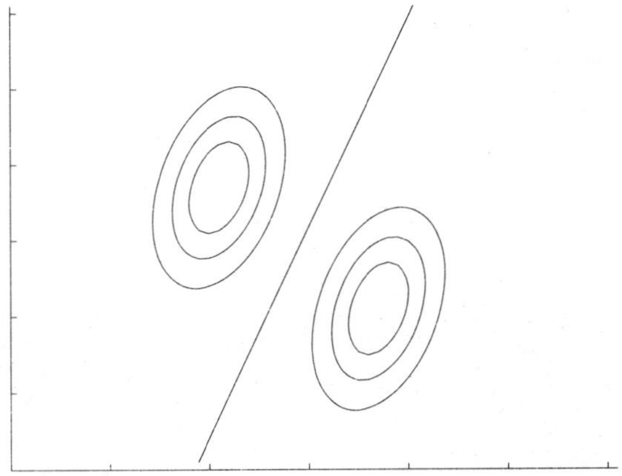

Figure 5.4 Covariances may be arbitary but shared by both classes.

toward the less likely class. Note that in this case, the quadratic term $\boldsymbol{x}^T\mathbf{S}^{-1}\boldsymbol{x}$ cancels since it is common in all discriminants, and the decision boundaries are linear, leading to a *linear discriminant* (figure 5.4) that can be written as

LINEAR DISCRIMINANT

$$g_i(\boldsymbol{x}) = \boldsymbol{w}_i^T\boldsymbol{x} + w_{i0} \tag{5.23}$$

where

$$\begin{aligned} \boldsymbol{w}_i &= \mathbf{S}^{-1}\boldsymbol{m}_i \\ w_{i0} &= -\frac{1}{2}\boldsymbol{m}_i^T\mathbf{S}^{-1}\boldsymbol{m}_i + \log \hat{P}(C_i) \end{aligned}$$

Decision regions of such a linear classifier are convex; namely, when two points are chosen arbitrarily in one decision region and are connected by a straight line, all the points on the line will lie in the region.

Further simplication may be possible by assuming all off-diagonals of the covariance matrix to be 0, thus assuming independent variables. This is the *naive Bayes' classifier* where $p(x_j|C_i)$ are univariate Gaussian. $\mathbf{S}$ and its inverse are diagonal, and we get

NAIVE BAYES' CLASSIFIER

$$g_i(\boldsymbol{x}) = -\frac{1}{2}\sum_{j=1}^{d}\left(\frac{x_j^t - m_{ij}}{s_j}\right)^2 + \log \hat{P}(C_i) \tag{5.24}$$

The term $(x_j^t - m_{ij})/s_j$ has the effect of normalization and measures the distance in terms of standard deviation units. Geometrically speaking,

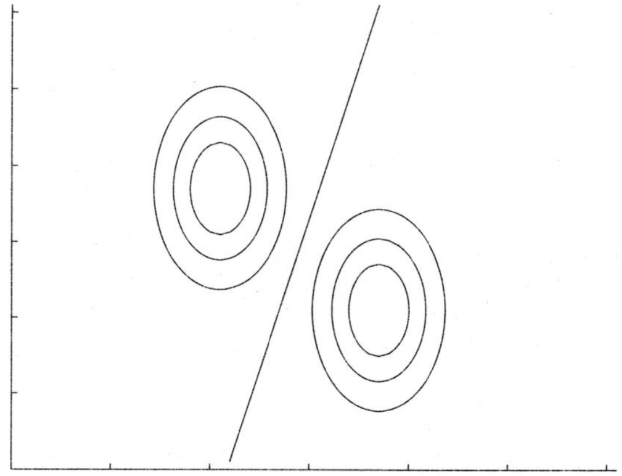

Figure 5.5 All classes have equal, diagonal covariance matrices, but variances are not equal.

classes are hyperellipsoidal and, because the covariances are zero, are axis-aligned (see figure 5.5). The number of parameters is $K \cdot d$ for the means and d for the variances. Thus the complexity of $\mathbf{S}$ is reduced from $\mathcal{O}(d^2)$ to $\mathcal{O}(d)$.

EUCLIDEAN DISTANCE

Simplifying even further, if we assume all variances to be equal, the Mahalanobis distance reduces to *Euclidean distance.* Geometrically, the distribution is shaped spherically, centered around the mean vector $\boldsymbol{m}_i$ (see figure 5.6). Then $|\mathbf{S}| = s^{2d}$ and $\mathbf{S}^{-1} = (1/s^2)\mathbf{I}$. The number of parameters in this case is $K \cdot d$ for the means and 1 for s^2.

$$g_i(\boldsymbol{x}) = -\frac{\|\boldsymbol{x} - \boldsymbol{m}_i\|^2}{2s^2} + \log \hat{P}(C_i) = -\frac{1}{2s^2}\sum_{j=1}^{d}(x_j^t - m_{ij})^2 + \log \hat{P}(C_i) \tag{5.25}$$

NEAREST MEAN CLASSIFIER

TEMPLATE MATCHING

If the priors are equal, we have $g_i(\boldsymbol{x}) = -\|\boldsymbol{x} - \boldsymbol{m}_i\|^2$. This is named the *nearest mean classifier* because it assigns the input to the class of the nearest mean. If each mean is thought of as the ideal prototype or template for the class, this is a *template matching* procedure. This can be expanded as

$$\begin{aligned} g_i(\boldsymbol{x}) &= -\|\boldsymbol{x} - \boldsymbol{m}_i\|^2 = -(\boldsymbol{x} - \boldsymbol{m}_i)^T(\boldsymbol{x} - \boldsymbol{m}_i) \\ &= -(\boldsymbol{x}^T\boldsymbol{x} - 2\boldsymbol{m}_i^T\boldsymbol{x} + \boldsymbol{m}_i^T\boldsymbol{m}_i) \end{aligned} \tag{5.26}$$

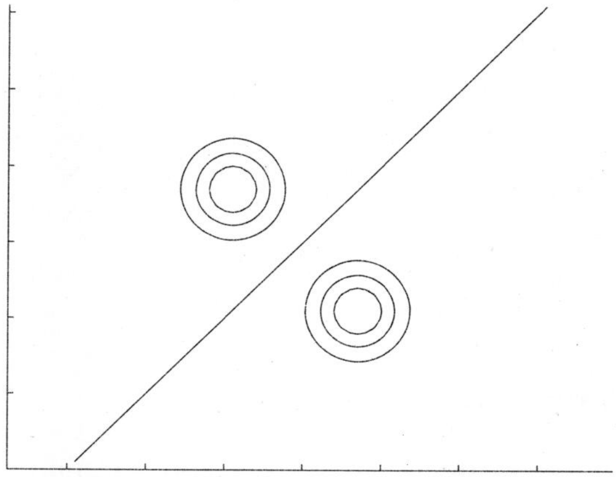

Figure 5.6 All classes have equal, diagonal covariance matrices of equal variances on both dimensions.

The first term, $\boldsymbol{x}^T\boldsymbol{x}$, is shared in all $g_i(\boldsymbol{x})$ and can be dropped, and we can write the discriminant function as

(5.27) $$g_i(\boldsymbol{x}) = \boldsymbol{w}_i^T\boldsymbol{x} + w_{i0}$$

where $\boldsymbol{w}_i = \boldsymbol{m}_i$ and $w_{i0} = -(1/2)\|\boldsymbol{m}_i\|^2$. If all $\boldsymbol{m}_i$ have similar norms, then this term can also be ignored and we can use

(5.28) $$g_i(\boldsymbol{x}) = \boldsymbol{m}_i^T\boldsymbol{x}$$

When the norms of $\boldsymbol{m}_i$ are comparable, dot product can also be used as the similarity measure instead of the (negative) Euclidean distance.

We can actually think of finding the best discriminant function as the task of finding the best distance function. This can be seen as another approach to classification: Instead of learning the discriminant functions, $g_i(\boldsymbol{x})$, we want to learn the suitable distance function $\mathcal{D}(\boldsymbol{x}_1, \boldsymbol{x}_2)$, such that for any $\boldsymbol{x}_1, \boldsymbol{x}_2, \boldsymbol{x}_3$, where $\boldsymbol{x}_1$ and $\boldsymbol{x}_2$ belong to the same class, and $\boldsymbol{x}_1$ and $\boldsymbol{x}_3$ belong to two different classes, we would like to have

$$\mathcal{D}(\boldsymbol{x}_1, \boldsymbol{x}_2) < \mathcal{D}(\boldsymbol{x}_1, \boldsymbol{x}_3)$$

Table 5.1 Reducing variance through simplifying assumptions

Assumption	Covariance matrix	No. of parameters
Shared, Hyperspheric	$\mathbf{S}_i = \mathbf{S} = s^2\mathbf{I}$	1
Shared, Axis-aligned	$\mathbf{S}_i = \mathbf{S}$, with $s_{ij} = 0$	d
Shared, Hyperellipsoidal	$\mathbf{S}_i = \mathbf{S}$	$d(d+1)/2$
Different, Hyperellipsoidal	$\mathbf{S}_i$	$K \cdot (d(d+1)/2)$

5.6 Tuning Complexity

In table 5.1, we see how the number of parameters of the covariance matrix may be reduced, trading off the comfort of a simple model with generality. This is another example of bias/variance dilemma. When we make simplifying assumptions about the covariance matrices and decrease the number of parameters to be estimated, we risk introducing bias (see figure 5.7). On the other hand, if no such assumption is made and the matrices are arbitrary, the quadratic discriminant may have large variance on small datasets. The ideal case depends on the complexity of the problem represented by the data at hand and the amount of data we have. When we have a small dataset, even if the covariance matrices are different, it may be better to assume a shared covariance matrix; a single covariance matrix has fewer parameters and it can be estimated using more data, that is, instances of all classes. This corresponds to using *linear discriminants*, which is very frequently used in classification and which we discuss in more detail in chapter 10.

Note that when we use Euclidean distance to measure similarity, we are assuming that all variables have the same variance and that they are independent. In many cases, this does not hold; for example, age and yearly income are in different units, and are dependent in many contexts. In such a case, the inputs may be separately z-normalized in a preprocessing stage (to have zero mean and unit variance), and then Euclidean distance can be used. On the other hand, sometimes even if the variables are dependent, it may be better to assume that they are independent and to use the naive Bayes' classifier, if we do not have enough data to calculate the dependency accurately.

REGULARIZED DISCRIMINANT ANALYSIS

Friedman (1989) proposed a method that combines all these as special cases, named *regularized discriminant analysis* (RDA). We remember

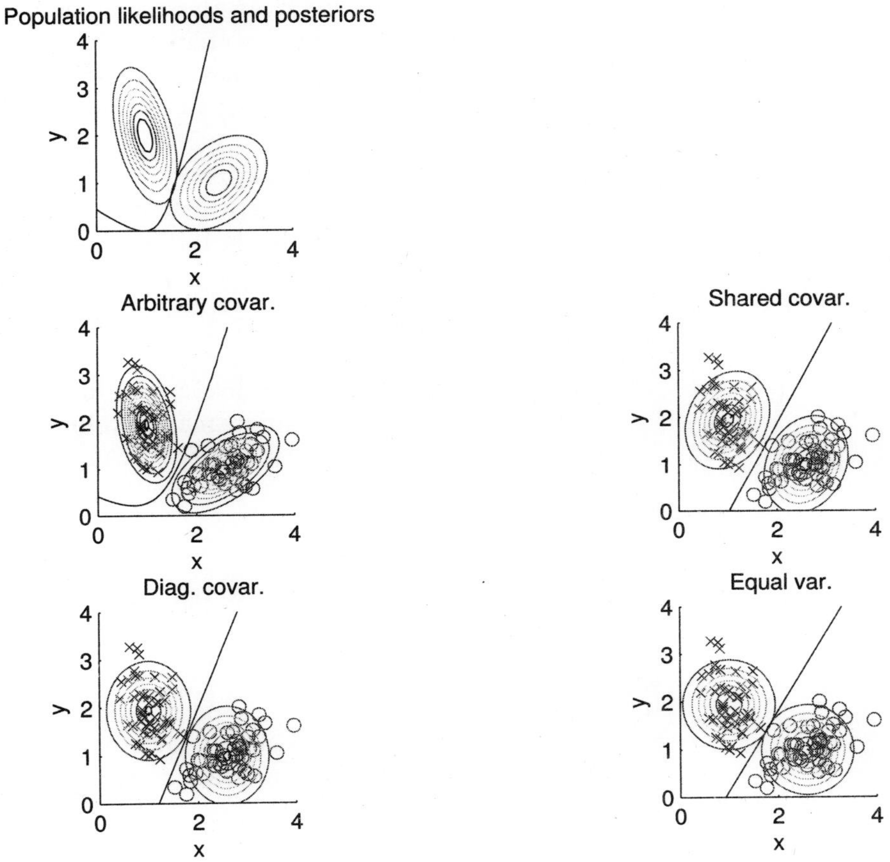

Figure 5.7 Different cases of the covariance matrices fitted to the same data lead to different boundaries.

that regularization corresponds to approaches where one starts with high variance and constrains toward lower variance, at the risk of increasing bias. In the case of parametric classification with Gaussian densities, the covariance matrices can be written as a weighted average of the three special cases:

$$\mathbf{S}_i' = \alpha\sigma^2\mathbf{I} + \beta\mathbf{S} + (1 - \alpha - \beta)\mathbf{S}_i \tag{5.29}$$

When $\alpha = \beta = 0$, this leads to a quadratic classifier. When $\alpha = 0$ and

$\beta = 1$, the covariance matrices are shared, and we get linear classifiers. When $\alpha = 1$ and $\beta = 0$, the covariance matrices are diagonal with σ^2 on the diagonals, and we get the nearest mean classifier. In between these extremes, we get a whole variety of classifiers where α, β are optimized by cross-validation.

Another approach to regularization, when the dataset is small, is one that uses a Bayesian approach by defining priors on $\boldsymbol{\mu}_i$ and $\mathbf{S}_i$ or that uses cross-validation to choose the best of the four cases given in table 5.1.

5.7 Discrete Features

In some applications, we have discrete attributes taking one of n different values. For example, an attribute may be color $\in$ {red, blue, green, black}, or another may be pixel $\in$ {on, off}. Let us say x_j are binary (Bernoulli) where

$$p_{ij} \equiv p(x_j = 1|C_i)$$

If x_j are independent binary variables, we have

$$p(\mathbf{x}|C_i) = \prod_{j=1}^{d} p_{ij}^{x_j}(1 - p_{ij})^{(1-x_j)}$$

This is another example of the naive Bayes' classifier where $p(x_j|C_i)$ are Bernoulli. The discriminant function is

$$\begin{aligned} g_i(\mathbf{x}) &= \log p(\mathbf{x}|C_i) + \log P(C_i) \\ &= \sum_j \left[x_j \log p_{ij} + (1 - x_j)\log(1 - p_{ij})\right] + \log P(C_i) \end{aligned} \tag{5.30}$$

which is linear. The estimator for p_{ij} is

$$\hat{p}_{ij} = \frac{\sum_t x_j^t r_i^t}{\sum_t r_i^t} \tag{5.31}$$

DOCUMENT CATEGORIZATION

BAG OF WORDS

This approach is used in *document categorization*, an example of which is classifying news reports into various categories, such as, politics, sports, fashion, and so forth. In the *bag of words* representation, we choose a priori d words that we believe give information regarding the class (Manning and Schütze 1999). For example, in news classification, words such as "missile," "athlete," and "couture" are useful, rather than ambiguous words such as "model," or even "runway." In this representation, each text is a d-dimensional binary vector where x_j is 1 if word j occurs in the document and is 0 otherwise. Note that this representation loses all ordering information of words, and hence the name *bag* of words.

After training, $\hat{p}_{ij}$ estimates the probability that word j occurs in document type i. Words whose probabilities are similar for different classes do not convey much information; for them to be useful, we would want the probability to be high for one class (or few) and low for all others; we are going to talk about this type of *feature selection* in chapter 6. Another example application of document categorization is *spam filtering* where there are two classes of emails as spam and legitimate. In bioinformatics, too, inputs are generally sequences of discrete items, whether base-pairs or amino acids.

SPAM FILTERING

In the general case, instead of binary features, let us say we have the multinomial x_j chosen from the set $\{v_1, v_2, \ldots, v_{n_j}\}$. We define new 0/1 dummy variables as

$$z_{jk}^t = \begin{cases} 1 & \text{if } x_j^t = v_k \\ 0 & \text{otherwise} \end{cases}$$

Let p_{ijk} denote the probability that x_j belonging to C_i takes value v_k:

$$p_{ijk} \equiv p(z_{jk} = 1|C_i) = p(x_j = v_k|C_i)$$

If the attributes are independent, we have

(5.32) $$p(\mathbf{x}|C_i) = \prod_{j=1}^{d} \prod_{k=1}^{n_j} p_{ijk}^{z_{jk}}$$

The discriminant function is then

(5.33) $$g_i(\mathbf{x}) = \sum_j \sum_k z_{jk} \log p_{ijk} + \log P(C_i)$$

The maximum likelihood estimator for p_{ijk} is

(5.34) $$\hat{p}_{ijk} = \frac{\sum_t z_{jk}^t r_i^t}{\sum_t r_i^t}$$

which can be plugged into equation 5.33 to give us the discriminant.

5.8 Multivariate Regression

MULTIVARIATE LINEAR REGRESSION

In *multivariate linear regression*, the numeric output r is assumed to be written as a linear function, that is, a weighted sum, of several input variables, $x_1, \ldots, x_d$, and noise. Actually in statistical literature, this is called *multiple* regression; statisticians use the term *multivariate* when there are multiple outputs. The multivariate linear model is

$$r^t = g(\mathbf{x}^t | w_0, w_1, \ldots, w_d) + \epsilon = w_0 + w_1 x_1^t + w_2 x_2^t + \cdots + w_d x_d^t + \epsilon \tag{5.35}$$

As in the univariate case, we assume ϵ to be normal with mean 0 and constant variance, and maximizing the likelihood is equivalent to minimizing the sum of squared errors:

$$E(w_0, w_1, \ldots, w_d | \mathcal{X}) = \frac{1}{2} \sum_t (r^t - w_0 - w_1 x_1^t - w_2 x_2^t - \cdots - w_d x_d^t)^2 \tag{5.36}$$

Taking the derivative with respect to the parameters, $w_j, j = 0, \ldots, d$, we get these *normal equations*:

$$\begin{aligned} \sum_t r^t &= N w_0 + w_1 \sum_t x_1^t + w_2 \sum_t x_2^t + \cdots + w_d \sum_t x_d^t \\ \sum_t x_1^t r^t &= w_0 \sum_t x_1^t + w_1 \sum_t (x_1^t)^2 + w_2 \sum_t x_1^t x_2^t + \cdots + w_d \sum_t x_1^t x_d^t \\ \sum_t x_2^t r^t &= w_0 \sum_t x_2^t + w_1 \sum_t x_1^t x_2^t + w_2 \sum_t (x_2^t)^2 + \cdots + w_d \sum_t x_2^t x_d^t \\ &\vdots \\ \sum_t x_d^t r^t &= w_0 \sum_t x_d^t + w_1 \sum_t x_d^t x_1^t + w_2 \sum_t x_d^t x_2^t + \cdots + w_d \sum_t (x_d^t)^2 \end{aligned} \tag{5.37}$$

Let us define the following vectors and matrix:

$$\mathbf{X} = \begin{bmatrix} 1 & x_1^1 & x_2^1 & \cdots & x_d^1 \\ 1 & x_1^2 & x_2^2 & \cdots & x_d^2 \\ \vdots & & & & \\ 1 & x_1^N & x_2^N & \cdots & x_d^N \end{bmatrix}, \boldsymbol{w} = \begin{bmatrix} w_0 \\ w_1 \\ \vdots \\ w_d, \end{bmatrix}, \boldsymbol{r} = \begin{bmatrix} r^1 \\ r^2 \\ \vdots \\ r^N \end{bmatrix}$$

Then the normal equations can be written as

$$\mathbf{X}^T \mathbf{X} \boldsymbol{w} = \mathbf{X}^T \boldsymbol{r} \tag{5.38}$$

and we can solve for the parameters as

$$\boldsymbol{w} = (\mathbf{X}^T \mathbf{X})^{-1} \mathbf{X}^T \boldsymbol{r} \tag{5.39}$$

This method is the same as we used for polynomial regression using one input. The two problems are the same if we define the variables as

MULTIVARIATE POLYNOMIAL REGRESSION

$x_1 = x, x_2 = x^2, \ldots, x_k = x^k$. This also gives us a hint as to how we can do *multivariate polynomial regression* if necessary (exercise 7), but unless d is small, in multivariate regression, we rarely use polynomials of an order higher than linear.

Actually using higher-order terms of inputs as additional inputs is only one possibility; we can define any nonlinear function of the original inputs using *basis functions.* For example, we can define new inputs $x_2 = \sin(x), x_3 = \exp(x^2)$ if we believe that such a transformation is useful. Then, using a linear model in this new augmented space will correspond to a nonlinear model in the original space. The same calculation will still be valid; we need only replace $\mathbf{X}$ with the data matrix after the basis functions are applied. As we will see later under various guises (e.g., multilayer perceptrons, support vector machines, Gaussian processes), this type of generalizing the linear model is frequently used.

One advantage of linear models is that after the regression, looking at the $w_j, j = 1, \ldots, d$, values, we can extract knowledge: First, by looking at the signs of w_j, we can see whether x_j have a positive or negative effect on the output. Second, if all x_j are in the same range, by looking at the absolute values of w_j, we can get an idea about how important a feature is, rank the features in terms of their importances, and even remove the features whose w_j are close to 0.

When there are multiple outputs, this can equivalently be defined as a set of independent single-output regression problems.

5.9 Notes

A good review text on linear algebra is Strang 2006. Harville 1997 is another excellent book that looks at matrix algebra from a statistical point of view.

One inconvenience with multivariate data is that when the number of dimensions is large, one cannot do a visual analysis. There are methods proposed in the statistical literature for displaying multivariate data; a review is given in Rencher 1995. One possibility is to plot variables two by two as bivariate scatter plots: If the data is multivariate normal, then the plot of any two variables should be roughly linear; this can be used as a visual test of multivariate normality. Another possibility that we discuss in chapter 6 is to project them to one or two dimensions and display there.

Most work on pattern recognition is done assuming multivariate normal densities. Sometimes such a discriminant is even called the Bayes' optimal classifier, but this is generally wrong; it is only optimal if the densities are indeed multivariate normal and if we have enough data to calculate the correct parameters from the data. Rencher 1995 discusses tests for assessing multivariate normality as well as tests for checking for equal covariance matrices. McLachlan 1992 discusses classification with multivariate normals and compares linear and quadratic discriminants.

One obvious restriction of multivariate normals is that it does not allow for data where some features are discrete. A variable with n possible values can be converted into n dummy 0/1 variables, but this increases dimensionality. One can do a dimensionality reduction in this n-dimensional space by a method explained in chapter 6 and thereby not increase dimensionality. Parametric classification for such cases of mixed features is discussed in detail in McLachlan 1992.

5.10 Exercises

1. Show equation 5.11.

   SOLUTION: Given that

$$\boldsymbol{\Sigma} = \begin{bmatrix} \sigma_1^2 & \rho\sigma_1\sigma_2 \\ \rho\sigma_1\sigma_2 & \sigma_2^2 \end{bmatrix}$$

   we have

$$\begin{aligned} |\boldsymbol{\Sigma}| &= \sigma_1^2\sigma_2^2 - \rho^2\sigma_1^2\sigma_2^2 = \sigma_1^2\sigma_2^2(1-\rho^2) \\ |\boldsymbol{\Sigma}|^{1/2} &= \sigma_1\sigma_2\sqrt{1-\rho^2} \\ \boldsymbol{\Sigma}^{-1} &= \frac{1}{\sigma_1^2\sigma_2^2(1-\rho^2)} \begin{bmatrix} \sigma_2^2 & -\rho\sigma_1\sigma_2 \\ -\rho\sigma_1\sigma_2 & \sigma_1^2 \end{bmatrix} \end{aligned}$$

   and $(\boldsymbol{x}-\boldsymbol{\mu})^T\boldsymbol{\Sigma}^{-1}(\boldsymbol{x}-\boldsymbol{\mu})$ can be expanded as

$$[x_1-\mu_1 \ x_2-\mu_2] \begin{bmatrix} \frac{\sigma_2^2}{\sigma_1^2\sigma_2^2(1-\rho^2)} & -\frac{\rho\sigma_1\sigma_2}{\sigma_1^2\sigma_2^2(1-\rho^2)} \\ -\frac{\rho\sigma_1\sigma_2}{\sigma_1^2\sigma_2^2(1-\rho^2)} & \frac{\sigma_1^2}{\sigma_1^2\sigma_2^2(1-\rho^2)} \end{bmatrix} \begin{bmatrix} x_1-\mu_1 \\ x_2-\mu_2 \end{bmatrix}$$

$$= \frac{1}{1-\rho^2}\left[\left(\frac{x_1-\mu_1}{\sigma_1}\right)^2 - 2\rho\left(\frac{x_1-\mu_1}{\sigma_1}\right)\left(\frac{x_2-\mu_2}{\sigma_2}\right) + \left(\frac{x_2-\mu_2}{\sigma_2}\right)^2\right]$$

2. Generate a sample from a multivariate normal density $\mathcal{N}(\boldsymbol{\mu}, \boldsymbol{\Sigma})$, calculate $\boldsymbol{m}$ and $\mathbf{S}$, and compare them with $\boldsymbol{\mu}$ and $\boldsymbol{\Sigma}$. Check how your estimates change as the sample size changes.

3. Generate samples from two multivariate normal densities $\mathcal{N}(\boldsymbol{\mu}_i, \boldsymbol{\Sigma}_i), i = 1, 2$, and calculate the Bayes' optimal discriminant for the four cases in table 5.1.
4. For a two-class problem, for the four cases of Gaussian densities in table 5.1, derive
$$\log \frac{P(C_1|\boldsymbol{x})}{P(C_2|\boldsymbol{x})}$$
5. Another possibility using Gaussian densities is to have them all diagonal but allow them to be different. Derive the discriminant for this case.
6. Let us say in two dimensions, we have two classes with exactly the same mean. What type of boundaries can be defined?
7. Let us say we have two variables x_1 and x_2 and we want to make a quadratic fit using them, namely,
$$f(x_1, x_2) = w_0 + w_1 x_1 + w_2 x_2 + w_3 x_1 x_2 + w_4 (x_1)^2 + w_5 (x_2)^2$$
How can we find $w_i, i = 0, \ldots, 5$, given a sample of $\mathcal{X} = \{x_1^t, x_2^t, r^t\}$?
SOLUTION: We write the fit as
$$f(x_1, x_2) = w_0 + w_1 z_1 + w_2 z_2 + w_3 z_3 + w_4 z_4 + w_5 z_5$$
where $z_1 = x_1$, $z_2 = x_2$, $z_3 = x_1 x_2$, $z_4 = (x_1)^2$, and $z_5 = (x_2)^2$. We can then use linear regression to learn $w_i, i = 0, \ldots, 5$. The linear fit in the five-dimensional $(z_1, z_2, z_3, z_4, z_5)$ space corresponds to a quadratic fit in the two-dimensional (x_1, x_2) space. We discuss such generalized linear models in more detail (and other nonlinear basis functions) in chapter 10.
8. In regression we saw that fitting a quadratic is equivalent to fitting a linear model with an extra input corresponding to the square of the input. Can we also do this in classification?
SOLUTION: Yes. We can define new, auxiliary variables corresponding to powers and cross-product terms and then use a linear model. For example, just as in exercise 7, we can define $z_1 = x_1$, $z_2 = x_2$, $z_3 = x_1 x_2$, $z_4 = (x_1)^2$, and $z_5 = (x_2)^2$ and then use a linear model to learn $w_i, i = 0, \ldots, 5$. The linear discriminant in the five-dimensional $(z_1, z_2, z_3, z_4, z_5)$ space corresponds to a quadratic discriminant in the two-dimensional (x_1, x_2) space.
9. In document clustering, ambiguity of words can be decreased by taking the context into account, for example, by considering pairs of words, as in "cocktail party" vs. "party elections." Discuss how this can be implemented.

5.11 References

Duda, R. O., P. E. Hart, and D. G. Stork. 2001. *Pattern Classification*, 2nd ed. New York: Wiley.

Friedman, J. H. 1989. "Regularized Discriminant Analysis." *Journal of American Statistical Association* 84:165–175.

Harville, D. A. 1997. *Matrix Algebra from a Statistician's Perspective.* New York: Springer.

Manning, C. D., and H. Schütze. 1999. *Foundations of Statistical Natural Language Processing.* Cambridge, MA: MIT Press.

McLachlan, G. J. 1992. *Discriminant Analysis and Statistical Pattern Recognition.* New York: Wiley.

Rencher, A. C. 1995. *Methods of Multivariate Analysis.* New York: Wiley.

Strang, G. 2006. *Linear Algebra and its Applications*, 4th ed. Boston: Cengage Learning.

6 Dimensionality Reduction

The complexity of any classifier or regressor depends on the number of inputs. This determines both the time and space complexity and the necessary number of training examples to train such a classifier or regressor. In this chapter, we discuss feature selection methods that choose a subset of important features pruning the rest and feature extraction methods that form fewer, new features from the original inputs.

6.1 Introduction

IN AN APPLICATION, whether it is classification or regression, observation data that we believe contain information are taken as inputs and fed to the system for decision making. Ideally, we should not need feature selection or extraction as a separate process; the classifier (or regressor) should be able to use whichever features are necessary, discarding the irrelevant. However, there are several reasons why we are interested in reducing dimensionality as a separate preprocessing step:

- In most learning algorithms, the complexity depends on the number of input dimensions, d, as well as on the size of the data sample, N, and for reduced memory and computation, we are interested in reducing the dimensionality of the problem. Decreasing d also decreases the complexity of the inference algorithm during testing.

- When an input is decided to be unnecessary, we save the cost of extracting it.

- Simpler models are more robust on small datasets. Simpler models have less variance, that is, they vary less depending on the particulars of a sample, including noise, outliers, and so forth.

- When data can be explained with fewer features, we get a better idea about the process that underlies the data and this allows knowledge extraction. These fewer features may be interpreted as *hidden* or *latent factors* that in combination generate the observed features.
- When data can be represented in a few dimensions without loss of information, it can be plotted and analyzed visually for structure and outliers.

There are two main methods for reducing dimensionality: feature selection and feature extraction. In *feature selection*, we are interested in finding k of the d dimensions that give us the most information, and we discard the other $(d - k)$ dimensions. We discuss *subset selection* as a feature selection method.

FEATURE SELECTION

In *feature extraction*, we are interested in finding a new set of k dimensions that are combinations of the original d dimensions. These methods may be supervised or unsupervised depending on whether or not they use the output information. The best known and most widely used feature extraction methods are *principal component analysis* and *linear discriminant analysis*, which are both linear projection methods, unsupervised and supervised respectively. Principal component analysis bears much similarity to two other unsupervised linear methods, which we also discuss—namely, *factor analysis* and *multidimensional scaling*. When we have not one but two sets of observed variables, *canonical correlation analysis* can be used to find the joint features that explain the dependency between the two. Examples of *nonlinear* dimensionality reduction we cover are *isometric feature mapping, locally linear embedding*, and *Laplacian eigenmaps*.

FEATURE EXTRACTION

6.2 Subset Selection

SUBSET SELECTION

In *subset selection*, we are interested in finding the best subset of the set of features. The best subset contains the least number of dimensions that most contribute to accuracy. We discard the remaining, unimportant dimensions. Using a suitable error function, this can be used in both regression and classification problems. There are 2^d possible subsets of d variables, but we cannot test for all of them unless d is small and we employ heuristics to get a reasonable (but not optimal) solution in reasonable (polynomial) time.

FORWARD SELECTION

There are two approaches: In *forward selection*, we start with no variables and add them one by one, at each step adding the one that decreases the error the most, until any further addition does not decrease the error (or decreases it only slightly). In *backward selection*, we start with all variables and remove them one by one, at each step removing the one that decreases the error the most (or increases it only slightly), until any further removal increases the error significantly. In either case, checking the error should be done on a validation set distinct from the training set because we want to test the generalization accuracy. With more features, generally we have lower training error, but not necessarily lower validation error.

BACKWARD SELECTION

Let us denote by F, a feature set of input dimensions, $x_i, i = 1, \ldots, d$. $E(F)$ denotes the error incurred on the validation sample when only the inputs in F are used. Depending on the application, the error is either the mean square error or misclassification error.

In *sequential forward selection*, we start with no features: $F = \emptyset$. At each step, for all possible x_i, we train our model on the training set and calculate $E(F \cup x_i)$ on the validation set. Then, we choose that input x_j that causes the least error

$$j = \arg\min_i E(F \cup x_i) \tag{6.1}$$

and we

$$\text{add } x_j \text{ to } F \text{ if } E(F \cup x_j) < E(F) \tag{6.2}$$

We stop if adding any feature does not decrease E. We may even decide to stop earlier if the decrease in error is too small, where there is a user-defined threshold that depends on the application constraints, trading off the importance of error and complexity. Adding another feature introduces the cost of observing the feature, as well as making the classifier/regressor more complex.

WRAPPER

This algorithm is also known as the *wrapper* approach, where the process of feature extraction is thought to "wrap" around the learner it uses as a subroutine (Kohavi and John 2007).

Let us see an example on the Iris data from the UCI repository; it has four inputs and three classes. There are fifty instances per class, and we use twenty for training and the remaining thirty for validation. We use the nearest mean as the classifier (see equation 5.26) in section 5.5. We start with a single feature; the plots of training data using single features separately are shown in figure 6.1. Using nearest mean in these one-dimensional spaces of features one to four lead to validation accuracies of 0.76, 0.57, 0.92, and 0.94, respectively. Hence, we select the fourth feature (F4) as our first feature. We then check whether adding another feature leads to improvement. The bivariate plots are shown in figure 6.2; the corresponding validation accuracies using the nearest mean classifier in these two-dimensional spaces are 0.87, 0.92, and 0.96 for (F1,F4), (F2,F4), and (F3,F4), respectively. Thus the third feature is added to as the second feature. Then we check whether adding the first feature or the second feature leads to further improvement; the validation accuracies of the nearest mean classifier in these three-dimensional spaces are both 0.94, and hence we stop with the third and fourth features as our selected features. Incidentally, using *all* four features, we get validation accuracy of 0.94—getting rid of the first two leads to an increase in accuracy.

Note that the features we select at the end depend heavily on the classifier we use. Another important point is that on small datasets, the selected features may also depend on the way data is split between training and validation data; hence on small datasets, it may be a better idea to do multiple, random training/validation splits and decide by looking at average validation performance—we will talk about such resampling methods in chapter 19.

This process of testing features one by one may be costly because to decrease the dimensions from d to k, we need to train and test the system $d + (d-1) + (d-2) + \cdots + (d-k)$ times, which is $\mathcal{O}(d^2)$. This is a local search procedure and does not guarantee finding the optimal subset, namely, the minimal subset causing the smallest error. For example, x_i and x_j by themselves may not be good but together may decrease the error a lot, but because this algorithm is greedy and adds attributes one by one, it may not be able to detect this. It is possible to add multiple features at a time, instead of a single one, at the expense of more computation. We can also backtrack and check which, if any, previously added feature can be removed after a current addition, thereby increasing the search space, but this increases complexity. In *floating search* methods (Pudil, Novovičová, and Kittler 1994), the number of added features and removed features can also change at each step.

FLOATING SEARCH

In *sequential backward selection*, we start with F containing all features

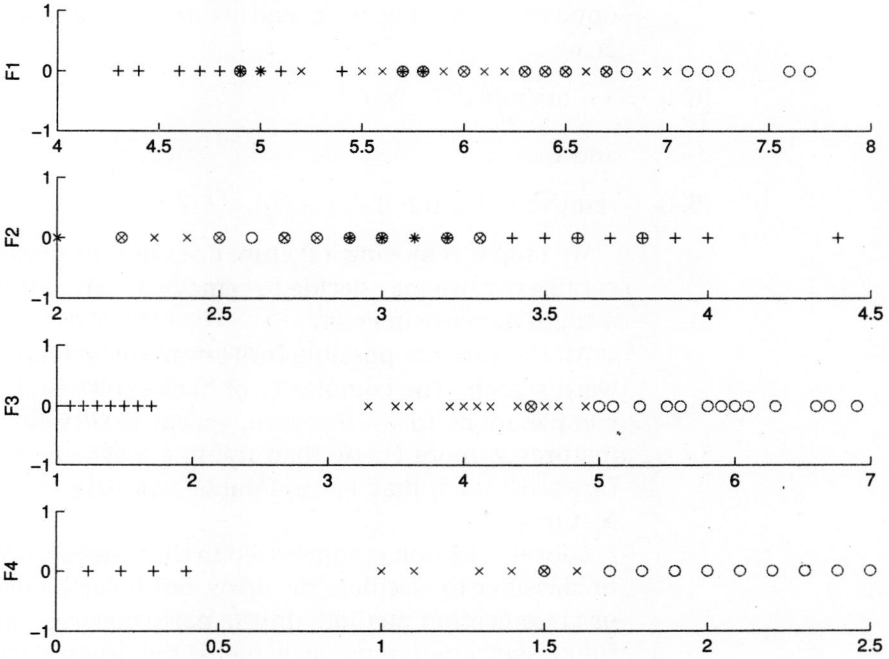

Figure 6.1 Plot of the training data for single features on Iris dataset; the three classes are shown with different symbols. It can be seen that F4 by itself allows quite good discrimination.

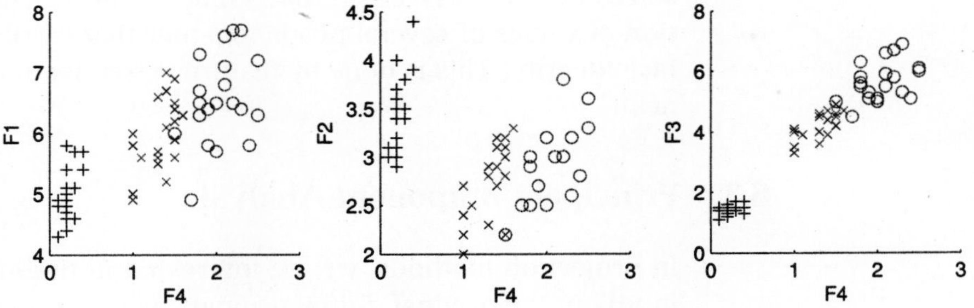

Figure 6.2 Plot of the training data with F4 as one feature, together with one of F1, F2, and F3. Using (F3, F4) leads to best separation.

and do a similar process except that we remove one attribute from F as opposed to adding to it, and we remove the one that causes the least error

$$j = \arg\min_i E(F - x_i) \tag{6.3}$$

and we

$$\text{remove } x_j \text{ from } F \text{ if } E(F - x_j) < E(F) \tag{6.4}$$

We stop if removing a feature does not decrease the error. To decrease complexity, we may decide to remove a feature if its removal causes only a slight increase in error.

All the variants possible for forward search are also possible for backward search. The complexity of backward search has the same order of complexity as forward search, except that training a system with more features is more costly than training a system with fewer features, and forward search may be preferable especially if we expect many useless features.

Subset selection is supervised in that outputs are used by the regressor or classifier to calculate the error, but it can be used with any regression or classification method. In the particular case of multivariate normals for classification, remember that if the original d-dimensional class densities are multivariate normal, then any subset is also multivariate normal and parametric classification can still be used with the advantage of $k \times k$ covariance matrices instead of $d \times d$.

In an application like face recognition, feature selection is not a good method for dimensionality reduction because individual pixels by themselves do not carry much discriminative information; it is the combination of values of several pixels together that carry information about the face identity. This is done by feature extraction methods that we discuss next.

6.3 Principal Component Analysis

In projection methods, we are interested in finding a mapping from the inputs in the original d-dimensional space to a new $(k < d)$-dimensional space, with minimum loss of information. The projection of $\boldsymbol{x}$ on the direction of $\boldsymbol{w}$ is

$$z = \boldsymbol{w}^T \boldsymbol{x} \tag{6.5}$$

PRINCIPAL COMPONENT ANALYSIS

Principal component analysis (PCA) is an unsupervised method in that it does not use the output information; the criterion to be maximized is the variance. The principal component is $\mathbf{w}_1$ such that the sample, after projection on to $\mathbf{w}_1$, is most spread out so that the difference between the sample points becomes most apparent. For a unique solution and to make the direction the important factor, we require $\|\mathbf{w}_1\| = 1$. We know from equation 5.14 that if $z_1 = \mathbf{w}_1^T \mathbf{x}$ with $\text{Cov}(\mathbf{x}) = \Sigma$, then

$$\text{Var}(z_1) = \mathbf{w}_1^T \Sigma \mathbf{w}_1$$

We seek $\mathbf{w}_1$ such that $\text{Var}(z_1)$ is maximized subject to the constraint that $\mathbf{w}_1^T \mathbf{w}_1 = 1$. Writing this as a Lagrange problem, we have

$$\max_{\mathbf{w}_1} \mathbf{w}_1^T \Sigma \mathbf{w}_1 - \alpha(\mathbf{w}_1^T \mathbf{w}_1 - 1) \tag{6.6}$$

Taking the derivative with respect to $\mathbf{w}_1$ and setting it equal to 0, we have

$$2\Sigma \mathbf{w}_1 - 2\alpha \mathbf{w}_1 = 0, \text{ and therefore } \Sigma \mathbf{w}_1 = \alpha \mathbf{w}_1$$

which holds if $\mathbf{w}_1$ is an eigenvector of Σ and α the corresponding eigenvalue. Because we want to maximize

$$\mathbf{w}_1^T \Sigma \mathbf{w}_1 = \alpha \mathbf{w}_1^T \mathbf{w}_1 = \alpha$$

we choose the eigenvector with the largest eigenvalue for the variance to be maximum. Therefore the principal component is the eigenvector of the covariance matrix of the input sample with the largest eigenvalue, $\lambda_1 = \alpha$.

The second principal component, $\mathbf{w}_2$, should also maximize variance, be of unit length, and be orthogonal to $\mathbf{w}_1$. This latter requirement is so that after projection $z_2 = \mathbf{w}_2^T \mathbf{x}$ is uncorrelated with z_1. For the second principal component, we have

$$\max_{\mathbf{w}_2} \mathbf{w}_2^T \Sigma \mathbf{w}_2 - \alpha(\mathbf{w}_2^T \mathbf{w}_2 - 1) - \beta(\mathbf{w}_2^T \mathbf{w}_1 - 0) \tag{6.7}$$

Taking the derivative with respect to $\mathbf{w}_2$ and setting it equal to 0, we have

$$2\Sigma \mathbf{w}_2 - 2\alpha \mathbf{w}_2 - \beta \mathbf{w}_1 = 0 \tag{6.8}$$

Premultiply by $\mathbf{w}_1^T$ and we get

$$2\mathbf{w}_1^T \Sigma \mathbf{w}_2 - 2\alpha \mathbf{w}_1^T \mathbf{w}_2 - \beta \mathbf{w}_1^T \mathbf{w}_1 = 0$$

Note that $w_1^T w_2 = 0$. $w_1^T \Sigma w_2$ is a scalar, equal to its transpose $w_2^T \Sigma w_1$ where, because w_1 is the leading eigenvector of Σ, $\Sigma w_1 = \lambda_1 w_1$. Therefore

$$w_1^T \Sigma w_2 = w_2^T \Sigma w_1 = \lambda_1 w_2^T w_1 = 0$$

Then $\beta = 0$ and equation 6.8 reduces to

$$\Sigma w_2 = \alpha w_2$$

which implies that w_2 should be the eigenvector of Σ with the second largest eigenvalue, $\lambda_2 = \alpha$. Similarly, we can show that the other dimensions are given by the eigenvectors with decreasing eigenvalues.

Because Σ is symmetric, for two different eigenvalues, the eigenvectors are orthogonal. If Σ is positive definite ($x^T \Sigma x > 0$, for all nonnull x), then all its eigenvalues are positive. If Σ is singular, then its rank, the effective dimensionality, is k with $k < d$ and $\lambda_i, i = k+1, \ldots, d$ are 0 (λ_i are sorted in descending order). The k eigenvectors with nonzero eigenvalues are the dimensions of the reduced space. The first eigenvector (the one with the largest eigenvalue), w_1, namely, the principal component, explains the largest part of the variance; the second explains the second largest; and so on.

We define

$$\mathbf{z} = \mathbf{W}^T (\mathbf{x} - \mathbf{m}) \tag{6.9}$$

where the k columns of $\mathbf{W}$ are the k leading eigenvectors of $\mathbf{S}$, the estimator to Σ. We subtract the sample mean m from x before projection to center the data on the origin. After this linear transformation, we get to a k-dimensional space whose dimensions are the eigenvectors, and the variances over these new dimensions are equal to the eigenvalues (see figure 6.3). To normalize variances, we can divide by the square roots of the eigenvalues.

Let us see another derivation: We want to find a matrix $\mathbf{W}$ such that when we have $z = \mathbf{W}^T x$ (assume without loss of generality that x are already centered), we will get $\text{Cov}(z) = \mathbf{D}$ where $\mathbf{D}$ is any diagonal matrix; that is, we would like to get uncorrelated z_i.

If we form a $(d \times d)$ matrix $\mathbf{C}$ whose ith column is the normalized eigenvector c_i of $\mathbf{S}$, then $\mathbf{C}^T\mathbf{C} = \mathbf{I}$ and

$$\begin{aligned}\mathbf{S} &= \mathbf{S}\mathbf{C}\mathbf{C}^T \\ &= \mathbf{S}(c_1, c_2, \ldots, c_d)\mathbf{C}^T\end{aligned}$$

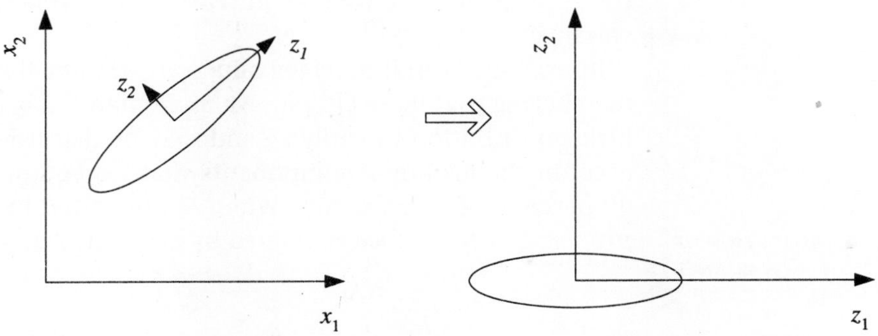

Figure 6.3 Principal component analysis centers the sample and then rotates the axes to line up with the directions of highest variance. If the variance on z_2 is too small, it can be ignored and we have dimensionality reduction from two to one.

$$
\begin{aligned}
&= (\mathbf{S}c_1, \mathbf{S}c_2, \ldots, \mathbf{S}c_d)C^T \\
&= (\lambda_1 \mathbf{c}_1, \lambda_2 \mathbf{c}_2, \ldots, \lambda_d \mathbf{c}_d)\mathbf{C}^T \\
&= \lambda_1 \mathbf{c}_1 \mathbf{c}_1^T + \cdots + \lambda_d \mathbf{c}_d \mathbf{c}_d^T \\
&= \mathbf{C}\mathbf{D}\mathbf{C}^T \qquad (6.10)
\end{aligned}
$$

SPECTRAL DECOMPOSITION

where $\mathbf{D}$ is a diagonal matrix whose diagonal elements are the eigenvalues, $\lambda_1, \ldots, \lambda_d$. This is called the *spectral decomposition* of $\mathbf{S}$. Since $\mathbf{C}$ is orthogonal and $\mathbf{C}\mathbf{C}^T = \mathbf{C}^T\mathbf{C} = \mathbf{I}$, we can multiply on the left by $\mathbf{C}^T$ and on the right by $\mathbf{C}$ to obtain

$$\mathbf{C}^T\mathbf{S}\mathbf{C} = \mathbf{D} \qquad (6.11)$$

We know that if $\boldsymbol{z} = \mathbf{W}^T\boldsymbol{x}$, then $\text{Cov}(\boldsymbol{z}) = \mathbf{W}^T\mathbf{S}\mathbf{W}$, which we would like to be equal to a diagonal matrix. Then from equation 6.11, we see that we can set $\mathbf{W} = \mathbf{C}$.

Let us see an example to get some intuition (Rencher 1995): Assume we are given a class of students with grades on five courses and we want to order these students. That is, we want to project the data onto one dimension, such that the difference between the data points become most apparent. We can use PCA. The eigenvector with the highest eigenvalue is the direction that has the highest variance, that is, the direction on which the students are most spread out. This works better than taking the average because we take into account correlations and differences in variances.

In practice even if all eigenvalues are greater than 0, if $|\mathbf{S}|$ is small, remembering that $|\mathbf{S}| = \prod_{i=1}^{d} \lambda_i$, we understand that some eigenvalues have little contribution to variance and may be discarded. Then, we take into account the leading k components that explain more than, for example, 90 percent, of the variance. When λ_i are sorted in descending order, the *proportion of variance* explained by the k principal components is

PROPORTION OF VARIANCE

$$\frac{\lambda_1 + \lambda_2 + \cdots + \lambda_k}{\lambda_1 + \lambda_2 + \cdots + \lambda_k + \cdots + \lambda_d}$$

If the dimensions are highly correlated, there will be a small number of eigenvectors with large eigenvalues and k will be much smaller than d and a large reduction in dimensionality may be attained. This is typically the case in many image and speech processing tasks where nearby inputs (in space or time) are highly correlated. If the dimensions are not correlated, k will be as large as d and there is no gain through PCA.

SCREE GRAPH

Scree graph is the plot of variance explained as a function of the number of eigenvectors kept (see figure 6.4). By visually analyzing it, one can also decide on k. At the "elbow," adding another eigenvector does not significantly increase the variance explained.

Another possibility is to ignore the eigenvectors whose eigenvalues are less than the average input variance. Given that $\sum_i \lambda_i = \sum_i s_i^2$ (equal to the *trace* of $\mathbf{S}$, denoted as $\text{tr}(\mathbf{S})$), the average eigenvalue is equal to the average input variance. When we keep only the eigenvectors with eigenvalues greater than the average eigenvalue, we keep only those that have variance higher than the average input variance.

If the variances of the original x_i dimensions vary considerably, they affect the direction of the principal components more than the correlations, so a common procedure is to preprocess the data so that each dimension has mean 0 and unit variance, before using PCA. Or, one may use the eigenvectors of the correlation matrix, $\mathbf{R}$, instead of the covariance matrix, $\mathbf{S}$, for the correlations to be effective and not the individual variances.

PCA explains variance and is sensitive to outliers: A few points distant from the center would have a large effect on the variances and thus the eigenvectors. *Robust estimation* methods allow calculating parameters in the presence of outliers. A simple method is to calculate the Mahalanobis distance of the data points, discarding the isolated data points that are

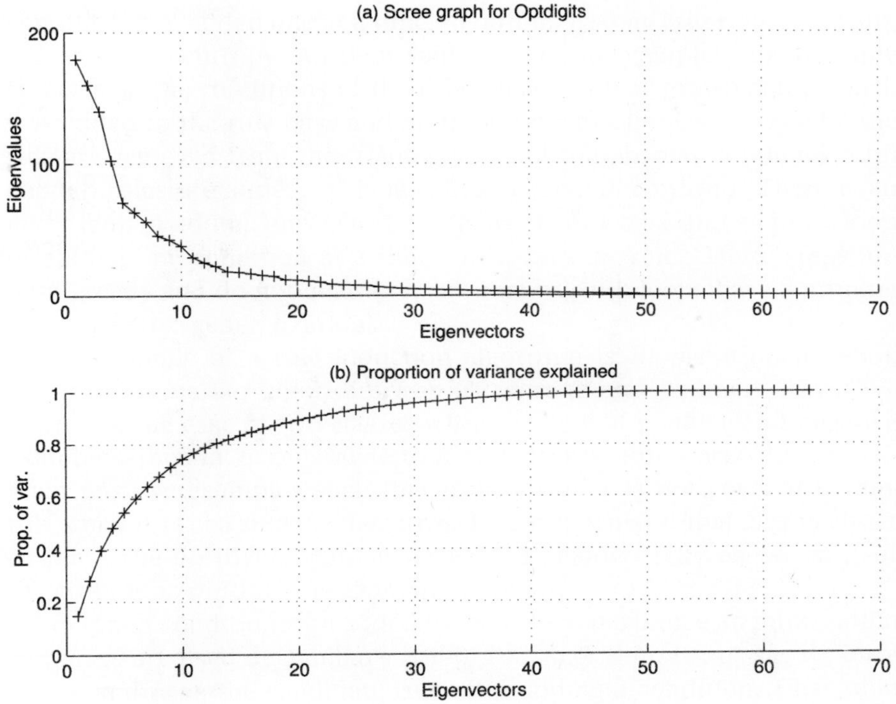

Figure 6.4 (a) Scree graph. (b) Proportion of variance explained is given for the Optdigits dataset from the UCI Repository. This is a handwritten digit dataset with ten classes and sixty-four dimensional inputs. The first twenty eigenvectors explain 90 percent of the variance.

far away.

If the first two principal components explain a large percentage of the variance, we can do *visual analysis*: We can plot the data in this two-dimensional space (figure 6.5) and search visually for structure, groups, outliers, normality, and so forth. This plot gives a better pictorial description of the sample than a plot of any two of the original variables. By looking at the dimensions of the principal components, we can also try to recover meaningful underlying variables that describe the data. For example, in image applications where the inputs are images, the eigenvectors can also be displayed as images and can be seen as templates for important features; they are typically named "*eigenfaces*," "*eigendigits*,"

EIGENFACES
EIGENDIGITS

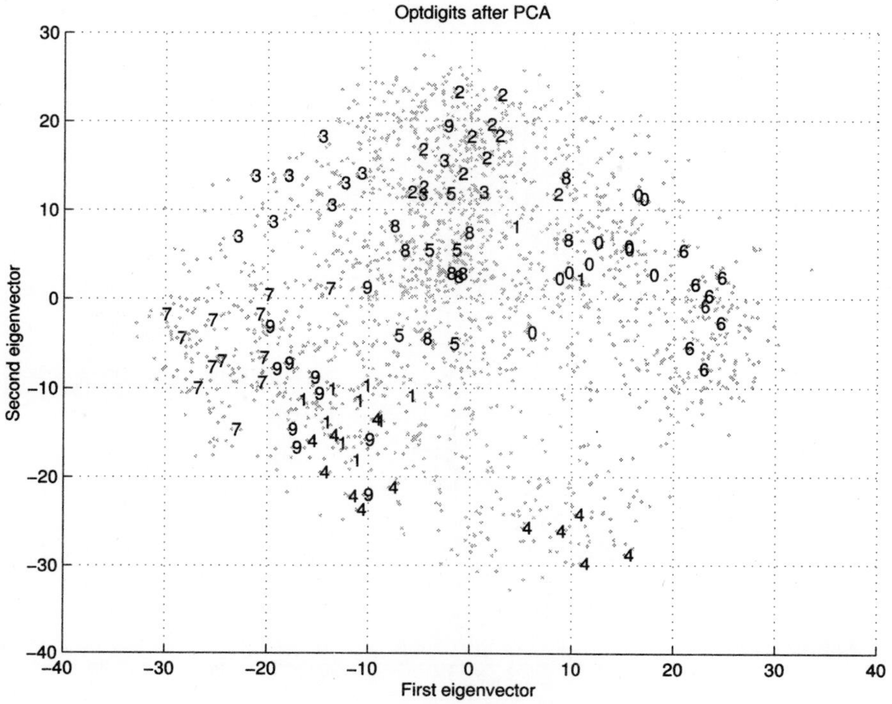

Figure 6.5 Optdigits data plotted in the space of two principal components. Only the labels of a hundred data points are shown to minimize the ink-to-noise ratio.

and so forth (Turk and Pentland 1991).

We know from equation 5.15 that if $\boldsymbol{x} \sim \mathcal{N}_d(\boldsymbol{\mu}, \boldsymbol{\Sigma})$, then after projection $\mathbf{W}^T\boldsymbol{x} \sim \mathcal{N}_k(\mathbf{W}^T\boldsymbol{\mu}, \mathbf{W}^T\boldsymbol{\Sigma}\mathbf{W})$. If the sample contains d-variate normals, then it projects to k-variate normals allowing us to do parametric discrimination in this lower-dimensional space. Because z_j are uncorrelated, the new covariance matrices will be diagonal, and if they are normalized to have unit variance, Euclidean distance can be used in this new space, leading to a simple classifier.

Instance $\boldsymbol{x}^t$ is projected to the z-space as

$$\boldsymbol{z}^t = \mathbf{W}^T(\boldsymbol{x}^t - \boldsymbol{\mu})$$

When $\mathbf{W}$ is an orthogonal matrix such that $\mathbf{W}\mathbf{W}^T = \mathbf{I}$, it can be backprojected to the original space as

$$\hat{\boldsymbol{x}}^t = \mathbf{W}\mathbf{z}^t + \boldsymbol{\mu}$$

$\hat{\boldsymbol{x}}^t$ is the reconstruction of $\boldsymbol{x}^t$ from its representation in the z-space. It is known that among all orthogonal linear projections, PCA minimizes the *reconstruction error*, which is the distance between the instance and its reconstruction from the lower-dimensional space:

RECONSTRUCTION ERROR

$$\sum_t \|\boldsymbol{x}^t - \hat{\boldsymbol{x}}^t\|^2 \quad (6.12)$$

As we discussed earlier, the contribution of each eigenvector is given by its eigenvalue, and hence it makes sense to keep the eigenvectors with the highest eigenvalues; if for dimensionality reduction we discard some eigenvectors with nonzero eigenvalues, there will be a reconstruction error and its magnitude will depend on the discarded eigenvalues. In a visual recognition application—for example, face recognition—displaying $\hat{\boldsymbol{x}}^t$ allows a visual check for information loss during PCA.

PCA is unsupervised and does not use output information. It is a one-group procedure. However, in the case of classification, there are multiple groups. *Karhunen-Loève expansion* allows using class information; for example, instead of using the covariance matrix of the whole sample, we can estimate separate class covariance matrices, take their average (weighted by the priors) as the covariance matrix, and use its eigenvectors.

KARHUNEN-LOÈVE EXPANSION

In *common principal components* (Flury 1988), we assume that the principal components are the same for each class whereas the variances of these components differ for different classes:

COMMON PRINCIPAL COMPONENTS

$$\mathbf{S}_i = \mathbf{C}\mathbf{D}_i\mathbf{C}^T$$

This allows pooling data and is a regularization method whose complexity is less than that of a common covariance matrix for all classes, while still allowing differentiation of $\mathbf{S}_i$. A related approach is *flexible discriminant analysis* (Hastie, Tibshirani, and Buja 1994), which does a linear projection to a lower-dimensional space where all features are uncorrelated and then uses a minimum distance classifier.

FLEXIBLE DISCRIMINANT ANALYSIS

6.4 Feature Embedding

Remember that $\mathbf{X}$ is the $N \times d$ data matrix where N is the number of instances and d is the input dimensionality. The covariance matrix of $\boldsymbol{x}$

is $d \times d$ and is equal to $\mathbf{X}^T\mathbf{X}$ if $\mathbf{X}$ is centered to have zero mean (without loss of generality). Principal component analysis uses the eigenvectors of $\mathbf{X}^T\mathbf{X}$. Remember that the spectral decomposition is

$$\mathbf{X}^T\mathbf{X} = \mathbf{W}\mathbf{D}\mathbf{W}^T \tag{6.13}$$

where $\mathbf{W}$ is $d \times d$ and contains the eigenvectors of $\mathbf{X}^T\mathbf{X}$ in its columns and $\mathbf{D}$ is a $d \times d$ diagonal matrix with the corresponding eigenvalues. We assume that the eigenvectors are sorted according to their eigenvalues so that the first column of $\mathbf{W}$ is the eigenvector with the largest eigenvalue in D_{11}, and so on. If $\mathbf{X}^T\mathbf{X}$ has rank $k < d$, then $D_{ii} = 0$ for $i > k$.

Let us say we want to reduce dimensionality to $k < d$. In PCA, as we saw before, we take the first k columns of $\mathbf{W}$ (with the highest eigenvalues). Let us denote them by $\boldsymbol{w}_i$ and their eigenvalues by $\lambda_i, i = 1, \ldots, k$. We map to the new k-dimensional space by taking a dot product of the original inputs with the eigenvectors:

$$z_i^t = \boldsymbol{w}_i^T \boldsymbol{x}^t,\ i = 1, \ldots, k, t = 1, \ldots, N \tag{6.14}$$

Given that λ_i and $\boldsymbol{w}_i$ are the eigenvalues and eigenvectors of $\mathbf{X}^T\mathbf{X}$, for any $i \leq k$, we have

$$(\mathbf{X}^T\mathbf{X})\boldsymbol{w}_i = \lambda_i \boldsymbol{w}_i$$

Premultiplying by $\mathbf{X}$, we find

$$(\mathbf{X}\mathbf{X}^T)\mathbf{X}\boldsymbol{w}_i = \lambda_i \mathbf{X}\boldsymbol{w}_i$$

Hence, $\mathbf{X}\boldsymbol{w}_i$ must be the eigenvectors of $\mathbf{X}\mathbf{X}^T$ with the same eigenvalues (Chatfield and Collins 1980). Note that $\mathbf{X}^T\mathbf{X}$ is $d \times d$, whereas $\mathbf{X}\mathbf{X}^T$ is $N \times N$.

Let us write *its* spectral decomposition:

$$\mathbf{X}\mathbf{X}^T = \mathbf{V}\mathbf{E}\mathbf{V}^T \tag{6.15}$$

$\mathbf{V}$ is the $N \times N$ matrix containing the eigenvectors of $\mathbf{X}\mathbf{X}^T$ in its columns, and $\mathbf{E}$ is the $N \times N$ diagonal matrix with the corresponding eigenvalues. The N-dimensional eigenvectors of $\mathbf{X}\mathbf{X}^T$ are the coordinates in the new space. We call this *feature embedding*.

FEATURE EMBEDDING

One caution here: Eigenvectors are usually normalized to have unit length, so if the eigenvectors of $\mathbf{X}\mathbf{X}^T$ are $\boldsymbol{v}_i$ (with the same eigenvalues), we have

$$\boldsymbol{v}_i = \mathbf{X}\boldsymbol{w}_i / \lambda_i, i = 1, \ldots, k$$

because the sum of squares of $\mathbf{X}\boldsymbol{w}_i$ is λ_i. So if we have $\boldsymbol{v}_i$ (column i of $\mathbf{V}$) calculated and we want to get $\mathbf{X}\boldsymbol{w}_i$, that is, do what PCA does, we should multiply with the square root of the eigenvalue:

$$z_i^t = \mathbf{V}_{ti}\sqrt{\mathbf{E}_{tt}},\ t = 1,\ldots,N, i = 1,\ldots,k \tag{6.16}$$

When $d < N$, as is generally the case, it is simpler to work with $\mathbf{X}^T\mathbf{X}$, that is, use PCA. Sometimes $d > N$ and it is easier to work with $\mathbf{X}\mathbf{X}^T$, which is $N \times N$. For example, in the eigenfaces approach (Turk and Pentland 1991), face images are $256\times256 = 65,536$-dimensional and there are only forty face images (four images each from ten people). Note that the rank can never exceed $\min(d, N)$; that is, in this face recognition example, even though the covariance matrix is $65,536 \times 65,536$, we know that the rank (the number of eigenvectors with eigenvalues greater than 0) can never exceed forty. Hence we can work with the 40×40 matrix instead and use the new coordinates in this forty-dimensional space; for example, do recognition using the nearest mean classifier (Turk and Pentland 1991). The same is also true in most bioinformatics applications where we may have long gene sequences but a small sample. In text clustering, the number of possible words may be much more than the number of documents, and in a movie recommendation system, the number of movies may be much more than the customers.

There is a caveat, though: In the case of PCA, we learn projection vectors, and we can map any new test $\boldsymbol{x}$ to the new space by taking dot products with the eigenvectors—we have a model for projection. We cannot do this with feature embedding, because we do not have projection vectors—we do not learn a projection model but get the coordinates directly. If we have new test data, we should add them to $\mathbf{X}$ and redo the calculation.

The element (i, j) of $\mathbf{X}\mathbf{X}^T$ is equal to the dot product of instances i and j; that is, $(\boldsymbol{x}^i)^T(\boldsymbol{x}^j)$, where $i, j = 1,\ldots,N$. If we consider dot product as measuring the similarity between vectors, we can consider $\mathbf{X}\mathbf{X}^T$ as an $N \times N$ matrix of pairwise similarities. From this perspective, we can consider feature embedding as a method of placing instances in a k-dimensional space such that pairwise similarities in the new space respect the original pairwise similarities. We will revisit this idea later: In section 6.7, we discuss multidimensional scaling where we use the Euclidean distance between vectors instead of the dot product, and in sections 6.10 and 6.12, we discuss Isomap and Laplacian eigenmaps respectively where we consider non-Euclidean measures of (dis)similarity.

6.5 Factor Analysis

In PCA, from the original dimensions $x_i, i = 1, \ldots, d$, we form a new set of variables $\boldsymbol{z}$ that are linear combinations of x_i:

$$\boldsymbol{z} = \mathbf{W}^T(\boldsymbol{x} - \boldsymbol{\mu})$$

FACTOR ANALYSIS
LATENT FACTORS

In *factor analysis* (FA), we assume that there is a set of unobservable, *latent factors* $z_j, j = 1, \ldots, k$, which when acting in combination *generate* $\boldsymbol{x}$. Thus the direction is opposite that of PCA (see figure 6.6). The goal is to characterize the dependency among the observed variables by means of a smaller number of factors.

Suppose there is a group of variables that have high correlation among themselves and low correlation with all the other variables. Then there may be a single underlying factor that gave rise to these variables. If the other variables can be similarly grouped into subsets, then a few factors can represent these groups of variables. Though factor analysis always partitions the variables into factor clusters, whether the factors mean anything, or really exist, is open to question.

FA, like PCA, is a one-group procedure and is unsupervised. The aim is to model the data in a smaller dimensional space without loss of information. In FA, this is measured as the correlation between variables.

As in PCA, we have a sample $\mathcal{X} = \{\boldsymbol{x}^t\}_t$ drawn from some unknown probability density with $E[\boldsymbol{x}] = \boldsymbol{\mu}$ and $\text{Cov}(\boldsymbol{x}) = \boldsymbol{\Sigma}$. We assume that the factors are unit normals, $E[z_j] = 0, \text{Var}(z_j) = 1$, and are uncorrelated, $\text{Cov}(z_i, z_j) = 0, i \neq j$. To explain what is not explained by the factors, there is an added source for each input which we denote by ϵ_i. It is assumed to be zero-mean, $E[\epsilon_i] = 0$, and have some unknown variance, $\text{Var}(\epsilon_i) = \psi_i$. These specific sources are uncorrelated among themselves, $\text{Cov}(\epsilon_i, \epsilon_j) = 0, i \neq j$, and are also uncorrelated with the factors, $\text{Cov}(\epsilon_i, z_j) = 0, \forall i, j$.

FA assumes that each input dimension, $x_i, i = 1, \ldots, d$, can be written as a weighted sum of the $k < d$ factors, $z_j, j = 1, \ldots, k$, plus the residual term (see figure 6.7):

$$x_i - \mu_i = v_{i1}z_1 + v_{i2}z_2 + \cdots + v_{ik}z_k + \epsilon_i, \forall i = 1, \ldots, d$$

(6.17) $$x_i - \mu_i = \sum_{j=1}^{k} v_{ij}z_j + \epsilon_i$$

This can be written in vector-matrix form as

(6.18) $$\boldsymbol{x} - \boldsymbol{\mu} = \mathbf{V}\boldsymbol{z} + \boldsymbol{\epsilon}$$

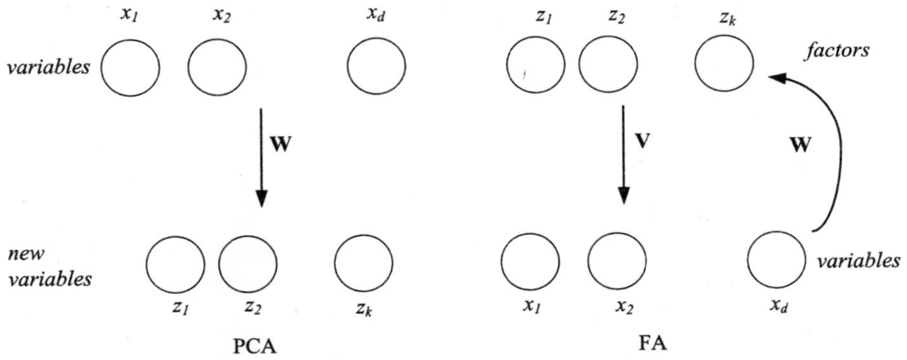

Figure 6.6 Principal component analysis generates new variables that are linear combinations of the original input variables. In factor analysis, however, we posit that there are factors that when linearly combined generate the input variables.

where **V** is the $d \times k$ matrix of weights, called *factor loadings.* From now on, we are going to assume that $\boldsymbol{\mu} = \mathbf{0}$ without loss of generality; we can always add $\boldsymbol{\mu}$ after projection. Given that $\text{Var}(z_j) = 1$ and $\text{Var}(\epsilon_i) = \psi_i$

(6.19) $$\text{Var}(x_i) = v_{i1}^2 + v_{i2}^2 + \cdots + v_{ik}^2 + \psi_i$$

$\sum_{j=1}^k v_{ij}^2$ is the part of the variance explained by the common factors and ψ_i is the variance specific to x_i.

In vector-matrix form, we have

(6.20) $$\begin{aligned}\boldsymbol{\Sigma} = \text{Cov}(\boldsymbol{x}) &= \text{Cov}(\mathbf{Vz} + \boldsymbol{\epsilon}) \\ &= \text{Cov}(\mathbf{Vz}) + \text{Cov}(\boldsymbol{\epsilon}) \\ &= \mathbf{V}\text{Cov}(\mathbf{z})\mathbf{V}^T + \boldsymbol{\Psi}\end{aligned}$$

(6.21) $$= \mathbf{VV}^T + \boldsymbol{\Psi}$$

where $\boldsymbol{\Psi}$ is a diagonal matrix with ψ_i on the diagonals. Because the factors are uncorrelated unit normals, we have $\text{Cov}(\mathbf{z}) = \mathbf{I}$. With two factors, for example,

$$\text{Cov}(x_1, x_2) = v_{11}v_{21} + v_{12}v_{22}$$

If x_1 and x_2 have high covariance, then they are related through a factor. If it is the first factor, then v_{11} and v_{21} will both be high; if it is the second factor, then v_{12} and v_{22} will both be high. In either case, the sum

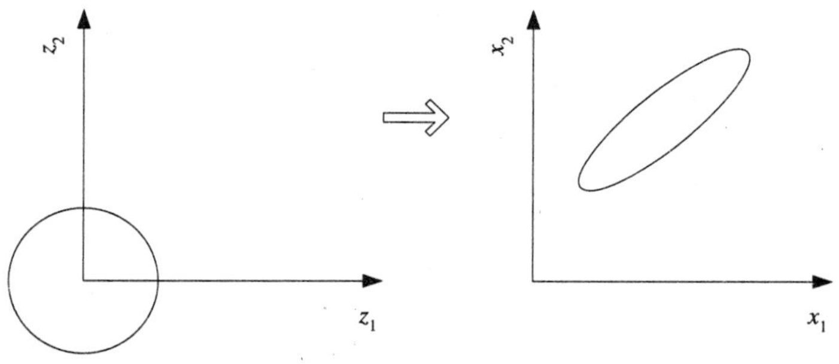

Figure 6.7 Factors are independent unit normals that are stretched, rotated, and translated to make up the inputs.

$v_{11}v_{21} + v_{12}v_{22}$ will be high. If the covariance is low, then x_1 and x_2 depend on different factors and in the products in the sum, one term will be high and the other will be low and the sum will be low.

We see that

$$\text{Cov}(x_1, z_2) = \text{Cov}(v_{12}z_2, z_2) = v_{12}\text{Var}(z_2) = v_{12}$$

Thus $\text{Cov}(\boldsymbol{x}, \boldsymbol{z}) = \mathbf{V}$, and we see that the loadings represent the correlations of variables with the factors.

Given $\mathbf{S}$, the estimator of $\boldsymbol{\Sigma}$, we would like to find $\mathbf{V}$ and $\boldsymbol{\Psi}$ such that

$$\mathbf{S} = \mathbf{V}\mathbf{V}^T + \boldsymbol{\Psi}$$

If there are only a few factors, that is, if $\mathbf{V}$ has few columns, then we have a simplified structure for $\mathbf{S}$, as $\mathbf{V}$ is $d \times k$ and $\boldsymbol{\Psi}$ has d values, thus reducing the number of parameters from d^2 to $d \cdot k + d$.

Since $\boldsymbol{\Psi}$ is diagonal, covariances are represented by $\mathbf{V}$. Note that PCA does not allow a separate $\boldsymbol{\Psi}$ and it tries to account for both the covariances *and* the variances. When all ψ_i are equal, namely, $\boldsymbol{\Psi} = \psi\mathbf{I}$, we get

PROBABILISTIC PCA

probabilistic PCA (Tipping and Bishop 1999) and the conventional PCA is when ψ_i are 0.

Let us now see how we can find the factor loadings and the specific variances: Let us first ignore $\boldsymbol{\Psi}$. Then, from its spectral decomposition, we know that we have

$$\mathbf{S} = \mathbf{C}\mathbf{D}\mathbf{C}^T = \mathbf{C}\mathbf{D}^{1/2}\mathbf{D}^{1/2}\mathbf{C}^T = (\mathbf{C}\mathbf{D}^{1/2})(\mathbf{C}\mathbf{D}^{1/2})^T$$

where we take only k of the eigenvectors by looking at the proportion of variance explained so that $\mathbf{C}$ is the $d \times k$ matrix of eigenvectors and $\mathbf{D}^{1/2}$

is the $k \times k$ diagonal matrix with the square roots of the eigenvalues on its diagonals. Thus we have

(6.22) $$\mathbf{V} = \mathbf{C}\mathbf{D}^{1/2}$$

We can find ψ_j from equation 6.19 as

(6.23) $$\psi_i = s_i^2 - \sum_{j=1}^{k} v_{ij}^2$$

Note that when $\mathbf{V}$ is multiplied with any orthogonal matrix—namely, having the property $\mathbf{T}\mathbf{T}^T = \mathbf{I}$—that is another valid solution and thus the solution is not unique.

$$\mathbf{S} = (\mathbf{V}\mathbf{T})(\mathbf{V}\mathbf{T})^T = \mathbf{V}\mathbf{T}\mathbf{T}^T\mathbf{V}^T = \mathbf{V}\mathbf{I}\mathbf{V}^T = \mathbf{V}\mathbf{V}^T$$

If $\mathbf{T}$ is an orthogonal matrix, the distance to the origin does not change. If $\boldsymbol{z} = \mathbf{T}\boldsymbol{x}$, then

$$\boldsymbol{z}^T\boldsymbol{z} = (\mathbf{T}\boldsymbol{x})^T(\mathbf{T}\boldsymbol{x}) = \boldsymbol{x}^T\mathbf{T}^T\mathbf{T}\boldsymbol{x} = \boldsymbol{x}^T\boldsymbol{x}$$

Multiplying with an orthogonal matrix has the effect of rotating the axes and allows us to choose the set of axes most interpretable (Rencher 1995). In two dimensions,

$$\mathbf{T} = \begin{pmatrix} \cos\phi & -\sin\phi \\ \sin\phi & \cos\phi \end{pmatrix}$$

rotates the axes by ϕ. There are two types of rotation: In orthogonal rotation the factors are still orthogonal after the rotation, and in oblique rotation the factors are allowed to become correlated. The factors are rotated to give the maximum loading on as few factors as possible for each variable, to make the factors interpretable. However, interpretability is subjective and should not be used to force one's prejudices on the data.

There are two uses of factor analysis: It can be used for knowledge extraction when we find the loadings and try to express the variables using fewer factors. It can also be used for dimensionality reduction when $k < d$. We already saw how the first one is done. Now, let us see how factor analysis can be used for dimensionality reduction.

When we are interested in dimensionality reduction, we need to be able to find the factor scores, z_j, from x_i. We want to find the loadings w_{ji} such that

(6.24) $$z_j = \sum_{i=1}^{d} w_{ji}x_i + \epsilon_j, j = 1, \ldots, k$$

where x_i are centered to have mean 0. In vector form, for observation t, this can be written as

$$\mathbf{z}^t = \mathbf{W}^T\mathbf{x}^t + \boldsymbol{\epsilon}, \forall t = 1,\ldots,N$$

This is a linear model with d inputs and k outputs. Its transpose can be written as

$$(\mathbf{z}^t)^T = (\mathbf{x}^t)^T\mathbf{W} + \boldsymbol{\epsilon}^T, \forall t = 1,\ldots,N$$

Given that we have a sample of N observations, we write

$$\mathbf{Z} = \mathbf{X}\mathbf{W} + \Xi \tag{6.25}$$

where $\mathbf{Z}$ is $N \times k$ of factors, $\mathbf{X}$ is $N \times d$ of (centered) observations, and Ξ is $N \times k$ of zero-mean noise. This is multivariate linear regression with multiple outputs, and we know from section 5.8 that $\mathbf{W}$ can be found as

$$\mathbf{W} = (\mathbf{X}^T\mathbf{X})^{-1}\mathbf{X}^T\mathbf{Z}$$

but we do not know $\mathbf{Z}$; it is what we would like to calculate. We multiply and divide both sides by $N-1$ and obtain

$$\begin{aligned}
\mathbf{W} &= (N-1)(\mathbf{X}^T\mathbf{X})^{-1}\frac{\mathbf{X}^T\mathbf{Z}}{N-1} \\
&= \left(\frac{\mathbf{X}^T\mathbf{X}}{N-1}\right)^{-1}\frac{\mathbf{X}^T\mathbf{Z}}{N-1} \\
&= \mathbf{S}^{-1}\mathbf{V} \qquad (6.26)
\end{aligned}$$

and placing equation 6.26 in equation 6.25, we write

$$\mathbf{Z} = \mathbf{X}\mathbf{W} = \mathbf{X}\mathbf{S}^{-1}\mathbf{V} \tag{6.27}$$

assuming that $\mathbf{S}$ is nonsingular. One can use $\mathbf{R}$ instead of $\mathbf{S}$ when x_i are normalized to have unit variance.

For dimensionality reduction, FA offers no advantage over PCA except the interpretability of factors allowing the identification of common causes, a simple explanation, and knowledge extraction. For example, in the context of speech recognition, $\boldsymbol{x}$ corresponds to the acoustic signal, but we know that it is the result of the (nonlinear) interaction of a small number of *articulators*, namely, jaw, tongue, velum, lips, and mouth, which are positioned appropriately to shape the air as it comes out of the lungs and generate the speech sound. If a speech signal could be transformed to this articulatory space, then recognition would be much easier. Using such generative models is one of the current research directions for speech recognition; in chapter 14, we discuss how such models can be represented as a graphical model.

6.6 Singular Value Decomposition and Matrix Factorization

Given the $N \times d$ data matrix $\mathbf{X}$, we work with $\mathbf{X}^T\mathbf{X}$ if $d < N$ or work with $\mathbf{X}\mathbf{X}^T$ if $N < d$. Both are square matrices and in either case, the spectral decomposition gives us $\mathbf{Q}\mathbf{\Lambda}\mathbf{Q}^T$ where the eigenvector matrix $\mathbf{Q}$ is orthogonal ($\mathbf{Q}^T\mathbf{Q} = \mathbf{I}$) and $\mathbf{\Lambda}$ contains the eigenvalues on its diagonal.

SINGULAR VALUE DECOMPOSITION

The *singular value decomposition* allows us to decompose any $N \times d$ *rectangular* matrix (Strang 2006):

(6.28)
$$\mathbf{X} = \mathbf{V}\mathbf{A}\mathbf{W}^T$$

where the $N \times N$ matrix $\mathbf{V}$ contains the eigenvectors of $\mathbf{X}\mathbf{X}^T$ in its columns, the $d \times d$ matrix $\mathbf{W}$ contains the eigenvectors of $\mathbf{X}^T\mathbf{X}$ in its columns, and the $N \times d$ matrix $\mathbf{A}$ contains the $k = \min(N, d)$ *singular values*, $a_i, i = 1, \dots, k$ on its diagonal that are the square roots of the nonzero eigenvalues of both $\mathbf{X}\mathbf{X}^T$ and $\mathbf{X}^T\mathbf{X}$; the rest of $\mathbf{A}$ is zero. $\mathbf{V}$ and $\mathbf{W}^T$ are orthogonal matrices (but not necessarily transposes of each other).

$$\begin{aligned}
\mathbf{X}\mathbf{X}^T &= (\mathbf{V}\mathbf{A}\mathbf{W}^T)(\mathbf{V}\mathbf{A}\mathbf{W}^T)^T = \mathbf{V}\mathbf{A}\mathbf{W}^T\mathbf{W}\mathbf{A}^T\mathbf{V}^T = \mathbf{V}\mathbf{E}\mathbf{V}^T \\
\mathbf{X}^T\mathbf{X} &= (\mathbf{V}\mathbf{A}\mathbf{W}^T)^T(\mathbf{V}\mathbf{A}\mathbf{W}^T) = \mathbf{W}\mathbf{A}^T\mathbf{V}^T\mathbf{V}\mathbf{A}\mathbf{W}^T = \mathbf{W}\mathbf{D}\mathbf{W}^T
\end{aligned}$$

where $\mathbf{E} = \mathbf{A}\mathbf{A}^T$ and $\mathbf{D} = \mathbf{A}^T\mathbf{A}$. They are of different sizes but are both square and contain $a_i^2, i = 1, \dots, k$ on their diagonal and zero elsewhere.

Just as in equation 6.10, we can write

(6.29)
$$\mathbf{X} = \boldsymbol{u}_1 a_1 \boldsymbol{v}_1^T + \boldsymbol{u}_2 a_2 \boldsymbol{v}_2^T + \cdots + \boldsymbol{u}_k a_k \boldsymbol{v}_k^T$$

We can ignore the corresponding $\boldsymbol{u}_i, \boldsymbol{v}_i$ of very small, though nonzero, a_i and can still reconstruct $\mathbf{X}$ without too much error.

MATRIX FACTORIZATION

In *matrix factorization*, we write a large matrix as a product of (generally) two matrices:

(6.30)
$$\mathbf{X} = \mathbf{F}\mathbf{G}$$

where $\mathbf{X}$ is $N \times d$, $\mathbf{F}$ is $N \times k$, and $\mathbf{G}$ is $k \times d$. k is the dimensionality of the factor space and is hopefully much smaller than d and N. The idea is that although the data may be too large, either it is sparse, or there is high correlation and it can be represented in a space of fewer dimensions.

G defines factors in terms of the original attributes and **F** defines data instances in terms of these factors. For example, if **X** is a sample of N documents each using a bag of words representation with d words, each factor may be one topic or concept written using a certain subset of words and each document is a certain combination of such factors. This is called *latent semantic indexing* (Landauer, Laham, and Derr 2004). In *nonnegative* matrix factorization, the matrices are nonnegative and this allows representing a complex object in terms of its parts (Lee and Seung 1999).

LATENT SEMANTIC INDEXING

Let us take another example from retail where **X** is the consumer data. We have N customers and we sell d different products. $\mathbf{X}_{ti}$ corresponds to the amount of product i customer N has purchased. We know that customers do not buy things at random, their purchases depend on a number of factors, for example, their their household size and composition, income level, taste, and so on—these factors are generally hidden from us. In matrix factorization of consumer data, we assume that there are k such factors. **G** relates factors to products: $\mathbf{G}_j$ is a d-dimensional vector explaining the relationship between factor j and the products; namely, $\mathbf{G}_{ji}$ is proportional to the amount of product i bought due to factor j. Similarly, **F** relates customers to factors: $\mathbf{F}_t$ is the k-dimensional vector defining customer t in terms of the hidden factors; namely, $\mathbf{F}_{tj}$ is the belief that behavior of customer t is due to factor j. We can hence rewrite equation 6.30 as

$$\mathbf{X}_{ti} = \mathbf{F}_t^T \mathbf{G}_i = \sum_{j=1}^{k} \mathbf{F}_{tj} \mathbf{G}_{ji} \quad (6.31)$$

That is, to calculate the total amount, we take a sum over all such factors where for each, we multiply our belief that the customer is affected by that factor and the amount of product due to that factor—see figure 6.8.

6.7 Multidimensional Scaling

Let us say for N points, we are given the distances between pairs of points, d_{ij}, for all $i, j = 1, \ldots, N$. We do not know the exact coordinates of the points, their dimensionality, or how the distances are calculated.

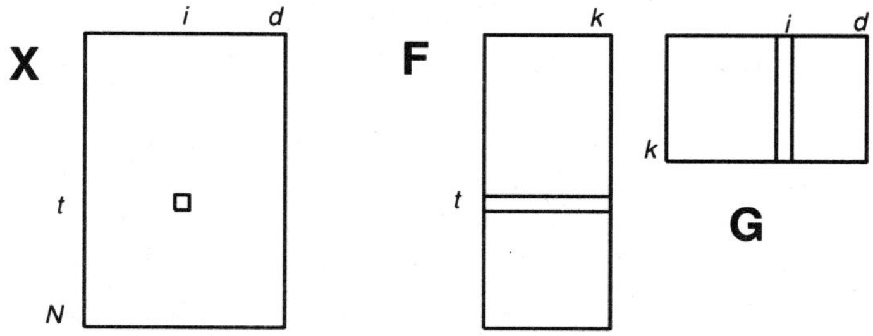

Figure 6.8 Matrix factorization. $\mathbf{X}$ is the $N \times d$ data matrix. $\mathbf{F}$ is $N \times k$ and its row t defines instance t in terms of the k hidden factors. $\mathbf{G}$ is $k \times d$ and explains factors in terms of the d observed variables. To get $\mathbf{X}_{ti}$, we consider all k factors by taking a weighted sum over them.

MULTIDIMENSIONAL SCALING

Multidimensional scaling (MDS) is the method for placing these points in a low—for example, two-dimensional—space such that the Euclidean distance between them there is as close as possible to d_{ij}, the given distances in the original space. Thus it requires a projection from some unknown dimensional space to, for example, two dimensions.

In the archetypical example of multidimensional scaling, we take the road travel distances between cities, and after applying MDS, we get an approximation to the map. The map is distorted such that in parts of the country with geographical obstacles like mountains and lakes where the road travel distance deviates much from the direct bird-flight path (Euclidean distance), the map is stretched out to accommodate longer distances (see figure 6.9). The map is centered on the origin, but the solution is still not unique. We can get any rotated or mirror image version.

MDS can be used for dimensionality reduction by calculating pairwise Euclidean distances in the d-dimensional $\boldsymbol{x}$ space and giving this as input to MDS, which then projects it to a lower-dimensional space so as to preserve these distances.

Let us say we have a sample $\mathcal{X} = \{\boldsymbol{x}^t\}_{t=1}^N$ as usual, where $\boldsymbol{x}^t \in \Re^d$. For two points r and s, the squared Euclidean distance between them is

$$
\begin{aligned}
d_{rs}^2 &= \|\boldsymbol{x}^r - \boldsymbol{x}^s\|^2 = \sum_{j=1}^d (x_j^r - x_j^s)^2 = \sum_{j=1}^d (x_j^r)^2 - 2\sum_{j=1}^d x_j^r x_j^s + \sum_{j=1}^d (x_j^s)^2 \\
&= b_{rr} + b_{ss} - 2b_{rs} \qquad (6.32)
\end{aligned}
$$

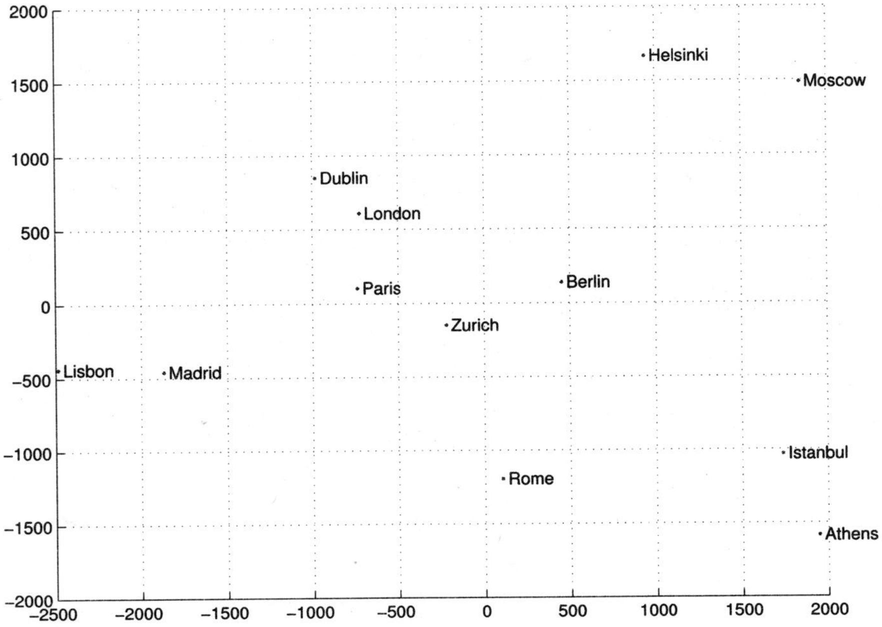

Figure 6.9 Map of Europe drawn by MDS. Pairwise road travel distances between these cities are given as input, and MDS places them in two dimensions such that these distances are preserved as well as possible.

where b_{rs} is defined as

$$b_{rs} = \sum_{j=1}^{d} x_j^r x_j^s \tag{6.33}$$

To constrain the solution, we center the data at the origin and assume

$$\sum_{t=1}^{N} x_j^t = 0, \forall j = 1, \dots, d$$

Then, summing up equation 6.32 on r, s, and both r and s, and defining

$$T = \sum_{t=1}^{N} b_{tt} = \sum_t \sum_j (x_j^t)^2$$

we get

$$\sum_r d_{rs}^2 = T + N b_{ss}$$

$$\sum_s d_{rs}^2 = Nb_{rr} + T$$
$$\sum_r \sum_s d_{rs}^2 = 2NT$$

When we define

$$d_{\bullet s}^2 = \frac{1}{N}\sum_r d_{rs}^2 \ , \ d_{r\bullet}^2 = \frac{1}{N}\sum_s d_{rs}^2 \ , \ d_{\bullet\bullet}^2 = \frac{1}{N^2}\sum_r\sum_s d_{rs}^2$$

and using equation 6.32, we get

$$b_{rs} = \frac{1}{2}(d_{r\bullet}^2 + d_{\bullet s}^2 - d_{\bullet\bullet}^2 - d_{rs}^2) \tag{6.34}$$

Having now calculated b_{rs} and knowing that $\mathbf{B} = \mathbf{X}\mathbf{X}^T$ as defined in equation 6.33, we can use feature embedding (section 6.4). We know from the spectral decomposition that $\mathbf{X} = \mathbf{C}\mathbf{D}^{1/2}$ can be used as an approximation for $\mathbf{X}$, where $\mathbf{C}$ is the matrix whose columns are the eigenvectors of $\mathbf{B}$ and $\mathbf{D}^{1/2}$ is a diagonal matrix with square roots of the eigenvalues on the diagonals. Looking at the eigenvalues of $\mathbf{B}$, we decide on a dimensionality k lower than d (and N), as we did in PCA and FA. Let us say $\boldsymbol{c}_j$ are the eigenvectors with λ_j as the corresponding eigenvalues. Note that $\boldsymbol{c}_j$ is N-dimensional. Then we get the new dimensions as

$$z_j^t = \sqrt{\lambda_j} c_j^t, j = 1, \ldots, k, t = 1, \ldots, N \tag{6.35}$$

That is, the new coordinates of instance t are given by the tth elements of the eigenvectors, $\boldsymbol{c}_j, j = 1, \ldots, k$, after normalization.

We know that principal component analysis and feature embedding do the same job. This shows that PCA does the same work with MDS and does it more cheaply if $d < N$. PCA done on the correlation matrix rather than the covariance matrix equals doing MDS with standardized Euclidean distances where each variable has unit variance.

In the general case, we want to find a mapping $\boldsymbol{z} = \boldsymbol{g}(\boldsymbol{x}|\theta)$, where $\boldsymbol{z} \in \Re^k, \boldsymbol{x} \in \Re^d$, and $\boldsymbol{g}(\boldsymbol{x}|\theta)$ is the mapping function from d to k dimensions defined up to a set of parameters θ. Classical MDS, which we discussed previously, corresponds to a linear transformation

$$\boldsymbol{z} = \boldsymbol{g}(\boldsymbol{x}|\mathbf{W}) = \mathbf{W}^T\boldsymbol{x} \tag{6.36}$$

but in a general case, a nonlinear mapping can also be used; this is called

SAMMON MAPPING

Sammon mapping. The normalized error in mapping is called the *Sam-*

mon stress and is defined as

$$
\begin{aligned}
E(\theta|\mathcal{X}) &= \sum_{r,s} \frac{(\|\boldsymbol{z}^r - \boldsymbol{z}^s\| - \|\boldsymbol{x}^r - \boldsymbol{x}^s\|)^2}{\|\boldsymbol{x}^r - \boldsymbol{x}^s\|^2} \\
&= \sum_{r,s} \frac{(\|\boldsymbol{g}(\boldsymbol{x}^r|\theta) - \boldsymbol{g}(\boldsymbol{x}^s|\theta)\| - \|\boldsymbol{x}^r - \boldsymbol{x}^s\|)^2}{\|\boldsymbol{x}^r - \boldsymbol{x}^s\|^2} \quad (6.37)
\end{aligned}
$$

One can use any regression method for $\boldsymbol{g}(\cdot|\theta)$ and estimate θ to minimize the stress on the training data $\mathcal{X}$. If $\boldsymbol{g}(\cdot)$ is nonlinear in $\boldsymbol{x}$, this will then correspond to a nonlinear dimensionality reduction.

In the case of classification, one can include class information in the distance (see Webb 1999) as

$$d'_{rs} = (1 - \alpha)d_{rs} + \alpha c_{rs}$$

where c_{rs} is the "distance" between the classes $\boldsymbol{x}^r$ and $\boldsymbol{x}^s$ belong to. This interclass distance should be supplied subjectively and α is optimized using cross-validation.

6.8 Linear Discriminant Analysis

LINEAR DISCRIMINANT ANALYSIS

Linear discriminant analysis (LDA) is a supervised method for dimensionality reduction for classification problems. We start with the case where there are two classes, then generalize to $K > 2$ classes.

Given samples from two classes C_1 and C_2, we want to find the direction, as defined by a vector $\boldsymbol{w}$, such that when the data are projected onto $\boldsymbol{w}$, the examples from the two classes are as well separated as possible. As we saw before,

$$z = \boldsymbol{w}^T\boldsymbol{x} \quad (6.38)$$

is the projection of $\boldsymbol{x}$ onto $\boldsymbol{w}$ and thus is a dimensionality reduction from d to 1.

$\boldsymbol{m}_1$ and m_1 are the means of samples from C_1 before and after projection, respectively. Note that $\boldsymbol{m}_1 \in \Re^d$ and $m_1 \in \Re$. We are given a sample $\mathcal{X} = \{\boldsymbol{x}^t, r^t\}$ such that $r^t = 1$ if $\boldsymbol{x}^t \in C_1$ and $r^t = 0$ if $\boldsymbol{x}^t \in C_2$.

$$
\begin{aligned}
m_1 &= \frac{\sum_t \boldsymbol{w}^T\boldsymbol{x}^t r^t}{\sum_t r^t} = \boldsymbol{w}^T\boldsymbol{m}_1 \\
m_2 &= \frac{\sum_t \boldsymbol{w}^T\boldsymbol{x}^t(1 - r^t)}{\sum_t (1 - r^t)} = \boldsymbol{w}^T\boldsymbol{m}_2 \quad (6.39)
\end{aligned}
$$

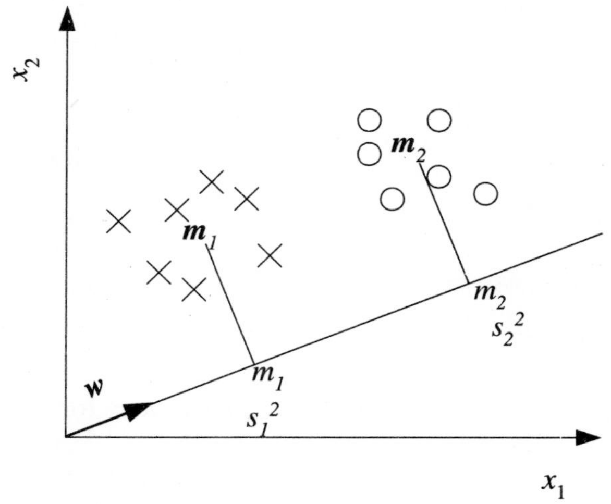

Figure 6.10 Two-dimensional, two-class data projected on $\boldsymbol{w}$.

SCATTER

The *scatter* of samples from C_1 and C_2 after projection are

$$
\begin{aligned}
s_1^2 &= \sum_t (\boldsymbol{w}^T \boldsymbol{x}^t - m_1)^2 r^t \\
s_2^2 &= \sum_t (\boldsymbol{w}^T \boldsymbol{x}^t - m_2)^2 (1 - r^t)
\end{aligned} \tag{6.40}
$$

FISHER'S LINEAR DISCRIMINANT

After projection, for the two classes to be well separated, we would like the means to be as far apart as possible and the examples of classes be scattered in as small a region as possible. So we want $|m_1 - m_2|$ to be large and $s_1^2 + s_2^2$ to be small (see figure 6.10). *Fisher's linear discriminant* is $\boldsymbol{w}$ that maximizes

$$
J(\boldsymbol{w}) = \frac{(m_1 - m_2)^2}{s_1^2 + s_2^2} \tag{6.41}
$$

Rewriting the numerator, we get

$$
\begin{aligned}
(m_1 - m_2)^2 &= (\boldsymbol{w}^T \boldsymbol{m}_1 - \boldsymbol{w}^T \boldsymbol{m}_2)^2 \\
&= \boldsymbol{w}^T (\boldsymbol{m}_1 - \boldsymbol{m}_2)(\boldsymbol{m}_1 - \boldsymbol{m}_2)^T \boldsymbol{w} \\
&= \boldsymbol{w}^T \mathbf{S}_B \boldsymbol{w}
\end{aligned} \tag{6.42}
$$

BETWEEN-CLASS SCATTER MATRIX

where $\mathbf{S}_B = (\boldsymbol{m}_1 - \boldsymbol{m}_2)(\boldsymbol{m}_1 - \boldsymbol{m}_2)^T$ is the *between-class scatter matrix*. The denominator is the sum of scatter of examples of classes around their means after projection and can be rewritten as

$$\begin{aligned} s_1^2 &= \sum_t (\boldsymbol{w}^T \boldsymbol{x}^t - m_1)^2 r^t \\ &= \sum_t \boldsymbol{w}^T (\boldsymbol{x}^t - \boldsymbol{m}_1)(\boldsymbol{x}^t - \boldsymbol{m}_1)^T \boldsymbol{w} r^t \\ &= \boldsymbol{w}^T \mathbf{S}_1 \boldsymbol{w} \end{aligned} \tag{6.43}$$

where

$$\mathbf{S}_1 = \sum_t r^t (\boldsymbol{x}^t - \boldsymbol{m}_1)(\boldsymbol{x}^t - \boldsymbol{m}_1)^T \tag{6.44}$$

WITHIN-CLASS SCATTER MATRIX

is the *within-class scatter matrix* for C_1. $\mathbf{S}_1 / \sum_t r^t$ is the estimator of $\boldsymbol{\Sigma}_1$. Similarly, $s_2^2 = \boldsymbol{w}^T \mathbf{S}_2 \boldsymbol{w}$ with $\mathbf{S}_2 = \sum_t (1 - r^t)(\boldsymbol{x}^t - \boldsymbol{m}_2)(\boldsymbol{x}^t - \boldsymbol{m}_2)^T$, and we get

$$s_1^2 + s_2^2 = \boldsymbol{w}^T \mathbf{S}_W \boldsymbol{w}$$

where $\mathbf{S}_W = \mathbf{S}_1 + \mathbf{S}_2$ is the total within-class scatter. Note that $s_1^2 + s_2^2$ divided by the total number of samples is the variance of the pooled data. Equation 6.41 can be rewritten as

$$J(\boldsymbol{w}) = \frac{\boldsymbol{w}^T \mathbf{S}_B \boldsymbol{w}}{\boldsymbol{w}^T \mathbf{S}_W \boldsymbol{w}} = \frac{|\boldsymbol{w}^T (\boldsymbol{m}_1 - \boldsymbol{m}_2)|^2}{\boldsymbol{w}^T \mathbf{S}_W \boldsymbol{w}} \tag{6.45}$$

Taking the derivative of J with respect to $\boldsymbol{w}$ and setting it equal to 0, we get

$$\frac{\boldsymbol{w}^T (\boldsymbol{m}_1 - \boldsymbol{m}_2)}{\boldsymbol{w}^T \mathbf{S}_W \boldsymbol{w}} 2 \left((\boldsymbol{m}_1 - \boldsymbol{m}_2) - \frac{\boldsymbol{w}^T (\boldsymbol{m}_1 - \boldsymbol{m}_2)}{\boldsymbol{w}^T \mathbf{S}_W \boldsymbol{w}} \mathbf{S}_W \boldsymbol{w} \right) = 0$$

Given that $\boldsymbol{w}^T (\boldsymbol{m}_1 - \boldsymbol{m}_2) / \boldsymbol{w}^T \mathbf{S}_W \boldsymbol{w}$ is a constant, we have

$$\boldsymbol{w} = c \mathbf{S}_W^{-1} (\boldsymbol{m}_1 - \boldsymbol{m}_2) \tag{6.46}$$

where c is some constant. Because it is the direction that is important for us and not the magnitude, we can just take $c = 1$ and find $\boldsymbol{w}$.

Remember that when $p(\boldsymbol{x}|C_i) \sim \mathcal{N}(\boldsymbol{\mu}_i, \boldsymbol{\Sigma})$, we have a linear discriminant where $\boldsymbol{w} = \boldsymbol{\Sigma}^{-1}(\boldsymbol{\mu}_1 - \boldsymbol{\mu}_2)$, and we see that Fisher's linear discriminant is optimal if the classes are normally distributed. Under the same assumption, a threshold, w_0, can also be calculated to separate the two classes. But Fisher's linear discriminant can be used even when the classes are not normal. We have projected the samples from d dimensions to 1,

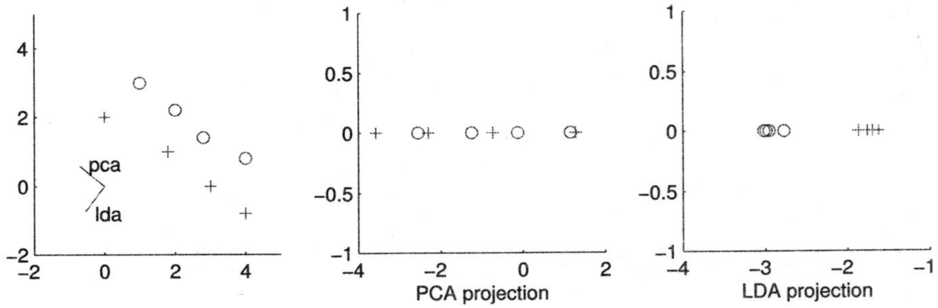

Figure 6.11 Two-dimensional synthetic data, directions found by PCA and LDA and projections along these directions are shown. LDA uses class information and as expected, does a much better job in terms of class separation.

and any classification method can be used afterward. In figure 6.11, we see two-dimensional synthetic data with two classes. As we see, and as expected, because it uses the class information, LDA direction is superior to the PCA direction in terms of the ease of discrimination afterwards.

In the case of $K > 2$ classes, we want to find the matrix $\mathbf{W}$ such that

$$\boldsymbol{z} = \mathbf{W}^T \boldsymbol{x} \tag{6.47}$$

where $\boldsymbol{z}$ is k-dimensional and $\mathbf{W}$ is $d \times k$. The within-class scatter matrix for C_i is

$$\mathbf{S}_i = \sum_t r_i^t (\boldsymbol{x}^t - \boldsymbol{m}_i)(\boldsymbol{x}^t - \boldsymbol{m}_i)^T \tag{6.48}$$

where $r_i^t = 1$ if $\boldsymbol{x}^t \in C_i$ and 0 otherwise. The total within-class scatter is

$$\mathbf{S}_W = \sum_{i=1}^{K} \mathbf{S}_i \tag{6.49}$$

When there are $K > 2$ classes, the scatter of the means is calculated as how much they are scattered around the overall mean

$$\boldsymbol{m} = \frac{1}{K} \sum_{i=1}^{K} \boldsymbol{m}_i \tag{6.50}$$

and the between-class scatter matrix is

$$\mathbf{S}_B = \sum_{i=1}^{K} N_i (\boldsymbol{m}_i - \boldsymbol{m})(\boldsymbol{m}_i - \boldsymbol{m})^T \tag{6.51}$$

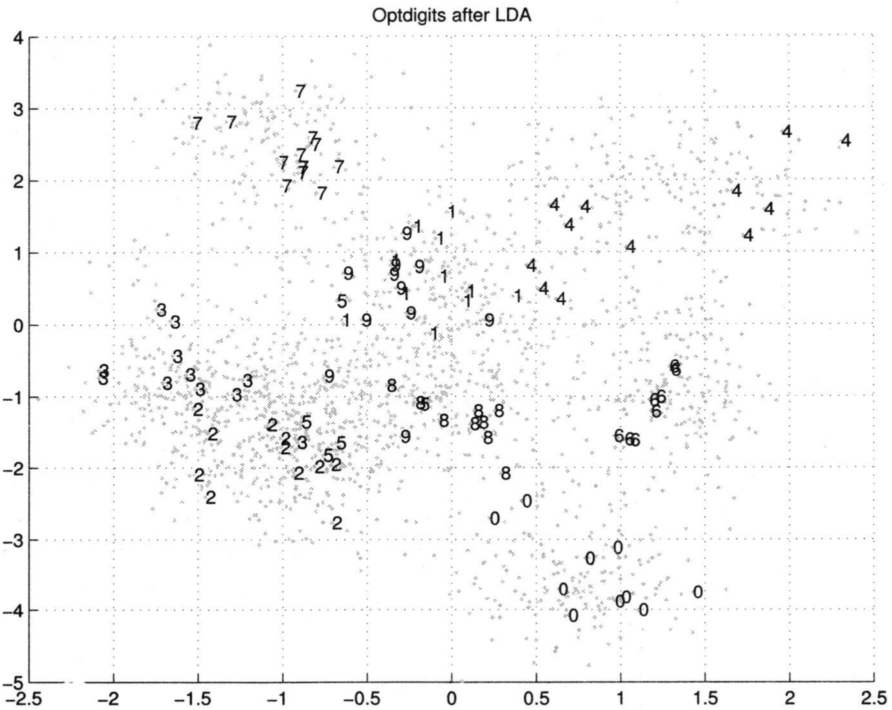

Figure 6.12 Optdigits data plotted in the space of the first two dimensions found by LDA. Comparing this with figure 6.5, we see that LDA, as expected, leads to a better separation of classes than PCA. Even in this two-dimensional space (there are nine altogether), we can discern separate clouds for different classes.

with $N_i = \sum_t r_i^t$. The between-class scatter matrix after projection is $\mathbf{W}^T\mathbf{S}_B\mathbf{W}$ and the within-class scatter matrix after projection is $\mathbf{W}^T\mathbf{S}_W\mathbf{W}$. These are both $k \times k$ matrices. We want the first scatter to be large, that is, after the projection, in the new k-dimensional space we want class means to be as far apart from each other as possible. We want the second scatter to be small, that is, after the projection, we want samples from the same class to be as close to their mean as possible. For a scatter (or covariance) matrix, a measure of spread is the determinant, remembering that the determinant is the product of eigenvalues and that an eigenvalue gives the variance along its eigenvector (component). Thus we are interested in the matrix $\mathbf{W}$ that maximizes

$$J(\mathbf{W}) = \frac{|\mathbf{W}^T \mathbf{S}_B \mathbf{W}|}{|\mathbf{W}^T \mathbf{S}_W \mathbf{W}|} \tag{6.52}$$

The largest eigenvectors of $\mathbf{S}_W^{-1}\mathbf{S}_B$ are the solution. $\mathbf{S}_B$ is the sum of K matrices of rank 1, namely, $(\boldsymbol{m}_i - \boldsymbol{m})(\boldsymbol{m}_i - \boldsymbol{m})^T$, and only $K - 1$ of them are independent. Therefore, $\mathbf{S}_B$ has a maximum rank of $K - 1$ and we take $k = K - 1$. Thus we define a new lower, $(K - 1)$-dimensional space where the discriminant is then to be constructed (see figure 6.12). Though LDA uses class separability as its goodness criterion, any classification method can be used in this new space for estimating the discriminants.

We see that to be able to apply LDA, $\mathbf{S}_W$ should be invertible. If this is not the case, we can first use PCA to get rid of singularity and then apply LDA to its result; however, we should make sure that PCA does not reduce dimensionality so much that LDA does not have anything left to work on.

6.9 Canonical Correlation Analysis

In all the methods discussed previously, we assume we have a single source of data returning us a single set of observations. Sometimes, for the same object or event, we have two types of variables. For example, in speech recognition, in addition to the acoustic information, we may also have the visual information of the lip movements while the word is uttered; in retrieval, we may have image data and text annotations. Frequently, these two sets of variables are correlated, and we want to take this correlation into account while reducing dimensionality to a joint space. This is the idea in *canonical correlation analysis* (CCA) (Rencher 1995).

CANONICAL CORRELATION ANALYSIS

Let us say we have a dataset with two sets of variables $\mathcal{X} = \{\boldsymbol{x}^t, \boldsymbol{y}^t\}_{t=1}^N$ where $\boldsymbol{x}^t \in \Re^d$ and $\boldsymbol{y}^t \in \Re^e$. Note that both of these are inputs and this is an unsupervised problem; if there is a required output for classification or regression, that is handled afterward as in PCA (section 6.3).

The *canonical correlation* is measured as the amount of correlation between the $\boldsymbol{x}$ dimensions and the $\boldsymbol{y}$ dimensions. Let us define a notation: $\mathbf{S}_{xx} = \text{Cov}(\boldsymbol{x}) = E[(\boldsymbol{x} - \boldsymbol{\mu}_x)^2]$ is the covariance matrix of the $\boldsymbol{x}$ dimensions and is $d \times d$—this is the $\boldsymbol{\Sigma}$ matrix that we use frequently, in PCA for example. Now, we also have the $e \times e$ covariance matrix of the $\boldsymbol{y}$, namely, $\mathbf{S}_{yy} = \text{Cov}(\boldsymbol{y})$. We also have the two cross-covariance matrices, namely,

$\mathbf{S}_{xy} = \text{Cov}(\boldsymbol{x}, \boldsymbol{y}) = E[(\boldsymbol{x} - \boldsymbol{\mu}_x)(\boldsymbol{y} - \boldsymbol{\mu}_y)]$, which is $d \times e$, and the other cross-covariance matrix $\mathbf{S}_{yx} = \text{Cov}(\boldsymbol{y}, \boldsymbol{x}) = E[(\boldsymbol{y} - \boldsymbol{\mu}_y)(\boldsymbol{x} - \boldsymbol{\mu}_x)]$, which is $e \times d$.

We are interested in the two vectors $\boldsymbol{w}$ and $\boldsymbol{v}$ such that when $\boldsymbol{x}$ is projected along $\boldsymbol{w}$ and $\boldsymbol{y}$ is projected along $\boldsymbol{v}$, we have maximum correlation. That is, we want to maximize

$$\rho = \text{Corr}(\boldsymbol{w}^T\boldsymbol{x}, \boldsymbol{v}^T\boldsymbol{y}) = \frac{\text{Cov}(\boldsymbol{w}^T\boldsymbol{x}, \boldsymbol{v}^T\boldsymbol{y})}{\sqrt{\text{Var}(\boldsymbol{w}^T\boldsymbol{x})}\sqrt{\text{Var}(\boldsymbol{v}^T\boldsymbol{y})}}$$

$$= \frac{\boldsymbol{w}^T\text{Cov}(\boldsymbol{x}, \boldsymbol{y})\boldsymbol{v}}{\sqrt{\boldsymbol{w}^T\text{Var}(\boldsymbol{x})\boldsymbol{w}}\sqrt{\boldsymbol{v}^T\text{Var}(\boldsymbol{y})\boldsymbol{v}}} = \frac{\boldsymbol{w}^T\mathbf{S}_{xy}\boldsymbol{v}}{\sqrt{\boldsymbol{w}^T\mathbf{S}_{xx}\boldsymbol{w}}\sqrt{\boldsymbol{v}^T\mathbf{S}_{yy}\boldsymbol{v}}} \quad (6.53)$$

Equally, we can say that what we want is to maximize $\boldsymbol{w}^T\mathbf{S}_{xy}\boldsymbol{v}$ subject to $\boldsymbol{w}^T\mathbf{S}_{xx}\boldsymbol{w} = 1$ and $\boldsymbol{v}^T\mathbf{S}_{yy}\boldsymbol{v} = 1$. Writing these as Lagrangian terms as we do in PCA and then taking derivatives with respect to $\boldsymbol{w}$ and $\boldsymbol{v}$ and setting them equal to 0, we see that $\boldsymbol{w}$ should be an eigenvector of $\mathbf{S}_{xx}^{-1}\mathbf{S}_{xy}\mathbf{S}_{yy}^{-1}\mathbf{S}_{yx}$ and similarly $\boldsymbol{v}$ should be an eigenvector of $\mathbf{S}_{yy}^{-1}\mathbf{S}_{yx}\mathbf{S}_{xx}^{-1}\mathbf{S}_{xy}$ (Hardoon, Szedmak, and Shawe-Taylor 2004).

Because we are interested in maximizing the correlation, we choose the two eigenvectors with the highest eigenvalues—let us call them $\boldsymbol{w}_1$ and $\boldsymbol{v}_1$—and the amount of correlation is equal to their (shared) eigenvalue λ_1. The eigenvalues of **AB** are the same as those of **BA** as long as **AB** and **BA** are square, but the eigenvectors are not the same: $\boldsymbol{w}_1$ is d-dimensional whereas $\boldsymbol{v}_1$ is e-dimensional.

Just as we do in PCA, we can decide how many pairs of eigenvectors $(\boldsymbol{w}_i, \boldsymbol{v}_i)$ to use by looking at the relative value of the corresponding eigenvalue:

$$\frac{\lambda_i}{\sum_{j=1}^{s}\lambda_j}$$

where $s = \min(d, e)$ is the maximum possible rank. We need to keep enough of them to conserve the correlation in the data.

Let us say we choose k as the dimensionality, then we get the *canonical variates* by projecting the training instances along them:

$$a_i^t = \boldsymbol{w}_i^T\boldsymbol{x}^t, b_i^t = \boldsymbol{v}_i^T\boldsymbol{y}^t, i = 1, \ldots, k \quad (6.54)$$

which we can write in matrix form as

$$\boldsymbol{a}^t = \mathbf{W}^T\boldsymbol{x}^t, \boldsymbol{b}^t = \mathbf{V}^T\boldsymbol{y}^t \quad (6.55)$$

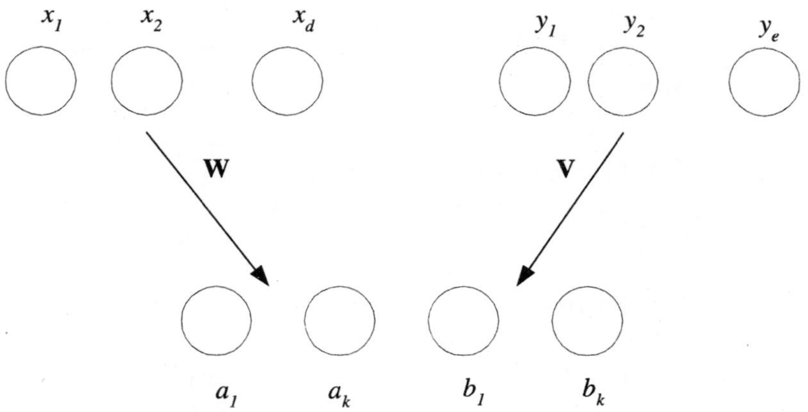

Figure 6.13 Canonical correlation analysis uses two sets of variables $\boldsymbol{x}$ and $\boldsymbol{y}$ and projects each so that the correlation after projections is maximized.

where $\mathbf{W}$ is the $d \times k$ matrix whose columns are $\boldsymbol{w}_i$ and $\mathbf{V}$ is the $e \times k$ matrix whose columns are $\boldsymbol{v}_i$ (figure 6.13). This vector of (a_i, b_i) pairs now constitutes our new, lower-dimensional representation that we can then use, for example, for classification. These new features are nonredundant: The values of a_i are uncorrelated, and each a_i is uncorrelated with all $b_j, j \neq i$.

For CCA to make sense, the two sets of variables need to be dependent. In the case of retrieval, for example, Hardoon, Szedmak, and Shawe-Taylor 2004, there is dependence: The word "sky" is associated with a lot of blue color in the image, so it makes sense to use CCA. But this is not always the case. For example, in user authentication, we may have the signature and iris images, but there is no reason to assume any dependence between them. In such a case, it would be better to do dimensionality reduction separately on signature and iris images, hence recovering dependence between features in the same set. It only makes sense to use CCA if we can also assume dependence between features of separate sets. Rencher (1995) discusses tests to check whether $\mathbf{S}_{xy} = \mathbf{0}$, that is, whether $\boldsymbol{x}$ and $\boldsymbol{y}$ are independent. One interesting note is that if $\boldsymbol{x}$ are the observed variables and if class labels are given as $\boldsymbol{y}$ using 1-of-K encoding, CCA finds the same solution as Fisher's LDA (section 6.8).

In factor analysis, we give a generative interpretation of dimensionality reduction: We assume that there are hidden variables z that in combination cause the observed variables x. Here, we can similarly think of hidden variables that generate x *and* y; actually, we may consider a and b together constituting z, the representation in the latent space.

It is possible to generalize CCA for more than two sets of variables. Bach and Jordan (2005) give a probabilistic interpretation of CCA where more than two sets of variables are possible.

6.10 Isomap

Principal component analysis, which we discussed in section 6.3, works when the data lies in a linear subspace. However, this may not hold in many applications. Take, for example, face recognition where a face is represented as a two-dimensional, say 100×100 image. In this case, each face is a point in $10,000$ dimensions. Now let us say that we take a series of pictures as a person slowly rotates his or her head from right to left. The sequence of face images we capture follows a trajectory in the $10,000$-dimensional space, and this is not linear. Now consider the faces of many people. The trajectories of all their faces as they rotate their faces define a manifold in the $10,000$-dimensional space, and this is what we want to model. The similarity between two faces cannot simply be written in terms of the sum of the pixel differences, and hence Euclidean distance is not a good metric. It may even be the case that images of two different people with the same pose have smaller Euclidean distance between them than the images of two different poses of the same person. This is not what we want. What should count is the distance along the manifold, which is called the *geodesic distance*. *Isometric feature mapping* (Isomap) (Tenenbaum, de Silva, and Langford 2000) estimates this distance and applies multidimensional scaling (section 6.7), using it for dimensionality reduction.

GEODESIC DISTANCE
ISOMETRIC FEATURE MAPPING

Isomap uses the geodesic distances between all pairs of data points. For neighboring points that are close in the input space, Euclidean distance can be used; for small changes in pose, the manifold is locally linear. For faraway points, geodesic distance is approximated by the sum of the distances between the points along the way over the manifold. This is done by defining a graph whose nodes correspond to the N data points and whose edges connect neighboring points (those with distance less than some ϵ or one of the n nearest) with weights corresponding

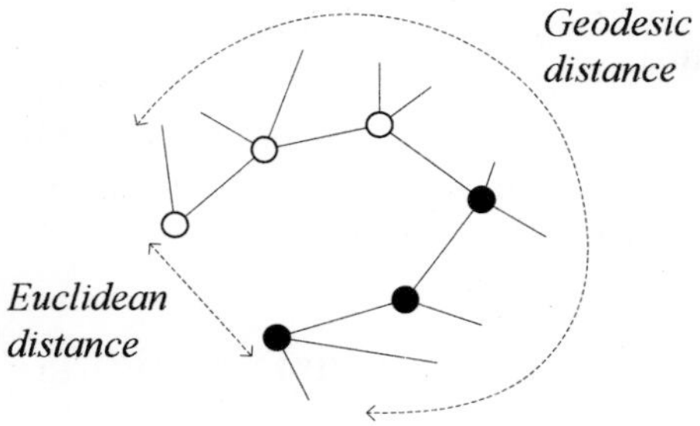

Figure 6.14 Geodesic distance is calculated along the manifold as opposed to the Euclidean distance that does not use this information. After multidimensional scaling, these two instances from two classes will be mapped to faraway positions in the new space, though they are close in the original space.

to Euclidean distances. The geodesic distance between any two points is calculated as the length of the shortest path between the corresponding two nodes. For two points that are not close by, we need to hop over a number of intermediate points along the way, and therefore the distance will be the distance along the manifold, approximated as the sum of local Euclidean distances (see figure 6.14).

Two nodes r and s are connected if $\|\boldsymbol{x}^r - \boldsymbol{x}^s\| < \epsilon$ (while making sure that the graph is connected), or if $\boldsymbol{x}^s$ is one of the n neighbors of $\boldsymbol{x}^r$ (while making sure that the distance matrix is symmetric), and we set the edge length to $\|\boldsymbol{x}^r - \boldsymbol{x}^s\|$. For any two nodes r and s, d_{rs} is the length of the shortest path between them. We then apply MDS on d_{rs} to reduce dimensionality to k using feature embedding by observing the proportion of variance explained. This will have the effect of placing r and s that are far apart in the geodesic space also far apart in the new k-dimensional space even if they are close in terms of Euclidean distance in the original d-dimensional space.

It is clear that the graph distances provide a better approximation as the number of points increases, though there is the trade-off of longer execution time; if time is critical, one can subsample and use a subset of "landmark points" to make the algorithm faster. The parameter ϵ needs to be carefully tuned; if it is too small, there may be more than one connected component, and if it is too large, "shortcut" edges may be added that corrupt the low-dimensional embedding (Balasubramanian et al. 2002).

One problem with Isomap, as with MDS, because it uses feature embedding, is that it places the N points in a low-dimensional space, but it does not learn a general mapping function that will allow mapping a new test point; the new point should be added to the dataset and the whole algorithm needs to be run once more using $N + 1$ instances.

6.11 Locally Linear Embedding

LOCALLY LINEAR EMBEDDING

Locally linear embedding (LLE) recovers global nonlinear structure from locally linear fits (Roweis and Saul 2000). The idea is that each local patch of the manifold can be approximated linearly and given enough data, each point can be written as a linear, weighted sum of its neighbors (again either defined using a given number of neighbors, n, or distance threshold, ϵ). Given $\boldsymbol{x}^r$ and its neighbors $\boldsymbol{x}^s_{(r)}$ in the original space, one can find the reconstruction weights $\mathbf{W}_{rs}$ that minimize the error function

$$\mathcal{E}^w(\mathbf{W}|\mathcal{X}) = \sum_r \|\boldsymbol{x}^r - \sum_s \mathbf{W}_{rs}\boldsymbol{x}^s_{(r)}\|^2 \tag{6.56}$$

using least squares subject to $\mathbf{W}_{rr} = 0, \forall r$ and $\sum_s \mathbf{W}_{rs} = 1$.

The idea in LLE is that the reconstruction weights $\mathbf{W}_{rs}$ reflect the intrinsic geometric properties of the data that we expect to be also valid for local patches of the manifold, that is, the new space we are mapping the instances to (see figure 6.15). The second step of LLE is hence to now keep the weights $\mathbf{W}_{rs}$ fixed and let the new coordinates $\boldsymbol{z}^r$ take whatever values they need respecting the interpoint constraints given by the weights:

$$\mathcal{E}^z(\mathcal{Z}|\mathbf{W}) = \sum_r \|\boldsymbol{z}^r - \sum_s \mathbf{W}_{rs}\boldsymbol{z}^s\|^2 \tag{6.57}$$

Nearby points in the original d-dimensional space should remain close and similarly colocated with respect to one another in the new, k-dimensional space. Equation 6.57 can be rewritten as

$$\mathcal{E}^z(\mathcal{Z}|\mathbf{W}) = \sum_{r,s} \mathbf{M}_{rs}(\boldsymbol{z}^r)^T\boldsymbol{z}^s \tag{6.58}$$

where

$$\mathbf{M}_{rs} = \delta_{rs} - \mathbf{W}_{rs} - \mathbf{W}_{sr} + \sum_i \mathbf{W}_{ir}\mathbf{W}_{is} \tag{6.59}$$

M is sparse (only a small percentage of data points are neighbors of a data point: $n \ll N$), symmetric, and positive semidefinite. As in other

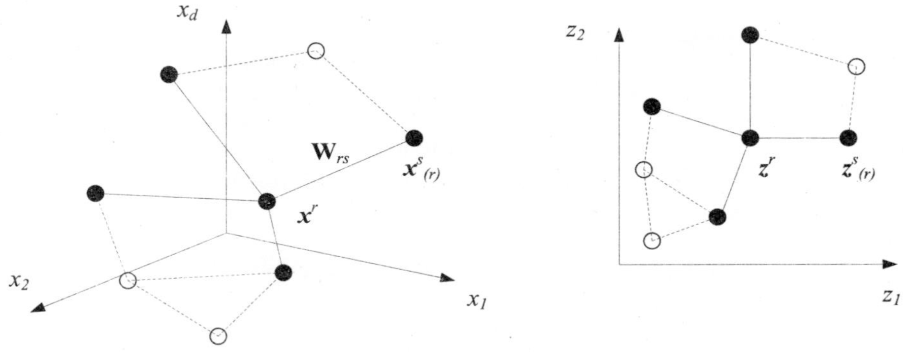

Figure 6.15 Local linear embedding first learns the constraints in the original space and next places the points in the new space respecting those constraints. The constraints are learned using the immediate neighbors (shown with continuous lines) but also propagate to second-order neighbors (shown dashed).

dimensionality reduction methods, we require that the data be centered at the origin, $E[\mathbf{z}] = 0$, and that the new coordinates be uncorrelated and unit length: $\text{Cov}(\mathbf{z}) = \mathbf{I}$. The solution to equation 6.58 subject to these two constraints is given by the $k+1$ eigenvectors with the smallest eigenvalues; we ignore the lowest one and the other k eigenvectors give us the new coordinates.

Because the n neighbors span a space of dimensionality $n - 1$ (you need distances to three points to uniquely specify your location in two dimensions), LLE can reduce dimensionality up to $k \le n-1$. It is observed (Saul and Roweis 2003) that some margin between k and n is necessary to obtain a good embedding. Note that if n (or ϵ) is small, the graph (that is constructed by connecting each instance to its neighbors) may no longer be connected and it may be necessary to run LLE separately on separate components to find separate manifolds in different parts of the input space. On the other hand, if n (or ϵ) is taken large, some neighbors may be too far for the local linearity assumption to hold and this may corrupt the embedding. It is possible to use different n (or ϵ) in different parts of the input space based on some prior knowledge, but how this can be done is open to research (Saul and Roweis 2003).

As with Isomap, LLE solution is the set of new coordinates for the N points, but we do not learn a mapping and hence cannot find $\mathbf{z}'$ for a new $\mathbf{x}'$. There are two solutions to this:

1. Using the same idea, one can find the n neighbors of $\mathbf{x}'$ in the original d-dimensional space and first learn the reconstruction weights $\mathbf{w}_j$ that minimizes

(6.60) $$\mathcal{E}^w(\mathbf{w}|\mathcal{X}) = \|\mathbf{x}' - \sum_s \mathbf{w}_s \mathbf{x}^s\|^2$$

   and then use them to reconstruct $\mathbf{z}'$ in the new k-dimensional space:

(6.61) $$\mathbf{z}' = \sum_s \mathbf{w}_s \mathbf{z}^s$$

   Note that this approach can also be used to interpolate from an Isomap (or MDS) solution. The drawback however is the need to store the whole set of $\{\mathbf{x}^t, \mathbf{z}^t\}_{t=1}^N$.

2. Using $\mathcal{X} = \{\mathbf{x}^t, \mathbf{z}^t\}_{t=1}^N$ as a training set, one can train any regressor, $\boldsymbol{g}(\mathbf{x}^t|\theta)$—for example, a multilayer perceptron (chapter 11)—as a generalizer to approximate $\mathbf{z}^t$ from $\mathbf{x}^t$, whose parameters θ is learned to minimize the regression error:

(6.62) $$\mathcal{E}(\theta|\mathcal{X}) = \sum_t \|\mathbf{z}^t - \boldsymbol{g}(\mathbf{x}^t|\theta)\|^2$$

   Once training is done, we can calculate $\mathbf{z}' = \boldsymbol{g}(\mathbf{x}'|\theta)$. The model $\boldsymbol{g}(\cdot)$ should be carefully chosen to be able to learn the mapping. There may no longer be a unique optimum and hence there are all the usual problems related to minimization, that is, initialization, local optima, convergence, and so on.

In both Isomap and LLE, there is local information that is propagated over neighbors to get a global solution. In Isomap, the geodesic distance is the sum of local distances; in LLE, the final optimization in placing $\mathbf{z}^t$ takes into account all local $\mathbf{W}_{rs}$ values. Let us say a and b are neighbors and b and c are neighbors. Though a and c may not be neighbors, there is dependence between a and c either through the graph, $d_{ac} = d_{ab} + d_{bc}$, or the weights $\mathbf{W}_{ab}$ and $\mathbf{W}_{bc}$. In both algorithms, the global nonlinear organization is found by integrating local linear constraints that overlap partially.

6.12 Laplacian Eigenmaps

Consider the data instance $\mathbf{x}^r \in \Re^d, r = 1, \ldots, N$ and its projection $\mathbf{z}^r \in \Re^k$. Let us say that we are given a similarity value B_{rs} between pairs of instances possibly calculated in some high-dimensional space such that it takes its maximum value if r and s are the same and decreases as they become dissimilar. Assume that the minimum possible value is 0 and that it is symmetric: $B_{rs} = B_{sr}$ (Belkin and Nyogi 2003). The aim is to

$$\min \sum_{r,s} \|\mathbf{z}^r - \mathbf{z}^s\|^2 B_{rs} \tag{6.63}$$

Two instances that should be similar, that is, r and s whose B_{rs} is high, should be placed nearby in the new space; hence $\mathbf{z}^r$ and $\mathbf{z}^s$ should be close. Whereas the more they are dissimilar, the less we care for their relative position in the new space. B_{rs} are calculated in the original space; for example, if we use the dot product, the method would work similar to the way multidimensional scaling does:

$$B_{rs} = (\mathbf{x}^r)^T \mathbf{x}_s$$

LAPLACIAN EIGENMAPS

But what is done in *Laplacian eigenmaps*, similar to Isomap and LLE, is that we care for similarities only locally (Belkin and Nyogi 2003). We define a neighborhood either through some maximum ϵ distance between $\mathbf{x}^r$ and $\mathbf{x}^s$, or a k-nearest neighborhood, and outside of that we set B_{rs} to 0. In the neighborhood, we use the Gaussian kernel to convert Euclidean distance to a similarity value:

$$B_{rs} = \exp\left[-\frac{\|\mathbf{x}^r - \mathbf{x}^s\|^2}{2\sigma^2}\right]$$

for some user-defined σ value. $\mathbf{B}$ can be seen as defining a weighted graph.

For the case of $k = 1$ (we reduce dimensionality to 1), we can rewrite equation 6.63 as

$$\begin{aligned}
\min \quad & \frac{1}{2}\sum_{r,s}(z_r - z_s)^2 B_{rs} \\
= \quad & \frac{1}{2}\left(\sum_{r,s} B_{rs} z_r^2 - 2\sum_{r,s} B_{rs} z_r z_s + \sum_{r,s} B_{rs}(z_s)^2\right) \\
= \quad & \frac{1}{2}\left(\sum_{r} d_r z_r^2 - 2\sum_{r,s} B_{rs} z_r z_s + \sum_{s} d_s z_s^2\right)
\end{aligned}$$

$$= \sum_r d_r z_r^2 - \sum_r \sum_s B_{rs} z_r z_s$$

$$\text{(6.64)} \quad = \mathbf{z}^T \mathbf{D} \mathbf{z} - \mathbf{z}^T \mathbf{B} \mathbf{z}$$

where $d_r = \sum_s B_{rs}$. **D** is the diagonal matrix of d_r, and $\boldsymbol{z}$ is the N-dimensional column vector whose dimension r, z_r is the new coordinate for $\boldsymbol{x}^r$. We define the *graph Laplacian*

$$\text{(6.65)} \quad \mathbf{L} = \mathbf{D} - \mathbf{B}$$

and the aim is to minimize $\boldsymbol{z}^T \mathbf{L} \boldsymbol{z}$. For a unique solution, we require $\|\boldsymbol{z}\| = 1$. Just as in feature embedding, we get the coordinates in the new space directly without any extra projection and it can be shown that $\boldsymbol{z}$ should be an eigenvector of **L**, and because we want to minimize, we choose the eigenvector with the smallest eigenvalue. Note, however, that there is at least one eigenvector with eigenvalue 0 and that should be ignored. That eigenvector has all its elements equal to each other: $\boldsymbol{c} = (1/\sqrt{N})\mathbf{1}^T$. The corresponding eigenvalue is 0 because

$$\mathbf{L}\boldsymbol{c} = \mathbf{D}\boldsymbol{c} - \mathbf{B}\boldsymbol{c} = 0$$

D has row sums in its diagonal, and the dot product of a row of **B** and **1** also takes a weighted sum; in this case, for equation 6.64 to be 0, with B_{ij} nonnegative, z_i and z_j should be equal for all pairs of i, j, and for the norm to be 1, all should be $1/\sqrt{N}$. So, we need to skip the eigenvector with eigenvalue 0 and if we want to reduce dimensionality to $k > 1$, we need to take the next k.

The Laplacian eigenmap is a feature embedding method; that is, we find the coordinates in the new space directly and have no explicit model for mapping that we can later use for new instances.

We can compare equation 6.63 with equation 6.37 (Sammon stress in MDS). Here, the similarity in the original space is represented implicitly in B_{rs} whereas in MDS, it is explicitly written as $\|\boldsymbol{x}^r - \boldsymbol{x}^s\|$. Another difference is that in MDS, we check for similarity between all pairs, whereas here the constraints are local (which are then propagated because those local neighborhoods partially overlap—as in Isomap and LLE).

For the four-dimensional Iris data, results after projection to two dimensions are given for MDS and Laplacian eigenmaps in figure 6.16. MDS here is equivalent to PCA, whereas we see that the Laplacian eigenmap projects similar instances nearby in the new space. This is why this method is a good way to preprocess the data before clustering; *spectral clustering*, which we discuss in section 7.7, uses this idea.

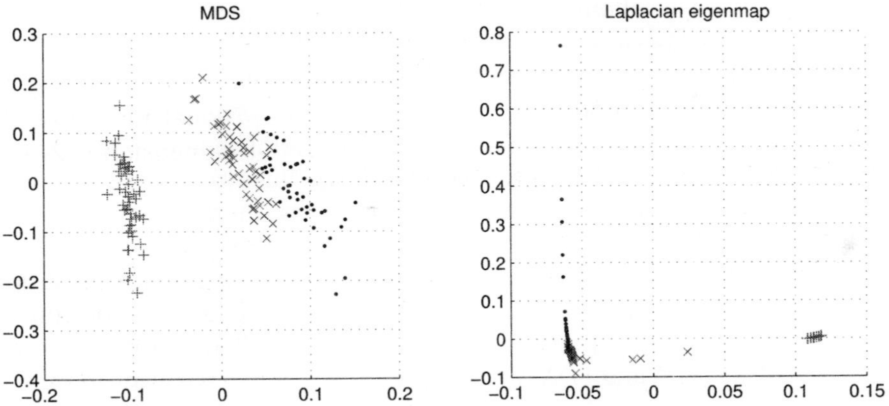

Figure 6.16 Iris data reduced to two dimensions using multidimensional scaling and Laplacian eigenmaps. The latter leads to a more dense placement of similar instances.

6.13 Notes

Subset selection in regression is discussed in Miller 1990. The forward and backward search procedures we discussed are local search procedures. Fukunaga and Narendra (1977) proposed a branch and bound procedure. At considerable more expense, you can use a stochastic procedure like simulated annealing or genetic algorithms to search more widely in the the search space.

There are also *filtering* algorithms for feature selection where heuristic measures are used to calculate the "relevance" of a feature in a preprocessing stage without actually using the learner. For example, in the case of classification, instead of training a classifier and testing it at each step, one can use a separability measure, like the one used in linear discriminant analysis, to measure the quality of the new space in separating classes from each other (McLachlan 1992). With the cost of computation going down, it is best to include the learner in the loop because there is no guarantee that the heuristic used by the filter will match the bias of the learner that uses the features; no heuristic can replace the actual validation accuracy. A survey of feature selection methods is given by Guyon and Elisseeff (2003).

Projection methods work with numeric inputs, and discrete variables should be represented by 0/1 dummy variables, whereas subset selection can use discrete inputs directly. Finding the eigenvectors and eigenvalues is quite straightforward and is part of any linear algebra package. Factor analysis was introduced by the British psychologist Charles Spearman to find the single factor for intelligence which explains the correlation between scores on various intelligence tests. The existence of such a single factor, called g, is highly disputed. More information on multidimensional scaling can be found in Cox and Cox 1994.

The projection methods we discussed are batch procedures in that they require that the whole sample be given before the projection directions are found. Mao and Jain (1995) discuss online procedures for doing PCA and LDA, where instances are given one by one and updates are done as new instances arrive. Another possibility for doing a nonlinear projection is when the estimator in Sammon mapping is taken as a nonlinear function, for example, a multilayer perceptron (section 11.11) (Mao and Jain 1995). It is also possible but much harder to do nonlinear factor analysis. When the models are nonlinear, it is difficult to come up with the right nonlinear model. You also need to use complicated optimization and approximation methods to solve for the model parameters.

Laplacian eigenmaps use the idea of feature embedding such that given pairwise similarities are preserved; the same idea is also used in kernel machines where pairwise similarities are given by a kernel function, and in chapter 13, we talk about "kernel" PCA, LDA, and CCA. Just as we implement polynomial regression by using linear regression where we consider high-order terms as additional inputs (section 5.8), we can do nonlinear dimensionality reduction by mapping to a new space by using nonlinear basis functions. That is the idea in kernel methods that allow us to go further than dot product or Euclidean distance for similarity calculation.

RECOMMENDATION SYSTEMS

Matrix decomposition methods are quite popular in various big data applications because they allow us to explain a large data matrix using smaller matrices. One example application is *recommendation systems* where we may have millions of movies and millions of customers and entries are customer ratings. Note that most entries will be missing and the aim is to fill in those missing values and then do a recommendation based on those predicted values (Koren, Bell, and Volinsky 2009).

There is a trade-off between feature extraction and decision making. If the feature extractor is good, the task of the classifier (or regressor) becomes trivial, for example, when the class code is extracted as a new feature from the existing features. On the other hand, if the classifier is good enough, then there is no need for feature extraction; it does its automatic feature selection or combination internally. We live between these two ideal worlds.

There exist algorithms that do some feature selection internally, though in a limited way. Decision trees (chapter 9) do feature selection while generating the decision tree, and multilayer perceptrons (chapter 11) do nonlinear feature extraction in the hidden nodes. We expect to see more development along this line in embedding feature extraction in the actual step of classification/regression.

6.14 Exercises

1. Assuming that the classes are normally distributed, in subset selection, when one variable is added or removed, how can the new discriminant be calculated quickly? For example, how can the new $\mathbf{S}_{new}^{-1}$ be calculated from $\mathbf{S}_{old}^{-1}$?
2. Using Optdigits from the UCI repository, implement PCA. For various number of eigenvectors, reconstruct the digit images and calculate the reconstruction error (equation 6.12).
3. Plot the map of your state/country using MDS, given the road travel distances as input.
4. In Sammon mapping, if the mapping is linear, namely, $g(\mathbf{x}|\mathbf{W}) = \mathbf{W}^T\mathbf{x}$, how can $\mathbf{W}$ that minimizes the Sammon stress be calculated?
5. In figure 6.11, we see a synthetic two-dimensional data where LDA does a better job than PCA. Draw a similar dataset where PCA and LDA find the same good direction. Draw another where neither PCA nor LDA find a good direction.
6. Redo exercise 3, this time using Isomap where two cities are connected only if there is a direct road between them that does not pass through any other city.
7. In Isomap, instead of using Euclidean distance, we can also use Mahalanobis distance between neighboring points. What are the advantages and disadvantages of this approach, if any?
8. Multidimensional scaling can work as long as we have the pairwise distances between objects. We do not actually need to represent the objects as vectors at all as long as we have some measure of similarity. Can you give an example?

   SOLUTION: Let us say we have a database of documents. Then if d_{rs} denotes the number of terms that documents r and s share, we can use MDS to map these documents to a lower-dimensional space, for example, to visualize them and check for structure. Note that here we can count the number of shared terms without needing to explicitly represent the documents as vectors using, for example, the bag of words representation.

9. How can we incorporate class information into Isomap or LLE such that instances of the same class are mapped to nearby locations in the new space?

   SOLUTION: We can include an additional penalty term in calculating distances for instances belonging to different classes; MDS will then map instances of the same class to nearby points.

10. In factor analysis, how can we find the remaining ones if we already know some of the factors?

    SOLUTION: If we already know some of the factors, we can find their loadings by regression and then remove their effect from the data. We will then get the residual of what is not explained by those factors and look for additional factors that can explain this residual.

11. Discuss an application where there are hidden factors (not necessarily linear) and where factor analysis would be expected to work well.

    SOLUTION: One example is the data of student grades at a university. The grade a student gets for a set of courses depends on a number of hidden factors—for example, the student's aptitude for the subject, the amount of time he/she can allocate to studying, the comfort of his/her lodging, and so on.

6.15 References

Balasubramanian, M., E. L. Schwartz, J. B. Tenenbaum, V. de Silva, and J. C. Langford. 2002. "The Isomap Algorithm and Topological Stability." *Science* 295:7.

Bach, F., and M. I. Jordan. 2005. *A Probabilistic Interpretation of Canonical Correlation Analysis.* Technical Report 688, Department of Statistics, University of California, Berkeley.

Belkin, M., and P. Niyogi. 2003. "Laplacian Eigenmaps for Dimensionality Reduction and Data Representation." *Neural Computation* 15:1373–1396.

Chatfield, C., and A. J. Collins. 1980. *Introduction to Multivariate Analysis.* London: Chapman and Hall.

Cox, T. F., and M. A. A. Cox. 1994. *Multidimensional Scaling.* London: Chapman and Hall.

Flury, B. 1988. *Common Principal Components and Related Multivariate Models.* New York: Wiley.

Fukunaga, K., and P. M. Narendra. 1977. "A Branch and Bound Algorithm for Feature Subset Selection." *IEEE Transactions on Computers* C-26:917–922.

Guyon, I., and A. Elisseeff. 2003. "An Introduction to Variable and Feature Selection." *Journal of Machine Learning Research* 3:1157–1182.

Hardoon, D. R., S. Szedmak, J. Shawe-Taylor. 2004. "Canonical Correlation Analysis: An Overview with Application to Learning Methods." *Neural Computation* 16:2639–2664.

Hastie, T. J., R. J. Tibshirani, and A. Buja. 1994. "Flexible Discriminant Analysis by Optimal Scoring." *Journal of the American Statistical Association* 89:1255–1270.

Kohavi, R., and G. John. 1997. "Wrappers for Feature Subset Selection." *Artificial Intelligence* 97:273–324.

Koren, Y., R. Bell, and C. Volinsky. 2009. "Matrix Factorization Techniques for Recommender Systems." *IEEE Computer* 42 (8): 30–37.

Landauer, T. K., D. Laham, and M. Derr. 2004. "From Paragraph to Graph: Latent Semantic Analysis for Information Visualization." *Proceedings of the National Academy of Sciences* 101 (suppl. 1): 5214–5219.

Lee, D. D., and H. S. Seung. 1999. "Learning the Parts of Objects by Non-Negative Matrix Factorization," *Nature* 401 (6755): 788–791.

Mao, J., and A. K. Jain. 1995. "Artificial Neural Networks for Feature Extraction and Multivariate Data Projection." *IEEE Transactions on Neural Networks* 6: 296–317.

McLachlan, G. J. 1992. *Discriminant Analysis and Statistical Pattern Recognition.* New York: Wiley.

Miller, A. J. 1990. *Subset Selection in Regression.* London: Chapman and Hall.

Pudil, P., J. Novovičová, and J. Kittler. 1994. "Floating Search Methods in Feature Selection." *Pattern Recognition Letters* 15:1119–1125.

Rencher, A. C. 1995. *Methods of Multivariate Analysis.* New York: Wiley.

Roweis, S. T., and L. K. Saul. 2000. "Nonlinear Dimensionality Reduction by Locally Linear Embedding." *Science* 290:2323–2326.

Saul, K. K., and S. T. Roweis. 2003. "Think Globally, Fit Locally: Unsupervised Learning of Low Dimensional Manifolds." *Journal of Machine Learning Research* 4:119–155.

Strang, G. 2006. *Linear Algebra and Its Applications,* 4th ed. Boston: Cengage Learning.

Tenenbaum, J. B., V. de Silva, and J. C. Langford. 2000. "A Global Geometric Framework for Nonlinear Dimensionality Reduction." *Science* 290:2319–2323.

Tipping, M. E., and C. M. Bishop. 1999. "Probabilistic Principal Component Analysis." *Journal of the Royal Statistical Society Series B* 61:611–622.

Turk, M., and A. Pentland. 1991. "Eigenfaces for Recognition." *Journal of Cognitive Neuroscience* 3:71–86.

Webb, A. 1999. *Statistical Pattern Recognition.* London: Arnold.

7 Clustering

In the parametric approach, we assumed that the sample comes from a known distribution. In cases when such an assumption is untenable, we relax this assumption and use a semiparametric approach that allows a mixture of distributions to be used for estimating the input sample. Clustering methods allow learning the mixture parameters from data. In addition to probabilistic modeling, we discuss vector quantization, spectral clustering, and hierarchical clustering.

7.1 Introduction

IN CHAPTERS 4 and 5, we discussed the parametric method for density estimation where we assumed that the sample $\mathcal{X}$ is drawn from some parametric family, for example, Gaussian. In parametric classification, this corresponds to assuming a certain density for the class densities $p(\mathbf{x}|C_i)$. The advantage of any parametric approach is that given a model, the problem reduces to the estimation of a small number of parameters, which, in the case of density estimation, are the sufficient statistics of the density, for example, the mean and covariance in the case of Gaussian densities.

Though parametric approaches are used quite frequently, assuming a rigid parametric model may be a source of bias in many applications where this assumption does not hold. We thus need more flexible models. In particular, assuming Gaussian density corresponds to assuming that the sample, for example, instances of a class, forms one single group in the d-dimensional space, and as we saw in chapter 5, the center and the shape of this group is given by the mean and the covariance respectively.

In many applications, however, the sample is not one group; there may be several groups. Consider the case of optical character recognition: There are two ways of writing the digit 7; the American writing is '7', whereas the European writing style has a horizontal bar in the middle (to tell it apart from the European '1', which keeps the small stroke on top in handwriting). In such a case, when the sample contains examples from both continents, the class for the digit 7 should be represented as the disjunction of two groups. If each of these groups can be represented by a Gaussian, the class can be represented by a *mixture* of two Gaussians, one for each writing style.

A similar example is in speech recognition where the same word can be uttered in different ways, due to different pronounciation, accent, gender, age, and so forth. Thus when there is not a single, universal prototype, all these different ways should be represented in the density to be statistically correct.

SEMIPARAMETRIC DENSITY ESTIMATION

We call this approach *semiparametric density estimation*, as we still assume a parametric model for each group in the sample. We discuss the *nonparametric* approach in chapter 8, which is used when there is no structure to the data and even a mixture model is not applicable. In this chapter, we focus on density estimation and defer supervised learning to chapter 12.

7.2 Mixture Densities

MIXTURE DENSITY

The *mixture density* is written as

$$p(\mathbf{x}) = \sum_{i=1}^{k} p(\mathbf{x}|\mathcal{G}_i)P(\mathcal{G}_i) \tag{7.1}$$

MIXTURE COMPONENTS GROUPS CLUSTERS COMPONENT DENSITIES MIXTURE PROPORTIONS

where $\mathcal{G}_i$ are the *mixture components*. They are also called *group* or *clusters*. $p(\mathbf{x}|\mathcal{G}_i)$ are the *component densities* and $P(\mathcal{G}_i)$ are the *mixture proportions*. The number of components, k, is a hyperparameter and should be specified beforehand. Given a sample and k, learning corresponds to estimating the component densities and proportions. When we assume that the component densities obey a parametric model, we need only estimate their parameters. If the component densities are multivariate Gaussian, we have $p(\mathbf{x}|\mathcal{G}_i) \sim \mathcal{N}(\boldsymbol{\mu}_i, \Sigma_i)$, and $\Phi = \{P(\mathcal{G}_i), \boldsymbol{\mu}_i, \Sigma_i\}_{i=1}^{k}$ are the parameters that should be estimated from the iid sample $\mathcal{X} = \{\mathbf{x}^t\}_t$.

Parametric classification is a bona fide mixture model where groups, $\mathcal{G}_i$, correspond to classes, C_i, component densities $p(\mathbf{x}|\mathcal{G}_i)$ correspond to class densities $p(\mathbf{x}|C_i)$, and $P(\mathcal{G}_i)$ correspond to class priors, $P(C_i)$:

$$p(\mathbf{x}) = \sum_{i=1}^{K} p(\mathbf{x}|C_i)P(C_i)$$

In this *supervised* case, we know how many groups there are and learning the parameters is trivial because we are given the labels, namely, which instance belongs to which class (component). We remember from chapter 5 that when we are given the sample $\mathcal{X} = \{\mathbf{x}^t, \mathbf{r}^t\}_{t=1}^N$, where $r_i^t = 1$ if $\mathbf{x}^t \in C_i$ and 0 otherwise, the parameters can be calculated using maximum likelihood. When each class is Gaussian distributed, we have a Gaussian mixture, and the parameters are estimated as

(7.2)
$$\begin{aligned} \hat{P}(C_i) &= \frac{\sum_t r_i^t}{N} \\ \mathbf{m}_i &= \frac{\sum_t r_i^t \mathbf{x}^t}{\sum_t r_i^t} \\ \mathbf{S}_i &= \frac{\sum_t r_i^t (\mathbf{x}^t - \mathbf{m}_i)(\mathbf{x}^t - \mathbf{m}_i)^T}{\sum_t r_i^t} \end{aligned}$$

The difference in this chapter is that the sample is $\mathcal{X} = \{\mathbf{x}^t\}_t$: We have an *unsupervised learning* problem. We are given only $\mathbf{x}^t$ and not the labels $\mathbf{r}^t$, that is, we do not know which $\mathbf{x}^t$ comes from which component. So we should estimate both: First, we should estimate the labels, r_i^t, the component that a given instance belongs to; and, second, once we estimate the labels, we should estimate the parameters of the components given the set of instances belonging to them. We first discuss a simple algorithm, k-means clustering, for this purpose and later on show that it is a special case of the *expectation-maximization* (EM) algorithm.

7.3 k-Means Clustering

Let us say we have an image that is stored with 24 bits/pixel and can have up to 16 million colors. Assume we have a color screen with 8 bits/pixel that can display only 256 colors. We want to find the best 256 colors among all 16 million colors such that the image using only the 256 colors in the palette looks as close as possible to the original image. This is *color quantization* where we map from high to lower resolution. In the general

COLOR QUANTIZATION

case, the aim is to map from a continuous space to a discrete space; this process is called *vector quantization*.

VECTOR QUANTIZATION

Of course we can always quantize uniformly, but this wastes the colormap by assigning entries to colors not existing in the image, or would not assign extra entries to colors frequently used in the image. For example, if the image is a seascape, we expect to see many shades of blue and maybe no red. So the distribution of the colormap entries should reflect the original density as close as possible placing many entries in high-density regions, discarding regions where there is no data.

REFERENCE VECTORS

Let us say we have a sample of $\mathcal{X} = \{\boldsymbol{x}^t\}_{t=1}^N$. We have k *reference vectors*, $\boldsymbol{m}_j, j = 1, \ldots, k$. In our example of color quantization, $\boldsymbol{x}^t$ are the image pixel values in 24 bits and $\boldsymbol{m}_j$ are the color map entries also in 24 bits, with $k = 256$.

Assume for now that we somehow have the $\boldsymbol{m}_j$ values; we discuss how to learn them shortly. Then in displaying the image, given the pixel, $\boldsymbol{x}^t$, we represent it with the most similar entry, $\boldsymbol{m}_i$ in the color map, satisfying

$$\|\boldsymbol{x}^t - \boldsymbol{m}_i\| = \min_j \|\boldsymbol{x}^t - \boldsymbol{m}_j\|$$

CODEBOOK VECTORS

CODE WORDS

COMPRESSION

That is, instead of the original data value, we use the closest value we have in the alphabet of reference vectors. $\boldsymbol{m}_i$ are also called *codebook vectors* or *code words*, because this is a process of *encoding/decoding* (see figure 7.1): Going from $\boldsymbol{x}^t$ to i is a process of encoding the data using the codebook of $\boldsymbol{m}_i, i = 1, \ldots, k$ and, on the receiving end, generating $\boldsymbol{m}_i$ from i is decoding. Quantization also allows *compression*: For example, instead of using 24 bits to store (or transfer over a communication line) each $\boldsymbol{x}^t$, we can just store/transfer its index i in the colormap using 8 bits to index any one of 256, and we get a compression rate of almost 3; there is also the color map to store/transfer.

RECONSTRUCTION ERROR

Let us see how we can calculate $\boldsymbol{m}_i$: When $\boldsymbol{x}^t$ is represented by $\boldsymbol{m}_i$, there is an error that is proportional to the distance, $\|\boldsymbol{x}^t - \boldsymbol{m}_i\|$. For the new image to look like the original image, we should have these distances as small as possible for all pixels. The total *reconstruction error* is defined as

$$E(\{\boldsymbol{m}_i\}_{i=1}^k | \mathcal{X}) = \sum_t \sum_i b_i^t \|\boldsymbol{x}^t - \boldsymbol{m}_i\|^2 \tag{7.3}$$

where

$$b_i^t = \begin{cases} 1 & \text{if } \|\boldsymbol{x}^t - \boldsymbol{m}_i\| = \min_j \|\boldsymbol{x}^t - \boldsymbol{m}_j\| \\ 0 & \text{otherwise} \end{cases} \tag{7.4}$$

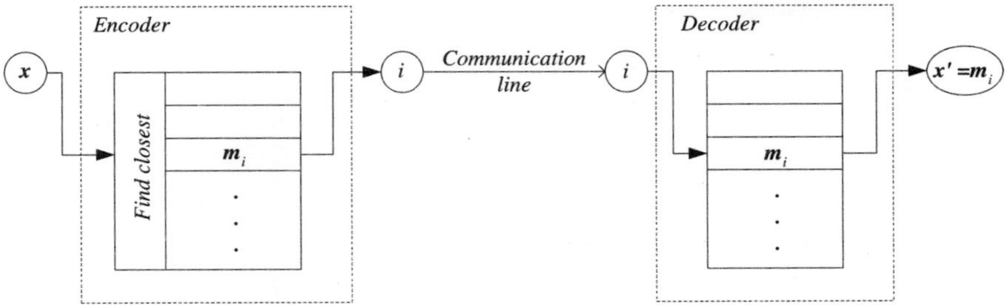

Figure 7.1 Given $\boldsymbol{x}$, the encoder sends the index of the closest code word and the decoder generates the code word with the received index as $\boldsymbol{x}'$. Error is $\|\boldsymbol{x}' - \boldsymbol{x}\|^2$.

k-MEANS CLUSTERING

The best reference vectors are those that minimize the total reconstruction error. b_i^t also depend on $\boldsymbol{m}_i$, and we cannot solve this optimization problem analytically. We have an iterative procedure named *k-means clustering* for this: First, we start with some $\boldsymbol{m}_i$ initialized randomly. Then at each iteration, we first use equation 7.4 and calculate b_i^t for all $\boldsymbol{x}^t$, which are the *estimated labels*; if b_i^t is 1, we say that $\boldsymbol{x}^t$ belongs to the group of $\boldsymbol{m}_i$. Then, once we have these labels, we minimize equation 7.3. Taking its derivative with respect to $\boldsymbol{m}_i$ and setting it to 0, we get

$$\boldsymbol{m}_i = \frac{\sum_t b_i^t \boldsymbol{x}^t}{\sum_t b_i^t} \tag{7.5}$$

The reference vector is set to the mean of all the instances that it represents. Note that this is the same as the formula for the mean in equation 7.2, except that we place the estimated labels b_i^t in place of the labels r_i^t. This is an iterative procedure because once we calculate the new $\boldsymbol{m}_i$, b_i^t change and need to be recalculated, which in turn affect $\boldsymbol{m}_i$. These two steps are repeated until $\boldsymbol{m}_i$ stabilize (see figure 7.2). The pseudocode of the *k*-means algorithm is given in figure 7.3.

One disadvantage is that this is a local search procedure, and the final $\boldsymbol{m}_i$ highly depend on the initial $\boldsymbol{m}_i$. There are various methods for initialization:

- We can simply take randomly selected k instances as the initial $\boldsymbol{m}_i$.
- The mean of all data can be calculated and small random vectors may be added to the mean to get the k initial $\boldsymbol{m}_i$.

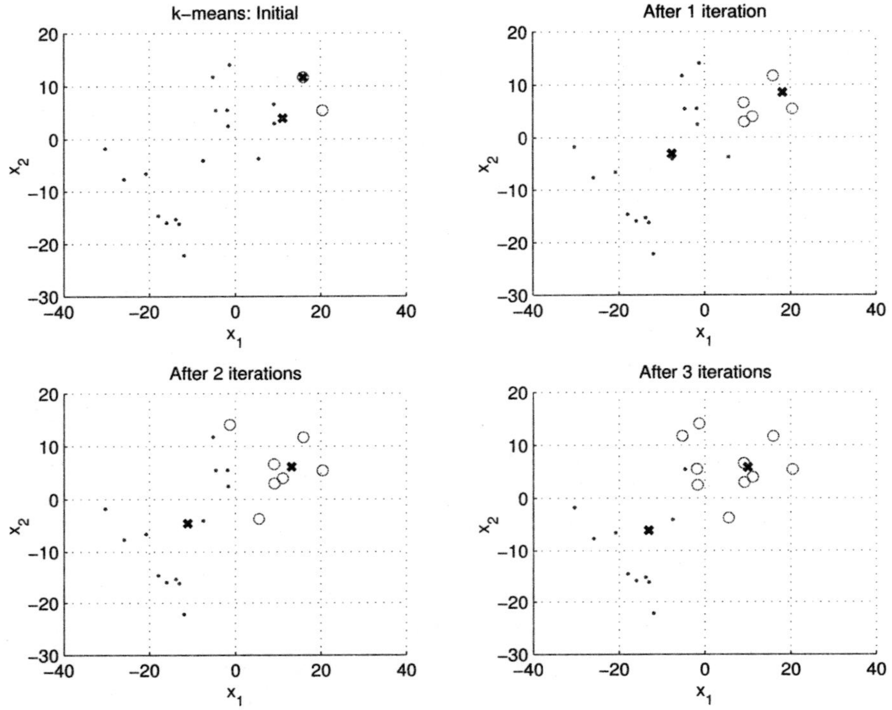

Figure 7.2 Evolution of k-means. Crosses indicate center positions. Data points are marked depending on the closest center.

- We can calculate the principal component, divide its range into k equal intervals, partitioning the data into k groups, and then take the means of these groups as the initial centers.

After convergence, all the centers should cover some subset of the data instances and be useful; therefore, it is best to initialize centers where we believe there is data.

LEADER CLUSTER ALGORITHM

There are also algorithms for adding new centers *incrementally* or deleting empty ones. In *leader cluster algorithm*, an instance that is far away from existing centers (defined by a threshold value) causes the creation of a new center at that point (we discuss such a neural network algorithm, ART, in chapter 12). Or, a center that covers a large number of instances ($\sum_t b_i^t / N > \theta$) can be split into two (by adding a small random vector to

Initialize $\boldsymbol{m}_i, i = 1, \ldots, k$, for example, to k random $\boldsymbol{x}^t$
Repeat
  For all $\boldsymbol{x}^t \in \mathcal{X}$
    $b_i^t \leftarrow \begin{cases} 1 & \text{if } \|\boldsymbol{x}^t - \boldsymbol{m}_i\| = \min_j \|\boldsymbol{x}^t - \boldsymbol{m}_j\| \\ 0 & \text{otherwise} \end{cases}$
  For all $\boldsymbol{m}_i, i = 1, \ldots, k$
    $\boldsymbol{m}_i \leftarrow \sum_t b_i^t \boldsymbol{x}^t / \sum_t b_i^t$
Until $\boldsymbol{m}_i$ converge

Figure 7.3 k-means algorithm.

one of the two copies to make them different). Similarly, a center that covers too few instances can be removed and restarted from some other part of the input space.

k-means algorithm is for clustering, that is, for finding groups in the data, where the groups are represented by their centers, which are the typical representatives of the groups. Vector quantization is one application of clustering, but clustering is also used for *preprocessing* before a later stage of classification or regression. Given $\boldsymbol{x}^t$, when we calculate b_i^t, we do a mapping from the original space to the k-dimensional space, that is, to one of the corners of the k-dimensional hypercube. A regression or discriminant function can then be learned in this new space; we discuss such methods in chapter 12.

7.4 Expectation-Maximization Algorithm

In k-means, we approached clustering as the problem of finding codebook vectors that minimize the total reconstruction error. In this section, our approach is probabilistic and we look for the component density parameters that maximize the likelihood of the sample. Using the mixture model of equation 7.1, the log likelihood given the sample $\mathcal{X} = \{\boldsymbol{x}^t\}_t$ is

$$\begin{aligned} \mathcal{L}(\Phi|\mathcal{X}) &= \log \prod_t p(\boldsymbol{x}^t|\Phi) \\ &= \sum_t \log \sum_{i=1}^{k} p(\boldsymbol{x}^t|\mathcal{G}_i)P(\mathcal{G}_i) \end{aligned} \tag{7.6}$$

where Φ includes the priors $P(\mathcal{G}_i)$ and also the sufficient statistics of the component densities $p(\mathbf{x}^t|\mathcal{G}_i)$. Unfortunately, we cannot solve for the parameters analytically and need to resort to iterative optimization.

EXPECTATION-MAXIMIZATION

The *expectation-maximization* algorithm (Dempster, Laird, and Rubin 1977; Redner and Walker 1984) is used in maximum likelihood estimation where the problem involves two sets of random variables of which one, X, is observable and the other, Z, is hidden. The goal of the algorithm is to find the parameter vector Φ that maximizes the likelihood of the observed values of X, $\mathcal{L}(\Phi|\mathcal{X})$. But in cases where this is not feasible, we associate the extra *hidden variables* Z and express the underlying model using both, to maximize the likelihood of the joint distribution of X and Z, the *complete* likelihood $\mathcal{L}_C(\Phi|\mathcal{X},\mathcal{Z})$.

Since the Z values are not observed, we cannot work directly with the complete data likelihood $\mathcal{L}_C$; instead, we work with its expectation, $\mathcal{Q}$, given $\mathcal{X}$ and the current parameter values Φ^l, where l indexes iteration. This is the *expectation* (E) step of the algorithm. Then in the *maximization* (M) step, we look for the new parameter values, Φ^{l+1}, that maximize this. Thus

$$\begin{aligned}\text{E-step} &: \mathcal{Q}(\Phi|\Phi^l) = E[\mathcal{L}_C(\Phi|\mathcal{X},\mathcal{Z})|\mathcal{X},\Phi^l]\\ \text{M-step} &: \Phi^{l+1} = \arg\max_{\Phi}\mathcal{Q}(\Phi|\Phi^l)\end{aligned}$$

Dempster, Laird, and Rubin (1977) proved that an increase in $\mathcal{Q}$ implies an increase in the incomplete likelihood

$$\mathcal{L}(\Phi^{l+1}|\mathcal{X}) \geq \mathcal{L}(\Phi^l|\mathcal{X})$$

In the case of mixtures, the hidden variables are the sources of observations, namely, which observation belongs to which component. If these were given, for example, as class labels in a supervised setting, we would know which parameters to adjust to fit that data point. The EM algorithm works as follows: in the E-step we estimate these labels given our current knowledge of components, and in the M-step we update our component knowledge given the labels estimated in the E-step. These two steps are the same as the two steps of k-means; calculation of b_i^t (E-step) and reestimation of $\boldsymbol{m}_i$ (M-step).

We define a vector of *indicator variables* $\mathbf{z}^t = \{z_1^t, \ldots, z_k^t\}$ where $z_i^t = 1$ if $\mathbf{x}^t$ belongs to cluster $\mathcal{G}_i$, and 0 otherwise. $\mathbf{z}$ is a multinomial distribution from k categories with prior probabilities π_i, shorthand for $P(\mathcal{G}_i)$.

Then

(7.7) $$P(\mathbf{z}^t) = \prod_{i=1}^{k} \pi_i^{z_i^t}$$

The likelihood of an observation $\mathbf{x}^t$ is equal to its probability specified by the component that generated it:

(7.8) $$p(\mathbf{x}^t|\mathbf{z}^t) = \prod_{i=1}^{k} p_i(\mathbf{x}^t)^{z_i^t}$$

$p_i(\mathbf{x}^t)$ is shorthand for $p(\mathbf{x}^t|\mathcal{G}_i)$. The joint density is

$$p(\mathbf{x}^t, \mathbf{z}^t) = P(\mathbf{z}^t)p(\mathbf{x}^t|\mathbf{z}^t)$$

and the complete data likelihood of the iid sample $\mathcal{X}$ is

$$\begin{aligned}
\mathcal{L}_C(\Phi|\mathcal{X}, \mathcal{Z}) &= \log \prod_t p(\mathbf{x}^t, \mathbf{z}^t|\Phi) \\
&= \sum_t \log p(\mathbf{x}^t, \mathbf{z}^t|\Phi) \\
&= \sum_t \log P(\mathbf{z}^t|\Phi) + \log p(\mathbf{x}^t|\mathbf{z}^t, \Phi) \\
&= \sum_t \sum_i z_i^t [\log \pi_i + \log p_i(\mathbf{x}^t|\Phi)]
\end{aligned}$$

E-step: We define

$$\begin{aligned}
\mathcal{Q}(\Phi|\Phi^l) &\equiv E\left[\log P(X, Z)|\mathcal{X}, \Phi^l\right] \\
&= E\left[\mathcal{L}_C(\Phi|\mathcal{X}, \mathcal{Z})|\mathcal{X}, \Phi^l)\right] \\
&= \sum_t \sum_i E[z_i^t|\mathcal{X}, \Phi^l][\log \pi_i + \log p_i(\mathbf{x}^t|\Phi^l)]
\end{aligned}$$

where

$$\begin{aligned}
E[z_i^t|\mathcal{X}, \Phi^l] &= E[z_i^t|\mathbf{x}^t, \Phi^l] \quad \mathbf{x}^t \text{ are iid} \\
&= P(z_i^t = 1|\mathbf{x}^t, \Phi^l) \quad z_i^t \text{ is a 0/1 random variable} \\
&= \frac{p(\mathbf{x}^t|z_i^t = 1, \Phi^l)P(z_i^t = 1|\Phi^l)}{p(\mathbf{x}^t|\Phi^l)} \quad \text{Bayes' rule} \\
&= \frac{p_i(\mathbf{x}^t|\Phi^l)\pi_i}{\sum_j p_j(\mathbf{x}^t|\Phi^l)\pi_j} \\
&= \frac{p(\mathbf{x}^t|\mathcal{G}_i, \Phi^l)P(\mathcal{G}_i)}{\sum_j p(\mathbf{x}^t|\mathcal{G}_j, \Phi^l)P(\mathcal{G}_j)} \\
&= P(\mathcal{G}_i|\mathbf{x}^t, \Phi^l) \equiv h_i^t
\end{aligned} \tag{7.9}$$

We see that the expected value of the hidden variable, $E[z_i^t]$, is the posterior probability that $\mathbf{x}^t$ is generated by component $\mathcal{G}_i$. Because this is a probability, it is between 0 and 1 and is a "soft" label, as opposed to the 0/1 "hard" label of k-means.

M-step: We maximize $\mathcal{Q}$ to get the next set of parameter values Φ^{l+1}:

$$\Phi^{l+1} = \arg\max_{\Phi} \mathcal{Q}(\Phi|\Phi^l)$$

which is

$$\begin{aligned} \mathcal{Q}(\Phi|\Phi^l) &= \sum_t \sum_i h_i^t [\log \pi_i + \log p_i(\mathbf{x}^t|\Phi^l)] \\ &= \sum_t \sum_i h_i^t \log \pi_i + \sum_t \sum_i h_i^t \log p_i(\mathbf{x}^t|\Phi^l) \end{aligned} \tag{7.10}$$

The second term is independent of π_i and using the constraint that $\sum_i \pi_i = 1$ as the Lagrangian, we solve for

$$\nabla_{\pi_i} \sum_t \sum_i h_i^t \log \pi_i - \lambda \left(\sum_i \pi_i - 1 \right) = 0$$

and get

$$\pi_i = \frac{\sum_t h_i^t}{N} \tag{7.11}$$

which is analogous to the calculation of priors in equation 7.2.

Similarly, the first term of equation 7.10 is independent of the components and can be dropped while estimating the parameters of the components. We solve for

$$\nabla_{\Phi} \sum_t \sum_i h_i^t \log p_i(\mathbf{x}^t|\Phi) = 0 \tag{7.12}$$

If we assume Gaussian components, $\hat{p}_i(\mathbf{x}^t|\Phi) \sim \mathcal{N}(\mathbf{m}_i, \mathbf{S}_i)$, the M-step is

$$\begin{aligned} \mathbf{m}_i^{l+1} &= \frac{\sum_t h_i^t \mathbf{x}^t}{\sum_t h_i^t} \\ \mathbf{S}_i^{l+1} &= \frac{\sum_t h_i^t (\mathbf{x}^t - \mathbf{m}_i^{l+1})(\mathbf{x}^t - \mathbf{m}_i^{l+1})^T}{\sum_t h_i^t} \end{aligned} \tag{7.13}$$

where, for Gaussian components in the E-step, we calculate

$$h_i^t = \frac{\pi_i |\mathbf{S}_i|^{-1/2} \exp[-(1/2)(\mathbf{x}^t - \mathbf{m}_i)^T \mathbf{S}_i^{-1} (\mathbf{x}^t - \mathbf{m}_i)]}{\sum_j \pi_j |\mathbf{S}_j|^{-1/2} \exp[-(1/2)(\mathbf{x}^t - \mathbf{m}_j)^T \mathbf{S}_j^{-1} (\mathbf{x}^t - \mathbf{m}_j)]} \tag{7.14}$$

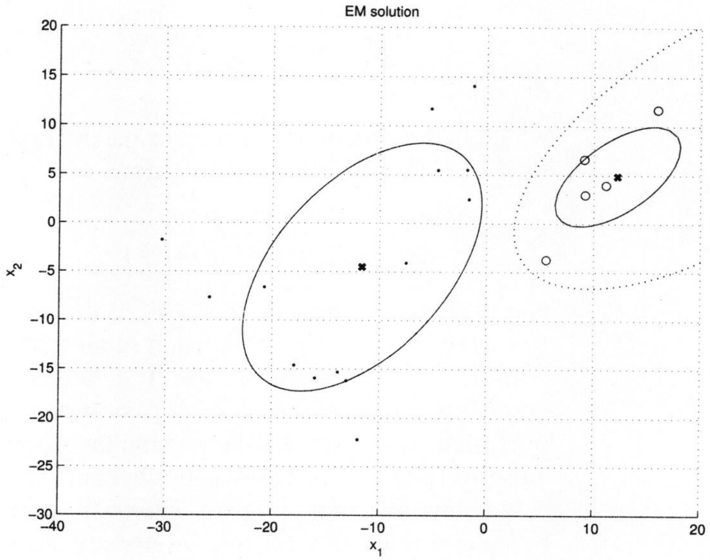

Figure 7.4 Data points and the fitted Gaussians by EM, initialized by one k-means iteration of figure 7.2. Unlike in k-means, as can be seen, EM allows estimating the covariance matrices. The data points labeled by greater h_i, the contours of the estimated Gaussian densities, and the separating curve of $h_i = 0.5$ (dashed line) are shown.

Again, the similarity between equations 7.13 and 7.2 is not accidental; the estimated soft labels h_i^t replace the actual (unknown) labels r_i^t.

EM is initalized by k-means. After a few iterations of k-means, we get the estimates for the centers $\boldsymbol{m}_i$, and using the instances covered by each center, we estimate the $\mathbf{S}_i$ and $\sum_t b_i^t / N$ give us the π_i. We run EM from that point on, as shown in figure 7.4.

Just as in parametric classification (section 5.5), with small samples and large dimensionality we can regularize by making simplifying assumptions. When $\hat{p}_i(\mathbf{x}^t|\Phi) \sim \mathcal{N}(\boldsymbol{m}_i, \mathbf{S})$, the case of a shared covariance matrix, equation 7.12 reduces to

$$\min_{\boldsymbol{m}_i, \mathbf{S}} \sum_t \sum_i h_i^t (\mathbf{x}^t - \boldsymbol{m}_i)^T \mathbf{S}^{-1} (\mathbf{x}^t - \boldsymbol{m}_i) \tag{7.15}$$

When $\hat{p}_i(\mathbf{x}^t|\Phi) \sim \mathcal{N}(\boldsymbol{m}_i, s^2\mathbf{I})$, the case of a shared diagonal matrix, we have

$$\min_{\boldsymbol{m}_i, s} \sum_t \sum_i h_i^t \frac{\|\boldsymbol{x}^t - \boldsymbol{m}_i\|^2}{s^2} \tag{7.16}$$

which is the reconstruction error we defined in k-means clustering (equation 7.3). The difference is that now

$$h_i^t = \frac{\exp\left[-(1/2s^2)\|\boldsymbol{x}^t - \boldsymbol{m}_i\|^2\right]}{\sum_j \exp\left[-(1/2s^2)\|\boldsymbol{x}^t - \boldsymbol{m}_j\|^2\right]} \tag{7.17}$$

is a probability between 0 and 1. b_i^t of k-means clustering makes a hard 0/1 decision, whereas h_i^t is a *soft label* that assigns the input to a cluster with a certain probability. When h_i^t are used instead of b_i^t, an instance contributes to the update of parameters of all components, to each proportional to that probability. This is especially useful if the instance is close to the midpoint between two centers.

We thus see that k-means clustering is a special case of EM applied to Gaussian mixtures where inputs are assumed independent with equal and shared variances, all components have equal priors, and labels are hardened. k-means thus pave the input density with circles, whereas EM in the general case uses ellipses of arbitrary shapes, orientations, and coverage proportions.

7.5 Mixtures of Latent Variable Models

When full covariance matrices are used with Gaussian mixtures, even if there is no singularity, one risks overfitting if the input dimensionality is high and the sample is small. To decrease the number of parameters, assuming a common covariance matrix may not be right since clusters may really have different shapes. Assuming diagonal matrices is even more risky because it removes all correlations.

The alternative is to do dimensionality reduction in the clusters. This decreases the number of parameters while still capturing the correlations. The number of free parameters is controlled through the dimensionality of the reduced space.

When we do factor analysis (section 6.5) in the clusters, we look for *latent* or *hidden variables* or *factors* that generate the data in the clusters (Bishop 1999):

$$p(\boldsymbol{x}^t|\mathcal{G}_i) \sim \mathcal{N}(\boldsymbol{m}_i, \mathbf{V}_i\mathbf{V}_i^T + \boldsymbol{\Psi}_i) \tag{7.18}$$

where $\mathbf{V}_i$ and $\mathbf{\Psi}_i$ are the factor loadings and specific variances of cluster $\mathcal{G}_i$. Rubin and Thayer (1982) give EM equations for factor analysis. It is possible to extend this in mixture models to find *mixtures of factor analyzers* (Ghahramani and Hinton 1997). In the E-step, in equation 7.9, we use equation 7.18, and in the M-step, we solve equation 7.12 for $\mathbf{V}_i$ and $\mathbf{\Psi}_i$ instead of $\mathbf{S}_i$. Similarly, one can also do PCA in groups, which is called *mixtures of probabilistic principal component analyzers* (Tipping and Bishop 1999).

MIXTURES OF FACTOR ANALYZERS

MIXTURES OF PROBABILISTIC PRINCIPAL COMPONENT ANALYZERS

We can of course use EM to learn $\mathbf{S}_i$ and then do FA or PCA separately in each cluster, but doing EM is better because it couples these two steps of clustering and dimensionality reduction and does a soft partitioning. An instance contributes to the calculation of the latent variables of all groups, weighted by h_i^t.

7.6 Supervised Learning after Clustering

Clustering, just as the dimensionality reduction methods discussed in chapter 6, can be used for two purposes. First, it can be used for data exploration, to understand the structure of data. Second, it can be used to map data to a new space where supervised learning is easier.

Dimensionality reduction methods are used to find correlations between variables and thus group variables; clustering methods, on the other hand, are used to find similarities between instances and thus group instances. If such groups are found, these may be named (by application experts) and their attributes be defined. One can choose the group mean as the representative prototype of instances in the group, or the possible range of attributes can be written. This allows a simpler description of the data. For example, if the customers of a company seem to fall in one of k groups, called *segments*, customers being defined in terms of their demographic attributes and transactions with the company, then a better understanding of the customer base will be provided that will allow the company to provide different strategies for different types of customers; this is part of *customer relationship management* (CRM). Likewise, the company will also be able to develop strategies for those customers who do not fall in any large group, and who may require attention—for example, churning customers.

CUSTOMER SEGMENTATION

CUSTOMER RELATIONSHIP MANAGEMENT

Frequently, clustering is also used as a preprocessing stage. Just like the dimensionality reduction methods of chapter 6 allowed us to make a mapping to a new space, after clustering, we also map to a new k-dimensional space where the dimensions are h_i (or b_i at the risk of loss of information). In a supervised setting, we can then learn the discriminant or regression function in this new space. The difference from dimensionality reduction methods like PCA however is that k, the dimensionality of the new space, can be larger than d, the original dimensionality.

When we use a method like PCA, where the new dimensions are combinations of the original dimensions, to represent any instance in the new space, all dimensions contribute; that is, all z_j are nonzero. In the case of a method like clustering where the new dimensions are defined locally, there are many more new dimensions, b_j, but only one (or if we use h_j, few) of them have a nonzero value. In the former case, where there are few dimensions but all contribute, we have a *distributed representation*; in the latter case, where there are many dimensions but few contribute, we have a *local representation*.

DISTRIBUTED VS. LOCAL REPRESENTATION

One advantage of preceding a supervised learner with unsupervised clustering or dimensionality reduction is that the latter does not need labeled data. Labeling the data is costly. We can use a large amount of unlabeled data for learning the cluster parameters and then use a smaller labeled data to learn the second stage of classification or regression. Unsupervised learning is called "learning what normally happens" (Barrow 1989). When followed by a supervised learner, we first learn what normally happens and then learn what that means. We discuss such methods in chapter 12.

MIXTURE OF MIXTURES

In the case of classification, when each class is a mixture model composed of a number of components, the whole density is a *mixture of mixtures*:

$$
\begin{aligned}
p(\mathbf{x}|C_i) &= \sum_{j=1}^{k_i} p(\mathbf{x}|\mathcal{G}_{ij})P(\mathcal{G}_{ij}) \\
p(\mathbf{x}) &= \sum_{i=1}^{K} p(\mathbf{x}|C_i)P(C_i)
\end{aligned}
$$

where k_i is the number of components making up $p(\mathbf{x}|C_i)$ and $\mathcal{G}_{ij}$ is the component j of class i. Note that different classes may need different number of components. Learning the parameters of components is done separately for each class (probably after some regularization) as we discussed previously. This is better than fitting many components to data from all classes and then labeling them later with classes.

7.7 Spectral Clustering

Instead of clustering in the original space, a possibility is to first map the data to a new space with reduced dimensionality such that similarities are made more apparent and then cluster in there. Any feature selection or extraction method can be used for this purpose, and one such method is the Laplacian eigenmaps of section 6.12, where the aim is to place the data instances in such a way that given pairwise similarities are preserved.

After such a mapping, points that are similar are placed nearby, and this is expected to enhance the performance of clustering—for example, by using k-means. This is the idea behind *spectral clustering* (von Luxburg 2007). There are hence two steps:

SPECTRAL CLUSTERING

1. In the original space, we define a local neighborhood (by either fixing the number of neighbors or a distance threshold), and then for instances that are in the same neighborhood, we define a similarity measure—for example, using the Gaussian kernel—that is inversely proportional to the distance between them. Remember that instances not in the same local neighborhood are assigned a similarity of 0 and hence can be placed anywhere with respect to each other. Given this Laplacian, instances are positioned in the new space using feature embedding.

2. We run k-means clustering with the new data coordinates in this new space.

We remember from section 6.12 that when $\mathbf{B}$ is the matrix of pairwise similarities and $\mathbf{D}$ is the diagonal degree matrix with $d_i = \sum_j B_{ij}$ on the diagonals, the graph Laplacian is defined as

$$\mathbf{L} = \mathbf{D} - \mathbf{B}$$

This is the unnormalized Laplacian. There are two ways to normalize. One is closely related to the random walk (Shi and Malik 2000) and the other constructs a symmetric matrix (Ng, Jordan, and Weiss 2002). They may lead to better performance in clustering:

$$\begin{aligned}\mathbf{L}_{rw} &= \mathbf{I} - \mathbf{D}^{-1}\mathbf{B}\\ \mathbf{L}_{sym} &= \mathbf{I} - \mathbf{D}^{-1/2}\mathbf{B}\mathbf{D}^{-1/2}\end{aligned}$$

It is always a good idea to do dimensionality reduction before clustering using Euclidean distance if there are redundant or correlated features. Using Laplacian eigenmaps makes more sense than multidimensional scaling proper or principal components analysis because those two check for the preservation of pairwise similarities between *all* pairs of instances whereas here with Laplacian eigenmaps, we care about preserving the similarity between neighboring instances only and in a manner that is inversely proportional to the distance between them. This has the effect that instances that are nearby in the original space, probably within the same cluster, will be placed very close in the new space, thus making the work of k-means easier, whereas those that are some distance away, probably belonging to different clusters, will be placed far apart. The graph should always be connected; that is, the local neighborhood should be large enough to connect clusters. Remember that the number of eigenvectors with eigenvalue 0 is the number of components and that it should be 1.

Note that though similarities are local, they propagate. Consider three instances, a, b, and c. Let us say a and b lie in the same neighborhood and so do b and c, but not a and c. Still, because a and b will be placed nearby and b and c will be placed nearby, a will lie close to c too, and they will probably be assigned to the same cluster. Consider now a and d that are not in the neighborhood with too many intermediate nodes between them; these two will not be placed nearby and it is very unlikely that they will be assigned to the same cluster.

Depending on which graph Laplacian is used and depending on the neighborhood size or the spread of the Gaussian, different results can be obtained, so one should always try for different parameters (von Luxburg 2009).

7.8 Hierarchical Clustering

We discussed clustering from a probabilistic point of view as fitting a mixture model to the data, or in terms of finding code words minimizing reconstruction error. There are also methods for clustering that use only similarities of instances, without any other requirement on the data; the aim is to find groups such that instances in a group are more similar to each other than instances in different groups. This is the approach taken by *hierarchical clustering*.

HIERARCHICAL CLUSTERING

This needs the use of a similarity, or equivalently a distance, measure defined between instances. Generally Euclidean distance is used, where we have to make sure that all attributes have the same scale. This is a special case of the *Minkowksi distance* with $p = 2$:

$$d_m(\boldsymbol{x}^r, \boldsymbol{x}^s) = \left[\sum_{j=1}^{d} (x_j^r - x_j^s)^p\right]^{1/p}$$

City-block distance is easier to calculate:

$$d_{cb}(\boldsymbol{x}^r, \boldsymbol{x}^s) = \sum_{j=1}^{d} |x_j^r - x_j^s|$$

AGGLOMERATIVE CLUSTERING

DIVISIVE CLUSTERING

An *agglomerative clustering* algorithm starts with N groups, each initially containing one training instance, merging similar groups to form larger groups, until there is a single one. A *divisive clustering* algorithm goes in the other direction, starting with a single group and dividing large groups into smaller groups, until each group contains a single instance.

SINGLE-LINK CLUSTERING

At each iteration of an agglomerative algorithm, we choose the two closest groups to merge. In *single-link clustering*, this distance is defined as the smallest distance between all possible pair of elements of the two groups:

(7.19) $$d(\mathcal{G}_i, \mathcal{G}_j) = \min_{\boldsymbol{x}^r \in \mathcal{G}_i, \boldsymbol{x}^s \in \mathcal{G}_j} d(\boldsymbol{x}^r, \boldsymbol{x}^s)$$

Consider a weighted, completely connected graph with nodes corresponding to instances and edges between nodes with weights equal to the distances between the instances. Then the single-link method corresponds to constructing the minimal spanning tree of this graph.

COMPLETE-LINK CLUSTERING

In *complete-link clustering*, the distance between two groups is taken as the largest distance between all possible pairs:

(7.20) $$d(\mathcal{G}_i, \mathcal{G}_j) = \max_{\boldsymbol{x}^r \in \mathcal{G}_i, \boldsymbol{x}^s \in \mathcal{G}_j} d(\boldsymbol{x}^r, \boldsymbol{x}^s)$$

These are the two most frequently used measures to choose the two closest groups to merge. Other possibilities are the average-link method that uses the average of distances between all pairs and the centroid distance that measures the distance between the centroids (means) of the two groups.

DENDROGRAM

Once an agglomerative method is run, the result is generally drawn as a hierarchical structure known as the *dendrogram*. This is a tree where

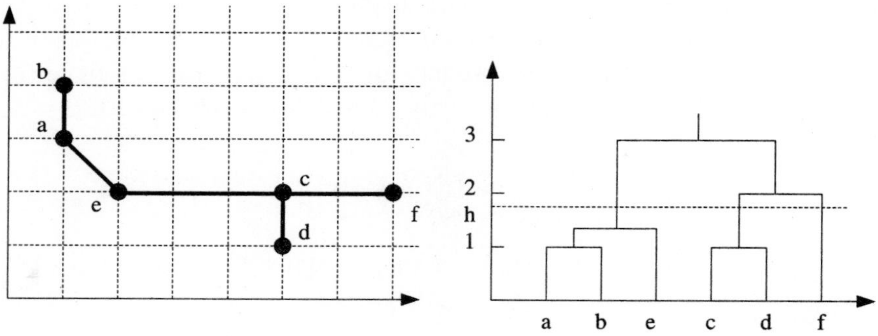

Figure 7.5 A two-dimensional dataset and the dendrogram showing the result of single-link clustering is shown. Note that leaves of the tree are ordered so that no branches cross. The tree is then intersected at a desired value of h to get the clusters.

leaves correspond to instances, which are grouped in the order in which they are merged. An example is given in figure 7.5. The tree can then be intersected at any level to get the wanted number of groups.

Single-link and complete-link methods calculate the distance between groups differently that affect the clusters and the dendrogram. In the single-link method, two instances are grouped together at level h if the distance between them is less than h, or if there is an intermediate sequence of instances between them such that the distance between consecutive instances is less than h. On the other hand, in the complete-link method, all instances in a group have a distance less than h between them. Single-link clusters may be elongated due to this "chaining" effect. (In figure 7.5, what if there were an instance halfway between e and c?) Complete-link clusters tend to be more compact.

7.9 Choosing the Number of Clusters

Like any learning method, clustering also has its knob to adjust complexity; it is k, the number of clusters. Given any k, clustering will always find k centers, whether they really are meaningful groups, or whether they are imposed by the method we use. There are various ways we can use to fine-tune k:

- In some applications such as color quantization, k is defined by the application.
- Plotting the data in two dimensions using PCA may be used in uncovering the structure of data and the number of clusters in the data.
- An incremental approach may also help: Setting a maximum allowed distance is equivalent to setting a maximum allowed reconstruction error per instance.
- In some applications, validation of the groups can be done manually by checking whether clusters actually code meaningful groups of the data. For example, in a data mining application, application experts may do this check. In color quantization, we may inspect the image visually to check its quality (despite the fact that our eyes and brain do not analyze an image pixel by pixel).

Depending on what type of clustering method we use, we can plot the reconstruction error or log likelihood as a function of k and look for the "elbow." After a large enough k, the algorithm will start dividing groups, in which case there will not be a large decrease in the reconstruction error or large increase in the log likelihood. Similarly, in hierarchical clustering, by looking at the differences between levels in the tree, we can decide on a good split.

7.10 Notes

Mixture models are frequently used in statistics. Dedicated textbooks are those by Titterington, Smith, and Makov (1985) and McLachlan and Basford (1988). McLachlan and Krishnan (1997) discuss recent developments in the EM algorithm, how its convergence can be accelerated, and various variants. In signal processing, k-means is called the *Linde-Buzo-Gray* (LBG) algorithm (Gersho and Gray 1992). It is used frequently in both statistics and signal processing in a large variety of applications and has many variants, one of which is *fuzzy k-means.* The *fuzzy membership* of an input to a component is also a number between 0 and 1 (Bezdek and Pal 1995). Alpaydın (1998) compares k-means, fuzzy k-means, and EM on Gaussian mixtures. A comparison of EM and other learning algorithms for the learning of Gaussian mixture models is given by Xu and Jordan (1996). On small data samples, an alternative to simplifying assumptions

FUZZY k-MEANS

is to use a Bayesian approach (Ormoneit and Tresp 1996). Moerland (1999) compares mixtures of Gaussians and mixtures of latent variable models on a set of classification problems, showing the advantage of latent variable models empirically. A book on clustering methods is by Jain and Dubes (1988) and survey articles are by Jain, Murty, and Flynn (1999) and Xu and Wunsch (2005).

One of the advantages of spectral clustering and hierarchical clustering is that we do not need a vectorial representation of the instances, as long as we can define a similarity/distance measure between pairs of instances. The problem of representing an arbitrary data structure—documents, graphs, web pages, and so on—as a vector such that Euclidean distance is meaningful is always a tedious task and leads to artificial representations, such as the bag of words. Being able to use (dis)similarity measures directly defined on the original structure is always a good idea, and we will have the same advantage with kernel functions when we talk about kernel machines in chapter 13.

7.11 Exercises

1. In image compression, k-means can be used as follows: The image is divided into nonoverlapping $c \times c$ windows and these c^2-dimensional vectors make up the sample. For a given k, which is generally a power of two, we do k-means clustering. The reference vectors and the indices for each window is sent over the communication line. At the receiving end, the image is then reconstructed by reading from the table of reference vectors using the indices. Write the computer program that does this for different values of k and c. For each case, calculate the reconstruction error and the compression rate.

2. We can do k-means clustering, partition the instances, and then calculate $\mathbf{S}_i$ separately in each group. Why is this not a good idea?

   SOLUTION: There are basically two reasons: First, k-means does hard partitioning but it is always better to do a soft partitioning (using $h_i^t \in (0, 1)$ instead of $b_i^t \in \{0, 1\}$) so that instances (in between two clusters) can contribute to the parameters (the covariance matrix in this case) of more than one cluster allowing a smooth transition between clusters.

   Second, k-means proper uses the Euclidean distance and we remember that Euclidean distance implies features that have the same scale and are independent. Using $\mathbf{S}_i$ implies the use of Mahalanobis distance and hence taking care of differences in scale and dependencies.

3. Derive the M-step equations for $\mathbf{S}$ in the case of shared arbitrary covariance

matrix **S** (equation 7.15) and s^2 in the case of shared diagonal covariance matrix (equation 7.16).

4. Define a multivariate Bernoulli mixture where inputs are binary and derive the EM equations.

   SOLUTION: When the components are multivariate Bernouilli, we have binary vectors that are d-dimensional. Assuming that the dimensions are independent, we have (see section 5.7)

$$p_i(\mathbf{x}^t|\Phi) = \prod_{j=1}^{d} p_{ij}^{x_j^t}(1-p_{ij})^{1-x_j^t}$$

   where $\Phi^l = \{p_{i1}^l, p_{i2}^l, \ldots, p_{id}^l\}_{i=1}^k$. The E-step does not change (equation 7.9). In the M-step, for the component parameters $p_{ij}, i = 1, \ldots, k, j = 1, \ldots, d$, we maximize

$$\begin{aligned} \mathcal{Q}' &= \sum_t \sum_i h_i^t \log p_i(\mathbf{x}^t|\phi^l) \\ &= \sum_t \sum_i h_i^t \sum_j x_j^t \log p_{ij}^l + (1-x_j^t)\log(1-p_{ij}^l) \end{aligned}$$

   Taking the derivative with respect to p_{ij} and setting it equal to 0, we get

$$p_{ij}^{l+1} = \frac{\sum_t h_i^t x_j^t}{\sum_t h_j^t}$$

   Note that this is the same as in equation 5.31, except that estimated "soft" labels h_i^t replace the supervised labels r_i^t.

5. In the mixture of mixtures approach for classification, how can we fine-tune k_i, the number of components for class C_i?

6. EDIT DISTANCE — *Edit distance* between two strings—for example, gene sequences—is the number of character operations (insertions, deletions, substitutions) it takes to convert one string into another. List the advantages of doing spectral clustering using the edit distance as opposed to vanilla k-means using Euclidean distance on strings.

7. How can we do hierarchical clustering with binary input vectors—for example, for text clustering using the bag of words representation?

8. What are the similarities and differences between average-link clustering and k-means?

   SOLUTION: They both measure similarity by looking at the average of instances that fall in a cluster. Note, however, that in a hierarchical scheme, there are clusters at different resolutions.

9. In hierarchical clustering, how can we have locally adaptive distances? What are the advantages and disadvantages of this?

10. How can we make k-means robust to outliers?

    SOLUTION: An outlier is an instance that is very far from *all* centers. We would not want outliers to affect the solution. One possibility is to not take such instances into account when calculating the parameters—for example, means and covariances. Note that to detect an outlier, we can use the Mahalanobis distance or the likelihood, but we cannot use the posterior. We discuss a nonparametric method for detecting outliers in section 8.7.

11. Having generated a dendrogram, can we "prune" it?

7.12 References

Alpaydın, E. 1998. "Soft Vector Quantization and the EM Algorithm." *Neural Networks* 11:467–477.

Barrow, H. B. 1989. "Unsupervised Learning." *Neural Computation* 1:295–311.

Bezdek, J. C., and N. R. Pal. 1995. "Two Soft Relatives of Learning Vector Quantization." *Neural Networks* 8:729–743.

Bishop, C. M. 1999. "Latent Variable Models." In *Learning in Graphical Models*, ed. M. I. Jordan, 371–403. Cambridge, MA: MIT Press.

Dempster, A. P., N. M. Laird, and D. B. Rubin. 1977. "Maximum Likelihood from Incomplete Data via the EM Algorithm." *Journal of Royal Statistical Society* B 39:1–38.

Gersho, A., and R. M. Gray. 1992. *Vector Quantization and Signal Compression.* Boston: Kluwer.

Ghahramani, Z., and G. E. Hinton. 1997. *The EM Algorithm for Mixtures of Factor Analyzers.* Technical Report CRG TR-96-1, Department of Computer Science, University of Toronto (revised Feb. 1997).

Jain, A. K., and R. C. Dubes. 1988. *Algorithms for Clustering Data.* New York: Prentice Hall.

Jain, A. K., M. N. Murty, and P. J. Flynn. 1999. "Data Clustering: A Review." *ACM Computing Surveys* 31:264–323.

McLachlan, G. J., and K. E. Basford. 1988. *Mixture Models: Inference and Applications to Clustering.* New York: Marcel Dekker.

McLachlan, G. J., and T. Krishnan. 1997. *The EM Algorithm and Extensions.* New York: Wiley.

Moerland, P. 1999. "A Comparison of Mixture Models for Density Estimation." In *International Conference on Artificial Neural Networks*, ed. D. Willshaw and A. Murray, 25–30. London, UK: IEE Press.

Ng, A., M. I. Jordan, and Y. Weiss. 2002. "On Spectral Clustering: Analysis and an Algorithm." In *Advances in Neural Information Processing Systems 14*, ed. T. Dietterich, S. Becker, and Z. Ghahramani, 849–856. Cambridge, MA: MIT Press.

Ormoneit, D., and V. Tresp. 1996. "Improved Gaussian Mixture Density Estimates using Bayesian Penalty Terms and Network Averaging." In *Advances in Neural Information Processing Systems 8*, ed. D. S. Touretzky, M. C. Mozer, and M. E. Hasselmo, 542–548. Cambridge, MA: MIT Press.

Redner, R. A., and H. F. Walker. 1984. "Mixture Densities, Maximum Likelihood and the EM Algorithm." *SIAM Review* 26:195–239.

Rubin, D. B., and D. T. Thayer. 1982. "EM Algorithms for ML Factor Analysis." *Psychometrika* 47:69–76.

Shi, J., and J. Malik. 2000. "Normalized Cuts and Image Segmentation." *IEEE Transactions on Pattern Analysis and Machine Intelligence* 22:888–905.

Tipping, M. E., and C. M. Bishop. 1999. "Mixtures of Probabilistic Principal Component Analyzers." *Neural Computation* 11:443–482.

Titterington, D. M., A. F. M. Smith, and E. E. Makov. 1985. *Statistical Analysis of Finite Mixture Distributions.* New York: Wiley.

von Luxburg, U. 2007. "A Tutorial on Spectral Clustering." *Statistical Computing* 17:395–416.

Xu, L., and M. I. Jordan. 1996. "On Convergence Properties of the EM Algorithm for Gaussian Mixtures." *Neural Computation* 8:129–151.

Xu, R., and D. Wunsch II. 2005. "Survey of Clustering Algorithms." *IEEE Transactions on Neural Networks* 16:645–678.

8 Nonparametric Methods

In the previous chapters, we discussed the parametric and semiparametric approaches where we assumed that the data is drawn from one or a mixture of probability distributions of known form. Now, we discuss the nonparametric approach that is used when no such assumption can be made about the input density and the data speaks for itself. We consider the nonparametric approaches for density estimation, classification, outlier detection, and regression and see how the time and space complexity can be checked.

8.1 Introduction

IN PARAMETRIC methods, whether for density estimation, classification, or regression, we assume a model valid over the whole input space. In regression, for example, when we assume a linear model, we assume that for any input, the output is the same linear function of the input. In classification when we assume a normal density, we assume that all examples of the class are drawn from this same density. The advantage of a parametric method is that it reduces the problem of estimating a probability density function, discriminant, or regression function to estimating the values of a small number of parameters. Its disadvantage is that this assumption does not always hold and we may incur a large error if it does not. If we cannot make such assumptions and cannot come up with a parametric model, one possibility is to use a semiparametric mixture model as we saw in chapter 7 where the density is written as a disjunction of a small number of parametric models.

NONPARAMETRIC ESTIMATION

In *nonparametric estimation*, all we assume is that *similar inputs have similar outputs.* This is a reasonable assumption: The world is smooth, and functions, whether they are densities, discriminants, or regression functions, change slowly. Similar instances mean similar things. We all love our neighbors because they are so much like us.

Therefore, our algorithm is composed of finding the similar past instances from the training set using a suitable distance measure and interpolating from them to find the right output. Different nonparametric methods differ in the way they define similarity or interpolate from the similar training instances. In a parametric model, all of the training instances affect the final global estimate, whereas in the nonparametric case, there is no single global model; local models are estimated as they are needed, affected only by the nearby training instances.

Nonparametric methods do not assume any a priori parametric form for the underlying densities; in a looser interpretation, a nonparametric model is not fixed but its complexity depends on the size of the training set, or rather, the complexity of the problem inherent in the data.

INSTANCE-BASED MEMORY-BASED LEARNING

In machine learning literature, nonparametric methods are also called *instance-based* or *memory-based learning* algorithms, since what they do is store the training instances in a lookup table and interpolate from these. This implies that all of the training instances should be stored and storing all requires memory of $\mathcal{O}(N)$. Furthermore, given an input, similar ones should be found, and finding them requires computation of $\mathcal{O}(N)$. Such methods are also called *lazy* learning algorithms, because unlike the *eager* parametric models, they do not compute a model when they are given the training set but postpone the computation of the model until they are given a test instance. In the case of a parametric approach, the model is quite simple and has a small number of parameters, of order $\mathcal{O}(d)$, or $\mathcal{O}(d^2)$, and once these parameters are calculated from the training set, we keep the model and no longer need the training set to calculate the output. N is generally much larger than d (or d^2), and this increased need for memory and computation is the disadvantage of the nonparametric methods.

We start by estimating a density function, and discuss its use in classification. We then generalize the approach to regression.

8.2 Nonparametric Density Estimation

As usual in density estimation, we assume that the sample $\mathcal{X} = \{x^t\}_{t=1}^N$ is drawn independently from some unknown probability density $p(\cdot)$. $\hat{p}(\cdot)$

is our estimator of $p(\cdot)$. We start with the univariate case where x^t are scalars and later generalize to the multidimensional case.

The nonparametric estimator for the cumulative distribution function, $F(x)$, at point x is the proportion of sample points that are less than or equal to x

$$\hat{F}(x) = \frac{\#\{x^t \le x\}}{N} \tag{8.1}$$

where $\#\{x^t \le x\}$ denotes the number of training instances whose x^t is less than or equal to x. Similarly, the nonparametric estimate for the density function, which is the derivative of the cumulative distribution, can be calculated as

$$\hat{p}(x) = \frac{1}{h}\left[\frac{\#\{x^t \le x+h\} - \#\{x^t \le x\}}{N}\right] \tag{8.2}$$

h is the length of the interval and instances x^t that fall in this interval are assumed to be "close enough." The techniques given in this chapter are variants where different heuristics are used to determine the instances that are close and their effects on the estimate.

8.2.1 Histogram Estimator

HISTOGRAM

The oldest and most popular method is the *histogram* where the input space is divided into equal-sized intervals named *bins*. Given an origin x_o and a bin width h, the bins are the intervals $[x_o + mh, x_o + (m+1)h)$ for positive and negative integers m and the estimate is given as

$$\hat{p}(x) = \frac{\#\{x^t \text{ in the same bin as } x\}}{Nh} \tag{8.3}$$

In constructing the histogram, we have to choose both an origin and a bin width. The choice of origin affects the estimate near boundaries of bins, but it is mainly the bin width that has an effect on the estimate: With small bins, the estimate is spiky, and with larger bins, the estimate is smoother (see figure 8.1). The estimate is 0 if no instance falls in a bin and there are discontinuities at bin boundaries. Still, one advantage of the histogram is that once the bin estimates are calculated and stored, we do not need to retain the training set.

NAIVE ESTIMATOR

The *naive estimator* (Silverman 1986) frees us from setting an origin. It is defined as

$$\hat{p}(x) = \frac{\#\{x - h/2 < x^t \le x + h/2\}}{Nh} \tag{8.4}$$

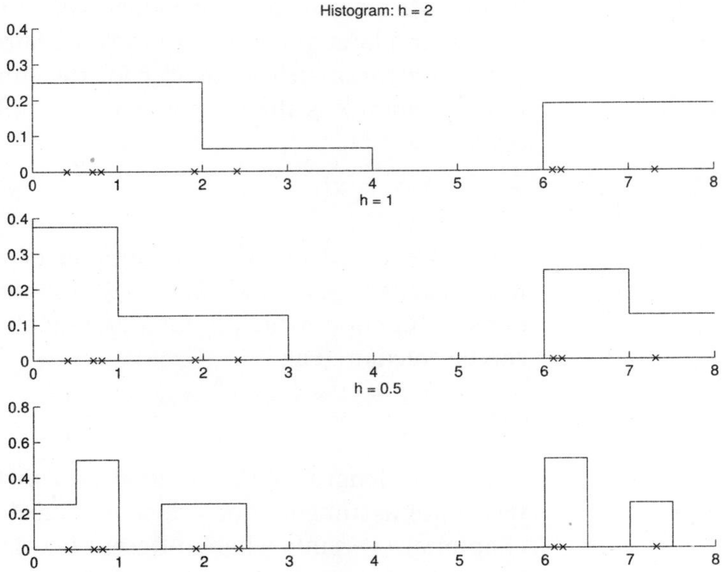

Figure 8.1 Histograms for various bin lengths. '×' denote data points.

and is equal to the histogram estimate where x is always at the center of a bin of size h (see figure 8.2). The estimator can also be written as

$$\hat{p}(x) = \frac{1}{Nh}\sum_{t=1}^{N} w\left(\frac{x - x^t}{h}\right) \tag{8.5}$$

with the *weight function* defined as

$$w(u) = \begin{cases} 1 & \text{if } |u| < 1/2 \\ 0 & \text{otherwise} \end{cases}$$

This is as if each x^t has a symmetric region of influence of size h around it and contributes 1 for an x falling in its region. Then the nonparametric estimate is just the sum of influences of x^t whose regions include x. Because this region of influence is "hard" (0 or 1), the estimate is not a continuous function and has jumps at $x^t \pm h/2$.

8.2.2 Kernel Estimator

KERNEL FUNCTION

To get a smooth estimate, we use a smooth weight function called a *kernel*

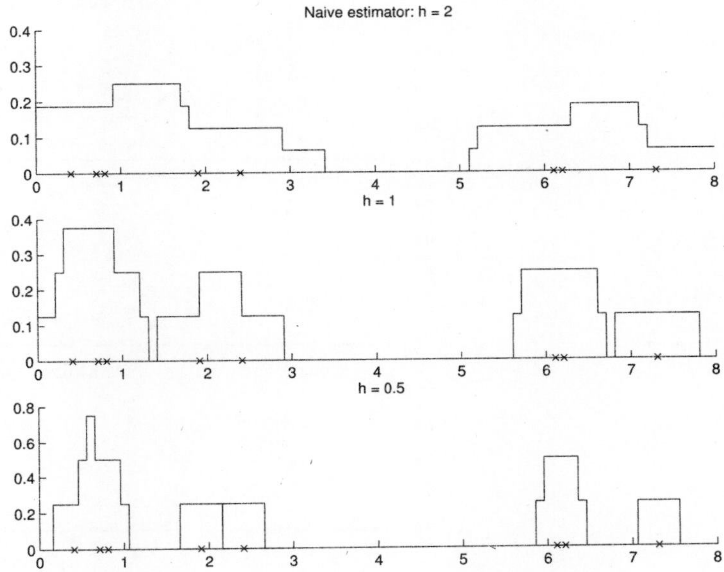

Figure 8.2 Naive estimate for various bin lengths.

function. The most popular is the Gaussian kernel:

$$K(u) = \frac{1}{\sqrt{2\pi}} \exp\left[-\frac{u^2}{2}\right] \tag{8.6}$$

KERNEL ESTIMATOR
PARZEN WINDOWS

The *kernel estimator*, also called *Parzen windows*, is defined as

$$\hat{p}(x) = \frac{1}{Nh}\sum_{t=1}^{N} K\left(\frac{x - x^t}{h}\right) \tag{8.7}$$

The kernel function $K(\cdot)$ determines the shape of the influences and the window width h determines the width. Just like the naive estimate is the sum of "boxes," the kernel estimate is the sum of "bumps." All the x^t have an effect on the estimate at x, and this effect decreases smoothly as $|x - x^t|$ increases.

To simplify calculation, $K(\cdot)$ can be taken to be 0 if $|x - x^t| > 3h$. There exist other kernels easier to compute that can be used, as long as $K(u)$ is maximum for $u = 0$ and decreasing symmetrically as $|u|$ increases.

When h is small, each training instance has a large effect in a small region and no effect on distant points. When h is larger, there is more

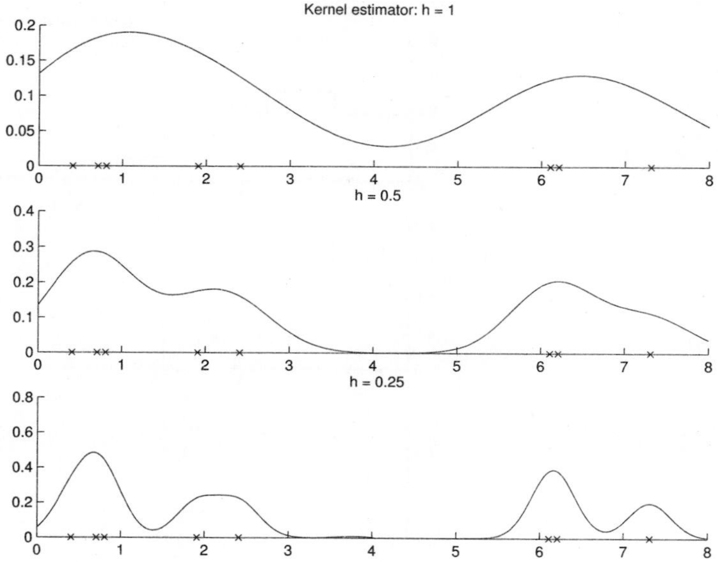

Figure 8.3 Kernel estimate for various bin lengths.

overlap of the kernels and we get a smoother estimate (see figure 8.3). If $K(\cdot)$ is everywhere nonnegative and integrates to 1, namely, if it is a legitimate density function, so will $\hat{p}(\cdot)$ be. Furthermore, $\hat{p}(\cdot)$ will inherit all the continuity and differentiability properties of the kernel $K(\cdot)$, so that, for example, if $K(\cdot)$ is Gaussian, then $\hat{p}(\cdot)$ will be smooth having all the derivatives.

One problem is that the window width is fixed across the entire input space. Various adaptive methods have been proposed to tailor h as a function of the density around x.

8.2.3 *k*-Nearest Neighbor Estimator

The nearest neighbor class of estimators adapts the amount of smoothing to the *local* density of data. The degree of smoothing is controlled by k, the number of neighbors taken into account, which is much smaller than N, the sample size. Let us define a distance between a and b, for example, $|a - b|$, and for each x, we define

$$d_1(x) \leq d_2(x) \leq \cdots \leq d_N(x)$$

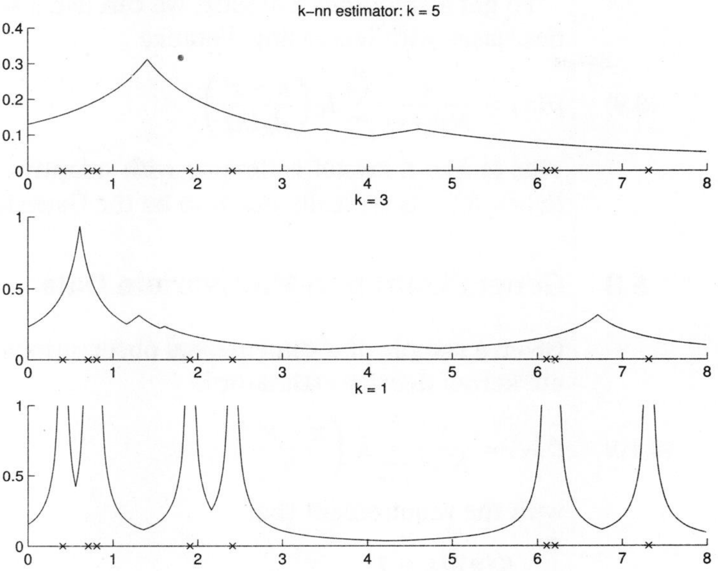

Figure 8.4 k-nearest neighbor estimate for various k values.

to be the distances arranged in ascending order, from x to the points in the sample: $d_1(x)$ is the distance to the nearest sample, $d_2(x)$ is the distance to the next nearest, and so on. If x^t are the data points, then we define $d_1(x) = \min_t |x - x^t|$, and if i is the index of the closest sample, namely, $i = \arg\min_t |x - x^t|$, then $d_2(x) = \min_{j \neq i} |x - x^j|$, and so forth.

k-NEAREST NEIGHBOR ESTIMATE

The *k-nearest neighbor* (k-nn) density estimate is

$$\hat{p}(x) = \frac{k}{2Nd_k(x)} \tag{8.8}$$

This is like a naive estimator with $h = 2d_k(x)$, the difference being that instead of fixing h and checking how many samples fall in the bin, we fix k, the number of observations to fall in the bin, and compute the bin size. Where density is high, bins are small, and where density is low, bins are larger (see figure 8.4).

The k-nn estimator is not continuous; its derivative has a discontinuity at all $\frac{1}{2}(x^{(j)} + x^{(j+k)})$ where $x^{(j)}$ are the order statistics of the sample. The k-nn is not a probability density function since it integrates to ∞, not 1.

To get a smoother estimate, we can use a kernel function whose effect decreases with increasing distance

$$\hat{p}(x) = \frac{1}{Nd_k(x)} \sum_{t=1}^{N} K\left(\frac{x - x^t}{d_k(x)}\right) \tag{8.9}$$

This is like a kernel estimator with adaptive smoothing parameter $h = d_k(x)$. $K(\cdot)$ is typically taken to be the Gaussian kernel.

8.3 Generalization to Multivariate Data

Given a sample of d-dimensional observations $\mathcal{X} = \{\boldsymbol{x}^t\}_{t=1}^N$, the multivariate kernel density estimator is

$$\hat{p}(\boldsymbol{x}) = \frac{1}{Nh^d} \sum_{t=1}^{N} K\left(\frac{\boldsymbol{x} - \boldsymbol{x}^t}{h}\right) \tag{8.10}$$

with the requirement that

$$\int_{\Re^d} K(\boldsymbol{x})d\boldsymbol{x} = 1$$

The obvious candidate is the multivariate Gaussian kernel:

$$K(\boldsymbol{u}) = \left(\frac{1}{\sqrt{2\pi}}\right)^d \exp\left[-\frac{\|\boldsymbol{u}\|^2}{2}\right] \tag{8.11}$$

CURSE OF DIMENSIONALITY

However, care should be applied to using nonparametric estimates in high-dimensional spaces because of the *curse of dimensionality*: Let us say $\boldsymbol{x}$ is eight-dimensional, and we use a histogram with ten bins per dimension, then there are 10^8 bins, and unless we have lots of data, most of these bins will be empty and the estimates in there will be 0. In high dimensions, the concept of "close" also becomes blurry so we should be careful in choosing h.

For example, the use of the Euclidean norm in equation 8.11 implies that the kernel is scaled equally on all dimensions. If the inputs are on different scales, they should be normalized to have the same variance. Still, this does not take correlations into account, and better results are achieved when the kernel has the same form as the underlying distribution

$$K(\boldsymbol{u}) = \frac{1}{(2\pi)^{d/2}|\mathbf{S}|^{1/2}} \exp\left[-\frac{1}{2}\boldsymbol{u}^T\mathbf{S}^{-1}\boldsymbol{u}\right] \tag{8.12}$$

where $\mathbf{S}$ is the sample covariance matrix. This corresponds to using Mahalanobis distance instead of the Euclidean distance.

8.4 Nonparametric Classification

When used for classification, we use the nonparametric approach to estimate the class-conditional densities, $p(\mathbf{x}|C_i)$. The kernel estimator of the class-conditional density is given as

$$\hat{p}(\mathbf{x}|C_i) = \frac{1}{N_i h^d} \sum_{t=1}^{N} K\left(\frac{\mathbf{x}-\mathbf{x}^t}{h}\right) r_i^t \tag{8.13}$$

where r_i^t is 1 if $\mathbf{x}^t \in C_i$ and 0 otherwise. N_i is the number of labeled instances belonging to C_i: $N_i = \sum_t r_i^t$. The MLE of the prior density is $\hat{P}(C_i) = N_i/N$. Then, the discriminant can be written as

$$\begin{aligned} g_i(\mathbf{x}) &= \hat{p}(\mathbf{x}|C_i)\hat{P}(C_i) \\ &= \frac{1}{Nh^d} \sum_{t=1}^{N} K\left(\frac{\mathbf{x}-\mathbf{x}^t}{h}\right) r_i^t \end{aligned} \tag{8.14}$$

and $\mathbf{x}$ is assigned to the class for which the discriminant takes its maximum. The common factor $1/(Nh^d)$ can be ignored. So each training instance votes for its class and has no effect on other classes; the weight of vote is given by the kernel function $K(\cdot)$, typically giving more weight to closer instances.

For the special case of k-nn estimator, we have

$$\hat{p}(\mathbf{x}|C_i) = \frac{k_i}{N_i V^k(\mathbf{x})} \tag{8.15}$$

where k_i is the number of neighbors out of the k nearest that belong to C_i and $V^k(\mathbf{x})$ is the volume of the d-dimensional hypersphere centered at $\mathbf{x}$, with radius $r = \|\mathbf{x} - \mathbf{x}_{(k)}\|$ where $\mathbf{x}_{(k)}$ is the k-th nearest observation to $\mathbf{x}$ (among all neighbors from all classes of $\mathbf{x}$): $V^k = r^d c_d$ with c_d as the volume of the unit sphere in d dimensions, for example, $c_1 = 2, c_2 = \pi, c_3 = 4\pi/3$, and so forth. Then

$$\hat{P}(C_i|\mathbf{x}) = \frac{\hat{p}(\mathbf{x}|C_i)\hat{P}(C_i)}{\hat{p}(\mathbf{x})} = \frac{k_i}{k} \tag{8.16}$$

k-NN CLASSIFIER

The *k-nn classifier* assigns the input to the class having most examples among the k neighbors of the input. All neighbors have equal vote, and the class having the maximum number of voters among the k neighbors is chosen. Ties are broken arbitrarily or a weighted vote is taken. k is generally taken to be an odd number to minimize ties: Confusion is

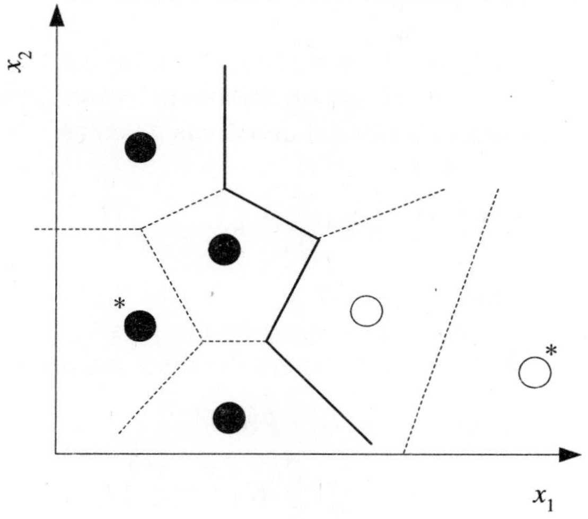

Figure 8.5 Dotted lines are the Voronoi tesselation and the straight line is the class discriminant. In condensed nearest neighbor, those instances that do not participate in defining the discriminant (marked by '*') can be removed without increasing the training error.

NEAREST NEIGHBOR CLASSIFIER

VORONOI TESSELATION

generally between two neighboring classes. A special case of k-nn is the *nearest neighbor classifier* where $k = 1$ and the input is assigned to the class of the nearest pattern. This divides the space in the form of a *Voronoi tesselation* (see figure 8.5).

8.5 Condensed Nearest Neighbor

Time and space complexity of nonparametric methods are proportional to the size of the training set, and *condensing* methods have been proposed to decrease the number of stored instances without degrading performance. The idea is to select the smallest subset $\mathcal{Z}$ of $\mathcal{X}$ such that when $\mathcal{Z}$ is used in place of $\mathcal{X}$, error does not increase (Dasarathy 1991).

CONDENSED NEAREST NEIGHBOR

The best-known and earliest method is *condensed nearest neighbor* where 1-nn is used as the nonparametric estimator for classification (Hart 1968). 1-nn approximates the discriminant in a piecewise linear manner, and only the instances that define the discriminant need be kept; an in-

```
Z ← ∅
Repeat
    For all x ∈ X (in random order)
        Find x' ∈ Z such that ||x − x'|| = min_{x^j ∈ Z} ||x − x^j||
        If class(x)≠class(x') add x to Z
Until Z does not change
```

Figure 8.6 Condensed nearest neighbor algorithm.

stance inside the class regions need not be stored as *its* nearest neighbor is of the same class and its absence does not cause any error (on the training set) (figure 8.5). Such a subset is called a consistent subset, and we would like to find the minimal consistent subset.

Hart proposed a greedy algorithm to find $\mathcal{Z}$ (figure 8.6). The algorithm starts with an empty $\mathcal{Z}$ and passing over the instances in $\mathcal{X}$ one by one in a random order, checks whether they can be classified correctly by 1-nn using the instances already stored in $\mathcal{Z}$. If an instance is misclassified, it is added to $\mathcal{Z}$; if it is correctly classified, $\mathcal{Z}$ is unchanged. We should pass over the training set a few times until no further instances are added. The algorithm does a local search and depending on the order in which the training instances are seen, different subsets may be found, which may have different accuracies on the validation data. Thus it does not guarantee finding the minimal consistent subset, which is known to be NP-complete (Wilfong 1992).

Condensed nearest neighbor is a greedy algorithm that aims to minimize training error and complexity, measured by the size of the stored subset. We can write an augmented error function

$$E'(\mathcal{Z}|\mathcal{X}) = E(\mathcal{X}|\mathcal{Z}) + \lambda|\mathcal{Z}| \tag{8.17}$$

where $E(\mathcal{X}|\mathcal{Z})$ is the error on $\mathcal{X}$ storing $\mathcal{Z}$. $|\mathcal{Z}|$ is the cardinality of $\mathcal{Z}$, and the second term penalizes complexity. As in any regularization scheme, λ represents the trade-off between the error and complexity such that for small λ, error becomes more important, and as λ gets larger, complex models are penalized more. Condensed nearest neighbor is one method to minimize equation 8.17, but other algorithms to optimize it can also be devised.

8.6 Distance-Based Classification

The k-nearest neighbor classifier assigns an instance to the class most heavily represented among its neighbors. It is based on the idea that the more similar the instances, the more likely it is that they belong to the same class. We can use the same approach for classification as long as we have a reasonable similarity or distance measure (Chen et al. 2009).

Most classification algorithms can be recast as a distance-based classifier. For example, in section 5.5, we saw the parametric approach with Gaussian classes, and there, we talked about the *nearest mean classifier* where we choose C_i if

$$\mathcal{D}(\boldsymbol{x}, \boldsymbol{m}_i) = \min_{j=1}^{K} \mathcal{D}(\boldsymbol{x}, \boldsymbol{m}_j) \tag{8.18}$$

In the case of hyperspheric Gaussians where dimensions are independent and all are in the same scale, the distance measure is the Euclidean:

$$\mathcal{D}(\boldsymbol{x}, \boldsymbol{m}_i) = \|\boldsymbol{x} - \boldsymbol{m}_i\|$$

Otherwise it is the Mahalanobis distance:

$$\mathcal{D}(\boldsymbol{x}, \boldsymbol{m}_i) = (\boldsymbol{x} - \boldsymbol{m}_i)^T \mathbf{S}_i^{-1} (\boldsymbol{x} - \boldsymbol{m}_i)$$

where $\mathbf{S}_i$ is the covariance matrix of C_i.

In the semiparametric approach where each class is written as a mixture of Gaussians, we can say roughly speaking that we choose C_i if among all cluster centers of all classes, one that belongs to C_i is the closest:

$$\min_{l=1}^{k_i} \mathcal{D}(\boldsymbol{x}, \boldsymbol{m}_{il}) = \min_{j=1}^{K} \min_{l=1}^{k_j} \mathcal{D}(\boldsymbol{x}, \boldsymbol{m}_{jl}) \tag{8.19}$$

where k_j is the number of clusters of C_j and $\boldsymbol{m}_{jl}$ denotes the center of cluster l of C_j. Again, the distance used is the Euclidean or Mahalanobis depending on the shape of the clusters.

The nonparametric case can be even more flexible: Instead of having a distance measure per class or per cluster, we can have a different one for each neighborhood, that is, for each small region in the input space. In other words, we can define *locally adaptive distance functions* that we can then use in classification, for example, with k-nn (Hastie and Tibshirani 1996; Domeniconi, Peng, and Gunopulos 2002; Ramanan and Baker 2011).

DISTANCE LEARNING

The idea of *distance learning* is to parameterize $\mathcal{D}(\boldsymbol{x}, \boldsymbol{x}^t | \theta)$, learn θ from a labeled sample in a supervised manner, and then use it with k-nn (Bellet, Habrard, and Sebban 2013). The most common approach is to use the Mahalanobis distance:

$$\mathcal{D}(\boldsymbol{x}, \boldsymbol{x}^t | \mathbf{M}) = (\boldsymbol{x} - \boldsymbol{x}^t)^T \mathbf{M} (\boldsymbol{x} - \boldsymbol{x}^t) \tag{8.20}$$

LARGE MARGIN NEAREST NEIGHBOR

where the parameter is the positive definite matrix $\mathbf{M}$. An example is the *large margin nearest neighbor* algorithm (Weinberger and Saul 2009) where $\mathbf{M}$ is estimated so that for all instances in the training set, the distance to a neighbor with the same label is always less than the distance to a neighbor with a different label—we discuss this algorithm in detail in section 13.13.

When the input dimensionality is high, to avoid overfitting, one approach is to add sparsity constraints on $\mathbf{M}$. The other approach is to use a low-rank approximation where we factor $\mathbf{M}$ as $\mathbf{L}^T\mathbf{L}$ and $\mathbf{L}$ is $k \times d$ with $k < d$. In this case:

$$\begin{aligned}
\mathcal{D}(\boldsymbol{x}, \boldsymbol{x}^t | \mathbf{M}) &= (\boldsymbol{x} - \boldsymbol{x}^t)^T \mathbf{M} (\boldsymbol{x} - \boldsymbol{x}^t) = (\boldsymbol{x} - \boldsymbol{x}^t)^T \mathbf{L}^T \mathbf{L} (\boldsymbol{x} - \boldsymbol{x}^t) \\
&= (\mathbf{L}(\boldsymbol{x} - \boldsymbol{x}^t))^T (\mathbf{L}(\boldsymbol{x} - \boldsymbol{x}^t)) = (\mathbf{L}\boldsymbol{x} - \mathbf{L}\boldsymbol{x}^t)^T (\mathbf{L}\boldsymbol{x} - \mathbf{L}\boldsymbol{x}^t) \\
&= (\mathbf{z} - \mathbf{z}^t)^T (\mathbf{z} - \mathbf{z}^t) = \|\mathbf{z} - \mathbf{z}^t\|^2
\end{aligned} \tag{8.21}$$

where $\mathbf{z} = \mathbf{L}\boldsymbol{x}$ is the k-dimensional projection of $\boldsymbol{x}$, and we learn $\mathbf{L}$ instead of $\mathbf{M}$. We see that the Mahalanobis distance in the original d-dimensional $\boldsymbol{x}$ space corresponds to the (squared) Euclidean distance in the new k-dimensional space. This implies the three-way relationship between distance estimation, dimensionality reduction, and feature extraction: The ideal distance measure is defined as the Euclidean distance in a new space whose (fewest) dimensions are extracted from the original inputs in the best possible way. This is demonstrated in figure 8.7.

HAMMING DISTANCE

With discrete data, *Hamming distance* that counts the number of nonmatching attributes can be used:

$$HD(\boldsymbol{x}, \boldsymbol{x}^t) = \sum_{j=1}^{d} 1(x_j \neq x_j^t) \tag{8.22}$$

where

$$1(a) = \begin{cases} 1 & \text{if } a \text{ is true} \\ 0 & \text{otherwise} \end{cases}$$

This framework can be used with application-dependent similarity or distance measures as well. We may have specialized similarity/distance

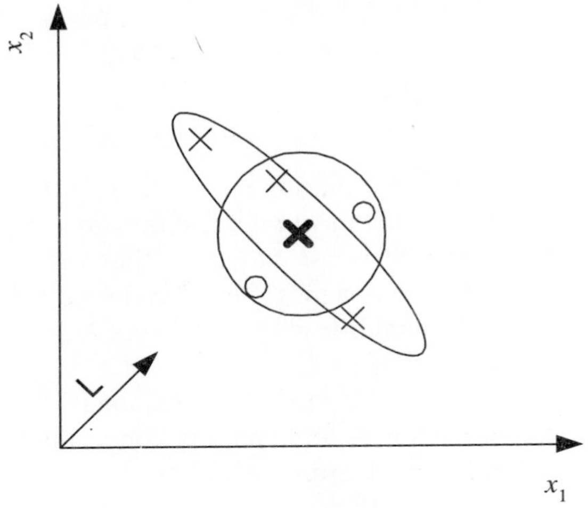

Figure 8.7 The use of Mahalanobis vs. Euclidean distance in k-nearest neighbor classification. There are two classes indicated by '$\circ$' and '$\times$'. The bold '$\times$' is the test instance and $k = 3$. Points that are of equal Euclidean distance define a circle that here leads to misclassification. We see that there is a certain correlation structure that can be captured by the Mahalanobis distance; it defines an ellipse and leads to correct classification. We also see that if the data is projected on the direction showed by L, we can do correct classification in that reduced one-dimensional space.

scores for matching image parts in vision, sequence alignment scores in bioinformatics, and document similarity measures in natural language processing; these can all be used without explicitly needing to represent those entities as vectors and using a general-purpose distance such as the Euclidean distance. In chapter 13, we will talk about kernel functions that have a similar role.

As long as we have a similarity score function between two instances $S(\boldsymbol{x}, \boldsymbol{x}^t)$, we can define a *similarity-based representation* $\boldsymbol{x}'$ of instance $\boldsymbol{x}$ as the N-dimensional vector of scores with all the training instances, $\boldsymbol{x}^t, t = 1, \ldots, N$:

$$\boldsymbol{x}' = [s(\boldsymbol{x}, \boldsymbol{x}^1), s(\boldsymbol{x}, \boldsymbol{x}^2), \ldots, s(\boldsymbol{x}, \boldsymbol{x}^N)]^T$$

This can then be used as a vector to be handled by any learner (Pekalska and Duin 2002); in the context of kernel machines, we will call this the *empirical kernel map* (section 13.7).

8.7 Outlier Detection

An *outlier, novelty,* or *anomaly* is an instance that is very much different from other instances in the sample. An outlier may indicate an abnormal behavior of the system; for example, in a dataset of credit card transactions, it may indicate fraud; in an image, outliers may indicate anomalies, for example, tumors; in a dataset of network traffic, outliers may be intrusion attempts; in a health-care scenario, an outlier indicates a significant deviation from patient's normal behavior. Outliers may also be recording errors—for example, due to faulty sensors—that should be detected and discarded to get reliable statistics.

OUTLIER DETECTION

Outlier detection is not generally cast as a supervised, two-class classification problem of seperating typical instances and outliers, because generally there are very few instances that can be labeled as outliers and they do not fit a consistent pattern that can be easily captured by a two-class classifier. Instead, it is the typical instances that are modeled; this is sometimes called *one-class classification.* Once we model the typical instances, any instance that does not fit the model (and this may occur in many different ways) is an anomaly. Another problem that generally occurs is that the data used to train the outlier detector is unlabeled and may contain outliers mixed with typical instances.

ONE-CLASS CLASSIFICATION

Outlier detection basically implies spotting what does not normally happen; that is, it is density estimation followed by checking for instances with too small probability under the estimated density. As usual, the fitted model can be parametric, semiparametric, or nonparametric. In the parametric case (section 5.4), for example, we can fit a Gaussian to the whole data and any instance having a low probability, or equally, with high Mahalanobis distance to the mean, is a candidate for being an outlier. In the semiparametric case (section 7.2), we fit, for example, a mixture of Gaussians and check whether an instance has small probability; this would be an instance that is far from its nearest cluster center or one that forms a cluster by itself.

Still when the data that is used for fitting the model itself includes outliers, it makes more sense to use a nonparametric density estimator, because the more parametric a model is, the less robust it will be to the

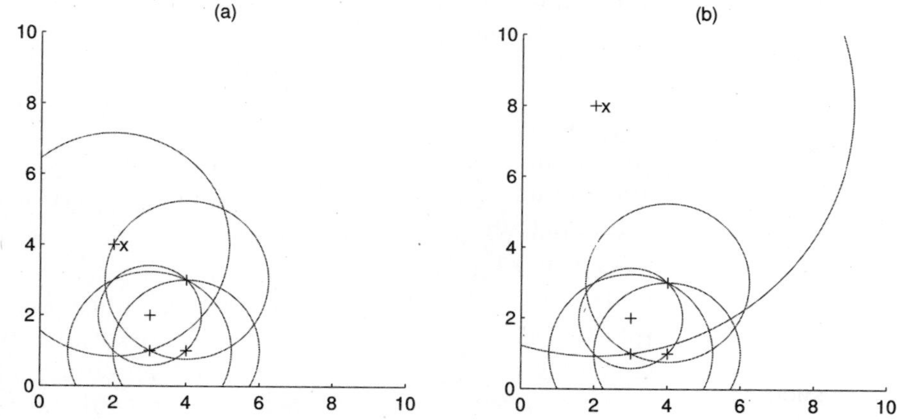

Figure 8.8 Training instances are shown by '+', '×' is the query, and the radius of the circle centered at an instance is equal to the distance to the third nearest neighbor. (a) LOF of '×' is close to 1 and it is not an outlier. (b) LOF of '×' is much larger than 1 and it is likely to be an outlier.

presence of outliers—for example, a single outlier may seriously corrupt the estimated mean and covariance of a Gaussian.

LOCAL OUTLIER FACTOR

In nonparametric density estimation, as we discussed in the preceding sections, the estimated probability is high where there are many training instances nearby and the probability decreases as the neighborhood becomes more sparse. One example is the *local outlier factor* that compares the denseness of the neighborhood of an instance with the average denseness of the neighborhoods of its neighbors (Breunig et al. 2000). Let us define $d_k(\boldsymbol{x})$ as the distance between instance $\boldsymbol{x}$ and its k-th nearest neighbor. Let us define $\mathcal{N}(\boldsymbol{x})$ as the set of training instances that are in the neighborhood of $\boldsymbol{x}$, for example, its k nearest neighbors. Consider $d_k(\boldsymbol{s})$ for $\boldsymbol{s} \in \mathcal{N}(\boldsymbol{x})$. We compare $d_k(\boldsymbol{x})$ with the average of $d_k(\boldsymbol{s})$ for such $\boldsymbol{s}$:

$$\text{LOF}(\boldsymbol{x}) = \frac{d_k(\boldsymbol{x})}{\sum_{\boldsymbol{s} \in \mathcal{N}(\boldsymbol{x})} d_k(\boldsymbol{s}) / |\mathcal{N}(\boldsymbol{x})|} \tag{8.23}$$

If LOF($\boldsymbol{x}$) is close to 1, $\boldsymbol{x}$ is not an outlier; as it gets larger, the probability that it is an outlier increases (see figure 8.8).

8.8 Nonparametric Regression: Smoothing Models

In regression, given the training set $\mathcal{X} = \{x^t, r^t\}$ where $r^t \in \Re$, we assume

$r^t = g(x^t) + \epsilon$

In parametric regression, we assume a polynomial of a certain order and compute its coefficients that minimize the sum of squared error on the training set. Nonparametric regression is used when no such polynomial can be assumed; we only assume that close x have close $g(x)$ values. As in nonparametric density estimation, given x, our approach is to find the neighborhood of x and average the r values in the neighborhood to calculate $\hat{g}(x)$. The nonparametric regression estimator is also called a *smoother* and the estimate is called a *smooth* (Härdle 1990). There are various methods for defining the neighborhood and averaging in the neighborhood, similar to methods in density estimation. We discuss the methods for the univariate x; they can be generalized to the multivariate case in a straightforward manner using multivariate kernels, as in density estimation.

SMOOTHER

8.8.1 Running Mean Smoother

If we define an origin and a bin width and average the r values in the bin as in the histogram, we get a *regressogram* (see figure 8.9)

REGRESSOGRAM

(8.24)
$$\hat{g}(x) = \frac{\sum_{t=1}^{N} b(x, x^t) r^t}{\sum_{t=1}^{N} b(x, x^t)}$$

where

$$b(x, x^t) = \begin{cases} 1 & \text{if } x^t \text{ is the same bin with } x \\ 0 & \text{otherwise} \end{cases}$$

Having discontinuities at bin boundaries is disturbing as is the need to fix an origin. As in the naive estimator, in the *running mean smoother*, we define a bin symmetric around x and average in there (figure 8.10).

RUNNING MEAN SMOOTHER

(8.25)
$$\hat{g}(x) = \frac{\sum_{t=1}^{N} w\left(\frac{x-x^t}{h}\right) r^t}{\sum_{t=1}^{N} w\left(\frac{x-x^t}{h}\right)}$$

where

$$w(u) = \begin{cases} 1 & \text{if } |u| < 1 \\ 0 & \text{otherwise} \end{cases}$$

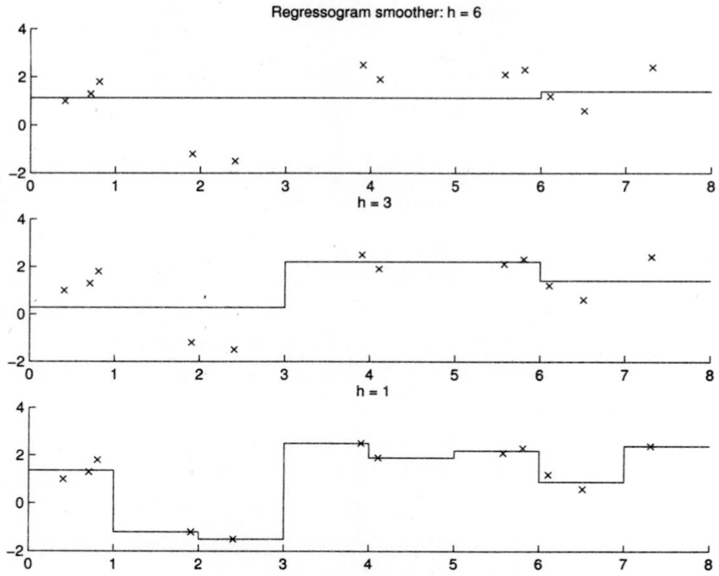

Figure 8.9 Regressograms for various bin lengths. '×' denote data points.

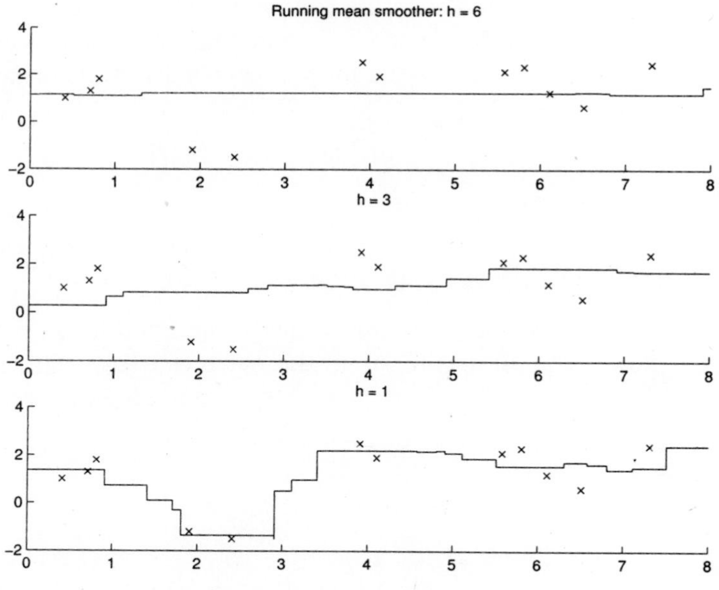

Figure 8.10 Running mean smooth for various bin lengths.

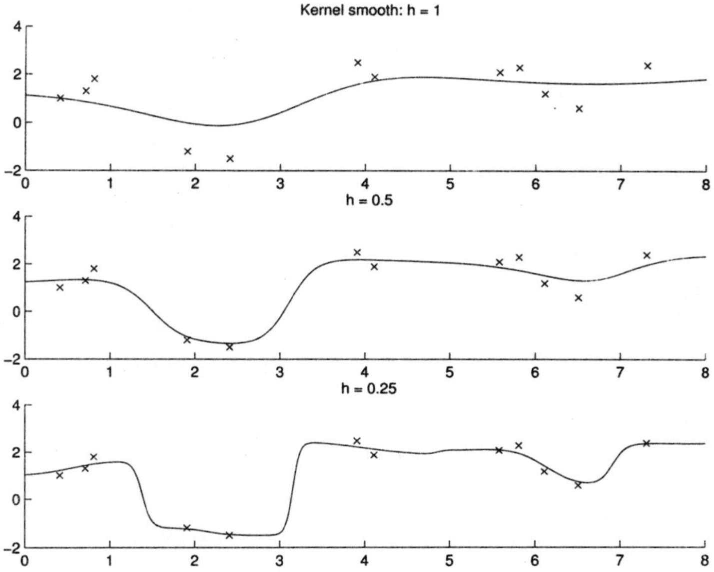

Figure 8.11 Kernel smooth for various bin lengths.

This method is especially popular with evenly spaced data, such as time series. In applications where there is noise, we can use the median of the r^t in the bin instead of their mean.

8.8.2 Kernel Smoother

KERNEL SMOOTHER

As in the kernel estimator, we can use a kernel giving less weight to further points, and we get the *kernel smoother* (see figure 8.11):

$$\hat{g}(x) = \frac{\sum_t K\left(\frac{x-x^t}{h}\right) r^t}{\sum_t K\left(\frac{x-x^t}{h}\right)} \tag{8.26}$$

k-NN SMOOTHER

Typically a Gaussian kernel $K(\cdot)$ is used. Instead of fixing h, we can fix k, the number of neighbors, adapting the estimate to the density around x, and get the *k-nn smoother.*

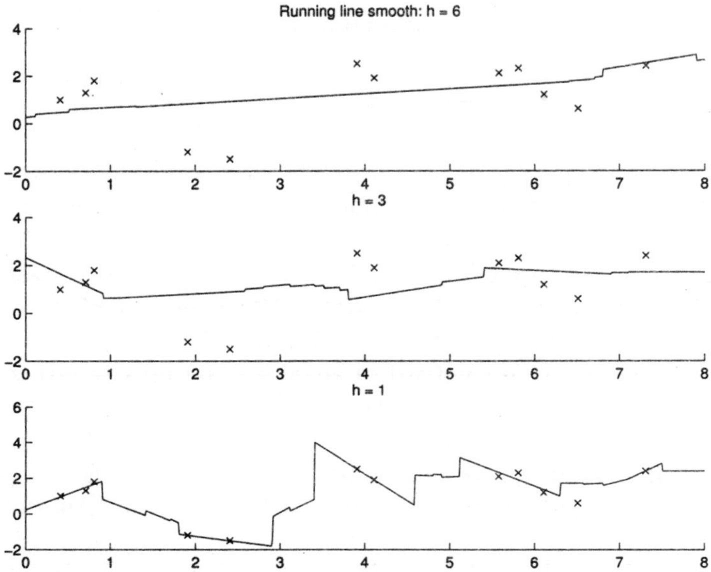

Figure 8.12 Running line smooth for various bin lengths.

8.8.3 Running Line Smoother

Instead of taking an average and giving a constant fit at a point, we can take into account one more term in the Taylor expansion and calculate a linear fit. In the *running line smoother*, we can use the data points in the neighborhood, as defined by h or k, and fit a local regression line (see figure 8.12).

RUNNING LINE SMOOTHER

In the *locally weighted running line smoother*, known as *loess*, instead of a hard definition of neighborhoods, we use kernel weighting such that distant points have less effect on error.

LOCALLY WEIGHTED RUNNING LINE SMOOTHER

8.9 How to Choose the Smoothing Parameter

In nonparametric methods, for density estimation or regression, the critical parameter is the smoothing parameter as used in bin width or kernel spread h, or the number of neighbors k. The aim is to have an estimate that is less variable than the data points. As we have discussed previously, one source of variability in the data is noise and the other is the variability in the unknown underlying function. We should smooth just enough to get rid of the effect of noise—not less, not more. With too large h or k, many instances contribute to the estimate at a point and we also smooth the variability due to the function (oversmoothing); with too small h or k, single instances have a large effect and we do not even smooth over the noise (undersmoothing). In other words, small h or k leads to small bias but large variance. Larger h or k decreases variance but increases bias. Geman, Bienenstock, and Doursat (1992) discuss bias and variance for nonparametric estimators.

This requirement is explicitly coded in a regularized cost function as used in *smoothing splines*:

SMOOTHING SPLINES

$$\sum_t [r^t - \hat{g}(x^t)]^2 + \lambda \int_a^b [\hat{g}''(x)]^2 dx \tag{8.27}$$

The first term is the error of fit. $[a, b]$ is the input range; $\hat{g}''(\cdot)$ is the *curvature* of the estimated function $\hat{g}(\cdot)$ and as such measures the variability. Thus the second term penalizes fast-varying estimates. λ trades off variability and error where, for example, with large λ, we get smoother estimates.

Cross-validation is used to tune h, k, or λ. In density estimation, we choose the parameter value that maximizes the likelihood of the validation set. In a supervised setting, trying a set of candidates on the training set (see figure 8.13), we choose the parameter value that minimizes the error on the validation set.

8.10 Notes

k-nearest neighbor and kernel-based estimation were proposed sixty years ago, but because of the need for large memory and computation, the approach was not popular for a long time (Aha, Kibler, and Albert 1991). With advances in parallel processing and with memory and computation getting cheaper, such methods have recently become more widely used. Textbooks on nonparametric estimation are Silverman 1986 and Scott 1992. Dasarathy 1991 is a collection of many papers on k-nn and editing/condensing rules; Aha 1997 is another collection.

The nonparametric methods are very easy to parallelize on a Single Instruction Multiple Data (SIMD) machine; each processor stores one training instance in its local memory and in parallel computes the kernel

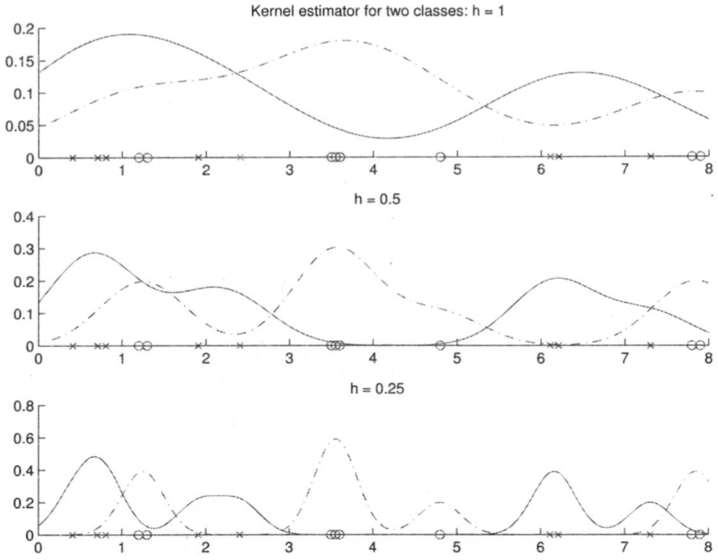

Figure 8.13 Kernel estimate for various bin lengths for a two-class problem. Plotted are the conditional densities, $p(x|C_i)$. It seems that the top one oversmooths and the bottom undersmooths, but whichever is the best will depend on where the validation data points are.

function value for that instance (Stanfill and Waltz 1986). Multiplying with a kernel function can be seen as a convolution, and we can use Fourier transformation to calculate the estimate more efficiently (Silverman 1986). It has also been shown that spline smoothing is equivalent to kernel smoothing.

CASE-BASED REASONING

In artificial intelligence, the nonparametric approach is called *case-based reasoning*. The output is found by interpolating from known similar past "cases." This also allows for some knowledge extraction: The given output can be justified by listing these similar past cases.

Due to its simplicity, k-nn is the most widely used nonparametric classification method and is quite successful in practice in a variety of applications. One nice property is that they can be used even with very few labeled instances; for example, in a forensic application, we may have only one face image per person.

It has been shown (Cover and Hart 1967; reviewed in Duda, Hart, and

Stork 2001) that in the large sample case when $N \to \infty$, the risk of nearest neighbor ($k = 1$) is never worse than twice the Bayes' risk (which is the best that can be achieved), and, in that respect, it is said that "half of the available information in an infinite collection of classified samples is contained in the nearest neighbor" (Cover and Hart 1967, 21). In the case of k-nn, it has been shown that the risk asymptotes to the Bayes' risk as k goes to infinity.

The most critical factor in nonparametric estimation is the distance metric used. With discrete attributes, we can simply use the Hamming distance where we just sum up the number of nonmatching attributes. More sophisticated distance functions are discussed in Wettschereck, Aha, and Mohri 1997 and Webb 1999.

Distance estimation or metric learning is a popular research area; see Bellet, Habrard, and Sebban 2013 for a comprehensive recent survey. The different ways similarity measures can be used in classification are discussed by Chen et al. (2009); examples of local distance methods in computer vision are given in Ramanan and Baker 2011.

Outlier/anomaly/novelty detection arises as an interesting problem in various contexts, from faults to frauds, and in detecting significant deviations from the past data, for example, churning customers. It is a very popular research area, and two comprehensive surveys include those by Hodge and Austin (2004) and Chandola, Banerjee, and Kumar (2009).

ADDITIVE MODELS

Nonparametric regression is discussed in detail in Härdle 1990. Hastie and Tibshirani (1990) discuss smoothing models and propose *additive models* where a multivariate function is written as a sum of univariate estimates. Locally weighted regression is discussed in Atkeson, Moore, and Schaal 1997. These models bear much similarity to radial basis functions and mixture of experts that we discuss in chapter 12.

In the condensed nearest neighbor algorithm, we saw that we can keep only a subset of the training instances, those that are close to the boundary, and we can define the discriminant using them only. This idea bears much similarity to the *support vector machines* that we discuss in chapter 13. There we also discuss various kernel functions to measure similarity between instances and how we can choose the best. Writing the prediction as a sum of the combined effects of training instances also underlies *Gaussian processes* (chapter 16), where a kernel function is called a *covariance function*.

8.11 Exercises

1. How can we have a smooth histogram?

   SOLUTION: We can interpolate between the two nearest bin centers. We can consider the bin centers as x^t, consider the histogram values as r^t, and use any interpolation scheme, linear or kernel-based.

2. Show equation 8.16.

   SOLUTION: Given that

   $$\hat{p}(\boldsymbol{x}|C_i) = \frac{k_i}{N_i V^k(\boldsymbol{x})} \quad \text{and} \quad \hat{P}(C_i) = \frac{N_i}{N}$$

   we can write

   $$\begin{aligned}\hat{P}(C_i|\boldsymbol{x}) &= \frac{\hat{p}(\boldsymbol{x}|C_i)\hat{P}(C_i)}{\sum_j \hat{p}(\boldsymbol{x}|C_j)\hat{P}(C_j)} = \frac{\frac{k_i}{N_i V^k(\boldsymbol{x})}\frac{N_i}{N}}{\sum_j \frac{k_j}{N_j V^k(\boldsymbol{x})}\frac{N_j}{N}} \\ &= \frac{k_i}{\sum_j k_j} = \frac{k_i}{k}\end{aligned}$$

3. Parametric regression (section 5.8) assumes Gaussian noise and hence is not robust to outliers; how can we make it more robust ?

4. How can we detect outliers after hierarchical clustering (section 7.8) ?

5. How does condensed nearest neighbor behave if $k > 1$?

   SOLUTION: When $k > 1$, to get full accuracy without any misclassification, it may be necessary to store an instance multiple times so that the correct class gets the majority of the votes. For example, if $k = 3$ and $\boldsymbol{x}$ has two neighbors both belonging to a different class, we need to store $\boldsymbol{x}$ twice (i.e., it gets added in two epochs), so that if $\boldsymbol{x}$ is seen during test, the majority (two in this case) out of three neighbors belong to the correct class.

6. In condensed nearest neighbor, an instance previously added to $\mathcal{Z}$ may no longer be necessary after a later addition. How can we find such instances that are no longer necessary?

7. In a regressogram, instead of averaging in a bin and doing a constant fit, we can use the instances falling in a bin and do a linear fit (see figure 8.14). Write the code and compare this with the regressogram proper.

8. Write the error function for loess discussed in section 8.8.3.

   SOLUTION: The output is calculated using a linear model $g(x) = ax+b$, where, in the running line smoother, we minimize

   $$E(a,b|x,\mathcal{X}) = \sum_t w\left(\frac{x-x^t}{h}\right)[r^t - (ax^t + b)]^2$$

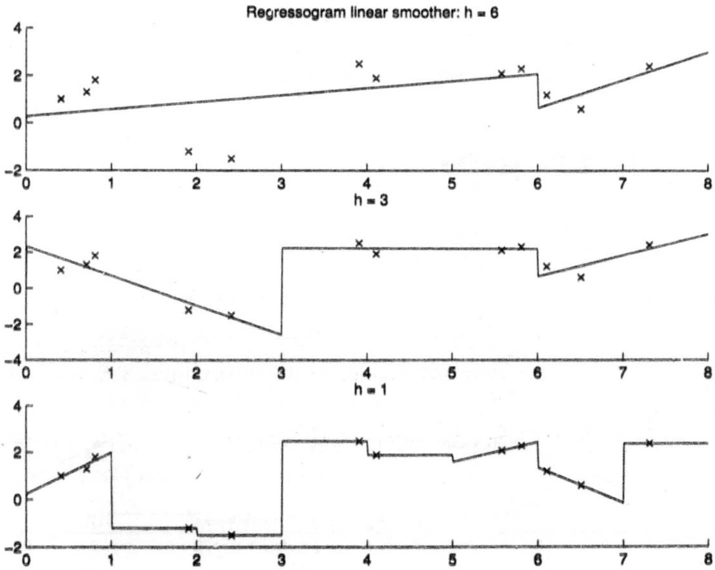

Figure 8.14 Regressograms with linear fits in bins for various bin lengths.

and

$$w(u) = \begin{cases} 1 & \text{if } |u| < 1 \\ 0 & \text{otherwise} \end{cases}$$

Note that we do not have one error function but rather, for each test input x, we have another error function taking into account only the data closest to x, which is minimized to fit a line in that neighborhood.

Loess is the weighted version of running line smoother where a kernel function $K(\cdot) \in (0,1)$ replaces the $w(\cdot) \in \{0,1\}$:

$$E(a, b|x, \mathcal{X}) = \sum_t K\left(\frac{x - x^t}{h}\right)[r^t - (ax^t + b)]^2$$

9. Propose an incremental version of the running mean estimator, which, like the condensed nearest neighbor, stores instances only when necessary.
10. Generalize kernel smoother to multivariate data.
11. In the running smoother, we can fit a constant, a line, or a higher-degree polynomial at a test point. How can we choose among them?
SOLUTION: By cross-validation.

12. In the running mean smoother, besides giving an estimate, can we also calculate a confidence interval indicating the variance (uncertainty) around the estimate at that point?

8.12 References

Aha, D. W., ed. 1997. Special Issue on Lazy Learning. *Artificial Intelligence Review* 11 (1–5): 7–423.

Aha, D. W., D. Kibler, and M. K. Albert. 1991. "Instance-Based Learning Algorithm." *Machine Learning* 6:37–66.

Atkeson, C. G., A. W. Moore, and S. Schaal. 1997. "Locally Weighted Learning." *Artificial Intelligence Review* 11:11–73.

Bellet, A., A. Habrard, and M. Sebban. 2013. "A Survey on Metric Learning for Feature Vectors and Structured Data." *arXiv:1306.6709v2.*

Breunig, M. M., H.-P. Kriegel, R. T. Ng, and J. Sander. 2000. "LOF: Identifying Density-Based Local Outliers." In *ACM SIGMOD International Conference on Management of Data*, 93–104. New York: ACM Press.

Chandola, V., A. Banerjee, and V. Kumar. 2009. "Anomaly Detection: A Survey." *ACM Computing Surveys* 41 (3): 15:1–15:58.

Chen, Y., E. K. Garcia, M. R. Gupta, A. Rahimi, and L. Cazzanti. 2009. "Similarity-Based Classification: Concepts and Algorithms." *Journal of Machine Learning Research* 11:747–776.

Cover, T. M., and P. E. Hart. 1967. "Nearest Neighbor Pattern Classification." *IEEE Transactions on Information Theory* 13:21–27.

Dasarathy, B. V. 1991. *Nearest Neighbor Norms: NN Pattern Classification Techniques.* Los Alamitos, CA: IEEE Computer Society Press.

Domeniconi, C., J. Peng, and D. Gunopulos. 2002. "Locally Adaptive Metric Nearest-Neighbor Classification." *IEEE Transactions on Pattern Analysis and Machine Intelligence* 24:1281–1285.

Duda, R. O., P. E. Hart, and D. G. Stork. 2001. *Pattern Classification*, 2nd ed. New York: Wiley.

Geman, S., E. Bienenstock, and R. Doursat. 1992. "Neural Networks and the Bias/Variance Dilemma." *Neural Computation* 4:1–58.

Härdle, W. 1990. *Applied Nonparametric Regression.* Cambridge, UK: Cambridge University Press.

Hart, P. E. 1968. "The Condensed Nearest Neighbor Rule." *IEEE Transactions on Information Theory* 14:515–516.

Hastie, T. J., and R. J. Tibshirani. 1990. *Generalized Additive Models.* London: Chapman and Hall.

Hastie, T. J., and R. J. Tibshirani. 1996. "Discriminant Adaptive Nearest Neighbor Classification." *IEEE Transactions on Pattern Analysis and Machine Intelligence* 18:607–616.

Hodge, V. J., and J. Austin. 2004. "A Survey of Outlier Detection Methodologies." *Artificial Intelligence Review* 22:85–126.

Pekalska, E., and R. P. W. Duin. 2002. "Dissimilarity Representations Allow for Building Good Classifiers." *Pattern Recognition Letters* 23:943–956.

Ramanan, D., and S. Baker. 2011. "Local Distance Functions: A Taxonomy, New Algorithms, and an Evaluation." *IEEE Transactions on Pattern Analysis and Machine Intelligence* 33:794–806.

Scott, D. W. 1992. *Multivariate Density Estimation.* New York: Wiley.

Silverman, B. W. 1986. *Density Estimation in Statistics and Data Analysis.* London: Chapman and Hall.

Stanfill, C., and D. Waltz. 1986. "Toward Memory-Based Reasoning." *Communications of the ACM* 29:1213–1228.

Webb, A. 1999. *Statistical Pattern Recognition.* London: Arnold.

Weinberger, K. Q., and L. K. Saul. 2009. "Distance Metric Learning for Large Margin Classification." *Journal of Machine Learning Research* 10:207–244.

Wettschereck, D., D. W. Aha, and T. Mohri. 1997. "A Review and Empirical Evaluation of Feature Weighting Methods for a Class of Lazy Learning Algorithms." *Artificial Intelligence Review* 11:273–314.

Wilfong, G. 1992. "Nearest Neighbor Problems." *International Journal on Computational Geometry and Applications* 2:383–416.

9 Decision Trees

A decision tree is a hierarchical data structure implementing the divide-and-conquer strategy. It is an efficient nonparametric method, which can be used for both classification and regression. We discuss learning algorithms that build the tree from a given labeled training sample, as well as how the tree can be converted to a set of simple rules that are easy to understand. Another possibility is to learn a rule base directly.

9.1 Introduction

IN PARAMETRIC estimation, we define a model over the whole input space and learn its parameters from all of the training data. Then we use the same model and the same parameter set for any test input. In nonparametric estimation, we divide the input space into local regions, defined by a distance measure like the Euclidean norm, and for each input, the corresponding local model computed from the training data in that region is used. In the instance-based models we discussed in chapter 8, given an input, identifying the local data defining the local model is costly; it requires calculating the distances from the given input to all of the training instances, which is $\mathcal{O}(N)$.

DECISION TREE

A *decision tree* is a hierarchical model for supervised learning whereby the local region is identified in a sequence of recursive splits in a smaller number of steps. A decision tree is composed of internal decision nodes and terminal leaves (see figure 9.1). Each *decision node m* implements a test function $f_m(\boldsymbol{x})$ with discrete outcomes labeling the branches. Given an input, at each node, a test is applied and one of the branches is taken depending on the outcome. This process starts at the root and is repeated

DECISION NODE

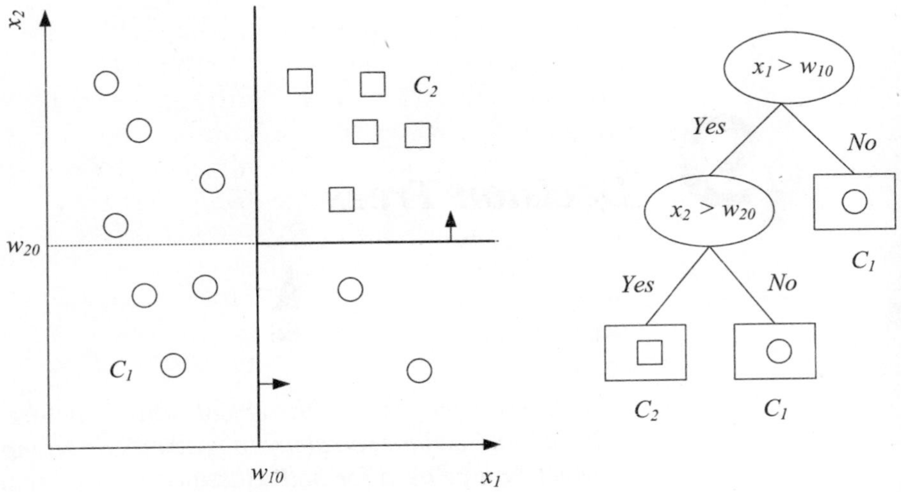

Figure 9.1 Example of a dataset and the corresponding decision tree. Oval nodes are the decision nodes and rectangles are leaf nodes. The univariate decision node splits along one axis, and successive splits are orthogonal to each other. After the first split, $\{\boldsymbol{x}|x_1 < w_{10}\}$ is pure and is not split further.

LEAF NODE

recursively until a *leaf node* is hit, at which point the value written in the leaf constitutes the output.

A decision tree is also a nonparametric model in the sense that we do not assume any parametric form for the class densities and the tree structure is not fixed a priori but the tree grows, branches and leaves are added, during learning depending on the complexity of the problem inherent in the data.

Each $f_m(\boldsymbol{x})$ defines a discriminant in the d-dimensional input space dividing it into smaller regions that are further subdivided as we take a path from the root down. $f_m(\cdot)$ is a simple function and when written down as a tree, a complex function is broken down into a series of simple decisions. Different decision tree methods assume different models for $f_m(\cdot)$, and the model class defines the shape of the discriminant and the shape of regions. Each leaf node has an output label, which in the case of classification is the class code and in regression is a numeric value. A leaf node defines a localized region in the input space where instances falling in this region have the same labels (in classification), or very similar numeric outputs (in regression). The boundaries of the regions are defined by the discriminants that are coded in the internal nodes on the path from the root to the leaf node.

The hierarchical placement of decisions allows a fast localization of the region covering an input. For example, if the decisions are binary, then in the best case, each decision eliminates half of the cases. If there are b regions, then in the best case, the correct region can be found in $\log_2 b$ decisions. Another advantage of the decision tree is interpretability. As we will see shortly, the tree can be converted to a set of *IF-THEN rules* that are easily understandable. For this reason, decision trees are very popular and sometimes preferred over more accurate but less interpretable methods.

We start with univariate trees where the test in a decision node uses only one input variable and we see how such trees can be constructed for classification and regression. We later generalize this to multivariate trees where all inputs can be used in an internal node.

9.2 Univariate Trees

UNIVARIATE TREE

In a *univariate tree*, in each internal node, the test uses only one of the input dimensions. If the used input dimension, x_j, is discrete, taking one of n possible values, the decision node checks the value of x_j and takes the corresponding branch, implementing an n-way split. For example, if an attribute is color $\in$ {red, blue, green}, then a node on that attribute has three branches, each one corresponding to one of the three possible values of the attribute.

A decision node has discrete branches and a numeric input should be discretized. If x_j is numeric (ordered), the test is a comparison

$$f_m(\mathbf{x}) : x_j > w_{m0} \tag{9.1}$$

BINARY SPLIT

where w_{m0} is a suitably chosen threshold value. The decision node divides the input space into two: $L_m = \{\mathbf{x}|x_j > w_{m0}\}$ and $R_m = \{\mathbf{x}|x_j \leq w_{m0}\}$; this is called a *binary split*. Successive decision nodes on a path from the root to a leaf further divide these into two using other attributes and generating splits orthogonal to each other. The leaf nodes define hyperrectangles in the input space (see figure 9.1).

Tree induction is the construction of the tree given a training sample. For a given training set, there exists many trees that code it with no error, and, for simplicity, we are interested in finding the smallest among them, where tree size is measured as the number of nodes in the tree and the complexity of the decision nodes. Finding the smallest tree is NP-complete (Quinlan 1986), and we are forced to use local search procedures based on heuristics that give reasonable trees in reasonable time.

Tree learning algorithms are greedy and, at each step, starting at the root with the complete training data, we look for the best split. This splits the training data into two or n, depending on whether the chosen attribute is numeric or discrete. We then continue splitting recursively with the corresponding subset until we do not need to split anymore, at which point a leaf node is created and labeled.

9.2.1 Classification Trees

CLASSIFICATION TREE
IMPURITY MEASURE

In the case of a decision tree for classification, namely, a *classification tree*, the goodness of a split is quantified by an *impurity measure*. A split is pure if after the split, for all branches, all the instances choosing a branch belong to the same class. Let us say for node m, N_m is the number of training instances reaching node m. For the root node, it is N. N_m^i of N_m belong to class C_i, with $\sum_i N_m^i = N_m$. Given that an instance reaches node m, the estimate for the probability of class C_i is

$$\hat{P}(C_i|x, m) \equiv p_m^i = \frac{N_m^i}{N_m} \tag{9.2}$$

Node m is pure if p_m^i for all i are either 0 or 1. It is 0 when none of the instances reaching node m are of class C_i, and it is 1 if all such instances are of C_i. If the split is pure, we do not need to split any further and can add a leaf node labeled with the class for which p_m^i is 1. One possible function to measure impurity is *entropy* (Quinlan 1986) (see figure 9.2):

ENTROPY

$$\mathcal{I}_m = -\sum_{i=1}^{K} p_m^i \log_2 p_m^i \tag{9.3}$$

where $0 \log 0 \equiv 0$. Entropy in information theory specifies the minimum number of bits needed to encode the class code of an instance. In a two-class problem, if $p^1 = 1$ and $p^2 = 0$, all examples are of C^1, and we do not need to send anything, and the entropy is 0. If $p^1 = p^2 = 0.5$, we need to send a bit to signal one of the two cases, and the entropy is 1. In between these two extremes, we can devise codes and use less than a bit per message by having shorter codes for the more likely class and

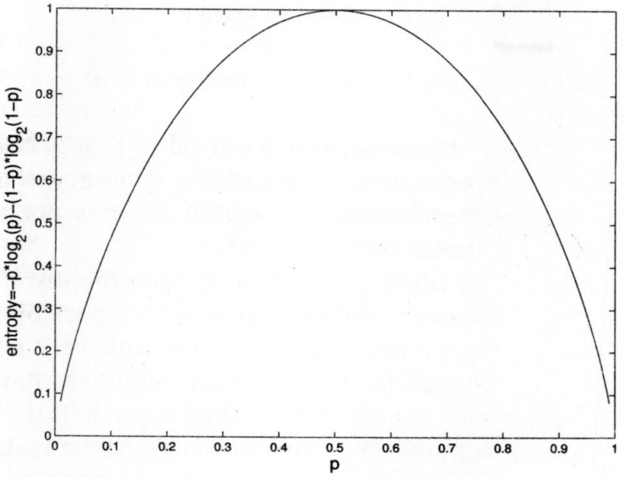

Figure 9.2 Entropy function for a two-class problem.

longer codes for the less likely. When there are $K > 2$ classes, the same discussion holds and the largest entropy is $\log_2 K$ when $p^i = 1/K$.

But entropy is not the only possible measure. For a two-class problem where $p^1 \equiv p$ and $p^2 = 1 - p$, $\phi(p, 1-p)$ is a nonnegative function measuring the impurity of a split if it satisfies the following properties (Devroye, Györfi, and Lugosi 1996):

- $\phi(1/2, 1/2) \geq \phi(p, 1-p)$, for any $p \in [0, 1]$.
- $\phi(0, 1) = \phi(1, 0) = 0$.
- $\phi(p, 1-p)$ is increasing in p on $[0, 1/2]$ and decreasing in p on $[1/2, 1]$.

Examples are

1. Entropy

(9.4) $$\phi(p, 1-p) = -p \log_2 p - (1-p) \log_2 (1-p)$$

Equation 9.3 is the generalization to $K > 2$ classes.

GINI INDEX

2. *Gini index* (Breiman et al. 1984)

(9.5) $$\phi(p, 1-p) = 2p(1-p)$$

3. Misclassification error

$$\phi(p, 1-p) = 1 - \max(p, 1-p) \tag{9.6}$$

These can be generalized to $K > 2$ classes, and the misclassification error can be generalized to minimum risk given a loss function (exercise 1). Research has shown that there is not a significant difference between these three measures.

If node m is not pure, then the instances should be split to decrease impurity, and there are multiple possible attributes on which we can split. For a numeric attribute, multiple split positions are possible. Among all, we look for the split that minimizes impurity after the split because we want to generate the smallest tree. If the subsets after the split are closer to pure, fewer splits (if any) will be needed afterward. Of course this is locally optimal, and we have no guarantee of finding the smallest decision tree.

Let us say at node m, N_{mj} of N_m take branch j; these are $\mathbf{x}^t$ for which the test $f_m(\mathbf{x}^t)$ returns outcome j. For a discrete attribute with n values, there are n outcomes, and for a numeric attribute, there are two outcomes ($n = 2$), in either case satisfying $\sum_{j=1}^{n} N_{mj} = N_m$. N_{mj}^i of N_{mj} belong to class C_i: $\sum_{i=1}^{K} N_{mj}^i = N_{mj}$. Similarly, $\sum_{j=1}^{n} N_{mj}^i = N_m^i$.

Then given that at node m, the test returns outcome j, the estimate for the probability of class C_i is

$$\hat{P}(C_i|\mathbf{x}, m, j) \equiv p_{mj}^i = \frac{N_{mj}^i}{N_{mj}} \tag{9.7}$$

and the total impurity after the split is given as

$$\mathcal{I}'_m = -\sum_{j=1}^{n} \frac{N_{mj}}{N_m} \sum_{i=1}^{K} p_{mj}^i \log_2 p_{mj}^i \tag{9.8}$$

In the case of a numeric attribute, to be able to calculate p_{mj}^i using equation 9.1, we also need to know w_{m0} for that node. There are $N_m - 1$ possible w_{m0} between N_m data points: We do not need to test for all (possibly infinite) points; it is enough to test, for example, at halfway between points. Note also that the best split is always between adjacent points belonging to different classes. So we try them, and the best in terms of purity is taken for the purity of the attribute. In the case of a discrete attribute, no such iteration is necessary.

```
GenerateTree(𝒳)
  If NodeEntropy(𝒳)< θ_I /* equation 9.3 */
    Create leaf labelled by majority class in 𝒳
    Return
  i ← SplitAttribute(𝒳)
  For each branch of x_i
    Find 𝒳_i falling in branch
    GenerateTree(𝒳_i)

SplitAttribute(𝒳)
  MinEnt← MAX
  For all attributes i = 1,...,d
    If x_i is discrete with n values
      Split 𝒳 into 𝒳_1,...,𝒳_n by x_i
      e ← SplitEntropy(𝒳_1,...,𝒳_n) /* equation 9.8 */
      If e<MinEnt MinEnt ← e; bestf ← i
    Else /* x_i is numeric */
      For all possible splits
        Split 𝒳 into 𝒳_1,𝒳_2 on x_i
        e←SplitEntropy(𝒳_1,𝒳_2)
        If e<MinEnt MinEnt ← e; bestf ← i
  Return bestf
```

Figure 9.3 Classification tree construction.

So for all attributes, discrete and numeric, and for a numeric attribute for all split positions, we calculate the impurity and choose the one that has the minimum entropy, for example, as measured by equation 9.8. Then tree construction continues recursively and in parallel for all the branches that are not pure, until all are pure. This is the basis of the *classification and regression tree* (CART) algorithm (Breiman et al. 1984), *ID3* algorithm (Quinlan 1986), and its extension *C4.5* (Quinlan 1993). The pseudocode of the algorithm is given in figure 9.3.

CLASSIFICATION AND REGRESSION TREE
ID3
C4.5

It can also be said that at each step during tree construction, we choose the split that causes the largest decrease in impurity, which is the difference between the impurity of data reaching node m (equation 9.3) and the total entropy of data reaching its branches after the split (equation 9.8).

One problem is that such splitting favors attributes with many values. When there are many values, there are many branches, and the impurity can be much less. For example, if we take training index t as an attribute, the impurity measure will choose that because then the impurity of each branch is 0, although it is not a reasonable feature. Nodes with many branches are complex and go against our idea of splitting class discriminants into simple decisions. Methods have been proposed to penalize such attributes and to balance the impurity drop and the branching factor.

When there is noise, growing the tree until it is purest, we may grow a very large tree and it overfits; for example, consider the case of a mislabeled instance amid a group of correctly labeled instances. To alleviate such overfitting, tree construction ends when nodes become pure enough, namely, a subset of data is not split further if $\mathcal{I} < \theta_I$. This implies that we do not require that p^i_{mj} be exactly 0 or 1 but close enough, with a threshold θ_p. In such a case, a leaf node is created and is labeled with the class having the highest p^i_{mj}.

θ_I (or θ_p) is the complexity parameter, like h or k of nonparametric estimation. When they are small, the variance is high and the tree grows large to reflect the training set accurately, and when they are large, variance is lower and a smaller tree roughly represents the training set and may have large bias. The ideal value depends on the cost of misclassification, as well as the costs of memory and computation.

It is generally advised that in a leaf, one stores the posterior probabilities of classes, instead of labeling the leaf with the class having the highest posterior. These probabilities may be required in later steps, for example, in calculating risks. Note that we do not need to store the instances reaching the node or the exact counts; just ratios suffice.

9.2.2 Regression Trees

REGRESSION TREE

A *regression tree* is constructed in almost the same manner as a classification tree, except that the impurity measure that is appropriate for classification is replaced by a measure appropriate for regression. Let us say for node m, $\mathcal{X}_m$ is the subset of $\mathcal{X}$ reaching node m; namely, it is the set of all $\boldsymbol{x} \in \mathcal{X}$ satisfying all the conditions in the decision nodes on the path from the root until node m. We define

$$b_m(\boldsymbol{x}) = \begin{cases} 1 & \text{if } \boldsymbol{x} \in \mathcal{X}_m\text{: } \boldsymbol{x} \text{ reaches node } m \\ 0 & \text{otherwise} \end{cases} \tag{9.9}$$

In regression, the goodness of a split is measured by the mean square error from the estimated value. Let us say g_m is the estimated value in node m.

$$E_m = \frac{1}{N_m}\sum_t (r^t - g_m)^2 b_m(\boldsymbol{x}^t) \tag{9.10}$$

where $N_m = |\mathcal{X}_m| = \sum_t b_m(\boldsymbol{x}^t)$.

In a node, we use the mean (median if there is too much noise) of the required outputs of instances reaching the node

$$g_m = \frac{\sum_t b_m(\boldsymbol{x}^t) r^t}{\sum_t b_m(\boldsymbol{x}^t)} \tag{9.11}$$

Then equation 9.10 corresponds to the variance at m. If at a node, the error is acceptable, that is, $E_m < \theta_r$, then a leaf node is created and it stores the g_m value. Just like the regressogram of chapter 8, this creates a piecewise constant approximation with discontinuities at leaf boundaries.

If the error is not acceptable, data reaching node m is split further such that the sum of the errors in the branches is minimum. As in classification, at each node, we look for the attribute (and split threshold for a numeric attribute) that minimizes the error, and then we continue recursively.

Let us define $\mathcal{X}_{mj}$ as the subset of $\mathcal{X}_m$ taking branch j: $\cup_{j=1}^n \mathcal{X}_{mj} = \mathcal{X}_m$. We define

$$b_{mj}(\boldsymbol{x}) = \begin{cases} 1 & \text{if } \boldsymbol{x} \in \mathcal{X}_{mj}\text{: } \boldsymbol{x} \text{ reaches node } m \text{ and takes branch } j \\ 0 & \text{otherwise} \end{cases} \tag{9.12}$$

g_{mj} is the estimated value in branch j of node m.

$$g_{mj} = \frac{\sum_t b_{mj}(\boldsymbol{x}^t) r^t}{\sum_t b_{mj}(\boldsymbol{x}^t)} \tag{9.13}$$

and the error after the split is

$$E'_m = \frac{1}{N_m}\sum_j \sum_t (r^t - g_{mj})^2 b_{mj}(\boldsymbol{x}^t) \tag{9.14}$$

The drop in error for any split is given as the difference between equation 9.10 and equation 9.14. We look for the split such that this drop is maximum or, equivalently, where equation 9.14 takes its minimum. The code given in figure 9.3 can be adapted to training a regression tree by replacing entropy calculations with mean square error and class labels with averages.

Mean square error is one possible error function; another is worst possible error

$$E_m = \max_j \max_t |r^t - g_{mj}| b_{mj}(\boldsymbol{x}^t) \tag{9.15}$$

and using this, we can guarantee that the error for any instance is never larger than a given threshold.

The acceptable error threshold is the complexity parameter; when it is small, we generate large trees and risk overfitting; when it is large, we underfit and smooth too much (see figures 9.4 and 9.5).

Similar to going from running mean to running line in nonparametric regression, instead of taking an average at a leaf that implements a constant fit, we can also do a linear regression fit over the instances choosing the leaf:

$$g_m(\boldsymbol{x}) = \boldsymbol{w}_m^T \boldsymbol{x} + w_{m0} \tag{9.16}$$

This makes the estimate in a leaf dependent on $\boldsymbol{x}$ and generates smaller trees, but there is the expense of extra computation at a leaf node.

9.3 Pruning

Frequently, a node is not split further if the number of training instances reaching a node is smaller than a certain percentage of the training set—for example, 5 percent—regardless of the impurity or error. The idea is that any decision based on too few instances causes variance and thus generalization error. Stopping tree construction early on before it is full is called *prepruning* the tree.

PREPRUNING

POSTPRUNING

Another possibility to get simpler trees is *postpruning*, which in practice works better than prepruning. We saw before that tree growing is greedy and at each step, we make a decision, namely, generate a decision node, and continue further on, never backtracking and trying out an alternative. The only exception is postpruning where we try to find and prune unnecessary subtrees.

PRUNING SET

In postpruning, we grow the tree full until all leaves are pure and we have no training error. We then find subtrees that cause overfitting and we prune them. From the initial labeled set, we set aside a *pruning set*, unused during training. For each subtree, we replace it with a leaf node

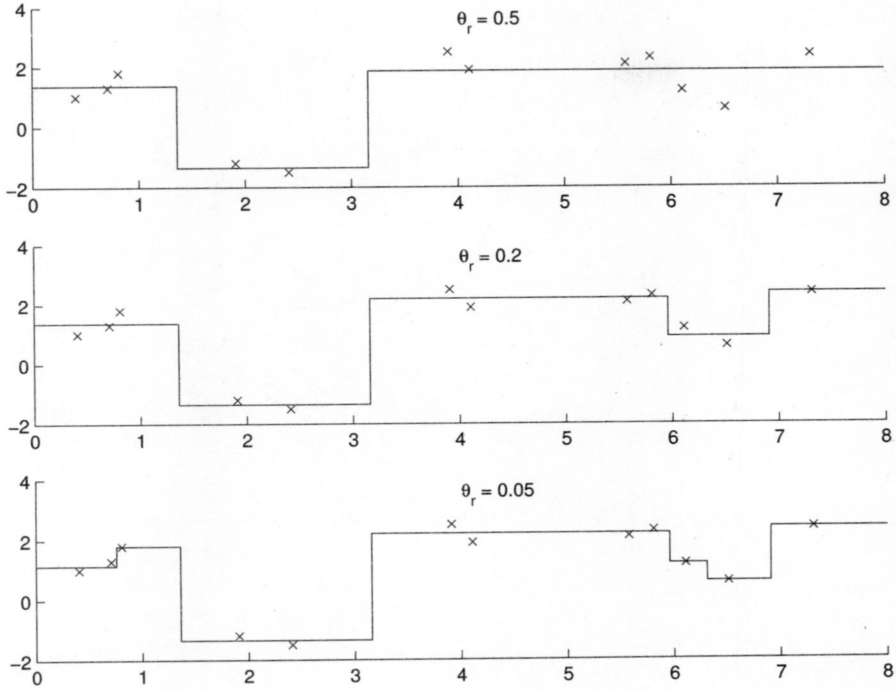

Figure 9.4 Regression tree smooths for various values of θ_r. The corresponding trees are given in figure 9.5.

labeled with the training instances covered by the subtree (appropriately for classification or regression). If the leaf node does not perform worse than the subtree on the pruning set, we prune the subtree and keep the leaf node because the additional complexity of the subtree is not justified; otherwise, we keep the subtree.

For example, in the third tree of figure 9.5, there is a subtree starting with condition $x < 6.31$. This subtree can be replaced by a leaf node of $y = 0.9$ (as in the second tree) if the error on the pruning set does not increase during the substitution. Note that the pruning set should not be confused with (and is distinct from) the validation set.

Comparing prepruning and postpruning, we can say that prepruning is faster but postpruning generally leads to more accurate trees.

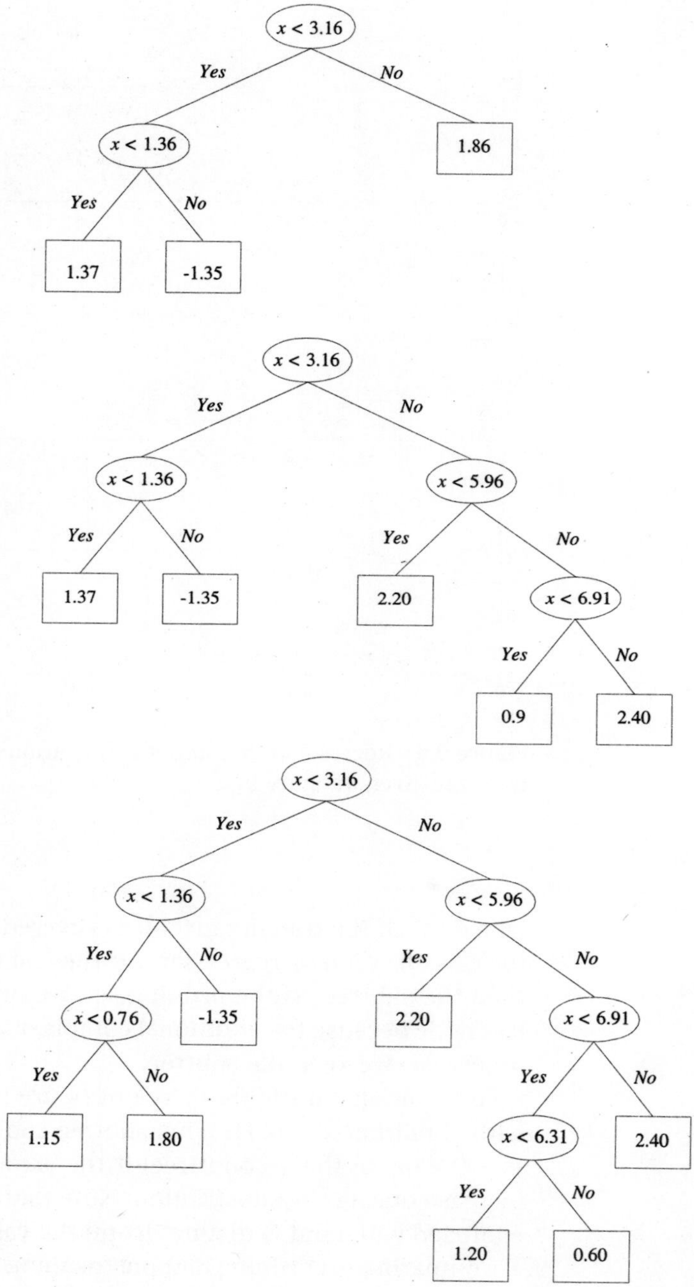

Figure 9.5 Regression trees implementing the smooths of figure 9.4 for various values of θ_r.

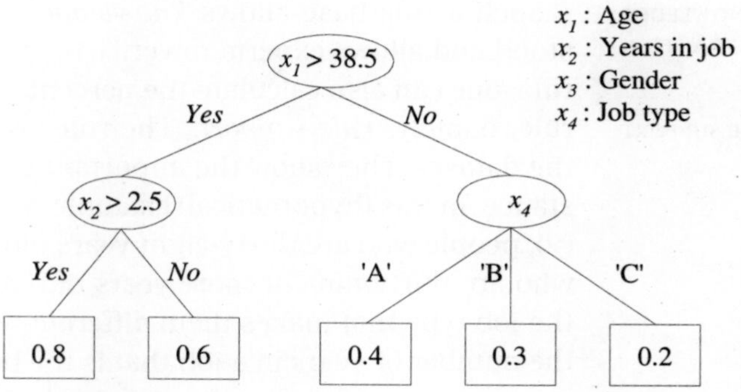

Figure 9.6 Example of a (hypothetical) decision tree. Each path from the root to a leaf can be written down as a conjunctive rule, composed of conditions defined by the decision nodes on the path.

9.4 Rule Extraction from Trees

A decision tree does its own feature extraction. The univariate tree only uses the necessary variables, and after the tree is built, certain features may not be used at all. We can also say that features closer to the root are more important globally. For example, the decision tree given in figure 9.6 uses x_1, x_2, and x_4, but not x_3. It is possible to use a decision tree for feature extraction: we build a tree and then take only those features used by the tree as inputs to another learning method.

INTERPRETABILITY

Another main advantage of decision trees is *interpretability*: The decision nodes carry conditions that are simple to understand. Each path from the root to a leaf corresponds to one conjunction of tests, as all those conditions should be satisfied to reach to the leaf. These paths together can be written down as a set of *IF-THEN rules*, called a *rule base*. One such method is *C4.5Rules* (Quinlan 1993).

IF-THEN RULES

For example, the decision tree of figure 9.6 can be written down as the following set of rules:

R1: IF (age > 38.5) AND (years-in-job > 2.5) THEN $y = 0.8$
R2: IF (age > 38.5) AND (years-in-job ≤ 2.5) THEN $y = 0.6$
R3: IF (age ≤ 38.5) AND (job-type = 'A') THEN $y = 0.4$
R4: IF (age ≤ 38.5) AND (job-type = 'B') THEN $y = 0.3$
R5: IF (age ≤ 38.5) AND (job-type = 'C') THEN $y = 0.2$

KNOWLEDGE EXTRACTION

RULE SUPPORT

Such a rule base allows *knowledge extraction*; it can be easily understood and allows experts to verify the model learned from data. For each rule, one can also calculate the percentage of training data covered by the rule, namely, *rule support*. The rules reflect the main characteristics of the dataset: They show the important features and split positions. For instance, in this (hypothetical) example, we see that in terms of our purpose (y), people who are thirty-eight years old or less are different from people who are thirty-nine or more years old. And among this latter group, it is the job type that makes them different, whereas in the former group, it is the number of years in a job that is the best discriminating characteristic.

In the case of a classification tree, there may be more than one leaf labeled with the same class. In such a case, these multiple conjunctive expressions corresponding to different paths can be combined as a disjunction (OR). The class region then corresponds to a union of these multiple patches, each patch corresponding to the region defined by one leaf. For example, class C_1 of figure 9.1 is written as

IF $(x \leq w_{10})$ OR $((x_1 > w_{10})$ AND $(x_2 \leq w_{20}))$ THEN C_1

PRUNING RULES

Pruning rules is possible for simplification. Pruning a subtree corresponds to pruning terms from a number of rules at the same time. It may be possible to prune a term from one rule without touching other rules. For example, in the previous rule set, for R3, if we see that all whose `job-type='A'` have outcomes close to 0.4, regardless of `age`, $R3$ can be pruned as

$R3'$: IF (job-type='A') THEN y =0.4

Note that after the rules are pruned, it may not be possible to write them back as a tree anymore.

9.5 Learning Rules from Data

RULE INDUCTION

As we have just seen, one way to get IF-THEN rules is to train a decision tree and convert it to rules. Another is to learn the rules directly. *Rule induction* works similar to tree induction except that rule induction does a depth-first search and generates one path (rule) at a time, whereas tree induction goes breadth-first and generates all paths simultaneously.

Rules are learned one at a time. Each rule is a conjunction of conditions on discrete or numeric attributes (as in decision trees) and these conditions are added one at a time, to optimize some criterion, for example, minimize entropy. A rule is said to *cover* an example if the example satisfies all the conditions of the rule. Once a rule is grown and pruned, it is added to the rule base and all the training examples covered by the rule are removed from the training set, and the process continues until enough rules are added. This is called *sequential covering*. There is an outer loop of adding one rule at a time to the rule base and an inner loop of adding one condition at a time to the current rule. These steps are both greedy and do not guarantee optimality. Both loops have a pruning step for better generalization.

SEQUENTIAL COVERING

RIPPER IREP

One example of a rule induction algorithm is *Ripper* (Cohen 1995), based on an earlier algorithm *Irep* (Fürnkranz and Widmer 1994). We start with the case of two classes where we talk of positive and negative examples, then later generalize to $K > 2$ classes. Rules are added to explain positive examples such that if an instance is not covered by any rule, then it is classified as negative. So a rule when it matches is either correct (true positive), or it causes a false positive. The pseudocode of the outer loop of Ripper is given in figure 9.7.

FOIL

In Ripper, conditions are added to the rule to maximize an information gain measure used in Quinlan's (1990) *Foil* algorithm. Let us say we have rule R and R' is the candidate rule after adding a condition. Change in gain is defined as

$$Gain(R', R) = s \cdot \left(\log_2 \frac{N'_+}{N'} - \log_2 \frac{N_+}{N}\right) \tag{9.17}$$

where N is the number of instances that are covered by R and N_+ is the number of true positives in them. N' and N'_+ are similarly defined for R'. s is the number of true positives in R, which are still true positives in R', after adding the condition. In terms of information theory, the change in gain measures the reduction in bits to encode a positive instance.

RULE VALUE METRIC

Conditions are added to a rule until it covers no negative example. Once a rule is grown, it is pruned back by deleting conditions in reverse order, to find the rule that maximizes the *rule value metric*

$$rvm(R) = \frac{p - n}{p + n} \tag{9.18}$$

where p and n are the number of true and false positives, respectively, on the pruning set, which is one-third of the data, having used two-thirds as the growing set.

```
Ripper(Pos,Neg,k)
    RuleSet ← LearnRuleSet(Pos,Neg)
    For k times
        RuleSet ← OptimizeRuleSet(RuleSet,Pos,Neg)
LearnRuleSet(Pos,Neg)
    RuleSet ← ∅
    DL ← DescLen(RuleSet,Pos,Neg)
    Repeat
        Rule ← LearnRule(Pos,Neg)
        Add Rule to RuleSet
        DL' ← DescLen(RuleSet,Pos,Neg)
        If DL'>DL+64
          PruneRuleSet(RuleSet,Pos,Neg)
          Return RuleSet
        If DL'<DL DL ← DL'
          Delete instances covered by Rule from Pos and Neg
    Until Pos = ∅
    Return RuleSet
PruneRuleSet(RuleSet,Pos,Neg)
    For each Rule ∈ RuleSet in reverse order
        DL ← DescLen(RuleSet,Pos,Neg)
        DL' ← DescLen(RuleSet-Rule,Pos,Neg)
        IF DL'<DL Delete Rule from RuleSet
    Return RuleSet
OptimizeRuleSet(RuleSet,Pos,Neg)
    For each Rule ∈ RuleSet
        DL0 ← DescLen(RuleSet,Pos,Neg)
        DL1 ← DescLen(RuleSet-Rule+
                ReplaceRule(RuleSet,Pos,Neg),Pos,Neg)
        DL2 ← DescLen(RuleSet-Rule+
                ReviseRule(RuleSet,Rule,Pos,Neg),Pos,Neg)
        If DL1=min(DL0,DL1,DL2)
                Delete Rule from RuleSet and
                        add ReplaceRule(RuleSet,Pos,Neg)
        Else If DL2=min(DL0,DL1,DL2)
                Delete Rule from RuleSet and
                        add ReviseRule(RuleSet,Rule,Pos,Neg)
    Return RuleSet
```

Figure 9.7 Ripper algorithm for learning rules. Only the outer loop is given; the inner loop is similar to adding nodes in a decision tree.

Once a rule is grown and pruned, all positive and negative training examples covered by the rule are removed from the training set. If there are remaining positive examples, rule induction continues. In the case of noise, we may stop early, namely, when a rule does not explain enough number of examples. To measure the worth of a rule, minimum description length (section 4.8) is used (Quinlan 1995). Typically, we stop if the description of the rule is not shorter than the description of instances it explains. The description length of a rule base is the sum of the description lengths of all the rules in the rule base, plus the description of instances not covered by the rule base. Ripper stops adding rules when the description length of the rule base is more than 64 bits larger than the best description length so far. Once the rule base is learned, we pass over the rules in reverse order to see if they can be removed without increasing the description length.

Rules in the rule base are also optimized after they are learned. Ripper considers two alternatives to a rule: One, called the replacement rule, starts from an empty rule, is grown, and is then pruned. The second, called the revision rule, starts with the rule as it is, is grown, and is then pruned. These two are compared with the original rule, and the shortest of three is added to the rule base. This optimization of the rule base can be done k times, typically twice.

When there are $K > 2$ classes, they are ordered in terms of their prior probabilities such that C_1 has the lowest prior probability and C_K has the highest. Then a sequence of two-class problems are defined such that, first, instances belonging to C_1 are taken as positive examples and instances of all other classes are taken as negative examples. Then, having learned C_1 and all its instances removed, it learns to separate C_2 from $C_3, \ldots, C_K$. This process is repeated until only C_K remains. The empty default rule is then labeled C_K, so that if an instance is not covered by any rule, it will be assigned to C_K.

For a training set of size N, Ripper's complexity is $\mathcal{O}(N \log^2 N)$ and is an algorithm that can be used on very large training sets (Dietterich 1997). The rules we learn are *propositional rules*. More expressive, *first-order rules* have variables in conditions, called *predicates*. A *predicate* is a function that returns true or false depending on the value of its argument. Predicates therefore allow defining relations between the values of attributes, which cannot be done by propositions (Mitchell 1997):

PROPOSITIONAL RULES

FIRST-ORDER RULES

IF Father(y, x) AND Female(y) THEN Daughter(x, y)

Such rules can be seen as programs in a logic programming language, such as Prolog, and learning them from data is called *inductive logic programming*. One such algorithm is Foil (Quinlan 1990).

INDUCTIVE LOGIC PROGRAMMING

BINDING

Assigning a value to a variable is called *binding*. A rule matches if there is a set of bindings to the variables existing in the training set. Learning first-order rules is similar to learning propositional rules with an outer loop of adding rules, and an inner loop of adding conditions to a rule, with prunings at the end of each loop. The difference is in the inner loop, where at each step we consider one predicate to add (instead of a proposition) and check the increase in the performance of the rule (Mitchell 1997). To calculate the performance of a rule, we consider all possible bindings of the variables, count the number of positive and negative bindings in the training set, and use, for example, equation 9.17. In this first-order case, we have predicates instead of propositions, so they should be previously defined, and the training set is a set of predicates known to be true.

9.6 Multivariate Trees

MULTIVARIATE TREE

In the case of a univariate tree, only one input dimension is used at a split. In a *multivariate tree*, at a decision node, all input dimensions can be used and thus it is more general. When all inputs are numeric, a binary linear multivariate node is defined as

$$f_m(\boldsymbol{x}) : \boldsymbol{w}_m^T \boldsymbol{x} + w_{m0} > 0 \quad (9.19)$$

Because the linear multivariate node takes a weighted sum, discrete attributes should be represented by 0/1 dummy numeric variables. Equation 9.19 defines a hyperplane with arbitrary orientation (see figure 9.8). Successive nodes on a path from the root to a leaf further divide these, and leaf nodes define polyhedra in the input space. The univariate node with a numeric feature is a special case when all but one of w_{mj} are 0. Thus the univariate numeric node of equation 9.1 also defines a linear discriminant but one that is orthogonal to axis x_j, intersecting it at w_{m0} and parallel to all other x_i. We therefore see that in a univariate node there are d possible orientations ($\boldsymbol{w}_m$) and $N_m - 1$ possible thresholds ($-w_{m0}$), making an exhaustive search possible. In a multivariate node, there are $2^d \binom{N_m}{d}$ possible hyperplanes (Murthy, Kasif, and Salzberg 1994) and an exhaustive search is no longer practical.

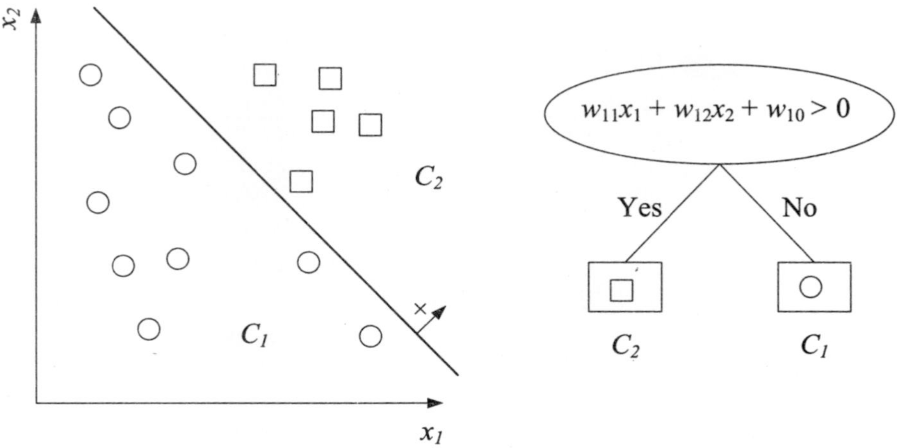

Figure 9.8 Example of a linear multivariate decision tree. The linear multivariate node can place an arbitrary hyperplane and thus is more general, whereas the univariate node is restricted to axis-aligned splits.

When we go from a univariate node to a linear multivariate node, the node becomes more flexible. It is possible to make it even more flexible by using a nonlinear multivariate node. For example, with a quadratic, we have

(9.20) $$f_m(\boldsymbol{x}) : \boldsymbol{x}^T \mathbf{W}_m \boldsymbol{x} + \boldsymbol{w}_m^T \boldsymbol{x} + w_{m0} > 0$$

Guo and Gelfand (1992) propose to use a multilayer perceptron (chapter 11) that is a linear sum of nonlinear basis functions, and this is another way of having nonlinear decision nodes. Another possibility is a

SPHERE NODE *sphere node* (Devroye, Györfi, and Lugosi 1996)

(9.21) $$f_m(\boldsymbol{x}) : \|\boldsymbol{x} - \boldsymbol{c}_m\| \le \alpha_m$$

where $\boldsymbol{c}_m$ is the center and α_m is the radius.

There are a number of algorithms proposed for learning multivariate decision trees for classification: The earliest is the multivariate version of the CART algorithm (Breiman et al. 1984), which fine-tunes the weights w_{mj} one by one to decrease impurity. CART also has a preprocessing stage to decrease dimensionality through subset selection (chapter 6) and reduce the complexity of the node. An algorithm with some extensions

OC1 to CART is the *OC1* algorithm (Murthy, Kasif, and Salzberg 1994). One possibility (Loh and Vanichsetakul 1988) is to assume that all classes are Gaussian with a common covariance matrix, thereby having linear discriminants separating each class from the others (chapter 5). In such a case, with K classes, each node has K branches and each branch carries the discriminant separating one class from the others. Brodley and Utgoff (1995) propose a method where the linear discriminants are trained to minimize classification error (chapter 10). Guo and Gelfand (1992) propose a heuristic to group $K > 2$ classes into two supergroups, and then binary multivariate trees can be learned. Loh and Shih (1997) use 2-means clustering (chapter 7) to group data into two. Yıldız and Alpaydın (2000) use LDA (chapter 6) to find the discriminant once the classes are grouped into two.

Any classifier approximates the real (unknown) discriminant choosing one hypothesis from its hypothesis class. When we use univariate nodes, our approximation uses piecewise, axis-aligned hyperplanes. With linear multivariate nodes, we can use arbitrary hyperplanes and do a better approximation using fewer nodes. If the underlying discriminant is curved, nonlinear nodes work better. The branching factor has a similar effect in that it specifies the number of discriminants that a node defines. A binary decision node with two branches defines one discriminant separating the input space into two. An n-way node separates into n. Thus, there is a dependency among the complexity of a node, the branching factor, and tree size. With simple nodes and low branching factors, one may grow large trees, but such trees, for example, with univariate binary nodes, are more interpretable. Linear multivariate nodes are more difficult to interpret. More complex nodes also require more data and are prone to overfitting as we get down the tree and have less and less data. If the nodes are complex and the tree is small, we also lose the main idea of the tree, which is that of dividing the problem into a set of simple problems. After all, we can have a very complex classifier in the root that separates all classes from each other, but then this will not be a tree!

9.7 Notes

Divide-and-conquer is a frequently used heuristic that has been used since the days of Caesar to break a complex problem, for example, Gaul, into a group of simpler problems. Trees are frequently used in computer science to decrease complexity from linear to log time. Decision trees were made popular in statistics in Breiman et al. 1984 and in machine learning in Quinlan 1986 and Quinlan 1993. Multivariate tree induction methods became popular more recently; a review and comparison on many datasets are given in Yıldız and Alpaydın 2000. Many researchers (e.g., Guo and Gelfand 1992), proposed to combine the simplicity of trees with the accuracy of multilayer perceptrons (chapter 11). Many studies, however, have concluded that the univariate trees are quite accurate and interpretable, and the additional complexity brought by linear (or nonlinear) multivariate nodes is hardly justified. A recent survey is given by Rokach and Maimon (2005).

OMNIVARIATE DECISION TREE

The *omnivariate decision tree* (Yıldız and Alpaydın 2001) is a hybrid tree architecture where the tree may have univariate, linear multivariate, or nonlinear multivariate nodes. The idea is that during construction, at each decision node, which corresponds to a different subproblem defined by the subset of the training data reaching that node, a different model may be appropriate and the appropriate one should be found and used. Using the same type of nodes everywhere corresponds to assuming that the same inductive bias is good in all parts of the input space. In an omnivariate tree, at each node, candidate nodes of different types are trained and compared using a statistical test (chapter 19) on a validation set to determine which one generalizes the best. The simpler one is chosen unless a more complex one is shown to have significantly higher accuracy. Results show that more complex nodes are used early in the tree, closer to the root, and as we go down the tree, simple univariate nodes suffice. As we get closer to the leaves, we have simpler problems and, at the same time, we have less data. In such a case, complex nodes overfit and are rejected by the statistical test. The number of nodes increases exponentially as we go down the tree; therefore, a large majority of the nodes are univariate and the overall complexity does not increase much.

Decision trees are used more frequently for classification than for regression. They are very popular: They learn and respond quickly, and are accurate in many domains (Murthy 1998). It is even the case that a decision tree is preferred over more accurate methods, because it is interpretable. When written down as a set of IF-THEN rules, the tree can be understood and the rules can be validated by human experts who have knowledge of the application domain.

It is generally recommended that a decision tree be tested and its accuracy be taken as a benchmark before more complicated algorithms are employed. Analysis of the tree also allows an understanding of the important features, and the univariate tree does its own automatic feature extraction. Another big advantage of the univariate tree is that it can use numeric and discrete features together, without needing to convert one type into the other.

The decision tree is a nonparametric method, similar to the instance-based methods discussed in chapter 8, but there are a number of differences:

- Each leaf node corresponds to a "bin," except that the bins need not be the same size (as in Parzen windows) or contain an equal number of training instances (as in k-nearest neighbor).
- The bin divisions are not done based only on similarity in the input space, but supervised output information through entropy or mean square error is also used.
- Another advantage of the decision tree is that, thanks to the tree structure, the leaf ("bin") is found much faster with smaller number of comparisons.
- The decision tree, once it is constructed, does not store all the training set but only the structure of the tree, the parameters of the decision nodes, and the output values in leaves; this implies that the space complexity is also much less, as opposed to instance-based nonparametric methods that store all training examples.

With a decision tree, a class need not have a single description to which all instances should match. It may have a number of possible descriptions that can even be disjoint in the input space.

The decision tree we discussed until now have *hard* decision nodes; that is, we take one of the branches depending on the test. We start from the root and follow a single path and stop at a leaf where we output the response value stored in that leaf. In a *soft decision tree*, however, we take *all* the branches but with different probabilities, and we follow in parallel all the paths and reach all the leaves, but with different probabilities. The output is the weighted average of all the outputs in all the leaves where the weights correspond to the probabilities accumulated over the paths; we will discuss this in section 12.9.

SOFT DECISION TREE

In chapter 17, we talk about combining multiple learners; one of the most popular models combined is a decision tree, and an ensemble of decision trees is called a *decision forest*. We will see that if we train not

DECISION FOREST

one but many decision trees, each on a random subset of training set or a random subset of the input features, and combine their predictions, overall accuracy can be significantly increased. This is the idea behind the *random forest* method.

RANDOM FOREST

The tree is different from the statistical models discussed in previous chapters. The tree codes directly the discriminants separating class instances without caring much for how those instances are distributed in the regions. The decision tree is *discriminant-based*, whereas the statistical methods are *likelihood-based* in that they explicitly estimate $p(\mathbf{x}|C_i)$ before using Bayes' rule and calculating the discriminant. Discriminant-based methods directly estimate the discriminants, bypassing the estimation of class densities. We further discuss such discriminant-based methods in the chapters ahead.

9.8 Exercises

1. Generalize the Gini index (equation 9.5) and the misclassification error (equation 9.6) for $K > 2$ classes. Generalize misclassification error to risk, taking a loss function into account.

   SOLUTION:

   - Gini index with $K > 2$ classes: $\phi(p_1, p_2, \ldots, p_K) = \sum_{i=1}^{K} \sum_{j<i} p_i p_j$
   - Misclassification error: $\phi(p_1, p_2, \ldots, p_K) = 1 - \max_{i=1}^{K} p_i$
   - Risk: $\phi_\Lambda(p_1, p_2, \ldots, p_K) = \min_{i=1}^{K} \sum_{k=1}^{K} \lambda_{ik} p_k$ where Λ is the $K \times K$ loss matrix.

2. For a numeric input, instead of a binary split, one can use a ternary split with two thresholds and three branches as

   $$x_j < w_{ma},\ w_{ma} \le x_j < w_{mb},\ x_j \ge w_{mb}$$

   Propose a modification of the tree induction method to learn the two thresholds, w_{ma}, w_{mb}. What are the advantages and the disadvantages of such a node over a binary node?

   SOLUTION: For the numeric attributes, instead of one split threshold, we need to try all possible pairs of split thresholds and choose the best. When there are two splits, there are three children, and in calculating the entropy after the splits, we need to sum up over the three sets corresponding to the instances taking the three branches.

   The complexity of finding the best pair is $\mathcal{O}(N_m^2)$ instead of $\mathcal{O}(N_m)$ and each node stores two thresholds instead of one and has three branches instead of two. The advantage is that one ternary node splits an input into three, whereas this requires two successive binary nodes. Which one is better depends on the data at hand; if we have hypotheses that require bounded intervals (e.g., rectangles), a ternary node may be advantageous.

3. Propose a tree induction algorithm with backtracking.

4. In generating a univariate tree, a discrete attribute with n possible values can be represented by n 0/1 dummy variables and then treated as n separate numeric attributes. What are the advantages and disadvantages of this approach?

5. Derive a learning algorithm for sphere trees (equation 9.21). Generalize to ellipsoid trees.

6. In a regression tree, we discussed that in a leaf node, instead of calculating the mean, we can do a linear regression fit and make the response at the leaf dependent on the input. Propose a similar method for classification trees.

   SOLUTION: This implies that at each leaf, we will have a linear classifier trained with instances reaching there. That linear classifier will generate posterior probabilities for the different classes, and those probabilities will be used in the entropy calculation. That is, it is not necessary for a leaf to be pure, that is, to contain instances of only one class; it is enough that the classifier in that leaf generates posterior probabilities close to 0 or 1.

7. Propose a rule induction algorithm for regression.

8. In regression trees, how can we get rid of discontinuities at the leaf boundaries?

9. Let us say that for a classification problem, we already have a trained decision tree. How can we use it in addition to the training set in constructing a k-nearest neighbor classifier?

   SOLUTION: The decision tree does feature selection, and we can use only the features used by the tree. The average number of instances per leaf also gives us information about a good k value.

10. In a multivariate tree, very probably, at each internal node, we will not be needing all the input variables. How can we decrease dimensionality at a node?

    SOLUTION: Each subtree handles a local region in the input space that can be explained by a small number of features. We can do feature selection or extraction using only the subset of the instances reaching that node. Ideally, as we go down the tree, we would expect to need fewer features.

9.9 References

Breiman, L., J. H. Friedman, R. A. Olshen, and C. J. Stone. 1984. *Classification and Regression Trees.* Belmont, CA: Wadsworth International Group.

Brodley, C. E., and P. E. Utgoff. 1995. "Multivariate Decision Trees." *Machine Learning* 19:45–77.

Cohen, W. 1995. "Fast Effective Rule Induction." In *Twelfth International Conference on Machine Learning,* ed. A. Prieditis and S. J. Russell, 115–123. San Mateo, CA: Morgan Kaufmann.

Devroye, L., L. Györfi, and G. Lugosi. 1996. *A Probabilistic Theory of Pattern Recognition.* New York: Springer.

Dietterich, T. G. 1997. "Machine Learning Research: Four Current Directions." *AI Magazine* 18:97–136.

Fürnkranz, J., and G. Widmer. 1994. "Incremental Reduced Error Pruning." In *Eleventh International Conference on Machine Learning,* ed. W. Cohen and H. Hirsh, 70–77. San Mateo, CA: Morgan Kaufmann.

Guo, H., and S. B. Gelfand. 1992. "Classification Trees with Neural Network Feature Extraction." *IEEE Transactions on Neural Networks* 3:923–933.

Loh, W.-Y., and Y. S. Shih. 1997. "Split Selection Methods for Classification Trees." *Statistica Sinica* 7:815–840.

Loh, W.-Y., and N. Vanichsetakul. 1988. "Tree-Structured Classification via Generalized Discriminant Analysis." *Journal of the American Statistical Association* 83:715–725.

Mitchell, T. 1997. *Machine Learning.* New York: McGraw-Hill.

Murthy, S. K. 1998. "Automatic Construction of Decision Trees from Data: A Multi-Disciplinary Survey." *Data Mining and Knowledge Discovery* 4:345–389.

Murthy, S. K., S. Kasif, and S. Salzberg. 1994. "A System for Induction of Oblique Decision Trees." *Journal of Artificial Intelligence Research* 2:1–32.

Quinlan, J. R. 1986. "Induction of Decision Trees." *Machine Learning* 1:81–106.

Quinlan, J. R. 1990. "Learning Logical Definitions from Relations." *Machine Learning* 5:239–266.

Quinlan, J. R. 1993. *C4.5: Programs for Machine Learning.* San Mateo, CA: Morgan Kaufmann.

Quinlan, J. R. 1995. "MDL and Categorical Theories (continued)." In *Twelfth International Conference on Machine Learning,* ed. A. Prieditis and S. J. Russell, 467–470. San Mateo, CA: Morgan Kaufmann.

Rokach, L., and O. Maimon. 2005. “Top-Down Induction of Decision Trees Classifiers—A Survey.” *IEEE Transactions on Systems, Man, and Cybernetics–Part C* 35:476–487.

Yıldız, O. T., and E. Alpaydın. 2000. “Linear Discriminant Trees.” In *Seventeenth International Conference on Machine Learning*, ed. P. Langley, 1175–1182. San Francisco: Morgan Kaufmann.

Yıldız, O. T., and E. Alpaydın. 2001. “Omnivariate Decision Trees.” *IEEE Transactions on Neural Networks* 12:1539–1546.

10 Linear Discrimination

In linear discrimination, we assume that instances of a class are linearly separable from instances of other classes. This is a discriminant-based approach that estimates the parameters of the linear discriminant directly from a given labeled sample.

10.1 Introduction

WE REMEMBER from the previous chapters that in classification we define a set of discriminant functions $g_j(\mathbf{x}), j = 1, \ldots, K$, and then we

$$\text{choose } C_i \text{ if } g_i(\mathbf{x}) = \max_{j=1}^{K} g_j(\mathbf{x})$$

Previously, when we discussed methods for classification, we first estimated the prior probabilities, $\hat{P}(C_i)$, and the class likelihoods, $\hat{p}(\mathbf{x}|C_i)$, then used Bayes' rule to calculate the posterior densities. We then defined the discriminant functions in terms of the posterior, for example,

$$g_i(\mathbf{x}) = \log \hat{P}(C_i|\mathbf{x})$$

LIKELIHOOD-BASED CLASSIFICATION

This is called *likelihood-based classification*, and we have previously discussed the parametric (chapter 5), semiparametric (chapter 7), and nonparametric (chapter 8) approaches to estimating the class likelihoods, $p(\mathbf{x}|C_i)$.

DISCRIMINANT-BASED CLASSIFICATION

We are now going to discuss *discriminant-based classification* where we assume a model directly for the discriminant, bypassing the estimation of likelihoods or posteriors. The discriminant-based approach, as we also saw for the case of decision trees in chapter 9, makes an assumption on the form of the discriminant between the classes and makes no assumption about, or requires no knowledge of the densities—for example, whether they are Gaussian, or whether the inputs are correlated, and so forth.

We define a model for the discriminant

$$g_i(\boldsymbol{x}|\Phi_i)$$

explicitly parameterized with the set of parameters Φ_i, as opposed to a likelihood-based scheme that has implicit parameters in defining the likelihood densities. This is a different inductive bias: Instead of making an assumption on the form of the class densities, we make an assumption on the form of the boundaries separating classes.

Learning is the optimization of the model parameters $\boldsymbol{\Phi}_i$ to maximize the quality of the separation, that is, the classification accuracy on a given labeled training set. This differs from the likelihood-based methods that search for the parameters that maximize sample likelihoods, separately for each class.

In the discriminant-based approach, we do not care about correctly estimating the densities inside class regions; all we care about is the correct estimation of the *boundaries* between the class regions. Those who advocate the discriminant-based approach (e.g., Vapnik 1995) state that estimating the class densities is a harder problem than estimating the class discriminants, and it does not make sense to solve a hard problem to solve an easier problem. This is of course true only when the discriminant can be approximated by a simple function.

In this chapter, we concern ourselves with the simplest case where the discriminant functions are linear in $\boldsymbol{x}$:

$$g_i(\boldsymbol{x}|\boldsymbol{w}_i, w_{i0}) = \boldsymbol{w}_i^T\boldsymbol{x} + w_{i0} = \sum_{j=1}^{d} w_{ij}x_j + w_{i0} \tag{10.1}$$

LINEAR DISCRIMINANT

The *linear discriminant* is used frequently mainly due to its simplicity: Both the space and time complexities are $\mathcal{O}(d)$. The linear model is easy to understand: the final output is a weighted sum of the input attributes x_j. The magnitude of the weight w_j shows the importance of x_j and its sign indicates if the effect is positive or negative. Most functions are additive in that the output is the sum of the effects of several attributes where the weights may be positive (enforcing) or negative (inhibiting). For example, when a customer applies for credit, financial institutions calculate the applicant's credit score that is generally written as a sum of the effects of various attributes; for example, yearly income has a positive effect (higher incomes increase the score).

In many applications, the linear discriminant is also quite accurate. We know, for example, that when classes are Gaussian with a shared covariance matrix, the optimal discriminant is linear. The linear discriminant, however, can be used even when this assumption does not hold, and the model parameters can be calculated without making any assumptions on the class densities. We should always use the linear discriminant before trying a more complicated model to make sure that the additional complexity is justified.

As always, we formulate the problem of finding a linear discriminant function as a search for the parameter values that minimize an error function. In particular, we concentrate on *gradient* methods for optimizing a criterion function.

10.2 Generalizing the Linear Model

QUADRATIC DISCRIMINANT

When a linear model is not flexible enough, we can use the *quadratic discriminant* function and increase complexity

$$g_i(\boldsymbol{x}|\mathbf{W}_i, \boldsymbol{w}_i, w_{i0}) = \boldsymbol{x}^T\mathbf{W}_i\boldsymbol{x} + \boldsymbol{w}_i\boldsymbol{x} + w_{i0} \tag{10.2}$$

but this approach is $O(d^2)$ and we again have the bias/variance dilemma: The quadratic model, though is more general, requires much larger training sets and may overfit on small samples.

HIGHER-ORDER TERMS

PRODUCT TERMS

An equivalent way is to preprocess the input by adding *higher-order terms*, also called *product terms*. For example, with two inputs x_1 and x_2, we can define new variables

$$z_1 = x_1, z_2 = x_2, z_3 = x_1^2, z_4 = x_2^2, z_5 = x_1x_2$$

and take $\boldsymbol{z} = [z_1, z_2, z_3, z_4, z_5]^T$ as the input. The linear function defined in the five-dimensional $\boldsymbol{z}$ space corresponds to a nonlinear function in the two-dimensional $\boldsymbol{x}$ space. Instead of defining a nonlinear function (discriminant or regression) in the original space, what we do is to define a suitable nonlinear transformation to a new space where the function can be written in a linear form.

We write the discriminant as

$$g_i(\boldsymbol{x}) = \sum_{j=1}^{k} w_j\phi_{ij}(\boldsymbol{x}) \tag{10.3}$$

BASIS FUNCTION

where $\phi_{ij}(\boldsymbol{x})$ are *basis functions*. Higher-order terms are only one set of possible basis functions; other examples are

- $\sin(x_1)$
- $\exp(-(x_1 - m)^2/c)$
- $\exp(-\|\boldsymbol{x} - \boldsymbol{m}\|^2/c)$
- $\log(x_2)$
- $1(x_1 > c)$
- $1(ax_1 + bx_2 > c)$

where m, a, b, c are scalars, $\boldsymbol{m}$ is a d-dimensional vector, and $1(b)$ returns 1 if b is true and returns 0 otherwise. The idea of writing a nonlinear function as a linear sum of nonlinear basis functions is an old idea and was originally called *potential functions* (Aizerman, Braverman, and Rozonoer 1964). Multilayer perceptrons (chapter 11) and radial basis functions (chapter 12) have the advantage that the parameters of the basis functions can be fine-tuned to the data during learning. In chapter 13, we discuss support vector machines that use kernel functions built from such basis functions.

POTENTIAL FUNCTION

10.3 Geometry of the Linear Discriminant

10.3.1 Two Classes

Let us start with the simpler case of two classes. In such a case, one discriminant function is sufficient:

$$
\begin{aligned}
g(\boldsymbol{x}) &= g_1(\boldsymbol{x}) - g_2(\boldsymbol{x}) \\
&= (\boldsymbol{w}_1^T\boldsymbol{x} + w_{10}) - (\boldsymbol{w}_2^T\boldsymbol{x} + w_{20}) \\
&= (\boldsymbol{w}_1 - \boldsymbol{w}_2)^T\boldsymbol{x} + (w_{10} - w_{20}) \\
&= \boldsymbol{w}^T\boldsymbol{x} + w_0
\end{aligned}
$$

and we

$$
\text{choose} \begin{cases} C_1 & \text{if } g(\boldsymbol{x}) > 0 \\ C_2 & \text{otherwise} \end{cases}
$$

WEIGHT VECTOR
THRESHOLD

This defines a hyperplane where $\boldsymbol{w}$ is the *weight vector* and w_0 is the *threshold*. This latter name comes from the fact that the decision rule can be rewritten as follows: Choose C_1 if $\boldsymbol{w}^T\boldsymbol{x} > -w_0$, and choose C_2

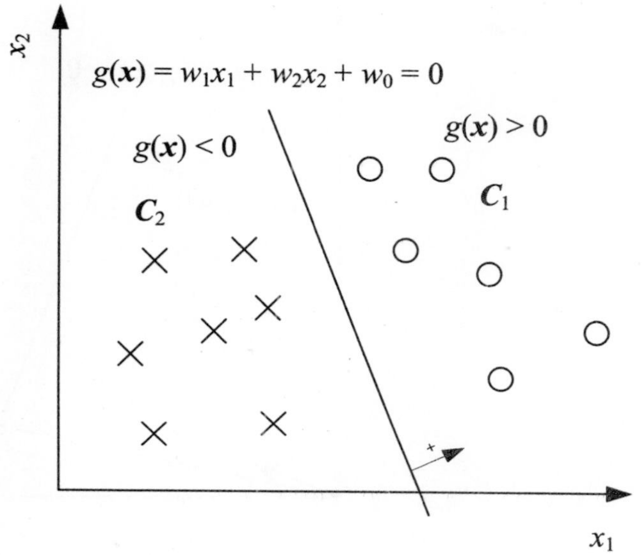

Figure 10.1 In the two-dimensional case, the linear discriminant is a line that separates the examples from two classes.

otherwise. The hyperplane divides the input space into two half-spaces: the decision region $\mathcal{R}_1$ for C_1 and $\mathcal{R}_2$ for C_2. Any $\boldsymbol{x}$ in $\mathcal{R}_1$ is on the *positive* side of the hyperplane and any $\boldsymbol{x}$ in $\mathcal{R}_2$ is on its *negative* side. When $\boldsymbol{x}$ is $\boldsymbol{0}$, $g(\boldsymbol{x}) = w_0$ and we see that if $w_0 > 0$, the origin is on the positive side of the hyperplane, and if $w_0 < 0$, the origin is on the negative side, and if $w_0 = 0$, the hyperplane passes through the origin (see figure 10.1).

Take two points $\boldsymbol{x}_1$ and $\boldsymbol{x}_2$ both on the decision surface; that is, $g(\boldsymbol{x}_1) = g(\boldsymbol{x}_2) = 0$, then

$$\begin{aligned}\boldsymbol{w}^T\boldsymbol{x}_1 + w_0 &= \boldsymbol{w}^T\boldsymbol{x}_2 + w_0 \\ \boldsymbol{w}^T(\boldsymbol{x}_1 - \boldsymbol{x}_2) &= 0\end{aligned}$$

and we see that $\boldsymbol{w}$ is normal to any vector lying on the hyperplane. Let us rewrite $\boldsymbol{x}$ as (Duda, Hart, and Stork 2001)

$$\boldsymbol{x} = \boldsymbol{x}_p + r\frac{\boldsymbol{w}}{\|\boldsymbol{w}\|}$$

where $\boldsymbol{x}_p$ is the normal projection of $\boldsymbol{x}$ onto the hyperplane and r gives us the distance from $\boldsymbol{x}$ to the hyperplane, negative if $\boldsymbol{x}$ is on the negative

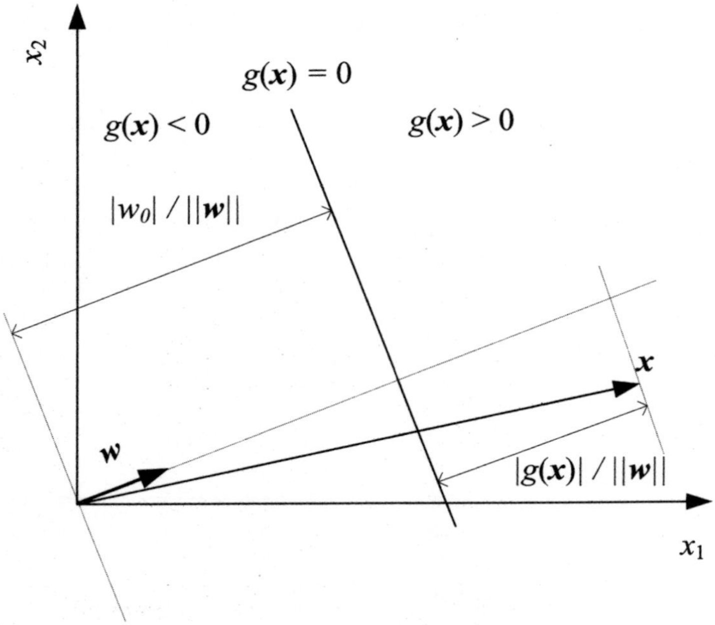

Figure 10.2 The geometric interpretation of the linear discriminant.

side, and positive if $\boldsymbol{x}$ is on the positive side (see figure 10.2). Calculating $g(\boldsymbol{x})$ and noting that $g(\boldsymbol{x}_p) = 0$, we have

(10.4) $$r = \frac{g(\boldsymbol{x})}{\|\boldsymbol{w}\|}$$

We see then that the distance to origin is

(10.5) $$r_0 = \frac{w_0}{\|\boldsymbol{w}\|}$$

Thus w_0 determines the location of the hyperplane with respect to the origin, and $\boldsymbol{w}$ determines its orientation.

10.3.2 Multiple Classes

When there are $K > 2$ classes, there are K discriminant functions. When they are linear, we have

(10.6) $$g_i(\boldsymbol{x}|\boldsymbol{w}_i, w_{i0}) = \boldsymbol{w}_i^T\boldsymbol{x} + w_{i0}$$

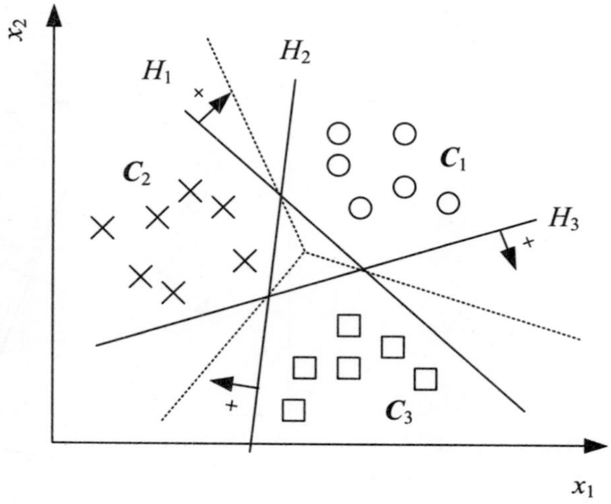

Figure 10.3 In linear classification, each hyperplane H_i separates the examples of C_i from the examples of all other classes. Thus for it to work, the classes should be linearly separable. Dotted lines are the induced boundaries of the linear classifier.

We are going to talk about learning later on but for now, we assume that the parameters, $\boldsymbol{w}_i, w_{i0}$, are computed so as to have

(10.7) $$g_i(\boldsymbol{x}|\boldsymbol{w}_i, w_{i0}) = \begin{cases} > 0 & \text{if } \boldsymbol{x} \in C_i \\ \leq 0 & \text{otherwise} \end{cases}$$

LINEARLY SEPARABLE CLASSES

for all $\boldsymbol{x}$ in the training set. Using such discriminant functions corresponds to assuming that all classes are *linearly separable*; that is, for each class C_i, there exists a hyperplane H_i such that all $\boldsymbol{x} \in C_i$ lie on its positive side and all $\boldsymbol{x} \in C_j, j \neq i$ lie on its negative side (see figure 10.3).

During testing, given $\boldsymbol{x}$, ideally, we should have only one $g_j(\boldsymbol{x}), j = 1, \ldots, K$ greater than 0 and all others should be less than 0, but this is not always the case: The positive half-spaces of the hyperplanes may overlap, or, we may have a case where all $g_j(\boldsymbol{x}) < 0$. These may be taken as *reject* cases, but the usual approach is to assign $\boldsymbol{x}$ to the class having the highest discriminant:

(10.8) Choose C_i if $g_i(\boldsymbol{x}) = \max_{j=1}^{K} g_j(\boldsymbol{x})$

Remembering that $|g_i(\boldsymbol{x})|/\|\boldsymbol{w}_i\|$ is the distance from the input point to the hyperplane, assuming that all $\boldsymbol{w}_i$ have similar length, this assigns the

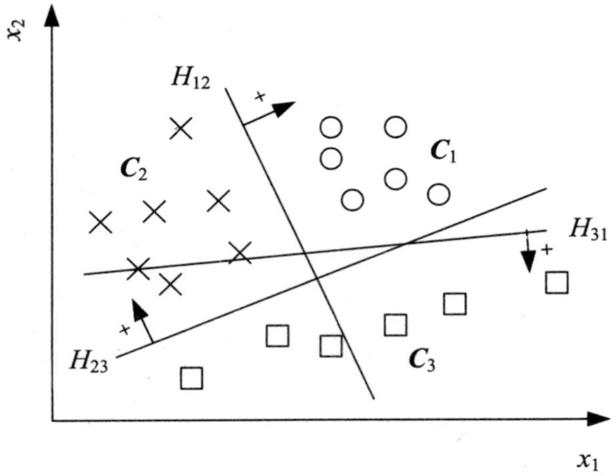

Figure 10.4 In pairwise linear separation, there is a separate hyperplane for each pair of classes. For an input to be assigned to C_1, it should be on the positive side of H_{12} and H_{13} (which is the negative side of H_{31}); we do not care about the value of H_{23}. In this case, C_1 is not linearly separable from other classes but is pairwise linearly separable.

point to the class (among all $g_j(\mathbf{x}) > 0$) to whose hyperplane the point is most distant. This is called a *linear classifier*, and geometrically it divides the feature space into K convex decision regions $\mathcal{R}_i$ (see figure 10.3).

LINEAR CLASSIFIER

10.4 Pairwise Separation

PAIRWISE SEPARATION

If the classes are not linearly separable, one approach is to divide it into a set of linear problems. One possibility is *pairwise separation* of classes (Duda, Hart, and Stork 2001). It uses $K(K-1)/2$ linear discriminants, $g_{ij}(\mathbf{x})$, one for every pair of distinct classes (see figure 10.4):

$$g_{ij}(\mathbf{x}|\mathbf{w}_{ij}, w_{ij0}) = \mathbf{w}_{ij}^T\mathbf{x} + w_{ij0}$$

The parameters $\mathbf{w}_{ij}, j \neq i$ are computed during training so as to have

$$(10.9) \quad g_{ij}(\mathbf{x}) = \begin{cases} > 0 & \text{if } \mathbf{x} \in C_i \\ \leq 0 & \text{if } \mathbf{x} \in C_j \quad i,j = 1,\ldots,K \text{ and } i \neq j \\ \text{don't care} & \text{otherwise} \end{cases}$$

that is, if $\boldsymbol{x}^t \in C_k$ where $k \neq i, k \neq j$, then $\boldsymbol{x}^t$ is not used during training of $g_{ij}(\boldsymbol{x})$.

During testing, we

$$\text{choose } C_i \text{ if } \forall j \neq i, g_{ij}(\boldsymbol{x}) > 0$$

In many cases, this may not be true for any i and if we do not want to reject such cases, we can relax the conjunction by using a summation and choosing the maximum of

$$g_i(\boldsymbol{x}) = \sum_{j \neq i} g_{ij}(\boldsymbol{x}) \tag{10.10}$$

Even if the classes are not linearly separable, if the classes are pairwise linearly separable—which is much more likely—pairwise separation can be used, leading to nonlinear separation of classes (see figure 10.4). This is another example of breaking down a complex (e.g., nonlinear) problem, into a set of simpler (e.g., linear) problems. We have already seen decision trees (chapter 9) that use this idea, and we will see more examples of this in chapter 17 on combining multiple models, for example, error-correcting output codes, and mixture of experts, where the number of linear models is less than $\mathcal{O}(K^2)$.

10.5 Parametric Discrimination Revisited

In chapter 5, we saw that if the class densities, $p(\boldsymbol{x}|C_i)$, are Gaussian and share a common covariance matrix, the discriminant function is linear

$$g_i(\boldsymbol{x}) = \boldsymbol{w}_i^T \boldsymbol{x} + w_{i0} \tag{10.11}$$

where the parameters can be analytically calculated as

$$\begin{aligned} \boldsymbol{w}_i &= \boldsymbol{\Sigma}^{-1}\boldsymbol{\mu}_i \\ w_{i0} &= -\frac{1}{2}\boldsymbol{\mu}_i^T \boldsymbol{\Sigma}^{-1}\boldsymbol{\mu}_i + \log P(C_i) \end{aligned} \tag{10.12}$$

Given a dataset, we first calculate the estimates for $\boldsymbol{\mu}_i$ and $\boldsymbol{\Sigma}$ and then plug the estimates, $\boldsymbol{m}_i$, $\mathbf{S}$, in equation 10.12 and calculate the parameters of the linear discriminant.

Let us again see the special case where there are two classes. We define $y \equiv P(C_1|\boldsymbol{x})$ and $P(C_2|\boldsymbol{x}) = 1 - y$. Then in classification, we

$$\text{choose } C_1 \text{ if } \begin{cases} y > 0.5 \\ \frac{y}{1-y} > 1 \\ \log \frac{y}{1-y} > 0 \end{cases} \quad \text{and } C_2 \text{ otherwise}$$

LOGIT
LOG ODDS

$\log y/(1-y)$ is known as the *logit* transformation or *log odds* of y. In the case of two normal classes sharing a common covariance matrix, the log odds is linear:

$$\begin{aligned} \text{logit}(P(C_1|\boldsymbol{x})) = \log \frac{P(C_1|\boldsymbol{x})}{1-P(C_1|\boldsymbol{x})} &= \log \frac{P(C_1|\boldsymbol{x})}{P(C_2|\boldsymbol{x})} \\ &= \log \frac{p(\boldsymbol{x}|C_1)}{p(\boldsymbol{x}|C_2)} + \log \frac{P(C_1)}{P(C_2)} \\ &= \log \frac{(2\pi)^{-d/2}|\boldsymbol{\Sigma}|^{-1/2}\exp[-(1/2)(\boldsymbol{x}-\boldsymbol{\mu}_1)^T\boldsymbol{\Sigma}^{-1}(\boldsymbol{x}-\boldsymbol{\mu}_1)]}{(2\pi)^{-d/2}|\boldsymbol{\Sigma}|^{-1/2}\exp[-(1/2)(\boldsymbol{x}-\boldsymbol{\mu}_2)^T\boldsymbol{\Sigma}^{-1}(\boldsymbol{x}-\boldsymbol{\mu}_2)]} + \log \frac{P(C_1)}{P(C_2)} \\ &= \boldsymbol{w}^T\boldsymbol{x} + w_0 \end{aligned} \tag{10.13}$$

where

$$\begin{aligned} \boldsymbol{w} &= \boldsymbol{\Sigma}^{-1}(\boldsymbol{\mu}_1 - \boldsymbol{\mu}_2) \\ w_0 &= -\frac{1}{2}(\boldsymbol{\mu}_1 + \boldsymbol{\mu}_2)^T\boldsymbol{\Sigma}^{-1}(\boldsymbol{\mu}_1 - \boldsymbol{\mu}_2) + \log \frac{P(C_1)}{P(C_2)} \end{aligned} \tag{10.14}$$

The inverse of logit

$$\log \frac{P(C_1|\boldsymbol{x})}{1-P(C_1|\boldsymbol{x})} = \boldsymbol{w}^T\boldsymbol{x} + w_0$$

LOGISTIC
SIGMOID

is the *logistic* function, also called the *sigmoid* function (see figure 10.5):

$$P(C_1|\boldsymbol{x}) = \text{sigmoid}(\boldsymbol{w}^T\boldsymbol{x} + w_0) = \frac{1}{1+\exp[-(\boldsymbol{w}^T\boldsymbol{x} + w_0)]} \tag{10.15}$$

During training, we estimate $\boldsymbol{m}_1, \boldsymbol{m}_2, \mathbf{S}$ and plug these estimates in equation 10.14 to calculate the discriminant parameters. During testing, given $\boldsymbol{x}$, we can either

1. calculate $g(\boldsymbol{x}) = \boldsymbol{w}^T\boldsymbol{x} + w_0$ and choose C_1 if $g(\boldsymbol{x}) > 0$, or
2. calculate $y = \text{sigmoid}(\boldsymbol{w}^T\boldsymbol{x} + w_0)$ and choose C_1 if $y > 0.5$,

because $\text{sigmoid}(0) = 0.5$. In this latter case, sigmoid transforms the discriminant value to a posterior probability. This is valid when there are two classes and one discriminant; we see in section 10.7 how we can estimate posterior probabilities for $K > 2$.

10.6 Gradient Descent

In likelihood-based classification, the parameters were the sufficient statistics of $p(\boldsymbol{x}|C_i)$ and $P(C_i)$, and the method we used to estimate the parameters is maximum likelihood. In the discriminant-based approach,

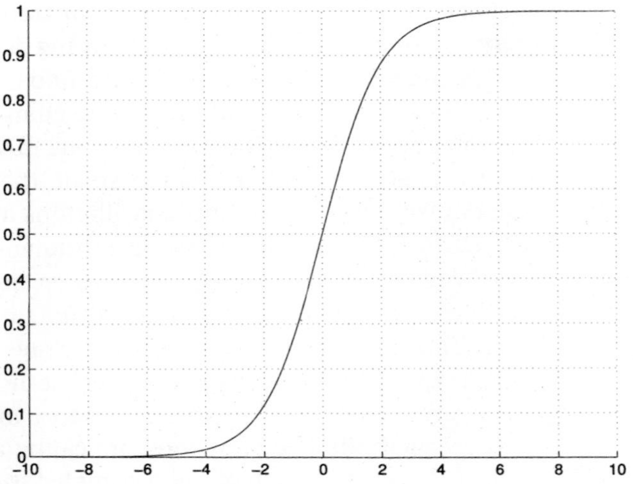

Figure 10.5 The logistic, or sigmoid, function.

the parameters are those of the discriminants, and they are optimized to minimize the classification error on the training set. When $\boldsymbol{w}$ denotes the set of parameters and $E(\boldsymbol{w}|\mathcal{X})$ is the error with parameters $\boldsymbol{w}$ on the given training set $\mathcal{X}$, we look for

$$\boldsymbol{w}^* = \arg\min_{\boldsymbol{w}} E(\boldsymbol{w}|\mathcal{X})$$

GRADIENT DESCENT
GRADIENT VECTOR

In many cases, some of which we will see shortly, there is no analytical solution and we need to resort to iterative optimization methods, the most commonly employed being that of *gradient descent*. When $E(\boldsymbol{w})$ is a differentiable function of a vector of variables, we have the *gradient vector* composed of the partial derivatives

$$\nabla_{\boldsymbol{w}} E = \left[\frac{\partial E}{\partial w_1}, \frac{\partial E}{\partial w_2}, \ldots, \frac{\partial E}{\partial w_d}\right]^T$$

and the *gradient descent* procedure to minimize E starts from a random $\boldsymbol{w}$, and at each step, updates $\boldsymbol{w}$, in the opposite direction of the gradient

$$\Delta w_i = -\eta \frac{\partial E}{\partial w_i}, \forall i \tag{10.16}$$

$$w_i = w_i + \Delta w_i \tag{10.17}$$

where η is called the *stepsize*, or *learning factor*, and determines how much to move in that direction. Gradient ascent is used to maximize a function and goes in the direction of the gradient. When we get to a minimum (or maximum), the derivative is 0 and the procedure terminates. This indicates that the procedure finds the nearest minimum that can be a local minimum, and there is no guarantee of finding the global minimum unless the function has only one minimum. The use of a good value for η is also critical; if it is too small, the convergence may be too slow, and a large value may cause oscillations and even divergence.

Throughout this book, we use gradient methods that are simple and quite effective. We keep in mind, however, that once a suitable model and an error function is defined, the optimization of the model parameters to minimize the error function can be done by using one of many possible techniques. There are second-order methods and conjugate gradient that converge faster, at the expense of more memory and computation. More costly methods like simulated annealing and genetic algorithms allow a more thorough search of the parameter space and do not depend as much on the initial point.

10.7 Logistic Discrimination

10.7.1 Two Classes

LOGISTIC DISCRIMINATION

In *logistic discrimination*, we do not model the class-conditional densities, $p(\boldsymbol{x}|C_i)$, but rather their ratio. Let us again start with two classes and assume that the log likelihood ratio is linear:

$$\log \frac{p(\boldsymbol{x}|C_1)}{p(\boldsymbol{x}|C_2)} = \boldsymbol{w}^T\boldsymbol{x} + w_0^o \tag{10.18}$$

This indeed holds when the class-conditional densities are normal (equation 10.13). But logistic discrimination has a wider scope of applicability; for example, $\boldsymbol{x}$ may be composed of discrete attributes or may be a mixture of continuous and discrete attributes.

Using Bayes' rule, we have

$$\begin{aligned}
\text{logit}(P(C_1|\boldsymbol{x})) &= \log \frac{P(C_1|\boldsymbol{x})}{1 - P(C_1|\boldsymbol{x})} \\
&= \log \frac{p(\boldsymbol{x}|C_1)}{p(\boldsymbol{x}|C_2)} + \log \frac{P(C_1)}{P(C_2)} \\
&= \boldsymbol{w}^T\boldsymbol{x} + w_0 \qquad (10.19)
\end{aligned}$$

where

(10.20) $$w_0 = w_0^o + \log \frac{P(C_1)}{P(C_2)}$$

Rearranging terms, we get the sigmoid function again:

(10.21) $$y = \hat{P}(C_1|\mathbf{x}) = \frac{1}{1 + \exp[-(\mathbf{w}^T\mathbf{x} + w_0)]}$$

as our estimator of $P(C_1|\mathbf{x})$.

Let us see how we can learn $\mathbf{w}$ and w_0. We are given a sample of two classes, $\mathcal{X} = \{\mathbf{x}^t, r^t\}$, where $r^t = 1$ if $\mathbf{x} \in C_1$ and $r^t = 0$ if $\mathbf{x} \in C_2$. We assume r^t, given $\mathbf{x}^t$, is Bernoulli with probability $y^t \equiv P(C_1|\mathbf{x}^t)$ as calculated in equation 10.21:

$$r^t|\mathbf{x}^t \sim \text{Bernoulli}(y^t)$$

Here, we see the difference from the likelihood-based methods where we modeled $p(\mathbf{x}|C_i)$; in the discriminant-based approach, we model directly $r|\mathbf{x}$. The sample likelihood is

(10.22) $$l(\mathbf{w}, w_0|\mathcal{X}) = \prod_t (y^t)^{(r^t)}(1 - y^t)^{(1-r^t)}$$

We know that when we have a likelihood function to maximize, we can always turn it into an error function to be minimized as $E = -\log l$, and

CROSS-ENTROPY

in our case, we have *cross-entropy*:

(10.23) $$E(\mathbf{w}, w_0|\mathcal{X}) = -\sum_t r^t \log y^t + (1 - r^t)\log(1 - y^t)$$

Because of the nonlinearity of the sigmoid function, we cannot solve directly and we use gradient descent to minimize cross-entropy, equivalent to maximizing the likelihood or the log likelihood. If $y = \text{sigmoid}(a) = 1/(1 + \exp(-a))$, its derivative is given as

$$\frac{dy}{da} = y(1 - y)$$

and we get the following update equations:

$$\begin{aligned}
\Delta w_j &= -\eta \frac{\partial E}{\partial w_j} = \eta \sum_t \left(\frac{r^t}{y^t} - \frac{1 - r^t}{1 - y^t}\right) y^t(1 - y^t)x_j^t \\
&= \eta \sum_t (r^t - y^t)x_j^t, j = 1, \ldots, d
\end{aligned}$$

(10.24) $$\Delta w_0 = -\eta \frac{\partial E}{\partial w_0} = \eta \sum_t (r^t - y^t)$$

```
For j = 0,...,d
    w_j ← rand(−0.01,0.01)
Repeat
    For j = 0,...,d
        Δw_j ← 0
    For t = 1,...,N
        o ← 0
        For j = 0,...,d
            o ← o + w_j x_j^t
        y ← sigmoid(o)
        For j = 0,...,d
            Δw_j ← Δw_j + (r^t − y) x_j^t
    For j = 0,...,d
        w_j ← w_j + η Δw_j
Until convergence
```

Figure 10.6 Logistic discrimination algorithm implementing gradient descent for the single output case with two classes. For w_0, we assume that there is an extra input x_0, which is always $+1$: $x_0^t \equiv +1, \forall t$.

It is best to initialize w_j with random values close to 0; generally they are drawn uniformly from the interval $[-0.01, 0.01]$. The reason for this is that if the initial w_j are large in magnitude, the weighted sum may also be large and may saturate the sigmoid. We see from figure 10.5 that if the initial weights are close to 0, the sum will stay in the middle region where the derivative is nonzero and an update can take place. If the weighted sum is large in magnitude (smaller than -5 or larger than $+5$), the derivative of the sigmoid will be almost 0 and weights will not be updated.

Pseudocode is given in figure 10.6. We see an example in figure 10.7 where the input is one-dimensional. Both the line $wx + w_0$ and its value after the sigmoid are shown as a function of learning iterations. We see that to get outputs of 0 and 1, the sigmoid hardens, which is achieved by increasing the magnitude of w, or $\|\mathbf{w}\|$ in the multivariate case.

Once training is complete and we have the final $\mathbf{w}$ and w_0, during testing, given $\mathbf{x}^t$, we calculate $y^t = \text{sigmoid}(\mathbf{w}^T\mathbf{x}^t + w_0)$ and we choose C_1 if $y^t > 0.5$ and choose C_2 otherwise. This implies that to minimize the number of misclassifications, we do not need to continue learning un-

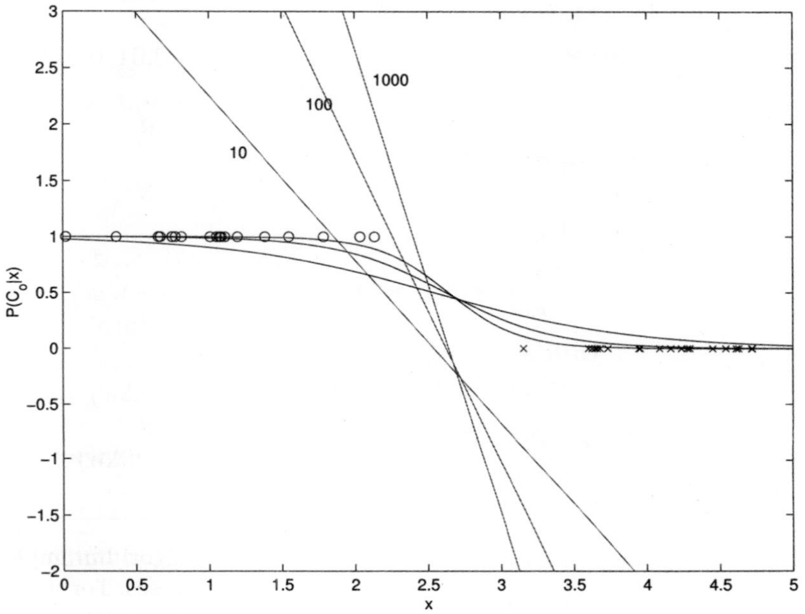

Figure 10.7 For a univariate two-class problem (shown with '∘' and '×'), the evolution of the line $wx + w_0$ and the sigmoid output after 10, 100, and 1,000 iterations over the sample.

til all y^t are 0 or 1, but only until y^t are less than or greater than 0.5, that is, on the correct side of the decision boundary. If we do continue training beyond this point, cross-entropy will continue decreasing ($|w_j|$ will continue increasing to harden the sigmoid), but the number of misclassifications will not decrease. Generally, we continue training until the number of misclassifications does not decrease (which will be 0 if the classes are linearly separable). Actually *stopping early* before we have 0 training error is a form of regularization. Because we start with weights almost 0 and they move away as training continues, stopping early corresponds to a model with more weights close to 0 and effectively fewer parameters.

EARLY STOPPING

Note that though we assumed the log ratio of the class densities are linear to derive the discriminant, we estimate directly the posterior and never explicitly estimate $p(\mathbf{x}|C_i)$ or $P(C_i)$.

10.7.2 Multiple Classes

Let us now generalize to $K > 2$ classes. We take one of the classes, for example, C_K, as the reference class and assume that

$$\log \frac{p(\boldsymbol{x}|C_i)}{p(\boldsymbol{x}|C_K)} = \boldsymbol{w}_i^T \boldsymbol{x} + w_{i0}^o \tag{10.25}$$

Then we have

$$\frac{P(C_i|\boldsymbol{x})}{P(C_K|\boldsymbol{x})} = \exp[\boldsymbol{w}_i^T \boldsymbol{x} + w_{i0}] \tag{10.26}$$

with $w_{i0} = w_{i0}^o + \log P(C_i)/P(C_K)$.

We see that

$$\begin{aligned} \sum_{i=1}^{K-1} \frac{P(C_i|\boldsymbol{x})}{P(C_K|\boldsymbol{x})} &= \frac{1 - P(C_K|\boldsymbol{x})}{P(C_K|\boldsymbol{x})} = \sum_{i=1}^{K-1} \exp[\boldsymbol{w}_i^T \boldsymbol{x} + w_{i0}] \\ &\Rightarrow \quad P(C_K|\boldsymbol{x}) = \frac{1}{1 + \sum_{i=1}^{K-1} \exp[\boldsymbol{w}_i^T \boldsymbol{x} + w_{i0}]} \end{aligned} \tag{10.27}$$

and also that

$$\begin{aligned} \frac{P(C_i|\boldsymbol{x})}{P(C_K|\boldsymbol{x})} &= \exp[\boldsymbol{w}_i^T \boldsymbol{x} + w_{i0}] \\ &\Rightarrow \quad P(C_i|\boldsymbol{x}) = \frac{\exp[\boldsymbol{w}_i^T \boldsymbol{x} + w_{i0}]}{1 + \sum_{j=1}^{K-1} \exp[\boldsymbol{w}_j^T \boldsymbol{x} + w_{j0}]}, \; i = 1, \dots, K-1 \end{aligned} \tag{10.28}$$

To treat all classes uniformly, we can write

$$y_i = \hat{P}(C_i|\boldsymbol{x}) = \frac{\exp[\boldsymbol{w}_i^T \boldsymbol{x} + w_{i0}]}{\sum_{j=1}^{K} \exp[\boldsymbol{w}_j^T \boldsymbol{x} + w_{j0}]}, \; i = 1, \dots, K \tag{10.29}$$

SOFTMAX

which is called the *softmax* function (Bridle 1990). If the weighted sum for one class is sufficiently larger than for the others, after it is boosted through exponentiation and normalization, its corresponding y_i will be close to 1 and the others will be close to 0. Thus it works like taking a maximum, except that it is differentiable; hence the name softmax. Softmax also guarantees that $\sum_i y_i = 1$.

Let us see how we can learn the parameters. In this case of $K > 2$ classes, each sample point is a multinomial trial with one draw; that is, $\boldsymbol{r}^t|\boldsymbol{x}^t \sim \text{Mult}_K(1, \boldsymbol{y}^t)$, where $y_i^t \equiv P(C_i|\boldsymbol{x}^t)$. The sample likelihood is

$$l(\{\boldsymbol{w}_i, w_{i0}\}_i|\mathcal{X}) = \prod_t \prod_i (y_i^t)^{r_i^t} \tag{10.30}$$

and the error function is again cross-entropy:

$$E(\{\mathbf{w}_i, w_{i0}\}_i|\mathcal{X}) = -\sum_t \sum_i r_i^t \log y_i^t \tag{10.31}$$

We again use gradient descent. If $y_i = \exp(a_i)/\sum_j \exp(a_j)$, we have

$$\frac{\partial y_i}{\partial a_j} = y_i(\delta_{ij} - y_j) \tag{10.32}$$

where δ_{ij} is the Kronecker delta, which is 1 if $i = j$ and 0 if $i \neq j$ (exercise 3). Given that $\sum_i r_i^t = 1$, we have the following update equations, for $j = 1, \ldots, K$

$$\begin{aligned}
\Delta \mathbf{w}_j &= \eta \sum_t \sum_i \frac{r_i^t}{y_i^t} y_i^t(\delta_{ij} - y_j^t)\mathbf{x}^t \\
&= \eta \sum_t \sum_i r_i^t(\delta_{ij} - y_j^t)\mathbf{x}^t \\
&= \eta \sum_t \left[\sum_i r_i^t \delta_{ij} - y_j^t \sum_i r_i^t \right] \mathbf{x}^t \\
&= \eta \sum_t (r_j^t - y_j^t)\mathbf{x}^t
\end{aligned}$$

$$\Delta w_{j0} = \eta \sum_t (r_j^t - y_j^t) \tag{10.33}$$

Note that because of the normalization in softmax, $\mathbf{w}_j$ and w_{j0} are affected not only by $\mathbf{x}^t \in C_j$ but also by $\mathbf{x}^t \in C_i, i \neq j$. The discriminants are updated so that the correct class has the highest weighted sum after softmax, and the other classes have their weighted sums as low as possible. Pseudocode is given in figure 10.8. For a two-dimensional example with three classes, the contour plot is given in figure 10.9, and the discriminants and the posterior probabilities in figure 10.10.

During testing, we calculate all $y_k, k = 1, \ldots, K$ and choose C_i if $y_i = \max_k y_k$. Again we do not need to continue training to minimize cross-entropy as much as possible; we train only until the correct class has the highest weighted sum, and therefore we can stop training earlier by checking the number of misclassifications.

When data are normally distributed, the logistic discriminant has a comparable error rate to the parametric, normal-based linear discriminant (McLachlan 1992). Logistic discrimination can still be used when the class-conditional densities are nonnormal or when they are not unimodal, as long as classes are linearly separable.

```
For i = 1,...,K
    For j = 0,...,d
        w_ij ← rand(−0.01, 0.01)
Repeat
    For i = 1,...,K
        For j = 0,...,d
            Δw_ij ← 0
    For t = 1,...,N
        For i = 1,...,K
            o_i ← 0
            For j = 0,...,d
                o_i ← o_i + w_ij x_j^t
        For i = 1,...,K
            y_i ← exp(o_i) / Σ_k exp(o_k)
        For i = 1,...,K
            For j = 0,...,d
                Δw_ij ← Δw_ij + (r_i^t − y_i) x_j^t
    For i = 1,...,K
        For j = 0,...,d
            w_ij ← w_ij + η Δw_ij
Until convergence
```

Figure 10.8 Logistic discrimination algorithm implementing gradient descent for the case with $K > 2$ classes. For generality, we take $x_0^t \equiv 1, \forall t$.

The ratio of class-conditional densities is of course not restricted to be linear (Anderson 1982; McLachlan 1992). Assuming a quadratic discriminant, we have

$$\log \frac{p(\mathbf{x}|C_i)}{p(\mathbf{x}|C_K)} = \mathbf{x}^T \mathbf{W}_i \mathbf{x} + \mathbf{w}_i^T \mathbf{x} + w_{i0} \tag{10.34}$$

corresponding to and generalizing parametric discrimination with multivariate normal class-conditionals having different covariance matrices. When d is large, just as we can simplify (regularize) $\mathbf{\Sigma}_i$, we can equally do it on $\mathbf{W}_i$ by taking only its leading eigenvectors into account.

As discussed in section 10.2, any specified function of the basic variables can be included as x-variates. One can, for example, write the dis-

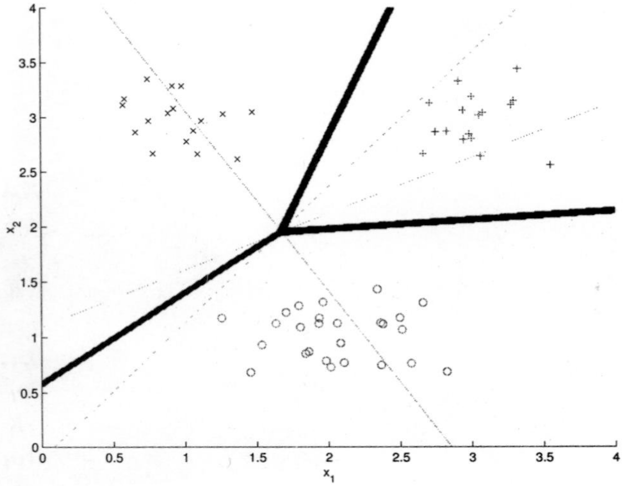

Figure 10.9 For a two-dimensional problem with three classes, the solution found by logistic discrimination. Thin lines are where $g_i(\mathbf{x}) = 0$, and the thick line is the boundary induced by the linear classifier choosing the maximum.

criminant as a linear sum of nonlinear basis functions

$$\log \frac{p(\mathbf{x}|C_i)}{p(\mathbf{x}|C_K)} = \mathbf{w}_i^T \boldsymbol{\phi}(\mathbf{x}) + w_{i0} \quad (10.35)$$

where $\boldsymbol{\phi}(\cdot)$ are the basis functions, which can be viewed as transformed variables. In neural network terminology, this is called a *multilayer perceptron* (chapter 11), and sigmoid is the most popular basis function. When a Gaussian basis function is used, the model is called *radial basis functions* (chapter 12). We can even use a completely nonparametric approach, for example, Parzen windows (chapter 8).

10.8 Discrimination by Regression

In regression, the probabilistic model is

$$r^t = y^t + \epsilon \quad (10.36)$$

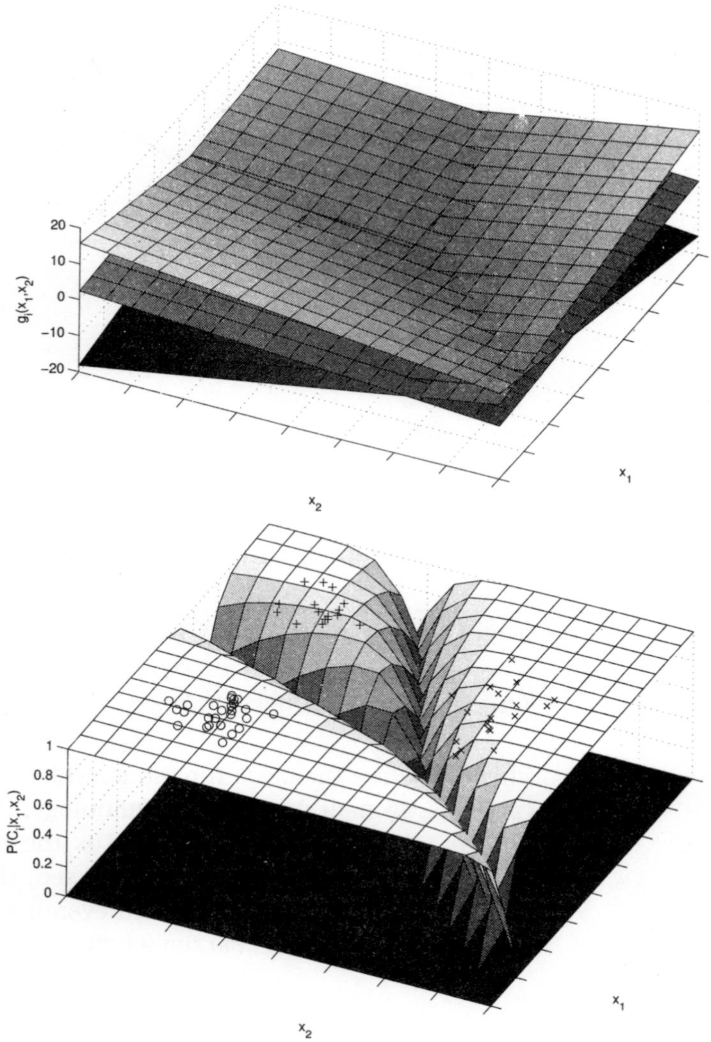

Figure 10.10 For the same example in figure 10.9, the linear discriminants (top), and the posterior probabilities after the softmax (bottom).

where $\epsilon \sim \mathcal{N}(0, \sigma^2)$. If $r^t \in \{0, 1\}$, y^t can be constrained to lie in this range using the sigmoid function. Assuming a linear model and two classes, we have

$$y^t = \text{sigmoid}(\mathbf{w}^T \mathbf{x}^t + w_0) = \frac{1}{1 + \exp[-(\mathbf{w}^T \mathbf{x}^t + w_0)]} \tag{10.37}$$

Then the sample likelihood in regression, assuming $r|\mathbf{x} \sim \mathcal{N}(y, \sigma^2)$, is

$$l(\mathbf{w}, w_0|\mathcal{X}) = \prod_t \frac{1}{\sqrt{2\pi}\sigma} \exp\left[-\frac{(r^t - y^t)^2}{2\sigma^2}\right] \tag{10.38}$$

Maximizing the log likelihood is minimizing the sum of square errors:

$$E(\mathbf{w}, w_0|\mathcal{X}) = \frac{1}{2}\sum_t (r^t - y^t)^2 \tag{10.39}$$

Using gradient descent, we get

$$\begin{aligned} \Delta \mathbf{w} &= \eta \sum_t (r^t - y^t) y^t (1 - y^t) \mathbf{x}^t \\ \Delta w_0 &= \eta \sum_t (r^t - y^t) y^t (1 - y^t) \end{aligned} \tag{10.40}$$

This method can also be used when there are $K > 2$ classes. The probabilistic model is

$$\mathbf{r}^t = \mathbf{y}^t + \boldsymbol{\epsilon} \tag{10.41}$$

where $\boldsymbol{\epsilon} \sim \mathcal{N}_K(0, \sigma^2 \mathbf{I}_K)$. Assuming a linear model for each class, we have

$$y_i^t = \text{sigmoid}(\mathbf{w}_i^T \mathbf{x}^t + w_{i0}) = \frac{1}{1 + \exp[-(\mathbf{w}_i^T \mathbf{x}^t + w_{i0})]} \tag{10.42}$$

Then the sample likelihood is

$$l(\{\mathbf{w}_i, w_{i0}\}_i|\mathcal{X}) = \prod_t \frac{1}{(2\pi)^{K/2}|\Sigma|^{1/2}} \exp\left[-\frac{\|\mathbf{r}^t - \mathbf{y}^t\|^2}{2\sigma^2}\right] \tag{10.43}$$

and the error function is

$$E(\{\mathbf{w}_i, w_{i0}\}_i|\mathcal{X}) = \frac{1}{2}\sum_t \|\mathbf{r}^t - \mathbf{y}^t\|^2 = \frac{1}{2}\sum_t \sum_i (r_i^t - y_i^t)^2 \tag{10.44}$$

The update equations for $i = 1, \ldots, K$, are

$$\begin{aligned} \Delta \mathbf{w}_i &= \eta \sum_t (r_i^t - y_i^t) y_i^t (1 - y_i^t) \mathbf{x}^t \\ \Delta w_{i0} &= \eta \sum_t (r_i^t - y_i^t) y_i^t (1 - y_i^t) \end{aligned} \tag{10.45}$$

But note that in doing so, we do not make use of the information that only one of y_i needs to be 1 and all others are 0, or that $\sum_i y_i = 1$. The softmax function of equation 10.29 allows us to incorporate this extra information we have due to the outputs' estimating class posterior probabilities. Using sigmoid outputs in $K > 2$ case, we treat y_i as if they are independent functions.

Note also that for a given class, if we use the regression approach, there will be updates until the right output is 1 and all others are 0. This is not in fact necessary because during testing, we are just going to choose the maximum anyway; it is enough to train only until the right output is larger than others, which is exactly what the softmax function does.

So this approach with multiple sigmoid outputs is more appropriate when the classes are *not* mutually exclusive and exhaustive. That is, for an $\mathbf{x}^t$, all r_i^t may be 0; namely, $\mathbf{x}^t$ does not belong to any of the classes, or more than one r_i^t may be 1, when classes overlap.

10.9 Learning to Rank

RANKING

Ranking is an application area of machine learning that is different from classification and regression, and is sort of between the two. Unlike classification and regression where there is an input $\mathbf{x}^t$ and a desired output r^t, in ranking we are asked to put two or more instances in the correct order (Liu 2011).

For example, let us say $\mathbf{x}^u$ and $\mathbf{x}^v$ represent two movies, and let us say that a user has enjoyed u more than v (in this case, we need to give higher rank to movies similar to u). This is labeled as $r^u \prec r^v$. What we learn is not a discriminant or a regression function but a *score function* $g(\mathbf{x}|\theta)$, and what is important are not the absolute values of $g(\mathbf{x}^u|\theta)$ and $g(\mathbf{x}^v|\theta)$, but that we need to give a higher score to $\mathbf{x}^u$ than $\mathbf{x}^v$; that is, $g(\mathbf{x}^u|\theta) > g(\mathbf{x}^v|\theta)$ should be satisfied for all such pairs of u and v.

As usual, we assume a certain model $g(\cdot)$ and we optimize its parameters θ so that all rank constraints are satisfied. Then, for example, to make a recommendation among the movies that the user has not yet seen, we choose the one with the highest score:

$$\text{Choose } u \text{ if } g(\mathbf{x}^u|\theta) = \max_t g(\mathbf{x}^t|\theta)$$

Sometimes, instead of only the topmost, we may want a list of the highest k.

We can note here the advantage and difference of a ranker. If users rate the movies they have seen as "enjoyed/not enjoyed," this will be a two-class classification problem and a classifier can be used, but taste is nuanced and a binary rating is very hard. On the other hand, if people rate their enjoyment of a movie on a scale of, say, 1 to 10, this will be a regression problem, but such absolute values are difficult to assign. It is more natural and easier for people to say that of the two movies they have watched, they like one more than the other, instead of a yes/no decision or a numeric value.

Ranking has many applications. In search engines, for example, given a query, we want to retrieve the most relevant documents. If we retrieve and display the current top ten candidates and then the user clicks the third one skipping the first two, we understand that the third should have been ranked higher than the first and the second. Such click logs are used to train rankers.

Sometimes reranking is used to improve the output of a ranker with additional information. For example, in speech recognition, an acoustic model can first be used to generate an ordered list of possible sentences, and then the N-best candidates can then be reranked using features from a language model; this can improve accuracy significantly (Shen and Joshi 2005).

A ranker can be trained in a number of different ways. For all (u, v) pairs where $r^u \prec r^v$ is defined, we have an error if $g(\boldsymbol{x}^v|\theta) > g(\boldsymbol{x}^u|\theta)$. Generally, we do not have a full ordering of all N^2 pairs but a subset, thereby defining a partial order. The sum of differences make up the error:

(10.46) $$E(\boldsymbol{w}|\{r^u, r^v\}) = \sum_{r^u \prec r^v} [g(\boldsymbol{x}^v|\theta) - g(\boldsymbol{x}^u|\theta)]_+$$

where a_+ is equal to a if $a \geq 0$ and 0 otherwise.

Let us use a linear model, as we do throughout this chapter:

(10.47) $$g(\boldsymbol{x}|\boldsymbol{w}) = \boldsymbol{w}^T\boldsymbol{x}$$

Because we do not care about the absolute values, we do not need w_0. The error in equation 10.46 becomes

(10.48) $$E(\boldsymbol{w}|\{r^u, r^v\}) = \sum_{r^u \prec r^v} \boldsymbol{w}^T(\boldsymbol{x}^v - \boldsymbol{x}^u)_+$$

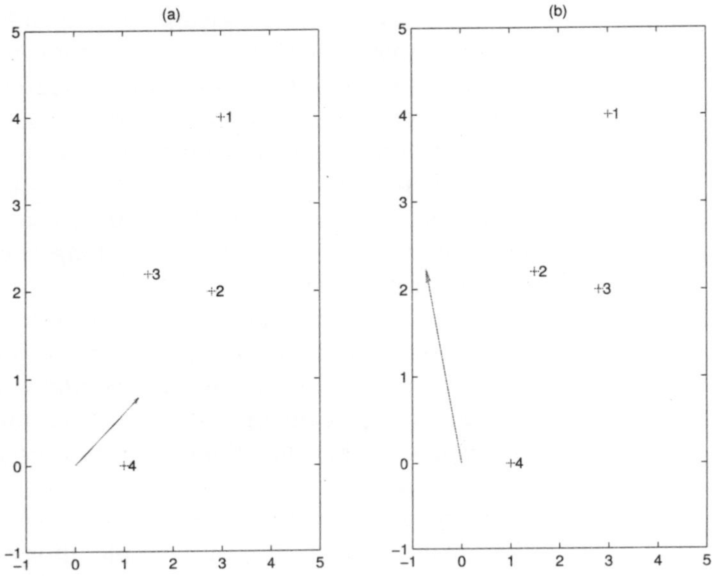

Figure 10.11 Sample ranking problems and solutions. Data points are indicated by '+' and the numbers next to them indicate the rank where 1 is the highest. We have a full ordering here. The arrow indicate the learned $\boldsymbol{w}$. In (a) and (b), we see two different ranking problems and the two corresponding solutions.

We can do an online update of $\boldsymbol{w}$ using gradient descent. For each $r^u \prec r^v$ where $g(\boldsymbol{x}^v|\theta) > g(\boldsymbol{x}^u|\theta)$, we do a small update:

(10.49) $$\Delta w_j = -\eta \frac{\partial E}{\partial w_j} = -\eta(\boldsymbol{x}_j^v - \boldsymbol{x}_j^u), j = 1, \ldots, d$$

$\boldsymbol{w}$ is chosen so that when the instances are projected onto $\boldsymbol{w}$, the correct orderings are obtained. In figure 10.11, we see example data and the projection directions learned. We see there that a slight change in the ranks may cause a big change in $\boldsymbol{w}$.

For error functions and gradient descent approaches in ranking and their use in practice, see Burges et al. 2005 and Shin and Josh 2005. Sometimes for confident decision, when $r^u \prec r^v$, we require that the output be not only larger, but larger with a margin, for example, $g(\boldsymbol{x}^u|\theta) > 1 + g(\boldsymbol{x}^u|\theta)$; we will see an example of this when we talk about learning to rank using kernel machines in section 13.11.

10.10 Notes

The linear discriminant, due to its simplicity, is the classifier most used in pattern recognition (Duda, Hart, and Stork 2001; McLachlan 1992). We discussed the case of Gaussian distributions with a common covariance matrix in chapter 4 and Fisher's linear discriminant in chapter 6, and in this chapter we discuss the logistic discriminant. In chapter 11, we discuss the perceptron that is the neural network implementation of the linear discriminant. In chapter 13, we discuss support vector machines, another type of linear discriminant.

Logistic discrimination is covered in more detail in Anderson 1982 and in McLachlan 1992. Logistic (sigmoid) is the inverse of logit, which is the *canonical link* in case of Bernoulli samples. Softmax is its generalization to multinomial samples. More information on such *generalized linear models* is given in McCullogh and Nelder 1989.

GENERALIZED LINEAR MODELS

Ranking has recently become a major application area of machine learning because of its use in search engines, information retrieval, and natural language processing. An extensive review of both important applications and machine learning algorithms is given in Liu 2011. The model we discussed here is a linear model; in section 13.11, we discuss how to learn a ranker using kernel machines where we get a nonlinear model with kernels that allow the integration of different measures of similarity.

Generalizing linear models by using nonlinear basis functions is a very old idea. We will discuss multilayer perceptrons (chapter 11) and radial basis functions (chapter 12) where the parameters of the basis functions can also be learned from data while learning the discriminant. Support vector machines (chapter 13) use kernel functions built from such basis functions.

10.11 Exercises

1. For each of the following basis functions, describe where it is nonzero:

   a. $\sin(x_1)$

   b. $\exp(-(x_1 - a)^2/c)$

   c. $\exp(-\|\boldsymbol{x} - \boldsymbol{a}\|^2/c)$

   d. $\log(x_2)$

   e. $1(x_1 > c)$

f. $1(ax_1 + bx_2 > c)$

2. For the two-dimensional case of figure 10.2, show equations 10.4 and 10.5.

3. Show that the derivative of the softmax, $y_i = \exp(a_i)/\sum_j \exp(a_j)$, is $\partial y_i/\partial a_j = y_i(\delta_{ij} - y_j)$, where δ_{ij} is 1 if $i = j$ and 0 otherwise.

4. With $K = 2$, show that using two softmax outputs is equal to using one sigmoid output.

   SOLUTION:

$$\begin{aligned} y_1 &= \frac{\exp o_1}{\exp o_1 + \exp o_2} = \frac{1}{1 + \exp(o_2 - o_1)} = \frac{1}{1 + \exp(-(o_1 - o_2))} \\ &= \text{sigmoid}(o_1 - o_2) \end{aligned}$$

   For example, if we have $o_1 = \boldsymbol{w}_1^T \boldsymbol{x}$, we have

$$y_1 = \frac{\exp \boldsymbol{w}_1^T \boldsymbol{x}}{\exp \boldsymbol{w}_1^T \boldsymbol{x} + \exp \boldsymbol{w}_2^T \boldsymbol{x}} = \text{sigmoid}(\boldsymbol{w}_1^T \boldsymbol{x} - \boldsymbol{w}_2^T \boldsymbol{x}) = \text{sigmoid}(\boldsymbol{w}^T \boldsymbol{x})$$

   where $\boldsymbol{w} \equiv \boldsymbol{w}_1 - \boldsymbol{w}_2$ and $y_2 = 1 - y_1$.

5. How can we learn $\mathbf{W}_i$ in equation 10.34?

   SOLUTION: For example, if we have two inputs x_1 and x_2, we have

$$\begin{aligned} \log \frac{p(x_1, x_2|C_i)}{p(x_1, x_2|C_K)} &= \mathbf{W}_{i11}x_1^2 + \mathbf{W}_{i12}x_1x_2 + \mathbf{W}_{i21}x_2x_1 + \mathbf{W}_{i22}x_2^2 \\ &+ w_{i1}x_1 + w_{i2}x_2 + w_{i0} \end{aligned}$$

   Then we can use gradient descent and take derivative with respect to any $\mathbf{W}_{jkl}$ to calculate an update rule:

$$\Delta \mathbf{W}_{jkl} = \eta \sum_t (r_j^t - y_j^t) x_k^t x_l^t$$

6. In using quadratic (or higher-order) discriminants as in equation 10.34, how can we keep variance under control?

7. What is the implication of the use of a single η for all x_j in gradient descent?

   SOLUTION: Using a single η for all x_j implies doing updates in the same scale, which in turn implies that all x_j are in the same scale. If they are not, it is a good idea to normalize all x_j, for example, by z-normalization, before training. Note that we need to save the scaling parameters for all inputs, so that the same scaling can also be done later to the test instances.

8. In the univariate case for classification as in figure 10.7, what do w and w_0 correspond to?

   SOLUTION: The slope and the intercept of the line, which are then fed to the sigmoid.

9. Let us say for univariate x, $x \in (2, 4)$ belong to C_1 and $x < 2$ or $x > 4$ belong to C_2. How can we separate the two classes using a linear discriminant?

   SOLUTION: We define an extra variable $z \equiv x^2$ and use the linear discriminant $w_2 z + w_1 x + w_0$ in the (z, x) space, which corresponds to a quadratic discriminant in the x space. For example, we can manually write

$$\text{Choose} \begin{cases} C_1 & \text{if } (x-3)^2 - 1 \leq 0 \\ C_2 & \text{otherwise} \end{cases}$$

   or rewrite it using a sigmoid (see figure 10.12):

$$\text{Choose} \begin{cases} C_1 & \text{if sigmoid}((x-3)^2 - 1) \leq 0.5 \\ C_2 & \text{otherwise} \end{cases}$$

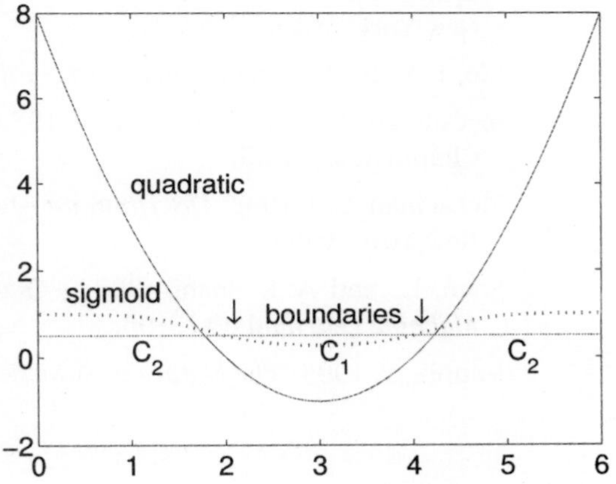

Figure 10.12 The quadratic discriminant, before and after the sigmoid. The boundaries are where the discriminant is 0 or where the sigmoid is 0.5.

   Or, we can use *two* linear discriminants in the x space, one separating at 2 and the other separating at 4, and then we can OR them. Such layered linear discriminants are discussed in chapter 11.

10. For the sample data in figure 10.11, define ranks such that a linear model would not be able to learn them. Explain how the model can be generalized so that they can be learned.

10.12 References

Aizerman, M. A., E. M. Braverman, and L. I. Rozonoer. 1964. "Theoretical Foundations of the Potential Function Method in Pattern Recognition Learning." *Automation and Remote Control* 25:821–837.

Anderson, J. A. 1982. "Logistic Discrimination." In *Handbook of Statistics*, Vol. 2, *Classification, Pattern Recognition and Reduction of Dimensionality*, ed. P. R. Krishnaiah and L. N. Kanal, 169–191. Amsterdam: North Holland.

Bridle, J. S. 1990. "Probabilistic Interpretation of Feedforward Classification Network Outputs with Relationships to Statistical Pattern Recognition." In *Neurocomputing: Algorithms, Architectures and Applications*, ed. F. Fogelman-Soulie and J. Herault, 227–236. Berlin: Springer.

Burges, C., T. Shaked, E. Renshaw, A. Lazier, M. Deeds, N. Hamilton, and G. Hullender. 2005. "Learning to Rank using Gradient Descent." In *22nd International Conference on Machine Learning*, 89–96, New York: ACM Press.

Duda, R. O., P. E. Hart, and D. G. Stork. 2001. *Pattern Classification*, 2nd ed. New York: Wiley.

Liu, T.-Y. 2011. *Learning to Rank for Information Retrieval.* Heidelberg: Springer.

McCullagh, P., and J. A. Nelder. 1989. *Generalized Linear Models.* London: Chapman and Hall.

McLachlan, G. J. 1992. *Discriminant Analysis and Statistical Pattern Recognition.* New York: Wiley.

Shen, L., and A. K. Joshi. 2005. "Ranking and Reranking with Perceptron." *Machine Learning* 60:73–96.

Vapnik, V. 1995. *The Nature of Statistical Learning Theory.* New York: Springer.

11 *Multilayer Perceptrons*

The multilayer perceptron is an artificial neural network structure and is a nonparametric estimator that can be used for classification and regression. We discuss the backpropagation algorithm to train a multilayer perceptron for a variety of applications.

11.1 Introduction

ARTIFICIAL NEURAL network models, one of which is the *perceptron* we discuss in this chapter, take their inspiration from the brain. There are cognitive scientists and neuroscientists whose aim is to understand the functioning of the brain (Posner 1989; Thagard 2005), and toward this aim, build models of the natural neural networks in the brain and make simulation studies.

ARTIFICIAL NEURAL NETWORKS

However, in engineering, our aim is not to understand the brain per se, but to build useful machines. We are interested in *artificial neural networks* because we believe that they may help us build better computer systems. The brain is an information processing device that has some incredible abilities and surpasses current engineering products in many domains—for example, vision, speech recognition, and learning, to name three. These applications have evident economic utility if implemented on machines. If we can understand how the brain performs these functions, we can define solutions to these tasks as formal algorithms and implement them on computers.

NEURONS

The human brain is quite different from a computer. Whereas a computer generally has one processor, the brain is composed of a very large (10^{11}) number of processing units, namely, *neurons*, operating in parallel. Though the details are not known, the processing units are believed to be much simpler and slower than a processor in a computer. What also makes the brain different, and is believed to provide its computational power, is the large connectivity. Neurons in the brain have connections, called *synapses*, to around 10^4 other neurons, all operating in parallel. In a computer, the processor is active and the memory is separate and passive, but it is believed that in the brain, both the processing and memory are distributed together over the network; processing is done by the neurons, and the memory is in the synapses between the neurons.

SYNAPSES

11.1.1 Understanding the Brain

According to Marr (1982), understanding an information processing system has three levels, called the *levels of analysis*:

LEVELS OF ANALYSIS

1. *Computational theory* corresponds to the goal of computation and an abstract definition of the task.

2. *Representation and algorithm* is about how the input and the output are represented and about the specification of the algorithm for the transformation from the input to the output.

3. *Hardware implementation* is the actual physical realization of the system.

One example is sorting: The computational theory is to order a given set of elements. The representation may use integers, and the algorithm may be Quicksort. After compilation, the executable code for a particular processor sorting integers represented in binary is one hardware implementation.

The idea is that for the same computational theory, there may be multiple representations and algorithms manipulating symbols in that representation. Similarly, for any given representation and algorithm, there may be multiple hardware implementations. We can use one of various sorting algorithms, and even the same algorithm can be compiled on computers with different processors and lead to different hardware implementations.

To take another example, '6', 'VI', and '110' are three different representations of the number six. There is a different algorithm for addition depending on the representation used. Digital computers use binary representation and have circuitry to add in this representation, which is one particular hardware implementation. Numbers are represented differently, and addition corresponds to a different set of instructions on an abacus, which is another hardware implementation. When we add two numbers in our head, we use another representation and an algorithm suitable to that representation, which is implemented by the neurons. But all these different hardware implementations—for example, us, abacus, digital computer—implement the same computational theory, addition.

The classic example is the difference between natural and artificial flying machines. A sparrow flaps its wings; a commercial airplane does not flap its wings but uses jet engines. The sparrow and the airplane are two hardware implementations built for different purposes, satisfying different constraints. But they both implement the same theory, which is aerodynamics.

The brain is one hardware implementation for learning or pattern recognition. If from this particular implementation, we can do reverse engineering and extract the representation and the algorithm used, and if from that in turn, we can get the computational theory, we can then use another representation and algorithm, and in turn a hardware implementation more suited to the means and constraints we have. One hopes our implementation will be cheaper, faster, and more accurate.

Just as the initial attempts to build flying machines looked very much like birds until we discovered aerodynamics, it is also expected that the first attempts to build structures possessing brain's abilities will look like the brain with networks of large numbers of processing units, until we discover the computational theory of intelligence. So it can be said that in understanding the brain, when we are working on artificial neural networks, we are at the representation and algorithm level.

Just as the feathers are irrelevant to flying, in time we may discover that neurons and synapses are irrelevant to intelligence. But until that time there is one other reason why we are interested in understanding the functioning of the brain, and that is related to parallel processing.

11.1.2 Neural Networks as a Paradigm for Parallel Processing

Since the 1980s, computer systems with thousands of processors have been commercially available. The software for such parallel architectures, however, has not advanced as quickly as hardware. The reason for this is that almost all our theory of computation up to that point was based on serial, one-processor machines. We are not able to use the parallel machines we have efficiently because we cannot program them efficiently.

PARALLEL PROCESSING

There are mainly two paradigms for *parallel processing*: In single instruction, multiple data (SIMD) machines, all processors execute the same instruction but on different pieces of data. In multiple instruction, multiple data (MIMD) machines, different processors may execute different instructions on different data. SIMD machines are easier to program because there is only one program to write. However, problems rarely have such a regular structure that they can be parallelized over a SIMD machine. MIMD machines are more general, but it is not an easy task to write separate programs for all the individual processors; additional problems are related to synchronization, data transfer between processors, and so forth. SIMD machines are also easier to build, and machines with more processors can be constructed if they are SIMD. In MIMD machines, processors are more complex, and a more complex communication network should be constructed for the processors to exchange data arbitrarily.

Assume now that we can have machines where processors are a little bit more complex than SIMD processors but not as complex as MIMD processors. Assume we have simple processors with a small amount of local memory where some parameters can be stored. Each processor implements a fixed function and executes the same instructions as SIMD processors; but by loading different values into the local memory, they can be doing different things and the whole operation can be distributed over such processors. We will then have what we can call neural instruction, multiple data (NIMD) machines, where each processor corresponds to a neuron, local parameters correspond to its synaptic weights, and the whole structure is a neural network. If the function implemented in each processor is simple and if the local memory is small, then many such processors can be fit on a single chip.

The problem now is to distribute a task over a network of such processors and to determine the local parameter values. This is where learning comes into play: We do not need to program such machines and determine the parameter values ourselves if such machines can learn from examples.

Thus, artificial neural networks are a way to make use of the parallel hardware we can build with current technology and—thanks to learning—they need not be programmed. Therefore, we also save ourselves the effort of programming them.

In this chapter, we discuss such structures and how they are trained.

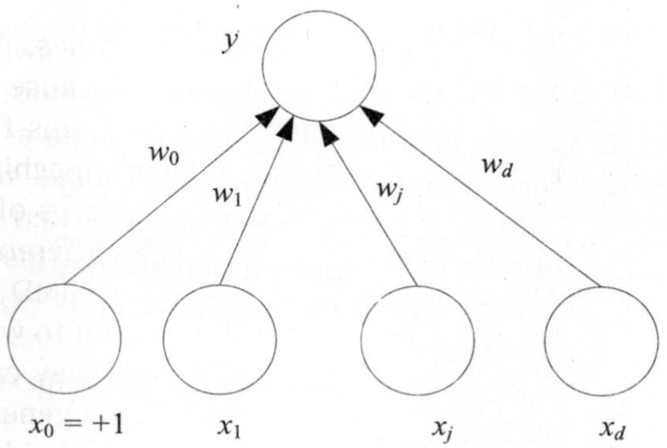

Figure 11.1 Simple perceptron. $x_j, j = 1, \ldots, d$ are the input units. x_0 is the bias unit that always has the value 1. y is the output unit. w_j is the weight of the directed connection from input x_j to the output.

Keep in mind that the operation of an artificial neural network is a mathematical function that can be implemented on a serial computer—as it generally is—and training the network is not much different from statistical techniques that we have discussed in the previous chapters. Thinking of this operation as being carried out on a network of simple processing units is meaningful only if we have the parallel hardware, and only if the network is so large that it cannot be simulated fast enough on a serial computer.

11.2 The Perceptron

PERCEPTRON

CONNECTION WEIGHT

SYNAPTIC WEIGHT

The *perceptron* is the basic processing element. It has inputs that may come from the environment or may be the outputs of other perceptrons. Associated with each input, $x_j \in \Re, j = 1, \ldots, d$, is a *connection weight*, or *synaptic weight* $w_j \in \Re$, and the output, y, in the simplest case is a weighted sum of the inputs (see figure 11.1):

$$y = \sum_{j=1}^{d} w_j x_j + w_0 \tag{11.1}$$

BIAS UNIT

w_0 is the intercept value to make the model more general; it is generally modeled as the weight coming from an extra *bias unit*, x_0, which is always

+1. We can write the output of the perceptron as a dot product

$$y = \mathbf{w}^T \mathbf{x} \tag{11.2}$$

where $\mathbf{w} = [w_0, w_1, \ldots, w_d]^T$ and $\mathbf{x} = [1, x_1, \ldots, x_d]^T$ are *augmented* vectors to include also the bias weight and input.

During testing, with given weights, $\mathbf{w}$, for input $\mathbf{x}$, we compute the output y. To implement a given task, we need to *learn* the weights $\mathbf{w}$, the parameters of the system, such that correct outputs are generated given the inputs.

When $d = 1$ and x is fed from the environment through an input unit, we have

$$y = wx + w_0$$

which is the equation of a line with w as the slope and w_0 as the intercept. Thus this perceptron with one input and one output can be used to implement a linear fit. With more than one input, the line becomes a (hyper)plane, and the perceptron with more than one input can be used to implement multivariate linear fit. Given a sample, the parameters w_j can be found by regression (see section 5.8).

The perceptron as defined in equation 11.1 defines a hyperplane and as such can be used to divide the input space into two: the half-space where it is positive and the half-space where it is negative (see chapter 10). By using it to implement a linear discriminant function, the perceptron can separate two classes by checking the sign of the output. If we define $s(\cdot)$ as the *threshold function*

THRESHOLD FUNCTION

$$s(a) = \begin{cases} 1 & \text{if } a > 0 \\ 0 & \text{otherwise} \end{cases} \tag{11.3}$$

then we can

$$\text{choose} \begin{cases} C_1 & \text{if } s(\mathbf{w}^T\mathbf{x}) > 0 \\ C_2 & \text{otherwise} \end{cases}$$

Remember that using a linear discriminant assumes that classes are linearly separable. That is to say, it is assumed that a hyperplane $\mathbf{w}^T\mathbf{x} = 0$ can be found that separates $\mathbf{x}^t \in C_1$ and $\mathbf{x}^t \in C_2$. If at a later stage we need the posterior probability—for example, to calculate risk—we need to use the sigmoid function at the output as

$$\begin{aligned} o &= \mathbf{w}^T\mathbf{x} \\ y &= \text{sigmoid}(o) = \frac{1}{1 + \exp[-\mathbf{w}^T\mathbf{x}]} \end{aligned} \tag{11.4}$$

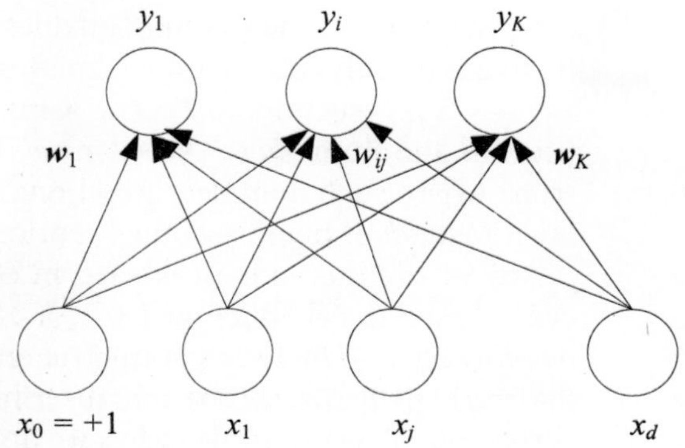

Figure 11.2 K parallel perceptrons. $x_j, j = 0, \ldots, d$ are the inputs and $y_i, i = 1, \ldots, K$ are the outputs. w_{ij} is the weight of the connection from input x_j to output y_i. Each output is a weighted sum of the inputs. When used for K-class classification problem, there is a postprocessing to choose the maximum, or softmax if we need the posterior probabilities.

When there are $K > 2$ outputs, there are K perceptrons, each of which has a weight vector $\mathbf{w}_i$ (see figure 11.2)

$$\begin{aligned} y_i &= \sum_{j=1}^{d} w_{ij}x_j + w_{i0} = \mathbf{w}_i^T \mathbf{x} \\ \mathbf{y} &= \mathbf{W}\mathbf{x} \end{aligned} \tag{11.5}$$

where w_{ij} is the weight from input x_j to output y_i. $\mathbf{W}$ is the $K \times (d + 1)$ weight matrix of w_{ij} whose rows are the weight vectors of the K perceptrons. When used for classification, during testing, we

$$\text{choose } C_i \text{ if } y_i = \max_k y_k$$

Each perceptron is a *local* function of its inputs and synaptic weights. In classification, if we need the posterior probabilities (instead of just the code of the winner class) and use the softmax, we need the values of all outputs. Implementing this as a neural network results in a two-stage process, where the first calculates the weighted sums, and the second calculates the softmax values; but we denote this as a single layer:

$$\begin{aligned} o_i &= \mathbf{w}_i^T \mathbf{x} \\ y_i &= \frac{\exp o_i}{\sum_k \exp o_k} \end{aligned} \tag{11.6}$$

Remember that by defining auxiliary inputs, the linear model can also be used for polynomial approximation; for example, define $x_3 = x_1^2, x_4 = x_2^2, x_5 = x_1 x_2$ (section 10.2). The same can also be used with perceptrons (Durbin and Rumelhart 1989). In section 11.5, we see multilayer perceptrons where such nonlinear functions are learned from data in a "hidden" layer instead of being assumed a priori.

Any of the methods discussed in chapter 10 on linear discrimination can be used to calculate $\mathbf{w}_i, i = 1, \ldots, K$ offline and then plugged into the network. These include parametric approach with a common covariance matrix, logistic discrimination, discrimination by regression, and support vector machines. In some cases, we do not have the whole sample at hand when training starts, and we need to iteratively update parameters as new examples arrive; we discuss this case of *online* learning in section 11.3.

Equation 11.5 defines a linear transformation from a d-dimensional space to a K-dimensional space and can also be used for dimensionality reduction if $K < d$. One can use any of the methods of chapter 6 to calculate $\mathbf{W}$ offline and then use the perceptrons to implement the transformation, for example, PCA. In such a case, we have a two-layer network where the first layer of perceptrons implements the linear transformation and the second layer implements the linear regression or classification in the new space. We note that because both are linear transformations, they can be combined and written down as a single layer. We will see the more interesting case where the first layer implements *nonlinear* dimensionality reduction in section 11.5.

11.3 Training a Perceptron

The perceptron defines a hyperplane, and the neural network perceptron is just a way of *implementing* the hyperplane. Given a data sample, the weight values can be calculated *offline* and then when they are plugged in, the perceptron can be used to calculate the output values.

In training neural networks, we generally use online learning where we are not given the whole sample, but we are given instances one by one and would like the network to update its parameters after each instance, adapting itself slowly in time. Such an approach is interesting for a number of reasons:

1. It saves us the cost of storing the training sample in an external memory and storing the intermediate results during optimization. An ap-

proach like support vector machines (chapter 13) may be quite costly with large samples, and in some applications, we may prefer a simpler approach where we do not need to store the whole sample and solve a complex optimization problem on it.

2. The problem may be changing in time, which means that the sample distribution is not fixed, and a training set cannot be chosen a priori. For example, we may be implementing a speech recognition system that adapts itself to its user.

3. There may be physical changes in the system. For example, in a robotic system, the components of the system may wear out, or sensors may degrade.

ONLINE LEARNING

In *online learning*, we do not write the error function over the whole sample but on individual instances. Starting from random initial weights, at each iteration we adjust the parameters a little bit to minimize the error, without forgetting what we have previously learned. If this error function is differentiable, we can use gradient descent.

For example, in regression the error on the single instance pair with index t, (x^t, r^t), is

$$E^t(\boldsymbol{w}|\boldsymbol{x}^t, r^t) = \frac{1}{2}(r^t - y^t)^2 = \frac{1}{2}[r^t - (\boldsymbol{w}^T\boldsymbol{x}^t)]^2$$

and for $j = 0, \ldots, d$, the online update is

$$\Delta w_j^t = \eta(r^t - y^t)x_j^t \tag{11.7}$$

where η is the learning factor, which is gradually decreased in time for convergence. This is known as *stochastic gradient descent*.

STOCHASTIC GRADIENT DESCENT

Similarly, update rules can be derived for classification problems using logistic discrimination where updates are done after each pattern, instead of summing them and doing the update after a complete pass over the training set. With two classes, for the single instance $(\boldsymbol{x}^t, \boldsymbol{r}^t)$ where $r_i^t = 1$ if $\boldsymbol{x}^t \in C_1$ and $r_i^t = 0$ if $\boldsymbol{x}^t \in C_2$, the single output is

$$y^t = \text{sigmoid}(\boldsymbol{w}^T\boldsymbol{x}^t)$$

and the cross-entropy is

$$E^t(\boldsymbol{w}|\boldsymbol{x}^t, \boldsymbol{r}^t) = -r^t \log y^t - (1 - r^t)\log(1 - y^t)$$

Using gradient descent, we get the following online update rule for $j = 0, \ldots, d$:

$$\Delta w_j^t = \eta(r^t - y^t)x_j^t \tag{11.8}$$

When there are $K > 2$ classes, for the single instance $(\boldsymbol{x}^t, \boldsymbol{r}^t)$ where $r_i^t = 1$ if $\boldsymbol{x}^t \in C_i$ and 0 otherwise, the outputs are

$$y_i^t = \frac{\exp \boldsymbol{w}_i^T \boldsymbol{x}^t}{\sum_k \exp \boldsymbol{w}_k^T \boldsymbol{x}^t}$$

and the cross-entropy is

$$E^t(\{\boldsymbol{w}_i\}_i | \boldsymbol{x}^t, \boldsymbol{r}^t) = -\sum_i r_i^t \log y_i^t$$

Using gradient descent, we get the following online update rule, for $i = 1, \ldots, K$, $j = 0, \ldots, d$:

$$\Delta w_{ij}^t = \eta(r_i^t - y_i^t)x_j^t \tag{11.9}$$

which is the same as the equations we saw in section 10.7 except that we do not sum over all of the instances but update after a single instance. The pseudocode of the algorithm is given in figure 11.3, which is the online version of figure 10.8.

Both equations 11.7 and 11.9 have the form

$$\text{Update} = \text{LearningFactor} \cdot (\text{DesiredOutput} - \text{ActualOutput}) \cdot \text{Input} \tag{11.10}$$

Let us try to get some insight into what this does. First, if the actual output is equal to the desired output, no update is done. When it is done, the magnitude of the update increases as the difference between the desired output and the actual output increases. We also see that if the actual output is less than the desired output, update is positive if the input is positive and negative if the input is negative. This has the effect of increasing the actual output and decreasing the difference. If the actual output is greater than the desired output, update is negative if the input is positive and positive if the input is negative; this decreases the actual output and makes it closer to the desired output.

When an update is done, its magnitude depends also on the input. If the input is close to 0, its effect on the actual output is small and therefore its weight is also updated by a small amount. The greater an input, the greater the update of its weight.

```
For i = 1,...,K
    For j = 0,...,d
        w_ij ← rand(−0.01,0.01)
Repeat
    For all (x^t, r^t) ∈ X in random order
        For i = 1,...,K
            o_i ← 0
            For j = 0,...,d
                o_i ← o_i + w_ij x_j^t
        For i = 1,...,K
            y_i ← exp(o_i) / Σ_k exp(o_k)
        For i = 1,...,K
            For j = 0,...,d
                w_ij ← w_ij + η(r_i^t − y_i) x_j^t
Until convergence
```

Figure 11.3 Perceptron training algorithm implementing stochastic online gradient descent for the case with $K > 2$ classes. This is the online version of the algorithm given in figure 10.8.

Finally, the magnitude of the update depends on the learning factor, η. If it is too large, updates depend too much on recent instances; it is as if the system has a very short memory. If this factor is small, many updates may be needed for convergence. In section 11.8.1, we discuss methods to speed up convergence.

11.4 Learning Boolean Functions

In a Boolean function, the inputs are binary and the output is 1 if the corresponding function value is true and 0 otherwise. Therefore, it can be seen as a two-class classification problem. As an example, for learning to AND two inputs, the table of inputs and required outputs is given in table 11.1. An example of a perceptron that implements AND and its geometric interpretation in two dimensions is given in figure 11.4. The discriminant is

$$y = s(x_1 + x_2 - 1.5)$$

Table 11.1 Input and output for the AND function

x_1	x_2	r
0	0	0
0	1	0
1	0	0
1	1	1

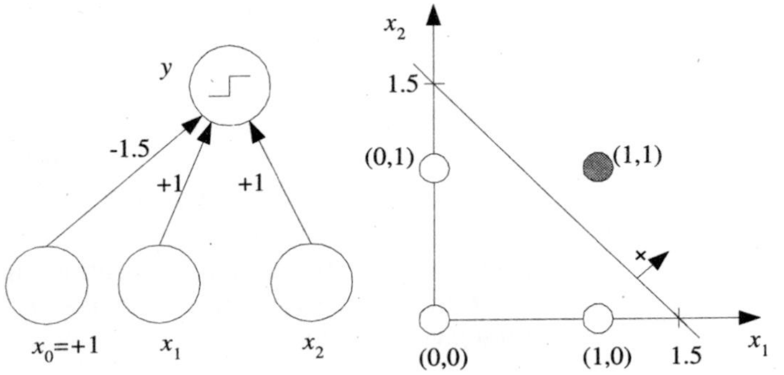

Figure 11.4 The perceptron that implements AND and its geometric interpretation.

that is, $\boldsymbol{x} = [1, x_1, x_2]^T$ and $\boldsymbol{w} = [-1.5, 1, 1]^T$. Note that $y = s(x_1+x_2-1.5)$ satisfies the four constraints given by the definition of AND function in table 11.1, for example, for $x_1 = 1, x_2 = 0$, $y = s(-0.5) = 0$. Similarly it can be shown that $y = s(x_1 + x_2 - 0.5)$ implements OR.

Though Boolean functions like AND and OR are linearly separable and are solvable using the perceptron, certain functions like XOR are not. The table of inputs and required outputs for XOR is given in table 11.2. As can be seen in figure 11.5, the problem is not linearly separable. This can also be proved by noting that there are no w_0, w_1, and w_2 values that satisfy the following set of inequalities:

$$
\begin{aligned}
& & w_0 &\le 0 \\
& w_2 + & w_0 &> 0 \\
w_1 + & & w_0 &> 0 \\
w_1 + & w_2 + & w_0 &\le 0
\end{aligned}
$$

Table 11.2 Input and output for the XOR function

x_1	x_2	r
0	0	0
0	1	1
1	0	1
1	1	0

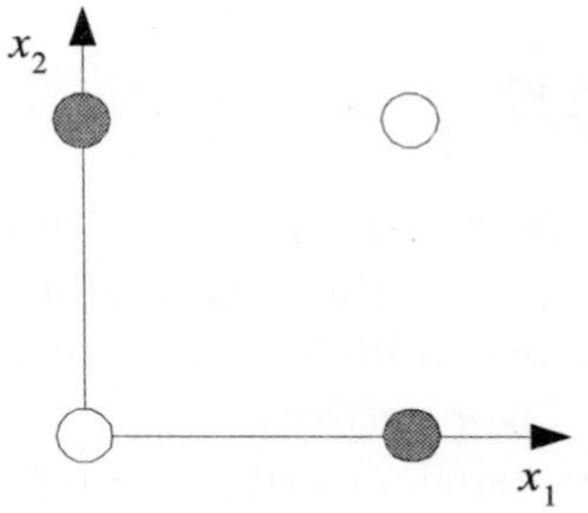

Figure 11.5 XOR problem is not linearly separable. We cannot draw a line where the empty circles are on one side and the filled circles on the other side.

This result should not be very surprising to us since the VC dimension of a line (in two dimensions) is three. With two binary inputs there are four cases, and thus we know that there exist problems with two inputs that are not solvable using a line; XOR is one of them.

11.5 Multilayer Perceptrons

A perceptron that has a single layer of weights can only approximate linear functions of the input and cannot solve problems like the XOR, where the discrimininant to be estimated is nonlinear. Similarly, a perceptron cannot be used for nonlinear regression. This limitation does not apply to feedforward networks with intermediate or *hidden layers* between the input and the output layers. If used for classification, such *multilayer perceptrons* (MLP) can implement nonlinear discriminants and, if used for regression, can approximate nonlinear functions of the input.

HIDDEN LAYERS

MULTILAYER PERCEPTRONS

Input $\boldsymbol{x}$ is fed to the input layer (including the bias), the "activation" propagates in the forward direction, and the values of the hidden units z_h are calculated (see figure 11.6). Each hidden unit is a perceptron by itself and applies the nonlinear sigmoid function to its weighted sum:

$$z_h = \text{sigmoid}(\boldsymbol{w}_h^T \boldsymbol{x}) = \frac{1}{1 + \exp\left[-\left(\sum_{j=1}^{d} w_{hj}x_j + w_{h0}\right)\right]}, \quad h = 1, \ldots, H \tag{11.11}$$

The output y_i are perceptrons in the second layer taking the hidden units as their inputs

$$y_i = \boldsymbol{v}_i^T \boldsymbol{z} = \sum_{h=1}^{H} v_{ih} z_h + v_{i0} \tag{11.12}$$

where there is also a bias unit in the hidden layer, which we denote by z_0, and v_{i0} are the bias weights. The input layer of x_j is not counted since no computation is done there and when there is a hidden layer, this is a two-layer network.

As usual, in a regression problem, there is no nonlinearity in the output layer in calculating y. In a two-class discrimination task, there is one sigmoid output unit and when there are $K > 2$ classes, there are K outputs with softmax as the output nonlinearity.

If the hidden units' outputs were linear, the hidden layer would be of no use: Linear combination of linear combinations is another linear combination. Sigmoid is the continuous, differentiable version of thresholding. We need differentiability because the learning equations we will see are gradient-based. Another sigmoid (S-shaped) nonlinear basis function that can be used is the hyperbolic tangent function, tanh, which ranges from -1 to $+1$, instead of 0 to $+1$. In practice, there is no difference between using the sigmoid and the tanh. Still another possibility is the Gaussian, which uses Euclidean distance instead of the dot product for similarity; we discuss such radial basis function networks in chapter 12.

The output is a linear combination of the nonlinear basis function values computed by the hidden units. It can be said that the hidden units make a nonlinear transformation from the d-dimensional input space to the H-dimensional space spanned by the hidden units, and, in this space, the second output layer implements a linear function.

One is not limited to having one hidden layer, and more hidden layers with their own incoming weights can be placed after the first hidden layer with sigmoid hidden units, thus calculating nonlinear functions of the

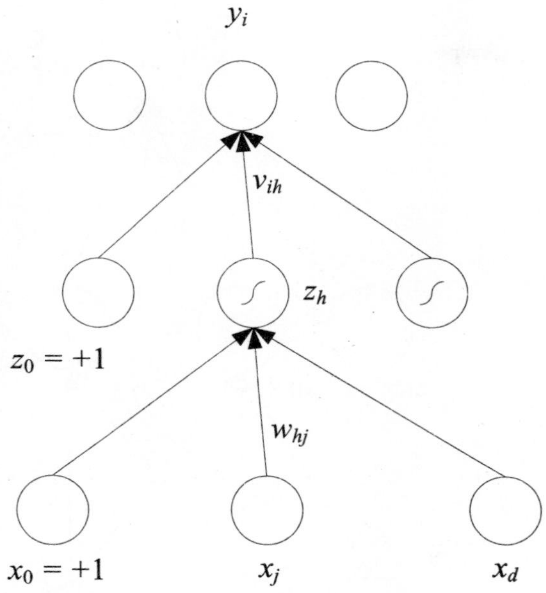

Figure 11.6 The structure of a multilayer perceptron. $x_j, j = 0, \ldots, d$ are the inputs and $z_h, h = 1, \ldots, H$ are the hidden units where H is the dimensionality of this hidden space. z_0 is the bias of the hidden layer. $y_i, i = 1, \ldots, K$ are the output units. w_{hj} are weights in the first layer, and v_{ih} are the weights in the second layer.

first layer of hidden units and implementing more complex functions of the inputs. In practice, people rarely go beyond one hidden layer since analyzing a network with many hidden layers is quite complicated; but sometimes when the hidden layer contains too many hidden units, it may be sensible to go to multiple hidden layers, preferring "long and narrow" networks to "short and fat" networks.

11.6 MLP as a Universal Approximator

We can represent any Boolean function as a disjunction of conjunctions, and such a Boolean expression can be implemented by a multilayer perceptron with one hidden layer. Each conjunction is implemented by one

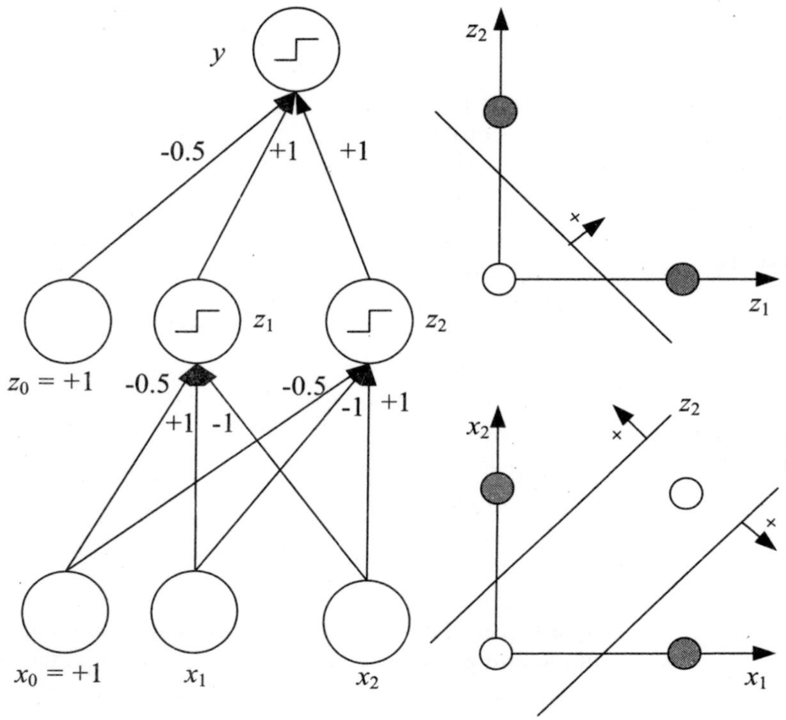

Figure 11.7 The multilayer perceptron that solves the XOR problem. The hidden units and the output have the threshold activation function with threshold at 0.

hidden unit and the disjunction by the output unit. For example,

$$x_1 \text{ XOR } x_2 = (x_1 \text{ AND } \sim x_2) \text{ OR } (\sim x_1 \text{ AND } x_2)$$

We have seen previously how to implement AND and OR using perceptrons. So two perceptrons can in parallel implement the two AND, and another perceptron on top can OR them together (see figure 11.7). We see that the first layer maps inputs from the (x_1, x_2) to the (z_1, z_2) space defined by the first-layer perceptrons. Note that both inputs, (0,0) and (1,1), are mapped to (0,0) in the (z_1, z_2) space, allowing linear separability in this second space.

Thus in the binary case, for every input combination where the output is 1, we define a hidden unit that checks for that particular conjunction of the input. The output layer then implements the disjunction. Note that this is just an existence proof, and such networks may not be practical as up to 2^d hidden units may be necessary when there are d inputs. Such an architecture implements table lookup and does not generalize.

UNIVERSAL APPROXIMATION

PIECEWISE CONSTANT APPROXIMATION

We can extend this to the case where inputs are continuous to show that similarly, any arbitrary function with continuous input and outputs can be approximated with a multilayer perceptron. The proof of *universal approximation* is easy with two hidden layers. For every input case or region, that region can be delimited by hyperplanes on all sides using hidden units on the first hidden layer. A hidden unit in the second layer then ANDs them together to bound the region. We then set the weight of the connection from that hidden unit to the output unit equal to the desired function value. This gives a *piecewise constant approximation* of the function; it corresponds to ignoring all the terms in the Taylor expansion except the constant term. Its accuracy may be increased to the desired value by increasing the number of hidden units and placing a finer grid on the input. Note that no formal bounds are given on the number of hidden units required. This property just reassures us that there is a solution; it does not help us in any other way. It has been proven that an MLP with *one* hidden layer (with an arbitrary number of hidden units) can learn any nonlinear function of the input (Hornik, Stinchcombe, and White 1989).

11.7 Backpropagation Algorithm

Training a multilayer perceptron is the same as training a perceptron; the only difference is that now the output is a nonlinear function of the input thanks to the nonlinear basis function in the hidden units. Considering the hidden units as inputs, the second layer is a perceptron and we already know how to update the parameters, v_{ij}, in this case, given the inputs z_h. For the first-layer weights, w_{hj}, we use the chain rule to calculate the gradient:

$$\frac{\partial E}{\partial w_{hj}} = \frac{\partial E}{\partial y_i}\frac{\partial y_i}{\partial z_h}\frac{\partial z_h}{\partial w_{hj}}$$

BACKPROPAGATION

It is as if the error propagates from the output y back to the inputs and hence the name *backpropagation* was coined (Rumelhart, Hinton, and Williams 1986a).

11.7.1 Nonlinear Regression

Let us first take the case of nonlinear regression (with a single output) calculated as

$$y^t = \sum_{h=1}^{H} v_h z_h^t + v_0 \tag{11.13}$$

with z_h computed by equation 11.11. The error function over the whole sample in regression is

$$E(\mathbf{W}, \mathbf{v}|\mathcal{X}) = \frac{1}{2}\sum_t (r^t - y^t)^2 \tag{11.14}$$

The second layer is a perceptron with hidden units as the inputs, and we use the least-squares rule to update the second-layer weights:

$$\Delta v_h = \eta \sum_t (r^t - y^t) z_h^t \tag{11.15}$$

The first layer also consists of perceptrons with the hidden units as the output units, but in updating the first-layer weights, we cannot use the least-squares rule directly because we do not have a desired output specified for the hidden units. This is where the chain rule comes into play. We write

$$\begin{aligned}
\Delta w_{hj} &= -\eta \frac{\partial E}{\partial w_{hj}} \\
&= -\eta \sum_t \frac{\partial E^t}{\partial y^t} \frac{\partial y^t}{\partial z_h^t} \frac{\partial z_h^t}{\partial w_{hj}} \\
&= -\eta \sum_t \underbrace{-(r^t - y^t)}_{\partial E^t/\partial y^t} \underbrace{v_h}_{\partial y^t/\partial z_h^t} \underbrace{z_h^t(1 - z_h^t)x_j^t}_{\partial z_h^t/\partial w_{hj}} \\
&= \eta \sum_t (r^t - y^t) v_h z_h^t (1 - z_h^t) x_j^t
\end{aligned} \tag{11.16}$$

The product of the first two terms $(r^t - y^t)v_h$ acts like the error term for hidden unit h. This error is *backpropagated* from the error to the hidden unit. $(r^t - y^t)$ is the error in the output, weighted by the "responsibility" of the hidden unit as given by its weight v_h. In the third term, $z_h(1 - z_h)$ is the derivative of the sigmoid and x_j^t is the derivative of the weighted sum with respect to the weight w_{hj}. Note that the change in the first-layer weight, Δw_{hj}, makes use of the second-layer weight, v_h. Therefore, we should calculate the changes in both layers and update the first-layer weights, making use of the *old* value of the second-layer weights, then update the second-layer weights.

Weights, w_{hj}, v_h are started from small random values initially, for example, in the range $[-0.01, 0.01]$, so as not to saturate the sigmoids. It is also a good idea to normalize the inputs so that they all have 0 mean and unit variance and have the same scale, since we use a single η parameter.

BATCH LEARNING

With the learning equations given here, for each pattern, we compute the direction in which each parameter needs be changed and the magnitude of this change. In *batch learning*, we accumulate these changes over all patterns and make the change once after a complete pass over the whole training set is made, as shown in the previous update equations.

EPOCH

It is also possible to have online learning, by updating the weights after each pattern, thereby implementing stochastic gradient descent. A complete pass over all the patterns in the training set is called an *epoch*. The learning factor, η, should be chosen smaller in this case and patterns should be scanned in a random order. Online learning converges faster because there may be similar patterns in the dataset, and the stochasticity has an effect like adding noise and may help escape local minima.

An example of training a multilayer perceptron for regression is shown in figure 11.8. As training continues, the MLP fit gets closer to the underlying function and error decreases (see figure 11.9). Figure 11.10 shows how the MLP fit is formed as a sum of the outputs of the hidden units.

It is also possible to have multiple output units, in which case a number of regression problems are learned at the same time. We have

$$y_i^t = \sum_{h=1}^{H} v_{ih} z_h^t + v_{i0} \tag{11.17}$$

and the error is

$$E(\mathbf{W}, \mathbf{V}|\mathcal{X}) = \frac{1}{2} \sum_t \sum_i (r_i^t - y_i^t)^2 \tag{11.18}$$

The batch update rules are then

$$\Delta v_{ih} = \eta \sum_t (r_i^t - y_i^t) z_h^t \tag{11.19}$$

$$\Delta w_{hj} = \eta \sum_t \left[\sum_i (r_i^t - y_i^t) v_{ih} \right] z_h^t (1 - z_h^t) x_j^t \tag{11.20}$$

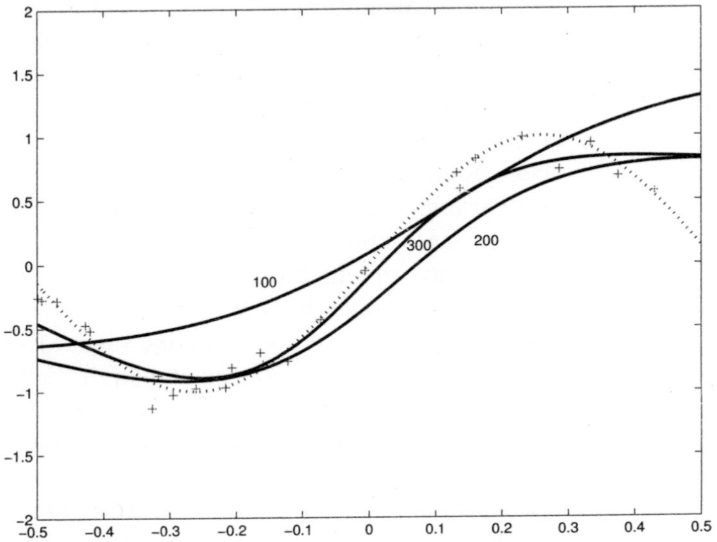

Figure 11.8 Sample training data shown as '+', where $x^t \sim U(-0.5, 0.5)$, and $y^t = f(x^t) + \mathcal{N}(0, 0.1)$. $f(x) = \sin(6x)$ is shown by a dashed line. The evolution of the fit of an MLP with two hidden units after 100, 200, and 300 epochs is drawn.

$\sum_i (r_i^t - y_i^t) v_{ih}$ is the accumulated backpropagated error of hidden unit h from all output units. Pseudocode is given in figure 11.11. Note that in this case, all output units share the same hidden units and thus use the same hidden representation, hence, we are assuming that corresponding to these different outputs, we have related prediction problems. An alternative is to train separate multilayer perceptrons for the separate regression problems, each with its own separate hidden units.

11.7.2 Two-Class Discrimination

When there are two classes, one output unit suffices:

$$y^t = \text{sigmoid}\left(\sum_{h=1}^{H} v_h z_h^t + v_0\right) \tag{11.21}$$

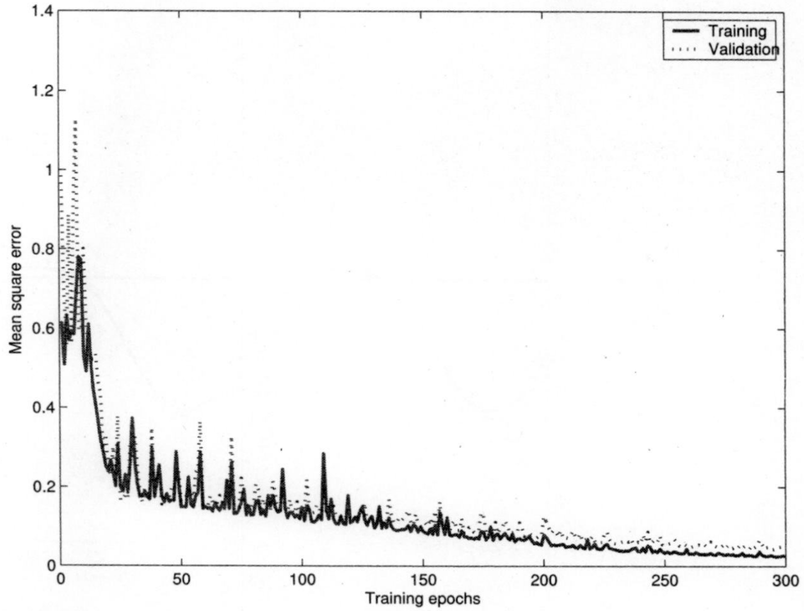

Figure 11.9 The mean square error on training and validation sets as a function of training epochs.

which approximates $P(C_1|\mathbf{x}^t)$ and $\hat{P}(C_2|\mathbf{x}^t) \equiv 1 - y^t$. We remember from section 10.7 that the error function in this case is

$$E(\mathbf{W}, \mathbf{v}|\mathcal{X}) = -\sum_t r^t \log y^t + (1 - r^t)\log(1 - y^t) \tag{11.22}$$

The update equations implementing gradient descent are

$$\Delta v_h = \eta \sum_t (r^t - y^t) z_h^t \tag{11.23}$$

$$\Delta w_{hj} = \eta \sum_t (r^t - y^t) v_h z_h^t (1 - z_h^t) x_j^t \tag{11.24}$$

As in the simple perceptron, the update equations for regression and classification are identical (which does not mean that the values are).

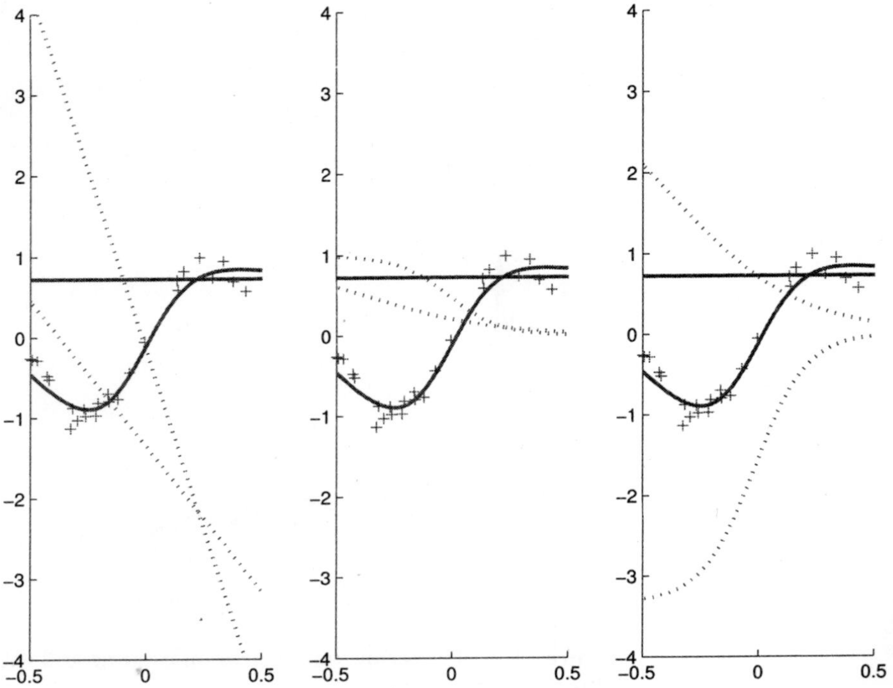

Figure 11.10 (a) The hyperplanes of the hidden unit weights on the first layer, (b) hidden unit outputs, and (c) hidden unit outputs multiplied by the weights on the second layer. Two sigmoid hidden units slightly displaced, one multiplied by a negative weight, when added, implement a bump. With more hidden units, a better approximation is attained (see figure 11.12).

11.7.3 Multiclass Discrimination

In a $(K > 2)$-class classification problem, there are K outputs

$$o_i^t = \sum_{h=1}^{H} v_{ih} z_h^t + v_{i0} \tag{11.25}$$

and we use softmax to indicate the dependency between classes; namely, they are mutually exclusive and exhaustive:

$$y_i^t = \frac{\exp o_i^t}{\sum_k \exp o_k^t} \tag{11.26}$$

```
Initialize all v_ih and w_hj to rand(-0.01,0.01)
Repeat
    For all (x^t, r^t) ∈ X in random order
        For h = 1,...,H
            z_h ← sigmoid(w_h^T x^t)
        For i = 1,...,K
            y_i = v_i^T z
        For i = 1,...,K
            Δv_i = η(r_i^t - y_i^t)z
        For h = 1,...,H
            Δw_h = η(Σ_i(r_i^t - y_i^t)v_ih)z_h(1 - z_h)x^t
        For i = 1,...,K
            v_i ← v_i + Δv_i
        For h = 1,...,H
            w_h ← w_h + Δw_h
Until convergence
```

Figure 11.11 Backpropagation algorithm for training a multilayer perceptron for regression with K outputs. This code can easily be adapted for two-class classification (by setting a single sigmoid output) and to $K > 2$ classification (by using softmax outputs).

where y_i approximates $P(C_i|\mathbf{x}^t)$. The error function is

$$E(\mathbf{W},\mathbf{V}|\mathcal{X}) = -\sum_t \sum_i r_i^t \log y_i^t \tag{11.27}$$

and we get the update equations using gradient descent:

$$\Delta v_{ih} = \eta \sum_t (r_i^t - y_i^t) z_h^t \tag{11.28}$$

$$\Delta w_{hj} = \eta \sum_t \left[\sum_i (r_i^t - y_i^t) v_{ih} \right] z_h^t (1 - z_h^t) x_j^t \tag{11.29}$$

Richard and Lippmann (1991) have shown that given a network of enough complexity and sufficient training data, a suitably trained multilayer perceptron estimates posterior probabilities.

11.7.4 Multiple Hidden Layers

As we saw before, it is possible to have multiple hidden layers each with its own weights and applying the sigmoid function to its weighted sum. For regression, let us say, if we have a multilayer perceptron with two hidden layers, we write

$$
\begin{aligned}
z_{1h} &= \text{sigmoid}(\boldsymbol{w}_{1h}^T \boldsymbol{x}) = \text{sigmoid}\left(\sum_{j=1}^{d} w_{1hj}x_j + w_{1h0}\right), \; h = 1, \ldots, H_1 \\
z_{2l} &= \text{sigmoid}(\boldsymbol{w}_{2l}^T \boldsymbol{z}_1) = \text{sigmoid}\left(\sum_{h=0}^{H_1} w_{2lh}z_{1h} + w_{2l0}\right), \; l = 1, \ldots, H_2 \\
y &= \boldsymbol{v}^T \boldsymbol{z}_2 = \sum_{l=1}^{H_2} v_l z_{2l} + v_0
\end{aligned}
$$

where $\boldsymbol{w}_{1h}$ and $\boldsymbol{w}_{2l}$ are the first- and second-layer weights, z_{1h} and z_{2h} are the units on the first and second hidden layers, and $\boldsymbol{v}$ are the third-layer weights. Training such a network is similar except that to train the first-layer weights, we need to backpropagate one more layer (exercise 5).

11.8 Training Procedures

11.8.1 Improving Convergence

Gradient descent has various advantages. It is simple. It is local; namely, the change in a weight uses only the values of the presynaptic and postsynaptic units and the error (suitably backpropagated). When online training is used, it does not need to store the training set and can adapt as the task to be learned changes. Because of these reasons, it can be (and is) implemented in hardware. But by itself, gradient descent converges slowly. When learning time is important, one can use more sophisticated optimization methods (Battiti 1992). Bishop (1995) discusses in detail the application of conjugate gradient and second-order methods to the training of multilayer perceptrons. However, there are two frequently used simple techniques that improve the performance of the gradient descent considerably, making gradient-based methods feasible in real applications.

Momentum

Let us say w_i is any weight in a multilayer perceptron in any layer, including the biases. At each parameter update, successive Δw_i^t values may be so different that large oscillations may occur and slow convergence. t is the time index that is the epoch number in batch learning and the iteration number in online learning. The idea is to take a running average by incorporating the previous update in the current change as if there is a MOMENTUM *momentum* due to previous updates:

$$\Delta w_i^t = -\eta \frac{\partial E^t}{\partial w_i} + \alpha \Delta w_i^{t-1} \tag{11.30}$$

α is generally taken between 0.5 and 1.0. This approach is especially useful when online learning is used, where as a result we get an effect of averaging and smooth the trajectory during convergence. The disadvantage is that the past Δw_i^{t-1} values should be stored in extra memory.

Adaptive Learning Rate

In gradient descent, the learning factor η determines the magnitude of change to be made in the parameter. It is generally taken between 0.0 and 1.0, mostly less than or equal to 0.2. It can be made adaptive for faster convergence, where it is kept large when learning takes place and is decreased when learning slows down:

$$\Delta \eta = \begin{cases} +a & \text{if } E^{t+\tau} < E^t \\ -b\eta & \text{otherwise} \end{cases} \tag{11.31}$$

Thus we increase η by a constant amount if the error on the training set decreases and decrease it geometrically if it increases. Because E may oscillate from one epoch to another, it is a better idea to take the average of the past few epochs as E^t.

11.8.2 Overtraining

A multilayer perceptron with d inputs, H hidden units, and K outputs has $H(d+1)$ weights in the first layer and $K(H+1)$ weights in the second layer. Both the space and time complexity of an MLP is $\mathcal{O}(H \cdot (K+d))$. When e denotes the number of training epochs, training time complexity is $\mathcal{O}(e \cdot H \cdot (K+d))$.

In an application, d and K are predefined and H is the parameter that we play with to tune the complexity of the model. We know from previous chapters that an overcomplex model memorizes the noise in the training set and does not generalize to the validation set. For example, we have previously seen this phenomenon in the case of polynomial regression where we noticed that in the presence of noise or small samples, increasing the polynomial order leads to worse generalization. Similarly in an MLP, when the number of hidden units is large, the generalization accuracy deteriorates (see figure 11.12), and the bias/variance dilemma also holds for the MLP, as it does for any statistical estimator (Geman, Bienenstock, and Doursat 1992).

A similar behavior happens when training is continued too long: As more training epochs are made, the error on the training set decreases, but the error on the validation set starts to increase beyond a certain point (see figure 11.13). Remember that initially all the weights are close to 0 and thus have little effect. As training continues, the most important weights start moving away from 0 and are utilized. But if training is continued further on to get less and less error on the training set, almost all weights are updated away from 0 and effectively become parameters. Thus as training continues, it is as if new parameters are added to the system, increasing the complexity and leading to poor generalization. Learning should be *stopped early* to alleviate this problem of *overtraining*. The optimal point to stop training, and the optimal number of hidden units, is determined through cross-validation, which involves testing the network's performance on validation data unseen during training.

EARLY STOPPING
OVERTRAINING

Because of the nonlinearity, the error function has many minima and gradient descent converges to the nearest minimum. To be able to assess expected error, the same network is trained a number of times starting from different initial weight values, and the average of the validation error is computed.

11.8.3 Structuring the Network

In some applications, we may believe that the input has a local structure. For example, in vision we know that nearby pixels are correlated and there are local features like edges and corners; any object, for example, a handwritten digit, may be defined as a combination of such primitives. Similarly, in speech, locality is in time and inputs close in time can be grouped as speech primitives. By combining these primitives, longer ut-

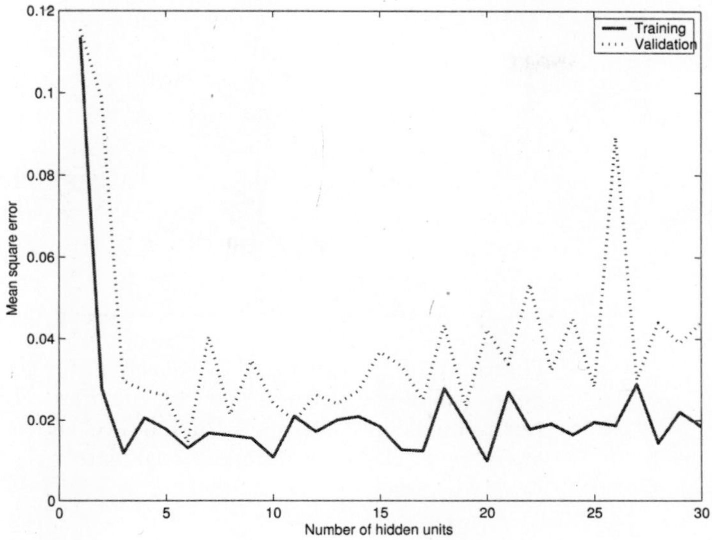

Figure 11.12 As complexity increases, training error is fixed but the validation error starts to increase and the network starts to overfit.

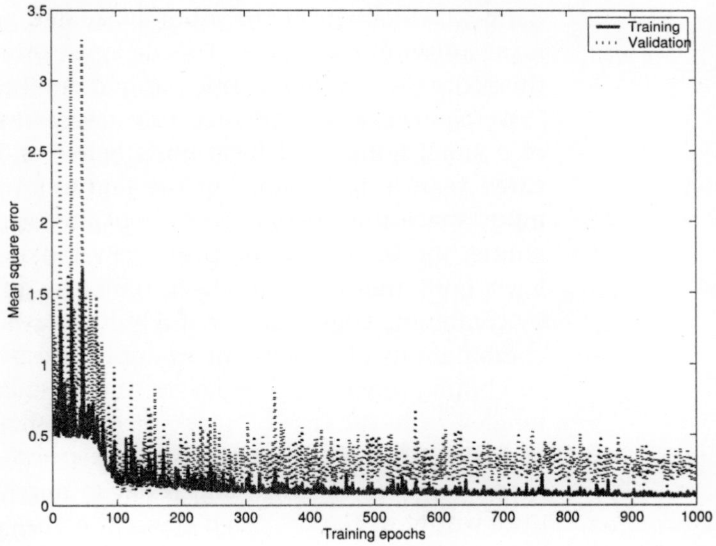

Figure 11.13 As training continues, the validation error starts to increase and the network starts to overfit.

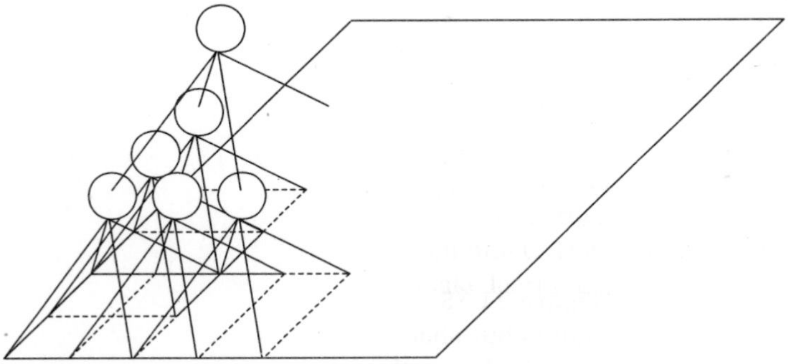

Figure 11.14 A structured MLP. Each unit is connected to a local group of units below it and checks for a particular feature—for example, edge, corner, and so forth—in vision. Only one hidden unit is shown for each region; typically there are many to check for different local features.

terances, for example, speech phonemes, may be defined. In such a case when designing the MLP, hidden units are not connected to all input units because not all inputs are correlated. Instead, we define hidden units that define a window over the input space and are connected to only a small local subset of the inputs. This decreases the number of connections and therefore the number of free parameters (Le Cun et al. 1989).

We can repeat this in successive layers where each layer is connected to a small number of local units below and checks for a more complicated feature by combining the features below in a larger part of the input space until we get to the output layer (see figure 11.14). For example, the input may be pixels. By looking at pixels, the first hidden layer units may learn to check for edges of various orientations. Then by combining edges, the second hidden layer units can learn to check for combinations of edges—for example, arcs, corners, line ends—and then combining them in upper layers, the units can look for semi-circles, rectangles, or in the case of a face recognition application, eyes, mouth, and so forth. This is the example of a *hierarchical cone* where features get more complex, abstract, and fewer in number as we go up the network until we get to classes. Such an architecture is called a *convolutional neural network* where the work of each hidden unit is considered to be a convolution of its input with its weight vector; an earlier similar architecture is the *neocognitron* (Fukushima 1980).

HIERARCHICAL CONE

CONVOLUTIONAL NEURAL NETWORK

NEOCOGNITRON

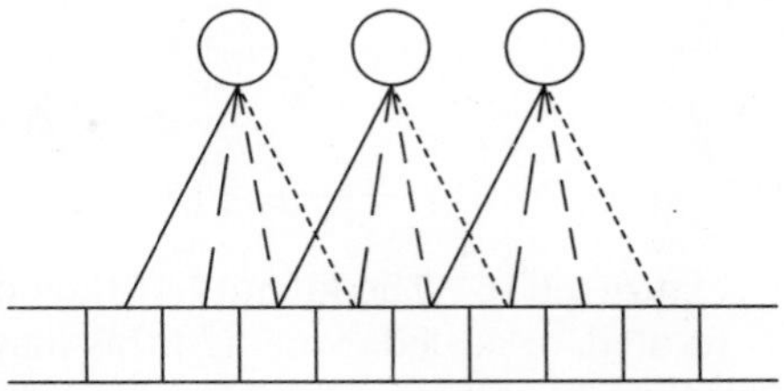

Figure 11.15 In weight sharing, different units have connections to different inputs but share the same weight value (denoted by line type). Only one set of units is shown; there should be multiple sets of units, each checking for different features.

WEIGHT SHARING

In such a case, we can further reduce the number of parameters by *weight sharing*. Taking the example of visual recognition again, we can see that when we look for features like oriented edges, they may be present in different parts of the input space. So instead of defining independent hidden units learning different features in different parts of the input space, we can have copies of the same hidden units looking at different parts of the input space (see figure 11.15). During learning, we calculate the gradients by taking different inputs, then we average these up and make a single update. This implies a single parameter that defines the weight on multiple connections. Also, because the update on a weight is based on gradients for several inputs, it is as if the training set is effectively multiplied.

11.8.4 Hints

The knowledge of local structure allows us to prestructure the multilayer network, and with weight sharing it has fewer parameters. The alternative of an MLP with completely connected layers has no such structure and is more difficult to train. Knowledge of any sort related to the application should be built into the network structure whenever possible.

HINTS

These are called *hints* (Abu-Mostafa 1995) and are the properties of the target function that are known to us independent of the training examples.

In image recognition, there are invariance hints: The identity of an object does not change when it is rotated, translated, or scaled (see figure 11.16). Hints are auxiliary information that can be used to guide the

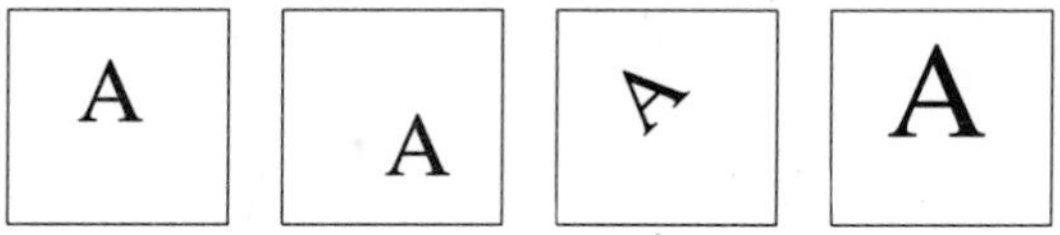

Figure 11.16 The identity of the object does not change when it is translated, rotated, or scaled. Note that this may not always be true, or may be true up to a point: 'b' and 'q' are rotated versions of each other. These are hints that can be incorporated into the learning process to make learning easier.

learning process and are especially useful when the training set is limited. There are different ways in which hints can be used:

VIRTUAL EXAMPLES

1. Hints can be used to create *virtual examples.* For example, knowing that the object is invariant to scale, from a given training example, we can generate multiple copies at different scales and add them to the training set with the same label. This has the advantage that we increase the training set and do not need to modify the learner in any way. The problem may be that too many examples may be needed for the learner to learn the invariance.

2. The invariance may be implemented as a preprocessing stage. For example, optical character readers have a preprocessing stage where the input character image is centered and normalized for size and slant. This is the easiest solution, when it is possible.

3. The hint may be incorporated into the network structure. Local structure and weight sharing, which we saw in section 11.8.3, is one example where we get invariance to small translations and rotations.

4. The hint may also be incorporated by modifying the error function. Let us say we know that $\boldsymbol{x}$ and $\boldsymbol{x}'$ are the same from the application's point of view, where $\boldsymbol{x}'$ may be a "virtual example" of $\boldsymbol{x}$. That is, $f(\boldsymbol{x}) = f(\boldsymbol{x}')$, when $f(\boldsymbol{x})$ is the function we would like to approximate. Let us denote by $g(\boldsymbol{x}|\theta)$, our approximation function, for example, an MLP where θ are its weights. Then, for all such pairs $(\boldsymbol{x}, \boldsymbol{x}')$, we define the penalty function

$$E_h = [g(\boldsymbol{x}|\theta) - g(\boldsymbol{x}'|\theta)]^2$$

and add it as an extra term to the usual error function:

$$E' = E + \lambda_h \cdot E_h$$

This is a penalty term penalizing the cases where our predictions do not obey the hint, and λ_h is the weight of such a penalty (Abu-Mostafa 1995).

Another example is the approximation hint: Let us say that for x, we do not know the exact value, $f(x)$, but we know that it is in the interval, $[a_x, b_x]$. Then our added penalty term is

$$E_h = \begin{cases} 0 & \text{if } g(x|\theta) \in [a_x, b_x] \\ (g(x) - a_x)^2 & \text{if } g(x|\theta) < a_x \\ (g(x) - b_x)^2 & \text{if } g(x|\theta) > b_x \end{cases}$$

This is similar to the error function used in support vector regression (section 13.10), which tolerates small approximation errors.

TANGENT PROP

Still another example is the *tangent prop* (Simard et al. 1992) where the transformation against which we are defining the hint—for example, rotation by an angle—is modeled by a function. The usual error function is modified (by adding another term) so as to allow parameters to move along this line of transformation without changing the error.

11.9 Tuning the Network Size

Previously we saw that when the network is too large and has too many free parameters, generalization may not be well. To find the optimal network size, the most common approach is to try many different architectures, train them all on the training set, and choose the one that generalizes best to the validation set. Another approach is to incorporate this *structural adaptation* into the learning algorithm. There are two ways this can be done:

STRUCTURAL ADAPTATION

1. In the *destructive* approach, we start with a large network and gradually remove units and/or connections that are not necessary.
2. In the *constructive* approach, we start with a small network and gradually add units and/or connections to improve performance.

WEIGHT DECAY

One destructive method is *weight decay* where the idea is to remove unnecessary connections. Ideally to be able to determine whether a unit or connection is necessary, we need to train once with and once without and check the difference in error on a separate validation set. This is costly since it should be done for all combinations of such units/connections.

Given that a connection is not used if its weight is 0, we give each connection a tendency to decay to 0 so that it disappears unless it is reinforced explicitly to decrease error. For any weight w_i in the network, we use the update rule:

$$\Delta w_i = -\eta \frac{\partial E}{\partial w_i} - \lambda w_i \tag{11.32}$$

This is equivalent to doing gradient descent on the error function with an added penalty term, penalizing networks with many nonzero weights:

$$E' = E + \frac{\lambda}{2} \sum_i w_i^2 \tag{11.33}$$

Simpler networks are better generalizers is a hint that we implement by adding a penalty term. Note that we are not saying that simple networks are always better than large networks; we are saying that if we have two networks that have the same training error, the simpler one—namely, the one with fewer weights—has a higher probability of better generalizing to the validation set.

The effect of the second term in equation 11.32 is like that of a spring that pulls each weight to 0. Starting from a value close to 0, unless the actual error gradient is large and causes an update, due to the second term, the weight will gradually decay to 0. λ is the parameter that determines the relative importances of the error on the training set and the complexity due to nonzero parameters and thus determines the speed of decay: With large λ, weights will be pulled to 0 no matter what the training error is; with small λ, there is not much penalty for nonzero weights. λ is fine-tuned using cross-validation.

DYNAMIC NODE CREATION

Instead of starting from a large network and *pruning* unnecessary connections or units, one can start from a small network and add units and associated connections should the need arise (figure 11.17). In *dynamic node creation* (Ash 1989), an MLP with one hidden layer with one hidden unit is trained and after convergence, if the error is still high, another hidden unit is added. The incoming weights of the newly added unit and its outgoing weight are initialized randomly and trained with the previ-

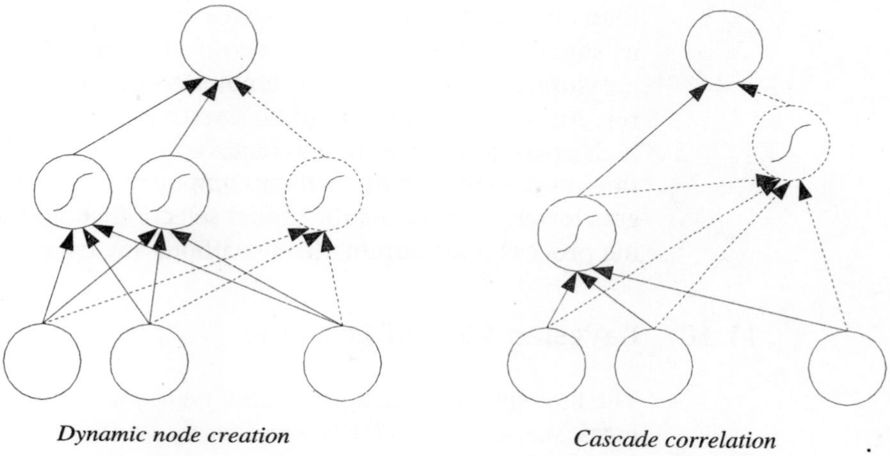

Figure 11.17 Two examples of constructive algorithms. Dynamic node creation adds a unit to an existing layer. Cascade correlation adds each unit as a new hidden layer connected to all the previous layers. Dashed lines denote the newly added unit/connections. Bias units/weights are omitted for clarity.

ously existing weights that are not reinitialized and continue from their previous values.

CASCADE CORRELATION

In *cascade correlation* (Fahlman and Lebiere 1990), each added unit is a new hidden unit in another hidden layer. Every hidden layer has only one unit that is connected to all of the hidden units preceding it and the inputs. The previously existing weights are frozen and are not trained; only the incoming and outgoing weights of the newly added unit are trained.

Dynamic node creation adds a new hidden unit to an existing hidden layer and never adds another hidden layer. Cascade correlation always adds a new hidden layer with a single unit. The ideal constructive method should be able to decide when to introduce a new hidden layer and when to add a unit to an existing layer. This is an open research problem.

Incremental algorithms are interesting because they correspond to modifying not only the parameters but also the model structure during learning. We can think of a space defined by the structure of the multilayer perceptron and operators corresponding to adding/removing unit(s) or layer(s) to move in this space (Aran et al. 2009). Incremental algorithms then do a search in this state space where operators are tried (according to some order) and accepted or rejected depending on some goodness measure, for example, some combination of complexity and validation error. Another example would be a setting in polynomial regression where high-order terms are added/removed during training automatically, fitting model complexity to data complexity. As the cost of computation gets lower, such automatic model selection should be a part of the learning process done automatically without any user interference.

11.10 Bayesian View of Learning

The Bayesian approach in training neural networks considers the parameters, namely, connection weights, w_i, as random variables drawn from a prior distribution $p(w_i)$ and computes the posterior probability given the data

$$p(\mathbf{w}|\mathcal{X}) = \frac{p(\mathcal{X}|\mathbf{w})p(\mathbf{w})}{p(\mathcal{X})} \tag{11.34}$$

where $\mathbf{w}$ is the vector of all weights of the network. The MAP estimate $\hat{\mathbf{w}}$ is the mode of the posterior

$$\hat{\mathbf{w}}_{MAP} = \arg\max_{\mathbf{w}} \log p(\mathbf{w}|\mathcal{X}) \tag{11.35}$$

Taking the log of equation 11.34, we get

$$\log p(\mathbf{w}|\mathcal{X}) = \log p(\mathcal{X}|\mathbf{w}) + \log p(\mathbf{w}) + C$$

The first term on the right is the log likelihood, and the second is the log of the prior. If the weights are independent and the prior is taken as Gaussian, $\mathcal{N}(0, 1/2\lambda)$

$$p(\mathbf{w}) = \prod_i p(w_i) \text{ where } p(w_i) = c \cdot \exp\left[-\frac{w_i^2}{2(1/2\lambda)}\right] \tag{11.36}$$

the MAP estimate minimizes the augmented error function

$$E' = E + \lambda \|\mathbf{w}\|^2 \tag{11.37}$$

where E is the usual classification or regression error (negative log likelihood). This augmented error is exactly the error function we used in weight decay (equation 11.33). Using a large λ assumes small variability in parameters, puts a larger force on them to be close to 0, and takes into account the prior more than the data; if λ is small, then the allowed variability of the parameters is larger. This approach of removing unnecessary parameters is known as *ridge regression* in statistics.

RIDGE REGRESSION

REGULARIZATION

This is another example of *regularization* with a cost function, combining the fit to data and model complexity

$$\text{cost} = \text{data-misfit} + \lambda \cdot \text{complexity} \tag{11.38}$$

The use of Bayesian estimation in training multilayer perceptrons is treated in MacKay 1992a, b. We are going to talk about Bayesian estimation in more detail in chapter 16.

Empirically, it has been seen that after training, most of the weights of a multilayer perceptron are distributed normally around 0, justifying the use of weight decay. But this may not always be the case. Nowlan and Hinton (1992) proposed *soft weight sharing* where weights are drawn from a mixture of Gaussians, allowing them to form multiple clusters, not one. Also, these clusters may be centered anywhere and not necessarily at 0, and have variances that are modifiable. This changes the prior of equation 11.36 to a mixture of $M \geq 2$ Gaussians

SOFT WEIGHT SHARING

$$p(w_i) = \sum_{j=1}^{M} \alpha_j p_j(w_i) \tag{11.39}$$

where α_j are the priors and $p_j(w_i) \sim \mathcal{N}(m_j, s_j^2)$ are the component Gaussians. M is set by the user and α_j, m_j, s_j are learned from the data. Using such a prior and augmenting the error function with its log during training, the weights converge to decrease error and also are grouped automatically to increase the log prior.

11.11 Dimensionality Reduction

In a multilayer perceptron, if the number of hidden units is less than the number of inputs, the first layer performs a dimensionality reduction. The form of this reduction and the new space spanned by the hidden units depend on what the MLP is trained for. If the MLP is for classification with output units following the hidden layer, then the new space is defined and the mapping is learned to minimize classification error (see figure 11.18).

We can get an idea of what the MLP is doing by analyzing the weights. We know that the dot product is maximum when the two vectors are

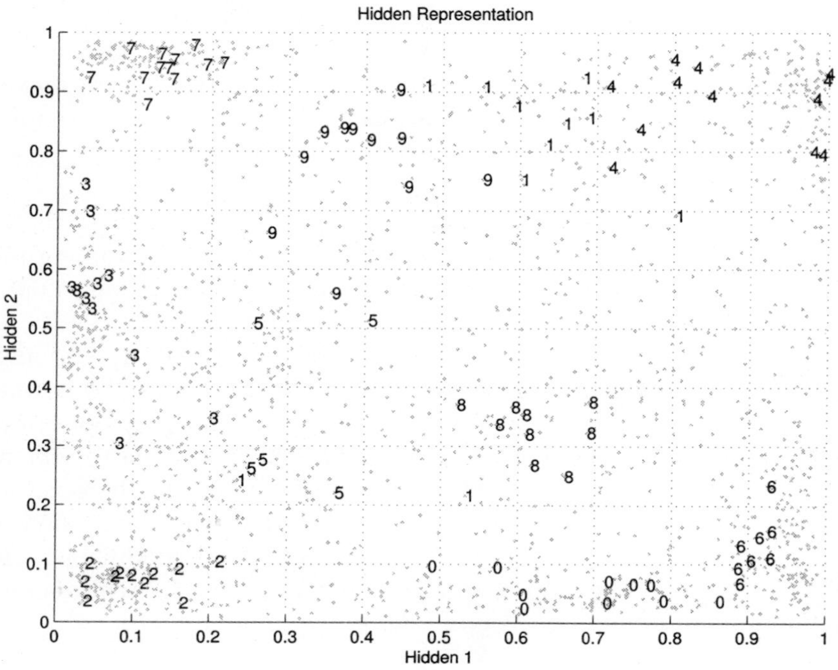

Figure 11.18 Optdigits data plotted in the space of the two hidden units of an MLP trained for classification. Only the labels of one hundred data points are shown. This MLP with sixty-four inputs, two hidden units, and ten outputs has 80 percent accuracy. Because of the sigmoid, hidden unit values are between 0 and 1 and classes are clustered around the corners. This plot can be compared with the plots in chapter 6, which are drawn using other dimensionality reduction methods on the same dataset.

identical. So we can think of each hidden unit as defining a template in its incoming weights, and by analyzing these templates, we can extract knowledge from a trained MLP. If the inputs are normalized, weights tell us of their relative importance. Such analysis is not easy but gives us some insight as to what the MLP is doing and allows us to peek into the black box.

AUTOENCODER

An interesting architecture is the *autoencoder* (Cottrell, Munro, and Zipser 1987), which is an MLP architecture where there are as many outputs as there are inputs, and the required outputs are defined to be equal

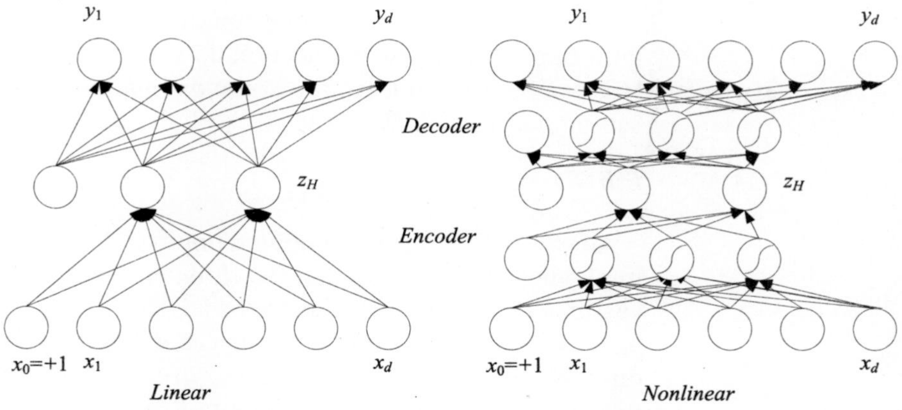

Figure 11.19 In the autoencoder, there are as many outputs as there are inputs and the desired outputs are the inputs. When the number of hidden units is less than the number of inputs, the MLP is trained to find the best coding of the inputs on the hidden units, performing dimensionality reduction. On the left, the first layer acts as an encoder and the second layer acts as the decoder. On the right, if the encoder and decoder are multilayer perceptrons with sigmoid hidden units, the network performs nonlinear dimensionality reduction.

to the inputs (see figure 11.19). To be able to reproduce the inputs again at the output layer, the MLP is forced to find the best representation of the inputs in the hidden layer. When the number of hidden units is less than the number of inputs, this implies dimensionality reduction. Once the training is done, the first layer from the input to the hidden layer acts as an encoder, and the values of the hidden units make up the encoded representation. The second layer from the hidden units to the output units acts as a decoder, reconstructing the original signal from its encoded representation.

It has been shown (Bourlard and Kamp 1988) that an autoencoder MLP with one hidden layer of units implements principal components analysis (section 6.3), except that the hidden unit weights are not the eigenvectors sorted in importance using the eigenvalues but span the same space as the H principal eigenvectors. If the encoder and decoder are not one layer but multilayer perceptrons with sigmoid nonlinearity in the hidden units, the encoder implements nonlinear dimensionality reduction. In section 11.13, we discuss "deep" networks composed of multiple nonlinear hidden layers.

Another way to use an MLP for dimensionality reduction is through multidimensional scaling (section 6.7). Mao and Jain (1995) show how an MLP can be used to learn the *Sammon mapping*. Recalling equation 6.37, Sammon stress is defined as

SAMMON MAPPING

$$E(\theta|\mathcal{X}) = \sum_{r,s}\left[\frac{\|\boldsymbol{g}(\boldsymbol{x}^r|\theta) - \boldsymbol{g}(\boldsymbol{x}^s|\theta)\| - \|\boldsymbol{x}^r - \boldsymbol{x}^s\|}{\|\boldsymbol{x}^r - \boldsymbol{x}^s\|}\right]^2 \quad (11.40)$$

An MLP with d inputs, H hidden units, and $k < d$ output units is used to implement $g(\boldsymbol{x}|\theta)$, mapping the d-dimensional input to a k-dimensional vector, where θ corresponds to the weights of the MLP. Given a dataset of $\mathcal{X} = \{\boldsymbol{x}^t\}_t$, we can use gradient descent to minimize the Sammon stress directly to learn the MLP, namely, $g(\boldsymbol{x}|\theta)$, such that the distances between the k-dimensional representations are as close as possible to the distances in the original space.

11.12 Learning Time

Until now, we have been concerned with cases where the input is fed once, all together. In some applications, the input is temporal where we need to learn a temporal sequence. In others, the output may also change in time. Examples are as follows:

- *Sequence recognition.* This is the assignment of a given sequence to one of several classes. Speech recognition is one example where the input signal sequence is the spoken speech and the output is the code of the word spoken. That is, the input changes in time but the output does not.
- *Sequence reproduction.* Here, after seeing part of a given sequence, the system should predict the rest. Time-series prediction is one example where the input is given but the output changes.
- *Temporal association.* This is the most general case where a particular output sequence is given as output after a specific input sequence. The input and output sequences may be different. Here both the input and the output change in time.

11.12.1 Time Delay Neural Networks

The easiest way to recognize a temporal sequence is by converting it to a spatial sequence. Then any method discussed up to this point can be uti-

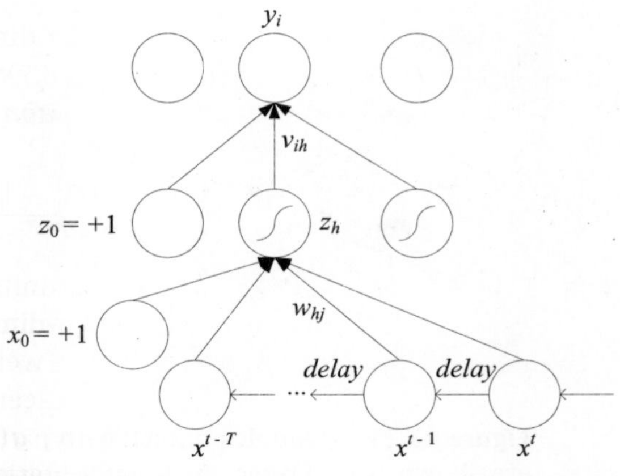

Figure 11.20 A time delay neural network. Inputs in a time window of length T are delayed in time until we can feed all T inputs as the input vector to the MLP.

TIME DELAY NEURAL NETWORK

lized for classification. In a *time delay neural network* (Waibel et al. 1989), previous inputs are delayed in time so as to synchronize with the final input, and all are fed together as input to the system (see figure 11.20). Backpropagation can then be used to train the weights. To extract features local in time, one can have layers of structured connections and weight sharing to get translation invariance in time. The main restriction of this architecture is that the size of the time window we slide over the sequence should be fixed a priori.

11.12.2 Recurrent Networks

RECURRENT NETWORK

In a *recurrent network*, additional to the feedforward connections, units have self-connections or connections to units in the previous layers. This recurrency acts as a short-term memory and lets the network remember what happened in the past.

Most frequently, one uses a partially recurrent network where a limited number of recurrent connections are added to a multilayer perceptron (see figure 11.21). This combines the advantage of the nonlinear approximation ability of a multilayer perceptron with the temporal representation ability of the recurrency, and such a network can be used to implement any of the three temporal association tasks. It is also possible to have hidden units in the recurrent backward connections, these being

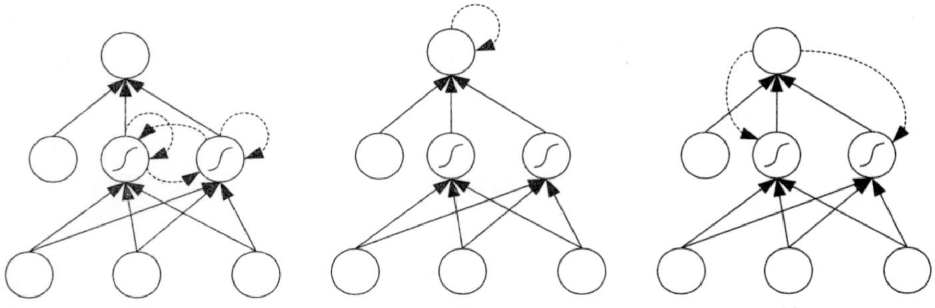

Figure 11.21 Examples of MLP with partial recurrency. Recurrent connections are shown with dashed lines: (a) self-connections in the hidden layer, (b) self-connections in the output layer, and (c) connections from the output to the hidden layer. Combinations of these are also possible.

known as *context units*. No formal results are known to determine how to choose the best architecture given a particular application.

UNFOLDING IN TIME

If the sequences have a small maximum length, then *unfolding in time* can be used to convert an arbitrary recurrent network to an equivalent feedforward network (see figure 11.22). A separate unit and connection is created for copies at different times. The resulting network can be trained with backpropagation with the additional requirement that all copies of each connection should remain identical. The solution, as in weight sharing, is to sum up the different weight changes in time and change the weight by the average. This is called *backpropagation through time* (Rumelhart, Hinton, and Willams 1986b). The problem with this approach is the memory requirement if the length of the sequence is large. *Real time recurrent learning* (Williams and Zipser 1989) is an algorithm for training recurrent networks without unfolding and has the advantage that it can use sequences of arbitrary length.

BACKPROPAGATION THROUGH TIME

REAL TIME RECURRENT LEARNING

11.13 Deep Learning

When a linear model is not sufficient, one possibility is to define new features that are nonlinear functions of the input, for example, higher-order terms, and then build a linear model in the space of those features; we discussed this in section 10.2. This requires us to know what such

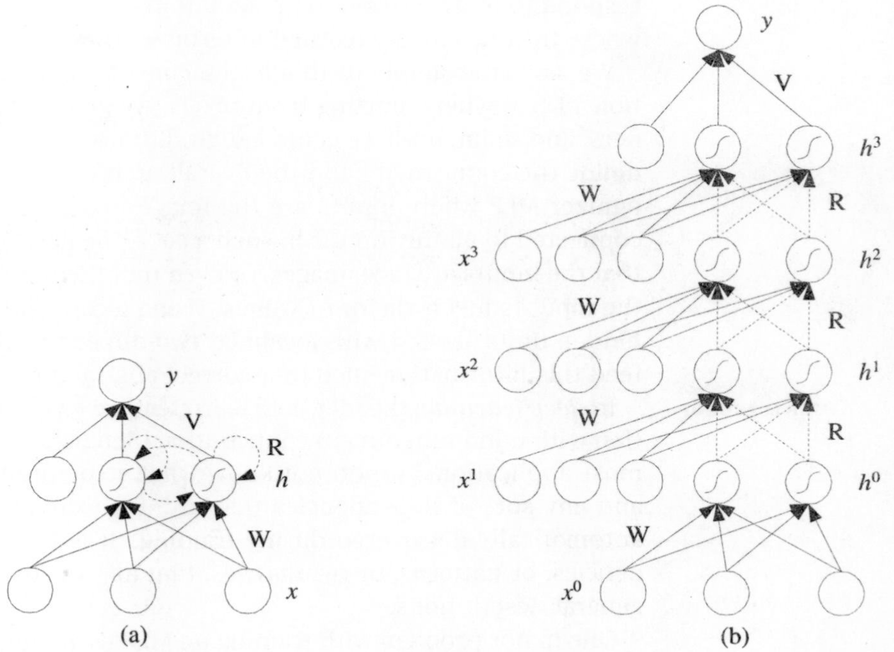

Figure 11.22 Backpropagation through time: (a) recurrent network, and (b) its equivalent unfolded network that behaves identically in four steps.

good basis functions are. Another possibility is to use one of the feature extraction methods we discussed in chapter 6 to learn the new space, for example, PCA or Isomap; such methods have the advantage that they are trained on data. Still, the best approach seems to be to use an MLP that extracts such features in its hidden layer; the MLP has the advantage that the first layer (feature extraction) and the second layer (how those features are combined to predict the output) are learned together in a coupled and supervised manner.

An MLP with one hidden layer has limited capacity, and using an MLP with multiple hidden layers can learn more complicated functions of the input. That is the idea behind *deep neural networks* where, starting from raw input, each hidden layer combines the values in its preceding layer and learns more complicated functions of the input.

DEEP NEURAL NETWORKS

Another aspect of deep networks is that successive hidden layers correspond to more abstract representations until we get to the output layer where the outputs are learned in terms of these most abstract concepts.

We saw an example of this in the convolutional neural networks (section 11.8.3) where starting from pixels, we get to edges, and then to corners, and so on, until we get to a digit. But user knowledge is necessary to define the connectivity and the overall architecture. Consider a face recognizer MLP where inputs are the image pixels and each hidden unit is connected to all the inputs; in such a case, the network has no knowledge that the inputs are face images, or even that the input is two-dimensional; the input is just a vector of values. Using a convolutional network where hidden units are fed with localized two-dimensional patches is a way to feed this information such that correct abstractions can be learned.

DEEP LEARNING

In *deep learning*, the idea is to learn feature levels of increasing abstraction with minimum human contribution (Bengio 2009). This is because in most applications, we do not know what structure there is in the input, and any sort of dependencies that are, for example, locality, should be automatically discovered during training. It is this extraction of dependencies, or patterns, or regularities, that allows abstraction and learning general descriptions.

One major problem with training an MLP with multiple hidden layers is that in backpropagating the error to an early layer, we need to multiply the derivatives in all the layers afterward and the gradient vanishes. This is also why unfolded recurrent neural networks (section 11.12.2) learn very slowly. This does not happen in convolutional neural networks because the fan-in and fan-out of hidden units are typically small.

A deep neural network is typically trained one layer at a time (Hinton and Salakhutdinov 2006). The aim of each layer is to extract the salient features in the data that is fed to it, and a method such as the autoencoder that we discussed in section 11.11 can be used for this purpose; there is the extra advantage that we can use unlabeled data for this purpose. So starting from the raw input, we train an autoencoder, and the encoded representation learned in its hidden layer is then used as input to train the next autoencoder and so on, until we get to the final layer that is trained in a supervised manner with the labeled data. Once all the layers are trained in this way one by one, they are all assembled and the whole network is fine-tuned with the labeled data.

If a lot of labeled data and a lot of computational power are available, the whole deep network can be trained in a supervised manner, but the consensus is that using an unsupervised method to initialize the weights works much better than random initialization—learning can be done much faster and with fewer labeled data.

Deep learning methods are attractive mainly because they need less manual interference. We do not need to craft the right features or suitable basis functions (or kernels—chapter 13), or worry about the right network architecture. Once we have data (and nowadays we have "big" data) and sufficient computation available, we just wait and let the learning algorithm discover all that is necessary by itself.

The idea of multiple layers of increasing abstraction that lies underneath deep learning is intuitive. Not only in vision—in handwritten digits or face images—but in many applications, we can think of layers of abstraction, and discovering such abstract representations would be informative; for example, it allows visualization and also a better description of the problem.

Consider machine translation. For example, starting with an English sentence, in multiple levels of processing and abstraction that are learned automatically from a very large corpus of English sentences to code the lexical, syntactic, and semantic rules of the English language, we would get to the most abstract representation. Now consider the same sentence in French. The levels of processing learned this time from a French corpus would be different, but if two sentences mean the same, at the most abstract, language-independent level, they should have very similar representations.

11.14 Notes

Research on artificial neural networks is as old as the digital computer. McCulloch and Pitts (1943) proposed the first mathematical model for the artificial neuron. Rosenblatt (1962) proposed the perceptron model and a learning algorithm in 1962. Minsky and Papert (1969) showed the limitation of single-layer perceptrons, for example, the XOR problem, and since there was no algorithm to train a multilayer perceptron with a hidden layer at that time, the work on artificial neural networks almost stopped except at a few places. The renaissance of neural networks came with the paper by Hopfield (1982). This was followed by the two-volume parallel distributed processing (PDP) book written by the PDP Research Group (Rumelhart, McClelland, and the PDP Research Group 1986). It seems as though backpropagation was invented independently in several places almost at the same time and the limitation of a single-layer perceptron no longer held.

Starting in the mid-1980s, there has been a huge explosion of work on artificial neural network models from various disciplines: physics, statistics, psychology, cognitive science, neuroscience, and lingustics, not to mention computer science, electrical engineering, and adaptive control. Perhaps the most important contribution of research on artificial neural networks is this synergy that bridged various disciplines, especially statistics and engineering. It is thanks to this that the field of machine learning is now well established.

The field is much more mature now; aims are more modest and better defined. One of the criticisms of backpropagation was that it was not biologically plausible! Though the term "neural network" is still widely used, it is generally understood that neural network models, for example, multilayer perceptrons, are nonparametric estimators and that the best way to analyze them is by using statistical methods.

PROJECTION PURSUIT

For example, a statistical method similar to the multilayer perceptron is *projection pursuit* (Friedman and Stuetzle 1981), which is written as

$$y = \sum_{h=1}^{H} \phi_h(\mathbf{w}_h^T \mathbf{x})$$

the difference being that each "hidden unit" has its own separate function, $\phi_h(\cdot)$, though in an MLP, all are fixed to be sigmoid. In chapter 12, we will see another neural network structure, named radial basis functions, which uses the Gaussian function at the hidden units.

There are various textbooks on artificial neural networks: Hertz, Krogh, and Palmer 1991, the earliest, is still readable. Bishop 1995 has a pattern recognition emphasis and discusses in detail various optimization algorithms that can be used for training, as well as the Bayesian approach, generalizing weight decay. Ripley 1996 analyzes neural networks from a statistical perspective.

Artificial neural networks, for example, multilayer perceptrons, have various successful applications. In addition to their various successful applications in adaptive control, speech recognition, and vision, two are noteworthy: Tesauro's TD-Gammon program (Tesauro 1994) uses reinforcement learning (chapter 18) to train a multilayer perceptron and plays backgammon at a master level. Pomerleau's ALVINN is a neural network that autonomously drives a van up to 20 miles per hour after learning by observing a driver for five minutes (Pomerleau 1991).

Research in neural networks has seen a major boost recently with the advent of deep learning and deep neural networks, and we see them applied in many areas, for example, finance, biology, natural language processing, and so on, with impressive results—see `deeplearning.net` for more information. With bigger data and cheaper processing hardware every year, they promise to be more popular in the near future.

11.15 Exercises

1. Show the perceptron that calculates NOT of its input.

   SOLUTION:

   $$y = s(-x + 0.5)$$

2. Show the perceptron that calculates NAND of its two inputs.
3. Show the perceptron that calculates the parity of its three inputs.

   SOLUTION:

   $$\begin{aligned} h_1 &= s(-x_1 - x_2 + 2x_3 - 1.5) \quad (001) \\ h_2 &= s(-x_1 + 2x_2 - x_3 - 1.5) \quad (010) \\ h_3 &= s(2x_1 - x_2 - x_3 - 1.5) \quad (100) \\ h_4 &= s(x_1 + x_2 + x_3 - 2.5) \quad (111) \\ y &= s(h_1 + h_2 + h_3 + h_4 - 0.5) \end{aligned}$$

   The four hidden units corresponding to the four cases of (x_1, x_2, x_3) values where the parity is 1, namely, 001, 010, 100, and 111. We then OR them to calculate the overall output. Note that another possibility is to calculate the three-bit parity in terms of two-bit parity (XOR) as $(x_1 \text{ XOR } x_2) \text{ XOR } x_3$.

4. Derive the update equations when the hidden units use tanh, instead of the sigmoid. Use the fact that $\tanh' = (1 - \tanh^2)$.
5. Derive the update equations for an MLP with two hidden layers.

   SOLUTION: Let us first define the forward equations:

   $$\begin{aligned} z_{1h} &= \text{sigmoid}(\mathbf{w}_{1h}^T \mathbf{x}) = \text{sigmoid}\left(\sum_{j=1}^{d} w_{1hj} x_j + w_{1h0}\right), \; h = 1, \ldots, H_1 \\ z_{2l} &= \text{sigmoid}(\mathbf{w}_{2l}^T \mathbf{z}_1) = \text{sigmoid}\left(\sum_{h=0}^{H_1} w_{2lh} z_{1h} + w_{2l0}\right), \; l = 1, \ldots, H_2 \\ y_i &= \mathbf{v}_i^T \mathbf{z}_2 = \sum_{l=1}^{H_2} v_{il} z_{2l} + v_0 \end{aligned}$$

Let us take the case of regression:

$$E = \frac{1}{2}\sum_t \sum_i (r_i^t - y_i^t)^2$$

We just backpropagate, that is, continue the chain rule, and we can write error in a layer as a function of the error in the layer that follows it, carrying the supervised error in the output layer to the layers before:

$$\begin{aligned} err_i &\equiv r_i^t - y_i^t \Rightarrow \Delta v_{il} = \eta \sum_t err_i z_{2l} \\ err_{2l} &\equiv \left[\sum_i err_i v_i\right] z_{2l}(1 - z_{2l}) \Rightarrow \Delta w_{2lh} = \eta \sum_t err_{2l} z_{1h} \\ err_{1h} &\equiv \left[\sum_l err_{2l} w_{2lh}\right] z_{1h}(1 - z_{1h}) \Rightarrow \Delta w_{1hj} = \eta \sum_t err_{1h} x_j \end{aligned}$$

6. Consider an MLP architecture with one hidden layer where there are also direct weights from the inputs directly to the output units. Explain when such a structure would be helpful and how it can be trained.
7. Parity is cyclic shift invariant; for example, "0101" and "1010" have the same parity. Propose a multilayer perceptron to learn the parity function using this hint.
8. In cascade correlation, what are the advantages of freezing the previously existing weights?
9. Derive the update equations for an MLP implementing Sammon mapping that minimizes Sammon stress (equation 11.40).
10. In section 11.6, we discuss how an MLP with two hidden layers can implement piecewise constant approximation. Show that if the weight in the last layer is not a constant but a linear function of the input, we can implement piecewise linear approximation.
11. Derive the update equations for soft weight sharing.

    SOLUTION: Assume a single-layer network for two-class classification for simplicity:

    $$y^t = \text{sigmoid}\left(\sum_i w_i x_i^t\right)$$

    the augmented error is

    $$E' = \log \sum_t r^t \log y^t + \lambda \sum_i \log \sum_{j=1}^{M} \alpha_j p_j(w_i)$$

where $p_j(w_i) \sim \mathcal{N}(m_j, s_j^2)$. Note that $\{w_i\}_i$ includes all the weights including the bias. When we use gradient descent, we get

$$\Delta w_i^t = \eta(r^t - y^t)x_i^t - \eta\lambda \sum_j \pi_j(w_i) \frac{(w_i - m_j)}{s_j^2}$$

where

$$\pi_j(w_i) = \frac{\alpha_j p_j(w_i)}{\sum_l \alpha_l p_l(w_i)}$$

is the posterior probability that w_i belongs to component j. The weight is updated to both decrease the cross-entropy and move it closer to the mean of the nearest Gaussian. Using such a scheme, we can also update the mixture parameters, for example:

$$\Delta m_j = \eta\lambda \sum_i \pi_j(w_i) \frac{(w_i - m_j)}{s_j^2}$$

$\pi_j(w_i)$ is close to 1 if it is highly probable that w_i comes from component j; in such a case, m_j is updated to be closer to the weight w_i it represents. This is an iterative clustering procedure, and we will discuss such methods in more detail in chapter 12; see for example, equation 12.5.

12. In the autoencoder network, how can we decide on the number of hidden units?
13. Incremental learning of the structure of a MLP can be viewed as a state space search. What are the operators? What is the goodness function? What type of search strategies are appropriate? Define these in such a way that dynamic node creation and cascade-correlation are special instantiations.
14. For the MLP given in figure 11.22, derive the update equations for the unfolded network.

11.16 References

Abu-Mostafa, Y. 1995. "Hints." *Neural Computation* 7:639–671.

Aran, O., O. T. Yıldız, and E. Alpaydın. 2009. "An Incremental Framework Based on Cross-Validation for Estimating the Architecture of a Multilayer Perceptron." *International Journal of Pattern Recognition and Artificial Intelligence* 23:159–190.

Ash, T. 1989. "Dynamic Node Creation in Backpropagation Networks." *Connection Science* 1:365–375.

Battiti, R. 1992. "First- and Second-Order Methods for Learning: Between Steepest Descent and Newton's Method." *Neural Computation* 4:141–166.

Bengio, Y. 2009. "Learning Deep Architectures for AI." *Foundations and Trends in Machine Learning* 2 (1): 1–127.

Bishop, C. M. 1995. *Neural Networks for Pattern Recognition.* Oxford: Oxford University Press.

Bourlard, H., and Y. Kamp. 1988. "Auto-Association by Multilayer Perceptrons and Singular Value Decomposition." *Biological Cybernetics* 59:291–294.

Cottrell, G. W., P. Munro, and D. Zipser. 1987. "Learning Internal Representations from Gray-Scale Images: An Example of Extensional Programming." In *Ninth Annual Conference of the Cognitive Science Society*, 462–473. Hillsdale, NJ: Erlbaum.

Durbin, R., and D. E. Rumelhart. 1989. "Product Units: A Computationally Powerful and Biologically Plausible Extension to Backpropagation Networks." *Neural Computation* 1:133–142.

Fahlman, S. E., and C. Lebiere. 1990. "The Cascade Correlation Architecture." In *Advances in Neural Information Processing Systems 2*, ed. D. S. Touretzky, 524–532. San Francisco: Morgan Kaufmann.

Friedman, J. H., and W. Stuetzle. 1981. "Projection Pursuit Regression." *Journal of the American Statistical Association* 76:817–823.

Fukushima, K. 1980. "Neocognitron: A Self-Organizing Neural Network Model for a Mechanism of Pattern Recognition Unaffected by Shift in Position." *Biological Cybernetics* 36:193–202.

Geman, S., E. Bienenstock, and R. Doursat. 1992. "Neural Networks and the Bias/Variance Dilemma." *Neural Computation* 4:1–58.

Hertz, J., A. Krogh, and R. G. Palmer. 1991. *Introduction to the Theory of Neural Computation.* Reading, MA: Addison-Wesley.

Hinton, G. E., and R. R. Salakhutdinov. 2006. "Reducing the dimensionality of data with neural networks." *Science* 313:504–507.

Hopfield, J. J. 1982. "Neural Networks and Physical Systems with Emergent Collective Computational Abilities." *Proceedings of the National Academy of Sciences USA* 79:2554–2558.

Hornik, K., M. Stinchcombe, and H. White. 1989. "Multilayer Feedforward Networks Are Universal Approximators." *Neural Networks* 2:359–366.

Le Cun, Y., B. Boser, J. S. Denker, D. Henderson, R. E. Howard, W. Hubbard, and L. D. Jackel. 1989. "Backpropagation Applied to Handwritten Zipcode Recognition." *Neural Computation* 1:541–551.

MacKay, D. J. C. 1992a. "Bayesian Interpolation." *Neural Computation* 4:415–447.

MacKay, D. J. C. 1992b. "A Practical Bayesian Framework for Backpropagation Networks" *Neural Computation* 4:448–472.

Mao, J., and A. K. Jain. 1995. "Artificial Neural Networks for Feature Extraction and Multivariate Data Projection." *IEEE Transactions on Neural Networks* 6:296–317.

Marr, D. 1982. *Vision.* New York: Freeman.

McCulloch, W. S., and W. Pitts. 1943. "A Logical Calculus of the Ideas Immenent in Nervous Activity." *Bulletin of Mathematical Biophysics* 5:115–133.

Minsky, M. L., and S. A. Papert. 1969. *Perceptrons.* Cambridge, MA: MIT Press. (Expanded ed. 1990.)

Nowlan, S. J., and G. E. Hinton. 1992. "Simplifying Neural Networks by Soft Weight Sharing." *Neural Computation* 4:473–493.

Pomerleau, D. A. 1991. "Efficient Training of Artificial Neural Networks for Autonomous Navigation." *Neural Computation* 3:88–97.

Posner, M. I., ed. 1989. *Foundations of Cognitive Science.* Cambridge, MA: MIT Press.

Richard, M. D., and R. P. Lippmann. 1991. "Neural Network Classifiers Estimate Bayesian *a Posteriori* Probabilities." *Neural Computation* 3:461–483.

Ripley, B. D. 1996. *Pattern Recognition and Neural Networks.* Cambridge, UK: Cambridge University Press.

Rosenblatt, F. 1962. *Principles of Neurodynamics: Perceptrons and the Theory of Brain Mechanisms.* New York: Spartan.

Rumelhart, D. E., G. E. Hinton, and R. J. Williams. 1986a. "Learning Representations by Backpropagating Errors." *Nature* 323:533–536.

Rumelhart, D. E., G. E. Hinton, and R. J. Williams. 1986b. "Learning Internal Representations by Error Propagation." In *Parallel Distributed Processing*, ed. D. E. Rumelhart, J. L. McClelland, and the PDP Research Group, 318–362. Cambridge, MA: MIT Press.

Rumelhart, D. E., J. L. McClelland, and the PDP Research Group, eds. 1986. *Parallel Distributed Processing.* Cambridge, MA: MIT Press.

Simard, P., B. Victorri, Y, Le Cun, and J. Denker. 1992. "Tangent Prop: A Formalism for Specifying Selected Invariances in an Adaptive Network." In *Advances in Neural Information Processing Systems 4*, ed. J. E. Moody, S. J. Hanson, and R. P. Lippman, 895–903. San Francisco: Morgan Kaufmann.

Tesauro, G. 1994. "TD-Gammon, a Self-Teaching Backgammon Program, Achieves Master-Level Play." *Neural Computation* 6:215–219.

Thagard, P. 2005. *Mind: Introduction to Cognitive Science.* 2nd ed. Cambridge, MA: MIT Press.

Waibel, A., T. Hanazawa, G. Hinton, K. Shikano, and K. Lang. 1989. "Phoneme Recognition Using Time-Delay Neural Networks." *IEEE Transactions on Acoustics, Speech, and Signal Processing* 37:328–339.

Williams, R. J., and D. Zipser. 1989. "A Learning Algorithm for Continually Running Fully Recurrent Neural Networks." *Neural Computation* 1:270–280.

12 Local Models

We continue our discussion of multilayer neural networks with models where the first layer contains locally receptive units that respond to instances in a localized region of the input space. The second layer on top learns the regression or classification function for these local regions. We discuss learning methods for finding the local regions of importance as well as the models responsible in there.

12.1 Introduction

ONE WAY to do function approximation is to divide the input space into local patches and learn a separate fit in each local patch. In chapter 7, we discussed statistical methods for clustering that allowed us to group input instances and model the input distribution. Competitive methods are neural network methods for online clustering. In this chapter, we discuss the online version of k-means, as well as two neural network extensions, adaptive resonance theory (ART), and the self-organizing map (SOM).

We then discuss how supervised learning is implemented once the inputs are localized. If the fit in a local patch is constant, then the technique is named the radial basis function (RBF) network; if it is a linear function of the input, it is called the mixture of experts (MoE). We discuss both regression and classification, and also compare this approach with MLP, which we discussed in chapter 11.

12.2 Competitive Learning

In chapter 7, we used the semiparametric Gaussian mixture density, which assumes that the input comes from one of k Gaussian sources. In this section, we make the same assumption that there are k groups (or clusters) in the data, but our approach is not probabilistic in that we do not enforce a parametric model for the sources. Another difference is that the learning methods we propose are online. We do not have the whole sample at hand during training; we receive instances one by one and update model parameters as we get them. The term *competitive learning* is used because it is as if these groups, or rather the units representing these groups, compete among themselves to be the one responsible for representing an instance. The model is also called *winner-take-all*; it is as if one group wins and gets updated, and the others are not updated at all.

COMPETITIVE LEARNING

WINNER-TAKE-ALL

These methods can be used by themselves for online clustering, as opposed to the batch methods discussed in chapter 7. An online method has the usual advantages that (1) we do not need extra memory to store the whole training set; (2) updates at each step are simple to implement, for example, in hardware; and (3) the input distribution may change in time and the model adapts itself to these changes automatically. If we were to use a batch algorithm, we would need to collect a new sample and run the batch method from scratch over the whole sample.

Starting in section 12.3, we will also discuss how such an approach can be followed by a supervised method to learn regression or classification problems. This will be a two-stage system that can be implemented by a two-layer network, where the first stage (-layer) models the input density and finds the responsible local model, and the second stage is that of the local model generating the final output.

12.2.1 Online k-Means

In equation 7.3, we defined the reconstruction error as

$$E(\{\boldsymbol{m}_i\}_{i=1}^k|\mathcal{X}) = \frac{1}{2}\sum_t \sum_i b_i^t \|\boldsymbol{x}^t - \boldsymbol{m}_i\|^2 \quad (12.1)$$

where

$$b_i^t = \begin{cases} 1 & \text{if } \|\boldsymbol{x}^t - \boldsymbol{m}_i\| = \min_l \|\boldsymbol{x}^t - \boldsymbol{m}_l\| \\ 0 & \text{otherwise} \end{cases} \quad (12.2)$$

$\mathcal{X} = \{\boldsymbol{x}^t\}_t$ is the sample and $\boldsymbol{m}_i, i = 1, \ldots, k$ are the cluster centers. b_i^t is 1 if $\boldsymbol{m}_i$ is the closest center to $\boldsymbol{x}^t$ in Euclidean distance. It is as if all $\boldsymbol{m}_l, l = 1, \ldots, k$ compete and $\boldsymbol{m}_i$ wins the competition because it is the closest.

The batch algorithm, k-means, updates the centers as

$$\boldsymbol{m}_i = \frac{\sum_t b_i^t \boldsymbol{x}^t}{\sum_t b_i^t} \tag{12.3}$$

which minimizes equation 12.1, once the winners are chosen using equation 12.2. As we saw before, these two steps of calculating b_i^t and updating $\boldsymbol{m}_i$ are iterated until convergence.

ONLINE k-MEANS

We can obtain *online k-means* by doing stochastic gradient descent, considering the instances one by one, and doing a small update at each step, not forgetting the effect of the previous updates. The reconstruction error for a single instance is

$$E^t(\{\boldsymbol{m}_i\}_{i=1}^k | \boldsymbol{x}^t) = \frac{1}{2}\sum_i b_i^t \|\boldsymbol{x}^t - \boldsymbol{m}_i\|^2 = \frac{1}{2}\sum_i \sum_{j=1}^d b_i^t (x_j^t - m_{ij})^2 \tag{12.4}$$

where b_i^t is defined as in equation 12.2. Using gradient descent on this, we get the following update rule for each instance $\boldsymbol{x}^t$:

$$\Delta m_{ij} = -\eta \frac{\partial E^t}{\partial m_{ij}} = \eta b_i^t (x_j^t - m_{ij}) \tag{12.5}$$

This moves the closest center (for which $b_i^t = 1$) toward the input by a factor given by η. The other centers have their $b_l^t, l \neq i$ equal to 0 and are not updated (see figure 12.1). A batch procedure can also be defined by summing up equation 12.5 over all t. Like in any gradient descent procedure, a momentum term can also be added. For convergence, η is gradually decreased to 0. But this implies the *stability-plasticity dilemma*: If η is decreased toward 0, the network becomes stable but we lose adaptivity to novel patterns that may occur in time because updates become too small. If we keep η large, $\boldsymbol{m}_i$ may oscillate.

STABILITY-PLASTICITY DILEMMA

The pseudocode of online k-means is given in figure 12.2. This is the online version of the batch algorithm given in figure 7.3.

The competitive network can be implemented as a one-layer recurrent network as shown in figure 12.3. The input layer contains the input vector $\boldsymbol{x}$; note that there is no bias unit. The values of the output units are the b_i and they are perceptrons:

$$b_i = \boldsymbol{m}_i^T \boldsymbol{x} \tag{12.6}$$

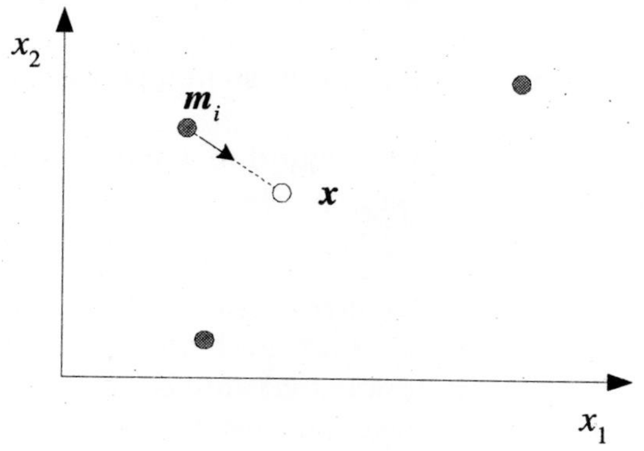

Figure 12.1 Shaded circles are the centers and the empty circle is the input instance. The online version of k-means moves the closest center along the direction of $(\boldsymbol{x} - \boldsymbol{m}_i)$ by a factor specified by η.

Then we need to choose the maximum of the b_i and set it equal to 1, and set the others, $b_l, l \neq i$ to 0. If we would like to do everything purely neural, that is, using a network of concurrently operating processing units, the choosing of the maximum can be implemented through *lateral inhibition*. As shown in figure 12.3, each unit has an excitatory recurrent connection (i.e., with a positive weight) to itself, and inhibitory recurrent connections (i.e., with negative weights) to the other output units. With an appropriate nonlinear activation function and positive and negative recurrent weight values, such a network, after some iterations, converges to a state where the maximum becomes 1 and all others become 0 (Grossberg 1980; Feldman and Ballard 1982).

LATERAL INHIBITION

The dot product used in equation 12.6 is a similarity measure, and we saw in section 5.5 (equation 5.26) that if $\boldsymbol{m}_i$ have the same norm, then the unit with the minimum Euclidean distance, $\|\boldsymbol{m}_i - \boldsymbol{x}\|$, is the same as the one with the maximum dot product, $\boldsymbol{m}_i^T \boldsymbol{x}$.

Here, and later when we discuss other competitive methods, we use the Euclidean distance, but we should keep in mind that using the Euclidean distance implies that all input attributes have the same variance and that they are not correlated. If this is not the case, this should be reflected in the distance measure, that is, by using the Mahalanobis distance, or suitable normalization should be done, for example, by PCA, at

> Initialize $\boldsymbol{m}_i, i = 1, \ldots, k$, for example, to k random $\boldsymbol{x}^t$
> Repeat
>   For all $\boldsymbol{x}^t \in \mathcal{X}$ in random order
> $i \leftarrow \arg\min_j \|\boldsymbol{x}^t - \boldsymbol{m}_j\|$
> $\boldsymbol{m}_i \leftarrow \boldsymbol{m}_i + \eta(\boldsymbol{x}^t - \boldsymbol{m}_i)$
> Until $\boldsymbol{m}_i$ converge

Figure 12.2 Online k-means algorithm. The batch version is given in figure 7.3.

a preprocessing stage before the Euclidean distance is used.

We can rewrite equation 12.5 as

$$\Delta m_{ij}^t = \eta b_i^t x_j^t - \eta b_i^t m_{ij} \tag{12.7}$$

Let us remember that m_{ij} is the weight of the connection from x_j to b_i. An update of the form, as we see in the first term

$$\Delta m_{ij}^t = \eta b_i^t x_j^t \tag{12.8}$$

HEBBIAN LEARNING

is *Hebbian learning*, which defines the update as the product of the values of the presynaptic and postsynaptic units. It was proposed as a model for neural plasticity: A synapse becomes more important if the units before and after the connection fire simultaneously, indicating that they are correlated. However, with only Hebbian learning, the weights grow without bound ($x_j^t \geq 0$), and we need a second force to decrease the weights that are not updated. One possibility is to explicitly normalize the weights to have $\|\boldsymbol{m}_i\| = 1$; if $\Delta m_{ij} > 0$ and $\Delta m_{il} = 0, l \neq j$, once we normalize $\boldsymbol{m}_i$ to unit length, m_{il} decrease. Another possibility is to introduce a weight decay term (Oja 1982), and the second term of equation 12.7 can be seen as such. Hertz, Krogh, and Palmer (1991) discuss competitive networks and Hebbian learning in more detail and show, for example, how such networks can learn to do PCA. Mao and Jain (1995) discuss online algorithms for PCA and LDA.

As we saw in chapter 7, one problem is to avoid dead centers, namely, the ones that are there but are not effectively utilized. In the case of competitive networks, this corresponds to centers that never win the competition because they are initialized far away from any input. There are various ways we can avoid this:

1. We can initialize $\boldsymbol{m}_i$ by randomly chosen input instances, and make sure that they start from where there is data.

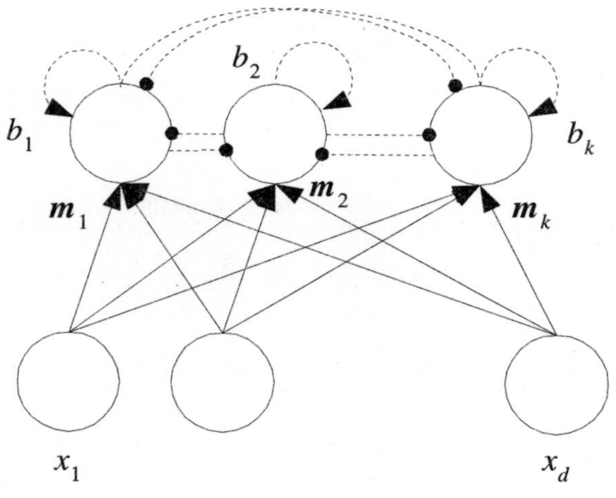

Figure 12.3 The winner-take-all competitive neural network, which is a network of k perceptrons with recurrent connections at the output. Dashed lines are recurrent connections, of which the ones that end with an arrow are excitatory and the ones that end with a circle are inhibitory. Each unit at the output reinforces its value and tries to suppress the other outputs. Under a suitable assignment of these recurrrent weights, the maximum suppresses all the others. This has the net effect that the one unit whose $\boldsymbol{m}_i$ is closest to $\boldsymbol{x}$ ends up with its b_i equal to 1 and all others, namely, $b_l, l \neq i$ are 0.

2. We can use a leader-cluster algorithm and add units one by one, always adding them at a place where they are needed. One example is the ART model, which we discuss in section 12.2.2.

3. When we update, we do not update only the center of the closest unit but some others as well. As they are updated, they also move toward the input, move gradually toward parts of the input space where there are inputs, and eventually win the competition. One example that we discuss in section 12.2.3 is SOM.

4. Another possibility is to introduce a *conscience* mechanism (DeSieno 1988): A unit that has won the competition recently feels guilty and allows others to win.

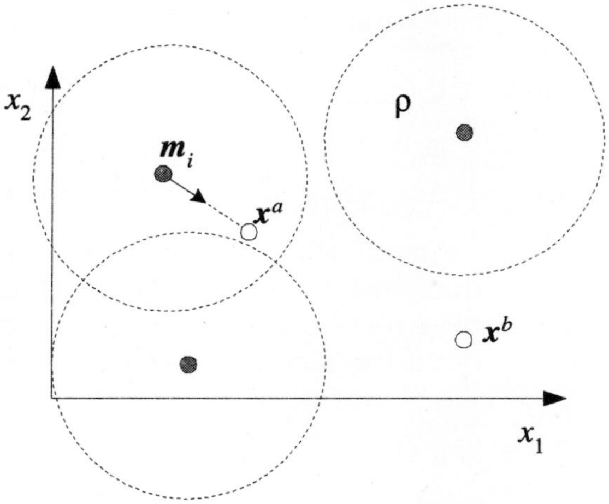

Figure 12.4 The distance from $\boldsymbol{x}^a$ to the closest center is less than the vigilance value ρ and the center is updated as in online k-means. However, $\boldsymbol{x}^b$ is not close enough to any of the centers and a new group should be created at that position.

12.2.2 Adaptive Resonance Theory

The number of groups, k, should be known and specified before the parameters can be calculated. Another approach is *incremental*, where one starts with a single group and adds new groups as they are needed. We discuss the *adaptive resonance theory* (ART) algorithm (Carpenter and Grossberg 1988) as an example of an incremental algorithm. In ART, given an input, all of the output units calculate their values and the one most similar to the input is chosen. This is the unit with the maximum value if the unit uses the dot product as in equation 12.6, or it is the unit with the minimum value if the unit uses the Euclidean distance.

ADAPTIVE RESONANCE THEORY

Let us assume that we use the Euclidean distance. If the minimum value is smaller than a certain threshold value, named the *vigilance*, the update is done as in online k-means. If this distance is larger than vigilance, a new output unit is added and its center is initialized with the instance. This defines a hypersphere whose radius is given by the vigilance defining the volume of scope of each unit; we add a new unit whenever we have an input that is not covered by any unit (see figure 12.4).

VIGILANCE

Denoting vigilance by ρ, we use the following equations at each update:

(12.9)
$$b_i = \|\boldsymbol{m}_i - \boldsymbol{x}^t\| = \min_{l=1}^{k} \|\boldsymbol{m}_l - \boldsymbol{x}^t\|$$

$$\begin{cases} \boldsymbol{m}_{k+1} \leftarrow \boldsymbol{x}^t & \text{if } b_i > \rho \\ \Delta\boldsymbol{m}_i = \eta(\boldsymbol{x}^t - \boldsymbol{m}_i) & \text{otherwise} \end{cases}$$

Putting a threshold on distance is equivalent to putting a threshold on the reconstruction error per instance, and if the distance is Euclidean and the error is defined as in equation 12.4, this indicates that the maximum reconstruction error allowed per instance is the square of vigilance.

12.2.3 Self-Organizing Maps

SELF-ORGANIZING MAP

One way to avoid having dead units is by updating not only the winner but also some of the other units as well. In the *self-organizing map* (SOM) proposed by Kohonen (1990, 1995), unit indices, namely, i as in $\boldsymbol{m}_i$, define a *neighborhood* for the units. When $\boldsymbol{m}_i$ is the closest center, in addition to $\boldsymbol{m}_i$, its neighbors are also updated. For example, if the neighborhood is of size 2, then $\boldsymbol{m}_{i-2}, \boldsymbol{m}_{i-1}, \boldsymbol{m}_{i+1}, \boldsymbol{m}_{i+2}$ are also updated but with less weight as the neighborhood increases. If i is the index of the closest center, the centers are updated as

(12.10)
$$\Delta\boldsymbol{m}_l = \eta\, e(l,i)(\boldsymbol{x}^t - \boldsymbol{m}_l)$$

where $e(l,i)$ is the *neighborhood function*. $e(l,i) = 1$ when $l = i$ and decreases as $|l - i|$ increases, for example, as a Gaussian, $\mathcal{N}(i,\sigma)$:

(12.11)
$$e(l,i) = \frac{1}{\sqrt{2\pi}\sigma} \exp\left[-\frac{(l-i)^2}{2\sigma^2}\right]$$

For convergence, the support of the neighborhood function decreases in time, for example, σ decreases, and at the end, only the winner is updated.

Because neighboring units are also moved toward the input, we avoid dead units since they get to win competition sometime later, after a little bit of initial help from their neighboring friends (see figure 12.5).

Updating the neighbors has the effect that, even if the centers are randomly initialized, because they are moved toward the same input together, once the system converges, units with neighboring indices will also be neighbors in the input space.

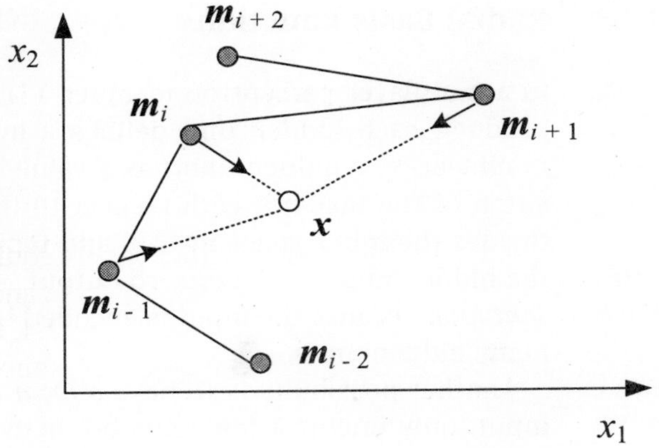

Figure 12.5 In the SOM, not only the closest unit but also its neighbors, in terms of indices, are moved toward the input. Here, neighborhood is 1; $\boldsymbol{m}_i$ and its 1-nearest neighbors are updated. Note here that $\boldsymbol{m}_{i+1}$ is far from $\boldsymbol{m}_i$, but as it is updated with $\boldsymbol{m}_i$, and as $\boldsymbol{m}_i$ will be updated when $\boldsymbol{m}_{i+1}$ is the winner, they will become neighbors in the input space as well.

In most applications, the units are organized as a two-dimensional *map*. That is, each unit will have two indices, $\boldsymbol{m}_{i,j}$, and the neighborhood will be defined in two dimensions. If $\boldsymbol{m}_{i,j}$ is the closest center, the centers are updated as

$$\Delta \boldsymbol{m}_{k,l} = \eta e(k,l,i,j)(\boldsymbol{x}^t - \boldsymbol{m}_{k,l}) \tag{12.12}$$

where the neighborhood function is now in two dimensions. After convergence, this forms a two-dimensional *topographical map* of the original d-dimensional input space. The map contains many units in parts of the space where density is high, and no unit will be dedicated to parts where there is no input. Once the map converges, inputs that are close in the original space are mapped to units that are close in the map. In this regard, the map can be interpreted as doing a nonlinear form of multidimensional scaling, mapping from the original $\boldsymbol{x}$ space to the two dimensions, (i, j). Similarly, if the map is one-dimensional, the units are placed on the curve of maximum density in the input space, as a *principal curve*.

TOPOGRAPHICAL MAP

12.3 Radial Basis Functions

In a multilayer perceptron (chapter 11) where hidden units use the dot product, each hidden unit defines a hyperplane and with the sigmoid nonlinearity, a hidden unit has a value between 0 and 1, coding the position of the instance with respect to the hyperplane. Each hyperplane divides the input space in two, and typically for a given input, many of the hidden units have nonzero output. This is called a *distributed representation* because the input is encoded by the simultaneous activation of many hidden units.

DISTRIBUTED REPRESENTATION

LOCAL REPRESENTATION

Another possibility is to have a *local representation* where for a given input, only one or a few units are active. It is as if these *locally tuned units* partition the input space among themselves and are selective to only certain inputs. The part of the input space where a unit has nonzero response is called its *receptive field*. The input space is then paved with such units.

RECEPTIVE FIELD

Neurons with such response characteristics are found in many parts of the cortex. For example, cells in the visual cortex respond selectively to stimulation that is both local in retinal position and local in angle of visual orientation. Such locally tuned cells are typically arranged in topogrophical cortical maps in which the values of the variables to which the cells respond vary by their position in the map, as in a SOM.

The concept of locality implies a distance function to measure the similarity between the given input $\boldsymbol{x}$ and the position of unit h, $\boldsymbol{m}_h$. Frequently this measure is taken as the Euclidean distance, $\|\boldsymbol{x} - \boldsymbol{m}_h\|$. The response function is chosen to have a maximum where $\boldsymbol{x} = \boldsymbol{m}_h$ and decreasing as they get less similar. Commonly we use the Gaussian function (see figure 12.6):

$$p_h^t = \exp\left[-\frac{\|\boldsymbol{x}^t - \boldsymbol{m}_h\|^2}{2s_h^2}\right] \tag{12.13}$$

Strictly speaking, this is not Gaussian density, but we use the same name anyway. $\boldsymbol{m}_j$ and s_j respectively denote the center and the spread of the local unit j, and as such define a radially symmetric basis function. One can use an elliptic one with different spreads on different dimensions, or even use the full Mahalanobis distance to allow correlated inputs, at the expense of using a more complicated model (exercise 2).

The idea in using such local basis functions is that in the input data, there are groups or clusters of instances and for each such cluster, we

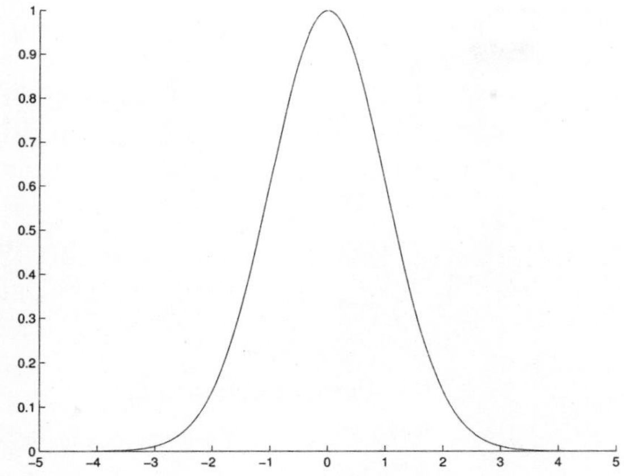

Figure 12.6 The one-dimensional form of the bell-shaped function used in the radial basis function network. This one has $m = 0$ and $s = 1$. It is like a Gaussian but it is not a density; it does not integrate to 1. It is nonzero between $(m - 3s, m + 3s)$, but a more conservative interval is $(m - 2s, m + 2s)$.

define a basis function, p_h^t, which becomes nonzero if instance $\boldsymbol{x}^t$ belongs to cluster h. One can use any of the online competitive methods discussed in section 12.2 to find the centers, $\boldsymbol{m}_h$. There is a simple and effective heuristic to find the spreads: Once we have the centers, for each cluster, we find the most distant instance covered by that cluster and set s_h to half its distance from the center. We could have used one-third, but we prefer to be conservative. We can also use the statistical clustering method, for example, EM on Gaussian mixtures, that we discussed in chapter 7 to find the cluster parameters, namely, means, variances (and covariances).

$p_h^t, h = 1, \ldots, H$ define a new H-dimensional space and form a new representation of $\boldsymbol{x}^t$. We can also use b_h^t (equation 12.2) to code the input but b_h^t are 0/1; p_h^t have the additional advantage that they code the distance to their center by a value in $(0, 1)$. How fast the value decays to 0 depends on s_h. Figure 12.7 gives an example and compares such a *local representation* with a *distributed* representation as used by the multilayer perceptron. Because Gaussians are local, typically we need many more local units than what we would need if we were to use a distributed representation, especially if the input is high-dimensional.

DISTRIBUTED VS LOCAL REPRESENTATION

In the case of supervised learning, we can then use this new local rep-

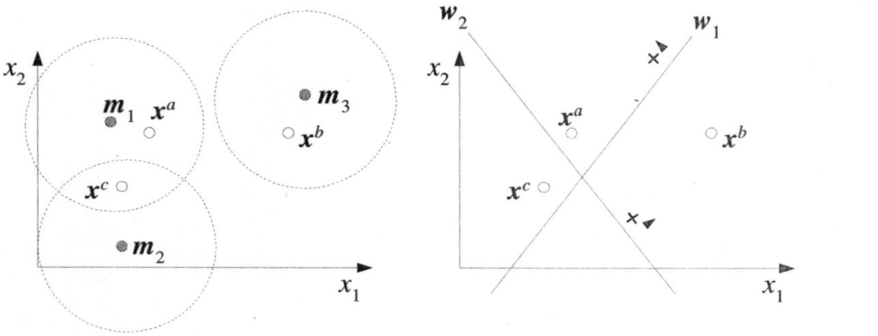

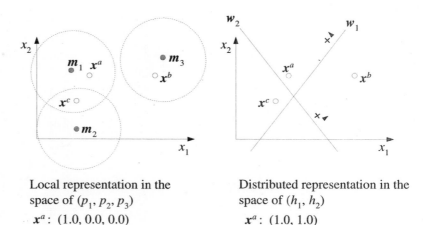

Local representation in the space of (p_1, p_2, p_3)

x^a : (1.0, 0.0, 0.0)
x^b : (0.0, 0.0, 1.0)
x^c : (1.0, 1.0, 0.0)

Distributed representation in the space of (h_1, h_2)

x^a : (1.0, 1.0)
x^b : (0.0, 1.0)
x^c : (1.0, 0.0)

Figure 12.7 The difference between local and distributed representations. The values are hard, 0/1, values. One can use soft values in $(0, 1)$ and get a more informative encoding. In the local representation, this is done by the Gaussian RBF that uses the distance to the center, $\boldsymbol{m}_i$, and in the distributed representation, this is done by the sigmoid that uses the distance to the hyperplane, $\boldsymbol{w}_i$.

resentation as the input. If we use a perceptron, we have

$$y^t = \sum_{h=1}^{H} w_h p_h^t + w_0 \tag{12.14}$$

RADIAL BASIS FUNCTION

where H is the number of basis functions. This structure is called a *radial basis function* (RBF) network (Broomhead and Lowe 1988; Moody and Darken 1989). Normally, people do not use RBF networks with more than one layer of Gaussian units. H is the complexity parameter, like the number of hidden units in a multilayer perceptron. Previously we denoted it by k, when it corresponded to the number of centers in the case of unsupervised learning.

Here, we see the advantage of using p_h instead of b_h. Because b_h are 0/1, if equation 12.14 contained b_h instead of the p_h, it would give a piecewise constant approximation with discontuinities at the unit region boundaries. p_h values are soft and lead to a smooth approximation, taking a weighted average while passing from one region to another. We can easily see that such a network is a universal approximator in that it can approximate any function with desired accuracy, given enough units. We can form a grid in the input space to our desired accuracy, define a unit that will be active for each cell, and set its outgoing weight, w_h, to the desired output value.

This architecture bears much similarity to the nonparametric estimators, for example, Parzen windows, we saw in chapter 8, and p_h may be seen as kernel functions. The difference is that now we do not have a kernel function over all training instances but group them using a clustering method to make do with fewer kernels. H, the number of units, is the complexity parameter, trading off simplicity and accuracy. With more units, we approximate the training data better, but we get a complex model and risk overfitting; too few may underfit. Again, the optimal value is determined by cross-validation.

Once $\boldsymbol{m}_h$ and s_h are given and fixed, p_h are also fixed. Then w_h can be trained easily batch or online. In the case of regression, this is a linear regression model (with p_h as the inputs) and the w_h can be solved analytically without any iteration (section 4.6). In the case of classification, we need to resort to an iterative procedure. We discussed learning methods for this in chapter 10 and do not repeat them here.

What we do here is a two-stage process: We use an unsupervised method for determining the centers, then build a supervised layer on top of that. This is called *hybrid learning*. We can also learn all parameters, including $\boldsymbol{m}_h$ and s_h, in a supervised manner. The radial basis function of equation 12.13 is differentiable and we can backpropagate, just as we backpropagated in a multilayer perceptron to update the first-layer weights. The structure is similar to a multilayer perceptron with p_h as the hidden units, $\boldsymbol{m}_h$ and s_h as the first-layer parameters, the Gaussian as the activation function in the hidden layer, and w_h as the second-layer weights (see figure 12.8).

HYBRID LEARNING

But before we discuss this, we should remember that training a two-layer network is slow. Hybrid learning trains one layer at a time and is faster. Another technique, called the *anchor* method, sets the centers to the randomly chosen patterns from the training set without any further update. It is adequate if there are many units.

ANCHOR

On the other hand, the accuracy normally is not as high as when a completely supervised method is used. Consider the case when the input is uniformly distributed. Then k-means clustering places the units uniformly. If the function is changing significantly in a small part of the

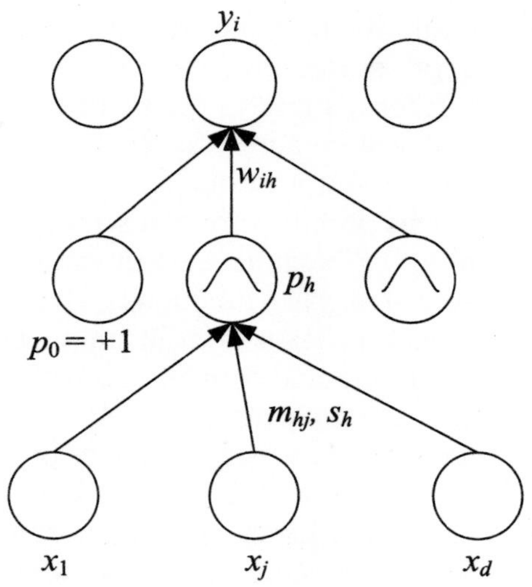

Figure 12.8 The RBF network where p_h are the hidden units using the bell-shaped activation function. $\boldsymbol{m}_h, s_h$ are the first-layer parameters, and $\boldsymbol{w}_i$ are the second-layer weights.

space, it is a better idea to have as many centers in places where the function changes fast, to make the error as small as possible; this is what the completely supervised method would do.

Let us discuss how all of the parameters can be trained in a fully supervised manner. The approach is the same as backpropagation applied to multilayer perceptrons. Let us see the case of regression with multiple outputs. The batch error is

$$E(\{\boldsymbol{m}_h, s_h, w_{ih}\}_{i,h}|\mathcal{X}) = \frac{1}{2}\sum_t \sum_i (r_i^t - y_i^t)^2 \tag{12.15}$$

where

$$y_i^t = \sum_{h=1}^{H} w_{ih} p_h^t + w_{i0} \tag{12.16}$$

Using gradient descent, we get the following update rule for the second-layer weights:

$$\Delta w_{ih} = \eta \sum_t (r_i^t - y_i^t) p_h^t \tag{12.17}$$

This is the usual perceptron update rule, with p_h as the inputs. Typically, p_h do not overlap much and at each iteration, only a few p_h are nonzero and only their w_h are updated. That is why RBF networks learn very fast, and faster than multilayer perceptrons that use a distributed representation.

Similarly, we can get the update equations for the centers and spreads by backpropagation (chain rule):

$$\Delta m_{hj} = \eta \sum_t \left[\sum_i (r_i^t - y_i^t) w_{ih} \right] p_h^t \frac{(x_j^t - m_{hj})}{s_h^2} \quad (12.18)$$

$$\Delta s_h = \eta \sum_t \left[\sum_i (r_i^t - y_i^t) w_{ih} \right] p_h^t \frac{\|\boldsymbol{x}^t - \boldsymbol{m}_h\|^2}{s_h^3} \quad (12.19)$$

Let us compare equation 12.18 with equation 12.5: First, here we use p_h instead of b_h, which means that not only the closest one but all units are updated, depending on their centers and spreads. Second, here the update is supervised and contains the backpropagated error term. The update depends not only on the input but also on the final error $(r_i^t - y_i^t)$, the effect of the unit on the output, w_{ih}, the activation of the unit, p_h, and the input, $(\boldsymbol{x} - \boldsymbol{m}_h)$.

In practice, equations 12.18 and 12.19 need some extra control. We need to explicitly check that s_h do not become very small or very large to be useless; we also need to check that $\boldsymbol{m}_h$ stay in the valid input range.

In the case of classification, we have

$$y_i^t = \frac{\exp\left[\sum_h w_{ih} p_h^t + w_{i0}\right]}{\sum_k \exp\left[\sum_h w_{kh} p_h^t + w_{k0}\right]} \quad (12.20)$$

and the cross-entropy error is

$$E(\{\boldsymbol{m}_h, s_h, w_{ih}\}_{i,h} | \mathcal{X}) = -\sum_t \sum_i r_i^t \log y_i^t \quad (12.21)$$

Update rules can similarly be derived using gradient descent (exercise 3).

Let us look again at equation 12.14. For any input, if p_h is nonzero, then it contributes w_h to the output. Its contribution is a constant fit, as given by w_h. Normally Gaussians do not overlap much, and one or two of them have a nonzero p_h value. In any case, only few units contribute to the output. w_0 is the constant offset and is added to the weighted sum of the active (nonzero) units. We also see that $y = w_0$ if all p_h are 0. We can therefore view w_0 as the "default" value of y: If no Gaussian is active, then the output is given by this value. So a possibility is to make this "default model" a more powerful "rule." For example, we can write

$$y^t = \underbrace{\sum_{h=1}^{H} w_h p_h^t}_{exceptions} + \underbrace{\boldsymbol{v}^T \boldsymbol{x}^t + v_0}_{rule} \tag{12.22}$$

In this case, the rule is linear: $\boldsymbol{v}^T \boldsymbol{x}^t + v_0$. When they are nonzero, Gaussians work as localized "exceptions" and modify the output to make up for the difference between the desired output and the rule output. Such a model can be trained in a supervised manner, and the rule can be trained together with the exceptions (exercise 4). We discuss a similar model, cascading, in section 17.11 where we see it as a combination of two learners, one general rule and the other formed by a set of exceptions.

12.4 Incorporating Rule-Based Knowledge

PRIOR KNOWLEDGE

The training of any learning system can be much simpler if we manage to incorporate *prior knowledge* to initialize the system. For example, prior knowledge may be available in the form of a set of rules that specify the input/output mapping that the model, for example, the RBF network, has to learn. This occurs frequently in industrial and medical applications where rules can be given by experts. Similarly, once a network has been trained, rules can be extracted from the solution in such a way as to better understand the solution to the problem.

The inclusion of prior knowledge has the additional advantage that if the network is required to extrapolate into regions of the input space where it has not seen any training data, it can rely on this prior knowledge. Furthermore, in many control applications, the network is required to make reasonable predictions right from the beginning. Before it has seen sufficient training data, it has to rely primarily on this prior knowledge.

In many applications we are typically told some basic rules that we try to follow in the beginning but that are then refined and altered through experience. The better our initial knowledge of a problem, the faster we can achieve good performance and the less training that is required.

Such inclusion of prior knowledge or extraction of learned knowledge is easy to do with RBF networks because the units are local. This makes RULE EXTRACTION *rule extraction* easier (Tresp, Hollatz, and Ahmad 1997). An example is

(12.23) IF $((x_1 \approx a)$ AND $(x_2 \approx b))$ OR $(x_3 \approx c)$ THEN $y = 0.1$

where $x_1 \approx a$ means "x_1 is approximately a." In the RBF framework, this rule is encoded by two Gaussian units as

$$p_1 = \exp\left[-\frac{(x_1-a)^2}{2s_1^2}\right] \cdot \exp\left[-\frac{(x_2-b)^2}{2s_2^2}\right] \text{ with } w_1 = 0.1$$

$$p_2 = \exp\left[-\frac{(x_3-c)^2}{2s_3^2}\right] \text{ with } w_2 = 0.1$$

"Approximately equal to" is modeled by a Gaussian where the center is the ideal value and the spread denotes the allowed difference around this ideal value. Conjunction is the product of two univariate Gaussians that is a bivariate Gaussian. Then, the first product term can be handled by a two-dimensional, namely, $\boldsymbol{x} = [x_1, x_2]$, Gaussian centered at (a, b), and the spreads on the two dimensions are given by s_1 and s_2. Disjunction is modeled by two separate Gaussians, each one handling one of the disjuncts.

Given labeled training data, the parameters of the RBF network so constructed can be fine-tuned after the initial construction, using a small value of η.

This formulation is related to the fuzzy logic approach where equation 12.23 is named a *fuzzy rule*. The Gaussian basis function that checks for approximate equality corresponds to a *fuzzy membership function* (Berthold 1999; Cherkassky and Mulier 1998).

FUZZY RULE

FUZZY MEMBERSHIP FUNCTION

12.5 Normalized Basis Functions

In equation 12.14, for an input, it is possible that all of the p_h are 0. In some applications, we may want to have a *normalization* step to make sure that the values of the local units sum up to 1, thus making sure that for any input there is at least one nonzero unit:

$$g_h^t = \frac{p_h^t}{\sum_{l=1}^H p_l^t} = \frac{\exp[-\|\boldsymbol{x}^t - \boldsymbol{m}_h\|^2/2s_h^2]}{\sum_l \exp[-\|\boldsymbol{x}^t - \boldsymbol{m}_l\|^2/2s_l^2]} \quad (12.24)$$

An example is given in figure 12.9. Taking p_h as $p(\boldsymbol{x}|h)$, g_h correspond to $p(h|\boldsymbol{x})$, the posterior probability that $\boldsymbol{x}$ belongs to unit h. It is as if

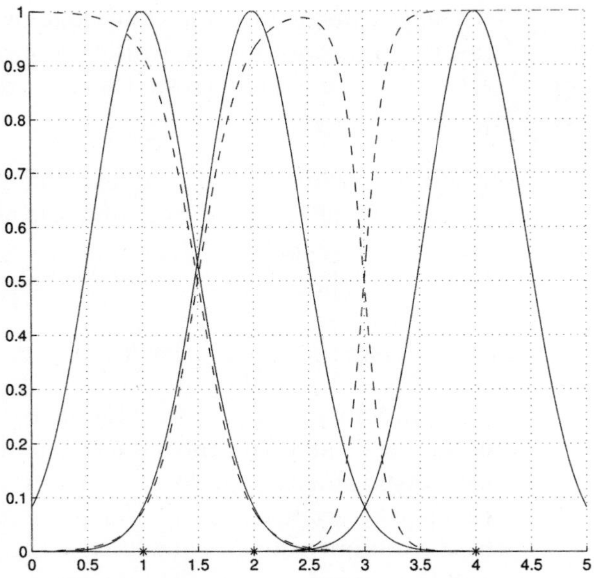

Figure 12.9 (-) Before and (- -) after normalization for three Gaussians whose centers are denoted by '*'. Note how the nonzero region of a unit depends also on the positions of other units. If the spreads are small, normalization implements a harder split; with large spreads, units overlap more.

the units divide the input space among themselves. We can think of g_h as a classifier in itself, choosing the responsible unit for a given input. This classification is done based on distance, as in a parametric Gaussian classifier (chapter 5).

The output is a weighted sum

$$y_i^t = \sum_{h=1}^{H} w_{ih} g_h^t \tag{12.25}$$

where there is no need for a bias term because there is at least one nonzero g_h for each $\boldsymbol{x}$. Using g_h instead of p_h does not introduce any extra parameters; it only couples the units together: p_h depends only on $\boldsymbol{m}_h$ and s_h, but g_h, because of normalization, depends on the centers and spreads of all of the units.

In the case of regression, we have the following update rules using gradient descent:

(12.26) $$\Delta w_{ih} = \eta \sum_t (r_i^t - y_i^t) g_h^t$$

(12.27) $$\Delta m_{hj} = \eta \sum_t \sum_i (r_i^t - y_i^t)(w_{ih} - y_i^t) g_h^t \frac{(x_j^t - m_{hj})}{s_h^2}$$

The update rule for s_h as well as the rules for classification can similarly be derived. Let us compare these with the update rules for the RBF with unnormalized Gaussians (equation 12.17). Here, we use g_h instead of p_h, which makes a unit's update dependent not only on its own parameters, but also on the centers and spreads of other units as well. Comparing equation 12.27 with equation 12.18, we see that instead of w_{ih}, we have $(w_{ih} - y_i^t)$, which shows the role of normalization on the output. The "responsible" unit wants to decrease the difference between its output, w_{ih}, and the final output, y_i^t, proportional to its responsibility, g_h.

12.6 Competitive Basis Functions

As we have seen up until now, in an RBF network the final output is determined as a weighted sum of the contributions of the local units. Though the units are local, it is the final weighted sum that is important and that we want to make as close as possible to the required output. For example, in regression we minimize equation 12.15, which is based on the probabilistic model

(12.28) $$p(\mathbf{r}^t|\mathbf{x}^t) = \prod_i \frac{1}{\sqrt{2\pi}\sigma} \exp\left[-\frac{(r_i^t - y_i^t)^2}{2\sigma^2}\right]$$

where y_i^t is given by equation 12.16 (unnormalized) or equation 12.25 (normalized). In either case, we can view the model as a *cooperative* one since the units cooperate to generate the final output, y_i^t. We now discuss the approach using *competitive basis functions* where we assume that the output is drawn from a mixture model

COMPETITIVE BASIS FUNCTIONS

(12.29) $$p(\mathbf{r}^t|\mathbf{x}^t) = \sum_{h=1}^{H} p(h|\mathbf{x}^t) p(\mathbf{r}^t|h, \mathbf{x}^t)$$

$p(h|\mathbf{x}^t)$ are the mixture proportions and $p(\mathbf{r}^t|h, \mathbf{x}^t)$ are the mixture components generating the output if that component is chosen. Note that both of these terms depend on the input $\mathbf{x}$.

The mixture proportions are

$$p(h|\boldsymbol{x}) = \frac{p(\boldsymbol{x}|h)p(h)}{\sum_l p(\boldsymbol{x}|l)p(l)} \tag{12.30}$$

$$g_h^t = \frac{a_h \exp[-\|\boldsymbol{x}^t - \boldsymbol{m}_h\|^2/2s_h^2]}{\sum_l a_l \exp[-\|\boldsymbol{x}^t - \boldsymbol{m}_l\|^2/2s_l^2]} \tag{12.31}$$

We generally assume a_h to be equal and ignore them. Let us first take the case of regression where the components are Gaussian. In equation 12.28, noise is added to the weighted sum; here, one component is chosen and noise is added to its output, y_{ih}^t.

Using the mixture model of equation 12.29, the log likelihood is

$$\mathcal{L}(\{\boldsymbol{m}_h, s_h, w_{ih}\}_{i,h}|\mathcal{X}) = \sum_t \log \sum_h g_h^t \exp\left[-\frac{1}{2}\sum_i (r_i^t - y_{ih}^t)^2\right] \tag{12.32}$$

where $y_{ih}^t = w_{ih}$ is the constant fit done by component h for output i, which, strictly speaking, does not depend on $\boldsymbol{x}$. (In section 12.8.2, we discuss the case of competitive mixture of experts where the local fit is a linear function of $\boldsymbol{x}$.) We see that if g_h^t is 1, then it is responsible for generating the right output and needs to minimize the squared error of its prediction, $\sum_i (r_i^t - y_{ih}^t)^2$.

Using gradient ascent to maximize the log likelihood, we get

$$\Delta w_{ih} = \eta \sum_t (r_i^t - y_{ih}^t) f_h^t \tag{12.33}$$

where

$$f_h^t = \frac{g_h^t \exp[-\frac{1}{2}\sum_i (r_i^t - y_{ih}^t)^2]}{\sum_l g_l^t \exp[-\frac{1}{2}\sum_i (r_i^t - y_{il}^t)^2]} \tag{12.34}$$

$$p(h|\boldsymbol{r}, \boldsymbol{x}) = \frac{p(h|\boldsymbol{x})p(\boldsymbol{r}|h, \boldsymbol{x})}{\sum_l p(l|\boldsymbol{x})p(\boldsymbol{r}|l, \boldsymbol{x})} \tag{12.35}$$

$g_h^t \equiv p(h|\boldsymbol{x}^t)$ is the posterior probability of unit h given the input, and it depends on the centers and spreads of all of the units. $f_h^t \equiv p(h|\boldsymbol{r}, \boldsymbol{x}^t)$ is the posterior probability of unit h given the input and the desired output, also taking the error into account in choosing the responsible unit.

Similarly, we can derive a rule to update the centers:

$$\Delta m_{hj} = \eta \sum_t (f_h^t - g_h^t) \frac{(x_j^t - m_{hj})}{s_h^2} \tag{12.36}$$

f_h is the posterior probability of unit h also taking the required output into account, whereas g_h is the posterior probability using only the input space information. Their difference is the error term for the centers. Δs_h can be similarly derived. In the cooperative case, there is no force on the units to be localized. To decrease the error, means and spreads can take any value; it is even possible sometimes for the spreads to increase and flatten out. In the competitive case, however, to increase the likelihood, units are forced to be localized with more separation between them and smaller spreads.

In classification, each component by itself is a multinomial. Then the log likelihood is

$$\mathcal{L}(\{\boldsymbol{m}_h, s_h, w_{ih}\}_{i,h}|\mathcal{X}) = \sum_t \log \sum_h g_h^t \prod_i (y_{ih}^t)^{r_i^t} \tag{12.37}$$

$$= \sum_t \log \sum_h g_h^t \exp\left[\sum_i r_i^t \log y_{ih}^t\right] \tag{12.38}$$

where

$$y_{ih}^t = \frac{\exp w_{ih}}{\sum_k \exp w_{kh}} \tag{12.39}$$

Update rules for w_{ih}, $\boldsymbol{m}_h$, and s_h can be derived using gradient ascent, which will include

$$f_h^t = \frac{g_h^t \exp[\sum_i r_i^t \log y_{ih}^t]}{\sum_l g_l^t \exp[\sum_i r_i^t \log y_{il}^t]} \tag{12.40}$$

In chapter 7, we discussed the EM algorithm for fitting Gaussian mixtures to data. It is possible to generalize EM for supervised learning as well. Actually, calculating f_h^t corresponds to the E-step. $f_h^t \equiv p(\boldsymbol{r}|h, \boldsymbol{x}^t)$ replaces $p(h|\boldsymbol{x}^t)$, which we used in the E-step in chapter 7 when the application was unsupervised. In the M-step for regression, we update the parameters as

$$\boldsymbol{m}_h = \frac{\sum_t f_h^t \boldsymbol{x}^t}{\sum_t f_h^t} \tag{12.41}$$

$$\mathbf{S}_h = \frac{\sum_t f_h^t (\boldsymbol{x}^t - \boldsymbol{m}_h)(\boldsymbol{x}^t - \boldsymbol{m}_h)^T}{\sum_t f_h^t} \tag{12.42}$$

$$w_{ih} = \frac{\sum_t f_h^t r_i^t}{\sum_t f_h^t} \tag{12.43}$$

We see that w_{ih} is a weighted average where weights are the posterior probabilities of units, given the input and the desired output. In the case of classification, the M-step has no analytical solution and we need to resort to an iterative procedure, for example, gradient ascent (Jordan and Jacobs 1994).

12.7 Learning Vector Quantization

Let us say we have H units for each class, already labeled by those classes. These units are initialized with random instances from their classes. At each iteration, we find the unit, $\boldsymbol{m}_i$, that is closest to the input instance in Euclidean distance and use the following update rule:

$$\begin{cases} \Delta \boldsymbol{m}_i = \eta(\boldsymbol{x}^t - \boldsymbol{m}_i) & \text{if } \boldsymbol{x}^t \text{ and } \boldsymbol{m}_i \text{ have the same class label} \\ \Delta \boldsymbol{m}_i = -\eta(\boldsymbol{x}^t - \boldsymbol{m}_i) & \text{otherwise} \end{cases} \tag{12.44}$$

If the closest center has the correct label, it is moved toward the input to better represent it. If it belongs to the wrong class, it is moved away from the input in the expectation that if it is moved sufficiently away, a center of the correct class will be the closest in a future iteration. This is the *learning vector quantization* (LVQ) model proposed by Kohonen (1990, 1995).

LEARNING VECTOR QUANTIZATION

The LVQ update equation is analogous to equation 12.36 where the direction in which the center is moved depends on the difference between two values: Our prediction of the winner unit based on the input distances and what the winner should be based on the required output.

12.8 The Mixture of Experts

In RBFs, corresponding to each local patch we give a constant fit. In the case where for any input, we have one g_h 1 and all others 0, we get a piecewise constant approximation where for output i, the local fit by patch h is given by w_{ih}. From the Taylor expansion, we know that at each point, the function can be written as

$$f(x) = f(a) + (x - a)f'(a) + \cdots \tag{12.45}$$

Thus a constant approximation is good if x is close enough to a and $f'(a)$ is close to 0—that is, if $f(x)$ is flat around a. If this is not the case, we need to divide the space into a large number of patches, which is particularly serious when the input dimensionality is high, due to the curse of dimensionality.

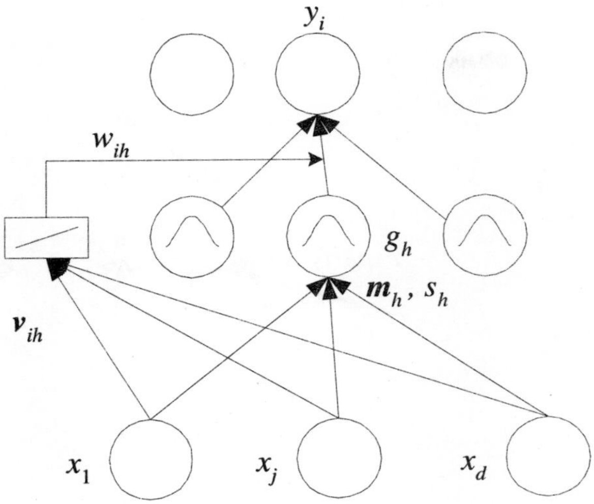

Figure 12.10 The mixture of experts can be seen as an RBF network where the second-layer weights are outputs of linear models. Only one linear model is shown for clarity.

PIECEWISE LINEAR APPROXIMATION

MIXTURE OF EXPERTS

An alternative is to have a *piecewise linear approximation* by taking into account the next term in the Taylor expansion, namely, the linear term. This is what is done by the *mixture of experts* (Jacobs et al. 1991). We write

$$y_i^t = \sum_{h=1}^{H} w_{ih} g_h^t \tag{12.46}$$

which is the same as equation 12.25 but here, w_{ih}, the contribution of patch h to output i is not a constant but a linear function of the input:

$$w_{ih}^t = \boldsymbol{v}_{ih}^T \boldsymbol{x}^t \tag{12.47}$$

$\boldsymbol{v}_{ih}$ is the parameter vector that defines the linear function and includes a bias term, making the mixture of experts a generalization of the RBF network. The unit activations can be taken as normalized RBFs:

$$g_h^t = \frac{\exp[-\|\boldsymbol{x}^t - \boldsymbol{m}_h\|^2/2s_h^2]}{\sum_l \exp[-\|\boldsymbol{x}^t - \boldsymbol{m}_l\|^2/2s_l^2]} \tag{12.48}$$

This can be seen as an RBF network except that the second-layer weights are not constants but are outputs of linear models (see figure 12.10). Ja-

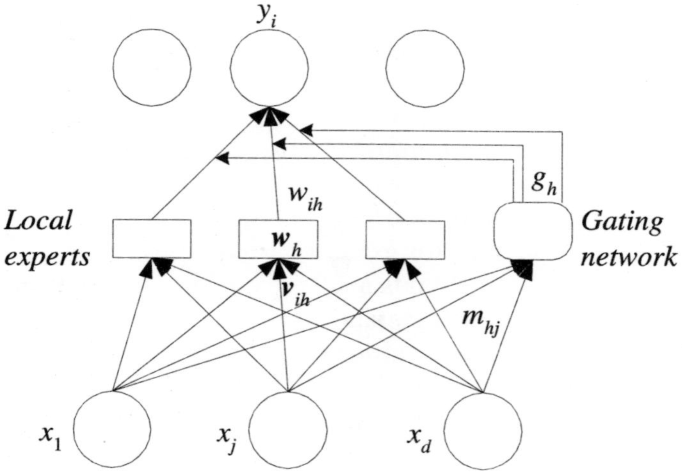

Figure 12.11 The mixture of experts can be seen as a model for combining multiple models. $\boldsymbol{w}_h$ are the models and the gating network is another model determining the weight of each model, as given by g_h. Viewed in this way, neither the experts nor the gating are restricted to be linear.

cobs et al. (1991) view this in another way: They consider $\boldsymbol{w}_h$ as linear models, each taking the input, and call them *experts*. g_h are considered to be the outputs of a *gating network*. The gating network works as a classifier does with its outputs summing to 1, assigning the input to one of the experts (see figure 12.11).

Considering the gating network in this manner, any classifier can be used in gating. When $\boldsymbol{x}$ is high-dimensional, using local Gaussian units may require a large number of experts and Jacobs et al. (1991) propose to take

$$g_h^t = \frac{\exp[\boldsymbol{m}_h^T \boldsymbol{x}^t]}{\sum_l \exp[\boldsymbol{m}_l^T \boldsymbol{x}^t]} \tag{12.49}$$

which is a linear classifier. Note that $\boldsymbol{m}_h$ are no longer centers but hyperplanes, and as such include bias values. This gating network is implementing a classification where it is dividing linearly the input region for which expert h is responsible from the expertise regions of other experts. As we will see again in chapter 17, the mixture of experts is a general architecture for combining multiple models; the experts and the gating may be nonlinear, for example, contain multilayer perceptrons, instead of linear perceptrons (exercise 6).

An architecture similar to the mixture of experts and running line smoother (section 8.8.3) has been proposed by Bottou and Vapnik (1992). In their approach, no training is done initially. When a test instance is given, a subset of the data close to the test instance is chosen from the training set (as in the k-nearest neighbor, but with a large k), a simple model, for example, a linear classifier, is trained with this local data, the prediction is made for the instance, and then the model is discarded. For the next instance, a new model is created, and so on. On a handwritten digit recognition application, this model has less error than the multilayer perceptron, k-nearest neighbor, and Parzen windows; the disadvantage is the need to train a new model on the fly for each test instance.

12.8.1 Cooperative Experts

In the cooperative case, y_i^t is given by equation 12.46, and we would like to make it as close as possible to the required output, r_i^t. In regression, the error function is

$$E(\{\boldsymbol{m}_h, s_h, w_{ih}\}_{i,h}|\mathcal{X}) = \frac{1}{2}\sum_t \sum_i (r_i^t - y_i^t)^2 \tag{12.50}$$

Using gradient descent, second-layer (expert) weight parameters are updated as

$$\Delta \boldsymbol{v}_{ih} = \eta \sum_t (r_i^t - y_i^t) g_h^t \boldsymbol{x}^t \tag{12.51}$$

Compared with equation 12.26, we see that the only difference is that this new update is a function of the input.

If we use softmax gating (equation 12.49), using gradient descent we have the following update rule for the hyperplanes:

$$\Delta m_{hj} = \eta \sum_t \sum_i (r_i^t - y_i^t)(w_{ih}^t - y_i^t) g_h^t x_j^t \tag{12.52}$$

If we use radial gating (equation 12.48), only the last term, $\partial p_h / \partial m_{hj}$, differs.

In classification, we have

$$y_i = \frac{\exp\left[\sum_h w_{ih} g_h^t\right]}{\sum_k \exp\left[\sum_h w_{kh} g_h^t\right]} \tag{12.53}$$

with $w_{ih} = \boldsymbol{v}_{ih}^T \boldsymbol{x}$, and update rules can be derived to minimize the cross-entropy using gradient descent (exercise 7).

12.8.2 Competitive Experts

Just like the competitive RBFs, we have

$$\mathcal{L}(\{\boldsymbol{m}_h, s_h, w_{ih}\}_{i,h}|\mathcal{X}) = \sum_t \log \sum_h g_h^t \exp\left[-\frac{1}{2}\sum_i (r_i^t - y_{ih}^t)^2\right] \tag{12.54}$$

where $y_{ih}^t = w_{ih}^t = \boldsymbol{v}_{ih}\boldsymbol{x}^t$. Using gradient ascent, we get

$$\Delta \boldsymbol{v}_{ih} = \eta \sum_t (r_i^t - y_{ih}^t) f_h^t \boldsymbol{x}^t \tag{12.55}$$

$$\Delta \boldsymbol{m}_h = \eta \sum_t (f_h^t - g_h^t) \boldsymbol{x}^t \tag{12.56}$$

assuming softmax gating as given in equation 12.49.

In classification, we have

$$\mathcal{L}(\{\boldsymbol{m}_h, s_h, w_{ih}\}_{i,h}|\mathcal{X}) = \sum_t \log \sum_h g_h^t \prod_i (y_{ih}^t)^{r_i^t} \tag{12.57}$$

$$= \sum_t \log \sum_h g_h^t \exp\left[\sum_i r_i^t \log y_{ih}^t\right] \tag{12.58}$$

where

$$y_{ih}^t = \frac{\exp w_{ih}^t}{\sum_k \exp w_{kh}^t} = \frac{\exp[\boldsymbol{v}_{ih}\boldsymbol{x}^t]}{\sum_k \exp[\boldsymbol{v}_{kh}\boldsymbol{x}^t]} \tag{12.59}$$

Jordan and Jacobs (1994) generalize EM for the competitive case with local linear models. Alpaydın and Jordan (1996) compare cooperative and competitive models for classification tasks and see that the cooperative model is generally more accurate but the competitive version learns faster. This is because in the cooperative case, models overlap more and implement a smoother approximation, and thus it is preferable in regression problems. The competitive model makes a harder split; generally only one expert is active for an input and therefore learning is faster.

12.9 Hierarchical Mixture of Experts

HIERARCHICAL MIXTURE OF EXPERTS

In figure 12.11, we see a set of experts and a gating network that chooses one of the experts as a function of the input. In a *hierarchical mixture of experts,* we replace each expert with a complete system of mixture of experts in a recursive manner (Jordan and Jacobs 1994). Once an architecture is chosen—namely, the depth, the experts, and the gating models—the whole tree can be learned from a labeled sample. Jordan and Jacobs (1994) derive both gradient descent and EM learning rules for such an architecture (see exercise 9).

We may also interpret this architecture as a decision tree (chapter 9) and its gating networks as decision nodes. In the decision trees we discussed earlier, a decision node makes a hard decision and takes one of the branches, so we take only one path from the root to one of the leaves. What we have here is a *soft decision tree* where, because the gating model returns us a probability, we take all the branches but with different probabilities; so we traverse all the paths to all the leaves and we take a weighted sum over all the leaf values where weights are equal to the product of the gating values on the path to each leaf. The advantage of this averaging is that the boundaries between leaf regions are no longer hard but there is a transition from one to the other and this smooths the response (İrsoy, Yıldız, and Alpaydın 2012).

12.10 Notes

An RBF network can be seen as a neural network, implemented by a network of simple processing units. It differs from a multilayer perceptron in that the first and second layers implement different functions. Omohundro (1987) discusses how local models can be implemented as neural networks and also addresses hierarchical data structures for fast localization of relevant local units. Specht (1991) shows how Parzen windows can be implemented as a neural network.

Platt (1991) proposed an incremental version of RBF where new units are added as necessary. Fritzke (1995) similarly proposed a growing version of SOM.

Lee (1991) compares k-nearest neighbor, multilayer perceptron, and RBF network on a handwritten digit recognition application and concludes that these three methods all have small error rates. RBF networks learn faster than backpropagation on a multilayer perceptron but use more parameters. Both of these methods are superior to the k-NN in terms of classification speed and memory need. Such practical constraints like time, memory, and computational complexity may be more important than small differences in error rate in real-world applications.

Kohonen's SOM (1990, 1995) was one of the most popular neural network methods, having been used in a variety of applications including exploratory data analysis and as a preprocessing stage before a supervised learner. One interesting and successful application is the traveling salesman problem (Angeniol, Vaubois, and Le Texier 1988). Just like the difference between k-means clustering and EM on Gaussian mixtures (chapter 7), *generative topographic mapping* (GTM) (Bishop, Svensén, and Williams 1998) is a probabilistic version of SOM that optimizes the log likelihood of the data using a mixture of Gaussians whose means are constrained to lie on a two-dimensional manifold (for topological ordering in low dimensions).

GENERATIVE TOPOGRAPHIC MAPPING

In an RBF network, once the centers and spreads are fixed (e.g., by choosing a random subset of training instances as centers, as in the anchor method), training the second layer is a linear model. This model is equivalent to support vector machines with Gaussian kernels where during learning the best subset of instances, named the *support vectors*, are chosen; we discuss them in chapter 13. Gaussian processes (chapter 16) where we interpolate from stored training instances are also similar.

12.11 Exercises

1. Show an RBF network that implements XOR.

   SOLUTION: There are two possibilities (see figure 12.12): (a) We can have two circular Gaussians centered on the two positive instances and the second layer ORs them, or (b) we can have one elliptic Gaussian centered on (0.5, 0.5) with negative correlation to cover the two positive instances.

2. Write down the RBF network that uses elliptic units instead of radial units as in equation 12.13.

   SOLUTION:

   $$p_h^t = \exp\left[-\frac{1}{2}(\boldsymbol{x}^t - \boldsymbol{m}_h)^T \mathbf{S}_h^{-1}(\boldsymbol{x}^t - \boldsymbol{m}_h)\right]$$

   where $\mathbf{S}_h$ is the local covariance matrix.

3. Derive the update equations for the RBF network for classification (equations 12.20 and 12.21).

4. Show how the system given in equation 12.22 can be trained.

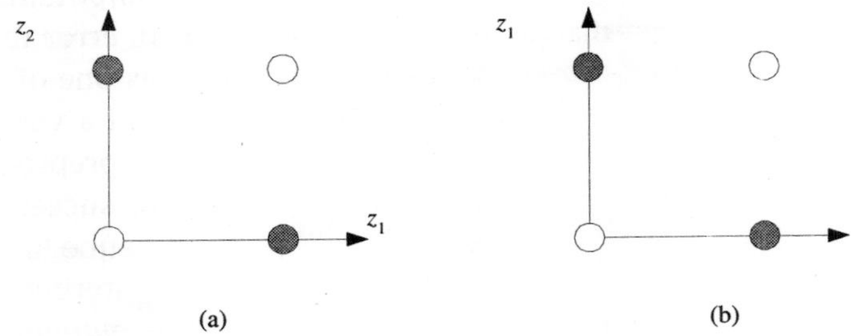

Figure 12.12 Two ways of implementing XOR with RBF.

5. Compare the number of parameters of a mixture of experts architecture with an RBF network.

   SOLUTION: With d inputs, K classes and H Gaussians, an RBF network needs $H \cdot d$ parameters for the centers, H parameters for the spreads and $(H+1)K$ parameters for the second-layer weights. For the case of the MoE, for each second-layer weight, we need a $d+1$ dimensional vector of the linear model, but there is no bias; hence we have $HK(d+1)$ parameters.

   Note that the number of parameters in the first layer is the same with RBF and it is the same whether we have Gaussian or softmax gating: For each hidden unit, in the case of Gaussian gating, we need d parameters for the center and 1 for the spread; in the case of softmax gating, the linear model has $d+1$ parameters (d inputs and a bias).

6. Formalize a mixture of experts architecture where the experts and the gating network are multilayer perceptrons. Derive the update equations for regression and classification.

7. Derive the update equations for the cooperative mixture of experts for classification.

8. Derive the update equations for the competitive mixture of experts for classification.

9. Formalize the hierarchical mixture of experts architecture with two levels. Derive the update equations using gradient descent for regression and classification.

   SOLUTION: The following is from Jordan and Jacobs 1994; notation is slightly changed to match the notation of the book.

   Let us see the case of regression with a single output: y is the overall output, y_i are the outputs on the first level, and y_{ij} are the outputs on the second level, which are the leaves in a model with two levels. Similarly, g_i are the gating outputs on the first level and $g_{j|i}$ are the outputs on the second level, that is, the gating value of expert j on the second level given that we have chosen the branch i on the first level:

$$
\begin{aligned}
y &= \sum_i g_i y_i \\
y_i &= \sum_j g_{j|i} y_{ij} \quad \text{and} \quad g_i = \frac{\exp \boldsymbol{m}_i^T \boldsymbol{x}}{\sum_k \exp \boldsymbol{m}_k^T \boldsymbol{x}} \\
y_{ij} &= \boldsymbol{v}_{ij}^T \boldsymbol{x} \quad \text{and} \quad g_{j|i} = \frac{\exp \boldsymbol{m}_{ij}^T \boldsymbol{x}}{\sum_l \exp \boldsymbol{m}_{il}^T \boldsymbol{x}}
\end{aligned}
$$

In regression, the error to be minimized is as follows (note that we are using a competitive version here):

$$
E = \sum_t \log \sum_i g_i^t \sum_j g_{j|i}^t \exp \left[-\frac{1}{2} (r^t - y_{ij}^t)^2 \right]
$$

and using gradient descent, we get the following update equations:

$$
\begin{aligned}
\Delta \boldsymbol{v}_{ij} &= \eta \sum_t f_i^t f_{j|i}^t (r^t - y^t) \boldsymbol{x}^t \\
\Delta \boldsymbol{m}_i &= \eta \sum_t (f_i^t - g_i^t) \boldsymbol{x}^t \\
\Delta \boldsymbol{m}_{ij} &= \eta \sum_t f_i^t (f_{j|i}^t - g_{j|i}^t) \boldsymbol{x}^t
\end{aligned}
$$

where we make use of the following posteriors:

$$
\begin{aligned}
f_i^t &= \frac{g_i^t \sum_j g_{j|i}^t \exp[-(1/2)(r^t - y_{ij}^t)^2]}{\sum_k g_k^t \sum_j g_{j|k}^t \exp[-(1/2)(r^t - y_{kj}^t)^2]} \\
f_{j|i}^t &= \frac{g_{j|i}^t \exp[-(1/2)(r^t - y_{ij}^t)^2]}{\sum_l g_{l|i}^t \exp[-(1/2)(r^t - y_{il}^t)^2]} \\
f_{ij}^t &= \frac{g_i^t g_{j|i}^t \exp[-(1/2)(r^t - y_{ij}^t)^2]}{\sum_k g_k^t \sum_l g_{l|k}^t \exp[-(1/2)(r^t - y_{kl}^t)^2]}
\end{aligned}
$$

Note how we multiply the gating values on the path starting from the root to a leaf expert.

For the case of classification with $K > 2$ classes, one possibility is to have K separate HMEs as above (having single output experts), whose outputs we softmax to maximize the log likelihood:

$$
\begin{aligned}
\mathcal{L} &= \sum_t \log \sum_i g_i^t \sum_j g_{j|i}^t \exp \left[\sum_c r_c^t \log p_c^t \right] \\
p_c^t &= \frac{\exp y_c^t}{\sum_k \exp y_k^t}
\end{aligned}
$$

where each y_c^t denotes the output of one single-output HME. The more interesting case of a single multiclass HME where experts have K softmax outputs is discussed in Waterhouse and Robinson 1994.

10. In the mixture of experts, because different experts specialize in different parts of the input space, they may need to focus on different inputs. Discuss how dimensionality can be locally reduced in the experts.

12.12 References

Alpaydın, E., and M. I. Jordan. 1996. "Local Linear Perceptrons for Classification." *IEEE Transactions on Neural Networks* 7:788–792.

Angeniol, B., G. Vaubois, and Y. Le Texier. 1988. "Self Organizing Feature Maps and the Travelling Salesman Problem." *Neural Networks* 1:289–293.

Berthold, M. 1999. "Fuzzy Logic." In *Intelligent Data Analysis: An Introduction,* ed. M. Berthold and D. J. Hand, 269–298. Berlin: Springer.

Bishop, C. M., M. Svensén, and C. K. I. Williams. 1998. "GTM: The Generative Topographic Mapping." *Neural Computation* 10:215–234.

Bottou, L., and V. Vapnik. 1992. "Local Learning Algorithms." *Neural Computation* 4:888–900.

Broomhead, D. S., and D. Lowe. 1988. "Multivariable Functional Interpolation and Adaptive Networks." *Complex Systems* 2:321–355.

Carpenter, G. A., and S. Grossberg. 1988. "The ART of Adaptive Pattern Recognition by a Self-Organizing Neural Network." *IEEE Computer* 21 (3): 77–88.

Cherkassky, V., and F. Mulier. 1998. *Learning from Data: Concepts, Theory, and Methods.* New York: Wiley.

DeSieno, D. 1988. "Adding a Conscience Mechanism to Competitive Learning." In *IEEE International Conference on Neural Networks,* 117–124. Piscataway, NJ: IEEE Press.

Feldman, J. A., and D. H. Ballard. 1982. "Connectionist Models and their Properties." *Cognitive Science* 6:205–254.

Fritzke, B. 1995. "Growing Cell Structures: A Self Organizing Network for Unsupervised and Supervised Training." *Neural Networks* 7:1441–1460.

Grossberg, S. 1980. "How Does the Brain Build a Cognitive Code?" *Psychological Review* 87:1–51.

Hertz, J., A. Krogh, and R. G. Palmer. 1991. *Introduction to the Theory of Neural Computation.* Reading, MA: Addison-Wesley.

İrsoy, O., O. T. Yıldız, and E. Alpaydın. 2012. "Soft Decision Trees." In *International Conference on Pattern Recognition*, 1819–1822. Piscataway, NJ: IEEE Press.

Jacobs, R. A., M. I. Jordan, S. J. Nowlan, and G. E. Hinton. 1991. "Adaptive Mixtures of Local Experts." *Neural Computation* 3:79–87.

Jordan, M. I., and R. A. Jacobs. 1994. "Hierarchical Mixtures of Experts and the EM Algorithm." *Neural Computation* 6:181–214.

Kohonen, T. 1990. "The Self-Organizing Map." *Proceedings of the IEEE* 78:1464–1480.

Kohonen, T. 1995. *Self-Organizing Maps.* Berlin: Springer.

Lee, Y. 1991. "Handwritten Digit Recognition Using *k*-Nearest Neighbor, Radial Basis Function, and Backpropagation Neural Networks." *Neural Computation* 3:440–449.

Mao, J., and A. K. Jain. 1995. "Artificial Neural Networks for Feature Extraction and Multivariate Data Projection." *IEEE Transactions on Neural Networks* 6:296–317.

Moody, J., and C. Darken. 1989. "Fast Learning in Networks of Locally-Tuned Processing Units." *Neural Computation* 1:281–294.

Oja, E. 1982. "A Simplified Neuron Model as a Principal Component Analyzer." *Journal of Mathematical Biology* 15:267–273.

Omohundro, S. M. 1987. "Efficient Algorithms with Neural Network Behavior." *Complex Systems* 1:273–347.

Platt, J. 1991. "A Resource Allocating Network for Function Interpolation." *Neural Computation* 3:213–225.

Specht, D. F. 1991. "A General Regression Neural Network." *IEEE Transactions on Neural Networks* 2:568–576.

Tresp, V., J. Hollatz, and S. Ahmad. 1997. "Representing Probabilistic Rules with Networks of Gaussian Basis Functions." *Machine Learning* 27:173–200.

Waterhouse, S. R., and A. J. Robinson. 1994. "Classification Using Hierarchical Mixtures of Experts." In *IEEE Workshop on Neural Networks for Signal Processing*, 177–186. Piscataway, NJ: IEEE Press.

13 *Kernel Machines*

Kernel machines are maximum margin methods that allow the model to be written as a sum of the influences of a subset of the training instances. These influences are given by application-specific similarity kernels, and we discuss "kernelized" classification, regression, ranking, outlier detection and dimensionality reduction, and how to choose and use kernels.

13.1 Introduction

We now discuss a different approach for linear classification and regression. We should not be surprised to have so many different methods even for the simple case of a linear model. Each learning algorithm has a different inductive bias, makes different assumptions, and defines a different objective function and thus may find a different linear model.

The model that we will discuss in this chapter, called the *support vector machine* (SVM), and later generalized under the name *kernel machine*, has been popular in recent years for a number of reasons:

1. It is a discriminant-based method and uses Vapnik's principle to never solve a more complex problem as a first step before the actual problem (Vapnik 1995). For example, in classification, when the task is to learn the discriminant, it is not necessary to estimate where the class densities $p(\boldsymbol{x}|C_i)$ or the exact posterior probability values $P(C_i|\boldsymbol{x})$; we only need to estimate where the class boundaries lie, that is, $\boldsymbol{x}$ where $P(C_i|\boldsymbol{x}) = P(C_j|\boldsymbol{x})$. Similarly, for outlier detection, we do not need to estimate the full density $p(\boldsymbol{x})$; we only need to find the boundary separating those $\boldsymbol{x}$ that have low $p(\boldsymbol{x})$, that is, $\boldsymbol{x}$ where $p(\boldsymbol{x}) < \theta$, for some threshold $\theta \in (0, 1)$.

2. After training, the parameter of the linear model, the weight vector, can be written down in terms of a subset of the training set, which are the so-called *support vectors.* In classification, these are the cases that are close to the boundary and as such, knowing them allows knowledge extraction: Those are the uncertain or erroneous cases that lie in the vicinity of the boundary between two classes. Their number gives us an estimate of the generalization error, and, as we see below, being able to write the model parameter in terms of a set of instances allows kernelization.

3. As we will see shortly, the output is written as a sum of the influences of support vectors and these are given by *kernel functions* that are application-specific measures of similarity between data instances. Previously, we talked about nonlinear basis functions allowing us to map the input to another space where a linear (smooth) solution is possible; the kernel function uses the same idea.

4. Typically in most learning algorithms, data points are represented as vectors, and either dot product (as in the multilayer perceptrons) or Euclidean distance (as in radial basis function networks) is used. A kernel function allows us to go beyond that. For example, G_1 and G_2 may be two graphs and $K(G_1, G_2)$ may correspond to the number of shared paths, which we can calculate without needing to represent G_1 or G_2 explicitly as vectors.

5. Kernel-based algorithms are formulated as convex optimization problems, and there is a single optimum that we can solve for analytically. Therefore we are no longer bothered with heuristics for learning rates, initializations, checking for convergence, and such. Of course, this does not mean that we do not have any hyperparameters for model selection; we do—any method needs them, to match the algorithm to the data at hand.

We start our discussion with the case of classification, and then generalize to regression, ranking, outlier (novelty) detection, and then dimensionality reduction. We see that in all cases basically we have the similar quadratic program template to maximize the separability, or *margin*, of instances subject to a constraint of the smoothness of solution. Solving for it, we get the support vectors. The kernel function defines the space according to its notion of similarity and a kernel function is good if we have better separation in its corresponding space.

13.2 Optimal Separating Hyperplane

Let us start again with two classes and use labels $-1/+1$ for the two classes. The sample is $\mathcal{X} = \{\boldsymbol{x}^t, r^t\}$ where $r^t = +1$ if $\boldsymbol{x}^t \in C_1$ and $r^t = -1$ if $\boldsymbol{x}^t \in C_2$. We would like to find $\boldsymbol{w}$ and w_0 such that

$$\begin{aligned} \boldsymbol{w}^T\boldsymbol{x}^t + w_0 \geq +1 \quad &\text{for} \quad r^t = +1 \\ \boldsymbol{w}^T\boldsymbol{x}^t + w_0 \leq -1 \quad &\text{for} \quad r^t = -1 \end{aligned}$$

which can be rewritten as

(13.1) $$r^t(\boldsymbol{w}^T\boldsymbol{x}^t + w_0) \geq +1$$

Note that we do not simply require

$$r^t(\boldsymbol{w}^T\boldsymbol{x}^t + w_0) \geq 0$$

Not only do we want the instances to be on the right side of the hyperplane, but we also want them some distance away, for better generalization. The distance from the hyperplane to the instances closest to it on either side is called the *margin*, which we want to maximize for best generalization.

MARGIN

Very early on, in section 2.1, we talked about the concept of the margin when we were talking about fitting a rectangle, and we said that it is better to take a rectangle halfway between S and G, to get a breathing space. This is so that in case noise shifts a test instance slightly, it will still be on the right side of the boundary.

OPTIMAL SEPARATING HYPERPLANE

Similarly, now that we are using the hypothesis class of lines, the *optimal separating hyperplane* is the one that maximizes the margin.

We remember from section 10.3 that the distance of $\boldsymbol{x}^t$ to the discriminant is

$$\frac{|\boldsymbol{w}^T\boldsymbol{x}^t + w_0|}{\|\boldsymbol{w}\|}$$

which, when $r^t \in \{-1, +1\}$, can be written as

$$\frac{r^t(\boldsymbol{w}^T\boldsymbol{x}^t + w_0)}{\|\boldsymbol{w}\|}$$

and we would like this to be at least some value ρ:

(13.2) $$\frac{r^t(\boldsymbol{w}^T\boldsymbol{x}^t + w_0)}{\|\boldsymbol{w}\|} \geq \rho, \forall t$$

We would like to maximize ρ but there are an infinite number of solutions that we can get by scaling $\boldsymbol{w}$ and for a unique solution, we fix $\rho\|\boldsymbol{w}\| = 1$ and thus, to maximize the margin, we minimize $\|\boldsymbol{w}\|$. The task can therefore be defined (see Cortes and Vapnik 1995; Vapnik 1995) as to

$$\min \frac{1}{2}\|\boldsymbol{w}\|^2 \text{ subject to } r^t(\boldsymbol{w}^T\boldsymbol{x}^t + w_0) \geq +1, \forall t \tag{13.3}$$

This is a standard quadratic optimization problem, whose complexity depends on d, and it can be solved directly to find $\boldsymbol{w}$ and w_0. Then, on both sides of the hyperplane, there will be instances that are $1/\|\boldsymbol{w}\|$ away from the hyperplane and the total margin will be $2/\|\boldsymbol{w}\|$.

We saw in section 10.2 that if the problem is not linearly separable, instead of fitting a nonlinear function, one trick is to map the problem to a new space by using nonlinear basis functions. It is generally the case that this new space has many more dimensions than the original space, and, in such a case, we are interested in a method whose complexity does not depend on the input dimensionality.

In finding the optimal hyperplane, we can convert the optimization problem to a form whose complexity depends on N, the number of training instances, and not on d. Another advantage of this new formulation is that it will allow us to rewrite the basis functions in terms of kernel functions, as we will see in section 13.5.

To get the new formulation, we first write equation 13.3 as an unconstrained problem using Lagrange multipliers α^t:

$$\begin{aligned} L_p &= \frac{1}{2}\|\boldsymbol{w}\|^2 - \sum_{t=1}^{N} \alpha^t[r^t(\boldsymbol{w}^T\boldsymbol{x}^t + w_0) - 1] \\ &= \frac{1}{2}\|\boldsymbol{w}\|^2 - \sum_t \alpha^t r^t(\boldsymbol{w}^T\boldsymbol{x}^t + w_0) + \sum_t \alpha^t \end{aligned} \tag{13.4}$$

This should be minimized with respect to $\boldsymbol{w}, w_0$ and maximized with respect to $\alpha^t \geq 0$. The saddle point gives the solution.

This is a convex quadratic optimization problem because the main term is convex and the linear constraints are also convex. Therefore, we can equivalently solve the dual problem, making use of the Karush-Kuhn-Tucker conditions. The dual is to *maximize* L_p with respect to α^t, subject to the constraints that the gradient of L_p with respect to $\boldsymbol{w}$ and w_0 are 0 and also that $\alpha^t \geq 0$:

(13.5) $$\frac{\partial L_p}{\partial \boldsymbol{w}} = 0 \quad \Rightarrow \quad \boldsymbol{w} = \sum_t \alpha^t r^t \boldsymbol{x}^t$$

(13.6) $$\frac{\partial L_p}{\partial w_0} = 0 \quad \Rightarrow \quad \sum_t \alpha^t r^t = 0$$

Plugging these into equation 13.4, we get the dual

$$\begin{aligned} L_d &= \frac{1}{2}(\boldsymbol{w}^T\boldsymbol{w}) - \boldsymbol{w}^T \sum_t \alpha^t r^t \boldsymbol{x}^t - w_0 \sum_t \alpha^t r^t + \sum_t \alpha^t \\ &= -\frac{1}{2}(\boldsymbol{w}^T\boldsymbol{w}) + \sum_t \alpha^t \\ &= -\frac{1}{2}\sum_t \sum_s \alpha^t \alpha^s r^t r^s (\boldsymbol{x}^t)^T \boldsymbol{x}^s + \sum_t \alpha^t \end{aligned} \quad (13.7)$$

which we maximize with respect to α^t only, subject to the constraints

$$\sum_t \alpha^t r^t = 0, \text{ and } \alpha^t \geq 0, \forall t$$

This can be solved using quadratic optimization methods. The size of the dual depends on N, sample size, and not on d, the input dimensionality. The upper bound for time complexity is $\mathcal{O}(N^3)$, and the upper bound for space complexity is $\mathcal{O}(N^2)$.

Once we solve for α^t, we see that though there are N of them, most vanish with $\alpha^t = 0$ and only a small percentage have $\alpha^t > 0$. The set of $\boldsymbol{x}^t$ whose $\alpha^t > 0$ are the *support vectors*, and as we see in equation 13.5, $\boldsymbol{w}$ is written as the weighted sum of these training instances that are selected as the support vectors. These are the $\boldsymbol{x}^t$ that satisfy

$$r^t(\boldsymbol{w}^T\boldsymbol{x}^t + w_0) = 1$$

and lie on the margin. We can use this fact to calculate w_0 from any support vector as

(13.8) $$w_0 = r^t - \boldsymbol{w}^T\boldsymbol{x}^t$$

For numerical stability, it is advised that this be done for all support vectors and an average be taken. The discriminant thus found is called the *support vector machine* (SVM) (see figure 13.1).

SUPPORT VECTOR MACHINE

The majority of the α^t are 0, for which $r^t(\boldsymbol{w}^T\boldsymbol{x}^t + w_0) > 1$. These are the $\boldsymbol{x}^t$ that lie more than sufficiently away from the discriminant,

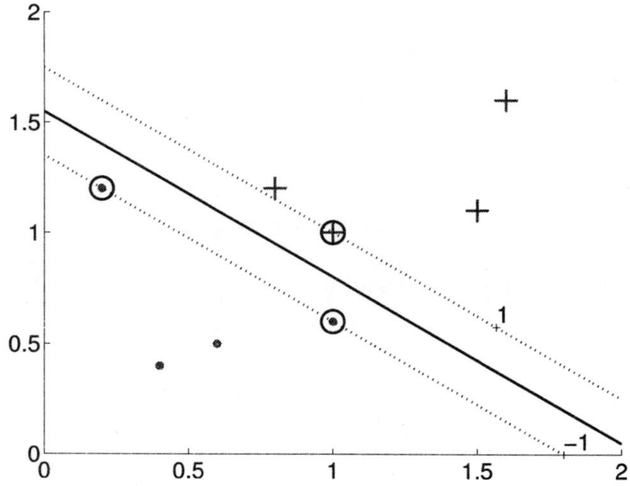

Figure 13.1 For a two-class problem where the instances of the classes are shown by plus signs and dots, the thick line is the boundary and the dashed lines define the margins on either side. Circled instances are the support vectors.

and they have no effect on the hyperplane. The instances that are not support vectors carry no information; even if any subset of them are removed, we would still get the same solution. From this perspective, the SVM algorithm can be likened to the condensed nearest neighbor algorithm (section 8.5), which stores only the instances neighboring (and hence constraining) the class discriminant.

Being a discriminant-based method, the SVM cares only about the instances close to the boundary and discards those that lie in the interior. Using this idea, it is possible to use a simpler classifier before the SVM to filter out a large portion of such instances, thereby decreasing the complexity of the optimization step of the SVM (exercise 1).

During testing, we do not enforce a margin. We calculate $g(\boldsymbol{x}) = \boldsymbol{w}^T\boldsymbol{x} + w_0$, and choose according to the sign of $g(\boldsymbol{x})$:

$$\text{Choose } C_1 \text{ if } g(\boldsymbol{x}) > 0 \text{ and } C_2 \text{ otherwise}$$

13.3 The Nonseparable Case: Soft Margin Hyperplane

If the data is not linearly separable, the algorithm we discussed earlier will not work. In such a case, if the two classes are not linearly separable such that there is no hyperplane to separate them, we look for the one that incurs the least error. We define *slack variables*, $\xi^t \geq 0$, which store the deviation from the margin. There are two types of deviation: An instance may lie on the wrong side of the hyperplane and be misclassified. Or, it may be on the right side but may lie in the margin, namely, not sufficiently away from the hyperplane. Relaxing equation 13.1, we require

SLACK VARIABLES

$$r^t(\boldsymbol{w}^T\boldsymbol{x}^t + w_0) \geq 1 - \xi^t \tag{13.9}$$

If $\xi^t = 0$, there is no problem with $\boldsymbol{x}^t$. If $0 < \xi^t < 1$, $\boldsymbol{x}^t$ is correctly classified but in the margin. If $\xi^t \geq 1$, $\boldsymbol{x}^t$ is misclassified (see figure 13.2). The number of misclassifications is $\#\{\xi^t > 1\}$, and the number of nonseparable points is $\#\{\xi_t > 0\}$. We define *soft error* as

SOFT ERROR

$$\sum_t \xi^t$$

and add this as a penalty term:

$$L_p = \frac{1}{2}\|\boldsymbol{w}\|^2 + C\sum_t \xi^t \tag{13.10}$$

subject to the constraint of equation 13.9. C is the penalty factor as in any regularization scheme trading off complexity, as measured by the L_2 norm of the weight vector (similar to weight decay in multilayer perceptrons; see sectiona 11.9 and 11.10), and data misfit, as measured by the number of nonseparable points. Note that we are penalizing not only the misclassified points but also the ones in the margin for better generalization, though these latter would be correctly classified during testing.

Adding the constraints, the Lagrangian of equation 13.4 then becomes

$$L_p = \frac{1}{2}\|\boldsymbol{w}\|^2 + C\sum_t \xi^t - \sum_t \alpha^t[r^t(\boldsymbol{w}^T\boldsymbol{x}^t + w_0) - 1 + \xi^t] - \sum_t \mu^t\xi^t \tag{13.11}$$

where μ_t are the new Lagrange parameters to guarantee the positivity of ξ^t. When we take the derivatives with respect to the parameters and set them to 0, we get

$$\frac{\partial L_p}{\partial \boldsymbol{w}} = \boldsymbol{w} - \sum_t \alpha^t r^t \boldsymbol{x}^t = 0 \Rightarrow \boldsymbol{w} = \sum_t \alpha^t r^t \boldsymbol{x}^t \tag{13.12}$$

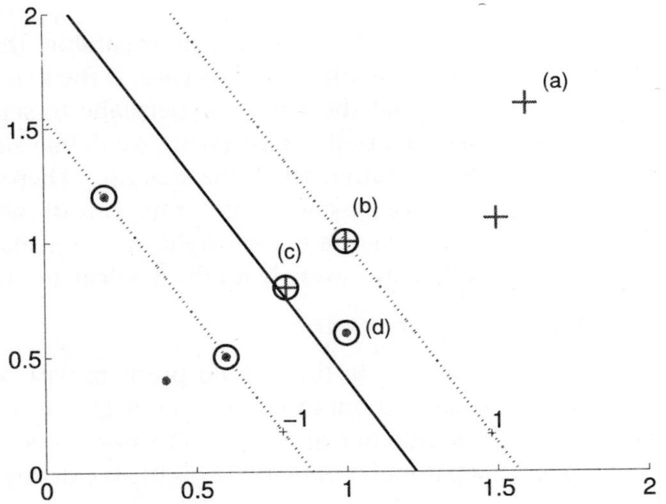

Figure 13.2 In classifying an instance, there are four possible cases: In (a), the instance is on the correct side and far away from the margin; $r^t g(\mathbf{x}^t) > 1$, $\xi^t = 0$. In (b), $\xi^t = 0$; it is on the right side and on the margin. In (c), $\xi^t = 1 - g(\mathbf{x}^t), 0 < \xi < 1$; it is on the right side but is in the margin and not sufficiently away. In (d), $\xi^t = 1 + g(\mathbf{x}^t) > 1$; it is on the wrong side—this is a misclassification. All cases except (a) are support vectors. In terms of the dual variable, in (a), $\alpha^t = 0$; in (b), $\alpha^t < C$; in (c) and (d), $\alpha^t = C$.

$$\frac{\partial L_p}{\partial w_0} = \sum_t \alpha^t r^t = 0 \tag{13.13}$$

$$\frac{\partial L_p}{\partial \xi^t} = C - \alpha^t - \mu^t = 0 \tag{13.14}$$

Since $\mu^t \geq 0$, this last implies that $0 \leq \alpha^t \leq C$. Plugging these into equation 13.11, we get the dual that we maximize with respect to α^t:

$$L_d = \sum_t \alpha^t - \frac{1}{2}\sum_t \sum_s \alpha^t \alpha^s r^t r^s (\mathbf{x}^t)^T \mathbf{x}^s \tag{13.15}$$

subject to

$$\sum_t \alpha^t r^t = 0 \text{ and } 0 \leq \alpha^t \leq C, \forall t$$

Solving this, we see that as in the separable case, instances that lie on the correct side of the boundary with sufficient margin vanish with their $\alpha^t = 0$ (see figure 13.2). The support vectors have their $\alpha^t > 0$ and they define $\boldsymbol{w}$, as given in equation 13.12. Of these, those whose $\alpha^t < C$ are the ones that are on the margin, and we can use them to calculate w_0; they have $\xi^t = 0$ and satisfy $r^t(\boldsymbol{w}^T\boldsymbol{x}^t + w_0) = 1$. Again, it is better to take an average over these w_0 estimates. Those instances that are in the margin or misclassified have their $\alpha^t = C$.

The nonseparable instances that we store as support vectors are the instances that we would have trouble correctly classifying if they were not in the training set; they would either be misclassified or classified correctly but not with enough confidence. We can say that the number of support vectors is an upper-bound estimate for the expected number of errors. And, actually, Vapnik (1995) has shown that the expected test error rate is

$$E_N[P(error)] \leq \frac{E_N[\text{\# of support vectors}]}{N}$$

where $E_N[\cdot]$ denotes expectation over training sets of size N. The nice implication of this is that it shows that the error rate depends on the number of support vectors and not on the input dimensionality.

Equation 13.9 implies that we define error if the instance is on the wrong side or if the margin is less than 1. This is called the *hinge loss*. If $y^t = \boldsymbol{w}^T\boldsymbol{x}^t + w_0$ is the output and r^t is the desired output, hinge loss is defined as

HINGE LOSS

$$L_{hinge}(y^t, r^t) = \begin{cases} 0 & \text{if } y^t r^t \geq 1 \\ 1 - y^t r^t & \text{otherwise} \end{cases} \tag{13.16}$$

In figure 13.3, we compare hinge loss with 0/1 loss, squared error, and cross-entropy. We see that unlike 0/1 loss, hinge loss also penalizes instances in the margin even though they may be on the correct side, and the loss increases linearly as the instance moves away on the wrong side. This is different from the squared loss that therefore is not as robust as the hinge loss. We see that cross-entropy minimized in logistic discrimination (section 10.7) or by the linear perceptron (section 11.3) is a good continuous approximation to the hinge loss.

C of equation 13.10 is the regularization parameter fine-tuned using cross-validation. It defines the trade-off between margin maximization and error minimization: If it is too large, we have a high penalty for nonseparable points, and we may store many support vectors and overfit.

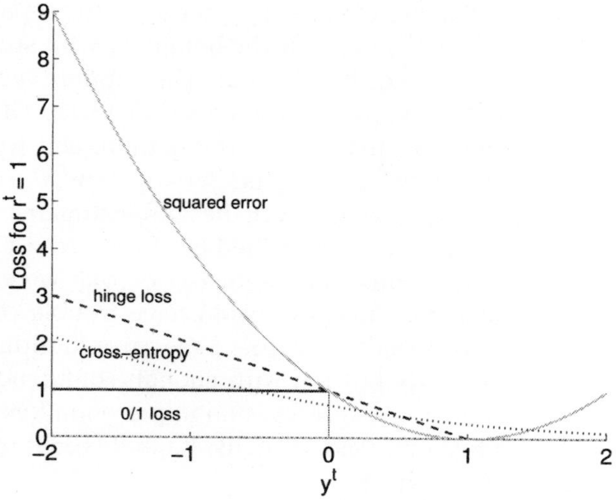

Figure 13.3 Comparison of different loss functions for $r^t = 1$: 0/1 loss is 0 if $y^t = 1$, 1 otherwise. Hinge loss is 0 if $y^t > 1$, $1 - y^t$ otherwise. Squared error is $(1 - y^t)^2$. Cross-entropy is $\log(1/(1 + \exp(-y^t)))$.

If it is too small, we may find too simple solutions that underfit. Typically, one chooses from $[10^{-6}, 10^{-5}, \ldots, 10^{+5}, 10^{+6}]$ in the log scale by looking at the accuracy on a validation set.

13.4 ν-SVM

There is another, equivalent formulation of the soft margin hyperplane that uses a parameter $\nu \in [0, 1]$ instead of C (Schölkopf et al. 2000). The objective function is

$$\min \frac{1}{2}\|\mathbf{w}\|^2 - \nu\rho + \frac{1}{N}\sum_t \xi^t \tag{13.17}$$

subject to

$$r^t(\mathbf{w}^T\mathbf{x}^t + w_0) \geq \rho - \xi^t,\ \xi^t \geq 0,\ \rho \geq 0 \tag{13.18}$$

ρ is a new parameter that is a variable of the optimization problem and scales the margin: The margin is now $2\rho/\|\mathbf{w}\|$. ν has been shown to be a lower bound on the fraction of support vectors and an upper bound on the fraction of instances having margin errors ($\sum_t \#\{\xi^t > 0\}$). The dual is

$$L_d = -\frac{1}{2}\sum_t \sum_s \alpha^t \alpha^s r^t r^s (\boldsymbol{x}^t)^T \boldsymbol{x}^s \tag{13.19}$$

subject to

$$\sum_t \alpha^t r^t = 0,\ 0 \le \alpha^t \le \frac{1}{N},\ \sum_t \alpha^t \ge \nu$$

When we compare equation 13.19 with equation 13.15, we see that the term $\sum_t \alpha^t$ no longer appears in the objective function but is now a constraint. By playing with ν, we can control the fraction of support vectors, and this is advocated to be more intuitive than playing with C.

13.5 Kernel Trick

Section 10.2 demonstrated that if the problem is nonlinear, instead of trying to fit a nonlinear model, we can map the problem to a new space by doing a nonlinear transformation using suitably chosen basis functions and then use a linear model in this new space. The linear model in the new space corresponds to a nonlinear model in the original space. This approach can be used in both classification and regression problems, and in the special case of classification, it can be used with any scheme. In the particular case of support vector machines, it leads to certain simplifications that we now discuss.

Let us say we have the new dimensions calculated through the basis functions

$$\boldsymbol{z} = \boldsymbol{\phi}(\boldsymbol{x}) \text{ where } z_j = \phi_j(\boldsymbol{x}), j = 1, \ldots, k$$

mapping from the d-dimensional $\boldsymbol{x}$ space to the k-dimensional $\boldsymbol{z}$ space where we write the discriminant as

$$\begin{aligned} g(\boldsymbol{z}) &= \boldsymbol{w}^T \boldsymbol{z} \\ g(\boldsymbol{x}) &= \boldsymbol{w}^T \boldsymbol{\phi}(\boldsymbol{x}) \\ &= \sum_{j=1}^{k} w_j \phi_j(\boldsymbol{x}) \end{aligned} \tag{13.20}$$

where we do not use a separate w_0; we assume that $z_1 = \phi_1(\boldsymbol{x}) \equiv 1$. Generally, k is much larger than d and k may also be larger than N, and there lies the advantage of using the dual form whose complexity depends on N, whereas if we used the primal it would depend on k. We also use the more general case of the soft margin hyperplane here because we have no guarantee that the problem is linearly separable in this new space.

The problem is the same

$$L_p = \frac{1}{2}\|\boldsymbol{w}\|^2 + C\sum_t \xi^t \tag{13.21}$$

except that now the constraints are defined in the new space

$$r^t \boldsymbol{w}^T \boldsymbol{\phi}(\boldsymbol{x}^t) \geq 1 - \xi^t \tag{13.22}$$

The Lagrangian is

$$L_p = \frac{1}{2}\|\boldsymbol{w}\|^2 + C\sum_t \xi^t - \sum_t \alpha^t \left[r^t \boldsymbol{w}^T \boldsymbol{\phi}(\boldsymbol{x}^t) - 1 + \xi^t\right] - \sum_t \mu^t \xi^t \tag{13.23}$$

When we take the derivatives with respect to the parameters and set them to 0, we get

$$\frac{\partial L_p}{\partial \boldsymbol{w}} = \boldsymbol{w} = \sum_t \alpha^t r^t \boldsymbol{\phi}(\boldsymbol{x}^t) \tag{13.24}$$

$$\frac{\partial L_p}{\partial \xi^t} = C - \alpha^t - \mu^t = 0 \tag{13.25}$$

The dual is now

$$L_d = \sum_t \alpha^t - \frac{1}{2}\sum_t \sum_s \alpha^t \alpha^s r^t r^s \boldsymbol{\phi}(\boldsymbol{x}^t)^T \boldsymbol{\phi}(\boldsymbol{x}^s) \tag{13.26}$$

subject to

$$\sum_t \alpha^t r^t = 0 \text{ and } 0 \leq \alpha^t \leq C, \forall t$$

KERNEL FUNCTION

The idea in *kernel machines* is to replace the inner product of basis functions, $\boldsymbol{\phi}(\boldsymbol{x}^t)^T \boldsymbol{\phi}(\boldsymbol{x}^s)$, by a *kernel function*, $K(\boldsymbol{x}^t, \boldsymbol{x}^s)$, between instances in the original input space. So instead of mapping two instances $\boldsymbol{x}^t$ and $\boldsymbol{x}^s$ to the $\boldsymbol{z}$-space and doing a dot product there, we directly apply the kernel function in the original space.

$$L_d = \sum_t \alpha^t - \frac{1}{2}\sum_t \sum_s \alpha^t \alpha^s r^t r^s K(\boldsymbol{x}^t, \boldsymbol{x}^s) \tag{13.27}$$

The kernel function also shows up in the discriminant

$$\begin{aligned} g(\boldsymbol{x}) &= \boldsymbol{w}^T \boldsymbol{\phi}(\boldsymbol{x}) = \sum_t \alpha^t r^t \boldsymbol{\phi}(\boldsymbol{x}^t)^T \boldsymbol{\phi}(\boldsymbol{x}) \\ &= \sum_t \alpha^t r^t K(\boldsymbol{x}^t, \boldsymbol{x}) \end{aligned} \quad (13.28)$$

This implies that if we have the kernel function, we do not need to map it to the new space at all. Actually, for any valid kernel, there does exist a corresponding mapping function, but it may be much simpler to use $K(\boldsymbol{x}^t, \boldsymbol{x})$ rather than calculating $\boldsymbol{\phi}(\boldsymbol{x}^t)$, $\boldsymbol{\phi}(\boldsymbol{x})$ and taking the dot product. Many algorithms have been *kernelized*, as we will see in later sections, and that is why we have the name "kernel machines."

KERNELIZATION

GRAM MATRIX

The matrix of kernel values, $\mathbf{K}$, where $\mathbf{K}_{ts} = K(\boldsymbol{x}^t, \boldsymbol{x}^s)$, is called the *Gram matrix*, which should be symmetric and positive semidefinite. Recently, it has become standard practice in sharing datasets to have available only the $\mathbf{K}$ matrices without providing $\boldsymbol{x}^t$ or $\boldsymbol{\phi}(\boldsymbol{x}^t)$. Especially in bioinformatics or natural language processing applications where $\boldsymbol{x}$ (or $\boldsymbol{\phi}(\boldsymbol{x})$) has hundreds or thousands of dimensions, storing/downloading the $N \times N$ matrix is much cheaper (Vert, Tsuda, and Schölkopf 2004); this, however, implies that we can use only those available for training/testing and cannot use the trained model to make predictions outside this dataset.

13.6 Vectorial Kernels

The most popular, general-purpose kernel functions are

- *polynomials* of degree q:

$$K(\boldsymbol{x}^t, \boldsymbol{x}) = (\boldsymbol{x}^T \boldsymbol{x}^t + 1)^q \quad (13.29)$$

where q is selected by the user. For example, when $q = 2$ and $d = 2$,

$$\begin{aligned} K(\boldsymbol{x}, \boldsymbol{y}) &= (\boldsymbol{x}^T \boldsymbol{y} + 1)^2 \\ &= (x_1 y_1 + x_2 y_2 + 1)^2 \\ &= 1 + 2x_1 y_1 + 2x_2 y_2 + 2x_1 x_2 y_1 y_2 + x_1^2 y_1^2 + x_2^2 y_2^2 \end{aligned}$$

corresponds to the inner product of the basis function (Cherkassky and Mulier 1998):

$$\boldsymbol{\phi}(\boldsymbol{x}) = [1, \sqrt{2}x_1, \sqrt{2}x_2, \sqrt{2}x_1 x_2, x_1^2, x_2^2]^T$$

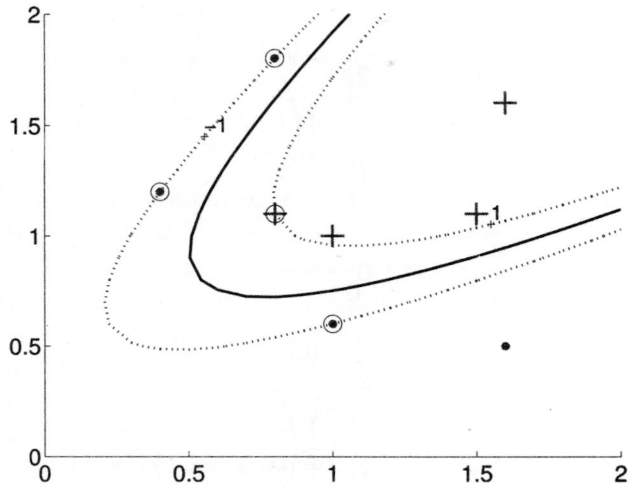

Figure 13.4 The discriminant and margins found by a polynomial kernel of degree 2. Circled instances are the support vectors.

An example is given in figure 13.4. When $q = 1$, we have the *linear kernel* that corresponds to the original formulation.

- *radial-basis functions*:

(13.30) $$K(\boldsymbol{x}^t, \boldsymbol{x}) = \exp\left[-\frac{\|\boldsymbol{x}^t - \boldsymbol{x}\|^2}{2s^2}\right]$$

defines a spherical kernel as in Parzen windows (chapter 8) where $\boldsymbol{x}^t$ is the center and s, supplied by the user, defines the radius. This is also similar to radial basis functions that we discuss in chapter 12.

An example is shown in figure 13.5 where we see that larger spreads smooth the boundary; the best value is found by cross-validation. Note that when there are two parameters to be optimized using cross-validation, for example, here C and s^2, one should do a grid (factorial) search in the two dimensions; we will discuss methods for searching the best combination of such factors in section 19.2.

One can have a Mahalanobis kernel, generalizing from the Euclidean distance:

(13.31) $$K(\boldsymbol{x}^t, \boldsymbol{x}) = \exp\left[-\frac{1}{2}(\boldsymbol{x}^t - \boldsymbol{x})^T \mathbf{S}^{-1}(\boldsymbol{x}^t - \boldsymbol{x})\right]$$

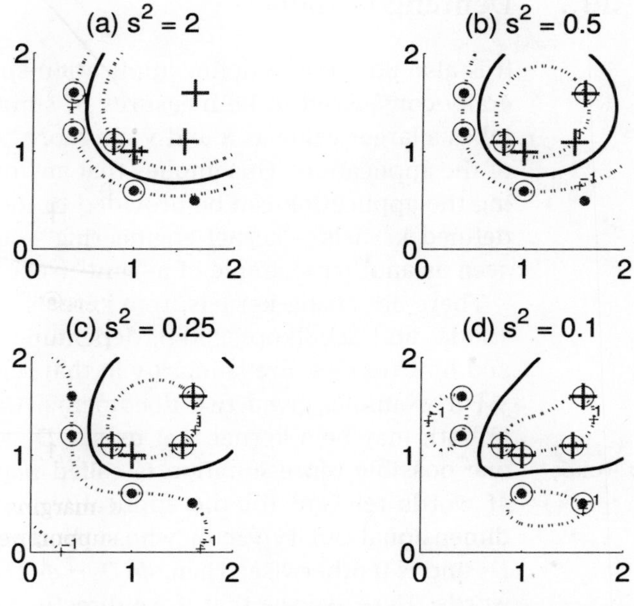

Figure 13.5 The boundary and margins found by the Gaussian kernel with different spread values, s^2. We get smoother boundaries with larger spreads.

where $\mathbf{S}$ is a covariance matrix. Or, in the most general case,

$$K(\boldsymbol{x}^t, \boldsymbol{x}) = \exp\left[-\frac{\mathcal{D}(\boldsymbol{x}^t, \boldsymbol{x})}{2s^2}\right] \tag{13.32}$$

for some distance function $\mathcal{D}(\boldsymbol{x}^t, \boldsymbol{x})$.

- *sigmoidal functions*:

$$K(\boldsymbol{x}^t, \boldsymbol{x}) = \tanh(2\boldsymbol{x}^T\boldsymbol{x}^t + 1) \tag{13.33}$$

where $\tanh(\cdot)$ has the same shape with sigmoid, except that it ranges between -1 and $+1$. This is similar to multilayer perceptrons that we discussed in chapter 11.

13.7 Defining Kernels

It is also possible to define application-specific kernels. Kernels are generally considered to be measures of similarity in the sense that $K(\boldsymbol{x}, \boldsymbol{y})$ takes a larger value as $\boldsymbol{x}$ and $\boldsymbol{y}$ are more "similar," from the point of view of the application. This implies that any prior knowledge we have regarding the application can be provided to the learner through appropriately defined kernels—"kernel engineering"—and such use of kernels can be seen as another example of a "hint" (section 11.8.4).

There are string kernels, tree kernels, graph kernels, and so on (Vert, Tsuda, and Schölkopf 2004), depending on how we represent the data and how we measure similarity in that representation.

BAG OF WORDS

For example, given two documents, the number of words appearing in both may be a kernel. Let us say D_1 and D_2 are two documents and one possible representation is called *bag of words* where we predefine M words relevant for the application, and we define $\boldsymbol{\phi}(D_1)$ as the M-dimensional binary vector whose dimension i is 1 if word i appears in D_1 and is 0 otherwise. Then, $\boldsymbol{\phi}(D_1)^T\boldsymbol{\phi}(D_2)$ counts the number of shared words. Here, we see that if we directly define and implement $K(D_1, D_2)$ as the number of shared words, we do not need to preselect M words and can use just any word in the vocabulary (of course, after discarding uninformative words like "of," "and," etc.) and we would not need to generate the bag-of-words representation explicitly and it would be as if we allowed M to be as large as we want.

EDIT DISTANCE

ALIGNMENT

Sometimes—for example, in bioinformatics applications—we can calculate a *similarity score* between two objects, which may not necessarily be positive semidefinite. Given two strings (of genes), a kernel measures the *edit distance*, namely, how many operations (insertions, deletions, substitutions) it takes to convert one string into another; this is also called *alignment*. In such a case, a trick is to define a set of M templates and represent an object as the M-dimensional vector of scores to all the templates. That is, if $\boldsymbol{m}_i, i = 1, \ldots, M$ are the templates and $s(\boldsymbol{x}^t, \boldsymbol{m}_i)$ is the score between $\boldsymbol{x}^t$ and $\boldsymbol{m}_i$, then we define

$$\boldsymbol{\phi}(\boldsymbol{x}^t) = [s(\boldsymbol{x}^t, \boldsymbol{m}_1), s(\boldsymbol{x}^t, \boldsymbol{m}_2), \ldots, s(\boldsymbol{x}^t, \boldsymbol{m}_M)]^T$$

EMPIRICAL KERNEL MAP

and we define the *empirical kernel map* as

$$K(\boldsymbol{x}^t, \boldsymbol{x}^s) = \boldsymbol{\phi}(\boldsymbol{x}^t)^T\boldsymbol{\phi}(\boldsymbol{x}^s)$$

which is a valid kernel.

Sometimes, we have a binary score function; for example, two proteins may interact or not, and we want to be able to generalize from this to scores for two arbitrary instances. In such a case, a trick is to define a graph where the nodes are the instances and two nodes are linked if they interact, that is, if the binary score returns 1. Then we say that two nodes that are not immediately linked are "similar" if the path between them is short or if they are connected by many paths. This converts pairwise local interactions to a global similarity measure, rather like defining a geodesic distance used in Isomap (section 6.10), and it is called the *diffusion kernel*.

DIFFUSION KERNEL

If $p(\mathbf{x})$ is a probability density, then

$$K(\mathbf{x}^t, \mathbf{x}) = p(\mathbf{x}^t)p(\mathbf{x})$$

is a valid kernel. This is used when $p(\mathbf{x})$ is a generative model for $\mathbf{x}$ measuring how likely it is that we see $\mathbf{x}$. For example, if $\mathbf{x}$ is a sequence, $p(\mathbf{x})$ can be a hidden Markov model (chapter 15). With this kernel, $K(\mathbf{x}^t, \mathbf{x})$ will take a high value if both $\mathbf{x}^t$ and $\mathbf{x}$ are likely to have been generated by the same model. It is also possible to parametrize the generative model as $p(\mathbf{x}|\theta)$ and learn θ from data; this is called the *Fisher kernel* (Jaakkola and Haussler 1998).

FISHER KERNEL

13.8 Multiple Kernel Learning

It is possible to construct new kernels by combining simpler kernels. If $K_1(\mathbf{x}, \mathbf{y})$ and $K_2(\mathbf{x}, \mathbf{y})$ are valid kernels and c a constant, then

$$K(\mathbf{x}, \mathbf{y}) = \begin{cases} cK_1(\mathbf{x}, \mathbf{y}) \\ K_1(\mathbf{x}, \mathbf{y}) + K_2(\mathbf{x}, \mathbf{y}) \\ K_1(\mathbf{x}, \mathbf{y}) \cdot K_2(\mathbf{x}, \mathbf{y}) \end{cases} \tag{13.34}$$

are also valid.

Different kernels may also be using different subsets of $\mathbf{x}$. We can therefore see combining kernels as another way to fuse information from different sources where each kernel measures similarity according to its domain. When we have input from two representations A and B

$$\begin{aligned} K_A(\mathbf{x}_A, \mathbf{y}_A) + K_B(\mathbf{x}_B, \mathbf{y}_B) &= \boldsymbol{\phi}_A(\mathbf{x}_A)^T \boldsymbol{\phi}_A(\mathbf{y}_A) + \boldsymbol{\phi}_B(\mathbf{x}_B)^T \boldsymbol{\phi}_B(\mathbf{y}_B) \\ &= \boldsymbol{\phi}(\mathbf{x})^T \boldsymbol{\phi}(\mathbf{y}) \\ &= K(\mathbf{x}, \mathbf{y}) \end{aligned} \tag{13.35}$$

where $\boldsymbol{x} = [\boldsymbol{x}_A, \boldsymbol{x}_B]$ is the concatenation of the two representations. That is, taking a sum of two kernels corresponds to doing a dot product in the concatenated feature vectors. One can generalize to a number of kernels

$$K(\boldsymbol{x}, \boldsymbol{y}) = \sum_{i=1}^{m} K_i(\boldsymbol{x}, \boldsymbol{y}) \tag{13.36}$$

which, similar to taking an average of classifiers (section 17.4), this time averages over kernels and frees us from the need to choose one particular kernel. It is also possible to take a weighted sum and also learn the weights from data (Lanckriet et al. 2004; Sonnenburg et al. 2006):

$$K(\boldsymbol{x}, \boldsymbol{y}) = \sum_{i=1}^{m} \eta_i K_i(\boldsymbol{x}, \boldsymbol{y}) \tag{13.37}$$

MULTIPLE KERNEL LEARNING

subject to $\eta_i \geq 0$, with or without the constraint of $\sum_i \eta_i = 1$, respectively known as convex or conic combination. This is called *multiple kernel learning* where we replace a single kernel with a weighted sum (Gönen and Alpaydın 2011). The single kernel objective function of equation 13.27 becomes

$$L_d = \sum_t \alpha^t - \frac{1}{2} \sum_t \sum_s \alpha^t \alpha^s r^t r^s \sum_i \eta_i K_i(\boldsymbol{x}^t, \boldsymbol{x}^s) \tag{13.38}$$

which we solve for both the support vector machine parameters α^t and the kernel weights η_i. Then, the combination of multiple kernels also appear in the discriminant

$$g(\boldsymbol{x}) = \sum_t \alpha^t r^t \sum_i \eta_i K_i(\boldsymbol{x}^t, \boldsymbol{x}) \tag{13.39}$$

After training, η_i will take values depending on how the corresponding kernel $K_i(\boldsymbol{x}^t, \boldsymbol{x})$ is useful in discriminating. It is also possible to localize kernels by defining kernel weights as a parameterized function of the input $\boldsymbol{x}$, rather like the gating function in mixture of experts (section 17.8)

$$g(\boldsymbol{x}) = \sum_t \alpha^t r^t \sum_i \eta_i(\boldsymbol{x}|\theta_i) K_i(\boldsymbol{x}^t, \boldsymbol{x}) \tag{13.40}$$

and the gating parameters θ_i are learned together with the support vector machine parameters (Gönen and Alpaydın 2008).

When we have information coming from multiple sources in different representations or modalities—for example, in speech recognition where we may have both acoustic and visual lip image—the usual approach is to feed them separately to different classifiers and then fuse the decisions; we will discuss methods for this in detail in chapter 17. Combining multiple kernels provides us with another way of integrating input from multiple sources, where there is a single classifier that uses different kernels for inputs of different sources, for which there are different notions of similarity (Noble 2004). The localized version can then seen be an extension of this where we can choose between sources, and hence similarity measures, depending on the input.

13.9 Multiclass Kernel Machines

When there are $K > 2$ classes, the straightforward, *one-vs.-all* way is to define K two-class problems, each one separating one class from all other classes combined and learn K support vector machines $g_i(\boldsymbol{x}), i = 1, \ldots, K$. That is, in training $g_i(\boldsymbol{x})$, examples of C_i are labeled $+1$ and examples of $C_k, k \neq i$ are labeled as -1. During testing, we calculate all $g_i(\boldsymbol{x})$ and choose the maximum.

Platt (1999) proposed to fit a sigmoid to the output of a single (2-class) SVM output to convert to a posterior probability. Similarly, one can train one layer of softmax outputs to minimize cross-entropy to generate $K > 2$ posterior probabilities (Mayoraz and Alpaydın 1999):

$$y_i(\boldsymbol{x}) = \sum_{j=1}^{K} v_{ij} f_j(\boldsymbol{x}) + v_{i0} \tag{13.41}$$

where $f_j(\boldsymbol{x})$ are the SVM outputs and y_i are the posterior probability outputs. Weights v_{ij} are trained to minimize cross-entropy. Note, however, that as in stacking (section 17.9), the data on which we train v_{ij} should be different from the data used to train the base SVMs $f_j(\boldsymbol{x})$, to alleviate overfitting.

Instead of the usual approach of building K two-class SVM classifiers to separate one from all the rest, as with any other classifier, one can build $K(K-1)/2$ *pairwise* classifiers (see also section 10.4), each $g_{ij}(\boldsymbol{x})$ taking examples of C_i with the label $+1$, examples of C_j with the label -1, and not using examples of the other classes. Separating classes in pairs is normally expected to be an easier job, with the additional advantage that because we use less data, the optimizations will be faster, noting however that we have $\mathcal{O}(K^2)$ discriminants to train instead of $\mathcal{O}(K)$.

In the general case, both one-vs.-all and pairwise separation are special cases of the *error-correcting output codes* (ECOC) that decompose a multiclass problem to a set of two-class problems (Dietterich and Bakiri 1995) (see also section 17.6). SVMs being two-class classifiers are ideally suited to this (Allwein, Schapire, and Singer 2000), and it is also possible to have an incremental approach where new two-class SVMs are added to better separate pairs of classes that are confused, to ameliorate a poor ECOC matrix (Mayoraz and Alpaydın 1999).

ERROR-CORRECTING OUTPUT CODES

Another possibility is to write a single *multiclass* optimization problem involving all classes (Weston and Watkins 1998):

$$\min \frac{1}{2}\sum_{i=1}^{K}\|\boldsymbol{w}_i\|^2 + C\sum_i\sum_t \xi_i^t \tag{13.42}$$

subject to

$$\boldsymbol{w}_{z^t}\boldsymbol{x}^t + w_{z^t0} \geq \boldsymbol{w}_i\boldsymbol{x}^t + w_{i0} + 2 - \xi_i^t, \forall i \neq z^t \text{ and } \xi_i^t \geq 0$$

where z^t contains the class index of $\boldsymbol{x}^t$. The regularization terms minimizes the norms of all hyperplanes simultaneously, and the constraints are there to make sure that the margin between the actual class and any other class is at least 2. The output for the correct class should be at least $+1$, the output of any other class should be at least -1, and the slack variables are defined to make up any difference.

Though this looks neat, the one-vs.-all approach is generally preferred because it solves K separate N variable problems whereas the multiclass formulation uses $K \cdot N$ variables.

13.10 Kernel Machines for Regression

Now let us see how support vector machines can be generalized for regression. We see that the same approach of defining acceptable margins, slacks, and a regularizing function that combines smoothness and error is also applicable here. We start with a linear model, and later on we see how we can use kernel functions here as well:

$$f(\boldsymbol{x}) = \boldsymbol{w}^T\boldsymbol{x} + w_0$$

In regression proper, we use the square of the difference as error:

$$e_2(r^t, f(\boldsymbol{x}^t)) = [r^t - f(\boldsymbol{x}^t)]^2$$

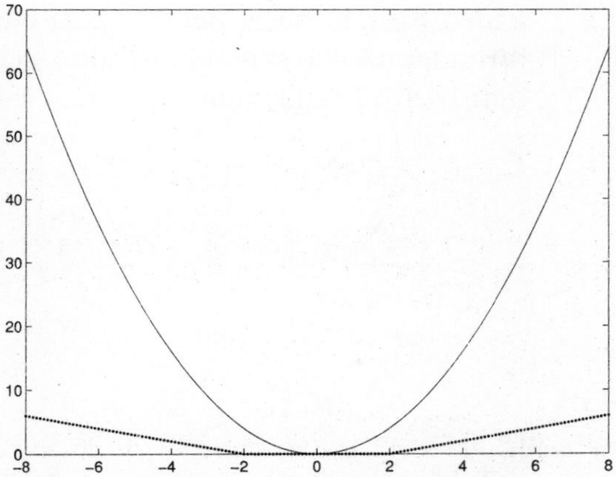

Figure 13.6 Quadratic and ϵ-sensitive error functions. We see that ϵ-sensitive error function is not affected by small errors and also is less affected by large errors and thus is more robust to outliers.

whereas in support vector regression, we use the ϵ-sensitive loss function:

$$e_\epsilon(r^t, f(\mathbf{x}^t)) = \begin{cases} 0 & \text{if } |r^t - f(\mathbf{x}^t)| < \epsilon \\ |r^t - f(\mathbf{x}^t)| - \epsilon & \text{otherwise} \end{cases} \tag{13.43}$$

which means that we tolerate errors up to ϵ and also that errors beyond have a linear effect and not a quadratic one. This error function is therefore more tolerant to noise and is thus more *robust* (see figure 13.6). As in the hinge loss, there is a region of no error, which causes sparseness.

ROBUST REGRESSION

Analogous to the soft margin hyperplane, we introduce slack variables to account for deviations out of the ϵ-zone and we get (Vapnik 1995)

$$\min \frac{1}{2}\|\mathbf{w}\|^2 + C\sum_t (\xi_+^t + \xi_-^t) \tag{13.44}$$

subject to

$$\begin{aligned} r^t - (\mathbf{w}^T\mathbf{x} + w_0) &\leq \epsilon + \xi_+^t \\ (\mathbf{w}^T\mathbf{x} + w_0) - r^t &\leq \epsilon + \xi_-^t \\ \xi_+^t, \xi_-^t &\geq 0 \end{aligned}$$

where we use two types of slack variables, for positive and negative deviations, to keep them positive. Actually, we can see this as two hinges added back to back, one for positive and one for negative slacks. This formulation corresponds to the ϵ-sensitive loss function given in equation 13.43. The Lagrangian is

$$\begin{aligned} L_p &= \frac{1}{2}\|\boldsymbol{w}\|^2 + C\sum_t(\xi_+^t + \xi_-^t) \\ &\quad - \sum_t \alpha_+^t \left[\epsilon + \xi_+^t - r^t + (\boldsymbol{w}^T\boldsymbol{x} + w_0)\right] \\ &\quad - \sum_t \alpha_-^t \left[\epsilon + \xi_-^t + r^t - (\boldsymbol{w}^T\boldsymbol{x} + w_0)\right] \\ &\quad - \sum_t(\mu_+^t\xi_+^t + \mu_-^t\xi_-^t) \end{aligned} \tag{13.45}$$

Taking the partial derivatives, we get

$$\frac{\partial L_p}{\partial \boldsymbol{w}} = \boldsymbol{w} - \sum_t(\alpha_+^t - \alpha_-^t)\boldsymbol{x}^t = 0 \Rightarrow \boldsymbol{w} = \sum_t(\alpha_+^t - \alpha_-^t)\boldsymbol{x}^t \tag{13.46}$$

$$\frac{\partial L_p}{\partial w_0} = \sum_t(\alpha_+^t - \alpha_-^t)\boldsymbol{x}^t = 0 \tag{13.47}$$

$$\frac{\partial L_p}{\partial \xi_+^t} = C - \alpha_+^t - \mu_+^t = 0 \tag{13.48}$$

$$\frac{\partial L_p}{\partial \xi_-^t} = C - \alpha_-^t - \mu_-^t = 0 \tag{13.49}$$

The dual is

$$\begin{aligned} L_d &= -\frac{1}{2}\sum_t\sum_s(\alpha_+^t - \alpha_-^t)(\alpha_+^s - \alpha_-^s)(\boldsymbol{x}^t)^T\boldsymbol{x}^s \\ &\quad -\epsilon\sum_t(\alpha_+^t + \alpha_-^t) + \sum_t r^t(\alpha_+^t - \alpha_-^t) \end{aligned} \tag{13.50}$$

subject to

$$0 \le \alpha_+^t \le C\,,\ 0 \le \alpha_-^t \le C\,,\ \sum_t(\alpha_+^t - \alpha_-^t) = 0$$

Once we solve this, we see that all instances that fall in the tube have $\alpha_+^t = \alpha_-^t = 0$; these are the instances that are fitted with enough precision (see figure 13.7). The support vectors satisfy either $\alpha_+^t > 0$ or $\alpha_-^t > 0$ and are of two types. They may be instances that are on the boundary of the tube (either α_+^t or α_-^t is between 0 and C), and we use these to calculate w_0. For example, assuming that $\alpha_+^t > 0$, we have $r^t = \boldsymbol{x}^T\boldsymbol{x}^t + w_0 + \epsilon$. Instances that fall outside the ϵ-tube are of the second type; these are

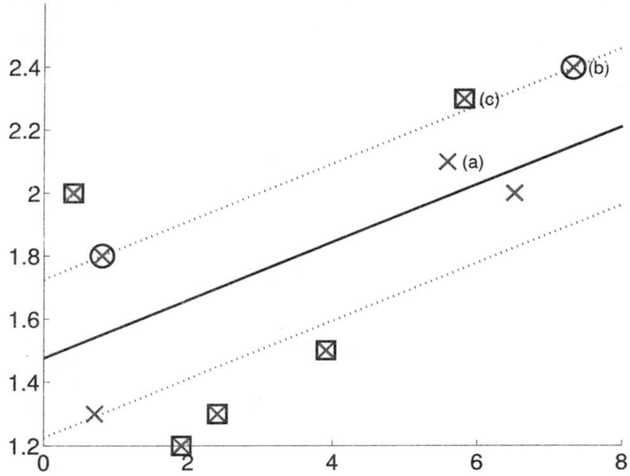

Figure 13.7 The fitted regression line to data points shown as crosses and the ϵ-tube are shown ($C = 10, \epsilon = 0.25$). There are three cases: In (a), the instance is in the tube; in (b), the instance is on the boundary of the tube (circled instances); in (c), it is outside the tube with a positive slack, that is, $\xi_+^t > 0$ (squared instances). (b) and (c) are support vectors. In terms of the dual variable, in (a), $\alpha_+^t = 0, \alpha_-^t = 0$, in (b), $\alpha_+^t < C$, and in (c), $\alpha_+^t = C$.

instances for which we do not have a good fit ($\alpha_+^t = C$), as shown in figure 13.7.

Using equation 13.46, we can write the fitted line as a weighted sum of the support vectors:

$$f(\boldsymbol{x}) = \boldsymbol{w}^T\boldsymbol{x} + w_0 = \sum_t (\alpha_+^t - \alpha_-^t)(\boldsymbol{x}^t)^T\boldsymbol{x} + w_0 \tag{13.51}$$

Again, the dot product $(\boldsymbol{x}^t)^T\boldsymbol{x}^s$ in equation 13.50 can be replaced with a kernel $K(\boldsymbol{x}^t, \boldsymbol{x}^s)$, and similarly $(\boldsymbol{x}^t)^T\boldsymbol{x}$ be replaced with $K(\boldsymbol{x}^t, \boldsymbol{x})$ and we can have a nonlinear fit. Using a polynomial kernel would be similar to fitting a polynomial (figure 13.8), and using a Gaussian kernel (figure 13.9) would be similar to nonparametric smoothing models (section 8.8) except that because of the sparsity of solution, we would not need the whole training set but only a subset.

There is also an equivalent ν-SVM formulation for regression (Schölkopf et al. 2000), where instead of fixing ϵ, we fix ν to bound the fraction of

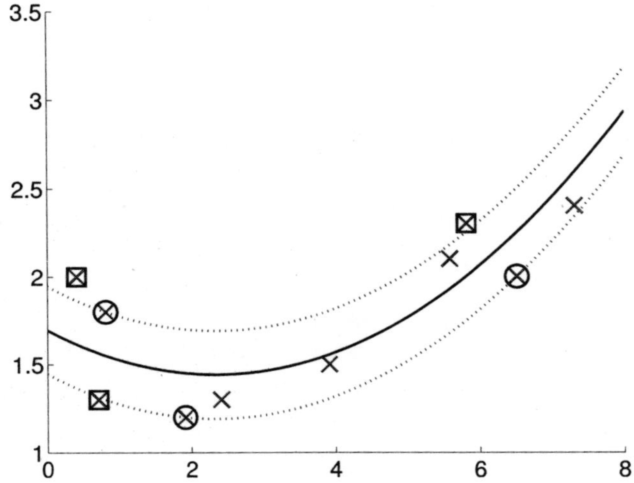

Figure 13.8 The fitted regression line and the ϵ-tube using a quadratic kernel are shown ($C = 10, \epsilon = 0.25$). Circled instances are the support vectors on the margins, squared instances are support vectors which are outliers.

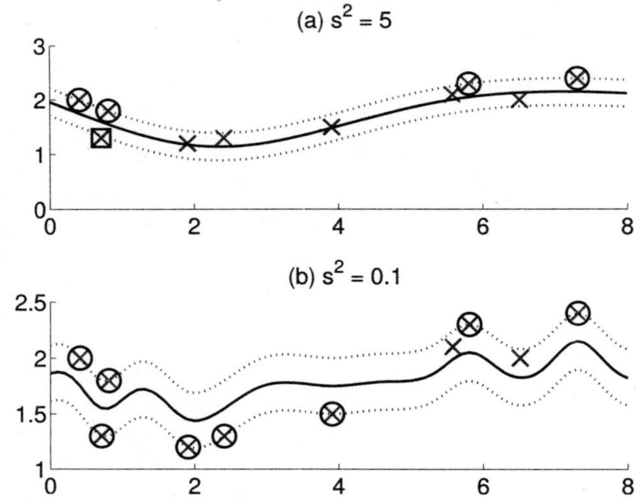

Figure 13.9 The fitted regression line and the ϵ-tube using a Gaussian kernel with two different spreads are shown ($C = 10, \epsilon = 0.25$). Circled instances are the support vectors on the margins, and squared instances are support vectors that are outliers.

support vectors. There is still a need for C though.

13.11 Kernel Machines for Ranking

Remember that in ranking, we have instances that need to be ordered in a certain way (Liu 2011). For example, we may have pairwise constraints such as $r^u \prec r^v$ which means that instance $\boldsymbol{x}^u$ should generate a higher score than $\boldsymbol{x}^v$. In section 10.9, we discuss how we can train a linear model for this purpose using gradient descent. We now discuss how we can do the same using support vector machines.

We consider each pairwise constraint as one data instance $t : r^u \prec r^v$ and minimize

$$L_p = \frac{1}{2}\|\boldsymbol{w}\|^2 + C\sum_t \xi^t \tag{13.52}$$

subject to

$$\begin{aligned} \boldsymbol{w}^T\boldsymbol{x}^u &\geq \boldsymbol{w}^T\boldsymbol{x}^v + 1 - \xi^t, \text{ for each } t : r^u \prec r^v \\ \xi^t &\geq 0 \end{aligned} \tag{13.53}$$

Equation 13.53 requires that the score for $\boldsymbol{x}^u$ be at least 1 unit more than the score for $\boldsymbol{x}^v$ and hence defines a margin. If the constraint is not satisfied, the slack variable is nonzero and equation 13.52 minimizes the sum of such slacks and the complexity term, which again corresponds to making the width of the margin as large as possible (Herbrich, Obermayer, and Graepel 2000; Joachims 2002). Note that the second term of the sum of slacks is the same as the error used in equation 10.46 except for the 1 unit margin, and the complexity term, as we discussed before, can be interpreted as a weight decay term on the linear model (see section 11.10).

Note that there is one constraint for each pair where an ordering is defined, and hence the number of such constraints is $\mathcal{O}(N^2)$. The constraint of equation 13.53 can also be written as

$$\boldsymbol{w}^T(\boldsymbol{x}^u - \boldsymbol{x}^v) \geq 1 - \xi^t$$

That is, we can view this as a two-class classification of pairwise differences, $\boldsymbol{x}^u - \boldsymbol{x}^v$. So by calculating such differences and labeling them as $r^t \in \{-1, +1\}$ depending on whether $r^v \prec r^u$ or $r^u \prec r^v$ respectively, any two-class kernel machine can be used to implement ranking. But this is not the most efficient way to implement, and faster methods have been proposed (Chapelle and Keerthi 2010).

The dual is

$$L_d = \sum_t \alpha^t - \frac{1}{2}\sum_t \sum_s \alpha^t \alpha^s (\mathbf{x}^u - \mathbf{x}^v)^T (\mathbf{x}^k - \mathbf{x}^l) \quad (13.54)$$

subject to $0 \leq \alpha^t \leq C$. Here, t and s are two pairwise constraints, such as $t : r^u \prec r^v$ and $s : r^k \prec r^l$. Solving this, for the constraints that are satisfied, we have $\xi^t = 0$ and $\alpha^t = 0$; for the ones that are satisfied but are in the margin, we have $0 < \xi^t < 1$ and $\alpha^t < C$; and for the ones that are not satisfied (and are misranked), we have $\xi^t > 1$ and $\alpha^t = C$.

For new test instance $\mathbf{x}$, the score is calculated as

$$g(\mathbf{x}) = \sum_t \alpha^t (\mathbf{x}^u - \mathbf{x}^v)^T \mathbf{x} \quad (13.55)$$

It is straightforward to write the kernelized version of the primal, dual, and score functions, and this is left to the reader (see exercise 7).

13.12 One-Class Kernel Machines

Support vector machines, originally proposed for classification, are extended to regression by defining slack variables for deviations around the regression line, instead of the discriminant. We now see how SVM can be used for a restricted type of unsupervised learning, namely, for estimating regions of high density. We are not doing a full density estimation; rather, we want to find a boundary (so that it reads like a classification problem) that separates volumes of high density from volumes of low density (Tax and Duin 1999). Such a boundary can then be used for *novelty* or *outlier detection*. This is also called *one-class classification*.

OUTLIER DETECTION
ONE-CLASS CLASSIFICATION

We consider a sphere with center $\boldsymbol{a}$ and radius R that we want to enclose as much as possible of the density, measured empirically as the enclosed training set percentage. At the same time, trading off with it, we want to find the smallest radius (see figure 13.10). We define slack variables for instances that lie outside (we only have one type of slack variable because we have examples from one class and we do not have any penalty for those inside), and we have a smoothness measure that is proportional to the radius:

$$\min R^2 + C\sum_t \xi^t \quad (13.56)$$

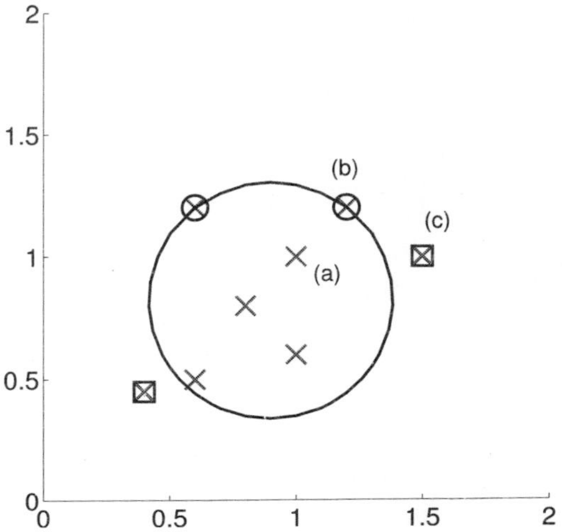

Figure 13.10 One-class support vector machine places the smoothest boundary (here using a linear kernel, the circle with the smallest radius) that encloses as much of the instances as possible. There are three possible cases: In (a), the instance is a typical instance. In (b), the instance falls on the boundary with $\xi^t = 0$; such instances define R. In (c), the instance is an outlier with $\xi^t > 0$. (b) and (c) are support vectors. In terms of the dual variable, we have, in (a), $\alpha^t = 0$; in (b), $0 < \alpha^t < C$; in (c), $\alpha^t = C$.

subject to

$$\|\boldsymbol{x}^t - \boldsymbol{a}\|^2 \le R^2 + \xi^t \text{ and } \xi^t \ge 0, \forall t$$

Adding the constraints, we get the Lagrangian, which we write keeping in mind that $\|\boldsymbol{x}^t - \boldsymbol{a}\|^2 = (\boldsymbol{x}^t - \boldsymbol{a})^T(\boldsymbol{x}^t - \boldsymbol{a})$:

(13.57) $$L_p = R^2 + C\sum_t \xi^t - \sum_t \alpha^t \left(R^2 + \xi^t - \left[(\boldsymbol{x}^t)^T\boldsymbol{x}^t - 2\boldsymbol{a}^T\boldsymbol{x}^t + \boldsymbol{a}^T\boldsymbol{a}\right]\right) - \sum_t \gamma^t\xi^t$$

with $\alpha^t \ge 0$ and $\gamma^t \ge 0$ being the Lagrange multipliers. Taking the derivative with respect to the parameters, we get

(13.58) $$\frac{\partial L}{\partial R} = 2R - 2R\sum_t \alpha^t = 0 \Rightarrow \sum_t \alpha^t = 1$$

(13.59) $$\frac{\partial L}{\partial \boldsymbol{a}} = \sum_t \alpha^t(2\boldsymbol{x}^t - 2\boldsymbol{a}) = 0 \Rightarrow \boldsymbol{a} = \sum_t \alpha^t\boldsymbol{x}^t$$

$$\frac{\partial L}{\partial \xi^t} = C - \alpha^t - \gamma^t = 0 \tag{13.60}$$

Since $\gamma^t \geq 0$, we can write this last as the constraint: $0 \leq \alpha^t \leq C$. Plugging these into equation 13.57, we get the dual that we maximize with respect to α^t:

$$L_d = \sum_t \alpha^t (\boldsymbol{x}^t)^T \boldsymbol{x}^t - \sum_t \sum_s \alpha^t \alpha^s (\boldsymbol{x}^t)^T \boldsymbol{x}^s \tag{13.61}$$

subject to

$$0 \leq \alpha^t \leq C \text{ and } \sum_t \alpha^t = 1$$

When we solve this, we again see that most of the instances vanish with their $\alpha^t = 0$; these are the typical, highly likely instances that fall inside the sphere (figure 13.10). There are two type of support vectors with $\alpha^t > 0$: There are instances that satisfy $0 < \alpha^t < C$ and lie on the boundary, $\|\boldsymbol{x}^t - \boldsymbol{a}\|^2 = R^2$ ($\xi^t = 0$), which we use to calculate R. Instances that satisfy $\alpha^t = C$ ($\xi^t > 0$) lie outside the boundary and are the outliers. From equation 13.59, we see that the center $\boldsymbol{a}$ is written as a weighted sum of the support vectors.

Then given a test input $\boldsymbol{x}$, we say that it is an outlier if

$$\|\boldsymbol{x} - \boldsymbol{a}\|^2 > R^2$$

or

$$\boldsymbol{x}^t \boldsymbol{x} - 2\boldsymbol{a}^T \boldsymbol{x} + \boldsymbol{a}^T \boldsymbol{a} > R^2$$

Using kernel functions, allow us to go beyond a sphere and define boundaries of arbitrary shapes. Replacing the dot product with a kernel function, we get (subject to the same constraints):

$$L_d = \sum_t \alpha^t K(\boldsymbol{x}^t, \boldsymbol{x}^t) - \sum_t \sum_s \alpha^t \alpha^s K(\boldsymbol{x}^t, \boldsymbol{x}^s) \tag{13.62}$$

For example, using a polynomial kernel of degree 2 allows arbitrary quadratic surfaces to be used. If we use a Gaussian kernel (equation 13.30), we have a union of local spheres. We reject $\boldsymbol{x}$ as an outlier if

$$K(\boldsymbol{x}, \boldsymbol{x}) - 2\sum_t \alpha^t K(\boldsymbol{x}, \boldsymbol{x}^t) + \sum_t \sum_s \alpha^t \alpha^s K(\boldsymbol{x}^t, \boldsymbol{x}^s) > R^2$$

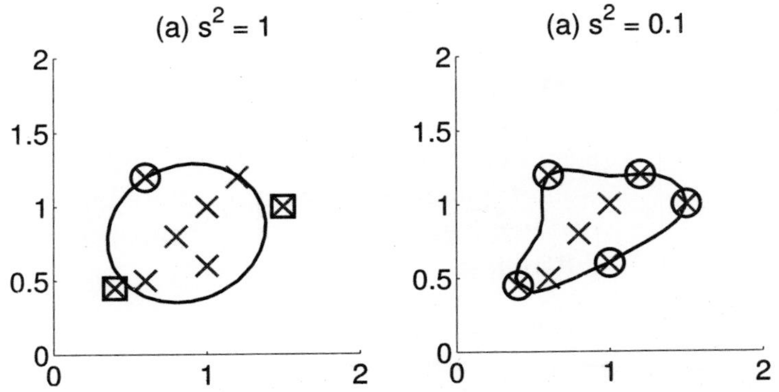

Figure 13.11 One-class support vector machine using a Gaussian kernel with different spreads.

The third term does not depend on $\boldsymbol{x}$ and is therefore a constant (we use this as an equality to solve for R where $\boldsymbol{x}$ is an instance on the margin). In the case of a Gaussian kernel where $K(\boldsymbol{x}, \boldsymbol{x}) = 1$, the condition reduces to

$$\sum_t \alpha^t K_G(\boldsymbol{x}, \boldsymbol{x}^t) < R_c$$

for some constant R_c, which is analogous to the kernel density estimator (section 8.2.2)—except for the sparseness of the solution—with a probability threshold R_c (see figure 13.11).

There is also an alternative, equivalent ν-SVM type of formulation of one-class support vector machines that uses the canonical $(1/2)\|\boldsymbol{w}\|^2$ type of smoothness (Schölkopf et al. 2001).

13.13 Large Margin Nearest Neighbor Classifier

In chapter 8, we discussed nonparametric methods where instead of fitting a global model to the data we interpolate from a subset of neighboring instances, and specifically in section 8.6, we covered the importance of using a good distance measure. We now discuss a method to learn a distance measure from the data. Strictly speaking, this is not a kernel machine, but it uses the idea of keeping a margin in ranking, as we noted in section 13.11.

The basic idea is to view k-nearest neighbor classification (section 8.4) as a ranking problem. Let us say the k-nearest neighbors of $\mathbf{x}^i$ contains two instances $\mathbf{x}^j$ and $\mathbf{x}^l$ such that $\mathbf{x}^i$ and $\mathbf{x}^j$ are of the same class and $\mathbf{x}^l$ belongs to another class. In such a case, we want a distance measure such that the distance between $\mathbf{x}^i$ and $\mathbf{x}^l$ is more than $\mathbf{x}^i$ and $\mathbf{x}^j$. Actually, we not only require that it be more but that there be a one-unit margin between them and if this is not satisfied, we have a slack variable for the difference:

$$\mathcal{D}(\mathbf{x}^i, \mathbf{x}^l) \geq \mathcal{D}(\mathbf{x}^i, \mathbf{x}^j) + 1 - \xi^{ijl}$$

The distance measure works as a score function in a ranking problem, and each $(\mathbf{x}^i, \mathbf{x}^j, \mathbf{x}^l)$ triple defines one ranking constraint as in equation 13.53.

LARGE MARGIN NEAREST NEIGHBOR

This is the basic idea behind the *large margin nearest neighbor* (LMNN) algorithm (Weinberger and Saul 2009). The error function minimized is

$$(1-\mu)\sum_{i,j} \mathcal{D}(\mathbf{x}^i, \mathbf{x}^j) + \mu \sum_{i,j,l} (1 - y_{il})\xi_{ijl} \tag{13.63}$$

subject to

$$\begin{aligned} \mathcal{D}(\mathbf{x}^i, \mathbf{x}^l) &\geq \mathcal{D}(\mathbf{x}^i, \mathbf{x}^j) + 1 - \xi^{ijl}, \text{ if } \boldsymbol{r}^i = \boldsymbol{r}^j \text{ and } \boldsymbol{r}^i \neq \boldsymbol{r}^l \\ \xi^{ijl} &\geq 0 \end{aligned} \tag{13.64}$$

Here, $\mathbf{x}^j$ is one of the k-nearest neighbors of $\mathbf{x}^i$ and they are of the same class: $\boldsymbol{r}^i = \boldsymbol{r}^j$—it is a *target* neighbor. $\mathbf{x}^l$ is also one of the k-nearest neighbors of $\mathbf{x}^i$; if they are of the same label, then y_{il} is set to 1 and we incur no loss; if they are of different classes, then $\mathbf{x}^l$ is an *impostor*, y_{il} is set to 0, and if the condition 13.64 is not satisfied, the slack defines a cost. The second term of equation 13.63 is the sum of such slacks. The first term is the total distance to all target neighbors and minimizing that has an effect of regularization—we want to keep the distances as small as possible.

In LMNN, Mahalanobis distance is used as the distance measure model:

$$\mathcal{D}(\mathbf{x}^i, \mathbf{x}^j | \mathbf{M}) = (\mathbf{x}^i - \mathbf{x}^j)^T \mathbf{M} (\mathbf{x}^i - \mathbf{x}^j) \tag{13.65}$$

and $\mathbf{M}$ matrix is the parameter that is to be optimized. Equation 13.63 defines a convex (more specifically, positive semi-definite) problem and hence has a unique minimum.

When the input dimensionality is high and there are few data, as we discuss in equation 8.21, we can regularize by factoring $\mathbf{M}$ as $\mathbf{L}^T\mathbf{L}$ where $\mathbf{L}$ is $k \times d$ with $k < d$:

$$\mathcal{D}(\boldsymbol{x}^i, \boldsymbol{x}^j|\mathbf{L}) = \|\mathbf{L}\boldsymbol{x}^i - \mathbf{L}\boldsymbol{x}^j\|^2 \tag{13.66}$$

$\mathbf{L}\boldsymbol{x}$ is the k-dimensional projection of $\boldsymbol{x}$, and Mahalanobis distance in the original d-dimensional $\boldsymbol{x}$ space corresponds to the (squared) Euclidean distance in the new k-dimensional space—see figure 8.7 for an example. If we plug equation 13.66 into equation 13.63 as the distance measure, we get the *large margin component analysis* (LMCA) algorithm (Torresani and Lee 2007); unfortunately, this is no longer a convex optimization problem, and if we use gradient descent, we get a locally optimal solution.

LARGE MARGIN COMPONENT ANALYSIS

13.14 Kernel Dimensionality Reduction

We know from section 6.3 that principal components analysis (PCA) reduces dimensionality by projecting on the eigenvectors of the covariance matrix $\boldsymbol{\Sigma}$ with the largest eigenvalues, which, if data instances are centered ($E[\boldsymbol{x}] = 0$), can be written as $\mathbf{X}^T\mathbf{X}$. In the kernelized version, we work in the space of $\boldsymbol{\phi}(\boldsymbol{x})$ instead of the original $\boldsymbol{x}$ and because, as usual, the dimensionality d of this new space may be much larger than the dataset size N, we prefer to work with the $N \times N$ matrix $\mathbf{X}\mathbf{X}^T$ and do feature embedding instead of working with the $d \times d$ matrix $\mathbf{X}^T\mathbf{X}$. The projected data matrix is $\boldsymbol{\Phi} = \boldsymbol{\phi}(\mathbf{X})$, and hence we work with the eigenvectors of $\boldsymbol{\Phi}^T\boldsymbol{\Phi}$ and hence the kernel matrix $\mathbf{K}$.

KERNEL PCA

Kernel PCA uses the eigenvectors and eigenvalues of the kernel matrix and this corresponds to doing a linear dimensionality reduction in the $\boldsymbol{\phi}(\boldsymbol{x})$ space. When $\boldsymbol{c}_i$ and λ_i are the corresponding eigenvectors and eigenvalues, the projected new k-dimensional values can be calculated as

$$z_j^t = \sqrt{\lambda_j}\boldsymbol{c}_j^t, j = 1, \ldots, k, \ t = 1, \ldots, N$$

An example is given in figure 13.12 where we first use a quadratic kernel and then decrease dimensionality to two (out of five) using kernel PCA and implement a linear SVM there. Note that in the general case (e.g., with a Gaussian kernel), the eigenvalues do not necessarily decay and there is no guarantee that we can reduce dimensionality using kernel PCA.

What we are doing here is multidimensional scaling (section 6.7) using kernel values as the similarity values. For example, by taking $k = 2$,

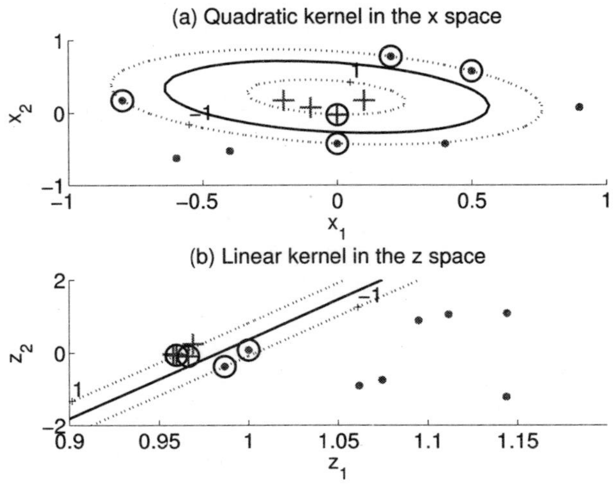

Figure 13.12 Instead of using a quadratic kernel in the original space (a), we can use kernel PCA on the quadratic kernel values to map to a two-dimensional new space where we use a linear discriminant (b); these two dimensions (out of five) explain 80 percent of the variance.

one can visualize the data in the space induced by the kernel matrix, which can give us information as to how similarity is defined by the used kernel. Linear discriminant analysis (LDA) (section 6.8) can similarly be kernelized (Müller et al. 2001). The kernelized version of canonical correlation analysis (CCA) (section 6.9) is discussed in Hardoon, Szedmak, Shawe-Taylor 2004.

In chapter 6, we discussed nonlinear dimensionality reduction methods, Isomap and LLE. In fact, by viewing the elements of the cost matrix in equation 6.58 as kernel evaluations for pairs of inputs, LLE can be seen as kernel PCA for a particular choice of kernel. The same also holds for Isomap when a kernel function is defined as a function of the geodesic distance on the graph.

13.15 Notes

The idea of generalizing linear models by mapping the data to a new space through nonlinear basis functions is old, but the novelty of support vector machines is that of integrating this into a learning algorithm whose parameters are defined in terms of a subset of data instances (the so-called *dual representation*), hence also without needing to explicitly evaluate the basis functions and thereby also limiting complexity by the size of the training set; this is also true for Gaussian processes where the kernel function is called the covariance function (section 16.9).

DUAL REPRESENTATION

The sparsity of the solution shows the advantage over nonparametric estimators, such as k-nearest neighbor and Parzen windows, or Gaussian processes, and the flexibility to use kernel functions allows working with nonvectorial data. Because there is a unique solution to the optimization problem, we do not need any iterative optimization procedure as we do in neural networks. Because of all these reasons, support vector machines are now considered to be the best, off-the-shelf learners and are widely used in many domains, especially bioinformatics (Schölkopf, Tsuda, and Vert 2004) and natural language processing applications, where an increasing number of tricks are being developed to derive kernels (Shawe-Taylor and Cristianini 2004).

The use of kernel functions implies a different data representation; we no longer define an instance (object/event) as a vector of attributes by itself, but in terms of how it is similar to or differs from other instances; this is akin to the difference between multidimensional scaling that uses a matrix of distances (without any need to know how they are calculated) and principal components analysis that uses vectors in some space.

The support vector machine is currently considered to be the best off-the-shelf learning algorithm and has been applied successfully in various domains. The fact that we are solving a convex problem and hence optimally and the idea of kernels that allow us to code our prior information has made it quite popular. There is a huge literature on the support vector machine and all types of kernel machines. The classic books are by Vapnik (1995, 1998) and Schölkopf and Smola (2002). Burges 1998 and Smola and Schölkopf 1998 are good tutorials on SVM classification and regression, respectively. Many free software packages are also available, and the ones that are most popular are SVMlight (Joachims 2008) and LIBSVM (Chang and Lin 2011).

13.16 Exercises

1. Propose a filtering algorithm to find training instances that are very unlikely to be support vectors.

   SOLUTION: Support vectors are those instances that are close to the boundaries. So if there is an instance surrounded by a large number of instances all of the same class, it will very probably not be chosen as a support vector. So, for example, we can do an 11-nearest neighbor search for all instances and if all its 11 neighbors are of the same class, we can prune that instance from the training set.

2. In equation 13.31, how can we estimate **S**?

   SOLUTION: We can calculate the covariance matrix of the data and use that as **S**. Another possibility is to have a local $\mathbf{S}^t$ for each support vector, and we can use a number of neighborhood data points to estimate it; we may need to take measures in such a case to make sure that **S** is not singular or decrease dimensionality is some way.

3. In the empirical kernel map, how can we choose the templates?

   SOLUTION: The easiest and most frequently used approach is to use all the training instances, and in such a case $\boldsymbol{\phi}(\cdot)$ is N-dimensional. We can decrease complexity and make the model more efficient by choosing a subset; we can use a randomly chosen subset, do some clustering, and use the cluster centers as templates (as in vector quantization), or use a subset that covers the input space well using as few instances as possible.

4. In the localized multiple kernel of equation 13.40, propose a suitable model for $\eta_i(\mathbf{x}|\theta_i)$ and discuss how it can be trained.

5. In kernel regression, what is the relation, if any, between ϵ and noise variance?

6. In kernel regression, what is the effect of using different ϵ on bias and variance?

   SOLUTION: ϵ is a smoothing parameter. When it is too large, we smooth too much, which reduces variance but risks increasing bias. If it is too small, the variance may be large and bias would be small.

7. Derive the kernelized version of the primal, dual, and the score functions for ranking..

   SOLUTION: The primal is

$$L_p = \frac{1}{2}\|\mathbf{w}\|^2 + C\sum_t \xi^t$$

   subject to

$$\begin{aligned} \mathbf{w}^T\boldsymbol{\phi}(\mathbf{x}^u - \mathbf{x}^v) &\geq 1 - \xi^t \\ \xi^t &\geq 0 \end{aligned}$$

The dual is

$$L_d = \sum_t \alpha^t - \frac{1}{2}\sum_t \sum_s \alpha^t \alpha^s K(\boldsymbol{x}^u - \boldsymbol{x}^v, \boldsymbol{x}^k - \boldsymbol{x}^l)$$

where $K(\boldsymbol{x}^u - \boldsymbol{x}^v, \boldsymbol{x}^k - \boldsymbol{x}^l) = \boldsymbol{\phi}(\boldsymbol{x}^u - \boldsymbol{x}^v)^T \boldsymbol{\phi}(\boldsymbol{x}^k - \boldsymbol{x}^l)$.

For new test instance $\boldsymbol{x}$, the score is calculated as

$$g(\boldsymbol{x}) = \sum_t \alpha^t K(\boldsymbol{x}^u - \boldsymbol{x}^v, \boldsymbol{x})$$

8. How can we use one-class SVM for classification?

   SOLUTION: We can use a separate one-class SVM for each class and then combine them to make a decision. For example, for each class C_i, we fit a one-class SVM to find parameters α_i^t:

   $$\sum_t \alpha_i^t K_G(\boldsymbol{x}, \boldsymbol{x}^t)$$

   and this then can be taken as an estimator for $p(\boldsymbol{x}|C_i)$. If the priors are more or less equal, we can simply choose the class having the largest value; otherwise we can use Bayes' rule for classification.

9. In a setting such as that in figure 13.12, use kernel PCA with a Gaussian kernel.

10. Let us say we have two representations for the same object and associated with each, we have a different kernel. How can we use both to implement a joint dimensionality reduction using kernel PCA?

13.17 References

Allwein, E. L., R. E. Schapire, and Y. Singer. 2000. "Reducing Multiclass to Binary: A Unifying Approach for Margin Classifiers." *Journal of Machine Learning Research* 1:113–141.

Burges, C. J. C. 1998. "A Tutorial on Support Vector Machines for Pattern Recognition." *Data Mining and Knowledge Discovery* 2:121–167.

Chang, C.-C., and C.-J. Lin. 2011. *LIBSVM: A Library for Support Vector Machines. ACM Transactions on Intelligent Systems and Technology* 2: 27:1–27:27.

Chapelle, O., and S. S. Keerthi. 2010. "Efficient Algorithms for Ranking with SVMs." *Information Retrieval* 11:201–215.

Cherkassky, V., and F. Mulier. 1998. *Learning from Data: Concepts, Theory, and Methods.* New York: Wiley.

Cortes, C., and V. Vapnik. 1995. "Support Vector Networks." *Machine Learning* 20:273–297.

Dietterich, T. G., and G. Bakiri. 1995. "Solving Multiclass Learning Problems via Error-Correcting Output Codes." *Journal of Artificial Intelligence Research* 2: 263–286.

Gönen, M., and E. Alpaydın. 2008. "Localized Multiple Kernel Learning." In *25th International Conference on Machine Learning*, ed. A. McCallum and S. Roweis, 352–359. Madison, WI: Omnipress.

Gönen, M., and E. Alpaydın. 2011. "Multiple Kernel Learning Algorithms." *Journal of Machine Learning Research* 12:2211–2268.

Hardoon, D. R., S. Szedmak, J. Shawe-Taylor. 2004. "Canonical Correlation Analysis: An Overview with Application to Learning Methods." *Neural Computation* 16:2639–2664.

Herbrich, R., K. Obermayer, and T. Graepel. 2000. "Large Margin Rank Boundaries for Ordinal Regression." In *Advances in Large Margin Classifiers*, ed. A. J. Smola, P. Bartlett, B. Schölkopf and D. Schuurmans, 115–132. Cambridge, MA: MIT Press.

Jaakkola, T., and D. Haussler. 1999. "Exploiting Generative Models in Discriminative Classifiers." In *Advances in Neural Information Processing Systems 11*, ed. M. J. Kearns, S. A. Solla, and D. A. Cohn, 487–493. Cambridge, MA: MIT Press.

Joachims, T. 2002. "Optimizing Search Engines using Clickthrough Data." In *ACM SIGKDD International Conference on Knowledge Discovery and Data Mining*, 133–142. New York, NY: ACM.

Joachims, T. 2008. *SVMlight*, `http://svmlight.joachims.org`.

Lanckriet, G. R. G, N. Cristianini, P. Bartlett, L. El Ghaoui, and M. I. Jordan. 2004. "Learning the Kernel Matrix with Semidefinite Programming." *Journal of Machine Learning Research* 5: 27–72.

Liu, T.-Y. 2011. *Learning to Rank for Information Retrieval.* Heidelberg: Springer.

Mayoraz, E., and E. Alpaydın. 1999. "Support Vector Machines for Multiclass Classification." In *Foundations and Tools for Neural Modeling, Proceedings of IWANN'99, LNCS 1606*, ed. J. Mira and J. V. Sanchez-Andres, 833–842. Berlin: Springer.

Müller, K. R., S. Mika, G. Rätsch, K. Tsuda, and B. Schölkopf. 2001. "An Introduction to Kernel-Based Learning Algorithms." *IEEE Transactions on Neural Networks* 12:181–201.

Noble, W. S. 2004. "Support Vector Machine Applications in Computational Biology." In *Kernel Methods in Computational Biology*, ed. B. Schölkopf, K. Tsuda, and J.-P. Vert, 71–92. Cambridge, MA: MIT Press.

Platt, J. 1999. "Probabilities for Support Vector Machines." In *Advances in Large Margin Classifiers*, ed. A. J. Smola, P. Bartlett, B. Schölkopf, and D. Schuurmans, 61–74. Cambridge, MA: MIT Press.

Schölkopf, B., J. Platt, J. Shawe-Taylor, A. J. Smola, and R. C. Williamson. 2001. "Estimating the Support of a High-Dimensional Distribution." *Neural Computation* 13:1443–1471.

Schölkopf, B., and A. J. Smola. 2002. *Learning with Kernels: Support Vector Machines, Regularization, Optimization, and Beyond.* Cambridge, MA: MIT Press.

Schölkopf, B., A. J. Smola, R. C. Williamson, and P. L. Bartlett. 2000. "New Support Vector Algorithms." *Neural Computation* 12:1207–1245.

Schölkopf, B., K. Tsuda, and J.-P. Vert, eds. 2004. *Kernel Methods in Computational Biology.* Cambridge, MA: MIT Press.

Shawe-Taylor, J., and N. Cristianini. 2004. *Kernel Methods for Pattern Analysis.* Cambridge, UK: Cambridge University Press.

Smola, A., and B. Schölkopf. 1998. *A Tutorial on Support Vector Regression,* NeuroCOLT TR-1998-030, Royal Holloway College, University of London, UK.

Sonnenburg, S., G. Rätsch, C. Schäfer, and B. Schölkopf. 2006. "Large Scale Multiple Kernel Learning." *Journal of Machine Learning Research* 7:1531–1565.

Tax, D. M. J., and R. P. W. Duin. 1999. "Support Vector Domain Description." *Pattern Recognition Letters* 20:1191–1199.

Torresani, L., and K. C. Lee. 2007. "Large Margin Component Analysis." In *Advances in Neural Information Processing Systems 19*, ed. B. Schölkopf, J. Platt, and T. Hoffman, 1385–1392. Cambridge, MA: MIT Press.

Vapnik, V. 1995. *The Nature of Statistical Learning Theory.* New York: Springer.

Vapnik, V. 1998. *Statistical Learning Theory.* New York: Wiley.

Vert, J.-P., K. Tsuda, and B. Schölkopf. 2004. "A Primer on Kernel Methods." In *Kernel Methods in Computational Biology*, ed. B. Schölkopf, K. Tsuda, and J.-P. Vert, 35–70. Cambridge, MA: MIT Press.

Weinberger, K. Q., and L. K. Saul. 2009. "Distance Metric Learning for Large Margin Classification." *Journal of Machine Learning Research* 10:207–244.

Weston, J., and C. Watkins. 1998. "Multiclass Support Vector Machines." *Technical Report CSD-TR-98-04*, Department of Computer Science, Royal Holloway, University of London.

14 *Graphical Models*

Graphical models represent the interaction between variables visually and have the advantage that inference over a large number of variables can be decomposed into a set of local calculations involving a small number of variables making use of conditional independencies. After some examples of inference by hand, we discuss the concept of d-separation and the belief propagation algorithm on a variety of graphs.

14.1 Introduction

GRAPHICAL MODELS
BAYESIAN NETWORKS
BELIEF NETWORKS
PROBABILISTIC NETWORKS

Graphical models, also called *Bayesian networks, belief networks*, or *probabilistic networks*, are composed of nodes and arcs between the nodes. Each node corresponds to a random variable, X, and has a value corresponding to the probability of the random variable, $P(X)$. If there is a directed arc from node X to node Y, this indicates that X has a *direct influence* on Y. This influence is specified by the conditional probability $P(Y|X)$. The network is a *directed acyclic graph* (DAG); namely, there are no cycles. The nodes and the arcs between the nodes define the *structure* of the network, and the conditional probabilities are the *parameters* given the structure.

DIRECTED ACYCLIC GRAPH

A simple example is given in figure 14.1, which models that rain causes the grass to get wet. It rains on 40 percent of the days and when it rains, there is a 90 percent chance that the grass gets wet; maybe 10 percent of the time it does not rain long enough for us to really consider the grass wet enough. The random variables in this example are binary; they are either true or false. There is a 20 percent probability that the grass gets wet without its actually raining, for example, when a sprinkler is used.

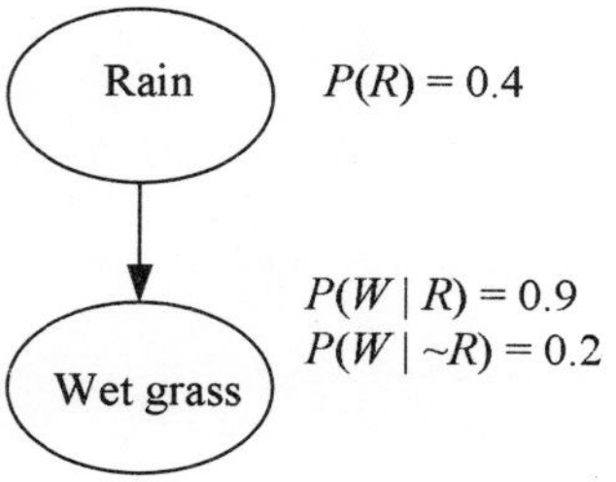

Figure 14.1 Bayesian network modeling that rain is the cause of wet grass.

We see that these three values completely specify the joint distribution of $P(R, W)$. If $P(R) = 0.4$, then $P(\sim R) = 0.6$, and similarly $P(\sim W|R) = 0.1$ and $P(\sim W|\sim R) = 0.8$. The joint is written as

$$P(R, W) = P(R)P(W|R)$$

We can calculate the individual (marginal) probability of wet grass by summing up over the possible values that its parent node can take:

$$\begin{aligned} P(W) &= \sum_R P(R, W) = P(W|R)P(R) + P(W|\sim R)P(\sim R) \\ &= 0.9 \cdot 0.4 + 0.2 \cdot 0.6 = 0.48 \end{aligned}$$

If we knew that it rained, the probability of wet grass would be 0.9; if we knew for sure that it did not, it would be as low as 0.2; not knowing whether it rained or not, the probability is 0.48.

CAUSAL GRAPH

Figure 14.1 shows a *causal graph* in that it explains that the cause of wet grass is rain. Bayes' rule allows us to invert the dependencies and have a *diagnosis*. For example, knowing that the grass is wet, the probability that it rained can be calculated as follows:

$$P(R|W) = \frac{P(W|R)P(R)}{P(W)} = 0.75$$

Knowing that the grass is wet increased the probability of rain from 0.4 to 0.75; this is because $P(W|R)$ is high and $P(W|\sim R)$ is low.

We form graphs by adding nodes and arcs and generate dependencies.

INDEPENDENCE

X and Y are *independent events* if

(14.1) $$p(X, Y) = P(X)P(Y)$$

CONDITIONAL INDEPENDENCE

X and Y are *conditionally independent events* given a third event Z if

(14.2) $P(X, Y|Z) = P(X|Z)P(Y|Z)$

which can also be rewritten as

(14.3) $P(X|Y, Z) = P(X|Z)$

In a graphical model, not all nodes are connected; actually, in general, a node is connected to only a small number of other nodes. Certain subgraphs imply conditional independence statements, and these allow us to break down a complex graph into smaller subsets in which inferences can be done locally and whose results are later propagated over the graph. There are three canonical cases and larger graphs are constructed using these as subgraphs.

14.2 Canonical Cases for Conditional Independence

Case 1: Head-to-Tail Connection

Three events may be connected serially, as seen in figure 14.2a. We see here that X and Z are independent given Y: Knowing Y tells Z everything; knowing the state of X does not add any extra knowledge for Z; we write $P(Z|Y, X) = P(Z|Y)$. We say that Y *blocks* the path from X to Z, or in other words, it *separates* them in the sense that if Y is removed, there is no path between X to Z. In this case, the joint is written as

(14.4) $P(X, Y, Z) = P(X)P(Y|X)P(Z|Y)$

Writing the joint this way implies independence:

(14.5) $$P(Z|X, Y) = \frac{P(X, Y, Z)}{P(X, Y)} = \frac{P(X)P(Y|X)P(Z|Y)}{P(X)P(Y|X)} = P(Z|Y)$$

Typically, X is the cause of Y and Y is the cause of Z. For example, as seen in figure 14.2b, X can be cloudy sky, Y can be rain, and Z can be wet grass. We can propagate information along the chain. If we do not know the state of cloudy, we have

$$\begin{aligned} P(R) &= P(R|C)P(C) + P(R|{\sim}C)P({\sim}C) = 0.38 \\ P(W) &= P(W|R)P(R) + P(W|{\sim}R)P({\sim}R) = 0.48 \end{aligned}$$

Let us say in the morning we see that the weather is cloudy; what can we say about the probability that the grass will be wet? To do this, we

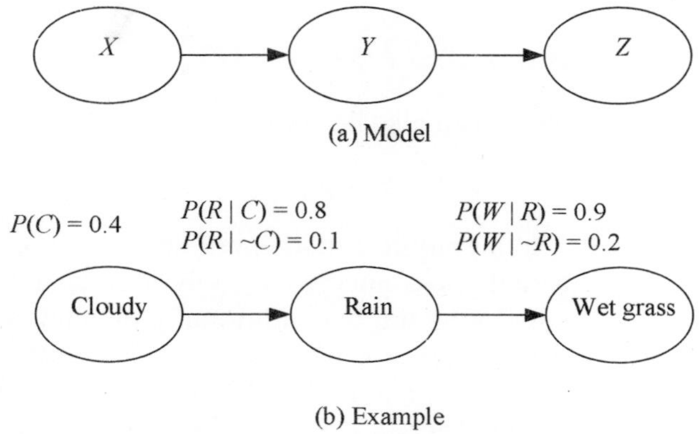

Figure 14.2 Head-to-tail connection. (a) Three nodes are connected serially. X and Z are independent given the intermediate node Y: $P(Z|Y,X) = P(Z|Y)$. (b) Example: Cloudy weather causes rain, which in turn causes wet grass.

need to propagate evidence first to the intermediate node R, and then to the query node W.

$$P(W|C) = P(W|R)P(R|C) + P(W|{\sim}R)P({\sim}R|C) = 0.76$$

Knowing that the weather is cloudy increased the probability of wet grass. We can also propagate evidence back using Bayes' rule. Let us say that we were traveling and on our return, see that our grass is wet; what is the probability that the weather was cloudy that day? We use Bayes' rule to invert the direction:

$$P(C|W) = \frac{P(W|C)P(C)}{P(W)} = 0.65$$

Knowing that the grass is wet increased the probability of cloudy weather from its default (prior) value of 0.4 to 0.65.

Case 2: Tail-to-Tail Connection

X may be the parent of two nodes Y and Z, as shown in figure 14.3a. The joint density is written as

$$P(X,Y,Z) = P(X)P(Y|X)P(Z|X) \tag{14.6}$$

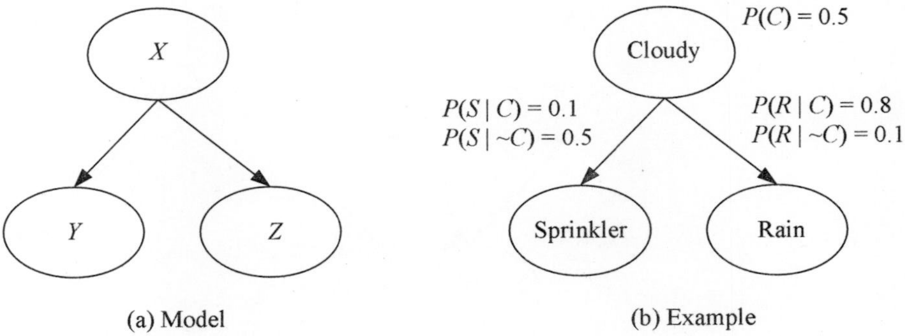

Figure 14.3 Tail-to-tail connection. X is the parent of two nodes Y and Z. The two child nodes are independent given the parent: $P(Y|X,Z) = P(Y|X)$. In the example, cloudy weather causes rain and also makes us less likely to turn the sprinkler on.

Normally Y and Z are dependent through X; given X, they become independent:

$$P(Y,Z|X) = \frac{P(X,Y,Z)}{P(X)} = \frac{P(X)P(Y|X)P(Z|X)}{P(X)} = P(Y|X)P(Z|X) \tag{14.7}$$

When its value is known, X blocks the path between Y and Z or, in other words, separates them.

In figure 14.3b, we see an example where cloudy weather influences both rain and the use of the sprinkler, one positively and the other negatively. Knowing that it rained, for example, we can invert the dependency using Bayes' rule and infer the cause:

$$\begin{aligned} P(C|R) &= \frac{P(R|C)P(C)}{P(R)} = \frac{P(R|C)P(C)}{\sum_C P(R,C)} \\ &= \frac{P(R|C)P(C)}{P(R|C)P(C) + P(R|{\sim}C)P({\sim}C)} = 0.89 \end{aligned} \tag{14.8}$$

Note that this value is larger than $P(C)$; knowing that it rained increased the probability that the weather is cloudy.

In figure 14.3a, if X is not known, knowing Y, for example, we can infer X that we can then use to infer Z. In figure 14.3b, knowing the state of the sprinkler has an effect on the probability that it rained. If we know that the sprinkler is on,

$$P(R|S) = \sum_C P(R,C|S) = P(R|C)P(C|S) + P(R|{\sim}C)P({\sim}C|S) \tag{14.9}$$

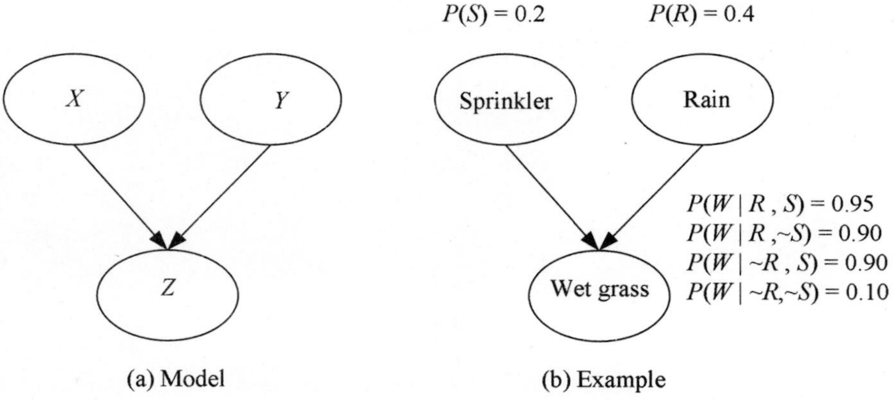

Figure 14.4 Head-to-head connection. A node has two parents that are independent unless the child is given. For example, an event may have two independent causes.

$$
\begin{aligned}
&= P(R|C)\frac{P(S|C)P(C)}{P(S)} + P(R|\sim C)\frac{P(S|\sim C)P(\sim C)}{P(S)} \\
&= 0.22
\end{aligned}
$$

This is less than $P(R) = 0.45$; that is, knowing that the sprinkler is on decreases the probability that it rained because sprinkler and rain happens for different states of cloudy weather. If the sprinkler is known to be off, using the same approach, we find that $P(R|\sim S) = 0.55$; the probability of rain increases this time.

Case 3: Head-to-Head Connection

In a head-to-head node, there are two parents X and Y to a single node Z, as shown in figure 14.4a. The joint density is written as

(14.10) $$P(X, Y, Z) = P(X)P(Y)P(Z|X, Y)$$

X and Y are independent: $P(X, Y) = P(X) \cdot P(Y)$ (exercise 2); they become dependent when Z is known. The concept of blocking or separation is different for this case: The path between X and Y is blocked, or they are separated, when Z is *not* observed; when Z (or any of its descendants) is observed, they are not blocked, separated, or independent.

We see, for example, in figure 14.4b that node W has two parents, R and S, and thus its probability is conditioned on the values of those two, $P(W|R,S)$.

Not knowing anything else, the probability that grass is wet is calculated by marginalizing over the joint:

$$\begin{aligned} P(W) &= \sum_{R,S} P(W,R,S) \\ &= P(W|R,S)P(R,S) + P(W|{\sim}R,S)P({\sim}R,S) \\ &\quad + P(W|R,{\sim}S)P(R,{\sim}S) + P(W|{\sim}R,{\sim}S)P({\sim}R,{\sim}S) \\ &= P(W|R,S)P(R)P(S) + P(W|{\sim}R,S)P({\sim}R)P(S) \\ &\quad + P(W|R,{\sim}S)P(R)P({\sim}S) + P(W|{\sim}R,{\sim}S)P({\sim}R)P({\sim}S) \\ &= 0.52 \end{aligned}$$

Now, let us say that we know that the sprinkler is on, and we check how this affects the probability. This is a causal (predictive) inference:

$$\begin{aligned} P(W|S) &= \sum_{R} P(W,R|S) \\ &= P(W|R,S)P(R|S) + P(W|{\sim}R,S)P({\sim}R|S) \\ &= P(W|R,S)P(R) + P(W|{\sim}R,S)P({\sim}R) \\ &= 0.92 \end{aligned}$$

We see that $P(W|S) > P(W)$; knowing that the sprinkler is on, the probability of wet grass increases.

We can also calculate the probability that the sprinkler is on, given that the grass is wet. This is a diagnostic inference.

$$P(S|W) = \frac{P(W|S)P(S)}{P(W)} = 0.35$$

$P(S|W) > P(S)$, that is, knowing that the grass is wet increased the probability of having the sprinkler on. Now let us assume that it rained. Then we have

$$\begin{aligned} P(S|R,W) &= \frac{P(W|R,S)P(S|R)}{P(W|R)} = \frac{P(W|R,S)P(S)}{P(W|R)} \\ &= 0.21 \end{aligned}$$

EXPLAINING AWAY

which is less than $P(S|W)$. This is called *explaining away*; given that we know it rained, the probability of the sprinkler causing the wet grass

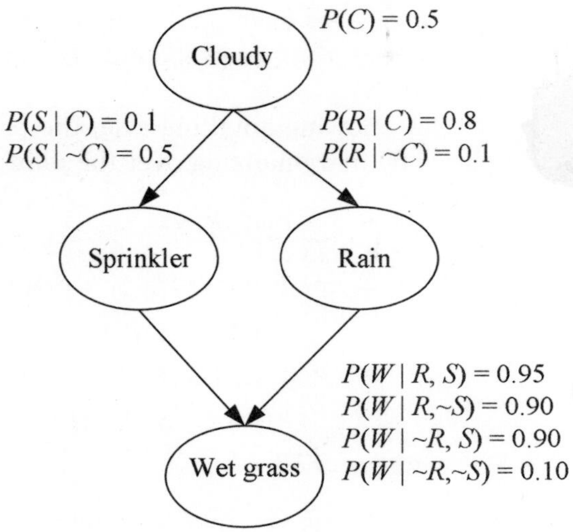

Figure 14.5 Larger graphs are formed by combining simpler subgraphs over which information is propagated using the implied conditional independencies.

decreases. Knowing that the grass is wet, rain and sprinkler become dependent. Similarly, $P(S|\sim R, W) > P(S|W)$. We see the same behavior when we compare $P(R|W)$ and $P(R|W, S)$ (exercise 3).

We can construct larger graphs by combining such subgraphs. For example, in figure 14.5 where we combine the two subgraphs, we can, for example, calculate the probability of having wet grass if it is cloudy:

$$\begin{aligned}
P(W|C) &= \sum_{R,S} P(W,R,S|C) \\
&= P(W,R,S|C) + P(W,\sim R,S|C) \\
&\quad + P(W,R,\sim S|C) + P(W,\sim R,\sim S|C) \\
&= P(W|R,S,C)P(R,S|C) \\
&\quad + P(W|\sim R,S,C)P(\sim R,S|C) \\
&\quad + P(W|R,\sim S,C)P(R,\sim S|C) \\
&\quad + P(W|\sim R,\sim S,C)P(\sim R,\sim S|C) \\
&= P(W|R,S)P(R|C)P(S|C) \\
&\quad + P(W|\sim R,S)P(\sim R|C)P(S|C) \\
&\quad + P(W|R,\sim S)P(R|C)P(\sim S|C)
\end{aligned}$$

$$+P(W|\sim R, \sim S)P(\sim R|C)P(\sim S|C)$$

where we have used that $P(W|R,S,C) = P(W|R,S)$; given R and S, W is independent of C: R and S between them block the path between W and C. Similarly, $P(R,S|C) = P(R|C)P(S|C)$; given C, R and S are independent. We see the advantage of Bayesian networks here, which explicitly encode independencies and allow breaking down inference into calculation over small groups of variables that are propagated from evidence nodes to query nodes.

We can calculate $P(C|W)$ and have a diagnostic inference:

$$P(C|W) = \frac{P(W|C)P(C)}{P(W)}$$

The graphical representation is visual and helps understanding. The network represents conditional independence statements and allows us to break down the problem of representing the joint distribution of many variables into *local* structures; this eases both analysis and computation. Figure 14.5 represents a joint density of four binary variables that would normally require fifteen values $(2^4 - 1)$ to be stored, whereas here there are only nine. If each node has a small number of parents, the complexity decreases from exponential to linear (in the number of nodes). As we have seen earlier, inference is also easier as the joint density is broken down into conditional densities of smaller groups of variables:

$$P(C,S,R,W) = P(C)P(S|C)P(R|C)P(W|S,R) \tag{14.11}$$

In the general case, when we have variables $X_1, \ldots, X_d$, we write

$$P(X_1, \ldots, X_d) = \prod_{i=1}^{d} P(X_i|\text{parents}(X_i)) \tag{14.12}$$

Then given any subset of X_i, namely, setting them to certain values due to evidence, we can calculate the probability distribution of some other subset of X_i by marginalizing over the joint. This is costly because it requires calculating an exponential number of joint probability combinations, even though each of them can be simplified as in equation 14.11. Note, however, that given the same evidence, for different X_i, we may be using the same intermediate values (products of conditional probabilities and sums for marginalization), and in section 14.5, we will discuss the belief propagation algorithm to do inference cheaply by doing the local intermediate calculations once which we can use multiple times for different query nodes.

Though in this example we use binary variables, it is straightforward to generalize for cases where the variables are discrete with any number of possible values (with m possible values and k parents, a table of size m^k is needed for the conditional probabilities), or they can be continuous (parameterized, e.g., $p(Y|x) \sim \mathcal{N}(\mu(x|\theta), \sigma^2)$; see figure 14.7).

One major advantage to using a Bayesian network is that we do not need to designate explicitly certain variables as input and certain others as output. The value of any set of variables can be established through evidence and the probabilities of any other set of variables can be inferred, and the difference between unsupervised and supervised learning becomes blurry. From this perspective, a graphical model can be thought of as a "probabilistic database" (Jordan 2004), a machine that can answer queries regarding the values of random variables.

HIDDEN VARIABLES

In a problem, there may also be *hidden variables* whose values are never known through evidence. The advantage of using hidden variables is that the dependency structure can be more easily defined. For example, in basket analysis when we want to find the dependencies among items sold, let us say we know that there is a dependency among "baby food," "diapers," and "milk" in that a customer buying one of these is very much likely to buy the other two. Instead of putting (noncausal) arcs among these three, we may designate a hidden node "baby at home" as the hidden cause of the consumption of these three items. When there are hidden nodes, their values are estimated given the values of observed nodes and filled in.

CAUSALITY

It should be stressed at this point that a link from a node X does not, and need not, always imply a *causality*. It only implies a *direct influence* of X over Y in the sense that the probability of Y is conditioned on the value of X, and two nodes may have a link between them even if there is no direct cause. It is preferable to have the causal relations in constructing the network by providing an explanation of how the data is generated (Pearl 2000) but such causes may not always be accessible.

14.3 Generative Models

GENERATIVE MODEL

Still, graphical models are frequently used to visualize *generative models* for representing the process that we believe has created the data. For example, for the case of classification, the corresponding graphical model is shown in figure 14.6a, with $\boldsymbol{x}$ as the input and C a multinomial variable

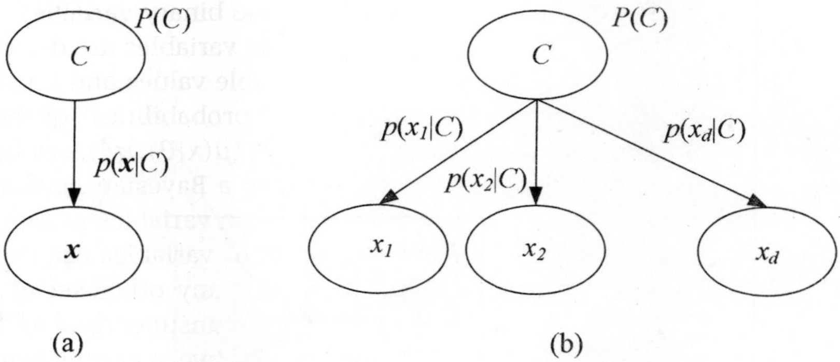

Figure 14.6 (a) Graphical model for classification. (b) Naive Bayes' classifier assumes independent inputs.

taking one of K states for the class code. It is as if we first pick a class C at random by sampling from $P(C)$, and then having fixed C, we pick an $\boldsymbol{x}$ by sampling from $p(\boldsymbol{x}|C)$. Bayes' rule inverts the generative direction and allows a diagnosis, as in the rain and wet grass case we saw in figure 14.1:

$$P(C|\boldsymbol{x}) = \frac{P(C)p(\boldsymbol{x}|C)}{P(\boldsymbol{x})}$$

Note that clustering is similar except that instead of the multinomial class indicator variable C we have the cluster indicator variable Z, and it is not observed during training. The E-step of the expectation-maximization algorithm (section 7.4) uses Bayes' rule to invert the arc and fills in the cluster indicator given the input.

If the inputs are independent, we have the graph shown in figure 14.6b, which is called the *naive Bayes' classifier*, because it ignores possible dependencies, namely, correlations, among the inputs and reduces a multivariate problem to a group of univariate problems:

NAIVE BAYES' CLASSIFIER

$$p(\boldsymbol{x}|C) = \prod_{j=1}^{d} p(x_j|C)$$

We have discussed classification for this case in sections 5.5 and 5.7 for numeric and discrete $\boldsymbol{x}$, respectively.

Linear regression can be visualized as a graphical model, as shown in figure 14.7. Input $\boldsymbol{x}^t$ is drawn from a prior $p(\boldsymbol{x})$, and the dependent variable r^t depends on the input $\boldsymbol{x}$ and the weights $\boldsymbol{w}$. Here, we define a

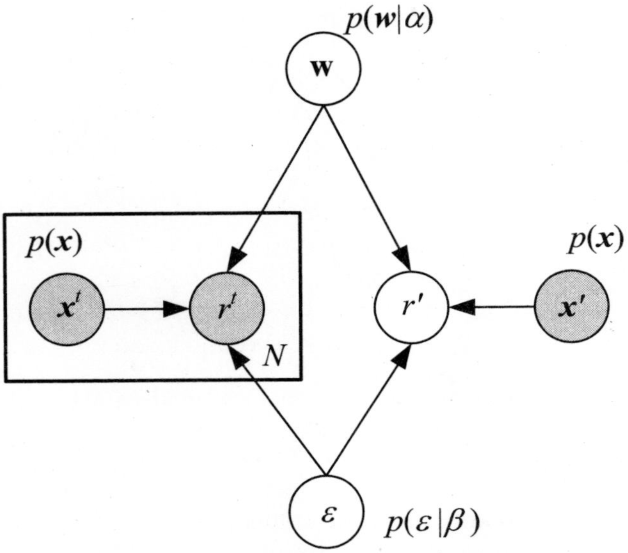

Figure 14.7 Graphical model for linear regression.

node for the weights $\boldsymbol{w}$ with a prior parameterized by α, namely, $p(\boldsymbol{w}) \sim \mathcal{N}(\mathbf{0}, \alpha^{-1}\mathbf{I})$. There is also a node for the noise ϵ variable, parameterized by β, namely, $p(\epsilon) \sim \mathcal{N}(0, \beta^{-1})$:

(14.13) $$p(r^t|\boldsymbol{x}^t, \boldsymbol{w}) \sim \mathcal{N}(\boldsymbol{w}^T\boldsymbol{x}^t, \beta^{-1})$$

There are N such pairs in the training set, which is shown by the rectangular *plate* in the figure—the plate corresponds to the training set $\mathcal{X}$. Given a new input $\boldsymbol{x}'$, the aim is to estimate r'. The weights $\boldsymbol{w}$ are not given but they can be estimated using the training set of $\mathcal{X}$ which we can divide as $[\mathbf{X}, \boldsymbol{r}]$.

In equation 14.9, where C is the cause of R and S, we write

$$P(R|S) = \sum_C P(R, C|S) = P(R|C)P(C|S) + P(R|{\sim}C)P({\sim}C|S)$$

filling in C using observed S and average over all possible values of C. Similarly here, we write

$$\begin{aligned} p(r'|\boldsymbol{x}', \boldsymbol{r}, \mathbf{X}) &= \int p(r'|\boldsymbol{x}', \boldsymbol{w})p(\boldsymbol{w}|\mathbf{X}, \boldsymbol{r})d\boldsymbol{w} \\ &= \int p(r'|\boldsymbol{x}', \boldsymbol{w})\frac{p(\boldsymbol{r}|\mathbf{X}, \boldsymbol{w})p(\boldsymbol{w})}{p(\boldsymbol{r})}d\boldsymbol{w} \end{aligned}$$

$$\propto \int p(r'|\mathbf{x}', \mathbf{w}) \prod_t p(r^t|\mathbf{x}^t, \mathbf{w}) p(\mathbf{w}) d\mathbf{w} \tag{14.14}$$

where the second line is due to Bayes' rule and the third line is due to the independence of instances in the training set.

Note that what we have in figure 14.7 is a Bayesian model where we designate parameter $\mathbf{w}$ as a random variable with a prior distribution. As we see in equation 14.14, what we are effectively doing is estimating the posterior $p(\mathbf{w}|\mathbf{X}, \mathbf{r})$ and then integrating over it. We began discussing this in section 4.4, and we discuss it in greater detail in chapter 16, for different generative models and different sets of parameters.

14.4 d-Separation

D-SEPARATION

BAYES' BALL

We now generalize the concept of blocking and separation under the name of *d-separation*, and we define it in a way so that for arbitrary subsets of nodes A, B, and C, we can check if A and B are independent given C. Jordan (2004) visualizes this as a ball bouncing over the graph and calls this the *Bayes' ball*. We set the nodes in C to their values, place a ball at each node in A, let the balls move around according to a set of rules, and check whether a ball reaches any node in B. If this is the case, they are dependent; otherwise, they are independent.

To check whether A and B are d-separated given C, we consider all possible paths between any node in A and any node in B. Any such path is *blocked* if

(a) the directions of the edges on the path either meet head-to-tail (case 1) or tail-to-tail (case 2) and the node is in C, or

(b) the directions of the edges on the path meet head-to-head (case 3) and neither that node nor any of its descendant is in C.

If all paths are blocked, we say that A and B are d-separated, that is, independent, given C; otherwise, they are dependent. Examples are given in figure 14.8.

14.5 Belief Propagation

Having discussed some inference examples by hand, we now are interested in an algorithm that can answer queries such as $P(X|E)$ where X

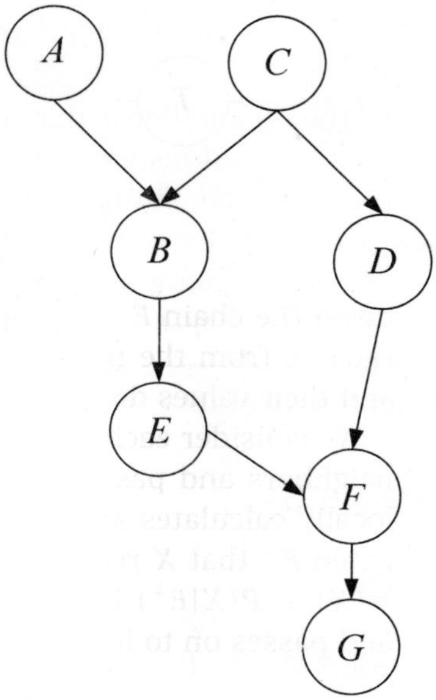

Figure 14.8 Examples of d-separation. The path $BCDF$ is blocked given C because C is a tail-to-tail node. $BEFG$ is blocked by F because F is a head-to-tail node. $BEFD$ is blocked unless F (or G) is given.

is any *query node* in the graph and E is any subset of *evidence nodes* whose values are set to certain value. Following Pearl (1988), we start with the simplest case of chains and gradually move on to more complex graphs. Our aim is to find the graph operation counterparts of probabilistic procedures such as Bayes' rule or marginalization, so that the task of inference can be mapped to general-purpose graph algorithms.

14.5.1 Chains

A *chain* is a sequence of head-to-tail nodes with one *root* node without any parent; all other nodes have exactly one parent node, and all nodes except the very last, *leaf*, have a single child. If evidence is in the ancestors of X, we can just do a diagnostic inference and propagate evidence down the chain; if evidence is in the descendants of X, we can do a causal inference and propagate upward using Bayes' rule. Let us see the general case where we have evidence in both directions, up the chain E^+ and

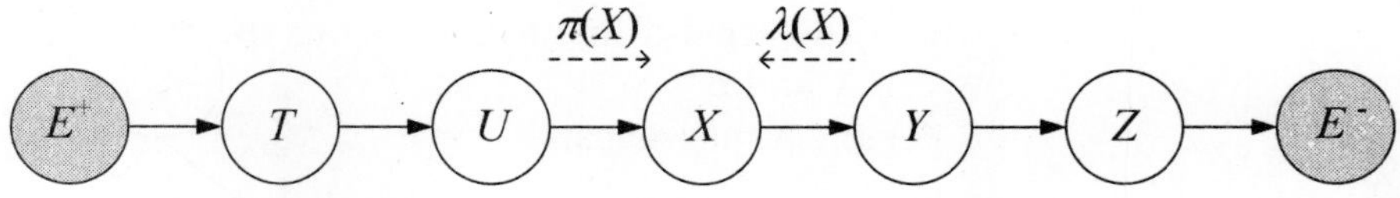

Figure 14.9 Inference along a chain.

down the chain E^- (see figure 14.9). Note that any evidence node separates X from the nodes on the chain on the other side of the evidence and their values do not affect $p(X)$; this is true in both directions.

We consider each node as a processor that receives messages from its neighbors and pass it along after some local calculation. Each node X locally calculates and stores two values: $\lambda(X) \equiv P(E^-|X)$ is the propagated E^- that X receives from its child and forwards to its parent, and $\pi(X) \equiv P(X|E^+)$ is the propagated E^+ that X receives from its parent and passes on to its child.

$$
\begin{aligned}
P(X|E) &= \frac{P(E|X)P(X)}{P(E)} = \frac{P(E^+,E^-|X)P(X)}{P(E)} \\
&= \frac{P(E^+|X)P(E^-|X)P(X)}{P(E)} \\
&= \frac{P(X|E^+)P(E^+)P(E^-|X)P(X)}{P(X)P(E)} \\
&= \alpha P(X|E^+)P(E^-|X) = \alpha\pi(X)\lambda(X) \qquad (14.15)
\end{aligned}
$$

for some normalizing constant α, not dependent on the value of X. The second line is there because E^+ and E^- are independent given X, and the third line is due to Bayes' rule.

If a node E is instantiated to a certain value $\tilde{e}$, $\lambda(\tilde{e}) \equiv 1$ and $\lambda(e) \equiv 0$, for $e \neq \tilde{e}$. The leaf node X that is not instantiated has its $\lambda(x) \equiv 1$, for all x values. The root node X that is not instantiated takes the prior probabilities as π values: $\pi(x) \equiv P(x), \forall x$.

Given these initial conditions, we can devise recursive formulas to propagate evidence along the chain.

For the π-messages, we have

$$
\begin{aligned}
\pi(X) &\equiv P(X|E^+) = \sum_U P(X|U,E^+)P(U|E^+) \\
&= \sum_U P(X|U)P(U|E^+) = \sum_U P(X|U)\pi(U) \qquad (14.16)
\end{aligned}
$$

where the second line follows from the fact that U blocks the path between X and E^+.

For the λ-messages, we have

$$\begin{aligned}\lambda(X) &\equiv P(E^-|X) = \sum_Y P(E^-|X,Y)P(Y|X) \\ &= \sum_Y P(E^-|Y)P(Y|X) = \sum_Y P(Y|X)\lambda(Y) \quad (14.17)\end{aligned}$$

where the second line follows from the fact that Y blocks the path between X and E^-.

When the evidence nodes are set to a value, they initiate traffic and nodes continue updating until there is convergence. Pearl (1988) views this as a parallel machine where each node is implemented by a processor that works in parallel with others and exchanges information through λ- and π-messages with its parent and child.

14.5.2 Trees

Chains are restrictive because each node can have only a single parent and a single child, that is, a single cause and a single symptom. In a *tree*, each node may have several children but all nodes, except the single root, have exactly one parent. The same belief propagation also applies here with the difference from chains being that a node receives different λ-messages from its children, $\lambda_Y(X)$ denoting the message X receives from its child Y, and sends different π-messages to its children, $\pi_Y(X)$ denoting the message X sends to its child Y.

Again, we divide possible evidence to two parts, E^- are nodes that are in the subtree rooted at the query node X, and E^+ are evidence nodes elsewhere (see figure 14.10). Note that this second need not be an ancestor of X but may also be in a subtree rooted at a sibling of X. The important point is that again X separates E^+ and E^- so that we can write $P(E^+,E^-|X) = P(E^+|X)P(E^-|X)$, and hence have

$$P(X|E) = \alpha\pi(X)\lambda(X)$$

where again α is a normalizing constant.

$\lambda(X)$ is the evidence in the subtree rooted at X, and if X has two children Y and Z, as shown in figure 14.10, it can be calculated as

$$\begin{aligned}\lambda(X) &\equiv P(E_X^-|X) = P(E_Y^-,E_Z^-|X) \\ &= P(E_Y^-|X)P(E_Z^-|X) = \lambda_Y(X)\lambda_Z(X) \quad (14.18)\end{aligned}$$

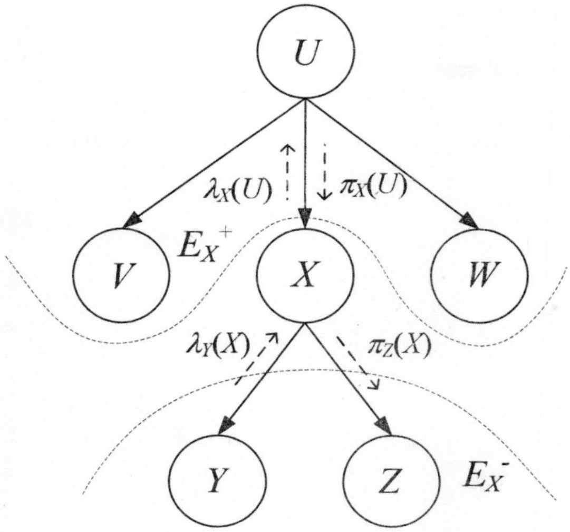

Figure 14.10 In a tree, a node may have several children but a single parent.

In the general case, if X has m children, $Y_j, j = 1, \ldots, m$, then we multiply all their λ values:

(14.19) $$\lambda(X) = \prod_{j=1}^{m} \lambda_{Y_j}(X)$$

Once X accumulates λ evidence from its children's λ-messages, it propagates it up to its parent:

(14.20) $$\lambda_X(U) = \sum_X \lambda(X) P(X|U)$$

Similarly and in the other direction, $\pi(X)$ is the evidence elsewhere that is accumulated in $P(U|E^+)$ and passed on to X as a π-message:

(14.21) $$\pi(X) \equiv P(X|E_X^+) = \sum_U P(X|U)P(U|E_X^+) = \sum_U P(X|U)\pi_X(U)$$

This calculated π value is then propagated down to X's children. Note that what Y receives from X is what X receives from its parent U and also from its other child Z; together they make up E_Y^+ (see figure 14.10):

$$\pi_Y(X) \quad \equiv \quad P(X|E_Y^+) = P(X|E_X^+, E_Z^-)$$

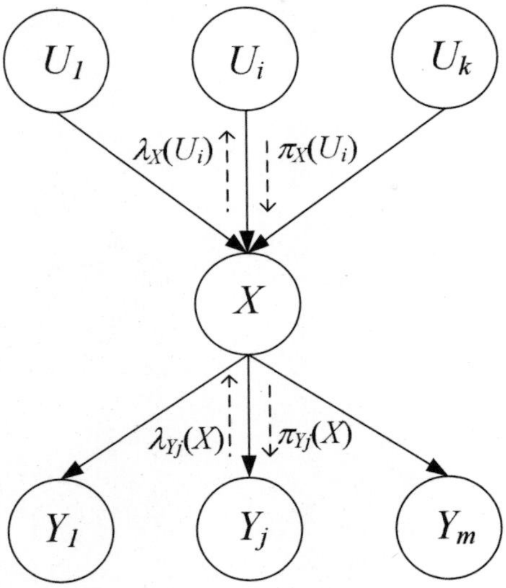

Figure 14.11 In a polytree, a node may have several children and several parents, but the graph is singly connected; that is, there is a single chain between U_i and Y_j passing through X.

$$= \frac{P(E_Z^-|X, E_X^+)P(X|E_X^+)}{P(E_Z^-)} = \frac{P(E_Z^-|X)P(X|E_X^+)}{P(E_Z^-)}$$

(14.22) $$= \alpha\lambda_Z(X)\pi(X)$$

Again, if Y has not one sibling Z but multiple, we need to take a product over all their λ values:

(14.23) $$\pi_{Y_j}(X) = \alpha \prod_{s \neq j} \lambda_{Y_s}(X)\pi(X)$$

14.5.3 Polytrees

POLYTREE

In a tree, a node has a single parent, that is, a single cause. In a *polytree*, a node may have multiple parents, but we require that the graph be singly connected, which means that there is a single chain between any two nodes. If we remove X, the graph will split into two components. This is necessary so that we can continue splitting E_X into E_X^+ and E_X^-, which are independent given X (see figure 14.11).

If X has multiple parents $U_i, i = 1, \dots, k$, it receives π-messages from all of them, $\pi_X(U_i)$, which it combines as follows:

$$\begin{aligned}\pi(X) &\equiv P(X|E_X^+) = P(X, E_{U_1X}^+, E_{U_2X}^+, \ldots, E_{U_kX}^+) \\ &= \sum_{U_1}\sum_{U_2}\cdots\sum_{U_k} P(X|U_1, U_2, \ldots, U_k)P(U_1|E_{U_1X}^+)\cdots P(U_k|E_{U_kX}^+) \\ &= \sum_{U_1}\sum_{U_2}\cdots\sum_{U_k} P(X|U_1, U_2, \ldots, U_k)\prod_{i=1}^{k}\pi_X(U_i) \qquad (14.24)\end{aligned}$$

and passes it on to its several children $Y_j, j = 1, \ldots, m$:

$$\pi_{Y_j}(X) = \alpha \prod_{s \neq j} \lambda_{Y_s}(X)\pi(X) \qquad (14.25)$$

In this case when X has multiple parents, a λ-message X passes on to one of its parents U_i combines not only the evidence X receives from its children but also the π-messages X receives from its other parents $U_r, r \neq i$; they together make up $E_{U_iX}^-$:

$$\begin{aligned}\lambda_X(U_i) &\equiv P(E_{U_iX}^-|X) \\ &= \sum_X \sum_{U_{r\neq i}} P(E_X^-, E_{U_{r\neq i}X}^+, X, U_{r\neq i}|U_i) \\ &= \sum_X \sum_{U_{r\neq i}} P(E_X^-, E_{U_{r\neq i}X}^+|X, U_{r\neq i}, U_i)P(X, U_{r\neq i}|U_i) \\ &= \sum_X \sum_{U_{r\neq i}} P(E_X^-|X)P(E_{U_{r\neq i}X}^+|U_{r\neq i})P(X|U_{r\neq i}, U_i)P(U_{r\neq i}|U_i) \\ &= \sum_X \sum_{U_{r\neq i}} P(E_X^-|X)\frac{P(U_{r\neq i}|E_{U_{r\neq i}X}^+)P(E_{U_{r\neq i}X}^+)}{P(U_{r\neq i})}P(X|U_{r\neq i}, U_i)P(U_{r\neq i}|U_i) \\ &= \beta\sum_X \sum_{U_{r\neq i}} P(E_X^-|X)P(U_{r\neq i}|E_{U_{r\neq i}X}^+)P(X|U_{r\neq i}, U_i) \\ &= \beta\sum_X \sum_{U_{r\neq i}} \lambda(X)\prod_{r\neq i}\pi_X(U_r)P(X|U_1, \ldots, U_k) \\ &= \beta\sum_X \lambda(X)\sum_{U_{r\neq i}} P(X|U_1, \ldots, U_k)\prod_{r\neq i}\pi_X(U_r) \qquad (14.26)\end{aligned}$$

As in a tree, to find its overall λ, the parent multiplies the λ-messages it receives from its children:

$$\lambda(X) = \prod_{j=1}^{m} \lambda_{Y_j}(X) \qquad (14.27)$$

In this case of multiple parents, we need to store and manipulate the conditional probability given all the parents, $p(X|U_1, \ldots, U_k)$, which is costly for large k. Approaches have been proposed to decrease the complexity from exponential in k to linear. For example, in a *noisy OR gate*, any of the parents is sufficient to cause the event and the likelihood does not decrease when multiple parent events occur. If the probability that X happens when only cause U_i happens is $1 - q_i$

NOISY OR

$$P(X|U_i, \sim U_{p \neq j}) = 1 - q_i \tag{14.28}$$

the probability that X happens when a subset T of them occur is calculated as

$$P(X|T) = 1 - \prod_{u_i \in T} q_i \tag{14.29}$$

For example, let us say wet grass has two causes, rain and a sprinkler, with $q_R = q_S = 0.1$; that is, both singly have a 90 percent probability of causing wet grass. Then, $P(W|R, \sim S) = 0.9$ and $P(W|R, S) = 0.99$.

Another possibility is to write the conditional probability as some function given a set of parameters, for example, as a linear model

$$P(X|U_1, \ldots, U_k, w_0, w_1, \ldots, w_k) = \text{sigmoid}\left(\sum_{i=1}^{k} w_i U_i + w_0\right) \tag{14.30}$$

where sigmoid guarantees that the output is a probability between 0 and 1. During training, we can learn the parameters $w_i, i = 0, \ldots, d$, for example, to maximize the likelihood on a sample.

14.5.4 Junction Trees

If there is a loop, that is, if there is a cycle in the underlying undirected graph—for example, if the parents of X share a common ancestor—the algorithm we discussed earlier does not work. In such a case, there is more than one path on which to propagate evidence and, for example, while evaluating the probability at X, we cannot say that X separates E into E_X^+ and E_X^- as causal (upward) and diagnostic (downward) evidence; removing X does not split the graph into two. Conditioning them on X does not make them independent and the two can interact through some other path not involving X.

We can still use the same algorithm if we can convert the graph to a polytree. We define *clique nodes* that correspond to a set of original variables and connect them so that they form a tree (see figure 14.12). We

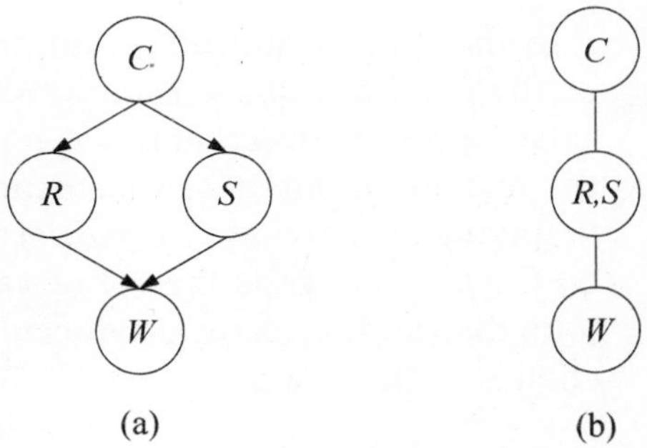

Figure 14.12 (a) A multiply connected graph, and (b) its corresponding junction tree with nodes clustered.

can then run the same belief propagation algorithm with some modifications. This is the basic idea behind the *junction tree algorithm* (Lauritzen and Spiegelhalter 1988; Jensen 1996; Jordan 2004).

JUNCTION TREE

14.6 Undirected Graphs: Markov Random Fields

Up to now, we have discussed directed graphs where the influences are undirectional and have used Bayes' rule to invert the arcs. If the influences are symmetric, we represent them using an undirected graphical model, also known as a *Markov random field.* For example, neighboring pixels in an image tend to have the same color—that is, are correlated—and this correlation goes both ways.

MARKOV RANDOM FIELD

Directed and undirected graphs define conditional independence differently, and, hence, there are probability distributions that are represented by a directed graph and not by an undirected graph, and vice versa (Pearl 1988).

Because there are no directions and hence no distinction between the head or the tail of an arc, the treatment of undirected graphs is simpler. For example, it is much easier to check if A and B are independent given C. We just check if after removing all nodes in C, we still have a path between a node in A and a node in B. If so, they are dependent, otherwise, if all paths between nodes in A and nodes in B pass through nodes in C such that removal of C leaves nodes of A and nodes of B in separate components, we have independence.

In the case of an undirected graph, we do not talk about the parent or the child but about *cliques*, which are sets of nodes such that there exists a link between any two nodes in the set. A *maximal* clique has the maximum number of elements. Instead of conditional probabilities (implying a direction), in undirected graphs we have *potential functions* $\psi_C(X_C)$ where X_C is the set of variables in clique C, and we define the joint distribution as the product of the potential functions of the maximal cliques of the graph

CLIQUE

POTENTIAL FUNCTION

$$p(X) = \frac{1}{Z}\prod_C \psi_C(X_C) \tag{14.31}$$

where Z is the normalization constant to make sure that $\sum_X p(X) = 1$:

$$Z = \sum_X \prod_C \psi_C(X) \tag{14.32}$$

It can be shown that a directed graph is already normalized (exercise 5).

Unlike in directed graphs, the potential functions in an undirected graph do not need to have a probabilistic interpretation, and one has more freedom in defining them. In general, we can view potential functions as expressing local constraints, that is, favoring some local configurations over others. For example, in an image, we can define a pairwise potential function between neighboring pixels, which takes a higher value if their colors are similar than the case when they are different (Bishop 2006). Then, setting some of the pixels to their values given as evidence, we can estimate the values of other pixels that are not known, for example, due to occlusion.

If we have the directed graph, it is easy to redraw it as an undirected graph, simply by dropping all the directions, and if a node has a single parent, we can set the pairwise potential function simply to the conditional probability. If the node has more than one parent, however, the "explaining away" phenomenon due to the head-to-head node makes the parents dependent, and hence we should have the parents in the same clique so that the clique potential includes all the parents. This is done by connecting all the parents of a node by links so that they are completely connected among them and form a clique. This is called "marrying" the parents, and the process is called *moralization*. Incidentally, moralization is one of the steps in generating a junction tree, which is undirected.

MORALIZATION

It is straightforward to adapt the belief propagation algorithm to work on undirected graphs, and it is easier because the potential function is

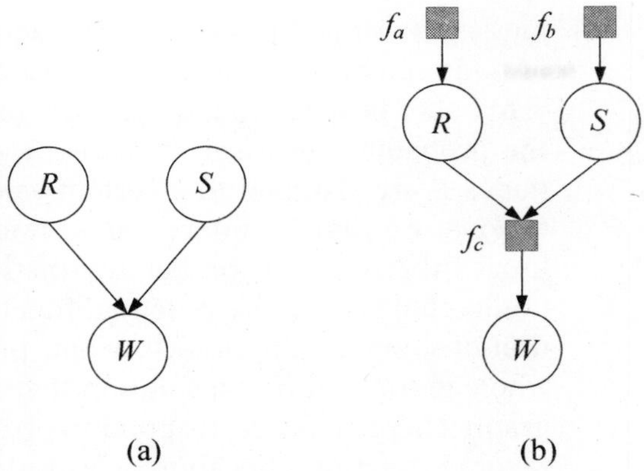

Figure 14.13 (a) A directed graph that would have a loop after moralization, and (b) its corresponding factor graph that is a tree. The three factors are $f_a(R) \equiv P(R)$, $f_b(S) \equiv P(S)$, and $f_c(R, S, W) \equiv P(W|R, S)$.

symmetric and we do not need to make a difference between causal and diagnostic evidence. Thus, we can do inference on undirected chains and trees. But in polytrees where a node has multiple parents and moralization necessarily creates loops, this would not work. One trick is to convert it to a *factor graph* that uses a second kind of *factor nodes* in addition to the variable nodes, and we write the joint distribution as a product of factors (Kschischang, Frey, and Loeliger 2001)

FACTOR GRAPH

$$p(X) = \frac{1}{Z} \prod_S f_S(X_S) \tag{14.33}$$

where X_s denotes a subset of the variable nodes used by factor S. Directed graphs are a special case where factors correspond to local conditional distributions, and undirected graphs are another special case where factors are potential functions over maximal cliques. The advantage is that, as we can see in figure 14.13, the tree structure can be kept even after moralization.

It is possible to generalize the belief propagation algorithm to work on factor graphs; this is called the *sum-product algorithm* (Bishop 2006; Jordan 2004) where there is the same idea of doing local computations once and propagating them through the graph as messages. The difference now is that there are two types of messages because there are two kinds of nodes, factors and variables, and we make a distinction between their

SUM-PRODUCT ALGORITHM

messages. Note, however, that a factor graph is bipartite, and one kind of node can have a close encounter only with the second kind.

In belief propagation, or the sum-product algorithm, the aim is to find the probability of a set of nodes X given that another set of evidence nodes E are clamped to a certain value, that is, $P(X|E)$. In some applications, we may be interested in finding the setting of all X that maximizes the full joint probability distribution $p(X)$. For example, in the undirected case where potential functions code locally consistent configurations, such an approach would propagate local constraints over the whole graph and find a solution that maximizes global consistency. In a graph where nodes correspond to pixels and pairwise potential functions favor correlation, this approach would implement noise removal (Bishop 2006). The algorithm for this, named the *max-product algorithm* (Bishop 2006; Jordan 2004) is the same as the sum-product algorithm where we take the maximum (choose the most likely value) rather than the sum (marginalize). This is analogous to the difference between the forward-backward procedure and the Viterbi algorithm in hidden Markov models that we discussed in chapter 15.

MAX-PRODUCT ALGORITHM

Note that the nodes need not correspond to low-level concepts like pixels; in a vision application, for instance, we may have nodes for corners of different types or lines of different orientations with potential functions checking for compatibility, so as to see if they can be part of the same interpretation—remember the Necker cube, for example—so that overall consistent solutions emerge after the consolidation of local evidences.

The complexity of the inference algorithms on polytrees or junction trees is determined by the maximum number of parents or the size of the largest clique, and when this is large, exact inference may be infeasible. In such a case, one needs to use an approximation or a sampling algorithm (Jordan 1999; Bishop 2006).

14.7 Learning the Structure of a Graphical Model

As in any approach, learning a graphical model has two parts. The first is the learning of parameters given a structure; this is relatively easier (Buntine 1996), and, in graphical models, conditional probability tables or their parameterizations (as in equation 14.30) can be trained to maximize the likelihood, or by using a Bayesian approach if suitable priors are known (chapter 16).

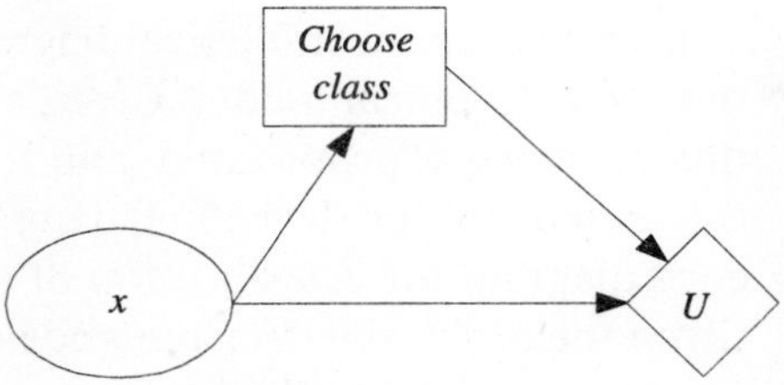

Figure 14.14 Influence diagram corresponding to classification. Depending on input x, a class is chosen that incurs a certain utility (risk).

The second, more difficult, and interesting part is to learn the graph structure (Cowell et al. 1999). This is basically a model selection problem, and just like the incremental approaches for learning the structure of a multilayer perceptron (section 11.9), we can see this as a search in the space of all possible graphs. One can, for example, consider operators that can add/remove arcs and/or hidden nodes and then do a search evaluating the improvement at each step (using parameter learning at each intermediate iteration). Note, however, that to check for overfitting, one should regularize properly, corresponding to a Bayesian approach with a prior that favors simpler graphs (Neapolitan 2004). However, because the state space is large, it is most helpful if there is a human expert who can manually define causal relationships among variables and creates subgraphs of small groups of variables.

In chapter 16, we discuss the Bayesian approach and in section 16.8, we discuss the nonparametric Bayesian methods where model structure can be made more complex in time as more data arrives.

14.8 Influence Diagrams

INFLUENCE DIAGRAMS

Just as in chapter 3, we generalized from probabilities to actions with risks, *influence diagrams* are graphical models that allow the generalization of graphical models to include decisions and utilities. An influence diagram contains *chance nodes* representing random variables that we use in graphical models (see figure 14.14). It also has decision nodes and a utility node. A *decision node* represents a choice of actions. A *utility node* is where the utility is calculated. Decisions may be based on chance nodes and may affect other chance nodes and the utility node.

Inference on an influence diagram is an extension to belief propagation on a graphical model. Given evidence on some of the chance nodes, this evidence is propagated, and for each possible decision, the utility is calculated and the decision having the highest utility is chosen. The influence diagram for classification of a given input is shown in figure 14.14. Given the input, the decision node decides on a class, and for each choice we incur a certain utility (risk).

14.9 Notes

Graphical models have two advantages. One is that we can visualize the interaction of variables and have a better understanding of the process, for example, by using a causal generative model. The second is that by finding graph operations that correspond to basic probabilistic procedures such as Bayes' rule or marginalization, the task of inference can be mapped to general-purpose graph algorithms that can be efficiently represented and implemented.

The idea of visual representation of variables and dependencies between them as a graph, and the related factorization of a complicated global function of many variables as a product of local functions involving a small subset of the variables for each, seems to be used in different domains in decision making, coding, and signal processing; Kschischang, Frey, and Loeliger (2001) give a review.

The complexity of the inference algorithms on polytrees or junction trees is determined by the maximum number of parents or the size of the largest clique, and when this is large exact inference may be infeasible. In such a case, one needs to use an approximation or a sampling algorithm. Variational approximations and Markov chain Monte Carlo (MCMC) algorithms are discussed in Jordan et al. 1999, MacKay 2003, Andrieu et al. 2003, Bishop 2006, and Murphy 2012.

Graphical models are especially suited to represent Bayesian approaches where in addition to nodes for observed variables, we also have nodes for hidden variables as well as the model parameters. We may also introduce a hierarchy where we have nodes for hyperparameters—that is, second-level parameters for the priors of the first-level parameters.

Thinking of data as sampled from a causal generative model that can be visualized as a graph can ease understanding and also inference in many domains. For example, in text categorization, generating a text may be thought of as the process whereby an author decides to write a document on a number of topics and then chooses a set of words for each topic. In bioinformatics, one area among many where a graphical approach used is the modeling of a *phylogenetic tree*; namely, it is a directed graph whose leaves are the current species, whose nonterminal nodes are past ancestors that split into multiple species during a speciation event, and whose conditional probabilities depend on the evolutionary distance between a species and its ancestor (Jordan 2004).

PHYLOGENETIC TREE

The hidden Markov model we discuss in chapter 15 is one type of graphical model where inputs are dependent sequentially, as in speech recognition, where a word is a particular sequence of basic speech sounds called phonemes (Ghahramani 2001). Such *dynamic graphical models* find applications in many areas where there is a temporal dimension, such as speech, music, and so on (Zweig 2003; Bilmes and Bartels 2005).

Graphical models are also used in computer vision—for example, in information retrieval (Barnard et al. 2003) and scene analysis (Sudderth et al. 2008). A review of the use of graphical models in bioinformatics (and related software) is given in Donkers and Tuyls 2008.

14.10 Exercises

1. With two independent inputs in a classification problem, that is, $p(x_1, x_2|C) = p(x_1|C)p(x_2|C)$, how can we calculate $p(x_1|x_2, C)$? Derive the formula for $p(x_j|C_i) \sim \mathcal{N}(\mu_{ij}, \sigma_{ij}^2)$.

2. For a head-to-head node, show that equation 14.10 implies $P(X, Y) = P(X) \cdot P(Y)$.

   SOLUTION: We know that $P(X, Y, Z) = P(Z|X, Y)P(X, Y)$, and if we also know that $P(X, Y, Z) = P(X)P(Y)P(Z|X, Y)$, we see that $P(X, Y) = P(X)P(Y)$.

3. In figure 14.4, calculate $P(R|W)$, $P(R|W, S)$, and $P(R|W, \sim S)$.

   SOLUTION:

$$
\begin{aligned}
P(R|W) &= \frac{P(R,W)}{P(W)} = \frac{\sum_S P(R,W,S)}{\sum_R \sum_S P(R,W,S)} \\
&= \frac{\sum_S P(R)P(S)P(W|R,S)}{\sum_R \sum_S P(R)P(S)P(W|R,S)} \\
P(R|W,S) &= \frac{P(R,W,S)}{P(W,S)} = \frac{P(R)P(S)P(W|R,S)}{\sum_R P(R)P(S)P(W|R,S)} \\
P(R|W,\sim S) &= \frac{P(R,W,\sim S)}{P(W,\sim S)} = \frac{P(R)P(\sim S)P(W|R,\sim S)}{\sum_R P(R)P(\sim S)P(W|R,\sim S)}
\end{aligned}
$$

4. In equation 14.30, X is binary. How do we need to modify it if X can take one of K discrete values?

   SOLUTION: Let us say there are $j = 1, \ldots, K$ states. Then, keeping the model linear, we need to parameterize each by a separate $\boldsymbol{w}_j$ and use softmax to map to probabilities:

$$P(X = j | U_1, \ldots, U_k, \{w_{ji}\}) = \frac{\exp \sum_{i=1}^{k} w_{ji} U_i + w_{j0}}{\sum_{l=1}^{K} \exp \sum_{i=1}^{k} w_{li} U_i + w_{l0}}$$

5. Show that in a directed graph where the joint distribution is written as equation 14.12, $\sum_{\boldsymbol{x}} p(\boldsymbol{x}) = 1$.

   SOLUTION: The terms cancel when we sum up over all possible values because these are probabilities. Let us, for example, take figure 14.3:

$$\begin{aligned}
P(X,Y,Z) &= P(X)P(Y|X)P(Z|X) \\
\sum_X \sum_Y \sum_Z P(X,Y,Z) &= \sum_X \sum_Y \sum_Z P(X)P(Y|X)P(Z|X) \\
&= \sum_X \sum_Y P(X)P(Y|X) \sum_Z P(Z|X) \\
&= \sum_X \sum_Y P(X)P(Y|X) \sum_Z \frac{P(Z,X)}{P(X)} \\
&= \sum_X \sum_Y P(X)P(Y|X) \frac{P(X)}{P(X)} \\
&= \sum_X \sum_Y P(X)P(Y|X) \\
&= \sum_X P(X) \sum_Y P(Y|X) = \sum_X P(X) = 1
\end{aligned}$$

6. Draw the Necker cube as a graphical model defining links to indicate mutually reinforcing or inhibiting relations between different corner interpretations.

   SOLUTION: We are going to have nodes corresponding to corners, and they take values depending on the interpretation; there will be positive, enforcing, excitatory connections between corners that are part of the same interpretation, and negative, inhibitory connections between corners that are part of different interpretations (see figure 14.15).

7. Write down the graphical model for linear logistic regression for two classes in the manner of figure 14.7.

8. Propose a suitable goodness measure that can be used in learning graph structure as a state-space search. What are suitable operators?

   SOLUTION: We need a *score function* that is the sum of two parts, one quantifying a goodness of fit, that is, how likely is the data given the model, and one quantifying the complexity of the graph, to alleviate overfitting. In measuring complexity, we must take into account the total number of nodes and

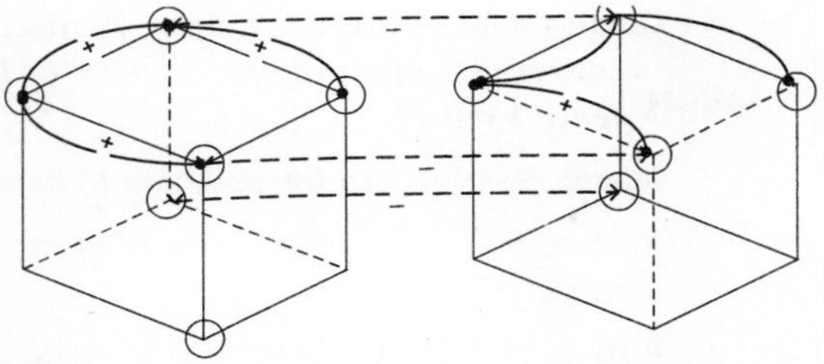

Figure 14.15 Two different interpretations of the Necker cube. Solid lines, marked by '+,' are excitatory and dashed lines, marked by '−,' are inhibitory.

the number of parameters needed to represent the conditional probability distributions. For example, we should try to have nodes with as few parents as possible. Possible operators are there to add/remove an edge and add/remove a hidden node.

9. Generally, in a newspaper, a reporter writes a series of articles on successive days related to the same topics as the story develops. How can we model this using a graphical model?

14.11 References

Andrieu, C., N. de Freitas, A. Doucet, and M. I. Jordan. 2003. "An Introduction to MCMC for Machine Learning." *Machine Learning* 50:5–43.

Barnard, K., P. Duygulu, D. Forsyth, N. de Freitas, D. M. Blei, and M. I. Jordan. 2003. "Matching Words and Pictures." *Journal of Machine Learning Research* 3:1107–1135.

Bilmes, J., and C. Bartels. 2005. "Graphical Model Architectures for Speech Recognition." *IEEE Signal Processing Magazine* 22:89–100.

Bishop, C. M. 2006. *Pattern Recognition and Machine Learning.* New York: Springer.

Buntine, W. 1996. "A Guide to the Literature on Learning Probabilistic Networks from Data." *IEEE Transactions on Knowledge and Data Engineering* 8:195–210.

Cowell, R. G., A. P. Dawid, S. L. Lauritzen, and D. J. Spiegelhalter. 1999. *Probabilistic Networks and Expert Systems.* New York: Springer.

Donkers, J., and K. Tuyls. 2008. "Belief Networks in Bioinformatics." In *Computational Intelligence in Bioinformatics*, ed. A. Kelemen, A. Abraham, and Y. Chen, 75–111. Berlin: Springer.

Ghahramani, Z. 2001. "An Introduction to Hidden Markov Models and Bayesian Networks." *International Journal of Pattern Recognition and Artificial Intelligence* 15:9–42.

Jensen, F. 1996. *An Introduction to Bayesian Networks.* New York: Springer.

Jordan, M. I., ed. 1999. *Learning in Graphical Models.* Cambridge, MA: MIT Press.

Jordan, M. I. 2004. "Graphical Models." *Statistical Science* 19:140–155.

Jordan, M. I., Z. Ghahramani, T. S. Jaakkola, and L. K. Saul. 1999. "An Introduction to Variational Methods for Graphical Models." In *Learning in Graphical Models*, ed. M. I. Jordan, 105–161. Cambridge, MA: MIT Press.

Kschischang, F. R., B. J. Frey, and H.-A. Loeliger. 2001. "Factor Graphs and the Sum-Product Algorithm." *IEEE Transactions on Information Theory* 47:498–519.

Lauritzen, S. L., and D. J. Spiegelhalter. 1988. "Local Computations with Probabilities on Graphical Structures and their Application to Expert Systems." *Journal of Royal Statistical Society B* 50:157–224.

MacKay, D. J. C. 2003. *Information Theory, Inference, and Learning Algorithms.* Cambridge, UK: Cambridge University Press.

Murphy, K. P. 2012. *Machine Learning: A Probabilistic Perspective.* Cambridge, MA: MIT Press.

Neapolitan, R. E. 2004. *Learning Bayesian Networks.* Upper Saddle River, NJ: Pearson.

Pearl, J. 1988. *Probabilistic Reasoning in Intelligent Systems: Networks of Plausible Inference.* San Francisco, CA: Morgan Kaufmann.

Pearl, J. 2000. *Causality: Models, Reasoning, and Inference.* Cambridge, UK: Cambridge University Press.

Sudderth, E. B., A. Torralba, W. T. Freeman, and A. S. Willsky. 2008. "Describing Visual Scenes Using Transformed Objects and Parts." *International Journal of Computer Vision* 77:291–330.

Zweig, G. 2003. "Bayesian Network Structures and Inference Techniques for Automatic Speech Recognition." *Computer Speech and Language* 17:173–193.

15 *Hidden Markov Models*

We relax the assumption that instances in a sample are independent and introduce Markov models to model input sequences as generated by a parametric random process. We discuss how this modeling is done as well as introduce an algorithm for learning the parameters of such a model from example sequences.

15.1 Introduction

UNTIL NOW, we assumed that the instances that constitute a sample are iid. This has the advantage that the likelihood of the sample is simply the product of the likelihoods of the individual instances. This assumption, however, is not valid in applications where successive instances are dependent. For example, in a word successive letters are dependent; in English 'h' is very likely to follow 't' but not 'x'. Such processes where there is a *sequence* of observations—for example, letters in a word, base pairs in a DNA sequence—cannot be modeled as simple probability distributions. A similar example is speech recognition where speech utterances are composed of speech primitives called phonemes; only certain sequences of phonemes are allowed, which are the words of the language. At a higher level, words can be written or spoken in certain sequences to form a sentence as defined by the syntactic and semantic rules of the language.

A sequence can be characterized as being generated by a *parametric random process*. In this chapter, we discuss how this modeling is done and also how the parameters of such a model can be learned from a training sample of example sequences.

15.2 Discrete Markov Processes

Consider a system that at any time is in one of a set of N distinct states: $S_1, S_2, \ldots, S_N$. The state at time t is denoted as $q_t, t = 1, 2, \ldots$, so, for example, $q_t = S_i$ means that at time t, the system is in state S_i. Though we write "time" as if this should be a temporal sequence, the methodology is valid for any sequencing, be it in time, space, position on the DNA string, and so forth.

At regularly spaced discrete times, the system moves to a state with a given probability, depending on the values of the previous states:

$$P(q_{t+1} = S_j | q_t = S_i, q_{t-1} = S_k, \cdots)$$

MARKOV MODEL

For the special case of a first-order *Markov model*, the state at time $t+1$ depends only on state at time t, regardless of the states in the previous times:

$$P(q_{t+1} = S_j | q_t = S_i, q_{t-1} = S_k, \cdots) = P(q_{t+1} = S_j | q_t = S_i) \quad (15.1)$$

This corresponds to saying that, given the present state, the future is independent of the past. This is just a mathematical version of the saying, Today is the first day of the rest of your life.

TRANSITION PROBABILITY

We further simplify the model—that is, regularize—by assuming that the *transition probability* from S_i to S_j is independent of time:

$$a_{ij} \equiv P(q_{t+1} = S_j | q_t = S_i) \quad (15.2)$$

satisfying

$$a_{ij} \geq 0 \text{ and } \sum_{j=1}^{N} a_{ij} = 1 \quad (15.3)$$

So, going from S_i to S_j has the same probability no matter when it happens, or where it happens in the observation sequence. $\mathbf{A} = [a_{ij}]$ is a $N \times N$ matrix whose rows sum to 1.

STOCHASTIC AUTOMATON

This can be seen as a *stochastic automaton* (see figure 15.1). From each state S_i, the system moves to state S_j with probability a_{ij}, and this probability is the same for any t. The only special case is the first state.

INITIAL PROBABILITY

We define the *initial probability*, π_i, which is the probability that the first state in the sequence is S_i:

$$\pi_i \equiv P(q_1 = S_i) \quad (15.4)$$

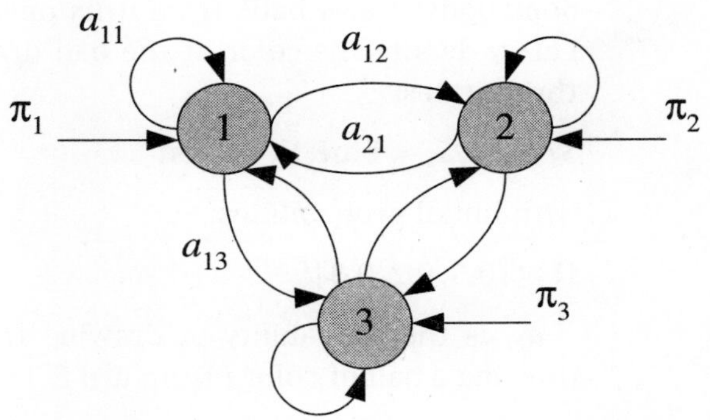

Figure 15.1 Example of a Markov model with three states. This is a stochastic automaton where π_i is the probability that the system starts in state S_i, and a_{ij} is the probability that the system moves from state S_i to state S_j.

satisfying

$$\sum_{i=1}^{N} \pi_i = 1 \tag{15.5}$$

$\mathbf{\Pi} = [\pi_i]$ is a vector of N elements that sum to 1.

OBSERVABLE MARKOV MODEL

In an *observable Markov model,* the states are observable. At any time t, we know q_t, and as the system moves from one state to another, we get an observation sequence that is a sequence of states. The output of the process is the set of states at each instant of time where each state corresponds to a physical observable event.

We have an observation sequence O that is the state sequence $O = Q = \{q_1 q_2 \cdots q_T\}$, whose probability is given as

$$P(O = Q|\mathbf{A}, \mathbf{\Pi}) = P(q_1) \prod_{t=2}^{T} P(q_t|q_{t-1}) = \pi_{q_1} a_{q_1 q_2} \cdots a_{q_{T-1} q_T} \tag{15.6}$$

π_{q_1} is the probability that the first state is q_1, $a_{q_1 q_2}$ is the probability of going from q_1 to q_2, and so on. We multiply these probabilities to get the probability of the whole sequence.

Let us now see an example (Rabiner and Juang 1986) to help us demonstrate. Assume we have N urns where each urn contains balls of only one color. So there is an urn of red balls, another of blue balls, and so forth.

Somebody draws balls from urns one by one and shows us their color. Let q_t denote the color of the ball drawn at time t. Let us say we have three states:

S_1 : red, S_2 = blue, S_3 : green

with initial probabilities:

$\mathbf{\Pi} = [0.5, 0.2, 0.3]^T$

a_{ij} is the probability of drawing from urn j (a ball of color j) after drawing a ball of color i from urn i. The transition matrix is, for example,

$$\mathbf{A} = \begin{bmatrix} 0.4 & 0.3 & 0.3 \\ 0.2 & 0.6 & 0.2 \\ 0.1 & 0.1 & 0.8 \end{bmatrix}$$

Given $\mathbf{\Pi}$ and $\mathbf{A}$, it is easy to generate K random sequences each of length T. Let us see how we can calculate the probability of a sequence. Assume that the first four balls are "red, red, green, green." This corresponds to the observation sequence $O = \{S_1, S_1, S_3, S_3\}$. Its probability is

$$\begin{aligned} P(O|\mathbf{A}, \mathbf{\Pi}) &= P(S_1) \cdot P(S_1|S_1) \cdot P(S_3|S_1) \cdot P(S_3|S_3) \\ &= \pi_1 \cdot a_{11} \cdot a_{13} \cdot a_{33} \\ &= 0.5 \cdot 0.4 \cdot 0.3 \cdot 0.8 = 0.048 \end{aligned} \tag{15.7}$$

Now, let us see how we can learn the parameters, $\mathbf{\Pi}, \mathbf{A}$. Given K sequences of length T, where q_t^k is the state at time t of sequence k, the initial probability estimate is the number of sequences starting with S_i divided by the number of sequences:

$$\hat{\pi}_i = \frac{\#\{\text{sequences starting with } S_i\}}{\#\{\text{sequences}\}} = \frac{\sum_k 1(q_1^k = S_i)}{K} \tag{15.8}$$

where $1(b)$ is 1 if b is true and 0 otherwise.

As for the transition probabilities, the estimate for a_{ij} is the number of transitions from S_i to S_j divided by the total number of transitions from S_i over all sequences:

$$\hat{a}_{ij} = \frac{\#\{\text{transitions from } S_i \text{ to } S_j\}}{\#\{\text{transitions from } S_i\}} = \frac{\sum_k \sum_{t=1}^{T-1} 1(q_t^k = S_i \text{ and } q_{t+1}^k = S_j)}{\sum_k \sum_{t=1}^{T-1} 1(q_t^k = S_i)} \tag{15.9}$$

$\hat{a}_{12}$ is the number of times a blue ball follows a red ball divided by the total number of red ball draws over all sequences.

15.3 Hidden Markov Models

HIDDEN MARKOV MODEL

In a *hidden Markov model* (HMM), the states are not observable, but when we visit a state, an observation is recorded that is a probabilistic function of the state. We assume a discrete observation in each state from the set $\{v_1, v_2, \ldots, v_M\}$:

$$b_j(m) \equiv P(O_t = v_m | q_t = S_j) \tag{15.10}$$

OBSERVATION PROBABILITY
EMISSION PROBABILITY

$b_j(m)$ is the *observation probability*, or *emission probability*, that we observe the value $v_m, m = 1, \ldots, M$ in state S_j. We again assume a homogeneous model in which the probabilities do not depend on t. The values thus observed constitute the observation sequence O. The state sequence Q is not observed, that is what makes the model "hidden," but it should be inferred from the observation sequence O. Note that there are typically many different state sequences Q that could have generated the same observation sequence O, but with different probabilities; just as, given an iid sample from a normal distribution, there are an infinite number of (μ, σ) value pairs possible, we are interested in the one having the highest likelihood of generating the sample.

Note also that in this case of a hidden Markov model, there are two sources of randomness. In addition to randomly moving from one state to another, the observation in a state is also random.

Let us go back to our example. The hidden case corresponds to the urn-and-ball example where each urn contains balls of different colors. Let $b_j(m)$ denote the probability of drawing a ball of color m from urn j. We again observe a sequence of ball colors but without knowing the sequence of urns from which the balls were drawn. So it is as if now the urns are placed behind a curtain and somebody picks a ball at random from one of the urns and shows us only the ball, without showing us the urn from which it is picked. The ball is returned to the urn to keep the probabilities the same. The number of ball colors may be different from the number of urns. For example, let us say we have three urns and the observation sequence is

$$O = \{\text{red, red, green, blue, yellow}\}$$

In the previous case, knowing the observation (ball color), we knew the state (urn) exactly because there were separate urns for separate colors and each urn contained balls of only one color. The observable model is a special case of the hidden model where $M = N$ and $b_j(m)$ is 1 if $j = m$

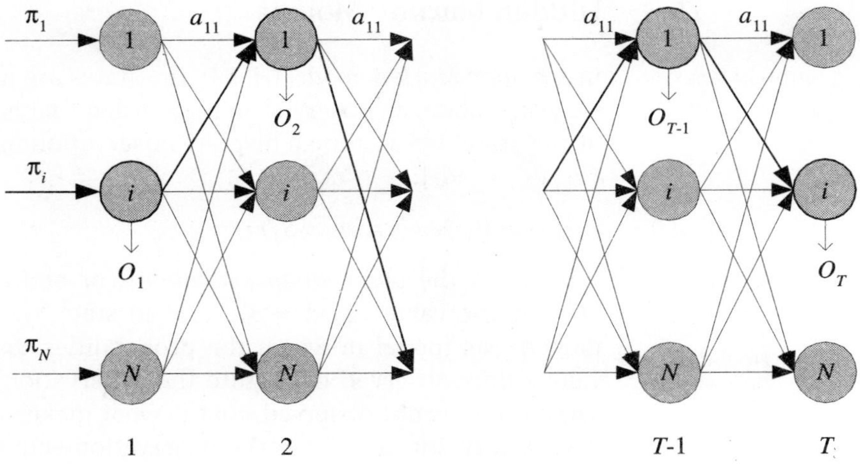

Figure 15.2 An HMM unfolded in time as a lattice (or trellis) showing all the possible trajectories. One path, shown in thicker lines, is the actual (unknown) state trajectory that generated the observation sequence.

and 0 otherwise. But in the case of a hidden model, a ball could have been picked from any urn. In this case, for the same observation sequence O, there may be many possible state sequences Q that could have generated O (see figure 15.2).

To summarize and formalize, an HMM has the following elements:

1. N: Number of states in the model

$$S = \{S_1, S_2, \ldots, S_N\}$$

2. M: Number of distinct observation symbols in the *alphabet*

$$V = \{v_1, v_2, \ldots, v_M\}$$

3. State transition probabilities:

$$\mathbf{A} = [a_{ij}] \text{ where } a_{ij} \equiv P(q_{t+1} = S_j | q_t = S_i)$$

4. Observation probabilities:

$$\mathbf{B} = [b_j(m)] \text{ where } b_j(m) \equiv P(O_t = v_m | q_t = S_j)$$

5. Initial state probabilities:

$$\Pi = [\pi_i] \text{ where } \pi_i \equiv P(q_1 = S_i)$$

N and M are implicitly defined in the other parameters so $\lambda = (\mathbf{A}, \mathbf{B}, \mathbf{\Pi})$ is taken as the parameter set of an HMM. Given λ, the model can be used to generate an arbitrary number of observation sequences of arbitrary length, but as usual, we are interested in the other direction, that of estimating the parameters of the model given a training set of sequences.

15.4 Three Basic Problems of HMMs

Given a number of sequences of observations, we are interested in three problems:

1. Given a model λ, we would like to evaluate the probability of any given observation sequence, $O = \{O_1 O_2 \cdots O_T\}$, namely, $P(O|\lambda)$.

2. Given a model λ and an observation sequence O, we would like to find out the state sequence $Q = \{q_1 q_2 \cdots q_T\}$, which has the highest probability of generating O; namely, we want to find Q^* that maximizes $P(Q|O, \lambda)$.

3. Given a training set of observation sequences, $\mathcal{X} = \{O^k\}_k$, we would like to learn the model that maximizes the probability of generating $\mathcal{X}$; namely, we want to find λ^* that maximizes $P(\mathcal{X}|\lambda)$.

Let us see solutions to these one by one, with each solution used to solve the next problem, until we get to calculating λ or learning a model from data.

15.5 Evaluation Problem

Given an observation sequence $O = \{O_1 O_2 \cdots O_T\}$ and a state sequence $Q = \{q_1 q_2 \cdots q_T\}$, the probability of observing O given the state sequence Q is simply

$$P(O|Q, \lambda) = \prod_{t=1}^{T} P(O_t|q_t, \lambda) = b_{q_1}(O_1) \cdot b_{q_2}(O_2) \cdots b_{q_T}(O_T) \tag{15.11}$$

which we cannot calculate because we do not know the state sequence. The probability of the state sequence Q is

$$P(Q|\lambda) = P(q_1)\prod_{t=2}^{T} P(q_t|q_{t-1}) = \pi_{q_1} a_{q_1q_2} \cdots a_{q_{T-1}q_T} \tag{15.12}$$

Then the joint probability is

$$\begin{aligned} P(O,Q|\lambda) &= P(q_1)\prod_{t=2}^{T} P(q_t|q_{t-1}) \prod_{t=1}^{T} P(O_t|q_t) \\ &= \pi_{q_1} b_{q_1}(O_1) a_{q_1q_2} b_{q_2}(O_2) \cdots a_{q_{T-1}q_T} b_{q_T}(O_T) \end{aligned} \tag{15.13}$$

We can compute $P(O|\lambda)$ by marginalizing over the joint, namely, by summing up over all possible Q:

$$P(O|\lambda) = \sum_{\text{all possible } Q} P(O,Q|\lambda)$$

However, this is not practical since there are N^T possible Q, assuming that all the probabilities are nonzero. Fortunately, there is an efficient procedure to calculate $P(O|\lambda)$, which is called the *forward-backward procedure* (see figure 15.3). It is based on the idea of dividing the observation sequence into two parts: the first one starting from time 1 until time t, and the second one from time $t+1$ until T.

FORWARD-BACKWARD PROCEDURE

We define the *forward variable* $\alpha_t(i)$ as the probability of observing the partial sequence $\{O_1 \cdots O_t\}$ until time t and being in S_i at time t, given the model λ:

FORWARD VARIABLE

$$\alpha_t(i) \equiv P(O_1 \cdots O_t, q_t = S_i|\lambda) \tag{15.14}$$

The nice thing about this is that it can be calculated recursively by accumulating results on the way.

- Initialization:

$$\begin{aligned} \alpha_1(i) &\equiv P(O_1, q_1 = S_i|\lambda) \\ &= P(O_1|q_1 = S_i, \lambda)P(q_1 = S_i|\lambda) \\ &= \pi_i b_i(O_1) \end{aligned} \tag{15.15}$$

- Recursion (see figure 15.3a):

$$\alpha_{t+1}(j) \equiv P(O_1 \cdots O_{t+1}, q_{t+1} = S_j|\lambda)$$

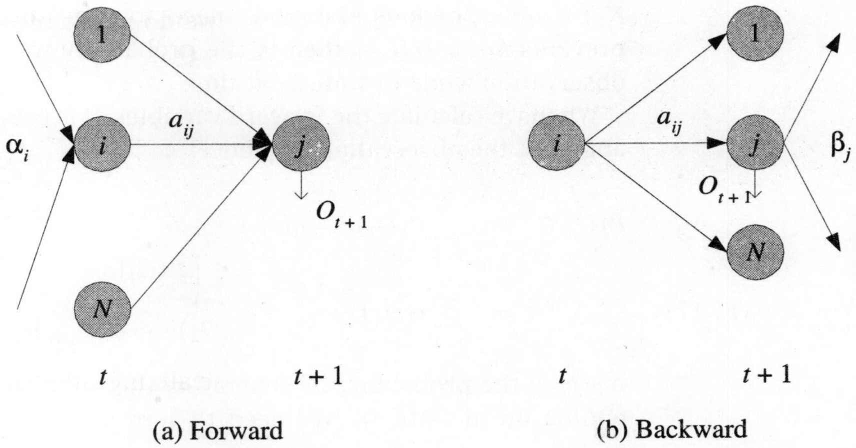

Figure 15.3 Forward-backward procedure: (a) computation of $\alpha_t(j)$ and (b) computation of $\beta_t(i)$.

$$
\begin{aligned}
&= P(O_1 \cdots O_{t+1} | q_{t+1} = S_j, \lambda) P(q_{t+1} = S_j | \lambda) \\
&= P(O_1 \cdots O_t | q_{t+1} = S_j, \lambda) P(O_{t+1} | q_{t+1} = S_j, \lambda) P(q_{t+1} = S_j | \lambda) \\
&= P(O_1 \cdots O_t, q_{t+1} = S_j | \lambda) P(O_{t+1} | q_{t+1} = S_j, \lambda) \\
&= P(O_{t+1} | q_{t+1} = S_j, \lambda) \sum_i P(O_1 \cdots O_t, q_t = S_i, q_{t+1} = S_j | \lambda) \\
&= P(O_{t+1} | q_{t+1} = S_j, \lambda) \\
&\quad \sum_i P(O_1 \cdots O_t, q_{t+1} = S_j | q_t = S_i, \lambda) P(q_t = S_i | \lambda) \\
&= P(O_{t+1} | q_{t+1} = S_j, \lambda) \\
&\quad \sum_i P(O_1 \cdots O_t | q_t = S_i, \lambda) P(q_{t+1} = S_j | q_t = S_i, \lambda) P(q_t = S_i | \lambda) \\
&= P(O_{t+1} | q_{t+1} = S_j, \lambda) \\
&\quad \sum_i P(O_1 \cdots O_t, q_t = S_i | \lambda) P(q_{t+1} = S_j | q_t = S_i, \lambda)
\end{aligned}
$$

$$
(15.16) \qquad = \left[\sum_{i=1}^{N} \alpha_t(i) a_{ij} \right] b_j(O_{t+1})
$$

$\alpha_t(i)$ explains the first t observations and ends in state S_i. We multiply this by the probability a_{ij} to move to state S_j, and because there are

N possible previous states, we need to sum up over all such possible previous S_i. $b_j(O_{t+1})$ then is the probability we generate the $(t+1)$st observation while in state S_j at time $t+1$.

When we calculate the forward variables, it is easy to calculate the probability of the observation sequence:

$$\begin{aligned} P(O|\lambda) &= \sum_{i=1}^{N} P(O, q_T = S_i|\lambda) \\ &= \sum_{i=1}^{N} \alpha_T(i) \qquad (15.17) \end{aligned}$$

$\alpha_T(i)$ is the probability of generating the full observation sequence and ending up in state S_i. We need to sum up over all such possible final states.

Computing $\alpha_t(i)$ is $\mathcal{O}(N^2T)$, and this solves our first evaluation problem in a reasonable amount of time. We do not need it now but let us similarly define the *backward variable*, $\beta_t(i)$, which is the probability of being in S_i at time t and observing the partial sequence $O_{t+1} \cdots O_T$:

BACKWARD VARIABLE

$$\beta_t(i) \equiv P(O_{t+1} \cdots O_T | q_t = S_i, \lambda) \qquad (15.18)$$

This can again be recursively computed as follows, this time going in the backward direction:

- Initialization (arbitrarily to 1):

$$\beta_T(i) = 1$$

- Recursion (see figure 15.3b):

$$\begin{aligned} \beta_t(i) &\equiv P(O_{t+1} \cdots O_T | q_t = S_i, \lambda) \\ &= \sum_j P(O_{t+1} \cdots O_T, q_{t+1} = S_j | q_t = S_i, \lambda) \\ &= \sum_j P(O_{t+1} \cdots O_T | q_{t+1} = S_j, q_t = S_i, \lambda) P(q_{t+1} = S_j | q_t = S_i, \lambda) \\ &= \sum_j P(O_{t+1} | q_{t+1} = S_j, q_t = S_i, \lambda) \\ &\quad P(O_{t+2} \cdots O_T | q_{t+1} = S_j, q_t = S_i, \lambda) P(q_{t+1} = S_j | q_t = S_i, \lambda) \\ &= \sum_j P(O_{t+1} | q_{t+1} = S_j, \lambda) \end{aligned}$$

$$P(O_{t+2}\cdots O_T|q_{t+1}=S_j,\lambda)P(q_{t+1}=S_j|q_t=S_i,\lambda)$$

$$(15.19)\qquad = \sum_{j=1}^{N} a_{ij}b_j(O_{t+1})\beta_{t+1}(j)$$

When in state S_i, we can go to N possible next states S_j, each with probability a_{ij}. While there, we generate the $(t+1)$st observation and $\beta_{t+1}(j)$ explains all the observations after time $t+1$, continuing from there.

One word of caution about implementation is necessary here: Both α_t and β_t values are calculated by multiplying small probabilities, and with long sequences we risk getting underflow. To avoid this, at each time step, we normalize $\alpha_t(i)$ by multiplying it with

$$c_t = \frac{1}{\sum_j \alpha_t(j)}$$

We also normalize $\beta_t(i)$ by multiplying it with the same c_t ($\beta_t(i)$ do not sum to 1). We cannot use equation 15.17 after normalization; instead, we have (Rabiner 1989)

$$(15.20)\qquad P(O|\lambda) = \frac{1}{\prod_t c_t} \text{ or } \log P(O|\lambda) = -\sum_t \log c_t$$

15.6 Finding the State Sequence

We now move on to the second problem, that of finding the state sequence $Q = \{q_1q_2\cdots q_T\}$ having the highest probability of generating the observation sequence $O = \{O_1O_2\cdots O_T\}$, given the model λ.

Let us define $\gamma_t(i)$ as the probability of being in state S_i at time t, given O and λ, which can be computed as follows:

$$(15.21)\qquad \gamma_t(i) \equiv P(q_t=S_i|O,\lambda)$$

$$= \frac{P(O|q_t=S_i,\lambda)P(q_t=S_i|\lambda)}{P(O|\lambda)}$$

$$= \frac{P(O_1\cdots O_t|q_t=S_i,\lambda)P(O_{t+1}\cdots O_T|q_t=S_i,\lambda)P(q_t=S_i|\lambda)}{\sum_{j=1}^{N} P(O,q_t=S_j|\lambda)}$$

$$= \frac{P(O_1\cdots O_t,q_t=S_i|\lambda)P(O_{t+1}\cdots O_T|q_t=S_i,\lambda)}{\sum_{j=1}^{N} P(O|q_t=S_j,\lambda)P(q_t=S_j|\lambda)}$$

$$(15.22)\qquad = \frac{\alpha_t(i)\beta_t(i)}{\sum_{j=1}^{N}\alpha_t(j)\beta_t(j)}$$

Here we see how nicely $\alpha_t(i)$ and $\beta_t(i)$ split the sequence between them: The forward variable $\alpha_t(i)$ explains the starting part of the sequence until time t and ends in S_i, and the backward variable $\beta_t(i)$ takes it from there and explains the ending part until time T.

The numerator $\alpha_t(i)\beta_t(i)$ explains the whole sequence given that at time t, the system is in state S_i. We need to normalize by dividing this over all possible intermediate states that can be traversed at time t, and guarantee that $\sum_i \gamma_t(i) = 1$.

To find the state sequence, for each time step t, we can choose the state that has the highest probability:

$$q_t^* = \arg\max_i \gamma_t(i) \tag{15.23}$$

but this may choose S_i and S_j as the most probable states at time t and $t+1$ even when $a_{ij} = 0$. To find the single best state *sequence* (path), we use the *Viterbi algorithm*, based on dynamic programming, which takes such transition probabilities into account.

VITERBI ALGORITHM

Given state sequence $Q = q_1 q_2 \cdots q_T$ and observation sequence $O = O_1 \cdots O_T$, we define $\delta_t(i)$ as the probability of the highest probability path at time t that accounts for the first t observations and ends in S_i:

$$\delta_t(i) \equiv \max_{q_1 q_2 \cdots q_{t-1}} p(q_1 q_2 \cdots q_{t-1}, q_t = S_i, O_1 \cdots O_t | \lambda) \tag{15.24}$$

Then we can recursively calculate $\delta_{t+1}(i)$ and the optimal path can be read by backtracking from T, choosing the most probable at each instant. The algorithm is as follows:

1. Initialization:

$$\begin{aligned} \delta_1(i) &= \pi_i b_i(O_1) \\ \psi_1(i) &= 0 \end{aligned}$$

2. Recursion:

$$\begin{aligned} \delta_t(j) &= \max_i \delta_{t-1}(i) a_{ij} \cdot b_j(O_t) \\ \psi_t(j) &= \arg\max_i \delta_{t-1}(i) a_{ij} \end{aligned}$$

3. Termination:

$$\begin{aligned} p^* &= \max_i \delta_T(i) \\ q_T^* &= \arg\max_i \delta_T(i) \end{aligned}$$

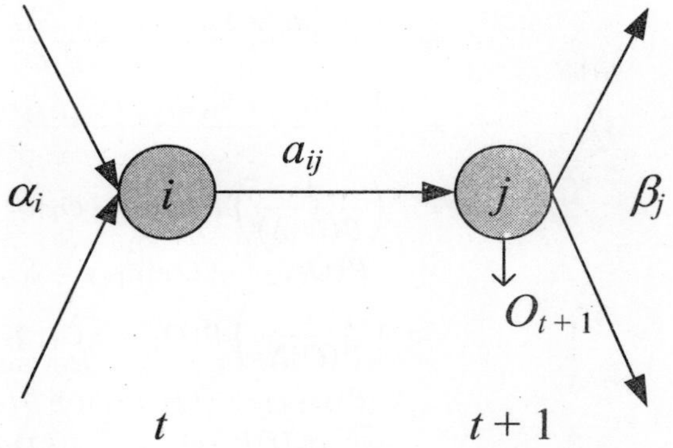

Figure 15.4 Computation of arc probabilities, $\xi_t(i,j)$.

4. Path (state sequence) backtracking:

$$q_t^* = \psi_{t+1}(q_{t+1}^*),\ t = T-1, T-2, \ldots, 1$$

Using the lattice structure of figure 15.2, $\psi_t(j)$ keeps track of the state that maximizes $\delta_t(j)$ at time $t-1$, that is, the best previous state. The Viterbi algorithm has the same complexity with the forward phase, where instead of the sum, we take the maximum at each step.

15.7 Learning Model Parameters

We now move on to the third problem, learning an HMM from data. The approach is maximum likelihood, and we would like to calculate λ^* that maximizes the likelihood of the sample of training sequences, $\mathcal{X} = \{O^k\}_{k=1}^K$, namely, $P(\mathcal{X}|\lambda)$. We start by defining a new variable that will become handy later on.

We define $\xi_t(i,j)$ as the probability of being in S_i at time t and in S_j at time $t+1$, given the whole observation O and λ:

(15.25) $$\xi_t(i,j) \equiv P(q_t = S_i, q_{t+1} = S_j | O, \lambda)$$

which can be computed as follows (see figure 15.4):

$$\xi_t(i,j) \equiv P(q_t = S_i, q_{t+1} = S_j | O, \lambda)$$

$$
\begin{aligned}
&= \frac{P(O|q_t = S_i, q_{t+1} = S_j, \lambda)P(q_t = S_i, q_{t+1} = S_j|\lambda)}{P(O|\lambda)} \\
&= \frac{P(O|q_t = S_i, q_{t+1} = S_j, \lambda)P(q_{t+1} = S_j|q_t = S_i, \lambda)P(q_t = S_i|\lambda)}{P(O|\lambda)} \\
&= \left(\frac{1}{P(O|\lambda)}\right) P(O_1 \cdots O_t|q_t = S_i, \lambda)P(O_{t+1}|q_{t+1} = S_j, \lambda) \\
&\quad P(O_{t+2} \cdots O_T|q_{t+1} = S_j, \lambda)a_{ij}P(q_t = S_i|\lambda) \\
&= \left(\frac{1}{P(O|\lambda)}\right) P(O_1 \cdots O_t, q_t = S_i|\lambda)P(O_{t+1}|q_{t+1} = S_j, \lambda) \\
&\quad P(O_{t+2} \cdots O_T|q_{t+1} = S_j, \lambda)a_{ij} \\
&= \frac{\alpha_t(i)b_j(O_{t+1})\beta_{t+1}(j)a_{ij}}{\sum_k \sum_l P(q_t = S_k, q_{t+1} = S_l, O|\lambda)}
\end{aligned}
$$

(15.26)
$$
= \frac{\alpha_t(i)a_{ij}b_j(O_{t+1})\beta_{t+1}(j)}{\sum_k \sum_l \alpha_t(k)a_{kl}b_l(O_{t+1})\beta_{t+1}(l)}
$$

$\alpha_t(i)$ explains the first t observations and ends in state S_i at time t. We move on to state S_j with probability a_{ij}, generate the $(t+1)$st observation, and continue from S_j at time $t+1$ to generate the rest of the observation sequence. We normalize by dividing for all such possible pairs that can be visited at time t and $t+1$.

If we want, we can also calculate the probability of being in state S_i at time t by marginalizing over the arc probabilities for all possible next states:

(15.27)
$$
\gamma_t(i) = \sum_{j=1}^{N} \xi_t(i, j)
$$

Note that if the Markov model were not hidden but observable, both $\gamma_t(i)$ and $\xi_t(i, j)$ would be 0/1. In this case when they are not, we estimate them with posterior probabilities that give us *soft counts*. This is just like the difference between supervised classification and unsupervised clustering where we did and did not know the class labels, respectively. In unsupervised clustering using EM (section 7.4), not knowing the class labels, we estimated them first (in the E-step) and calculated the parameters with these estimates (in the M-step).

SOFT COUNTS

BAUM-WELCH ALGORITHM

Similarly here we have the *Baum-Welch algorithm*, which is an EM procedure. At each iteration, first in the E-step, we compute $\xi_t(i, j)$ and $\gamma_t(i)$ values given the current $\lambda = (\mathbf{A}, \mathbf{B}, \mathbf{\Pi})$, and then in the M-step, we recalculate λ given $\xi_t(i, j)$ and $\gamma_t(i)$. These two steps are alternated until convergence during which, it has been shown, $P(O|\lambda)$ never decreases.

Assume indicator variables z_i^t as

$$z_i^t = \begin{cases} 1 & \text{if } q_t = S_i \\ 0 & \text{otherwise} \end{cases} \tag{15.28}$$

and

$$z_{ij}^t = \begin{cases} 1 & \text{if } q_t = S_i \text{ and } q_{t+1} = S_j \\ 0 & \text{otherwise} \end{cases} \tag{15.29}$$

These are 0/1 in the case of an observable Markov model and are hidden random variables in the case of an HMM. In this latter case, we estimate them in the E-step as

$$\begin{aligned} E[z_i^t] &= \gamma_t(i) \\ E[z_{ij}^t] &= \xi_t(i,j) \end{aligned} \tag{15.30}$$

In the M-step, we calculate the parameters given these estimated values. The expected number of transitions from S_i to S_j is $\sum_t \xi_t(i,j)$ and the total number of transitions from S_i is $\sum_t \gamma_t(i)$. The ratio of these two gives us the probability of transition from S_i to S_j at any time:

$$\hat{a}_{ij} = \frac{\sum_{t=1}^{T-1} \xi_t(i,j)}{\sum_{t=1}^{T-1} \gamma_t(i)} \tag{15.31}$$

Note that this is the same as equation 15.9, except that the actual counts are replaced by estimated soft counts.

The probability of observing v_m in S_j is the expected number of times v_m is observed when the system is in S_j over the total number of times the system is in S_j:

$$\hat{b}_j(m) = \frac{\sum_{t=1}^{T} \gamma_t(j) 1(O_t = v_m)}{\sum_{t=1}^{T} \gamma_t(j)} \tag{15.32}$$

When there are multiple observation sequences

$$\mathcal{X} = \{O^k\}_{k=1}^K$$

which we assume to be independent

$$P(\mathcal{X}|\lambda) = \prod_{k=1}^{K} P(O^k|\lambda)$$

the parameters are now averages over all observations in all sequences:

$$
\begin{aligned}
\hat{a}_{ij} &= \frac{\sum_{k=1}^{K}\sum_{t=1}^{T_k-1}\xi_t^k(i,j)}{\sum_{k=1}^{K}\sum_{t=1}^{T_k-1}\gamma_t^k(i)} \\
\hat{b}_j(m) &= \frac{\sum_{k=1}^{K}\sum_{t=1}^{T_k}\gamma_t^k(j)1(O_t^k = v_m)}{\sum_{k=1}^{K}\sum_{t=1}^{T_k}\gamma_t^k(j)} \\
\hat{\pi}_i &= \frac{\sum_{k=1}^{K}\gamma_1^k(i)}{K}
\end{aligned} \tag{15.33}
$$

15.8 Continuous Observations

In our discussion, we assumed discrete observations modeled as a multinomial

$$P(O_t|q_t = S_j, \lambda) = \prod_{m=1}^{M} b_j(m)^{r_m^t} \tag{15.34}$$

where

$$r_m^t = \begin{cases} 1 & \text{if } O_t = v_m \\ 0 & \text{otherwise} \end{cases} \tag{15.35}$$

If the inputs are continuous, one possibility is to discretize them and then use these discrete values as observations. Typically, a vector quantizer (section 7.3) is used for this purpose of converting continuous values to the discrete index of the closest reference vector. For example, in speech recognition, a word utterance is divided into short speech segments corresponding to phonemes or part of phonemes; after preprocessing, these are discretized using a vector quantizer and an HMM is then used to model a word utterance as a sequence of them.

We remember that k-means used for vector quantization is the hard version of a Gaussian mixture model:

$$p(O_t|q_t = S_j, \lambda) = \sum_{l=1}^{L} P(G_l)p(O_t|q_t = S_j, G_l, \lambda) \tag{15.36}$$

where

$$p(O_t|q_t = S_j, G_l, \lambda) \sim \mathcal{N}(\boldsymbol{\mu}_l, \boldsymbol{\Sigma}_l) \tag{15.37}$$

and the observations are kept continuous. In this case of Gaussian mixtures, EM equations can be derived for the component parameters (with suitable regularization to keep the number of parameters in check) and the mixture proportions (Rabiner 1989).

Let us see the case of a scalar continuous observation, $O_t \in \Re$. The easiest is to assume a normal distribution:

$$p(O_t|q_t = S_j, \lambda) \sim \mathcal{N}(\mu_j, \sigma_j^2) \tag{15.38}$$

which implies that in state S_j, the observation is drawn from a normal with mean μ_j and variance σ_j^2. The M-step equations in this case are

$$\begin{aligned} \hat{\mu}_j &= \frac{\sum_t \gamma_t(j) O_t}{\sum_t \gamma_t(j)} \\ \hat{\sigma}_j^2 &= \frac{\sum_t \gamma_t(j)(O_t - \hat{\mu}_j)^2}{\sum_t \gamma_t(j)} \end{aligned} \tag{15.39}$$

15.9 The HMM as a Graphical Model

We discussed graphical models in chapter 14, and the hidden Markov model can also be depicted as a graphical model. The three successive states q_{t-2}, q_{t-1}, q_t correspond to the three states on a chain in a first-order Markov model. The state at time t, q_t, depends only on the state at time $t-1$, q_{t-1}, and given q_{t-1}, q_t is independent of q_{t-2}

$$P(q_t|q_{t-1}, q_{t-2}) = P(q_t|q_{t-1})$$

as given by the state transition probability matrix $\mathbf{A}$ (see figure 15.5). Each hidden variable generates a discrete observation that is observed, as given by the observation probability matrix $\mathbf{B}$. The forward-backward procedure of hidden Markov models we discuss in this chapter is an application of belief propagation that we discussed in section 14.5.

Continuing with the graphical formalism, different HMM types can be devised and depicted as different graphical models. In figure 15.6a, an

INPUT-OUTPUT HMM

input-output HMM is shown where there are two separate observed input-output sequences and there is also a sequence of hidden states (Bengio and Frasconi 1996). In some applications this is the case, namely, additional to the observation sequence O_t, we have an input sequence, x_t, and we know that the observation depends also on the input. In such a case, we condition the observation O_t in state S_j on the input x^t and write $P(O_t|q_t = S_j, x_t)$. When the observations are numeric, for example, we replace equation 15.38 with a generalized model

$$p(O_t|q_t = S_j, x_t, \lambda) \sim \mathcal{N}(g_j(x^t|\theta_j), \sigma_j^2) \tag{15.40}$$

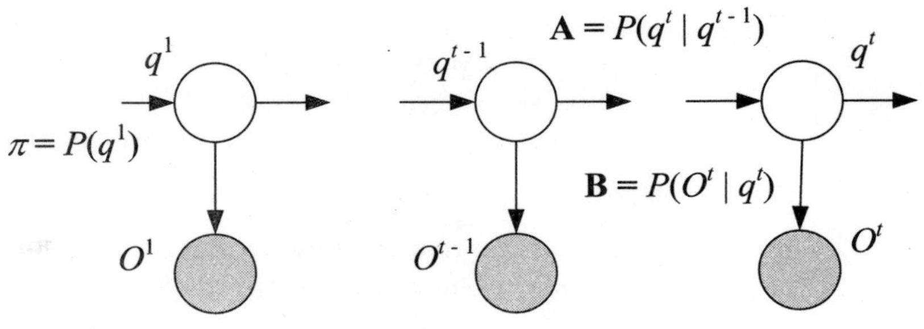

Figure 15.5 A hidden Markov model can be drawn as a graphical model where q^t are the hidden states and shaded O^t are observed.

where, for example, assuming a linear model, we have

$$g_j(x^t|w_j, w_{j0}) = w_j x^t + w_{j0} \tag{15.41}$$

If the observations are discrete and multinomial, we have a classifier taking x^t as input and generating a 1-of-M output, or we can generate posterior class probabilities and keep the observations continuous.

Similarly, the state transition probabilities can also be conditioned on the input, namely, $P(q_{t+1} = S_j | q_t = S_i, x_t)$, which is implemented by a classifier choosing the state at time $t + 1$ as a function of the state at time t and the input. This is a *Markov mixture of experts* (Meila and Jordan 1996) and is a generalization of the mixture of experts architecture (section 12.8) where the gating network keeps track of the decision it made in the previous time step. This has the advantage that the model is no longer homogeneous; different observation and transition probabilities are used at different time steps. There is still a single model for each state, parameterized by θ_j, but it generates different transition or observation probabilities depending on the input seen. It is possible that the input is not a single value but a window around time t making the input a vector; this allows handling applications where the input and observation sequences have different lengths.

MARKOV MIXTURE OF EXPERTS

Even if there is no other explicit input sequence, an HMM with input can be used by generating an "input" through some prespecified function of previous observations

$$\mathbf{x}_t = \boldsymbol{f}(O_{t-\tau}, \ldots, O_{t-1})$$

thereby providing a window of size τ of contextual input.

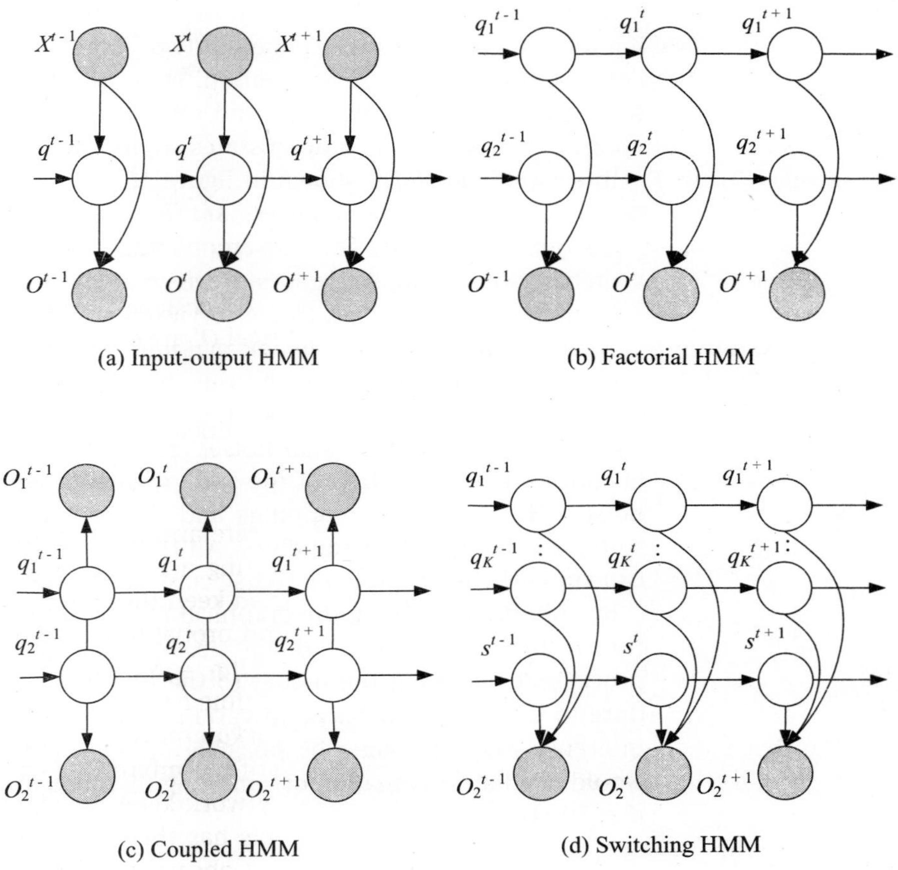

Figure 15.6 Different types of HMM model different assumptions about the way the observed data (shown shaded) is generated from Markov sequences of latent variables.

FACTORIAL HMM

PEDIGREE

Another HMM type that can be easily visualized is a *factorial HMM*, where there are multiple separate hidden sequences that interact to generate a single observation sequence. An example is a *pedigree* that displays the parent-child relationship (Jordan 2004); figure 15.6b models *meiosis* where the two sequences correspond to the chromosomes of the father and the mother (which are independent), and at each locus (gene), the offspring receives one allele from the father and the other allele from the mother.

COUPLED HMM

A *coupled HMM*, shown in figure 15.6c, models two parallel but interacting hidden sequences that generate two parallel observation sequences. For example, in speech recognition, we may have one observed acoustic sequence of uttered words and one observed visual sequence of lip images, each having its hidden states where the two are dependent.

SWITCHING HMM

In a *switching HMM*, shown in figure 15.6d, there are K parallel independent hidden state sequences, and the state variable S at any one time picks one of them and the chosen one generates the output. That is, we switch between state sequences as we go along.

LINEAR DYNAMICAL SYSTEM

KALMAN FILTER

In HMM proper, though the observation may be continuous, the state variable is discrete; in a *linear dynamical system*, also known as the *Kalman filter*, both the state and the observations are continuous. In the basic case, the state at time t is a linear function of the state at $t-1$ with additive zero-mean Gaussian noise, and, at each state, the observation is another linear function of the state with additive zero-mean Gaussian noise. The two linear mappings and the covariances of the two noise sources make up the parameters. All HMM variants we discussed earlier can similarly be generalized to use continuous states.

By suitably modifying the graphical model, we can adapt the architecture to the characteristics of the process that generates the data. This process of matching the model to the data is a model selection procedure to best trade off bias and variance. The disadvantage is that exact inference may no longer be possible on such extended HMMs, and we would need approximation or sampling methods (Ghahramani 2001; Jordan 2004).

15.10 Model Selection in HMMs

Just like any model, the complexity of an HMM should be tuned so as to balance its complexity with the size and properties of the data at hand. One possibility is to tune the topology of the HMM. In a fully connected (ergodic) HMM, there is transition from a state to any other state, which makes $\mathbf{A}$ a full $N \times N$ matrix. In some applications, only certain transitions are allowed, with the disallowed transitions having their $a_{ij} = 0$. When there are fewer possible next states, $N' < N$, the complexity of forward-backward passes and the Viterbi procedure is $\mathcal{O}(NN'T)$ instead of $\mathcal{O}(N^2T)$.

LEFT-TO-RIGHT HMMS

For example, in speech recognition, *left-to-right HMMs* are used, which have their states ordered in time so that as time increases, the state index increases or stays the same. Such a constraint allows modeling sequences whose properties change over time as in speech, and when we get to a state, we know approximately the states preceding it. There is the property that we never move to a state with a smaller index, namely, $a_{ij} = 0$, for $j < i$. Large changes in state indices are not allowed either, namely, $a_{ij} = 0$, for $j > i + \tau$. The example of the left-to-right HMM given in figure 15.7 with $\tau = 2$ has the state transition matrix

$$\mathbf{A} = \begin{bmatrix} a_{11} & a_{12} & a_{13} & 0 \\ 0 & a_{22} & a_{23} & a_{24} \\ 0 & 0 & a_{33} & a_{34} \\ 0 & 0 & 0 & a_{44} \end{bmatrix}$$

Another factor that determines the complexity of an HMM is the number of states N. Because the states are hidden, their number is not known and should be chosen before training. This is determined using prior information and can be fine-tuned by cross-validation, namely, by checking the likelihood of validation sequences.

When used for classification, we have a set of HMMs, each one modeling the sequences belonging to one class. For example, in spoken word recognition, examples of each word train a separate model, λ_i. Given a new word utterance O to classify, all of the separate word models are evaluated to calculate $P(O|\lambda_i)$. We then use Bayes' rule to get the posterior probabilities

(15.42) $$P(\lambda_i|O) = \frac{P(O|\lambda_i)P(\lambda_i)}{\sum_j P(O|\lambda_j)P(\lambda_j)}$$

where $P(\lambda_i)$ is the prior probability of word i. The utterance is assigned to the word having the highest posterior. This is the likelihood-based approach; there is also work on discriminative HMM trained directly to maximize the posterior probabilities. When there are several pronunciations of the same word, these are defined as parallel paths in the HMM for the word.

In the case of a continuous input like speech, the difficult task is that of segmenting the signal into small discrete observations. Typically, *phones* are used that are taken as the primitive parts, and combining them, longer sequences (e.g., words) are formed. Each phone is recognized in parallel (by the vector quantizer), then the HMM is used to combine them serially. If the speech primitives are simple, then the HMM becomes complex and vice versa. In connected speech recognition where the words are

PHONES

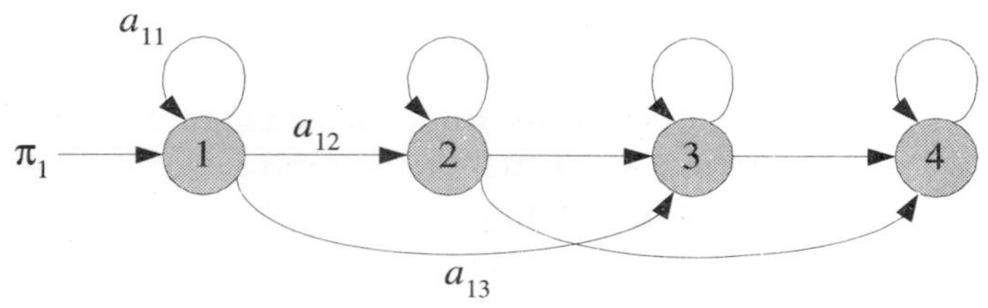

Figure 15.7 Example of a left-to-right HMM.

not uttered one by one with clear pauses between them, there is a hierarchy of HMMs at several levels; one combines phones to recognize words, another combines words to recognize sentences by building a language model, and so forth.

Hybrid neural network/HMM models were also used for speech recognition (Morgan and Bourlard 1995). In such a model, a multilayer perceptron (chapter 11) is used to capture temporally local but possibly complex and nonlinear primitives, for example, phones, while the HMM is used to learn the temporal structure. The neural network acts as a preprocessor and translates the raw observations in a time window to a form that is easier to model than the output of a vector quantizer.

An HMM can be visualized as a graphical model and evaluation in an HMM is a special case of the belief propagation algorithm that we discuss in chapter 14. The reason we devote a special chapter is the widespread successful use of this particular model, especially in automatic speech recognition. But the basic HMM architecture can be extended—for example, by having multiple sequences, or by introducing hidden (latent) variables, as we discuss in section 15.9.

In chapter 16, we discuss the Bayesian approach and in section 16.8, we discuss the nonparametric Bayesian methods where the model structure can be made more complex over time as more data arrives. One application of that is the *infinite HMM* (Beal, Ghahramani, and Rasmussen 2002).

15.11 Notes

The HMM is a mature technology, and there are HMM-based commercial speech recognition systems in actual use (Rabiner and Juang 1993; Jelinek 1997). In section 11.12, we discussed how to train multilayer perceptrons for recognizing sequences. HMMs have the advantage over time delay neural networks in that no time window needs to be defined a priori, and they train better than recurrent neural networks. HMMs are applied to diverse sequence recognition tasks. Applications of HMMs to bioinformatics is given in Baldi and Brunak 1998, and to natural language processing in Manning and Schütze 1999. It is also applied to online handwritten character recognition, which differs from optical recognition in that the writer writes on a touch-sensitive pad and the input is a sequence of (x, y) coordinates of the pen tip as it moves over the pad and is not a static image. Bengio et al. (1995) explain a hybrid system for online recognition where an MLP recognizes individual characters, and an HMM combines them to recognize words. Various applications of the HMM and several extensions, for example, discriminative HMMs, are discussed in Bengio 1999. A more recent survey of what HMMs can and cannot do is Bilmes 2006.

In any such recognition system, one critical point is to decide how much to do things in parallel and what to leave to serial processing. In speech recognition, phonemes may be recognized by a parallel system that corresponds to assuming that all the phoneme sound is uttered in one time step. The word is then recognized serially by combining the phonemes. In an alternative system, phonemes themselves may be designed as a sequence of simpler speech sounds, if the same phoneme has many versions, for example, depending on the previous and following phonemes. Doing things in parallel is good but only to a degree; one should find the ideal balance of parallel and serial processing. To be able to call anyone at the touch of a button, we would need millions of buttons on our telephone; instead, we have ten buttons and we press them in a sequence to dial the number.

We discussed graphical models in chapter 14, and we know that HMMs can be considered a special class of graphical models and inference and learning operations on HMMs are analogous to their counterparts in graphical models (Smyth, Heckerman, and Jordan 1997). There are various extensions to HMMs, such as *factorial HMMs*, where at each time step, there are a number of states that collectively generate the observation and *tree-structured HMMs* where there is a hierarchy of states. The general formalism also allows us to treat continuous as well as discrete states, known as *linear dynamical systems*. For some of these models, exact inference is not possible and one needs to use approximation or sampling methods (Ghahramani 2001).

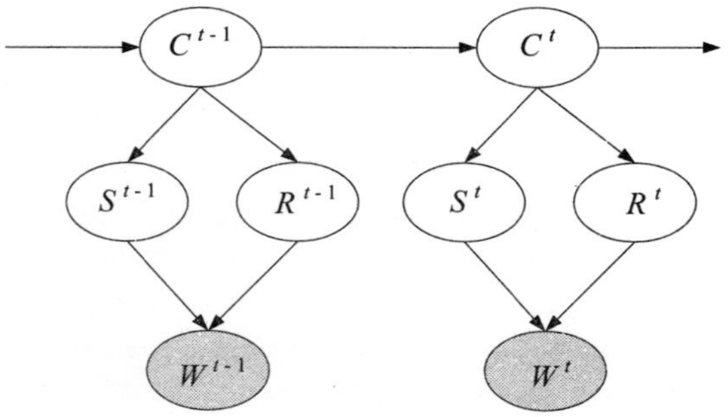

Figure 15.8 A dynamic version where we have a chain of graphs to show dependency in weather on consecutive days.

Actually, any graphical model can be extended in time by unfolding it in time and adding dependencies between successive copies. In fact, a hidden Markov model is nothing but a sequence of clustering problems where the cluster index at time t is dependent not only on observation at time t but also on the index at time $t - 1$, and the Baum-Welch algorithm is expectation-maximization extended to also include this dependency in time. In section 6.5, we discussed factor analysis where a small number of hidden factors generate the observation; similarly, a linear dynamical system may be viewed as a sequence of such factor analysis models where the current factors also depend on the previous factors.

This dynamic dependency may be added when needed. For example, figure 14.5 models the cause of wet grass for a particular day; if we believe that yesterday's weather has an influence on today's weather (and we should—it tends to be cloudy on successive days, then sunny for a number of days, and so on), we can have the dynamic graphical model shown in figure 15.8 where we model this dependency.

15.12 Exercises

1. Given the observable Markov model with three states, S_1, S_2, S_3, initial probabilities

   $\mathbf{\Pi} = [0.5, 0.2, 0.3]^T$

and transition probabilities

$$\mathbf{A} = \begin{bmatrix} 0.4 & 0.3 & 0.3 \\ 0.2 & 0.6 & 0.2 \\ 0.1 & 0.1 & 0.8 \end{bmatrix}$$

generate 100 sequences of 1,000 states.

2. Using the data generated by the previous exercise, estimate Π, $\mathbf{A}$ and compare with the parameters used to generate the data.

3. Formalize a second-order Markov model. What are the parameters? How can we calculate the probability of a given state sequence? How can the parameters be learned for the case of an observable model?

   SOLUTION: In a second-order model, the current state depends on the two previous states:

   $a_{ijk} \equiv P(q_{t+2} = S_k | q_{t+1} = S_j, q_t = S_i)$

   Initial state probability defines the probability of the first state:

   $\pi_i \equiv P(q_1 = S_i)$

   We also need parameters to define the probability of the second state given the first state:

   $\theta_{ij} \equiv P(q_2 = S_j | q_1 = S_i)$

   Given a second-order observable MM with parameters $\lambda = (\Pi, \Theta, \mathbf{A})$, the probability of an observed state sequence is

$$\begin{aligned} P(O = Q|\lambda) &= P(q_1)P(q_2|q_1)\prod_{t=3}^{T} P(q_t|q_{t-1}, q_{t-2}) \\ &= \pi_{q_1}\theta_{q_2 q_1} a_{q_3 q_2 q_1} a_{q_4 q_3 q_2} \cdots a_{q_T q_{T-1} q_{T-2}} \end{aligned}$$

   The probabilities are estimated as proportions:

$$\begin{aligned} \hat{\pi}_i &= \frac{\sum_k 1(q_1^k = S_i)}{K} \\ \hat{\theta}_{ij} &= \frac{\sum_k 1(q_2^k = S_j \text{ and } q_1^k = S_i)}{\sum_k 1(q_1^k = S_i)} \\ \hat{a}_{ijk} &= \frac{\sum_k \sum_{t=3}^{T} 1(q_t^k = S_k \text{ and } q_{t-1}^k = S_j \text{ and } q_{t-2}^k = S_i)}{\sum_k \sum_{t=3}^{T} 1(q_{t-1}^k = S_j \text{ and } q_{t-2}^k = S_i)} \end{aligned}$$

4. Show that any second- (or higher-order) Markov model can be converted to a first-order Markov model.

   SOLUTION: In a second-order model, each state depends on the two previous states. We can define a new set of states corresponding to the Cartesian product of the original set of states with itself. A first-order model defined on this new N^2 states corrresponds to a second-order model defined on the original N states.

5. Some researchers define a Markov model as generating an observation while traversing an arc, instead of on arrival at a state. Is this model any more powerful than what we have discussed?

   SOLUTION: Similar to the case of the previous exercise, if the output depends not only on the current state but also on the next state, we can define new states corresponding to this pair and have the output generated by this (joint) state.

6. Generate training and validation sequences from an HMM of your choosing. Then train different HMMs by varying the number of hidden states on the same training set and calculate the validation likelihoods. Observe how the validation likelihood changes as the number of states increases.

7. If in equation 15.38 we have multivariate observations, what will the M-step equations be?

   SOLUTION: If we have d-dimensional $\boldsymbol{O}_t \in \Re^d$, drawn from d-variate Gaussians with their mean vectors and covariance matrices

   $$p(\boldsymbol{O}_t|q_t = S_j, \lambda) \sim \mathcal{N}(\boldsymbol{\mu}_j, \boldsymbol{\Sigma}_j)$$

   the M-step equations are

   $$\hat{\boldsymbol{\mu}}_j = \frac{\sum_t \gamma_t(j)\boldsymbol{O}_t}{\sum_t \gamma_t(j)}$$

   $$\hat{\boldsymbol{\Sigma}}_j = \frac{\sum_t \gamma_t(j)(\boldsymbol{O}_t - \hat{\boldsymbol{\mu}}_j)(\boldsymbol{O}_t - \hat{\boldsymbol{\mu}}_j)^T}{\sum_t \gamma_t(j)}$$

8. Consider the urn-and-ball example where we draw *without replacement.* How will it be different?

   SOLUTION: If we draw without replacement, then at each iteration, the number of balls change, which means that the observation probabilities, **B**, change. We will no longer have a homogenous model.

9. Let us say at any time we have two observations from two different alphabets; for example, let us say we are observing the values of two currencies every day. How can we implement this using HMM?

   SOLUTION: In such a case, what we have is a hidden state generating two different observations. That is, we have two **B**, each trained with its own observation sequence. These two observations then need to be combined to estimate **A** and π.

10. How can we have an incremental HMM where we add new hidden states when necessary?

    SOLUTION: Again, this is a state space search. Our aim may be to maximize validation log likelihood, and an operator allows us to add a hidden state. We do then a forward search. There are structure learning algorithms for the more general case of graphical models, which we discussed in chapter 14.

15.13 References

Baldi, P., and S. Brunak. 1998. *Bioinformatics: The Machine Learning Approach.* Cambridge, MA: MIT Press.

Beal, M. J., Z. Ghahramani, and C. E. Rasmussen. 2002. "The Infinite Hidden Markov Model." In *Advances in Neural Information Processing Systems 14*, ed. T. G. Dietterich, S. Becker, and Z. Ghahramani, 577–585. Cambridge, MA: MIT Press.

Bengio, Y. 1999. "Markovian Models for Sequential Data." *Neural Computing Surveys* 2: 129–162.

Bengio, Y., and P. Frasconi. 1996. "Input-Output HMMs for Sequence Processing." *IEEE Transactions on Neural Networks* 7:1231–1249.

Bengio, Y., Y. Le Cun, C. Nohl, and C. Burges. 1995. "LeRec: A NN/HMM Hybrid for On-line Handwriting Recognition." *Neural Computation* 7:1289–1303.

Bilmes, J. A. 2006. "What HMMs Can Do." *IEICE Transactions on Information and Systems* E89-D:869–891.

Ghahramani, Z. 2001. "An Introduction to Hidden Markov Models and Bayesian Networks." *International Journal of Pattern Recognition and Artificial Intelligence* 15:9–42.

Jelinek, F. 1997. *Statistical Methods for Speech Recognition.* Cambridge, MA: MIT Press.

Jordan, M. I. 2004. "Graphical Models." *Statistical Science* 19:140–155.

Manning, C. D., and H. Schütze. 1999. *Foundations of Statistical Natural Language Processing.* Cambridge, MA: MIT Press.

Meila, M., and M. I. Jordan. 1996. "Learning Fine Motion by Markov Mixtures of Experts." In *Advances in Neural Information Processing Systems 8*, ed. D. S. Touretzky, M. C. Mozer, and M. E. Hasselmo, 1003–1009. Cambridge, MA: MIT Press.

Morgan, N., and H. Bourlard. 1995. "Continuous Speech Recognition: An Introduction to the Hybrid HMM/Connectionist Approach." *IEEE Signal Processing Magazine* 12:25–42.

Smyth, P., D. Heckerman, and M. I. Jordan. 1997. "Probabilistic Independence Networks for Hidden Markov Probability Models." *Neural Computation* 9:227–269.

Rabiner, L. R. 1989. "A Tutorial on Hidden Markov Models and Selected Applications in Speech Recognition." *Proceedings of the IEEE* 77:257–286.

Rabiner, L. R., and B. H. Juang. 1986. "An Introduction to Hidden Markov Models." *IEEE Acoustics, Speech, and Signal Processing Magazine* 3:4–16.

Rabiner, L. R., and B. H. Juang. 1993. *Fundamentals of Speech Recognition.* New York: Prentice Hall.

16 *Bayesian Estimation*

In the Bayesian approach, we consider parameters as random variables with a distribution allowing us to model our uncertainty in estimating them. We continue from where we left off in section 4.4 and discuss estimating both the parameters of a distribution and the parameters of a model for regression, classification, clustering, or dimensionality reduction. We also discuss nonparametric Bayesian modeling where model complexity is not fixed but depends on the data.

16.1 Introduction

BAYESIAN ESTIMATION, which we introduced in section 4.4, treats a parameter θ as a random variable with a probability distribution. The maximum likelihood approach we discussed in section 4.2 treats a parameter as an unknown constant. For example, if the parameter we want to estimate is the mean μ, its maximum likelihood estimator is the sample average $\overline{X}$. We calculate $\overline{X}$ over our training set, plug it in our model, and use it, for example, for classification. However, we know that especially with small samples, the maximum likelihood estimator can be a poor estimator and has variance—as the training set varies, we may calculate different values of $\overline{X}$, which in turn may lead to different discriminants with different generalization accuracies.

In Bayesian estimation, we make use of the fact that we have uncertainty in estimating θ and instead of a single θ_{ML}, we use all θ weighted by our estimated distribution, $p(\theta|\mathcal{X})$. That is, we average over our uncertainty in estimating θ.

While estimating $p(\theta|\mathcal{X})$, we can make use of the prior information we

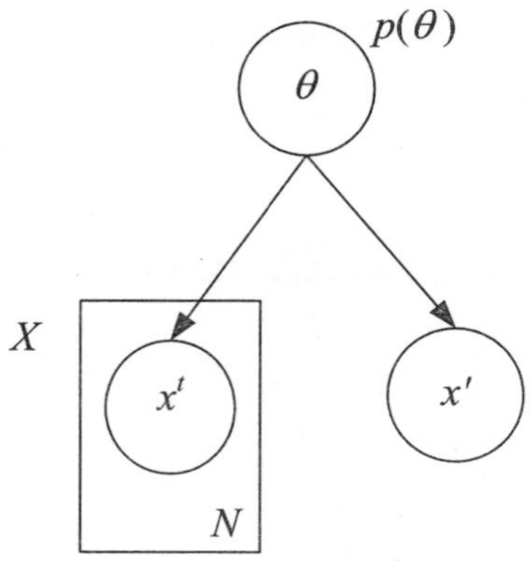

Figure 16.1 The generative graphical model (see chapter 14). The arcs are in the direction of sampling; first we pick θ from $p(\theta)$, and then we generate data by sampling from $p(x|\theta)$. The rectangular *plate* contains N independent instances drawn, and they make up the training set $\mathcal{X}$. The new x' is independently drawn given θ. This is the iid assumption. If θ is not known, they are dependent. We infer θ from the past instances using Bayes' rule, which is then used to make inference about the new x'.

may have regarding the value of the parameter. Such prior beliefs are especially important when we have a small sample (and when the variance of the maximum likelihood estimator is high). In such a case, we are interested in combining what the data tells us, namely, the value calculated from the sample, and our prior information. As we first discussed in section 4.4, we code this information using a *prior probability* distribution. For example, before looking at a sample to estimate the mean, we may have some prior belief that it is close to 2, between 1 and 3, and in such a case, we write $p(\mu)$ in such a way that the bulk of the density lies in the interval $[1, 3]$.

PRIOR PROBABILITY

Using Bayes' rule, we combine the prior and the likelihood and calculate the *posterior probability* distribution:

POSTERIOR PROBABILITY

$$p(\theta|\mathcal{X}) = \frac{p(\theta)p(\mathcal{X}|\theta)}{p(\mathcal{X})} \tag{16.1}$$

Here, $p(\theta)$ is the prior density; it is what we know regarding the possible values that θ may take *before* looking at the sample. $p(\mathcal{X}|\theta)$ is the *sample likelihood*; it tells us how likely our sample $\mathcal{X}$ is if the parameter of the distribution takes the value θ. For example, if the instances in our sample are between 5 and 10, such a sample is likely if μ is 7 but is less likely if μ is 3 and even less likely if μ is 1. $p(\mathcal{X})$ in the denominator is a normalizer to make sure that the *posterior* $p(\theta|\mathcal{X})$ integrates to 1. It is called the posterior probability because it tells us how likely θ takes a certain value *after* looking at the sample. The Bayes' rule takes the prior distribution, combines it with what the data reveals, and generates the posterior distribution. We then use this posterior distribution later for making inference.

Let us say that we have a past sample $\mathcal{X} = \{\boldsymbol{x}^t\}_{t=1}^N$ drawn from sone distribution with unknown parameter θ. We can then draw one more instance x', and we would like to calculate its probability distribution. We can visualize this as a graphical model (chapter 14) as shown in figure 16.1. What is shown here is a *generative model* representing how the data is generated. We first sample θ from $p(\theta)$ and then sample from $p(x|\theta)$ to first generate the training instances $\boldsymbol{x}^t$ and also the new test x'.

GENERATIVE MODEL

We write the joint as

$$p(x', \mathcal{X}, \theta) = p(\theta)p(\mathcal{X}|\theta)p(x'|\theta)$$

We can estimate the probability distribution for the new x given the sample $\mathcal{X}$:

$$\begin{aligned} p(x'|\mathcal{X}) &= \frac{p(x', \mathcal{X})}{p(\mathcal{X})} = \frac{\int p(x', \mathcal{X}, \theta)d\theta}{p(\mathcal{X})} = \frac{\int p(\theta)p(\mathcal{X}|\theta)p(x'|\theta)d\theta}{p(\mathcal{X})} \\ &= \int p(x'|\theta)p(\theta|\mathcal{X})d\theta \end{aligned} \tag{16.2}$$

In calculating $p(\theta|\mathcal{X})$, Bayes' rule inverts the direction of the arc and makes a diagnostic inference. This inferred (posterior) distribution is then used to derive a predictive distribution for new x.

We see that our estimate is a weighted sum (we replace $\int d\theta$ by $\sum_\theta$ if θ is discrete valued) of estimates using all possible values of θ weighted by how likely each θ is, given the sample $\mathcal{X}$.

This is the *full Bayesian treatment* and it may not be possible if the posterior is not easy to integrate. As we saw in section 4.4, in the case of the *maximum a posteriori (MAP) estimate*, we use the mode of the posterior:

MAXIMUM A POSTERIORI (MAP) ESTIMATE

$$\theta_{MAP} = \arg\max_\theta p(\theta|\mathcal{X}) \text{ and } p_{MAP}(x'|\mathcal{X}) = p(x'|\theta_{MAP})$$

The MAP estimate corresponds to assuming that the posterior makes a very narrow peak around a single point, that is, the mode. If the prior

$p(\theta)$ is uniform over all θ, then the mode of the posterior $p(\theta|\mathcal{X})$ and the mode of the likelihood $p(\mathcal{X}|\theta)$ are at the same point, and the MAP estimate is equal to the maximum likelihood (ML) estimate:

$$\theta_{ML} = \arg\max_{\theta} p(\mathcal{X}|\theta) \text{ and } p_{ML}(x'|\mathcal{X}) = p(x'|\theta_{ML})$$

This implies that using ML corresponds to assuming no a priori distinction between different values of θ.

Basically, the Bayesian approach has two advantages:

1. The prior helps us ignore the values that θ is unlikely to take and concentrate on the region where it is likely to lie. Even a weak prior with long tails can be very helpful.

2. Instead of using a single θ estimate in prediction, we generate a set of possible θ values (as defined by the posterior) and use all of them in prediction, weighted by how likely they are.

If we use the MAP estimate instead of integrating over θ, we make use of the first advantage but not the second—if we use the ML estimate, we lose both advantages. If we use an uninformative (uniform) prior, we make use of the second advantage but not the first. Actually it is this second advantage, rather than the first, that makes the Bayesian approach interesting, and in chapter 17, we discuss combining multiple models where we see methods that are very similar, though not always Bayesian.

This approach can be used in different types of distributions and for different types of applications. The parameter θ can be the parameter of a distribution. For example, in classification, it can be the unknown class mean, for which we define a prior and get its posterior; then, we get a different discriminant for each possible value of the mean and hence the Bayesian approach will average over all possible discriminants whereas in the ML approach there is a single mean estimate and hence a single discriminant.

The unknown parameter, as we will see shortly, can also be the parameters of a fitted model. For example, in linear regression, we can define a prior distribution on the slope and the intercept parameters and calculate a posterior on them, that is, a distribution over lines. We will then be averaging over the prediction of all possible lines, weighted by how likely they are as specified by their prior weights and how well they fit the given data.

One of the most critical aspects of Bayesian estimation is evaluating the integral in equation 16.2. For some cases, we can calculate it, but mostly we cannot, and in such cases, we need to approximate it, and we will see methods for this in the next few sections, namely, Laplace and variational approximations, and Markov chain Monte Carlo (MCMC) sampling.

Now, let us see these and other applications of the Bayesian approach in more detail, starting from simple and incrementally making them more complex.

16.2 Bayesian Estimation of the Parameters of a Discrete Distribution

16.2.1 $K > 2$ States: Dirichlet Distribution

Let us say that each instance is a multinomial variable taking one of K distinct states (section 4.2.2). We say $x_i^t = 1$ if instance t is in state i and $x_j^t = 0, \forall j \neq i$. The parameters are the probabilities of states, $\boldsymbol{q} = [q_1, q_2, \ldots, q_K]^T$ with $q_i, i = 1, \ldots, K$ satisfying $q_i \geq 0, \forall i$ and $\sum_i q_i = 1$.

For example, x^t may correspond to news documents and states may correspond to K different news categories: sports, politics, arts, and so on. The probabilities q_i then correspond to the proportions of different news categories, and priors on them allow us to code our prior beliefs in these proportions; for example, we may expect to have more news related to sports than news related to arts.

The sample likelihood is

$$p(\mathcal{X}|\boldsymbol{q}) = \prod_{t=1}^{N} \prod_{i=1}^{K} q_i^{x_i^t}$$

DIRICHLET DISTRIBUTION

The prior distribution of $\boldsymbol{q}$ is the *Dirichlet distribution*:

$$\text{Dirichlet}(\boldsymbol{q}|\boldsymbol{\alpha}) = \frac{\Gamma(\alpha_0)}{\Gamma(\alpha_1)\cdots\Gamma(\alpha_K)} \prod_{i=1}^{K} q_i^{\alpha_i - 1}$$

GAMMA FUNCTION

where $\boldsymbol{\alpha} = [\alpha_1, \ldots, \alpha_K]^T$ and $\alpha_0 = \sum_i \alpha_i$. α_i, the parameters of the prior, are called the *hyperparameters*. $\Gamma(x)$ is the *gamma function* defined as

$$\Gamma(x) \equiv \int_0^\infty u^{x-1} e^{-u} du$$

Given the prior and the likelihood, we can derive the posterior:

$$p(\boldsymbol{q}|\mathcal{X}) \propto p(\mathcal{X}|\boldsymbol{q})p(\boldsymbol{q}|\boldsymbol{\alpha})$$

(16.3) $$\propto \prod_i q_i^{\alpha_i+N_i-1}$$

where $N_i = \sum_{t=1}^{N} x_i^t$. We see that the posterior has the same form as the prior, and we call such a prior a *conjugate prior*. Both the prior and the likelihood have the form of product of powers of q_i, and we combine them to make up the posterior:

CONJUGATE PRIOR

$$p(\boldsymbol{q}|\mathcal{X}) = \frac{\Gamma(\alpha_0+N)}{\Gamma(\alpha_1+N_1)\cdots\Gamma(\alpha_K+N_K)}\prod_{i=1}^{K} q_i^{\alpha_i+N_i-1}$$

(16.4) $$= \text{Dirichlet}(\boldsymbol{q}|\boldsymbol{\alpha}+\boldsymbol{n})$$

where $\boldsymbol{n} = [N_1, \ldots, N_K]^T$ and $\sum_i N_i = N$.

Looking at equation 16.3, we can bring an interpretation to the hyperparameters α_i (Bishop 2006). Just as n_i are counts of occurrences of state i in a sample of N, we can view α_i as counts of occurences of state i in some imaginary sample of α_0 instances. In defining the prior, we are subjectively saying the following: In a sample of α_0, I would expect α_i of them to belong to state i. Note that larger α_0 implies that we have a higher confidence (a more peaked distribution) in our subjective proportions: Saying that I expect to have 60 out of 100 occurrences belong to state 1 has higher confidence than saying that I expect to have 6 out of 10. The posterior then is another Dirichlet that sums up the counts of the occurences of states, imagined and actual, given by the prior and the likelihood, respectively.

The conjugacy has a nice implication. In a sequential setting where we receive a sequence of instances, because the posterior and the prior have the same form, the current posterior accumulates information from all past instances and becomes the prior for the next instance.

16.2.2 $K = 2$ States: Beta Distribution

When the variable is binary, $x^t \in \{0, 1\}$, the multinomial sample becomes Bernoulli:

$$p(\mathcal{X}|q) = \prod_t q^{x^t}(1-q)^{1-x^t}$$

BETA DISTRIBUTION

and the Dirichlet prior reduces to the *beta distribution*:

$$\text{beta}(q|\alpha,\beta) = \frac{\Gamma(\alpha+\beta)}{\Gamma(\alpha)\Gamma(\beta)}q^{\alpha-1}(1-q)^{\beta-1}$$

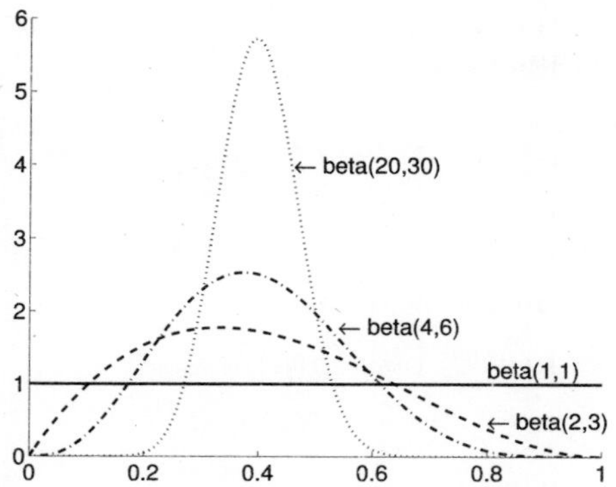

Figure 16.2 Plots of beta distributions for different sets of (α, β).

For example, x^t may be 0 or 1 depending on whether email with index t in a random sample of size N is legitimate or spam, respectively. Then defining a prior on q allows us to define a prior belief on the spam probability: I would expect, on the average, $\alpha/(\alpha+\beta)$ of my emails to be spam.

Beta is a conjugate prior, and for the posterior we get

$$p(q|A, N, \alpha, \beta) \propto q^{A+\alpha-1}(1-p)^{N-A+\beta-1}$$

where $A = \sum_t x^t$, and we see again that we combine the occurrences in the imaginary and the actual samples. Note that when $\alpha = \beta = 1$, we have a uniform prior and the posterior has the same shape as the likelihood. As the two counts, whether α and β for the prior or $\alpha+A$ and $\beta+N-A$ for the posterior, increase and their difference increases, we get a distribution that is more peaked with smaller variance (see figure 16.2). As we see more data (imagined or actual), the variance decreases.

16.3 Bayesian Estimation of the Parameters of a Gaussian Distribution

16.3.1 Univariate Case: Unknown Mean, Known Variance

We now consider the case where instances are Gaussian distributed. Let us start with the univariate case, $p(x) \sim \mathcal{N}(\mu, \sigma^2)$, where the parameters are μ and σ^2; we discussed this briefly in section 4.4. The sample likelihood is

$$p(\mathcal{X}|\mu, \sigma^2) = \prod_t \frac{1}{\sqrt{2\pi}\sigma} \exp\left[-\frac{(x^t - \mu)^2}{2\sigma^2}\right] \quad (16.5)$$

The conjugate prior for μ is Gaussian, $p(\mu) \sim \mathcal{N}(\mu_0^2, \sigma_0^2)$, and we write the posterior as

$$\begin{aligned} p(\mu|\mathcal{X}) &\propto p(\mu)p(\mathcal{X}|\mu) \\ &\sim \mathcal{N}(\mu_N, \sigma_N^2) \end{aligned}$$

where

$$\mu_N = \frac{\sigma^2}{N\sigma_0^2 + \sigma^2}\mu_0 + \frac{N\sigma_0^2}{N\sigma_0^2 + \sigma^2}m \quad (16.6)$$

$$\frac{1}{\sigma_N^2} = \frac{1}{\sigma_0^2} + \frac{N}{\sigma^2} \quad (16.7)$$

where $m = \sum_t x^t/N$ is the sample average. We see that the mean of the posterior density (which is the MAP estimate), μ_N, is a weighted average of the prior mean μ_0 and the sample mean m, with weights being inversely proportional to their variances (see figure 16.3 for an example). Note that because both coefficients are between 0 and 1 and sum to 1, μ_N is always between μ_0 and m. When the sample size N or the variance of the prior σ_0^2 is large, the posterior mean is close to m, relying more on the information provided by the sample. When σ_0^2 is small—that is, when we have little prior uncertainty regarding the correct value of μ, or when we have a small sample—our prior guess μ_0 has higher effect.

σ_N gets smaller when either of σ_0 or σ gets smaller or if N is larger. Note also that σ_N is smaller than both σ_0 and $\sigma/\sqrt{N}$, that is, the posterior variance is smaller than both prior variance and that of m. Incorporating both results in a better posterior estimate than using any of the prior or sample alone.

If σ^2 is known, for new x, we can integrate over this posterior to make a prediction:

$$\begin{aligned} p(x|\mathcal{X}) &= \int p(x|\mu)p(\mu|\mathcal{X})d\mu \\ &\sim \mathcal{N}(\mu_N, \sigma_N^2 + \sigma^2) \quad (16.8) \end{aligned}$$

We see that x is still Gaussian, that it is centered at the posterior mean, and that its variance now includes the uncertainty due to the estimation

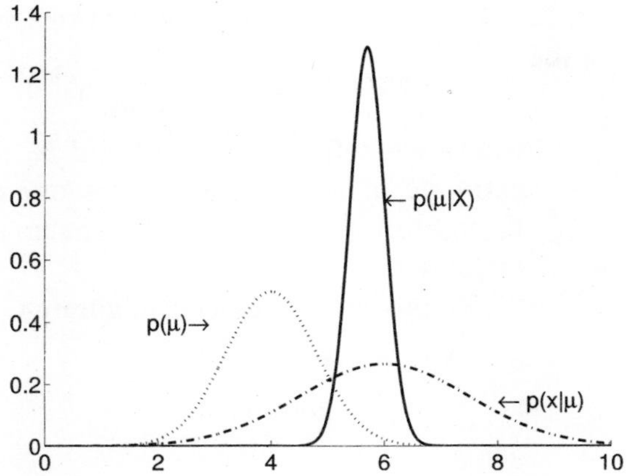

Figure 16.3 Twenty data points are drawn from $p(x) \sim \mathcal{N}(6, 1.5^2)$, prior is $p(\mu) \sim \mathcal{N}(4, 0.8^2)$, and posterior is then $p(\mu|\mathcal{X}) \sim \mathcal{N}(5.7, 0.3^2)$.

of the mean and the new sampled instance x. We can write $x = \mu + x'$ where $x' \sim \mathcal{N}(0, \sigma^2)$; then $E[x] = E[\mu] + E[x'] = \mu_N$ and $\text{Var}(x) = \text{Var}(\mu) + \text{Var}(x') = \sigma_N^2 + \sigma^2$, where this last follows from the fact that the new x' is an independent draw.

Once we get a distribution for $p(x|\mathcal{X})$, we can use it for different purposes. For example in classification, this approach corresponds to assuming Gaussian classes where means have a Gaussian prior and they are trained using $\mathcal{X}_i$, the subset of $\mathcal{X}$ labeled by class C_i. Then, $p(x|\mathcal{X}_i)$ as calculated above, corresponds to $p(x|C_i)$, which we combine with prior $P(C_i)$ to get the posterior and hence a discriminant.

16.3.2 Univariate Case: Unknown Mean, Unknown Variance

If we do not know σ^2, we also need to estimate it. For the case of variance, we work with the *precision*, the reciprocal of the variance, $\lambda \equiv 1/\sigma^2$. Using this, the sample likelihood is written as

PRECISION

$$
\begin{aligned}
p(\mathcal{X}|\lambda) &= \prod_t \frac{\lambda^{1/2}}{\sqrt{2\pi}} \exp\left[-\frac{\lambda}{2}(x^t - \mu)^2\right] \\
&= \lambda^{N/2}(2\pi)^{-N/2} \exp\left[-\frac{\lambda}{2}\sum_t (x^t - \mu)^2\right] \qquad (16.9)
\end{aligned}
$$

GAMMA DISTRIBUTION

The conjugate prior for the precision is the *gamma distribution*:

$$p(\lambda) \sim \text{gamma}(a_0, b_0) = \frac{1}{\Gamma(a_0)} b_0^{a_0} \lambda^{a_0 - 1} \exp(-b_0 \lambda)$$

where we define $a_0 \equiv \nu_0/2$ and $b_0 \equiv (\nu_0/2)s_0^2$ such that s_0^2 is our prior estimate of variance and ν_0 is our confidence in this prior—it may be thought of as the size of the imaginary sample on which we believe s_0^2 is estimated.

The posterior then is also gamma:

$$\begin{aligned} p(\lambda|\mathcal{X}) &\propto p(\mathcal{X}|\lambda)p(\lambda) \\ &\sim \text{gamma}(a_N, b_N) \end{aligned}$$

where

$$\begin{aligned} a_N &= a_0 + N/2 = \frac{\nu_0 + N}{2} \\ b_N &= b_0 + \frac{N}{2}s^2 = \frac{\nu_0}{2}s_0^2 + \frac{N}{2}s^2 \end{aligned} \tag{16.10}$$

where $s^2 = \sum_t (x^t - \mu)^2/N$ is the sample variance. Again, we see that posterior estimates are weighted sum of priors and sample statistics.

To make a prediction for new x, when both μ and σ^2 are unknown, we need the joint posterior that we write as

$$p(\mu, \lambda) = p(\mu|\lambda)p(\lambda)$$

where $p(\lambda) \sim \text{gamma}(a_0, b_0)$ and $p(\mu|\lambda) \sim \mathcal{N}(\mu_0, 1/(\kappa_0\lambda))$. Here again, κ_0 may be thought of as the size of the imaginary sample and as such it defines our confidence in the prior. The conjugate prior for the joint in this case is called the *normal-gamma distribution*

NORMAL-GAMMA DISTRIBUTION

$$\begin{aligned} p(\mu, \lambda) &\sim \text{normal-gamma}(\mu_0, \kappa_0, a_0, b_0) \\ &= \mathcal{N}(\mu, 1/(\kappa_0\lambda)) \cdot \text{gamma}(a_0, b_0) \end{aligned}$$

The posterior is

$$p(\mu, \lambda|\mathcal{X}) \sim \text{normal-gamma}(\mu_N, \kappa_N, a_N, b_N) \tag{16.11}$$

where

$$\begin{aligned} \kappa_N &= \kappa_0 + N \\ \mu_N &= \frac{\kappa_0\mu_0 + Nm}{\kappa_N} \\ a_N &= a_0 + N/2 \\ b_N &= b_0 + \frac{N}{2}s^2 + \frac{\kappa_0 N}{2\kappa_N}(m - \mu_0)^2 \end{aligned} \tag{16.12}$$

To make a prediction for new x, we integrate over the posterior:

$$p(x|\mathcal{X}) = \int\int p(x|\mu,\lambda)p(\mu,\lambda|\mathcal{X})d\mu d\lambda \tag{16.13}$$

$$\sim t_{2a_N}\left(\mu_N, \frac{b_N(\kappa_N+1)}{a_N\kappa_N}\right) \tag{16.14}$$

That is, we get a (nonstandardized) t distribution having the given mean and variance values with $2a_N$ degrees of freedom. In equation 16.8, we have a Gaussian distribution; here the mean is the same but because σ^2 is unknown, its estimation adds uncertainty, and we get a t distribution with wider tails. Sometimes, equivalently, instead of modeling the precision λ, we model σ^2 and for this, we can use the inverse gamma or the inverse chi-squared distribution; see Murphy 2007.

16.3.3 Multivariate Case: Unknown Mean, Unknown Covariance

If we have multivariate $\boldsymbol{x} \in \Re^d$, we use exactly the same approach, except for the fact that we need to use the multivariate versions of the distributions (Murphy 2012). We have

$$p(\boldsymbol{x}) \sim \mathcal{N}_d(\boldsymbol{\mu}, \boldsymbol{\Lambda})$$

PRECISION MATRIX

where $\boldsymbol{\Lambda} \equiv \boldsymbol{\Sigma}^{-1}$ is the *precision matrix*. We use a Gaussian prior (conditioned on $\boldsymbol{\Lambda}$) for the mean:

$$p(\boldsymbol{\mu}|\boldsymbol{\Lambda}) \sim \mathcal{N}_d(\boldsymbol{\mu}_0, (1/\kappa_0)\boldsymbol{\Lambda})$$

WISHART DISTRIBUTION

and for the precision matrix, the multivariate version of the gamma distribution is called the *Wishart distribution*:

$$p(\boldsymbol{\Lambda}) \sim \text{Wishart}(\nu_0, \mathbf{V}_0)$$

where ν_0, as with κ_0, corresponds to the strength of our prior belief.

NORMAL-WISHART DISTRIBUTION

The conjugate joint prior is the *normal-Wishart distribution*:

$$p(\mu, \boldsymbol{\Lambda}) = p(\boldsymbol{\mu}|\boldsymbol{\Lambda})p(\boldsymbol{\Lambda})$$

$$\sim \text{normal-Wishart}(\boldsymbol{\mu}_0, \kappa_0, \nu_0, \mathbf{V}_0) \tag{16.15}$$

and the posterior is

$$p(\mu, \boldsymbol{\Lambda}|\mathcal{X}) \sim \text{normal-Wishart}(\boldsymbol{\mu}_N, \kappa_N, \nu_N, \mathbf{V}_N)$$

where

$$\begin{aligned} \kappa_N &= \kappa_0 + N \\ \boldsymbol{\mu}_N &= \frac{\kappa_0 \boldsymbol{\mu}_0 + N\boldsymbol{m}}{\kappa_N} \\ \nu_N &= \nu_0 + N \\ \mathbf{V}_N &= \left(\mathbf{V}_0^{-1} + \mathbf{C} + \frac{\kappa_0 N}{\kappa_N}(\boldsymbol{m} - \boldsymbol{\mu}_0)(\boldsymbol{m} - \boldsymbol{\mu}_0)^T\right)^{-1} \end{aligned} \tag{16.16}$$

and $\mathbf{C} = \sum_t (\boldsymbol{x}^t - \boldsymbol{m})(\boldsymbol{x}^t - \boldsymbol{m})^T$ is the scatter matrix.

To make a prediction for new $\mathbf{x}$, we integrate over the joint posterior:

$$p(\mathbf{x}|\mathcal{X}) = \int\int p(\mathbf{x}|\boldsymbol{\mu}, \boldsymbol{\Lambda})p(\boldsymbol{\mu}, \boldsymbol{\Lambda}|\mathcal{X})d\boldsymbol{\mu}d\boldsymbol{\Lambda} \tag{16.17}$$

$$\sim t_{\nu_N - d + 1}\left(\boldsymbol{\mu}_N, \frac{\kappa_N + 1}{\kappa_N(\nu_N - d + 1)}(\mathbf{V}_N)^{-1}\right) \tag{16.18}$$

That is, we get a (nonstandardized) multivariate t distribution having this mean and covariance with $\nu_N - d + 1$ degrees of freedom.

16.4 Bayesian Estimation of the Parameters of a Function

We now discuss the case where we estimate the parameters, not of a distribution, but some function of the input, for regression or classification. Again, our approach is to consider these parameters as random variables with a prior distribution and use Bayes' rule to calculate a posterior distribution. We can then either evaluate the full integral, approximate it, or use the MAP estimate.

16.4.1 Regression

Let us take the case of a linear regression model:

$$r = \mathbf{w}^T\mathbf{x} + \epsilon \text{ where } \epsilon \sim \mathcal{N}(0, 1/\beta) \tag{16.19}$$

where β is the precision of the additive noise (assume that one of the d inputs is always $+1$).

The parameters are the weights $\mathbf{w}$ and we have a sample $\mathcal{X} = \{\mathbf{x}^t, r^t\}_{t=1}^N$ where $\mathbf{x} \in \Re^d$ and $r^t \in \Re$. We can break it down into a matrix of inputs and a vector of desired outputs as $\mathcal{X} = [\mathbf{X}, \boldsymbol{r}]$ where $\mathbf{X}$ is $N \times d$ and $\boldsymbol{r}$ is $N \times 1$. From equation 16.19, we have

$$p(r^t|\mathbf{x}^t, \mathbf{w}, \beta) \sim \mathcal{N}(\mathbf{w}^T\mathbf{x}, 1/\beta)$$

We saw previously in section 4.6 that the log likelihood is

$$\begin{aligned}\mathcal{L}(\boldsymbol{w}|\mathcal{X}) \equiv \log p(\mathcal{X}|\boldsymbol{w}) &= \log p(\boldsymbol{r},\mathbf{X}|\boldsymbol{w}) \\ &= \log p(\boldsymbol{r}|\mathbf{X},\boldsymbol{w}) + \log p(\mathbf{X})\end{aligned}$$

where the second term is a constant, independent of the parameters. We expand the first term as

$$\begin{aligned}\log p(\boldsymbol{r}|\mathbf{X},\boldsymbol{w},\beta) &= \log \prod_t p(r^t|\boldsymbol{x}^t,\boldsymbol{w},\beta) \\ &= -N\log(\sqrt{2\pi}) + N\log\sqrt{\beta} - \frac{\beta}{2}\sum_t (r^t - \boldsymbol{w}^T\boldsymbol{x}^t)^2 \qquad (16.20)\end{aligned}$$

For the case of the ML estimate, we find $\boldsymbol{w}$ that maximizes this, or equivalently, minimizes the last term that is the sum of the squared error. It can be rewritten as

$$\begin{aligned}E &= \sum_{t=1}^{N}(r^t - \boldsymbol{w}^T\boldsymbol{x}^t)^2 = (\boldsymbol{r} - \mathbf{X}\boldsymbol{w})^T(\boldsymbol{r} - \mathbf{X}\boldsymbol{w}) \\ &= \boldsymbol{r}^T\boldsymbol{r} - 2\boldsymbol{w}^T\mathbf{X}^T\boldsymbol{r} + \boldsymbol{w}^T\mathbf{X}^T\mathbf{X}\boldsymbol{w}\end{aligned}$$

Taking the derivative with respect to $\boldsymbol{w}$ and setting it to 0

$$-2\mathbf{X}^T\boldsymbol{r} + 2\mathbf{X}^T\mathbf{X}\boldsymbol{w} = 0 \Rightarrow \mathbf{X}^T\mathbf{X}\boldsymbol{w} = \mathbf{X}^T\boldsymbol{r}$$

we get the maximum likelihood estimator (we have previously derived this in section 5.8):

$$\boldsymbol{w}_{ML} = (\mathbf{X}^T\mathbf{X})^{-1}\mathbf{X}^T\boldsymbol{r} \qquad (16.21)$$

Having calculated the parameters, we can now do prediction. Given new input $\boldsymbol{x}'$, the response is calculated as

$$r' = \boldsymbol{w}_{ML}^T\boldsymbol{x}' \qquad (16.22)$$

In the general case, for any model, $g(\boldsymbol{x}|\boldsymbol{w})$, for example, a multilayer perceptron where $\boldsymbol{w}$ are all the weights, we minimize, for example, using gradient descent:

$$E(\mathcal{X}|\boldsymbol{w}) = [r^t - g(x^t|\mathbf{w})]^2$$

and $\boldsymbol{w}_{LSQ}$ that minimizes it is called the *least squares estimator.* Then for new x', the prediction is calculated as

$$r' = g(\boldsymbol{x}'|\boldsymbol{w}_{LSQ})$$

In the case of the Bayesian approach, we define a Gaussian prior for the parameters:

$$p(\boldsymbol{w}) \sim \mathcal{N}(\mathbf{0}, (1/\alpha)\mathbf{I})$$

which is a conjugate prior, and for the posterior, we get

$$p(\boldsymbol{w}|\mathcal{X}, \boldsymbol{r}) \sim \mathcal{N}(\boldsymbol{\mu}_N, \boldsymbol{\Sigma}_N)$$

where

(16.23)
$$\begin{aligned} \boldsymbol{\mu}_N &= \beta \boldsymbol{\Sigma}_N \mathbf{X}^T \boldsymbol{r} \\ \boldsymbol{\Sigma}_N &= (\alpha \mathbf{I} + \beta \mathbf{X}^T \mathbf{X})^{-1} \end{aligned}$$

To calculate the output for new $\boldsymbol{x}'$, we integrate over the full posterior

$$r' = \int (\boldsymbol{w}^T \boldsymbol{x}') p(\boldsymbol{w}|\mathcal{X}, \boldsymbol{r}) d\boldsymbol{w}$$

The graphical model for this is shown in figure 14.7.

If we want to use a point estimate, the MAP estimator is

(16.24)
$$\boldsymbol{w}_{MAP} = \boldsymbol{\mu}_N = \beta(\alpha \mathbf{I} + \beta \mathbf{X}^T \mathbf{X})^{-1} \mathbf{X}^T \boldsymbol{r}$$

and in calculating the output for input $\boldsymbol{x}'$, we replace the density with a single point, namely, the mean:

$$r' = \boldsymbol{w}_{MAP}^T \boldsymbol{x}'$$

We can also calculate the variance of our estimate:

(16.25)
$$\text{Var}(r') = 1/\beta + (\boldsymbol{x}')^T \boldsymbol{\Sigma}_N \boldsymbol{x}'$$

Comparing equation 16.24 with the ML estimate of equation 16.21, this can be seen as regularization—that is, we add a constant α to the diagonal to better condition the matrix to be inverted.

The prior, $p(\boldsymbol{w}) \sim \mathcal{N}(\mathbf{0}, (1/\alpha)\mathbf{I})$, says that we expect the parameters to be close to 0 with spread inversely proportional to α. When $\alpha \to 0$, we have a flat prior and the MAP estimate converges to the ML estimate.

We see in figure 16.4 that if we increase α, we force parameters to be closer to 0 and the posterior distribution moves closer to the origin and shrinks. If we decrease β, we assume noise with higher variance and the posterior also has higher variance.

If we take the log of the posterior, we have

$$\begin{aligned} \log p(\boldsymbol{w}|\mathbf{X}, \boldsymbol{r}) &\propto \log p(\boldsymbol{r}|\boldsymbol{w}, \mathbf{X}) + \log p(\boldsymbol{w}) \\ &= -\frac{\beta}{2} \sum_t (r^t - \boldsymbol{w}^T \boldsymbol{x}^t)^2 - \frac{\alpha}{2} \boldsymbol{w}^T \boldsymbol{w} + c \end{aligned}$$

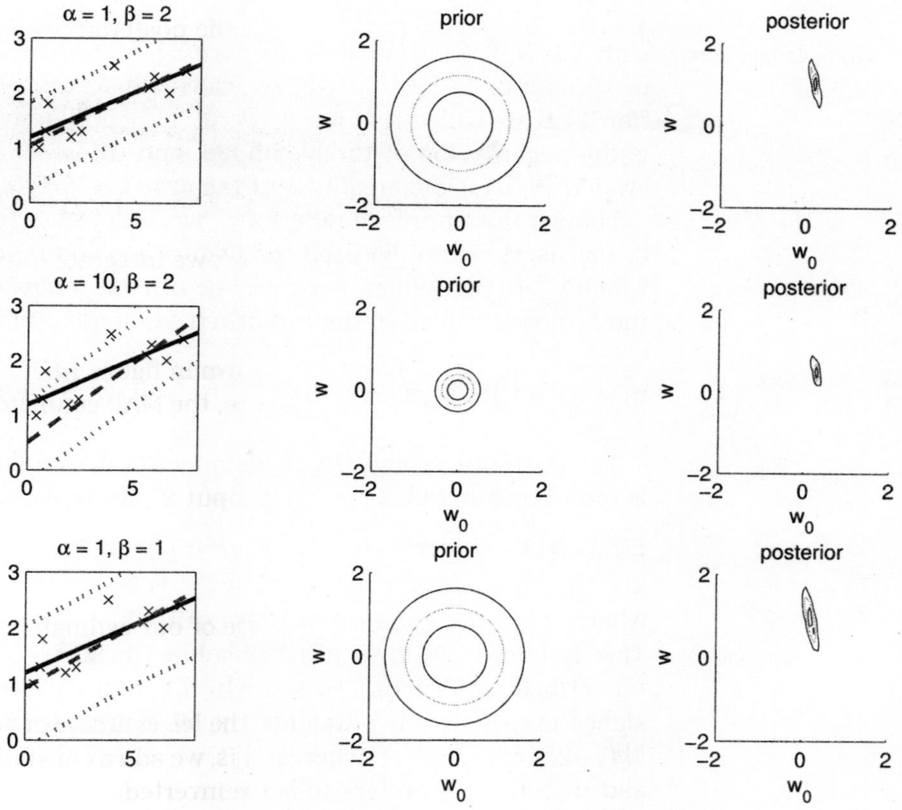

Figure 16.4 Bayesian linear regression for different values of α and β. To the left: crosses that are the data points and the straight line that is the ML solution. The MAP solution with one standard deviation error bars are also shown dashed. Center: prior density centered at 0 and variance $1/\alpha$. To the right: posterior density whose mean is the MAP solution. We see that when α is increased, the variance of the prior shrinks and the line moves closer to the flat 0 line. When β is decreased, more noise is assumed and the posterior density has higher variance.

which we maximize to find the MAP estimate. In the general case, given our model $g(\mathbf{x}|\mathbf{w})$, we can write an augmented error function

$$E_{ridge}(\mathbf{w}|\mathcal{X}) = \sum_t [r^t - g(\mathbf{x}^t|\mathbf{w})]^2 + \lambda \sum_i w_i^2$$

RIDGE REGRESSION

with $\lambda \equiv \alpha/\beta$. This is known as *parameter shrinkage* or *ridge regression* in statistics. In section 4.8, we called this *regularization*, and in section 11.9, we called this *weight decay* in neural networks. The first term is the negative log of the likelihood, and the second term penalizes w_i away from 0 (as dictated by α of the prior).

LAPLACIAN PRIOR

Though this approach reduces $\sum_i w_i^2$, it does not force individual w_i to 0; that is, it cannot be used for feature selection, namely, to determine which x_i are redundant. For this, one can use a *Laplacian prior* that uses the L_1 norm instead of the L_2 norm (Figueiredo 2003):

$$p(\mathbf{w}|\alpha) = \prod_i \frac{\alpha}{2} \exp(-\alpha|w_i|) = \left(\frac{\alpha}{2}\right)^d \exp\left(-\alpha \sum_i |w_i|\right)$$

The posterior probability is no longer Gaussian and the MAP estimate is found by minimizing

$$E_{lasso}(\mathbf{w}|\mathcal{X}) = \sum_t (r^t - \mathbf{w}^T\mathbf{x}^t)^2 + 2\sigma^2\alpha \sum_i |w_i|$$

LASSO

where σ^2 is the variance of noise (for which we plug in our estimate). This is known as *lasso* (least absolute shrinkage and selection operator) (Tibshirani 1996). To see why L_1 induces sparseness, let us consider the case with two weights $[w_1, w_2]^T$ (Figueiredo 2003): $\|[1, 0^T\|_2 = \|[1/\sqrt{2}, 1/\sqrt{2}]^T\|_2 = 1$, whereas $\|[1,0]^T\|_1 = 1 < \|[1/\sqrt{2}, 1/\sqrt{2}]^T\|_1 = \sqrt{2}$, and therefore L_1 prefers to set w_2 to 0 and use a large w_1, rather than having small values for both.

16.4.2 Regression with Prior on Noise Precision

Above, we assume that β, the precision of noise, is known and $\mathbf{w}$ is the only parameter we integrated on. If we do not know β, we can also define a prior on it. Just as we do in section 16.3, we can define a gamma prior:

$$p(\beta) \sim \text{gamma}(a_0, b_0)$$

and a prior on $\mathbf{w}$ conditioned on β:

$$p(\mathbf{w}|\beta) \sim \mathcal{N}(\boldsymbol{\mu}_0, \beta\Sigma_0)$$

If $\boldsymbol{\mu}_0 = \mathbf{0}$ and $\Sigma_0 = \alpha\mathbf{I}$, we get ridge regression, as we discussed above. We now can write a conjugate normal-gamma prior on parameters $\boldsymbol{w}$ and β:

$$p(\boldsymbol{w}, \beta) = p(\beta)p(\boldsymbol{w}|\beta) \sim \text{normal-gamma}(\boldsymbol{\mu}_0, \Sigma_0, a_0, b_0)$$

It can be shown (Hoff 2009) that the posterior is

$$p(\boldsymbol{w}, \beta|\mathbf{X}, \boldsymbol{r}) \sim \text{normal-gamma}(\boldsymbol{\mu}_N, \Sigma_N, a_N, b_N)$$

where

$$\begin{aligned} \Sigma_N &= (\mathbf{X}^T\mathbf{X} + \Sigma_0)^{-1} \\ \boldsymbol{\mu}_N &= \Sigma_N(\mathbf{X}^T\boldsymbol{r} + \Sigma_0\boldsymbol{\mu}_0) \\ a_N &= a_0 + N/2 \\ b_N &= b_0 + \frac{1}{2}(\boldsymbol{r}^T\boldsymbol{r} + \boldsymbol{\mu}_0^T\Sigma_0\boldsymbol{\mu}_0 - \boldsymbol{\mu}_N^T\Sigma_N\boldsymbol{\mu}_N) \end{aligned} \tag{16.26}$$

An example is given in figure 16.5 where we fit a polynomial of different degrees on a small set of instances—$\boldsymbol{w}$ corresponds to the vector of coefficients of the polynomial. We see that the maximum likelihood starts to overfit as the degree is increased.

MARKOV CHAIN MONTE CARLO SAMPLING

We use *Markov chain Monte Carlo sampling* to get the Bayesian fit as follows: We draw a β value from $p(\beta) \sim \text{gamma}(a_N, b_N)$, and then we draw a $\boldsymbol{w}$ from $p(\boldsymbol{w}|\beta) \sim \mathcal{N}(\boldsymbol{\mu}_N, \beta\Sigma_N)$, which gives us one sampled model from the posterior $p(\boldsymbol{w}, \beta)$. Ten such samples are drawn for each degree, as shown in figure 16.5. The thick line is the average of those ten models and is an approximation of the full integral; we see that even with ten samples, we get a reasonable and very smooth fit to the data. Note that any of the sampled models from the posterior is not necessarily any better than the maximum likelihood estimator; it is the averaging that leads to a smoother and hence better fit.

16.4.3 The Use of Basis/Kernel Functions

Using the Bayes' estimate of equation 16.23, the prediction is written as

$$\begin{aligned} r' &= (\boldsymbol{x}')^T\boldsymbol{w} \\ &= \beta(\boldsymbol{x}')^T\Sigma_N\mathbf{X}^T\boldsymbol{r} \\ &= \sum_t \beta(\boldsymbol{x}')^T\Sigma_N\boldsymbol{x}^t r^t \end{aligned}$$

DUAL REPRESENTATION

This is the *dual representation*. When we can write the parameter in

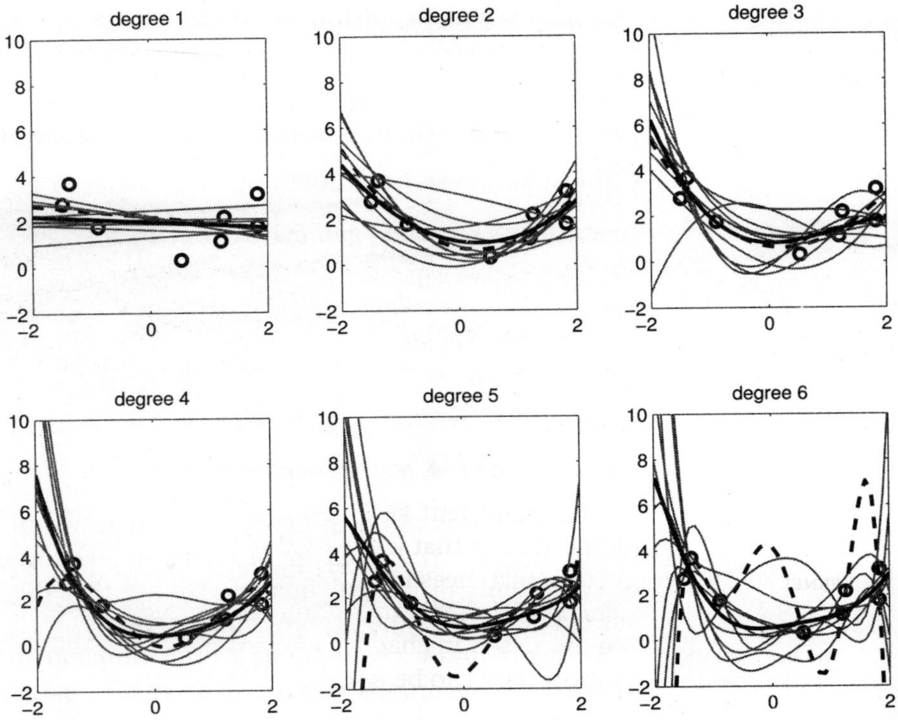

Figure 16.5 Bayesian polynomial regression example. Circles are the data points and the dashed line is the maximum likelihood fit, which overfits as the degree of the polynomial is increased. Thin lines are ten samples from the posterior $p(\mathbf{w}, \beta)$ and the thick line is their average.

terms of the training data, or a subset of it as in support vector machines (chapter 13), we can write the prediction as a function of the current input and past data. We can rewrite this as

$$r' = \sum_t K(\mathbf{x}', \mathbf{x}^t) r^t \tag{16.27}$$

where we define

$$K(\mathbf{x}', \mathbf{x}^t) = \beta(\mathbf{x}')^T \Sigma_N \mathbf{x}^t \tag{16.28}$$

We know that we can generalize the linear kernel of equation 16.28 by using a nonlinear *basis function* $\phi(\mathbf{x})$ to map to a new space where we

BASIS FUNCTION

fit the linear model. In such a case, instead of the d-dimensional $\boldsymbol{x}$ we have the k-dimensional $\boldsymbol{\phi}(\boldsymbol{x})$ where k is the number of basis functions and instead of $N \times d$ data matrix $\mathbf{X}$, we have $N \times k$ image of the basis functions $\boldsymbol{\Phi}$.

During test, we have

$$\begin{aligned} r' &= \boldsymbol{\phi}(\boldsymbol{x}')^T \boldsymbol{w} \text{ where } \boldsymbol{w} = \beta \Sigma_N^{\phi} \boldsymbol{\Phi}^T \boldsymbol{r} \text{ and } \Sigma_N^{\phi} = \left(\alpha \mathbf{I} + \beta \boldsymbol{\Phi}^T \boldsymbol{\Phi}\right)^{-1} \\ &= \beta \boldsymbol{\phi}(\boldsymbol{x}')^T \Sigma_N^{\phi} \boldsymbol{\Phi}^T \boldsymbol{r} \\ &= \sum_t \beta \boldsymbol{\phi}(\boldsymbol{x}')^T \Sigma_N^{\phi} \boldsymbol{\phi}(\boldsymbol{x}^t) r^t \\ &= \sum_t K(\boldsymbol{x}', \boldsymbol{x}^t) r^t \qquad (16.29) \end{aligned}$$

where we define

$$K(\boldsymbol{x}', \boldsymbol{x}^t) = \beta \boldsymbol{\phi}(\boldsymbol{x}')^T \Sigma_N^{\phi} \boldsymbol{\phi}(\boldsymbol{x}^t) \qquad (16.30)$$

KERNEL FUNCTION

as the equivalent kernel. This is the dual representation in the space of $\boldsymbol{\phi}(\boldsymbol{x})$. We see that we can write our estimate as a weighted sum of the effects of instances in the training set where the effect is given by the *kernel function* $K(\boldsymbol{x}', \boldsymbol{x}^t)$; this is similar to the nonparametric kernel smoothers we discussed in chapter 8, or the kernel machines of chapter 13.

Error bars can be defined using

$$\text{Var}(r') = \beta^{-1} + \boldsymbol{\phi}(\boldsymbol{x}')^T \Sigma_N^{\phi} \boldsymbol{\phi}(\boldsymbol{x}')$$

An example is given in figure 16.6 for the linear, quadratic, and sixth-degree kernels. This is equivalent to the polynomial regression we see in figure 16.5, except that here we use the dual representation and the polynomial coefficients $\boldsymbol{w}$ are embedded in the kernel function. We see that just as in regression proper where we can work on the original $\boldsymbol{x}$ or $\boldsymbol{\phi}(\boldsymbol{x})$, in Bayesian regression too we can work on the preprocessed $\boldsymbol{\phi}(\boldsymbol{x})$, defining parameters in that space. Later on in this chapter, we are going to see Gaussian processes where we can define and use $K(\boldsymbol{x}, \boldsymbol{x}^t)$ directly without needing to calculate $\boldsymbol{\phi}(\boldsymbol{x})$.

16.4.4 Bayesian Classification

In a two-class problem, we have a single output, and assuming a linear model, we have

$$P(C_1|\boldsymbol{x}^t) = y^t = \text{sigmoid}(\boldsymbol{w}^T \boldsymbol{x}^t)$$

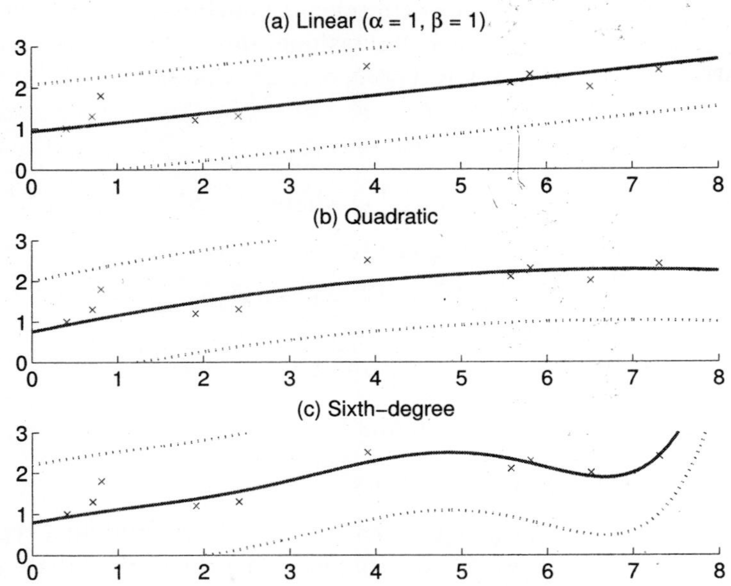

Figure 16.6 Bayesian regression using kernels with one standard deviation error bars: (a) linear: $\boldsymbol{\phi}(x) = [1, x]^T$, (b) quadratic: $\boldsymbol{\phi}(x) = [1, x, x^2]^T$, and (c) sixth degree: $\boldsymbol{\phi}(x) = [1, x, x^2, x^3, x^4, x^5, x^6]^T$.

The log likelihood of a Bernoulli sample is given as

$$\mathcal{L}(\boldsymbol{r}|\mathbf{X}) = \sum_t r^t \log y_t + (1 - r^t)\log(1 - y^t)$$

which we maximize, or minimize its negative log—the cross-entropy—to find the ML estimate, for example, using gradient descent. This is called *logistic discrimination* (section 10.7).

In the case of the Bayesian approach, we assume a Gaussian prior

$$p(\boldsymbol{w}) = \mathcal{N}(\boldsymbol{m}_0, \mathbf{S}_0) \tag{16.31}$$

and the log of the posterior is given as

$$\begin{aligned} \log p(\boldsymbol{w}|\boldsymbol{r}, \mathbf{X}) &\propto \log p(\boldsymbol{w}) + \log p(\boldsymbol{r}|\boldsymbol{w}, \mathbf{X}) \\ &= -\frac{1}{2}(\boldsymbol{w} - \boldsymbol{m}_0)^T \mathbf{S}_0^{-1}(\boldsymbol{w} - \boldsymbol{m}_0) \\ &\quad + \sum_t r^t \log y_t + (1 - r^t)\log(1 - y^t) + c \end{aligned} \tag{16.32}$$

This posterior distribution is no longer Gaussian, and we cannot integrate exactly. We can use *Laplace approximation*, which works as follows (MacKay 2003). Let us say we want to approximate some distribution $f(x)$, not necessarily normalized (to integrate to 1). In Laplace approximation, we find the mode of $f(x)$, x_0, fit a Gaussian $q(x)$ centered there with covariance given by the curvature of $f(x)$ around that mean, and then if we want to integrate, we integrate this fitted Gaussian instead.

LAPLACE APPROXIMATION

To find the variance of the Gaussian, we consider the Taylor expansion of $f(\cdot)$ at $x = x_0$

$$\log f(x) = \log f(x_0) - \frac{1}{2}a(x - x_0)^2 + \cdots$$

where

$$a \equiv -\frac{d}{dx^2}\log f(x)\Big|_{x=x_0}$$

Note that the first, linear term disappears because the first derivative is 0 at the mode. Taking exp, we have

$$f(x) = f(x_0)\exp\left[-\frac{a}{2}(x - x_0)^2\right]$$

To normalize $f(x)$, we consider that in a Gaussian distribution

$$\int \frac{1}{\sqrt{2\pi}(1/\sqrt{a})}\exp\left[-\frac{a}{2}(x - x_0)^2\right] = 1 \Rightarrow \int \exp\left[-\frac{a}{2}(x - x_0)^2\right] = \sqrt{a/2\pi}$$

and therefore

$$q(x) = \sqrt{a/2\pi}\exp\left[-\frac{a}{2}(x - x_0)^2\right] \sim \mathcal{N}(x_0, 1/a)$$

In the multivariate setting where $\boldsymbol{x} \in \Re^d$, we have

$$\log f(\boldsymbol{x}) = \log f(\boldsymbol{x}_0) - \frac{1}{2}(\boldsymbol{x} - \boldsymbol{x}_0)^T\mathbf{A}(\boldsymbol{x} - \boldsymbol{x}_0) + \cdots$$

where $\mathbf{A}$ is the (Hessian) matrix of second derivatives:

$$\mathbf{A} = -\nabla\nabla\log f(\boldsymbol{x})|_{\boldsymbol{x}=\boldsymbol{x}_0}$$

The Laplace approximation is then

$$f(\boldsymbol{x}) = \frac{|\mathbf{A}|^{1/2}}{(2\pi)^{d/2}}\exp\left[-\frac{1}{2}(\boldsymbol{x} - \boldsymbol{x}_0)^T\mathbf{A}(\boldsymbol{x} - \boldsymbol{x}_0)\right] \sim \mathcal{N}_d(\boldsymbol{x}_0, \mathbf{A}^{-1})$$

Having now discussed how to approximate, we can now use it for the posterior density. The MAP estimate, $\boldsymbol{w}_{MAP}$—the mode of $p(\boldsymbol{w}|\boldsymbol{r}, \mathbf{X})$—is taken as the mean, and the covariance matrix is given by the inverse of the matrix of the second derivatives of the negative log likelihood:

$$\mathbf{S}_N = -\nabla\nabla \log p(\boldsymbol{w}|\boldsymbol{r},\mathbf{X}) = \mathbf{S}_0^{-1} + \sum_t y^t(1-y^t)\boldsymbol{x}^t(\boldsymbol{x}^t)^T$$

We then integrate over this Gaussian to estimate the class probability:

$$P(C_1|\boldsymbol{x}) = y = \int \text{sigmoid}(\boldsymbol{w}^T\boldsymbol{x})q(\boldsymbol{w})d\boldsymbol{w}$$

where $q(\boldsymbol{w}) \sim \mathcal{N}(\boldsymbol{w}_{MAP}, \mathbf{S}_N^{-1})$. A further complication is that we cannot integrate analytically over a Gaussian convolved with a sigmoid. If we use the *probit function* instead, which has the same S-shape as the sigmoid, an analytical solution is possible (Bishop 2006).

PROBIT FUNCTION

16.5 Choosing a Prior

Defining the prior is the subjective part of Bayesian estimation and as such should be done with care. It is best to define robust priors with heavy tails so as not to limit the parameter space too much; in the extreme case of no prior preference, one can use an uninformative prior and methods have been proposed for this purpose, for example, Jeffreys prior (Murphy 2012). Sometimes our choice of a prior is also motivated by simplicity—for example, a conjugate prior makes inference quite easy.

One critical decision is when to take a parameter as a constant and when to define it as a random variable with a prior and to be integrated (averaged) out. For example, in section 16.4.1, we assume that we know the noise precision whereas in section 16.4.2, we assume we do not and define a gamma prior on it. Similarly for the spread of weights in linear regression, we assume a constant α value but can also define a prior on it and average it out if we want. Of course, this makes the prior more complicated and the whole inference more difficult but averaging over α should be preferred if we do not know what the good value for α is.

Another decision is how high to go in defining the priors. Let us say we have parameter θ and we define a posterior on it. In prediction, we have

$$\text{Level I: } p(x|\mathcal{X}) = \int p(x|\theta)p(\theta|\mathcal{X})d\theta$$

where $p(\theta|\mathcal{X}) \propto p(\mathcal{X}|\theta)p(\theta)$. If we believe that we cannot define a good

$p(\theta)$ but that it depends on some other variable, we can condition θ on a hyper parameter α and integrate it out:

$$\text{Level II: } p(x|\mathcal{X}) = \int p(x|\theta)p(\theta|\mathcal{X}, \alpha)p(\alpha)d\theta d\alpha$$

This is called a *hierarchical prior.* This really makes the inference rather difficult because we need to integrate on two levels. One shortcut is to test different values α on the data, choose the best α^*, and just use that value:

$$\text{Level II ML: } p(x|\mathcal{X}) = \int p(x|\theta)p(\theta|\mathcal{X}, \alpha^*)d\theta$$

This is called *level II maximum likelihood* or *empirical Bayes.*

16.6 Bayesian Model Comparison

Assume we have many models $\mathcal{M}_j$, each with its own set of parameters θ_j, and we want to compare these models. For example, in figure 16.5, we have polynomials of different degrees and let us say we want to check how well they fit the data.

For a given model $\mathcal{M}$ and parameter θ, the likelihood of data is $p(\mathcal{X}|\mathcal{M}, \theta)$.

MARGINAL LIKELIHOOD

To get the Bayesian *marginal likelihood* for a given model, we average over θ:

$$p(\mathcal{X}|\mathcal{M}) = \int p(\mathcal{X}|\theta, \mathcal{M})p(\theta|\mathcal{M})d\theta \quad (16.33)$$

MODEL EVIDENCE

This is also called *model evidence.* For example, in the polynomial regression example above, for a given degree, we have

$$p(\boldsymbol{r}|\mathbf{X}, \mathcal{M}) = \int\int p(\boldsymbol{r}|\mathbf{X}, \boldsymbol{w}, \beta, \mathcal{M})p(\boldsymbol{w}, \beta|\mathcal{M})d\boldsymbol{w}d\beta$$

where $p(\boldsymbol{w}, \beta|\mathcal{M})$ is the prior assumed for model $\mathcal{M}$. We can then calculate the posterior probability of a model given the data:

$$p(\mathcal{M}|\mathcal{X}) = \frac{p(\mathcal{X}|\mathcal{M})p(\mathcal{M})}{p(\mathcal{X})} \quad (16.34)$$

where $P(\mathcal{M})$ is the prior distribution defined over models. The nice property of the Bayesian approach is that even if those priors are taken uniform, the marginal likelihood, because it averages over all θ, favors simpler models. Let us assume we have models in increasing complexity, for example, polynomials with increasing degree.

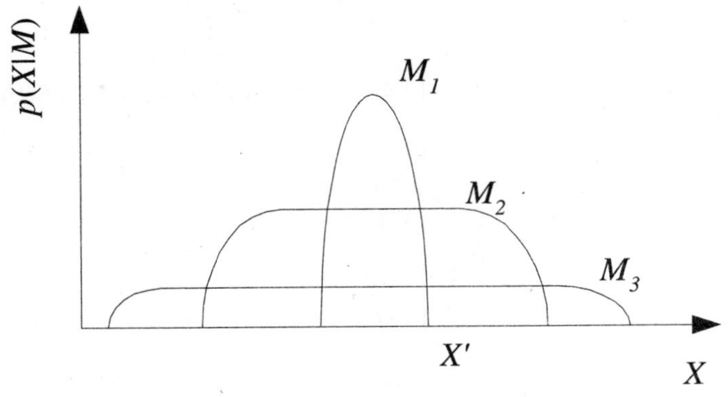

Figure 16.7 Bayesian model comparison favors simpler models. $\mathcal{M}_1$, $\mathcal{M}_2$, and $\mathcal{M}_3$ are three models in increasing complexity. The x axis is the space of all datasets with N instances. A complex model can fit more datasets but spreads itself thin over the space of all possible datasets of size N; a simpler model can fit fewer datasets but each with a heavier probability. For a particular dataset $\mathcal{X}'$, if both can fit, the simpler model will have higher marginal likelihood (MacKay 2003).

Let us say we have a dataset $\mathcal{X}$ with N instances. A more complex model will be able to fit more of such datasets reasonably well compared with a simpler model—consider choosing randomly three points in a plane; the number of such triples that can be fitted by a line is much fewer than the number of triples that can be fitted by a quadratic. Given that $\sum_{\mathcal{X}} p(\mathcal{X}|\mathcal{M}) = 1$, because for a complex model there are more possible $\mathcal{X}$ where it can make a reasonable fit, if there is a fit, the value of $p(\mathcal{X}'|\mathcal{M})$ for some particular $\mathcal{X}'$ is going to be smaller—see figure 16.7. Hence for a simpler model $p(\mathcal{M}|\mathcal{X})$ will be higher (even if we assume that the priors, $p(\mathcal{M})$, are equal); this is the Bayesian interpretation of Occam's razor (MacKay 2003).

For the polynomial fitting example of figure 16.5, a comparison of likelihood and the marginal likelihood is shown in figure 16.8. We see that likelihood increases when complexity increases, which implies overfitting, but the marginal likelihood increases until the correct degree and then starts decreasing; this is because there are many more complex models that fit badly to the data and they pull the likelihood down as

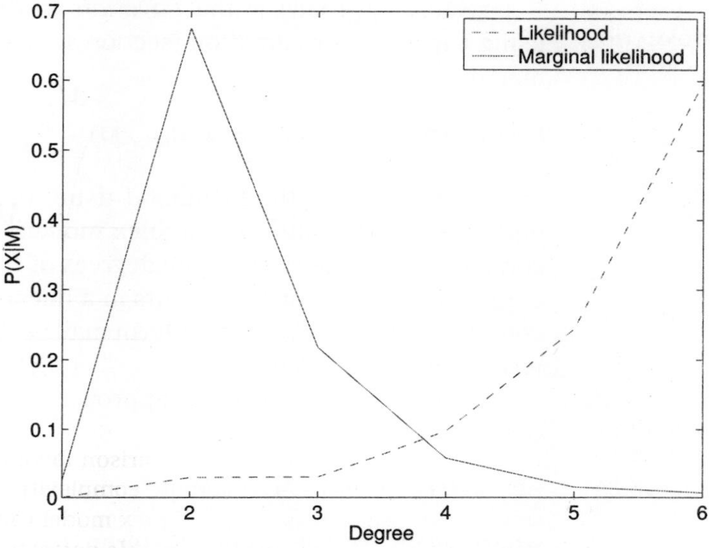

Figure 16.8 Likelihood versus marginal likelihood for the polynomial regression example. Though the likelihood increases as the degree of the polynomial increases, the marginal likelihood that averages over parameter values make a peak at the right complexity and then levels off.

we average over them.

If we have two models $\mathcal{M}_0$ and $\mathcal{M}_1$, we can compare them

$$\frac{P(\mathcal{M}_1|\mathcal{X})}{P(\mathcal{M}_0|\mathcal{X})} = \frac{P(\mathcal{X}|\mathcal{M}_1)}{P(\mathcal{X}|\mathcal{M}_0)} \frac{P(\mathcal{M}_1)}{P(\mathcal{M}_0)}$$

and we have higher belief in $\mathcal{M}_1$ if this ratio is higher than 1, and in $\mathcal{M}_0$ otherwise.

There are two important points here: One, the ratio of the two marginal likelihoods is called the *Bayes factor* and is enough for model selection even if the two priors are taken equal. Second, in the Bayesian approach, we do not choose among models and we do not do model selection; but in keeping with the spirit of the Bayesian approach, we average over their predictions rather than choosing one and discarding the rest. For instance, in the polynomial regression example above, rather than choosing one degree, it is best to take a weighted average over all degrees weighted by their marginal likelihoods.

BAYES FACTOR

BAYESIAN INFORMATION CRITERION

A related approach is the *Bayesian information criterion* (BIC) where using Laplace approximation (section 16.4.4), equation 16.33 is approximated as

$$\log p(\mathcal{X}|\mathcal{M}) \approx \text{BIC} \equiv \log p(\mathcal{X}|\theta_{ML}, \mathcal{M}) - \frac{|\mathcal{M}|}{2} \log N \tag{16.35}$$

The first term is the likelihood using the ML estimator and the second term is a penalty for complex models: $|\mathcal{M}|$ is a measure of model complexity, in other words, the degrees of freedom in the model—for example, the number of coefficients in a linear regression model. As model complexity increases, the first term may be higher but the second penalty term compensates for this.

AKAIKE'S INFORMATION CRITERION

A related, but not Bayesian, approach is *Akaike's information criterion* (AIC), which is written as

$$\text{AIC} \equiv \log p(\mathcal{X}|\theta_{ML}, \mathcal{M}) - |\mathcal{M}| \tag{16.36}$$

where again we see a penalty term that is proportional to the model complexity. It is important to note here that in such criteria, $|\mathcal{M}|$ represents the "effective" degrees of freedom and not simply the number of adjustable parameters in the model. For example in a multilayer perceptron (chapter 11), the effective degrees of freedom is much less than the number of adjustable connection weights.

One interpretation of the penalty term is as a term of "optimism" (Hastie, Tibshirani, and Friedman 2011). In a complex model, the ML estimator would overfit and hence be a very optimistic indicator of model performance; therefore, it should be cut back proportional to the model complexity.

16.7 Bayesian Estimation of a Mixture Model

In section 7.2, we discuss the mixture model where we write the density as a weighted sum of component densities. Let us remember equation 7.1:

$$p(\boldsymbol{x}) = \sum_{i=1}^{k} P(\mathcal{G}_i)p(\boldsymbol{x}|\mathcal{G}_i)$$

where $P(\mathcal{G}_i)$ are the mixture proportions and $p(\boldsymbol{x}|\mathcal{G}_i)$ are the component densities. For example, in Gaussian mixtures, we have $p(\boldsymbol{x}|\mathcal{G}_i) \sim$

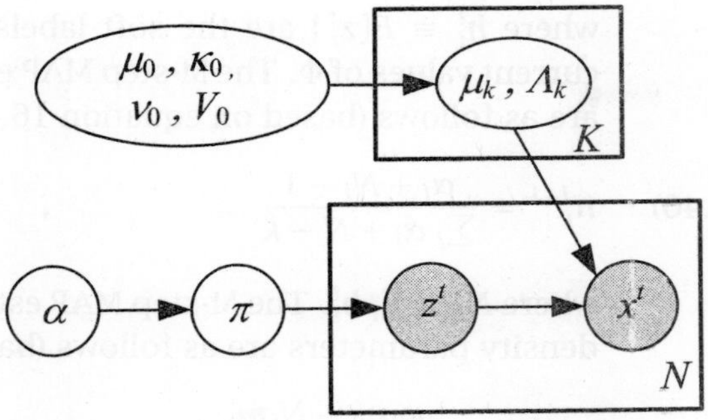

Figure 16.9 The generative graphical representation of a Gaussian mixture model.

$\mathcal{N}(\boldsymbol{\mu}_i, \Sigma_i)$, and defining $\pi_i \equiv P(\mathcal{G}_i)$, we have the parameter vector $\Phi = \{\pi_i, \boldsymbol{\mu}_i, \Sigma_i\}_{i=1}^k$ that we need to learn from data $\mathcal{X} = \{\boldsymbol{x}^t\}_{t=1}^N$.

In section 7.4, we discussed the EM algorithm that is a maximum likelihood procedure:

$$\Phi_{MLE} = \arg\max_{\Phi} \log p(\mathcal{X}|\Phi)$$

If we have a prior distribution $p(\Phi)$, we can devise a Bayesian approach. For example, the MAP estimator is

$$\Phi_{MAP} = \arg\max_{\Phi} \log p(\Phi|\mathcal{X}) = \arg\max_{\Phi} \log p(\mathcal{X}|\Phi) + \log p(\Phi) \tag{16.37}$$

Let us now write down the prior. Π_i are multinomial variables and for them, we can use a Dirichlet prior as we discuss in section 16.2.1. For the Gaussian components, for the mean and precision (inverse covariance) matrix, we can use a normal-Wishart prior as we discuss in section 16.3:

$$\begin{aligned} p(\Phi) &= p(\boldsymbol{\pi}) \prod_i p(\boldsymbol{\mu}_i, \Lambda_i) \\ &= \text{Dirichlet}(\boldsymbol{\pi}|\boldsymbol{\alpha}) \prod_i \text{normal-Wishart}(\boldsymbol{\mu}_0, \kappa_0, \nu_0, \mathbf{V}_0) \end{aligned} \tag{16.38}$$

So in using EM in this case, the E-step does not change, but in the M-step we maximize the posterior with this prior (Murphy 2012). Adding log of the posterior, equation 7.10 becomes

$$\begin{aligned} \mathcal{Q}(\Phi|\Phi^l) &= \sum_t \sum_i h_i^t \log \pi_i + \sum_t \sum_i h_i^t \log p_i(\boldsymbol{x}^t|\Phi^l) + \log p(\boldsymbol{\pi}) + \\ & \sum_i \log p(\boldsymbol{\mu}_i, \Lambda_i) \end{aligned} \tag{16.39}$$

where $h_i^t \equiv E[z_i^t]$ are the soft labels estimated in the E-step using the current values of Φ. The M-step MAP estimate for the mixture proportions are as follows (based on equation 16.4):

$$\pi_i^{l+1} = \frac{\alpha_i + N_i - 1}{\sum_i \alpha_i + N - k} \tag{16.40}$$

where $N_i = \sum_i h_i^t$. The M-step MAP estimates for the Gaussian component density parameters are as follows (based on equation 16.16):

$$\begin{aligned} \boldsymbol{\mu}_i^{l+1} &= \frac{\kappa_0 \boldsymbol{\mu}_0 + N_i \boldsymbol{m}_i}{\kappa_0 + N_i} \\ \boldsymbol{\Lambda}_i^{l+1} &= \left(\frac{\mathbf{V}_0^{-1} + \mathbf{C}_i + \mathbf{S}_i}{\nu_0 + N_i + d + 2} \right)^{-1} \end{aligned} \tag{16.41}$$

where $\boldsymbol{m}_i = \sum_t h_i^t / N_i$ is the component mean, $\mathbf{C}_i = \sum_t h_i^t (\boldsymbol{x}^t - \boldsymbol{m}_i)(\boldsymbol{x}^t - \boldsymbol{m}_i)^T$ is the within-scatter matrix for component i, and $\mathbf{S}_i = (\kappa_0 N_i)/(\kappa_0 + N_i)(\boldsymbol{m}_i - \boldsymbol{\mu}_0)(\boldsymbol{m}_i - \boldsymbol{\mu}_0)^T$ is the between-scatter of component i around the prior mean.

If we take $\alpha_i = 1/K$, this is a uniform prior. We can take $\kappa_0 = 0$ not to bias the mean estimates unless we do have some prior information about them. We can take $\mathbf{V}_0$ as the identity matrix and hence the MAP estimate has a regularizing effect.

The mixture density is shown as a generative graphical model in figure 16.9.

Once we know how to do basic blocks in a Bayesian manner, we can combine them to get more complicated models. For example, combining the mixture model we have here and the linear regression model we discuss in section 16.4.1, we can write the Bayesian version of the mixture of experts model (section 12.8) where we cluster the data into components and learn a separate linear regression model in each component at the same time. The posterior turns out to be rather nasty and Waterhouse et al. 1996 use variational approximation, which, roughly speaking, works as follows.

VARIATIONAL APPROXIMATION

We remember that in Laplace approximation, we approximate $p(\theta|\mathcal{X})$ by a Gaussian and integrate over the Gaussian instead. In *variational approximation*, we approximate the posterior by a density $q(\mathcal{Z}|\psi)$ whose parameters ψ are adjustable (Jordan et al. 1999; MacKay 2003; Bishop 2006). Hence, it is more general because we are not restricted to use a Gaussian density. Here, $\mathcal{Z}$ contains all the latent variables in the model *and* the parameters θ, and ψ of the approximating model $q(\mathcal{Z}|\psi)$ are adjusted such that $q(\mathcal{Z}|\psi)$ is as close as possible to $p(\mathcal{Z}|\mathcal{X})$.

KULLBACK-LEIBLER DISTANCE

We define as the *Kullback-Leibler distance* between the two:

(16.42) $$D_{\text{KL}}(q||p) = \sum_{\mathcal{Z}} q(\mathcal{Z}|\psi) \log \frac{q(\mathcal{Z}|\psi)}{p(\mathcal{Z}|\mathcal{X})}$$

To make life easier, the set of latent variables (including the parameters) is assumed to be partitioned into subsets $\mathcal{Z}_i, i = 1, \ldots, k$, such that the variational distribution can be factorized:

(16.43) $$q(\mathcal{Z}|\psi) = \prod_{i=1}^{k} q_i(\mathcal{Z}_i|\psi_i)$$

Adjustment of the parameters ψ_i in each factor is iterative, rather like the expectation-maximization algorithm we discussed in section 7.4. We start from (possibly random) initial values and while adjusting each, we use the expected values of the $\mathcal{Z}_j, j \neq i$ in a circular manner. This is called the *mean-field approximation.*

MEAN-FIELD APPROXIMATION

This factorization is an approximation. For example, in section 16.4.2 when we discuss regression, we write

$$p(\boldsymbol{w}, \beta) = p(\beta)p(\boldsymbol{w}|\beta)$$

because $\boldsymbol{w}$ is conditioned on β. A variational approximation would assume

$$p(\boldsymbol{w}, \beta) = p(\beta)p(\boldsymbol{w})$$

For example, in the mixture of experts model, the latent parameters are the component indices and the parameters are the parameters in the gating model, the regression weights in the local experts, the variance of the noise, and the hyperparameters of the priors for gating and regression weights; they are all factors (Waterhouse, MacKay, and Robinson 1996).

16.8 Nonparametric Bayesian Modeling

The models we discuss earlier in this chapter are all parametric, in the sense that we have models of fixed complexity with a set of parameters and these parameters are optimized using the data and the prior information. In chapter 8, we discussed nonparametric models where the training data makes up the model and hence model complexity depends on the size of the data. Now we address how such a nonparametric approach can be used in the Bayesian setting.

A nonparametric model does not mean that the model has no parameters; it means that the number of parameters is not fixed and that their number can grow depending on the size of the data, or better still, depending on the complexity of the regularity that underlies the data. Such models are also sometimes called *infinite* models, in the sense that their complexity can keep on increasing with more data. In section 11.9, we discuss incremental neural network models where new hidden units are added when necessary and network is grown during training, but usually in parametric learning, adjusting model complexity is handled in an outer loop by checking performance on a separate validation set. The nonparametric Bayesian approach includes model adjustment in parameter training by using a suitable prior (Gershman and Blei 2012). This makes such models more flexible, and would have normally made them prone to overfitting if not for the Bayesian approach that alleviates this risk.

Because it is the parameters that grow, the priors on such parameters should be able to handle that growth and we will discuss three example prior distributions for three different type of machine learning applications, namely, Gaussian processes for supervised learning, Dirichlet processes for clustering, and beta processes for dimensionality reduction.

16.9 Gaussian Processes

Let us say we have the linear model $y = \boldsymbol{w}^T\boldsymbol{x}$. Then, for each $\boldsymbol{w}$, we have one line. Given a prior distribution $p(\boldsymbol{w})$, we get a distribution of lines, or to be more specific, for any $\boldsymbol{w}$, we get a distribution of y values calculated at x as $y(\boldsymbol{x}|\boldsymbol{w})$ when $\boldsymbol{w}$ is sampled from $p(\boldsymbol{w})$, and this is what we mean when we talk about a *Gaussian process*. We know that if $p(\boldsymbol{w})$ is Gaussian, each y is a linear combination of Gaussians and is also Gaussian; in particular, we are interested in the joint distribution of y values calculated at the N input data points, $\boldsymbol{x}^t, t = 1, \ldots, N$ (MacKay 1998).

GAUSSIAN PROCESS

We assume a zero-mean Gaussian prior

$$p(\boldsymbol{w}) \sim \mathcal{N}(\mathbf{0}, (1/\alpha)\mathbf{I})$$

Given the $N \times d$ data points $\mathbf{X}$ and the $d \times 1$ weight vector, we write the

y outputs as

(16.44) $$y = \mathbf{X}w$$

which is N-variate Gaussian with

(16.45) $$\begin{aligned} E[y] &= \mathbf{X}E[w] = \mathbf{0} \\ \text{Cov}(y) &= E[yy^T] = \mathbf{X}E[ww^T]\mathbf{X}^T = \frac{1}{\alpha}\mathbf{X}\mathbf{X}^T \equiv \mathbf{K} \end{aligned}$$

where $\mathbf{K}$ is the (Gram) matrix with elements

$$K_{i,j} \equiv K(x^i, x^j) = \frac{(x^i)^T x^j}{\alpha}$$

COVARIANCE FUNCTION

This is known as the *covariance function* in the literature of Gaussian processes and the idea is the same as in kernel functions: If we use a set of basis functions $\boldsymbol{\phi}(x)$, we generalize from the dot product of the original inputs to the dot product of basis functions by a kernel

$$K_{i,j} = \frac{\boldsymbol{\phi}(x^i)^T \boldsymbol{\phi}(x^j)}{\alpha}$$

The actual observed output r is given by the line with added noise, $r = y + \epsilon$ where $\epsilon \sim \mathcal{N}(0, \beta^{-1})$. For all N data points, we write it as

(16.46) $$r \sim \mathcal{N}_N(\mathbf{0}, \mathbf{C}_N) \text{ where } \mathbf{C}_N = \beta^{-1}\mathbf{I} + \mathbf{K}$$

To make a prediction, we consider the new data as the $(N+1)$st data point pair (x', r'), and write the joint using all $N+1$ data points. We have

(16.47) $$r_{N+1} \sim \mathcal{N}_N(\mathbf{0}, \mathbf{C}_{N+1})$$

where

$$\mathbf{C}_{N+1} = \begin{bmatrix} \mathbf{C}_N & k \\ k^T & c \end{bmatrix}$$

with k being the $N \times 1$ dimensional vector of $K(x', x^t), t = 1, \ldots, N$ and $c = K(x', x') + \beta^{-1}$. Then to make a prediction, we calculate $p(r'|x', \mathbf{X}, r)$, which is Gaussian with

$$\begin{aligned} E[r'|x'] &= k^T \mathbf{C}_N^{-1} r \\ \text{Var}(r'|x') &= c - k^T \mathbf{C}_N^{-1} k \end{aligned}$$

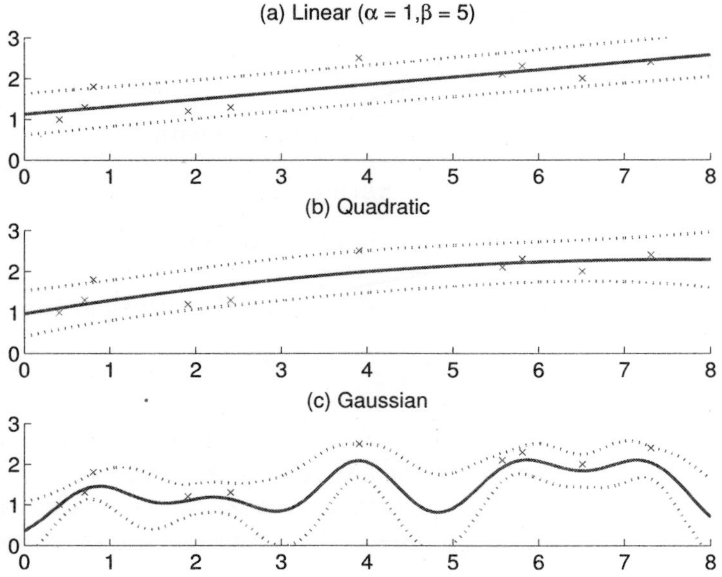

Figure 16.10 Gaussian process regression with one standard deviation error bars: (a) linear kernel, (b) quadratic kernel, and (c) Gaussian kernel with spread $s^2 = 0.5$.

An example shown in figure 16.10 uses linear, quadratic, and Gaussian kernels. The first two are defined as the dot product of their corresponding basis functions; the Gaussian kernel is defined directly as

$$K_G(\mathbf{x}^i, \mathbf{x}^j) = \exp\left[-\frac{\|\mathbf{x}^i - \mathbf{x}^j\|^2}{s^2}\right]$$

The mean, which is our point estimate (if we do not integrate over the full distribution), can also be written as a weighted sum of the kernel effects

(16.48) $$E[r'|\mathbf{x}'] = \sum_t a^t K(\mathbf{x}^t, \mathbf{x}')$$

where a^t is the tth component of $\mathbf{C}_N^{-1}\boldsymbol{r}$. Or, we can write it as a weighted sum of the outputs of the training data points where weights are given by the kernel function

(16.49) $$E[r'|\mathbf{x}'] = \sum_t r^t w^t$$

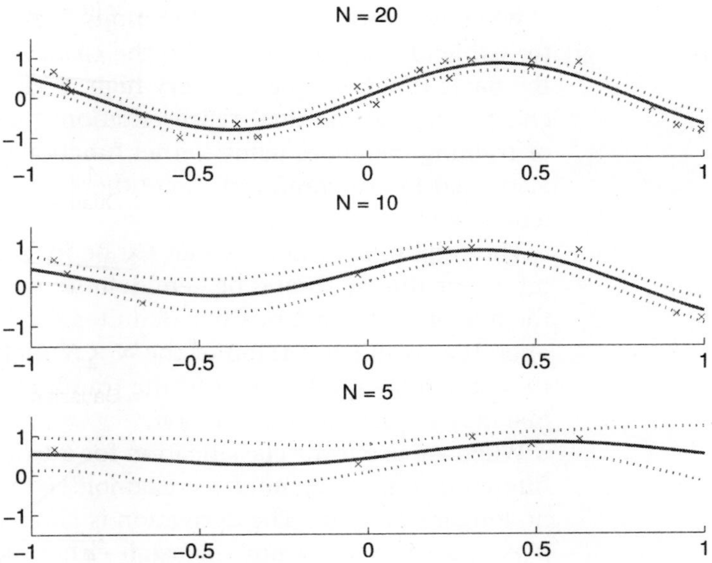

Figure 16.11 Gaussian process regression using a Gaussian kernel with $s^2 = 0.5$ and varying number of training data. We see how variance of the prediction is larger where there is few data.

where w^t is the tth component of $\boldsymbol{k}^T \mathbf{C}_N^{-1}$.

Note that we can also calculate the variance of a prediction at a point to get an idea about uncertainty in there, and it depends on the instances that affect the prediction in there. In the case of a Gaussian kernel, only instances within a locality are effective and prediction variance is high where there is little data in the vicinity (see figure 16.11).

Kernel functions can be defined and used for any application, as we have previously discussed in the context of kernel machines in chapter 13. The possibility of using kernel functions directly without needing to calculate or store the basis functions offers a great flexibility. Normally, given a training set, we first calculate the parameters, for example using equation 16.21, and then use the parameters to make predictions using equation 16.22, never needing the training set any more. This makes sense because generally the dimensionality of the parameters, which is generally $\mathcal{O}(d)$, is much lower than the size of the training set N.

When we work with basis functions, however, calculating the parameter explicitly may no longer be the case, because the dimensionality of the basis functions may be very high, even infinite. In such a case, it is cheaper to use the dual representation, taking into account the effects of training instances using kernel functions, as we do here. This idea is also used in nonparametric smoothers (chapter 8) and kernel machines (chapter 13).

The requirement here is that $\mathbf{C}_N$ be invertible and hence positive definite. For this, $\mathbf{K}$ should be semidefinite so that after adding $\beta^{-1} > 0$ to the diagonals, we get positive definiteness. We also see that the costliest operation is this inversion of the $N \times N$ matrix, which fortunately needs to be calculated only once (during training) and stored. Still, for large N, one may need an approximation.

When we use it for classification for a two-class problem, the output is filtered through a sigmoid, $y = \text{sigmoid}(\boldsymbol{w}^T\boldsymbol{x})$, and the distribution of y is no longer Gaussian. The derivation is similar except that the conditional $p(r_{N+1}|\boldsymbol{x}_{N+1}, \mathbf{X}, \boldsymbol{r})$ is not Gaussian either and we need to approximate, for example, using Laplace approximation (Bishop 2006; Rasmussen and Williams 2006).

16.10 Dirichlet Processes and Chinese Restaurants

To explain a Dirichlet process, let us start with a metaphor: There is a Chinese restaurant with a lot of tables. Customers enter one by one; we start with the first customer who sits at the first table, and any subsequent customer can either sit at one of the occupied tables or go and start a new table. The probability that a customer sits at an occupied table is proportional to the number of customers already sitting at the table, and the probability that he or she sits at a new table depends on a parameter α. This is called a *Chinese restaurant process*:

CHINESE RESTAURANT PROCESS

$$\begin{aligned} \text{Join existing table } i \text{ with } P(z_i = 1) &= \frac{n_i}{\alpha + n - 1}, i = 1, \ldots, k \\ \text{Start new table with } P(z_{k+1} = 1) &= \frac{\alpha}{\alpha + n - 1} \end{aligned}$$

where n_i is the number of customers already starting at table i, $n = \sum_{i=1}^{k} n_i$ is the total number of customers. α is the propensity to start a new table and is the parameter of the process. Note that at each step, the sitting arrangement of customers define a partition of integers 1 to n into k subsets. This is called a *Dirichlet process* with parameter α.

DIRICHLET PROCESS

We can apply this to clustering by making customer choices not only dependent on the table occupancies but also on the input. Let us say that this is not a Chinese restaurant but the dinner of a large conference, for example, NIPS. There is a large dining lounge with many tables, and in the evening, the conference participants enter the lounge one by one. They want to eat, but they also want to participate in interesting conversation. For that, they want to sit at a table where there are already many people sitting, but they also want to sit next to people having similar research interests. If they see no such table, they start a new table and expect incoming similar participants to find and join them.

Assume that instance/participant t is represented by a d-dimensional vector $\boldsymbol{x}^t$, and let us assume that such $\boldsymbol{x}^t$ are locally Gaussian distributed. This defines a Gaussian mixture over the whole space/dining lounge, and to have it Bayesian, we define priors on the parameters of the Gaussian components, as we discuss in section 16.7. To make it nonparametric, we define a Dirichlet process as the prior so a new component can be added when necessary, as follows:

$$\begin{aligned}
\text{Join component } i \text{ with } P(z_i^t = 1) &\propto \frac{n_i}{\alpha + n - 1} p(\boldsymbol{x}^t | \mathcal{X}_i), i = 1, \ldots, k \\
\text{Start new component with } P(z_{k+1}^t) &\propto \frac{\alpha}{\alpha + n - 1} p(\boldsymbol{x}^t)
\end{aligned}$$

$\mathcal{X}_i$ is the set of instances previously assigned to component i; using their data and the priors, we can calculate a posterior and integrating over it, we can calculate $p(\boldsymbol{x}^t | \mathcal{X}_i)$. Roughly speaking, the probability this new instance is assigned to component i will be high if there are already many instances in the component, that is, due to a high prior, or if $\boldsymbol{x}^t$ is similar to the instances already in $\mathcal{X}_i$. If none of the existing components have a high probability, a new component is added: $p(\boldsymbol{x}^t)$ is the marginal probability (integrated over the component parameter priors because there is no data).

Different α may lead to different numbers of clusters. To adjust α, we can use empirical Bayes, or also define a prior on it and average it out.

In chapter 7, when we talk about k-means clustering (section 7.3), we discuss leader-cluster algorithms where new clusters are added during training and as an example of that, in section 12.2.2, we discuss adaptive resonance theory where we add a new cluster if the distance to the center

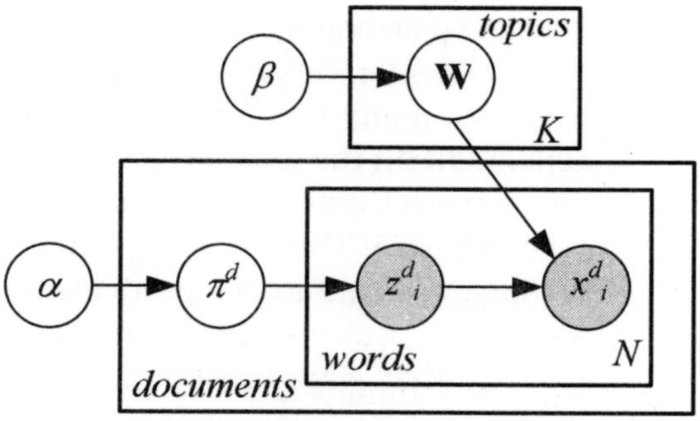

Figure 16.12 The graphical model for latent Dirichlet allocation.

of the nearest cluster is more than a vigilance value. What we have here is very similar: Assuming Gaussian components and diagonal covariance matrices, if the Euclidean distance to all clusters is high, all posteriors will be small and a new component will be added.

16.11 Latent Dirichlet Allocation

TOPIC MODELING

Let us see an application of the Bayesian approach in text processing, namely *topic modeling* (Blei 2012). In this age, there are digital repositories containing a very large number of documents—scientific articles, web pages, emails, blog posts, and so on—but finding a relevant topic for a query is very difficult, unless documents are manually annotated with topics, such as "arts," "sports," and so on. What we would like to is do this annotation automatically.

Assume we have a vocabulary with M words. Each document contains N words chosen from a number of topics in different proportions—that is, each document is a probability distribution over topics. A document may be partially "arts" and partially "politics," for example. Each topic in turn is defined as a mixture of the M words—that is, each topic corresponds to a probability distribution over words. For example, for the topic arts, the words "painting" and "sculpture" have a high probability, but the word "knee" has a low probability.

LATENT DIRICHLET ALLOCATION

In *latent Dirichlet allocation*, we define a generative process as follows (figure 16.12)—there are K topics, a vocabulary of M words, and all documents contain N words (Blei, Ng, and Jordan 2003):

To generate each document d, we first decide on the topics it will be about. These topic probabilities, $\pi_k^d, k = 1, \ldots, K$, define a multinomial distribution and are drawn from a Dirichlet prior with hyperparameter $\boldsymbol{\alpha}$ (section 16.2.1):

$$\boldsymbol{\pi}^d \sim \text{Dirichlet}_K(\boldsymbol{\alpha})$$

Once we know the topic distribution for document d, we generate its N words using it. In generating word i, first we decide on its particular topic by sampling from $\boldsymbol{\pi}$: We roll a die with K faces where face k has probability π_k. We define z_i^d as the outcome, it will be a value between 1 and K:

$$z_i^d \sim \text{Mult}_K(\boldsymbol{\pi}^d)$$

Now we know that in document d, the ith word will be about topic $z_i^d \in \{1, \ldots, K\}$. We have a $K \times M$ matrix of probabilities $\mathbf{W}$ whose row k, $\boldsymbol{w}_k \equiv [w_{k1}, \ldots, w_{KM}]^T$ gives us the probabilities of occurrences of the M words in topic k. So knowing that the topic for word i needs to come from topic z_i^d, we will sample from the multinomial distribution whose parameters are given by row z_i^d of $\mathbf{W}$ to get the word x_i^d (which is a value between 1 and M):

$$x_i^d \sim \text{Mult}_M(\boldsymbol{w}_{z_i^d})$$

This is a multinomial draw, and we define a Dirichlet prior with hyperparameter $\boldsymbol{\beta}$ on these rows of multinomial probabilities:

$$\boldsymbol{w}_k \sim \text{Dirichlet}(\boldsymbol{\beta})$$

This completes the process to generate one word. To generate the N words for the document, we do this N times; namely, for each word, we decide on a topic, then given the topic, we choose a word (inner plate in the figure). When we get to the next document, we sample another topic distribution $\boldsymbol{\pi}$ (outer plate), and then sample N words from that topic distribution.

On all the documents, we always use the same $\mathbf{W}$, and in learning, we are given a large corpus of documents, that is, only x_i^d values are observed. We can then write a posterior distribution as usual and learn $\mathbf{W}$, the word probabilities for topics shared across all documents.

Once $\mathbf{W}$ is learned, each of its rows correspond to one topic. By looking at the words with high probabilities, we can assign some meaning to these topics. Note, however, that we will always learn some $\mathbf{W}$; whether the rows will be meaningful or not is another matter.

The model we have just discussed is parametric, and its size is fixed; we can make it nonparametric by making K, the number of topics, which is the hidden complexity parameter, increase as necessary and adapt to data using a Dirichlet process. We need to be careful though. Each document contains N words that come from some topics, but we have several documents and they all need to share the same set of topics; that is, we need to tie the Dirichlets that generate the topics. For this, we define a hierarchy; we define a higher Dirichlet process from which we draw the Dirichlets for individual documents. This is a *hierarchical Dirichlet process* (Teh et al. 2006) that allows topics learned for one document be shared by all.

HIERARCHICAL DIRICHLET PROCESS

16.12 Beta Processes and Indian Buffets

Now let us see an application of the Bayesian approach to dimensionality reduction in factor analysis. Remember that given the $N \times d$ matrix of data $\mathbf{X}$, we want to find k features or latent factors, each of which are d-dimensional such that the data can be written as a linear combination of them. That is, we want to find $\mathbf{Z}$ and $\mathbf{A}$ such that

$$\mathbf{X} = \mathbf{Z}\mathbf{A}$$

where $\mathbf{A}$ is the $k \times d$ matrix whose row j is the d-dimensional feature vector (similar to the eigenvector in PCA (section 6.3) and $\mathbf{Z}$ is $N \times k$ matrix whose row t defines instance t as a vector of features.

Let us assume that z_j^t are binary and are drawn from Bernoulli distributions with probability μ_j:

$$z_j^t = \begin{cases} 1 & \text{with probability } \mu_j \\ 0 & \text{with probability } 1 - \mu_j \end{cases} \quad (16.50)$$

So z_j^t indicates the absence/presence of hidden factor j in constructing instance t. If the corresponding factor is present, row j of $\mathbf{A}$ is chosen and the sum of all such rows chosen make up row t of $\mathbf{X}$.

We are being Bayesian so we define priors. We define a Gaussian prior on $\mathbf{A}$ and a beta conjugate prior on μ_j of Bernoulli z_j^t:

$$\mu_j \sim \text{beta}(\alpha, 1) \quad (16.51)$$

where α is the hyperparameter. We can write down the posterior and estimate the matrix **A**. Looking at the rows of **A**, we can get an idea about what the hidden factors represent; for example, if k is small (e.g., 2), we can plot and visualize the data.

We assume a certain k; hence this model is parametric. We can make it nonparametric and allow k increase with more data (Griffiths and Ghahramani 2011). This defines a *beta process* and the corresponding metaphor is called the *Indian buffet process*, which defines a generative model that works as follows.

BETA PROCESS

INDIAN BUFFET PROCESS

There is an Indian restaurant with a buffet that contains k dishes and each customer can take a serving of any subset of these dishes. The first customer (instance) enters and takes servings of the first m dishes; we assume m is a random variable generated from a Poisson distribution with parameter α. Then each subsequent customer n can take a serving of any existing dish j with probability n_j/n where n_j is the number of customers before who took a serving of dish j, and once he or she is done sampling the existing dishes, that customer can also ask for Poisson(α/n) additional new dishes, hence growing the model. When applied to the context of latent factor model earlier, this corresponds to a model where the number of factors need not be fixed and instead grows as the complexity inherent in data grows.

16.13 Notes

Bayesian approaches are becoming more popular recently. The use of generative graphical models corresponds quite well to the Bayesian formalism, and we are seeing interesting applications in various domains from natural language processing to computer vision to bioinformatics.

The recent field of Bayesian nonparametrics is also interesting in that adapting model complexity is now a part of training and is not an outer loop of model complexity adjustment; we expect to see more work along this direction in the near future. One example of this is the infinite hidden Markov models (Beal, Ghahramani, and Rasmussen 2002) where the number of hidden states is automatically adjusted with more data.

Due to lack of space and the need to keep the chapter to a reasonable length, the approximation and sampling methods are not discussed in detail in this chapter; see MacKay 2003, Bishop 2006, or Murphy 2012 for more information about variational methods and Markov chain Monte Carlo sampling.

Bayesian approach is interesting and promising, and has already worked successfully in many cases, but it is far from completely supplanting the nonBayesian, or frequentist, approach. For tractability, generative models may be quite simple—for example, latent Dirichlet analysis loses the ordering or words—or the approximation methods may be hard to derive, and sampling methods slow to converge; hence frequentist shortcuts, (e.g., empirical Bayes), may be preferred in certain cases. Hence, it is best to look for an ideal compromise between the two worlds rather than fully committing to one.

16.14 Exercises

1. For the setting of figure 16.3, observe how the posterior changes as we change N, σ^2, and σ_0^2.
2. Let us denote by x the number of spam emails I receive in a random sample of n. Assume that the prior for q, the proportion of spam emails is uniform in $[0, 1]$. Find the posterior distribution for $p(q|x)$.
3. As above, except that assume that $p(q) \sim \mathcal{N}(\mu_0, \sigma_0^2)$. Also assume n is large so that you can use central limit theorem and approximate binomial by a Gaussian. Derive $p(q|x)$.
4. What is $\text{Var}(r')$ when the maximum likelihood estimator is used? Compare it with equation 16.25.
5. In figure 16.10, how does the fit change when we change s^2?

   SOLUTION: As usual, s is the smoothing parameter and we get smoother fits as we increase s.
6. Propose a filtering algorithm to choose a subset of the training set in Gaussian processes.

   SOLUTION: One nice property of Gaussian processes is that we can calculate the variance at a certain point. For any instance from the training set, we can calculate the leave-one-out estimate there and check whether the actual output is in, for example, the 95 percent prediction interval. If it is, this means that we do not need that instance and it can be left out. Those that cannot be pruned will be just like the support vectors in a kernel machine, namely, those instances that are stored and needed, to bound the total error of the fit.

ACTIVE LEARNING

7. *Active learning* is when the learner is able to generate x itself and ask a su-

pervisor to provide the corresponding r value during learning one by one, instead of passively being given a training set. How can we implement active learning using Gaussian processes? (Hint: Where do we have the largest uncertainty?)

SOLUTION: This is just like the previous exercise, except that we add instead of prune. Using the same logic, we can see that we need instances where the prediction interval is large. Given the variance as a function of $\boldsymbol{x}$, we search for its local maxima. In the case of a Gaussian kernel, we expect points that are distant from training data to have high variance, but this need not be the case for all kernels. While searching, we need to make sure that we do not go out of the valid input bounds.

8. Let us say we have a set of documents where for each document, we have one copy in English and one in French. How can we extend latent Dirichlet allocation for this case?

16.15 References

Beal, M. J., Z. Ghahramani, and C. E. Rasmussen. 2002. "The Infinite Hidden Markov Model." In *Advances in Neural Information Processing Systems 14*, ed. T. G. Dietterich, S. Becker, and Z. Ghahramani, 577–585. Cambridge, MA: MIT Press.

Bishop, C. M. 2006. *Pattern Recognition and Machine Learning.* New York: Springer.

Blei, D. M. 2012. "Probabilistic Topic Models." *Communications of the ACM* 55 (4): 77–84.

Blei, D. M., A. Y. Ng, and M. I. Jordan. 2003. "Latent Dirichlet Allocation." *Journal of Machine Intelligence* 3:993–1022.

Figueiredo, M. A. T. 2003. "Adaptive Sparseness for Supervised Learning." *IEEE Transactions on Pattern Analysis and Machine Intelligence* 25:1150–1159.

Gershman, S. J., and D. M. Blei. 2012. "A Tutorial on Bayesian Nonparametric Models." *Journal of Mathematical Psychology* 56:1–12.

Griffiths, T. L., and Z. Ghahramani. 2011. "The Indian Buffet Process: An Introduction and Review." *Journal of Machine Learning Research* 12:1185–1224.

Hastie, T., R. Tibshirani, and J. Friedman. 2011. *The Elements of Statistical Learning: Data Mining, Inference, and Prediction,* 2nd ed. New York: Springer.

Hoff, P. D. 2009. *A First Course in Bayesian Statistical Methods.* New York: Springer.

Jordan, M. I., Z. Ghahramani, T. S. Jaakkola, L. K. Saul. 1999. "An Introduction to Variational Methods for Graphical Models." *Machine Learning* 37:183–233.

MacKay, D. J. C. 1998. "Introduction to Gaussian Processes." In *Neural Networks and Machine Learning*, ed. C. M. Bishop, 133–166. Berlin: Springer.

MacKay, D. J. C. 2003. *Information Theory, Inference, and Learning Algorithms.* Cambridge, UK: Cambridge University Press.

Murphy, K. P. 2007. "Conjugate Bayesian Analysis of the Gaussian Distribution." `http://www.cs.ubc.ca/~murphyk/Papers/bayesGauss.pdf`.

Murphy, K. P. 2012. *Machine Learning: A Probabilistic Perspective.* Cambridge, MA: MIT Press.

Rasmussen, C. E. , and C. K. I. Williams. 2006. *Gaussian Processes for Machine Learning.* Cambridge, MA: MIT Press.

Teh, Y. W., M. I. Jordan, M. J. Beal, and D. M. Blei. 2006. "Hierarchical Dirichlet Processes." *Journal of Americal Statistical Association* 101: 1566–1581.

Tibshirani, R. 1996. "Regression Shrinkage and Selection via the Lasso." *Journal of the Royal Statistical Society B* 58: 267–288.

Waterhouse, S., D. MacKay, and T. Robinson. 1996. "Bayesian Methods for Mixture of Experts." In *Advances in Neural Information Processing Systems 8*, ed. D. S. Touretzky, M. C. Mozer, and M. E. Hasselmo, 351–357. Cambridge, MA: MIT Press.

17 *Combining Multiple Learners*

We discussed many different learning algorithms in the previous chapters. Though these are generally successful, no one single algorithm is always the most accurate. Now, we are going to discuss models composed of multiple learners that complement each other so that by combining them, we attain higher accuracy.

17.1 Rationale

IN ANY APPLICATION, we can use one of several learning algorithms, and with certain algorithms, there are hyperparameters that affect the final learner. For example, in a classification setting, we can use a parametric classifier or a multilayer perceptron, and, for example, with a multilayer perceptron, we should also decide on the number of hidden units. The No Free Lunch Theorem states that there is no single learning algorithm that in any domain always induces the most accurate learner. The usual approach is to try many and choose the one that performs the best on a separate validation set.

Each learning algorithm dictates a certain model that comes with a set of assumptions. This inductive bias leads to error if the assumptions do not hold for the data. Learning is an ill-posed problem and with finite data, each algorithm converges to a different solution and fails under different circumstances. The performance of a learner may be fine-tuned to get the highest possible accuracy on a validation set, but this fine-tuning is a complex task and still there are instances on which even the best learner is not accurate enough. The idea is that there may be another

BASE-LEARNER

learner that is accurate on these. By suitably combining multiple *base-learners* then, accuracy can be improved. Recently with computation and memory getting cheaper, such systems composed of multiple learners have become popular (Kuncheva 2004).

There are basically two questions here:

1. How do we generate base-learners that complement each other?
2. How do we combine the outputs of base-learners for maximum accuracy?

Our discussion in this chapter will answer these two related questions. We will see that model combination is not a trick that always increases accuracy; model combination does always increase time and space complexity of training and testing, and unless base-learners are trained carefully and their decisions combined smartly, we will only pay for this extra complexity without any significant gain in accuracy.

17.2 Generating Diverse Learners

DIVERSITY

Since there is no point in combining learners that always make similar decisions, the aim is to be able to find a set of *diverse* learners who differ in their decisions so that they complement each other. At the same time, there cannot be a gain in overall success unless the learners are accurate, at least in their domain of expertise. We therefore have this double task of maximizing individual accuracies and the diversity between learners. Let us now discuss the different ways to achieve this.

Different Algorithms

We can use different learning algorithms to train different base-learners. Different algorithms make different assumptions about the data and lead to different classifiers. For example, one base-learner may be parametric and another may be nonparametric. When we decide on a single algorithm, we give emphasis to a single method and ignore all others. Combining multiple learners based on multiple algorithms, we free ourselves from taking a decision and we no longer put all our eggs in one basket.

Different Hyperparameters

We can use the same learning algorithm but use it with different hyperparameters. Examples are the number of hidden units in a multilayer perceptron, k in k-nearest neighbor, error threshold in decision trees, the kernel function in support vector machines, and so forth. With a Gaussian parametric classifier, whether the covariance matrices are shared or not is a hyperparameter. If the optimization algorithm uses an iterative procedure such as gradient descent whose final state depends on the initial state, such as in backpropagation with multilayer perceptrons, the initial state, for example, the initial weights, is another hyperparameter. When we train multiple base-learners with different hyperparameter values, we average over this factor and reduce variance, and therefore error.

Different Input Representations

Separate base-learners may be using different *representations* of the same input object or event, making it possible to integrate different types of sensors/measurements/modalities. Different representations make different characteristics explicit allowing better identification. In many applications, there are multiple sources of information, and it is desirable to use all of these data to extract more information and achieve higher accuracy in prediction.

For example, in speech recognition, to recognize the uttered words, in addition to the acoustic input, we can also use the video image of the speaker's lips and shape of the mouth as the words are spoken. This is similar to *sensor fusion* where the data from different sensors are integrated to extract more information for a specific application. Another example is information, for example, image retrieval where in addition to the image itself, we may also have text annotation in the form of keywords. In such a case, we want to be able to combine both of these sources to find the right set of images; this is also sometimes called *multi-view learning*.

SENSOR FUSION

MULTI-VIEW LEARNING

The simplest approach is to concatenate all data vectors and treat it as one large vector from a single source, but this does not seem theoretically appropriate since this corresponds to modeling data as sampled from one multivariate statistical distribution. Moreover, larger input dimensionalities make the systems more complex and require larger samples for the estimators to be accurate. The approach we take is to make separate predictions based on different sources using separate base-learners, then combine their predictions.

Even if there is a single input representation, by choosing random subsets from it, we can have classifiers using different input features; this is

RANDOM SUBSPACE

called the *random subspace method* (Ho 1998). This has the effect that different learners will look at the same problem from different points of view and will be robust; it will also help reduce the curse of dimensionality because inputs are fewer dimensional.

Different Training Sets

Another possibility is to train different base-learners by different subsets of the training set. This can be done randomly by drawing random training sets from the given sample; this is called *bagging*. Or, the learners can be trained serially so that instances on which the preceding base-learners are not accurate are given more emphasis in training later base-learners; examples are *boosting* and *cascading*, which actively try to generate complementary learners, instead of leaving this to chance.

The partitioning of the training sample can also be done based on locality in the input space so that each base-learner is trained on instances in a certain local part of the input space; this is what is done by the *mixture of experts* that we discussed in chapter 12 but that we revisit in this context of combining multiple learners. Similarly, it is possible to define the main task in terms of a number of subtasks to be implemented by the base-learners, as is done by *error-correcting output codes*.

Diversity vs. Accuracy

One important note is that when we generate multiple base-learners, we want them to be reasonably accurate but do not require them to be very accurate individually, so they are not, and need not be, optimized separately for best accuracy. The base-learners are not chosen for their accuracy, but for their simplicity. We do require, however, that the base-learners be diverse, that is, accurate on different instances, specializing in subdomains of the problem. What we care for is the final accuracy when the base-learners are combined, rather than the accuracies of the base-learners we started from. Let us say we have a classifier that is 80 percent accurate. When we decide on a second classifier, we do not care for the overall accuracy; we care only about how accurate it is on the 20 percent that the first classifier misclassifies, as long as we know when to use which one.

This implies that the required accuracy and diversity of the learners also depend on how their decisions are to be combined, as we will discuss next. If, as in a voting scheme, a learner is consulted for all inputs, it should be accurate everywhere and diversity should be enforced everywhere; if we have a partioning of the input space into regions of expertise for different learners, diversity is already guaranteed by this partitioning and learners need to be accurate only in their own local domains.

17.3 Model Combination Schemes

There are also different ways the multiple base-learners are combined to generate the final output:

MULTIEXPERT COMBINATION

- *Multiexpert combination* methods have base-learners that work in *parallel.* These methods can in turn be divided into two:
  - In the *global* approach, also called *learner fusion,* given an input, all base-learners generate an output and all these outputs are used. Examples are *voting* and *stacking.*
  - In the *local* approach, or *learner selection,* for example, in *mixture of experts,* there is a *gating* model, which looks at the input and chooses one (or very few) of the learners as responsible for generating the output.

MULTISTAGE COMBINATION

- *Multistage combination* methods use a *serial* approach where the next base-learner is trained with or tested on only the instances where the previous base-learners are not accurate enough. The idea is that the base-learners (or the different representations they use) are sorted in increasing complexity so that a complex base-learner is not used (or its complex representation is not extracted) unless the preceding simpler base-learners are not confident. An example is *cascading.*

Let us say that we have L base-learners. We denote by $d_j(x)$ the prediction of base-learner $\mathcal{M}_j$ given the arbitrary dimensional input x. In the case of multiple representations, each $\mathcal{M}_j$ uses a different input representation x_j. The final prediction is calculated from the predictions of the base-learners:

$$y = f(d_1, d_2, \ldots, d_L|\Phi) \tag{17.1}$$

where $f(\cdot)$ is the combining function with Φ denoting its parameters.

When there are K outputs, for each learner there are $d_{ji}(x), i = 1, \ldots, K$, $j = 1, \ldots, L$, and, combining them, we also generate K values, $y_i, i =$

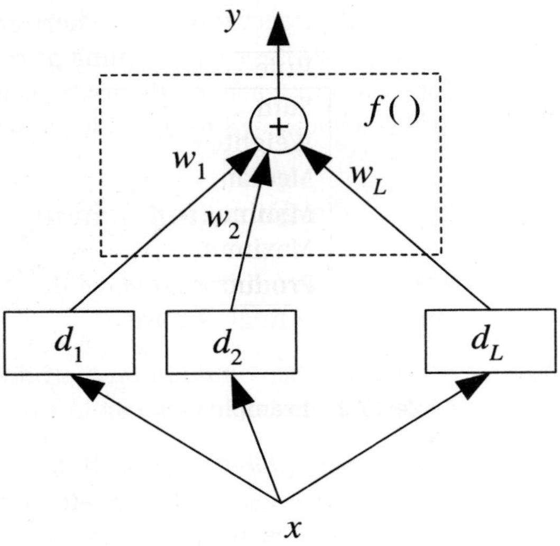

Figure 17.1 Base-learners are d_j and their outputs are combined using $f(\cdot)$. This is for a single output; in the case of classification, each base-learner has K outputs that are separately used to calculate y_i, and then we choose the maximum. Note that here all learners observe the same input; it may be the case that different learners observe different representations of the same input object or event.

$1, \ldots, K$ and then for example in classification, we choose the class with the maximum y_i value:

$$\text{Choose } C_i \text{ if } y_i = \max_{k=1}^{K} y_k$$

17.4 Voting

VOTING

The simplest way to combine multiple classifiers is by *voting*, which corresponds to taking a linear combination of the learners (see figure 17.1):

$$y_i = \sum_j w_j d_{ji} \text{ where } w_j \geq 0, \sum_j w_j = 1 \tag{17.2}$$

ENSEMBLES
LINEAR OPINION POOLS

This is also known as *ensembles* and *linear opinion pools*. In the simplest case, all learners are given equal weight and we have *simple voting*

Table 17.1 Classifier combination rules

Rule	Fusion function $f(\cdot)$
Sum	$y_i = \frac{1}{L}\sum_{j=1}^{L} d_{ji}$
Weighted sum	$y_i = \sum_j w_j d_{ji}, w_j \geq 0, \sum_j w_j = 1$
Median	$y_i = \text{median}_j d_{ji}$
Minimum	$y_i = \min_j d_{ji}$
Maximum	$y_i = \max_j d_{ji}$
Product	$y_i = \prod_j d_{ji}$

Table 17.2 Example of combination rules on three learners and three classes

	C_1	C_2	C_3
d_1	0.2	0.5	0.3
d_2	0.0	0.6	0.4
d_3	0.4	0.4	0.2
Sum	0.2	**0.5**	0.3
Median	0.2	**0.5**	0.4
Minimum	0.0	**0.4**	0.2
Maximum	0.4	**0.6**	0.4
Product	0.0	**0.12**	0.032

that corresponds to taking an average. Still, taking a (weighted) sum is only one of the possibilities and there are also other combination rules, as shown in table 17.1 (Kittler et al. 1998). If the outputs are not posterior probabilities, these rules require that outputs be normalized to the same scale (Jain, Nandakumar, and Ross 2005).

An example of the use of these rules is shown in table 17.2, which demonstrates the effects of different rules. Sum rule is the most intuitive and is the most widely used in practice. Median rule is more robust to outliers; minimum and maximum rules are pessimistic and optimistic, respectively. With the product rule, each learner has veto power; regardless of the other ones, if one learner has an output of 0, the overall output goes to 0. Note that after the combination rules, y_i do not necessarily sum up to 1.

In weighted sum, d_{ji} is the vote of learner j for class C_i and w_j is the weight of its vote. Simple voting is a special case where all voters have equal weight, namely, $w_j = 1/L$. In classification, this is called *plurality voting* where the class having the maximum number of votes is the winner. When there are two classes, this is *majority voting* where the winning class gets more than half of the votes (exercise 1). If the voters can also supply the additional information of how much they vote for each class (e.g., by the posterior probability), then after normalization, these can be used as weights in a *weighted voting* scheme. Equivalently, if d_{ji} are the class posterior probabilities, $P(C_i|x, \mathcal{M}_j)$, then we can just sum them up ($w_j = 1/L$) and choose the class with maximum y_i.

In the case of regression, simple or weighted averaging or median can be used to fuse the outputs of base-regressors. Median is more robust to noise than the average.

Another possible way to find w_j is to assess the accuracies of the learners (regressor or classifier) on a separate validation set and use that information to compute the weights, so that we give more weights to more accurate learners. These weights can also be learned from data, as we will discuss when we discuss stacked generalization in section 17.9.

Voting schemes can be seen as approximations under a Bayesian framework with weights approximating prior model probabilities, and model decisions approximating model-conditional likelihoods. This is *Bayesian model combination*—see section 16.6. For example, in classification we have $w_j \equiv P(\mathcal{M}_j)$, $d_{ji} = P(C_i|x, \mathcal{M}_j)$, and equation 17.2 corresponds to

BAYESIAN MODEL COMBINATION

(17.3)
$$P(C_i|x) = \sum_{\text{all models } \mathcal{M}_j} P(C_i|x, \mathcal{M}_j)P(\mathcal{M}_j)$$

Simple voting corresponds to a uniform prior. If we have a prior distribution preferring simpler models, this would give larger weights to them. We cannot integrate over all models; we only choose a subset for which we believe $P(\mathcal{M}_j)$ is high, or we can have another Bayesian step and calculate $P(\mathcal{M}_j|\mathcal{X})$, the probability of a model given the sample, and sample high probable models from this density.

Hansen and Salamon (1990) have shown that given independent two-class classifiers with success probability higher than 1/2, namely, better than random guessing, by taking a majority vote, the accuracy increases as the number of voting classifiers increases.

Let us assume that d_j are iid with expected value $E[d_j]$ and variance $\text{Var}(d_j)$, then when we take a simple average with $w_j = 1/L$, the expected value and variance of the output are

$$E[y] = E\left[\sum_j \frac{1}{L} d_j\right] = \frac{1}{L} L E[d_j] = E[d_j]$$

$$\text{Var}(y) = \text{Var}\left(\sum_j \frac{1}{L} d_j\right) = \frac{1}{L^2}\text{Var}\left(\sum_j d_j\right) = \frac{1}{L^2} L \text{Var}(d_j) = \frac{1}{L}\text{Var}(d_j) \quad (17.4)$$

We see that the expected value does not change, so the bias does not change. But variance, and therefore mean square error, decreases as the number of independent voters, L, increases. In the general case,

$$\text{Var}(y) = \frac{1}{L^2}\text{Var}\left(\sum_j d_j\right) = \frac{1}{L^2}\left[\sum_j \text{Var}(d_j) + 2\sum_j \sum_{i<j} \text{Cov}(d_j, d_i)\right] \quad (17.5)$$

which implies that if learners are positively correlated, variance (and error) increase. We can thus view using different algorithms and input features as efforts to decrease, if not completely eliminate, the positive correlation. In section 17.10, we discuss pruning methods to remove learners with high positive correlation fron an ensemble.

We also see here that further decrease in variance is possible if the voters are not independent but negatively correlated. The error then decreases if the accompanying increase in bias is not higher because these aims are contradictory; we cannot have a number of classifiers that are all accurate *and* negatively correlated. In mixture of experts for example, where learners are localized, the experts are negatively correlated but biased (Jacobs 1997).

If we view each base-learner as a random noise function added to the true discriminant/regression function and if these noise functions are uncorrelated with 0 mean, then the averaging of the individual estimates is like averaging over the noise. In this sense, voting has the effect of smoothing in the functional space and can be thought of as a regularizer with a smoothness assumption on the true function (Perrone 1993). We saw an example of this in figure 4.5d, where, averaging over models with large variance, we get a better fit than those of the individual models. This is the idea in voting: We vote over models with high variance and low bias so that after combination, the bias remains small and we reduce the variance by averaging. Even if the individual models are biased, the decrease in variance may offset this bias and still a decrease in error is possible.

17.5 Error-Correcting Output Codes

ERROR-CORRECTING OUTPUT CODES

In *error-correcting output codes* (ECOC) (Dietterich and Bakiri 1995), the main classification task is defined in terms of a number of subtasks that are implemented by the base-learners. The idea is that the original task of separating one class from all other classes may be a difficult problem. Instead, we want to define a set of simpler classification problems, each specializing in one aspect of the task, and combining these simpler classifiers, we get the final classifier.

Base-learners are binary classifiers having output $-1/+1$, and there is a *code matrix* $\mathbf{W}$ of $K \times L$ whose K rows are the binary codes of classes in terms of the L base-learners d_j. For example, if the second row of $\mathbf{W}$ is $[-1, +1, +1, -1]$, this means that for us to say an instance belongs to C_2, the instance should be on the negative side of d_1 and d_4, and on the positive side of d_2 and d_3. Similarly, the columns of the code matrix defines the task of the base-learners. For example, if the third column is $[-1, +1, +1]^T$, we understand that the task of the third base-learner, d_3, is to separate the instances of C_1 from the instances of C_2 and C_3 combined. This is how we form the training set of the base-learners. For example in this case, all instances labeled with C_2 and C_3 form $\mathcal{X}_3^+$ and instances labeled with C_1 form $\mathcal{X}_3^-$, and d_3 is trained so that $\boldsymbol{x}^t \in \mathcal{X}_3^+$ give output $+1$ and $\boldsymbol{x}^t \in \mathcal{X}_3^-$ give output -1.

The code matrix thus allows us to define a polychotomy ($K > 2$ classification problem) in terms of dichotomies ($K = 2$ classification problem), and it is a method that is applicable using any learning algorithm to implement the dichotomizer base-learners—for example, linear or multilayer perceptrons (with a single output), decision trees, or SVMs whose original definition is for two-class problems.

The typical one discriminant per class setting corresponds to the diagonal code matrix where $L = K$. For example, for $K = 4$, we have

$$\mathbf{W} = \begin{bmatrix} +1 & -1 & -1 & -1 \\ -1 & +1 & -1 & -1 \\ -1 & -1 & +1 & -1 \\ -1 & -1 & -1 & +1 \end{bmatrix}$$

The problem here is that if there is an error with one of the base-learners, there may be a misclassification because the class code words are so similar. So the approach in error-correcting codes is to have $L > K$ and increase the Hamming distance between the code words. One possibility is *pairwise separation* of classes where there is a separate base-learner to separate C_i from C_j, for $i < j$ (section 10.4). In this case, $L = K(K-1)/2$ and with $K = 4$, the code matrix is

$$\mathbf{W} = \begin{bmatrix} +1 & +1 & +1 & 0 & 0 & 0 \\ -1 & 0 & 0 & +1 & +1 & 0 \\ 0 & -1 & 0 & -1 & 0 & +1 \\ 0 & 0 & -1 & 0 & -1 & -1 \end{bmatrix}$$

where a 0 entry denotes "don't care." That is, d_1 is trained to separate C_1 from C_2 and does not use the training instances belonging to the other classes. Similarly, we say that an instance belongs to C_2 if $d_1 = -1$ and $d_4 = d_5 = +1$, and we do not consider the values of d_2, d_3, and d_6. The problem here is that L is $\mathcal{O}(K^2)$, and for large K pairwise separation may not be feasible.

If we can have L high, we can just randomly generate the code matrix with $-1/+1$ and this will work fine, but if we want to keep L low, we need to optimize $\mathbf{W}$. The approach is to set L beforehand and then find $\mathbf{W}$ such that the distances between rows, and at the same time the distances between columns, are as large as possible, in terms of Hamming distance. With K classes, there are $2^{(K-1)} - 1$ possible columns, namely, two-class problems. This is because K bits can be written in 2^K different ways and complements (e.g., "0101" and "1010," from our point of view, define the same discriminant) dividing the possible combinations by 2 and then subtracting 1 because a column of all 0s (or 1s) is useless. For example, when $K = 4$, we have

$$\mathbf{W} = \begin{bmatrix} -1 & -1 & -1 & -1 & -1 & -1 & -1 \\ -1 & -1 & -1 & +1 & +1 & +1 & +1 \\ -1 & +1 & +1 & -1 & -1 & +1 & +1 \\ +1 & -1 & +1 & -1 & +1 & -1 & +1 \end{bmatrix}$$

When K is large, for a given value of L, we look for L columns out of the $2^{(K-1)} - 1$. We would like these columns of $\mathbf{W}$ to be as different as possible so that the tasks to be learned by the base-learners are as different from each other as possible. At the same time, we would like the rows of $\mathbf{W}$ to be as different as possible so that we can have maximum error correction in case one or more base-learners fail.

ECOC can be written as a voting scheme where the entries of $\mathbf{W}$, w_{ij}, are considered as vote weights:

$$y_i = \sum_{j=1}^{L} w_{ij} d_j \tag{17.6}$$

and then we choose the class with the highest y_i. Taking a weighted sum and then choosing the maximum instead of checking for an exact match allows d_j to no longer need to be binary but to take a value between -1 and $+1$, carrying soft certainties instead of hard decisions. Note that a value p_j between 0 and 1, for example, a posterior probability, can be converted to a value d_j between -1 and $+1$ simply as

$$d_j = 2p_j - 1$$

The difference between equation 17.6 and the generic voting model of equation 17.2 is that the weights of votes can be different for different classes, namely, we no longer have w_j but w_{ij}, and also that $w_j \geq 0$ whereas w_{ij} are -1, 0, or $+1$.

One problem with ECOC is that because the code matrix **W** is set a priori, there is no guarantee that the subtasks as defined by the columns of **W** will be simple. Dietterich and Bakiri (1995) report that the dichotomizer trees may be larger than the polychotomizer trees and when multilayer perceptrons are used, there may be slower convergence by backpropagation.

17.6 Bagging

BAGGING

Bagging is a voting method whereby base-learners are made different by training them over slightly different training sets. Generating L slightly different samples from a given sample is done by bootstrap, where given a training set $\mathcal{X}$ of size N, we draw N instances randomly from $\mathcal{X}$ *with replacement.* Because sampling is done with replacement, it is possible that some instances are drawn more than once and that certain instances are not drawn at all. When this is done to generate L samples $\mathcal{X}_j, j = 1, \ldots, L$, these samples are similar because they are all drawn from the same original sample, but they are also slightly different due to chance. The base-learners d_j are trained with these L samples $\mathcal{X}_j$.

UNSTABLE ALGORITHM

A learning algorithm is an *unstable algorithm* if small changes in the training set causes a large difference in the generated learner, namely, the learning algorithm has high variance. Bagging, short for bootstrap aggregating, uses bootstrap to generate L training sets, trains L base-learners using an unstable learning procedure, and then, during testing, takes an average (Breiman 1996). Bagging can be used both for classification and regression. In the case of regression, to be more robust, one can take the median instead of the average when combining predictions.

We saw before that averaging reduces variance only if the positive correlation is small; an algorithm is stable if different runs of the same algorithm on resampled versions of the same dataset lead to learners with high positive correlation. Algorithms such as decision trees and multilayer perceptrons are unstable. Nearest neighbor is stable, but condensed nearest neighbor is unstable (Alpaydın 1997). If the original training set is large, then we may want to generate smaller sets of size $N' < N$ from them using bootstrap, since otherwise the bootstrap replicates $\mathcal{X}_j$ will be too similar, and d_j will be highly correlated.

17.7 Boosting

In bagging, generating complementary base-learners is left to chance and to the unstability of the learning method. In boosting, we actively try to generate complementary base-learners by training the next learner on the mistakes of the previous learners. The original *boosting* algorithm (Schapire 1990) combines three weak learners to generate a strong learner. A *weak learner* has error probability less than 1/2, which makes it better than random guessing on a two-class problem, and a *strong learner* has arbitrarily small error probability.

BOOSTING

WEAK LEARNER

STRONG LEARNER

Given a large training set, we randomly divide it into three. We use $\mathcal{X}_1$ and train d_1. We then take $\mathcal{X}_2$ and feed it to d_1. We take all instances misclassified by d_1 and also as many instances on which d_1 is correct from $\mathcal{X}_2$, and these together form the training set of d_2. We then take $\mathcal{X}_3$ and feed it to d_1 and d_2. The instances on which d_1 and d_2 disagree form the training set of d_3. During testing, given an instance, we give it to d_1 and d_2; if they agree, that is the response, otherwise the response of d_3 is taken as the output. Schapire (1990) has shown that this overall system has reduced error rate, and the error rate can arbitrarily be reduced by using such systems recursively, that is, a boosting system of three models used as d_j in a higher system.

Though it is quite successful, the disadvantage of the original boost-

Training:
  For all $\{x^t, r^t\}_{t=1}^N \in \mathcal{X}$, initialize $p_1^t = 1/N$
  For all base-learners $j = 1, \ldots, L$
    Randomly draw $\mathcal{X}_j$ from $\mathcal{X}$ with probabilities p_j^t
    Train d_j using $\mathcal{X}_j$
    For each (x^t, r^t), calculate $y_j^t \leftarrow d_j(x^t)$
    Calculate error rate: $\epsilon_j \leftarrow \sum_t p_j^t \cdot 1(y_j^t \neq r^t)$
    If $\epsilon_j > 1/2$, then $L \leftarrow j - 1$; stop
    $\beta_j \leftarrow \epsilon_j / (1 - \epsilon_j)$
    For each (x^t, r^t), decrease probabilities if correct:
      If $y_j^t = r^t$, then $p_{j+1}^t \leftarrow \beta_j p_j^t$ Else $p_{j+1}^t \leftarrow p_j^t$
    Normalize probabilities:
      $Z_j \leftarrow \sum_t p_{j+1}^t;\ \ p_{j+1}^t \leftarrow p_{j+1}^t / Z_j$
Testing:
  Given x, calculate $d_j(x), j = 1, \ldots, L$
  Calculate class outputs, $i = 1, \ldots, K$:
    $y_i = \sum_{j=1}^L \left(\log \frac{1}{\beta_j}\right) d_{ji}(x)$

Figure 17.2 AdaBoost algorithm.

ing method is that it requires a very large training sample. The sample should be divided into three and furthermore, the second and third classifiers are only trained on a subset on which the previous ones err. So unless one has a quite large training set, d_2 and d_3 will not have training sets of reasonable size. Drucker et al. (1994) use a set of 118,000 instances in boosting multilayer perceptrons for optical handwritten digit recognition.

ADABOOST

Freund and Schapire (1996) proposed a variant, named *AdaBoost*, short for adaptive boosting, that uses the same training set over and over and thus need not be large, but the classifiers should be simple so that they do not overfit. AdaBoost can also combine an arbitrary number of base-learners, not three.

Many variants of AdaBoost have been proposed; here, we discuss the original algorithm AdaBoost.M1 (see figure 17.2). The idea is to modify the probabilities of drawing the instances as a function of the error. Let us say p_j^t denotes the probability that the instance pair (x^t, r^t) is drawn to train the jth base-learner. Initially, all $p_1^t = 1/N$. Then we add new base-learners as follows, starting from $j = 1$: ϵ_j denotes the error rate of d_j. AdaBoost requires that learners are weak, that is, $\epsilon_j < 1/2, \forall j$; if not, we stop adding new base-learners. Note that this error rate is not on the original problem but on the dataset used at step j. We define $\beta_j = \epsilon_j/(1-\epsilon_j) < 1$, and we set $p^t_{j+1} = \beta_j p^t_j$ if d_j correctly classifies x^t; otherwise, $p^t_{j+1} = p^t_j$. Because p^t_{j+1} should be probabilities, there is a normalization where we divide p^t_{j+1} by $\sum_t p^t_{j+1}$, so that they sum up to 1. This has the effect that the probability of a correctly classified instance is decreased, and the probability of a misclassified instance increases. Then a new sample of the same size is drawn from the original sample according to these modified probabilities, p^t_{j+1}, with replacement, and is used to train d_{j+1}.

This has the effect that d_{j+1} focuses more on instances misclassified by d_j; that is why the base-learners are chosen to be simple and not accurate, since otherwise the next training sample would contain only a few outlier and noisy instances repeated many times over. For example, with decision trees, *decision stumps*, which are trees grown only one or two levels, are used. So it is clear that these would have bias but the decrease in variance is larger and the overall error decreases. An algorithm like the linear discriminant has low variance, and we cannot gain by AdaBoosting linear discriminants.

Once training is done, AdaBoost is a voting method. Given an instance, all d_j decide and a weighted vote is taken where weights are proportional to the base-learners' accuracies (on the training set): $w_j = \log(1/\beta_j)$. Freund and Schapire (1996) showed improved accuracy in twenty-two benchmark problems, equal accuracy in one problem, and worse accuracy in four problems.

MARGIN

Schapire et al. (1998) explain that the success of AdaBoost is due to its property of increasing the *margin*. If the margin increases, the training instances are better separated and an error is less likely. This makes AdaBoost's aim similar to that of support vector machines (chapter 13).

In AdaBoost, although different base-learners have slightly different training sets, this difference is not left to chance as in bagging, but is a function of the error of the previous base-learner. The actual performance of boosting on a particular problem is clearly dependent on the data and the base-learner. There should be enough training data and the base-learner should be weak but not too weak, and boosting is especially susceptible to noise and outliers.

AdaBoost has also been generalized to regression: One straightforward way, proposed by Avnimelech and Intrator (1997), checks for whether the prediction error is larger than a certain threshold, and if so marks it as error, then uses AdaBoost proper. In another version (Drucker 1997), probabilities are modified based on the magnitude of error, such that instances where the previous base-learner commits a large error, have a higher probability of being drawn to train the next base-learner. Weighted average, or median, is used to combine the predictions of the base-learners.

17.8 The Mixture of Experts Revisited

MIXTURE OF EXPERTS

In voting, the weights w_j are constant over the input space. In the *mixture of experts* architecture, which we previously discussed in section 12.8) as a local method, as an extension of radial basis functions, there is a gating network whose outputs are weights of the experts. This architecture can then be viewed as a voting method where the votes depend on the input, and may be different for different inputs. The competitive learning algorithm used by the mixture of experts localizes the base-learners such that each of them becomes an expert in a different part of the input space and have its weight, $w_j(x)$, close to 1 in its region of expertise. The final output is a weighted average as in voting

$$y = \sum_{j=1}^{L} w_j(x) d_j \tag{17.7}$$

except in this case, both the base-learners and the weights are a function of the input (see figure 17.3).

Jacobs (1997) has shown that in the mixture of experts architecture, experts are biased but are negatively correlated. As training proceeds, bias decreases and expert variances increase but at the same time as experts localize in different parts of the input space, their covariances get more and more negative, which, due to equation 17.5, decreases the total variance, and thus the error. In section 12.8, we considered the case where both experts and gating are linear functions but a nonlinear method, for example, a multilayer perceptron with hidden units, can also be used for both. This may decrease the expert biases but risks increasing expert variances and overfitting.

DYNAMIC CLASSIFIER SELECTION

In *dynamic classifier selection*, similar to the gating network of mixture of experts, there is first a system which takes a test input and estimates

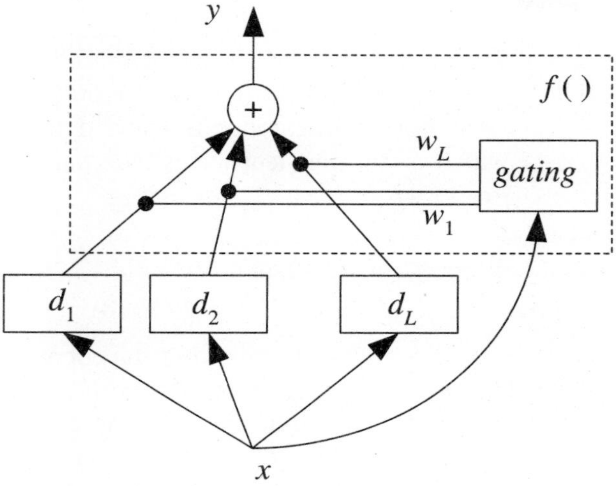

Figure 17.3 Mixture of experts is a voting method where the votes, as given by the gating system, are a function of the input. The combiner system f also includes this gating system.

the competence of base-classifiers in the vicinity of the input. It then picks the most competent to generate output and that output is given as the overall output. Woods, Kegelmeyer, and Bowyer (1997) find the k nearest training points of the test input, look at the accuracies of the base classifiers on those, and choose the one that performs the best on them. Only the selected base-classifier need be evaluated for that test input. To decrease variance, at the expense of more computation, one can take a vote over a few competent base-classifiers instead of using just a single one.

Note that in such a scheme, one should make sure that for any region of the input space, there is a competent base-classifier; this implies that there should be some partitioning of the learning of the input space among the base-classifiers. This is the nice property of mixture of experts, namely, the gating model that does the selection and the expert base-learners that it selects from are trained in a coupled manner. It would be straightforward to have a regression version of this dynamic learner selection algorithm (exercise 5).

17.9 Stacked Generalization

STACKED GENERALIZATION

Stacked generalization is a technique proposed by Wolpert (1992) that extends voting in that the way the output of the base-learners is combined need not be linear but is learned through a combiner system, $f(\cdot|\Phi)$, which is another learner, whose parameters Φ are also trained (see figure 17.4):

$$y = f(d_1, d_2, \ldots, d_L|\Phi) \tag{17.8}$$

The combiner learns what the correct output is when the base-learners give a certain output combination. We cannot train the combiner function on the training data because the base-learners may be memorizing the training set; the combiner system should actually learn how the base-learners make errors. Stacking is a means of estimating and correcting for the biases of the base-learners. Therefore, the combiner should be trained on data unused in training the base-learners.

If $f(\cdot|w_1, \ldots, w_L)$ is a linear model with constraints, $w_i \geq 0, \sum_j w_j = 1$, the optimal weights can be found by constrained regression, but of course we do not need to enforce this; in stacking, there is no restriction on the combiner function and unlike voting, $f(\cdot)$ can be nonlinear. For example, it may be implemented as a multilayer perceptron with Φ its connection weights.

The outputs of the base-learners d_j define a new L-dimensional space in which the output discriminant/regression function is learned by the combiner function.

In stacked generalization, we would like the base-learners to be as different as possible so that they will complement each other, and, for this, it is best if they are based on different learning algorithms. If we are combining classifiers that can generate continuous outputs, for example, posterior probabilities, it is better that they be the combined rather than hard decisions.

When we compare a trained combiner as we have in stacking, with a fixed rule such as in voting, we see that both have their advantages: A trained rule is more flexible and may have less bias, but adds extra parameters, risks introducing variance, and needs extra time and data for training. Note also that there is no need to normalize classifier outputs before stacking.

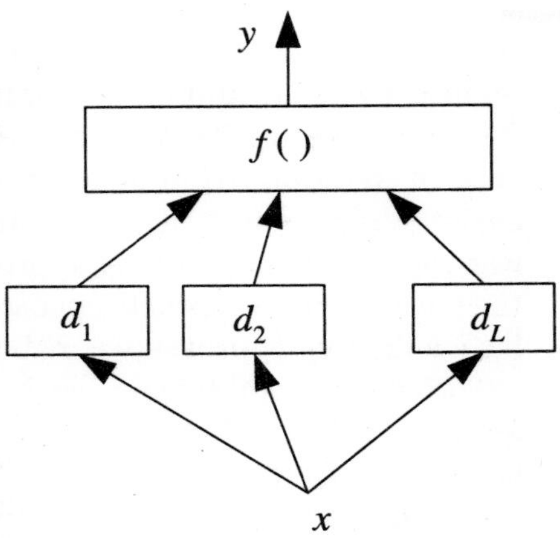

Figure 17.4 In stacked generalization, the combiner is another learner and is not restricted to being a linear combination as in voting.

17.10 Fine-Tuning an Ensemble

Model combination is not a magical formula that is always guaranteed to decrease error; base-learners should be diverse and accurate—that is, they should provide useful information. If a base-learner does not add to accuracy, it can be discarded; also, of the two base-learners that are highly correlated, one is not needed. Note that an inaccurate learner can worsen accuracy, for example, majority voting assumes more than half of the classifiers to be accurate for an input. Therefore, given a set of candidate base-learners, it may not be a good idea to use them as they are, and instead, we may want to do some preprocessing.

We can actually think of the outputs of our base-learners as forming a feature vector for the later stage of combination, and we remember from chapter 6 that we have the same problem with features. Some may be just useless, and some may be highly correlated. Hence, we can use the same ideas of feature selection and extraction here too. Our first approach is to select a subset from the set of base-learners, keeping some and discarding the rest, and the second approach is to define few, new, uncorrelated metalearners from the original base-learners.

17.10.1 Choosing a Subset of the Ensemble

ENSEMBLE SELECTION

Choosing a subset from an ensemble of base-learners is similar to input feature selection, and the possible approaches for *ensemble selection* are the same. We can have a forward/incremental/growing approach where at each iteration, from a set of candidate base-learners, we add to the ensemble the one that most improves accuracy, we can have a backward/decremental/pruning approach where at each iteration, we remove the base-learner whose absence leads to highest improvement, or we can have a floating approach where both additions and removals are allowed.

The combination scheme can be a fixed rule, such as voting, or it can be a trained stacker. Such a selection scheme would not include inaccurate learners, ones that are not diverse enough or are correlated (Caruana et al. 2004; Ruta and Gabrys 2005). So discarding the useless also decreases the overall complexity. Different learners may be using different representations, and such an approach also allows choosing the best complementary representations (Demir and Alpaydın 2005). Note that if we use a decision tree as the combiner, it acts both as a selector and a combiner (Ulaş et al. 2009).

17.10.2 Constructing Metalearners

No matter how we vary the learning algorithms, hyperparameters, resampled folds, or input features, we get positively correlated classifiers (Ulaş, Yıldız, and Alpaydın 2012), and postprocessing is needed to remove this correlation that may be harmful. One possibility is to discard some of the correlated ones, as we discussed earlier; another is to apply a feature extraction method where from the space of the outputs of base-learners, we go to a new, lower-dimensional space where we define uncorrelated metalearners that will also be fewer in number.

Merz (1999) proposes the SCANN algorithm that uses correspondence analysis—a variant of principal components analysis (section 6.3)—on the crisp outputs of base classifiers and combines them using the nearest mean classifier. Actually, any linear or nonlinear feature extraction method we discussed in chapter 6 can be used and its (preferrably continuous) output can be fed to any learner, as we do in stacking.

Let us say we have L learners each having K outputs. Then, for example, using principal component analysis, we can map from the $K \cdot L$-dimensional space to a new space of lower-dimensional, uncorrelated space of "eigenlearners" (Ulaş, Yıldız, and Alpaydın 2012). We can then train the combiner in this new space (using a separate dataset unused to train the base-learners and the dimensionality reducer). Actually, by looking at the coefficients of the eigenvectors, we can also understand the contribution of the base-learners and assess their utility.

It has been shown by Jacobs (1995) that L dependent learners are worth the same as L' independent learners where $L' \leq L$, and this is exactly the idea here. Another point to note is that rather than drastically discarding or keeping a subset of the ensemble, this approach uses all the base-learners, and hence all the information, but at the expense of more computation.

17.11 Cascading

The idea in cascaded classifiers is to have a *sequence* of base-classifiers d_j sorted in terms of their space or time complexity, or the cost of the representation they use, so that d_{j+1} is costlier than d_j (Kaynak and Alpaydın 2000). *Cascading* is a multistage method, and we use d_j only if all preceding learners, $d_k, k < j$ are not confident (see figure 17.5). For this, associated with each learner is a *confidence* w_j such that we say d_j is confident of its output and can be used if $w_j > \theta_j$ where $1/K < \theta_j \leq \theta_{j+1} < 1$ is the confidence threshold. In classification, the confidence function is set to the highest posterior: $w_j \equiv \max_i d_{ji}$; this is the strategy used for rejections (section 3.3).

CASCADING

We use learner d_j if all the preceding learners are not confident:

$$y_i = d_{ji} \text{ if } w_j > \theta_j \text{ and } \forall k < j, w_k < \theta_k \tag{17.9}$$

Starting with $j = 1$, given a training set, we train d_j. Then we find all instances from a separate validation set on which d_j is not confident, and these constitute the training set of d_{j+1}. Note that unlike in AdaBoost, we choose not only the misclassified instances but the ones for which the previous base-learner is not confident. This covers the misclassifications as well as the instances for which the posterior is not high enough; these are instances on the right side of the boundary but for which the distance to the discriminant, namely, the margin, is not large enough.

The idea is that an early simple classifier handles the majority of instances, and a more complex classifier is used only for a small percentage, thereby not significantly increasing the overall complexity. This is

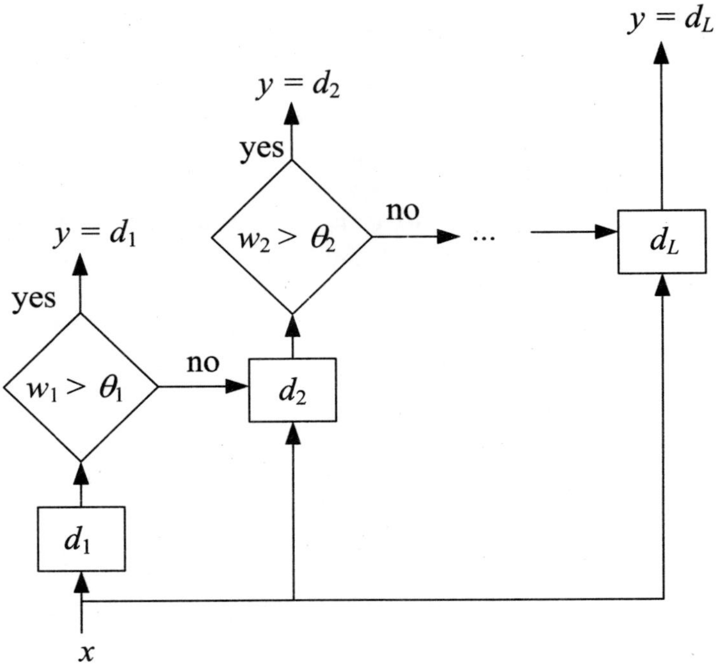

Figure 17.5 Cascading is a multistage method where there is a sequence of classifiers, and the next one is used only when the preceding ones are not confident.

contrary to the multiexpert methods like voting where all base-learners generate their output for any instance. If the problem space is complex, a few base-classifiers may be cascaded increasing the complexity at each stage. In order not to increase the number of base-classifiers, the few instances not covered by any are stored as they are and are treated by a nonparametric classifier, such as k-NN.

The inductive bias of cascading is that the classes can be explained by a small number of "rules" in increasing complexity, with an additional small set of "exceptions" not covered by the rules. The rules are implemented by simple base-classifiers, for example, perceptrons of increasing complexity, which learn general rules valid over the whole input space. Exceptions are localized instances and are best handled by a nonparametric model.

Cascading thus stands between the two extremes of parametric and nonparametric classification. The former—for example, a linear model—finds a single rule that should cover all the instances. A nonparametric classifier—for example, k-NN—stores the whole set of instances without generating any simple rule explaining them. Cascading generates a rule (or rules) to explain a large part of the instances as cheaply as possible and stores the rest as exceptions. This makes sense in a lot of learning applications. For example, most of the time the past tense of a verb in English is found by adding a "-d" or "-ed" to the verb; there are also irregular verbs—for example, "go"/"went"—that do not obey this rule.

17.12 Notes

The idea in combining learners is to divide a complex task into simpler tasks that are handled by separately trained base-learners. Each base-learner has its own task. If we had a large learner containing all the base-learners, then it would risk overfitting. For example, consider taking a vote over three multilayer perceptrons, each with a single hidden layer. If we combine them all together with the linear model combining their outputs, this is a large multilayer perceptron with two hidden layers. If we train this large model with the whole sample, it very probably overfits. When we train the three multilayer perceptrons separately, for example, using ECOC, bagging, and so forth, it is as if we define a required output for the second-layer hidden nodes of the large multilayer perceptron. This puts a constraint on what the overall learner should learn and simplifies learning.

One disadvantage of combining is that the combined system is not interpretable. For example, even though decision trees are interpretable, bagged or boosted trees are not interpretable. Error-correcting codes with their weights as $-1/0/+1$ allow some form of interpretability. Mayoraz and Moreira (1997) discuss incremental methods for learning the error-correcting output codes where base-learners are added when needed. Allwein, Schapire, and Singer (2000) discuss various methods for coding multiclass problems as two-class problems. Alpaydın and Mayoraz (1999) consider the application of ECOC where linear base-learners are combined to get nonlinear discriminants, and they also propose methods to learn the ECOC matrix from data.

The earliest and most intuitive approach is voting. Kittler et al. (1998) give a review of fixed rules and also discuss an application where multiple representations are combined. The task is person identification using three representations: frontal face image, face profile image, and voice. The error rate of the voting model is lower than the error rates when a single representation is used. Another application is given in Alimoğlu and Alpaydın 1997 where for improved handwritten digit recognition, two sources of information are combined: One is the temporal pen movement data as the digit is written on a touch-sensitive pad, and the other is the static two-dimensional bitmap image once the digit is written. In that application, the two classifiers using either of the two representations have around 5 percent error, but combining the two reduces the error rate to 3 percent. It is also seen that the critical stage is the design of the complementary learners and/or representations, the way they are combined is not as critical.

BIOMETRICS

Combining different modalities is used in *biometrics*, where the aim is authentication using different input sources, fingerprint, signature, face, and so on. In such a case, different classifiers use these modalities separately and their decisions are combined. This both improves accuracy and makes *spoofing* more difficult.

Noble (2004) makes a distinction between three type of combination strategies when we have information coming from multiple sources in different representations or modalities:

- In *early integration*, all these inputs are concatenated to form a single vector that is then fed to a single classifier. Previously we discussed why this is not a very good idea.

- In *late integration*, which we advocated in this chapter, different inputs are fed to separate classifiers whose outputs are then combined, by voting, stacking, or any other method we discussed.

MULTIPLE KERNEL LEARNING

- Kernel algorithms, which we discussed in chapter 13, allow a different method of integration that Noble (2004) calls *intermediate integration*, as being between early and late integration. This is the *multiple kernel learning* approach (see section 13.8) where there is a single kernel machine classifier that uses multiple kernels for different inputs and the combination is not in the input space as in early integration, or in the space of decisions as in late integration, but in the space of the basis functions that define the kernels. For different sources, there are different notions of similarity calculated by their kernels, and the classifier accumulates and uses them.

Some ensemble methods such as voting are similar to Bayesian averaging (chapter 16). For example when we do bagging and train the same model on different resampled training sets, we may consider them as being samples from the posterior distribution, but other combination methods such as mixture of experts and stacking go much beyond averaging over parameters or models.

When we are combining multiple views/representations, concatenating them is not really a good idea but one interesting possibility is to do some combined dimensionality reduction. We can consider a generative model (section 14.3) where we assume that there is a set of latent factors that generate these multiple views in parallel, and from the observed views, we can go back to that latent space and do classification there (Chen et al. 2012).

Combining multiple learners has been a popular topic in machine learning since the early 1990s, and research has been going on ever since. Kuncheva (2004) discusses different aspects of classifier combination; the book also includes a section on combination of multiple clustering results.

AdaBoosted decision trees are considered to be one of the best machine learning algorithms. There are also versions of AdaBoost where the next base-learner is trained on the residual of the previous base-learner (Hastie, Tibshirani, and Friedman 2001). Recently, it has been noticed that ensembles do not always improve accuracy and research has started to focus on the criteria that a good ensemble should satisfy or how to form a good one. A survey of the role of diversity in ensembles is given in Kuncheva 2005.

17.13 Exercises

1. If each base-learner is iid and correct with probability $p > 1/2$, what is the probability that a majority vote over L classifiers gives the correct answer?

   SOLUTION: It is given by a binomial distribution (see figure 17.6).

$$P(X \geq \lfloor L/2 \rfloor + 1) = \sum_{i=\lfloor L/2 \rfloor+1}^{L} \binom{L}{i} p^i (1-p)^{L-i}$$

2. In bagging, to generate the L training sets, what would be the effect of using L-fold cross-validation instead of bootstrap?
3. Propose an incremental algorithm for learning error-correcting output codes

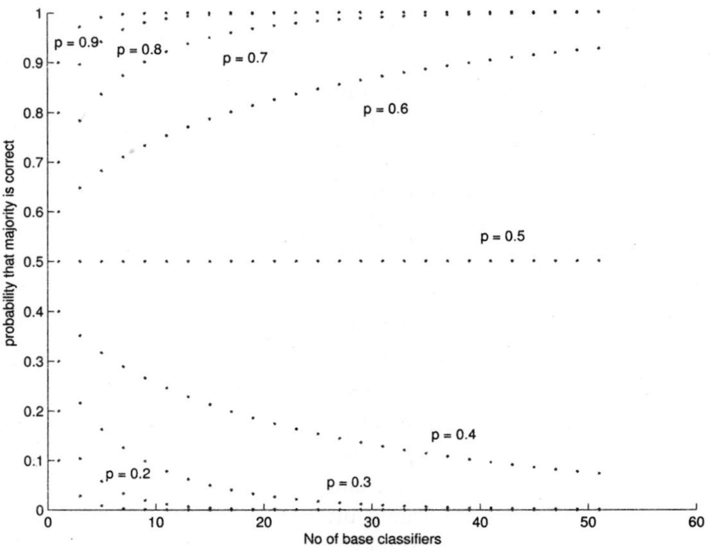

Figure 17.6 Probability that a majority vote is correct as a function of the number of base-learners for different p. The probabity increases only for $p > 0.5$.

where new two-class problems are added as they are needed to better solve the multiclass problem.

4. In the mixture of experts architecture, we can have different experts use different input representations. How can we design the gating network in such a case?

5. Propose a dynamic regressor selection algorithm.

6. What is the difference between voting and stacking using a linear perceptron as the combiner function?

   SOLUTION: If the voting system is also trained, the only difference would be that with stacking, the weights need not be positive or sum up to 1, and there is also a bias term. Of course, the main advantage of stacking is when the combiner is nonlinear.

7. In cascading, why do we require $\theta_{j+1} \geq \theta_j$?

   SOLUTION: Instances on which the confidence is less than θ_j have already been filtered out by d_j; we require the threshold to increase so that we can have higher confidences.

8. To be able to use cascading for regression, during testing, a regressor should

be able to say whether it is confident of its output. How can we implement this?

9. How can we combine the results of multiple clustering solutions?

   SOLUTION: The easiest is the following: Let us take any two training instances. Each clustering solution either places them in the same cluster or not; denote it as 1 and 0. The average of these counts over all clustering solutions is the overall probability that those two are in the same cluster (Kuncheva 2004).

10. In section 17.10, we discuss that if we use a decision tree as a combiner in stacking, it works both as a selector and a combiner. What are the other advantages and disadvantages?

    SOLUTION: A tree uses only a subset of the classifiers and not the whole. Using the tree is fast, and we need to evaluate only the nodes on our path, which may be short. See Ulaş et al. 2009 for more detail. The disadvantage is that the combiner cannot look at combinations of classifier decisions (assuming that the tree is univariate). Using a subset may also be harmful; we do not get the redundancy we need if some classifiers are faulty.

17.14 References

Alimoğlu, F., and E. Alpaydın. 1997. "Combining Multiple Representations and Classifiers for Pen-Based Handwritten Digit Recognition." In *Fourth International Conference on Document Analysis and Recognition*, 637–640. Los Alamitos, CA: IEEE Computer Society.

Allwein, E. L., R. E. Schapire, and Y. Singer. 2000. "Reducing Multiclass to Binary: A Unifying Approach for Margin Classifiers." *Journal of Machine Learning Research* 1:113–141.

Alpaydın, E. 1997. "Voting over Multiple Condensed Nearest Neighbors." *Artificial Intelligence Review* 11:115–132.

Alpaydın, E., and E. Mayoraz. 1999. "Learning Error-Correcting Output Codes from Data." In *Ninth International Conference on Artificial Neural Networks*, 743–748. London: IEE Press.

Avnimelech, R., and N. Intrator. 1997. "Boosting Regression Estimators." *Neural Computation* 11:499–520.

Breiman, L. 1996. "Bagging Predictors." *Machine Learning* 26:123–140.

Caruana, R., A. Niculescu-Mizil, G. Crew, and A. Ksikes. 2004. "Ensemble Selection from Libraries of Models." In *Twenty-First International Conference on Machine Learning*, ed. C. E. Brodley, 137–144. New York: ACM.

Chen, N., J. Zhu, F. Sun, and E. P. Xing. 2012. "Large-Margin Predictive Latent Subspace Learning for Multiview Data Analysis." *IEEE Transactions on Pattern Analysis and Machine Intelligence* 34:2365–2378.

Demir, C., and E. Alpaydın. 2005. "Cost-Conscious Classifier Ensembles." *Pattern Recognition Letters* 26:2206–2214.

Dietterich, T. G., and G. Bakiri. 1995. "Solving Multiclass Learning Problems via Error-Correcting Output Codes." *Journal of Artificial Intelligence Research* 2:263–286.

Drucker, H. 1997. "Improving Regressors using Boosting Techniques." In *Fourteenth International Conference on Machine Learning*, ed. D. H. Fisher, 107–115. San Mateo, CA: Morgan Kaufmann.

Drucker, H., C. Cortes, L. D. Jackel, Y. Le Cun, and V. Vapnik. 1994. "Boosting and Other Ensemble Methods." *Neural Computation* 6:1289–1301.

Freund, Y., and R. E. Schapire. 1996. "Experiments with a New Boosting Algorithm." In *Thirteenth International Conference on Machine Learning*, ed. L. Saitta, 148–156. San Mateo, CA: Morgan Kaufmann.

Hansen, L. K., and P. Salamon. 1990. "Neural Network Ensembles." *IEEE Transactions on Pattern Analysis and Machine Intelligence* 12:993–1001.

Hastie, T., R. Tibshirani, and J. Friedman. 2001. *The Elements of Statistical Learning: Data Mining, Inference, and Prediction.* New York: Springer.

Ho, T. K. 1998. "The Random Subspace Method for Constructing Decision Forests." *IEEE Transactions on Pattern Analysis and Machine Intelligence* 20:832–844.

Jacobs, R. A. 1995. "Methods for Combining Experts' Probability Assessments." *Neural Computation* 7:867–888.

Jacobs, R. A. 1997. "Bias/Variance Analyses for Mixtures-of-Experts Architectures." *Neural Computation* 9:369–383.

Jain, A., K. Nandakumar, and A. Ross. 2005. "Score Normalization in Multimodal Biometric Systems." *Pattern Recognition* 38:2270–2285.

Kaynak, C., and E. Alpaydın. 2000. "MultiStage Cascading of Multiple Classifiers: One Man's Noise is Another Man's Data." In *Seventeenth International Conference on Machine Learning*, ed. P. Langley, 455–462. San Francisco: Morgan Kaufmann.

Kittler, J., M. Hatef, R. P. W. Duin, and J. Matas. 1998. "On Combining Classifiers." *IEEE Transactions on Pattern Analysis and Machine Intelligence* 20:226–239.

Kuncheva, L. I. 2004. *Combining Pattern Classifiers: Methods and Algorithms.* Hoboken, NJ: Wiley.

Kuncheva, L. I. 2005. Special issue on Diversity in Multiple Classifier Systems. *Information Fusion* 6:1–115.

Mayoraz, E., and M. Moreira. 1997. "On the Decomposition of Polychotomies into Dichotomies." In *Fourteenth International Conference on Machine Learning*, ed. D. H. Fisher, 219–226. San Mateo, CA: Morgan Kaufmann.

Merz, C. J. 1999. "Using Correspondence Analysis to Combine Classifiers." *Machine Learning* 36:33–58.

Noble, W. S. 2004. "Support Vector Machine Applications in Computational Biology." In *Kernel Methods in Computational Biology*, ed. B. Schölkopf, K. Tsuda, and J.-P. Vert, 71–92. Cambridge, MA: MIT Press.

Özen, A., M. Gönen, E. Alpaydın, and T. Haliloğlu. 2009. "Machine Learning Integration for Predicting the Effect of Single Amino Acid Substitutions on Protein Stability." *BMC Structural Biology* 9 (66): 1–17.

Perrone, M. P. 1993. "Improving Regression Estimation: Averaging Methods for Variance Reduction with Extensions to General Convex Measure." Ph.D. thesis, Brown University.

Ruta, D., and B. Gabrys. 2005. "Classifier Selection for Majority Voting." *Information Fusion* 6:63–81.

Schapire, R. E. 1990. "The Strength of Weak Learnability." *Machine Learning* 5:197–227.

Schapire, R. E., Y. Freund, P. Bartlett, and W. S. Lee. 1998. "Boosting the Margin: A New Explanation for the Effectiveness of Voting Methods." *Annals of Statistics* 26:1651–1686.

Ulaş, A., M. Semerci, O. T. Yıldız, and E. Alpaydın. 2009. "Incremental Construction of Classifier and Discriminant Ensembles." *Information Sciences* 179:1298–1318.

Ulaş, A., O. T. Yıldız, and E. Alpaydın. 2012. "Eigenclassifiers for Combining Correlated Classifiers." *Information Sciences* 187:109–120.

Wolpert, D. H. 1992. "Stacked Generalization." *Neural Networks* 5:241–259.

Woods, K., W. P. Kegelmeyer Jr., and K. Bowyer. 1997. "Combination of Multiple Classifiers Using Local Accuracy Estimates." *IEEE Transactions on Pattern Analysis and Machine Intelligence* 19:405–410.

18 *Reinforcement Learning*

In reinforcement learning, the learner is a decision-making agent that takes actions in an environment and receives reward (or penalty) for its actions in trying to solve a problem. After a set of trial-and-error runs, it should learn the best policy, which is the sequence of actions that maximize the total reward.

18.1 Introduction

LET US SAY we want to build a machine that learns to play chess. In this case we cannot use a supervised learner for two reasons. First, it is very costly to have a teacher that will take us through many games and indicate us the best move for each position. Second, in many cases, there is no such thing as the best move; the goodness of a move depends on the moves that follow. A single move does not count; a sequence of moves is good if after playing them we win the game. The only feedback is at the end of the game when we win or lose the game.

Another example is a robot that is placed in a maze. The robot can move in one of the four compass directions and should make a sequence of movements to reach the exit. As long as the robot is in the maze, there is no feedback and the robot tries many moves until it reaches the exit and only then does it get a reward. In this case there is no opponent, but we can have a preference for shorter trajectories, implying that in this case we play against time.

These two applications have a number of points in common: There is a decision maker, called the *agent*, that is placed in an *environment* (see figure 18.1). In chess, the game-player is the decision maker and the environment is the board; in the second case, the maze is the environment

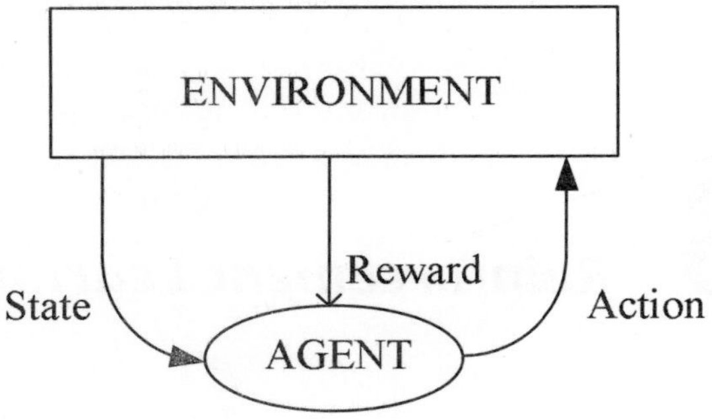

Figure 18.1 The agent interacts with an environment. At any state of the environment, the agent takes an action that changes the state and returns a reward.

of the robot. At any time, the environment is in a certain *state* that is one of a set of possible states—for example, the state of the board, the position of the robot in the maze. The decision maker has a set of *actions* possible: legal movement of pieces on the chess board, movement of the robot in possible directions without hitting the walls, and so forth. Once an action is chosen and taken, the state changes. The solution to the task requires a sequence of actions, and we get feedback, in the form of a *reward* rarely, generally only when the complete sequence is carried out. The reward defines the problem and is necessary if we want a *learning* agent. The learning agent learns the best sequence of actions to solve a problem where "best" is quantified as the sequence of actions that has the maximum cumulative reward. Such is the setting of *reinforcement learning*.

Reinforcement learning is different from the learning methods we discussed before in a number of respects. It is called "learning with a critic," as opposed to learning with a teacher which we have in supervised learning. A *critic* differs from a teacher in that it does not tell us what to do but only how well we have been doing in the past; the critic never informs in advance. The feedback from the critic is scarce and when it comes, it comes late. This leads to the *credit assignment* problem. After taking several actions and getting the reward, we would like to assess the individual actions we did in the past and find the moves that led us to win the reward so that we can record and recall them later on. As we see shortly, what a reinforcement learning program does is that it learns to generate

CRITIC

CREDIT ASSIGNMENT

an *internal value* for the intermediate states or actions in terms of how good they are in leading us to the goal and getting us to the real reward. Once such an internal reward mechanism is learned, the agent can just take the local actions to maximize it.

The solution to the task requires a *sequence* of actions, and from this perspective, we remember the Markov models we discussed in chapter 15. Indeed, we use a Markov decision process to model the agent. The difference is that in the case of Markov models, there is an external process that generates a sequence of signals, for exampie, speech, which we observe and model. In the current case, however, it is the agent that generates the sequence of actions. Previously, we also made a distinction between observable and hidden Markov models where the states are observed or hidden (and should be inferred) respectively. Similarly here, sometimes we have a partially observable Markov decision process in cases where the agent does not know its state exactly but should infer it with some uncertainty through observations using sensors. For example, in the case of a robot moving in a room, the robot may not know its exact position in the room, nor the exact location of obstacles nor the goal, and should make decisions through a limited image provided by a camera.

18.2 Single State Case: *K*-Armed Bandit

K-ARMED BANDIT

We start with a simple example. The K-*armed bandit* is a hypothetical slot machine with K levers. The action is to choose and pull one of the levers, and we win a certain amount of money that is the reward associated with the lever (action). The task is to decide which lever to pull to maximize the reward. This is a classification problem where we choose one of K. If this were supervised learning, then the teacher would tell us the correct class, namely, the lever leading to maximum earning. In this case of reinforcement learning, we can only try different levers and keep track of the best. This is a simplified reinforcement learning problem because there is only one state, or one slot machine, and we need only decide on the action. Another reason why this is simplified is that we immediately get a reward after a single action; the reward is not delayed, so we immediately see the value of our action.

Let us say $Q(a)$ is the value of action a. Initially, $Q(a) = 0$ for all a. When we try action a, we get reward $r_a \geq 0$. If rewards are deterministic, we always get the same r_a for any pull of a and in such a case, we can just set $Q(a) = r_a$. If we want to exploit, once we find an action a such that $Q(a) > 0$, we can keep choosing it and get r_a at each pull. However, it is quite possible that there is another lever with a higher reward, so we need to explore.

We can choose different actions and store $Q(a)$ for all a. Whenever we want to exploit, we can choose the action with the maximum value, that is,

$$\text{choose } a^* \text{ if } Q(a^*) = \max_a Q(a) \tag{18.1}$$

If rewards are not deterministic but stochastic, we get a different reward each time we choose the same action. The amount of the reward is defined by the probability distribution $p(r|a)$. In such a case, we define $Q_t(a)$ as the estimate of the value of action a at time t. It is an average of all rewards received when action a was chosen before time t. An online update can be defined as

$$Q_{t+1}(a) \leftarrow Q_t(a) + \eta[r_{t+1}(a) - Q_t(a)] \tag{18.2}$$

where $r_{t+1}(a)$ is the reward received after taking action a at time $(t+1)$st time.

Note that equation 18.2 is the *delta rule* that we have used on many occasions in the previous chapters: η is the learning factor (gradually decreased in time for convergence), r_{t+1} is the desired output, and $Q_t(a)$ is the current prediction. $Q_{t+1}(a)$ is the *expected* value of action a at time $t+1$ and converges to the mean of $p(r|a)$ as t increases.

The full reinforcement learning problem generalizes this simple case in a number of ways. First, we have several states. This corresponds to having several slot machines with different reward probabilities, $p(r|s_i, a_j)$, and we need to learn $Q(s_i, a_j)$, which is the value of taking action a_j when in state s_i. Second, the actions affect not only the reward but also the next state, and we move from one state to another. Third, the rewards are delayed and we need to be able to estimate immediate values from delayed rewards.

18.3 Elements of Reinforcement Learning

The learning decision maker is called the *agent*. The agent interacts with the *environment* that includes everything outside the agent. The agent has sensors to decide on its *state* in the environment and takes an *action* that modifies its state. When the agent takes an action, the environment provides a *reward.* Time is discrete as $t = 0, 1, 2, \ldots$, and $s_t \in S$ denotes the state of the agent at time t where S is the set of all possible states. $a_t \in \mathcal{A}(s_t)$ denotes the action that the agent takes at time t where $\mathcal{A}(s_t)$ is the set of possible actions in state s_t. When the agent in state s_t takes the action a_t, the clock ticks, reward $r_{t+1} \in \Re$ is received, and the agent moves to the next state, s_{t+1}. The problem is modeled using a *Markov decision process* (MDP). The reward and next state are sampled from their respective probability distributions, $p(r_{t+1}|s_t, a_t)$ and $P(s_{t+1}|s_t, a_t)$. Note that what we have is a *Markov* system where the state and reward in the next time step depend only on the current state and action. In some applications, reward and next state are deterministic, and for a certain state and action taken, there is one possible reward value and next state.

MARKOV DECISION PROCESS

Depending on the application, a certain state may be designated as the initial state and in some applications, there is also an absorbing terminal (goal) state where the search ends; all actions in this terminal state transition to itself with probability 1 and without any reward. The sequence of actions from the start to the terminal state is an *episode*, or a *trial.*

EPISODE

POLICY

The *policy*, π, defines the agent's behavior and is a mapping from the states of the environment to actions: $\pi : S \to \mathcal{A}$. The policy defines the action to be taken in any state s_t: $a_t = \pi(s_t)$. The *value* of a policy π, $V^\pi(s_t)$, is the expected cumulative reward that will be received while the agent follows the policy, starting from state s_t.

FINITE-HORIZON

In the *finite-horizon* or *episodic* model, the agent tries to maximize the expected reward for the next T steps:

$$V^\pi(s_t) = E[r_{t+1} + r_{t+2} + \cdots + r_{t+T}] = E\left[\sum_{i=1}^{T} r_{t+i}\right] \tag{18.3}$$

INFINITE-HORIZON

Certain tasks are continuing, and there is no prior fixed limit to the episode. In the *infinite-horizon* model, there is no sequence limit, but future rewards are discounted:

$$V^\pi(s_t) = E[r_{t+1} + \gamma r_{t+2} + \gamma^2 r_{t+3} + \cdots] = E\left[\sum_{i=1}^{\infty} \gamma^{i-1} r_{t+i}\right] \tag{18.4}$$

DISCOUNT RATE

where $0 \le \gamma < 1$ is the *discount rate* to keep the return finite. If $\gamma = 0$, then only the immediate reward counts. As γ approaches 1, rewards further in the future count more, and we say that the agent becomes more farsighted. γ is less than 1 because there generally is a time limit to the sequence of actions needed to solve the task. The agent may be a robot that runs on a battery. We prefer rewards sooner rather than later because we are not certain how long we will survive.

OPTIMAL POLICY

For each policy π, there is a $V^{\pi}(s_t)$, and we want to find the *optimal policy* π^* such that

$$V^*(s_t) = \max_{\pi} V^{\pi}(s_t), \forall s_t \tag{18.5}$$

In some applications, for example, in control, instead of working with the values of states, $V(s_t)$, we prefer to work with the values of state-action pairs, $Q(s_t, a_t)$. $V(s_t)$ denotes how good it is for the agent to be in state s_t, whereas $Q(s_t, a_t)$ denotes how good it is to perform action a_t when in state s_t. We define $Q^*(s_t, a_t)$ as the value, that is, the expected cumulative reward, of action a_t taken in state s_t and then obeying the optimal policy afterward. The value of a state is equal to the value of the best possible action:

$$\begin{aligned}
V^*(s_t) &= \max_{a_t} Q^*(s_t, a_t) \\
&= \max_{a_t} E\left[\sum_{i=1}^{\infty} \gamma^{i-1} r_{t+i}\right] \\
&= \max_{a_t} E\left[r_{t+1} + \gamma \sum_{i=1}^{\infty} \gamma^{i-1} r_{t+i+1}\right] \\
&= \max_{a_t} E\left[r_{t+1} + \gamma V^*(s_{t+1})\right]
\end{aligned}$$

$$V^*(s_t) = \max_{a_t} \left(E[r_{t+1}] + \gamma \sum_{s_{t+1}} P(s_{t+1}|s_t, a_t) V^*(s_{t+1}) \right) \tag{18.6}$$

To each possible next state s_{t+1}, we move with probability $P(s_{t+1}|s_t, a_t)$, and continuing from there using the optimal policy, the expected cumulative reward is $V^*(s_{t+1})$. We sum over all such possible next states, and we discount it because it is one time step later. Adding our immediate expected reward, we get the total expected cumulative reward for action a_t. We then choose the best of possible actions. Equation 18.6 is known as *Bellman's equation* (Bellman 1957). Similarly, we can also write

BELLMAN'S EQUATION

$$Q^*(s_t, a_t) = E[r_{t+1}] + \gamma \sum_{s_{t+1}} P(s_{t+1}|s_t, a_t) \max_{a_{t+1}} Q^*(s_{t+1}, a_{t+1}) \tag{18.7}$$

```
Initialize V(s) to arbitrary values
Repeat
    For all s ∈ S
        For all a ∈ A
            Q(s,a) ← E[r|s,a] + γ Σ_{s'∈S} P(s'|s,a)V(s')
        V(s) ← max_a Q(s,a)
Until V(s) converge
```

Figure 18.2 Value iteration algorithm for model-based learning.

Once we have $Q^*(s_t, a_t)$ values, we can then define our policy π as taking the action a_t^*, which has the highest value among all $Q^*(s_t, a_t)$:

(18.8) $$\pi^*(s_t) : \text{Choose } a_t^* \text{ where } Q^*(s_t, a_t^*) = \max_{a_t} Q^*(s_t, a_t)$$

This means that if we have the $Q^*(s_t, a_t)$ values, then by using a greedy search at each *local* step we get the optimal sequence of steps that maximizes the *cumulative* reward.

18.4 Model-Based Learning

We start with model-based learning where we completely know the environment model parameters, $p(r_{t+1}|s_t, a_t)$ and $P(s_{t+1}|s_t, a_t)$. In such a case, we do not need any exploration and can directly solve for the optimal value function and policy using dynamic programming. The optimal value function is unique and is the solution to the simultaneous equations given in equation 18.6. Once we have the optimal value function, the optimal policy is to choose the action that maximizes the value in the next state:

(18.9) $$\pi^*(s_t) = \arg\max_{a_t} \left(E[r_{t+1}|s_t, a_t] + \gamma \sum_{s_{t+1}\in S} P(s_{t+1}|s_t, a_t) V^*(s_t + 1) \right)$$

18.4.1 Value Iteration

VALUE ITERATION

To find the optimal policy, we can use the optimal value function, and there is an iterative algorithm called *value iteration* that has been shown to converge to the correct V^* values. Its pseudocode is given in figure 18.2.

```
Initialize a policy π' arbitrarily
Repeat
    π ← π'
    Compute the values using π by
        solving the linear equations
            V^π(s) = E[r|s,π(s)] + γ Σ_{s'∈S} P(s'|s,π(s))V^π(s')
    Improve the policy at each state
        π'(s) ← arg max_a(E[r|s,a] + γ Σ_{s'∈S} P(s'|s,a)V^π(s'))
Until π = π'
```

Figure 18.3 Policy iteration algorithm for model-based learning.

We say that the values converged if the maximum value difference between two iterations is less than a certain threshold δ:

$$\max_{s \in S} |V^{(l+1)}(s) - V^{(l)}(s)| < \delta$$

where l is the iteration counter. Because we care only about the actions with the maximum value, it is possible that the policy converges to the optimal one even before the values converge to their optimal values. Each iteration is $\mathcal{O}(|S|^2|\mathcal{A}|)$, but frequently there is only a small number $k < |S|$ of next possible states, so complexity decreases to $\mathcal{O}(k|S||\mathcal{A}|)$.

18.4.2 Policy Iteration

In policy iteration, we store and update the policy rather than doing this indirectly over the values. The pseudocode is given in figure 18.3. The idea is to start with a policy and improve it repeatedly until there is no change. The value function can be calculated by solving for the linear equations. We then check whether we can improve the policy by taking these into account. This step is guaranteed to improve the policy, and when no improvement is possible, the policy is guaranteed to be optimal. Each iteration of this algorithm takes $\mathcal{O}(|\mathcal{A}||S|^2 + |S|^3)$ time that is more than that of value iteration, but policy iteration needs fewer iterations than value iteration.

18.5 Temporal Difference Learning

Model is defined by the reward and next state probability distributions, and as we saw in section 18.4, when we know these, we can solve for the optimal policy using dynamic programming. However, these methods are costly, and we seldom have such perfect knowledge of the environment. The more interesting and realistic application of reinforcement learning is when we do not have the model. This requires exploration of the environment to query the model. We first discuss how this exploration is done and later see model-free learning algorithms for deterministic and nondeterministic cases. Though we are not going to assume a full knowledge of the environment model, we will however require that it be stationary.

TEMPORAL DIFFERENCE

As we will see shortly, when we explore and get to see the value of the next state and reward, we use this information to update the value of the current state. These algorithms are called *temporal difference* algorithms because what we do is look at the difference between our current estimate of the value of a state (or a state-action pair) and the discounted value of the next state and the reward received.

18.5.1 Exploration Strategies

To explore, one possibility is to use ϵ-*greedy* search where with probability ϵ, we choose one action uniformly randomly among all possible actions, namely, explore, and with probability $1 - \epsilon$, we choose the best action, namely, exploit. We do not want to continue exploring indefinitely but start exploiting once we do enough exploration; for this, we start with a high ϵ value and gradually decrease it. We need to make sure that our policy is *soft*, that is, the probability of choosing any action $a \in \mathcal{A}$ in state $s \in S$ is greater than 0.

We can choose probabilistically, using the softmax function to convert values to probabilities

$$P(a|s) = \frac{\exp Q(s,a)}{\sum_{b \in \mathcal{A}} \exp Q(s,b)} \tag{18.10}$$

and then sample according to these probabilities. To gradually move from exploration to exploitation, we can use a "temperature" variable T and define the probability of choosing action a as

$$P(a|s) = \frac{\exp[Q(s,a)/T]}{\sum_{b \in \mathcal{A}} \exp[Q(s,b)/T]} \tag{18.11}$$

When T is large, all probabilities are equal and we have exploration. When T is small, better actions are favored. So the strategy is to start with a large T and decrease it gradually, a procedure named *annealing*, which in this case moves from exploration to exploitation smoothly in time.

18.5.2 Deterministic Rewards and Actions

In model-free learning, we first discuss the simpler deterministic case, where at any state-action pair, there is a single reward and next state possible. In this case, equation 18.7 reduces to

$$Q(s_t, a_t) = r_{t+1} + \gamma \max_{a_{t+1}} Q(s_{t+1}, a_{t+1}) \tag{18.12}$$

and we simply use this as an assignment to update $Q(s_t, a_t)$. When in state s_t, we choose action a_t by one of the stochastic strategies we saw earlier, which returns a reward r_{t+1} and takes us to state s_{t+1}. We then update the value of *previous* action as

$$\hat{Q}(s_t, a_t) \leftarrow r_{t+1} + \gamma \max_{a_{t+1}} \hat{Q}(s_{t+1}, a_{t+1}) \tag{18.13}$$

where the hat denotes that the value is an estimate. $\hat{Q}(s_{t+1}, a_{t+1})$ is a later value and has a higher chance of being correct. We discount this by γ and add the immediate reward (if any) and take this as the new estimate for the previous $\hat{Q}(s_t, a_t)$. This is called a *backup* because it can be viewed as taking the estimated value of an action in the next time step and "backing it up" to revise the estimate for the value of a current action.

BACKUP

For now we assume that all $\hat{Q}(s, a)$ values are stored in a table; we will see later on how we can store this information more succinctly when $|S|$ and $|\mathcal{A}|$ are large.

Initially all $\hat{Q}(s_t, a_t)$ are 0, and they are updated in time as a result of trial episodes. Let us say we have a sequence of moves and at each move, we use equation 18.13 to update the estimate of the Q value of the previous state-action pair using the Q value of the current state-action pair. In the intermediate states, all rewards and therefore values are 0, so no update is done. When we get to the goal state, we get the reward r and then we can update the Q value of the previous state-action pair as γr. As for the preceding state-action pair, its immediate reward is 0 and the contribution from the next state-action pair is discounted by γ because it is one step later. Then in another episode, if we reach this

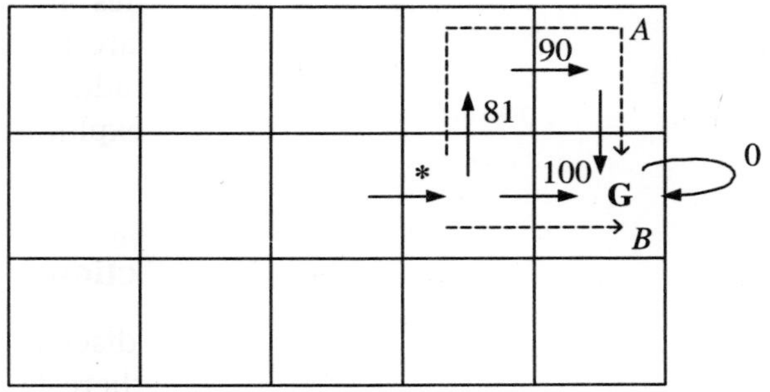

Figure 18.4 Example to show that Q values increase but never decrease. This is a deterministic grid-world where G is the goal state with reward 100, all other immediate rewards are 0, and $\gamma = 0.9$. Let us consider the Q value of the transition marked by asterisk, and let us just consider only the two paths A and B. Let us say that path A is seen before path B, then we have $\gamma \max(0, 81) = 72.9$; if afterward B is seen, a shorter path is found and the Q value becomes $\gamma \max(100, 81) = 90$. If B is seen before A, the Q value is $\gamma \max(100, 0) = 90$; then when A is seen, it does not change because $\gamma \max(100, 81) = 90$.

state, we can update the one preceding that as $\gamma^2 r$, and so on. This way, after many episodes, this information is backed up to earlier state-action pairs. Q values increase until they reach their optimal values as we find paths with higher cumulative reward, for example, shorter paths, but they never decrease (see figure 18.4).

Note that we do not know the reward or next state functions here. They are part of the environment, and it is as if we query them when we explore. We are not modeling them either, though that is another possibility. We just accept them as given and learn directly the optimal policy through the estimated value function.

18.5.3 Nondeterministic Rewards and Actions

If the rewards and the result of actions are not deterministic, then we have a probability distribution for the reward $p(r_{t+1}|s_t, a_t)$ from which rewards are sampled, and there is a probability distribution for the next state $P(s_{t+1}|s_t, a_t)$. These help us model the uncertainty in the system that may be due to forces we cannot control in the environment: for instance, our opponent in chess, the dice in backgammon, or our lack of

```
Initialize all Q(s,a) arbitrarily
For all episodes
    Initalize s
    Repeat
        Choose a using policy derived from Q, e.g., ϵ-greedy
        Take action a, observe r and s'
        Update Q(s,a):
            Q(s,a) ← Q(s,a) + η(r + γ max_a' Q(s',a') − Q(s,a))
        s ← s'
    Until s is terminal state
```

Figure 18.5 Q learning, which is an off-policy temporal difference algorithm.

knowledge of the system. For example, we may have an imperfect robot which sometimes fails to go in the intended direction and deviates, or advances shorter or longer than expected.

In such a case, we have

$$Q(s_t, a_t) = E[r_{t+1}] + \gamma \sum_{s_{t+1}} P(s_{t+1}|s_t, a_t) \max_{a_{t+1}} Q(s_{t+1}, a_{t+1}) \tag{18.14}$$

We cannot do a direct assignment in this case because for the same state and action, we may receive different rewards or move to different next states. What we do is keep a running average. This is known as the Q *learning* algorithm:

Q LEARNING

$$\hat{Q}(s_t, a_t) \leftarrow \hat{Q}(s_t, a_t) + \eta(r_{t+1} + \gamma \max_{a_{t+1}} \hat{Q}(s_{t+1}, a_{t+1}) - Q(s_t, a_t)) \tag{18.15}$$

We think of $r_{t+1} + \gamma \max_{a_{t+1}} \hat{Q}(s_{t+1}, a_{t+1})$ values as a sample of instances for each (s_t, a_t) pair and we would like $\hat{Q}(s_t, a_t)$ to converge to its mean. As usual η is gradually decreased in time for convergence, and it has been shown that this algorithm converges to the optimal Q^* values (Watkins and Dayan 1992). The pseudocode of the Q learning algorithm is given in figure 18.5.

We can also think of equation 18.15 as reducing the difference between the current Q value and the backed-up estimate, from one time step later. Such algorithms are called *temporal difference* (TD) algorithms (Sutton 1988).

TEMPORAL DIFFERENCE

OFF-POLICY

ON-POLICY

This is an *off-policy* method as the value of the best next action is used without using the policy. In an *on-policy* method, the policy is used to

```
Initialize all Q(s, a) arbitrarily
For all episodes
    Initalize s
    Choose a using policy derived from Q, e.g., ε-greedy
    Repeat
        Take action a, observe r and s'
        Choose a' using policy derived from Q, e.g., ε-greedy
        Update Q(s, a):
            Q(s, a) ← Q(s, a) + η(r + γQ(s', a') − Q(s, a))
        s ← s', a ← a'
    Until s is terminal state
```

Figure 18.6 Sarsa algorithm, which is an on-policy version of Q learning.

determine also the next action. The on-policy version of Q learning is the *Sarsa* algorithm whose pseudocode is given in figure 18.6. We see that instead of looking for all possible next actions a' and choosing the best, the on-policy Sarsa uses the policy derived from Q values to choose one next action a' and uses its Q value to calculate the temporal difference. On-policy methods estimate the value of a policy while using it to take actions. In off-policy methods, these are separated, and the policy used to generate behavior, called the *behavior* policy, may in fact be different from the policy that is evaluated and improved, called the *estimation* policy.

SARSA

Sarsa converges with probability 1 to the optimal policy and state-action values if a *GLIE policy* is employed to choose actions. A GLIE (greedy in the limit with infinite exploration) policy is where (1) all state-action pairs are visited an infinite number of times, and (2) the policy converges in the limit to the greedy policy (which can be arranged, e.g., with ϵ-greedy policies by setting $\epsilon = 1/t$).

The same idea of temporal difference can also be used to learn $V(s)$ values, instead of $Q(s, a)$. *TD learning* (Sutton 1988) uses the following update rule to update a state value:

TD LEARNING

(18.16) $$V(s_t) \leftarrow V(s_t) + \eta[r_{t+1} + \gamma V(s_{t+1}) - V(s_t)]$$

This again is the delta rule where $r_{t+1} + \gamma V(s_{t+1})$ is the better, later prediction and $V(s_t)$ is the current estimate. Their difference is the temporal difference, and the update is done to decrease this difference. The update factor η is gradually decreased, and TD is guaranteed to converge to the optimal value function $V^*(s)$.

18.5.4 Eligibility Traces

The previous algorithms are one-step—that is, the temporal difference is used to update only the previous value (of the state or state-action pair).

ELIGIBILITY TRACE

An *eligibility trace* is a record of the occurrence of past visits that enables us to implement temporal credit assignment, allowing us to update the values of previously occurring visits as well. We discuss how this is done with Sarsa to learn Q values; adapting this to learn V values is straightforward.

To store the eligibility trace, we require an additional memory variable associated with each state-action pair, $e(s, a)$, initialized to 0. When the state-action pair (s, a) is visited, namely, when we take action a in state s, its eligibility is set to 1; the eligibilities of all other state-action pairs are multiplied by $\gamma\lambda$. $0 \le \lambda \le 1$ is the trace decay parameter.

$$e_t(s, a) = \begin{cases} 1 & \text{if } s = s_t \text{ and } a = a_t, \\ \gamma\lambda e_{t-1}(s, a) & \text{otherwise} \end{cases} \tag{18.17}$$

If a state-action pair has never been visited, its eligibility remains 0; if it has been, as time passes and other state-actions are visited, its eligibility decays depending on the value of γ and λ (see figure 18.7).

We remember that in Sarsa, the temporal error at time t is

$$\delta_t = r_{t+1} + \gamma Q(s_{t+1}, a_{t+1}) - Q(s_t, a_t) \tag{18.18}$$

In Sarsa with an eligibility trace, named Sarsa(λ), *all* state-action pairs are updated as

$$Q(s, a) \leftarrow Q(s, a) + \eta\delta_t e_t(s, a), \ \forall s, a \tag{18.19}$$

This updates all eligible state-action pairs, where the update depends on how far they have occurred in the past. The value of λ defines the temporal credit: If $\lambda = 0$, only a one-step update is done. The algorithms we discussed in section 18.5.3 are such, and for this reason they are named $Q(0)$, Sarsa(0), or TD(0). As λ gets closer to 1, more of the previous steps are considered. When $\lambda = 1$, all previous steps are updated and the credit given to them falls only by γ per step. In online updating, all eligible values are updated immediately after each step; in offline updating, the updates are accumulated and a single update is done at

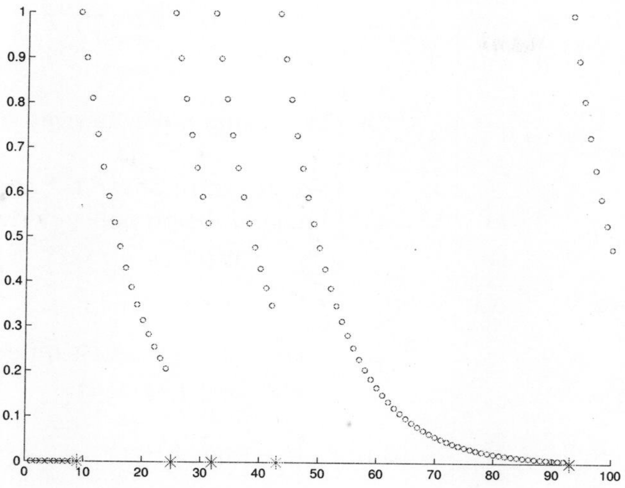

Figure 18.7 Example of an eligibility trace for a value. Visits are marked by an asterisk.

the end of the episode. Online updating takes more time but converges faster. The pseudocode for *Sarsa*(λ) is given in figure 18.8. $Q(\lambda)$ and TD(λ) algorithms can similarly be derived (Sutton and Barto 1998).

SARSA(λ)

18.6 Generalization

Until now, we assumed that the $Q(s, a)$ values (or $V(s)$, if we are estimating values of states) are stored in a lookup table, and the algorithms we considered earlier are called *tabular* algorithms. There are a number of problems with this approach: (1) when the number of states and the number of actions is large, the size of the table may become quite large; (2) states and actions may be continuous, for example, turning the steering wheel by a certain angle, and to use a table, they should be discretized which may cause error; and (3) when the search space is large, too many episodes may be needed to fill in all the entries of the table with acceptable accuracy.

Instead of storing the Q values as they are, we can consider this a regression problem. This is a supervised learning problem where we define a regressor $Q(s, a|\boldsymbol{\theta})$, taking s and a as inputs and parameterized by a

```
Initialize all Q(s,a) arbitrarily, e(s,a) ← 0, ∀s,a
For all episodes
    Initalize s
    Choose a using policy derived from Q, e.g., ε-greedy
    Repeat
        Take action a, observe r and s'
        Choose a' using policy derived from Q, e.g., ε-greedy
        δ ← r + γQ(s',a') − Q(s,a)
        e(s,a) ← 1
        For all s,a:
            Q(s,a) ← Q(s,a) + ηδe(s,a)
            e(s,a) ← γλe(s,a)
        s ← s', a ← a'
    Until s is terminal state
```

Figure 18.8 Sarsa(λ) algorithm.

vector of parameters, $\boldsymbol{\theta}$, to learn Q values. For example, this can be an artificial neural network with s and a as its inputs, one output, and $\boldsymbol{\theta}$ its connection weights.

A good function approximator has the usual advantages and solves the problems discussed previously. A good approximation may be achieved with a simple model without explicitly storing the training instances; it can use continuous inputs; and it allows generalization. If we know that similar (s, a) pairs have similar Q values, we can generalize from past cases and come up with good $Q(s, a)$ values even if that state-action pair has never been encountered before.

To be able to train the regressor, we need a training set. In the case of Sarsa(0), we saw before that we would like $Q(s_t, a_t)$ to get close to $r_{t+1} + \gamma Q(s_{t+1}, a_{t+1})$. So, we can form a set of training samples where the input is the state-action pair (s_t, a_t) and the required output is $r_{t+1} + \gamma Q(s_{t+1}, a_{t+1})$. We can write the squared error as

$$E^t(\boldsymbol{\theta}) = [r_{t+1} + \gamma Q(s_{t+1}, a_{t+1}) - Q(s_t, a_t)]^2 \tag{18.20}$$

Training sets can similarly be defined for $Q(0)$ and TD(0), where in the latter case we learn $V(s)$, and the required output is $r_{t+1} + \gamma V(s_{t+1})$.

Once such a set is ready, we can use any supervised learning algorithm for learning the training set.

If we are using a gradient descent method, as in training neural networks, the parameter vector is updated as

(18.21) $$\Delta\boldsymbol{\theta} = \eta[r_{t+1} + \gamma Q(s_{t+1}, a_{t+1}) - Q(s_t, a_t)]\nabla_{\boldsymbol{\theta}_t} Q(s_t, a_t)$$

This is a one-step update. In the case of Sarsa(λ), the eligibility trace is also taken into account:

(18.22) $$\Delta\boldsymbol{\theta} = \eta\delta_t \boldsymbol{e}_t$$

where the temporal difference error is

$$\delta_t = r_{t+1} + \gamma Q(s_{t+1}, a_{t+1}) - Q(s_t, a_t)$$

and the vector of eligibilities of parameters are updated as

(18.23) $$\boldsymbol{e}_t = \gamma\lambda \boldsymbol{e}_{t-1} + \nabla_{\boldsymbol{\theta}_t} Q(s_t, a_t)$$

with $\boldsymbol{e}_0$ all zeros. In the case of a tabular algorithm, the eligibilities are stored for the state-action pairs because they are the parameters (stored as a table). In the case of an estimator, eligibility is associated with the parameters of the estimator. We also note that this is very similar to the momentum method for stabilizing backpropagation (section 11.8.1). The difference is that in the case of momentum previous weight changes are remembered, whereas here previous gradient vectors are remembered. Depending on the model used for $Q(s_t, a_t)$, for example, a neural network, we plug its gradient vector in equation 18.23.

In theory, any regression method can be used to train the Q function, but the particular task has a number of requirements. First, it should allow generalization; that is, we really need to guarantee that similar states and actions have similar Q values. This also requires a good coding of s and a, as in any application, to make the similarities apparent. Second, reinforcement learning updates provide instances one by one and not as a whole training set, and the learning algorithm should be able to do individual updates to learn the new instance without forgetting what has been learned before. For example, a multilayer perceptron using backpropagation can be trained with a single instance only if a small learning rate is used. Or, such instances may be collected to form a training set and learned altogether but this slows down learning as no learning happens while a sufficiently large sample is being collected.

Because of these reasons, it seems a good idea to use local learners to learn the Q values. In such methods, for example, radial basis functions, information is localized and when a new instance is learned, only a local part of the learner is updated without possibly corrupting the information in another part. The same requirements apply if we are estimating the state values as $V(s_t|\boldsymbol{\theta})$.

18.7 Partially Observable States

18.7.1 The Setting

In certain applications, the agent does not know the state exactly. It is equipped with sensors that return an *observation*, which the agent then uses to estimate the state. Let us say we have a robot that navigates in a room. The robot may not know its exact location in the room, or what else is there in the room. The robot may have a camera with which sensory observations are recorded. This does not tell the robot its state exactly but gives some indication as to its likely state. For example, the robot may only know that there is an obstacle to its right.

The setting is like a Markov decision process, except that after taking an action a_t, the new state s_{t+1} is not known, but we have an observation o_{t+1} that is a stochastic function of s_t and a_t: $p(o_{t+1}|s_t, a_t)$. This is called a *partially observable MDP* (POMDP). If $o_{t+1} = s_{t+1}$, then POMDP reduces to the MDP. This is just like the distinction between observable and hidden Markov models and the solution is similar; that is, from the observation, we need to infer the state (or rather a probability distribution for the states) and then act based on this. If the agent believes that it is in state s_1 with probability 0.4 and in state s_2 with probability 0.6, then the value of any action is 0.4 times the value of the action in s_1 plus 0.6 times the value of the action in s_2.

PARTIALLY OBSERVABLE MDP

The Markov property does not hold for observations. The next state observation does not only depend on the current action and observation. When there is limited observation, two states may appear the same but are different and if these two states require different actions, this can lead to a loss of performance, as measured by the cumulative reward. The agent should somehow compress the past trajectory into a current unique state estimate. These past observations can also be taken into account by taking a past window of observations as input to the policy,

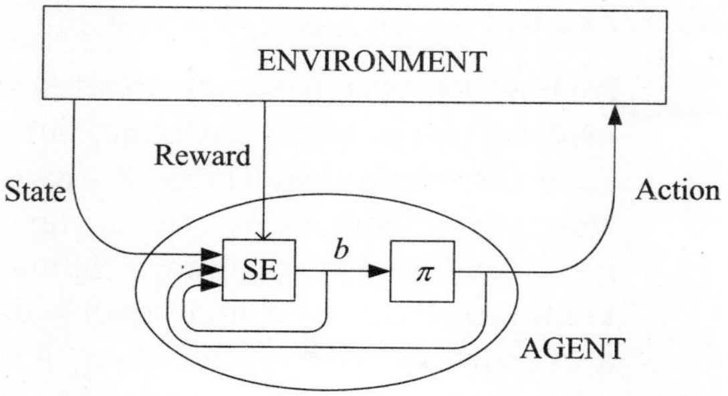

Figure 18.9 In the case of a partially observable environment, the agent has a state estimator (SE) that keeps an internal belief state b and the policy π generates actions based on the belief states.

or one can use a recurrent neural network (section 11.12.2) to maintain the state without forgetting past observations.

At any time, the agent may calculate the most likely state and take an action accordingly. Or it may take an action to gather information and reduce uncertainty, for example, search for a landmark, or stop to ask for direction. This implies the importance of the *value of information*, and indeed POMDPs can be modeled as *dynamic* influence diagrams (section 14.8). The agent chooses between actions based on the amount of information they provide, the amount of reward they produce, and how they change the state of the environment.

VALUE OF INFORMATION

To keep the process Markov, the agent keeps an internal *belief state* b_t that summarizes its experience (see figure 18.9). The agent has a *state estimator* that updates the belief state b_{t+1} based on the last action a_t, current observation o_{t+1}, and its previous belief state b_t. There is a policy π that generates the next action a_{t+1} based on this belief state, as opposed to the actual state that we had in a completely observable environment. The belief state is a probability distribution over states of the environment given the initial belief state (before we did any actions) and the past observation-action history of the agent (without leaving out any information that could improve agent's performance). Q learning in such a case involves the belief state-action pair values, instead of the actual state-action pairs:

BELIEF STATE

$$Q(b_t, a_t) = E[r_{t+1}] + \gamma \sum_{b_{t+1}} P(b_{t+1}|b_t, a_t)V(b_{t+1}) \tag{18.24}$$

18.7.2 Example: The Tiger Problem

We now discuss an example that is a slightly different version of the *Tiger problem* discussed in Kaelbling, Littman, and Cassandra 1998, modified as in the example in Thrun, Burgard, and Fox 2005. Let us say we are standing in front of two doors, one to our left and the other to other right, leading to two rooms. Behind one of the two doors, we do not know which, there is a crouching tiger, and behind the other, there is a treasure. If we open the door of the room where the tiger is, we get a large negative reward, and if we open the door of the treasure room, we get some positive reward. The hidden state, z_L, is the location of the tiger. Let us say p denotes the probability that tiger is in the room to the left and therefore, the tiger is in the room to the right with probability $1 - p$:

$$p \equiv P(z_L = 1)$$

The two actions are a_L and a_R, which respectively correspond to opening the left or the right door. The rewards are

$r(A, Z)$	Tiger left	Tiger right
Open left	−100	+80
Open right	+90	−100

We can calculate the expected reward for the two actions. There are no future rewards because the episode ends once we open one of the doors.

$$\begin{aligned} R(a_L) &= r(a_L, z_L)P(z_L) + r(a_L, z_R)P(z_R) = -100p + 80(1-p) \\ R(a_R) &= r(a_R, z_L)P(z_L) + r(a_R, z_R)P(z_R) = 90p - 100(1-p) \end{aligned}$$

Given these rewards, if p is close to 1, if we believe that there is a high chance that the tiger is on the left, the right action will be to choose the right door, and, similarly, for p close to 0, it is better to choose the left door.

The two intersect for p around 0.5, and there the expected reward is approximately −10. The fact that the expected reward is negative when p is around 0.5 (when we have uncertainty) indicates the importance of collecting information. If we can add sensors to to decrease uncertainty—that is, move p away from 0.5 to either close to 0 or close to 1—we can take actions with high positive rewards. That sensing action, a_S, may have a small negative reward: $R(a_S) = -1$; this may be considered as the cost of sensing or equivalent to discounting future reward by $\gamma < 1$ because we are postponing taking the real action (of opening one of the doors).

In such a case, the expected rewards and value of the best action are shown in figure 18.10a:

$$V = \max(a_L, a_R, a_S)$$

Let us say as sensory input, we use microphones to check whether the tiger is behind the left or the right door. But we have unreliable sensors (so that we still stay in the realm of partial observability). Let us say we can only detect tiger's presence with 0.7 probability:

$$P(o_L|z_L) = 0.7 \qquad P(o_L|z_R) = 0.3$$
$$P(o_R|z_L) = 0.3 \qquad P(o_R|z_R) = 0.7$$

If we sense o_L, our belief in the tiger's position changes:

$$p' = P(z_L|o_L) = \frac{P(o_L|z_L)P(z_L)}{p(o_L)} = \frac{0.7p}{0.7p + 0.3(1-p)}$$

The effect of this is shown in figure 18.10b where we plot $R(a_L|o_L)$. Sensing o_L turns opening the right door into a better action for a wider range. The better sensors we have (if the probability of correct sensing moves from 0.7 closer to 1), the larger this range gets (exercise 9). Similarly, as we see in figure 18.10c, if we sense o_R, this increases the chances of opening the left door. Note that sensing also decreases the range where there is a need to sense (once more).

The expected rewards for the actions in this case are

$$\begin{aligned}
R(a_L|o_L) &= r(a_L, z_L)P(z_L|o_L) + r(a_L, z_R)P(z_R|o_L) \\
&= -100p' + 80(1-p') \\
&= -100 \cdot \frac{0.7 \cdot p}{p(o_L)} + 80 \cdot \frac{0.3 \cdot (1-p)}{p(o_L)} \\
R(a_R|o_L) &= r(a_R, z_L)P(z_L|o_L) + r(a_R, z_R)P(z_R|o_L) \\
&= 90p' - 100(1-p') \\
&= 90 \cdot \frac{0.7 \cdot p}{p(o_L)} - 100 \cdot \frac{0.3 \cdot (1-p)}{p(o_L)} \\
R(a_S|o_L) &= -1
\end{aligned}$$

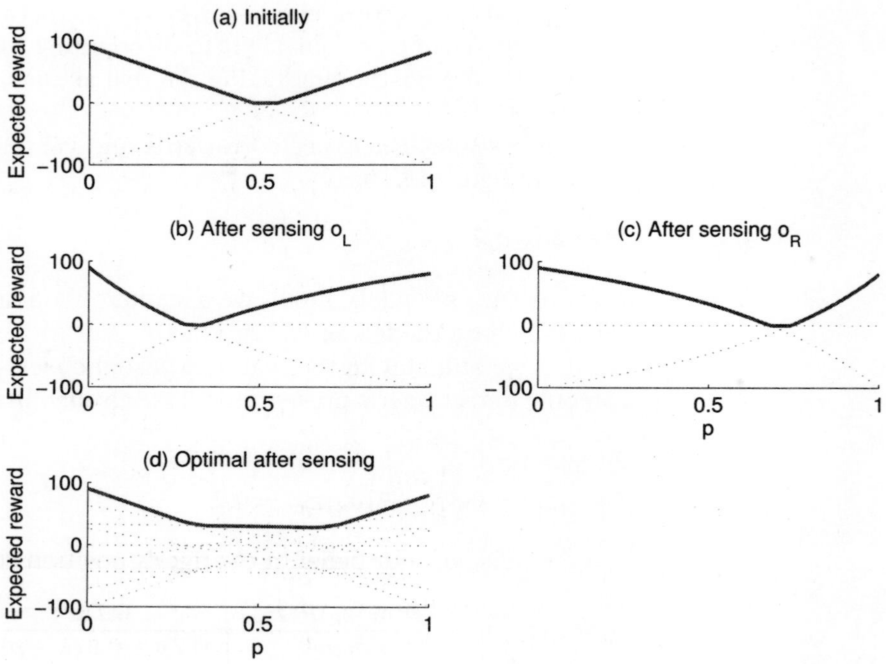

Figure 18.10 Expected rewards and the effect of sensing in the Tiger problem.

The best action is this case is the maximum of these three. Similarly, if we sense o_R, the expected rewards become

$$\begin{aligned} R(a_L|o_R) &= r(a_L, z_L)P(z_L|o_R) + r(a_L, z_R)P(z_R|o_R) \\ &= -100 \cdot \frac{0.3 \cdot p}{p(o_R)} + 80 \cdot \frac{0.7 \cdot (1-p)}{p(o_R)} \\ R(a_R|o_R) &= r(a_R, z_L)P(z_L|o_R) + r(a_R, z_R)P(z_R|o_R) \\ &= 90 \cdot \frac{0.3 \cdot p}{p(o_R)} - 100 \cdot \frac{0.7 \cdot (1-p)}{p(o_R)} \\ R(a_S|o_R) &= -1 \end{aligned}$$

To calculate the expected reward, we need to take average over both sensor readings weighted by their probabilities:

$$V' = \sum_j \left[\max_i R(a_i|o_j) \right] P(O_j)$$

$$
\begin{aligned}
&= \max(R(a_L|o_L), R(a_R|o_L), R(a_S|o_L))P(o_L) + \\
&\quad \max(R(a_L|o_R), R(a_R|o_R), R(a_S|o_R))P(o_R) \\
&= \max(-70p + 24(1-p), 63p - 30(1-p), -0.7p - 0.3(1-p)) + \\
&\quad \max(-30p + 56(1-p), 27p - 70(1-p), -0.3p - 0.7(1-p)) \\
&= \max\begin{pmatrix} -100p & +80(1-p) \\ -43p & -46(1-p) \\ 33p & +26(1-p) \\ 90p & -100(1-p) \end{pmatrix} \qquad (18.25)
\end{aligned}
$$

Note that when we multiply by $P(o_L)$, it cancels out and we get functions linear in p. These five lines and the piecewise function that corresponds to their maximum are shown in figure 18.10d. Note that the line, $-40p - 5(1-p)$, as well as the ones involving a_S, are beneath others for all values of p and can safely be pruned. The fact that figure 18.10d is better than figure 18.10a indicates the *value of information.*

VALUE OF INFORMATION

What we calculate here is the value of the best action had we chosen a_S. For example, the first line corresponds to choosing a_L after a_S. So to find the best decision with an episode of length two, we need to back this up by subtracting -1, which is the reward of a_S, and get the expected reward for the action of sense. Equivalently, we can consider this as waiting that has an immediate reward of 0 but discounts the future reward by some $\gamma < 1$. We also have the two usual actions of a_L and a_R and we choose the best of three; the two immediate actions and the one discounted future action.

Let us now make the problem more interesting, as in the example of Thrun, Burgard, and Fox 2005. Let us assume that there is a door between the two rooms and without us seeing, the tiger can move from one room to the other. Let us say that this is a restless tiger and it stays in the same room with probability 0.2 and moves to the other room with probability 0.8. This means that p should also be updated as

$$p' = 0.2p + 0.8(1-p)$$

and this updated p should be used in equation 18.25 while choosing the best action after having chosen a_S:

$$V' = \max\begin{pmatrix} -100p' & +80(1-p') \\ 33p' & +26(1-p') \\ 90p' & -100(1-p') \end{pmatrix}$$

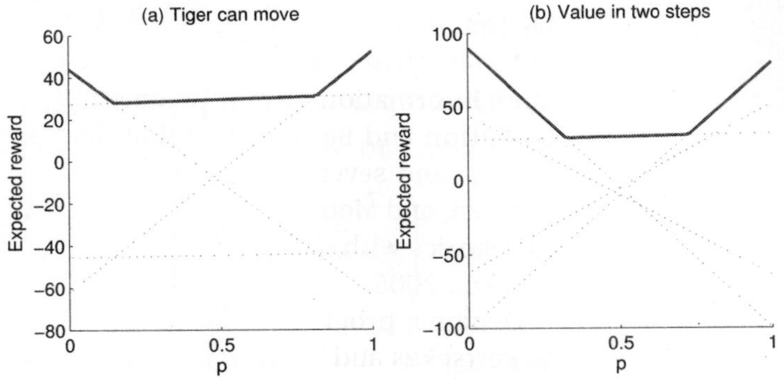

Figure 18.11 Expected rewards change (a) if the hidden state can change, and (b) when we consider episodes of length two.

Figure 18.11b corresponds to figure 18.10d with the updated p'. Now, when planning for episodes of length two, we have the two immediate actions of a_L and a_R, or we wait and sense when p changes and then we take the action and get its discounted reward (figure 18.11b):

$$V_2 = \max \begin{pmatrix} -100p & +80(1-p) \\ 90p & -100(1-p) \\ \multicolumn{2}{c}{\max V' - 1} \end{pmatrix}$$

We see that figure 18.11b is better than figure 18.10a; when wrong actions may lead to large penalty, it is better to defer judgment, look for extra information, and plan ahead. We can consider longer episodes by continuing the iterative updating of p and discounting by subtracting 1 and including the two immediate actions to calculate $V_t, t > 2$.

The algorithm we have just discussed where the value is represented by piecewise linear functions works only when the number of states, actions, observations, and the episode length are all finite. Even in applications where any of these is not small, or when any is continuous-valued, the complexity becomes high and we need to resort to approximate algorithms having reasonable complexity. Reviews of such algorithms are given in Hauskrecht 2000 and Thrun, Burgard, and Fox 2005.

18.8 Notes

More information on reinforcement learning can be found in the textbook by Sutton and Barto (1998) that discusses all the aspects, learning algorithms, and several applications. A comprehensive tutorial is Kaelbling, Littman, and Moore 1996. Recent work on reinforcement learning applied to robotics with some impressive applications is given in Thrun, Burgard, and Fox 2005.

Dynamic programming methods are discussed in Bertsekas 1987 and in Bertsekas and Tsitsiklis 1996, and TD(λ) and Q-learning can be seen as stochastic approximations to dynamic programming (Jaakkola, Jordan, and Singh 1994). Reinforcement learning has two advantages over classical dynamic programming: First, as they learn, they can focus on the parts of the space that are important and ignore the rest; and second, they can employ function approximation methods to represent knowledge that allows them to generalize and learn faster.

LEARNING AUTOMATA

A related field is that of *learning automata* (Narendra and Thathachar 1974), which are finite state machines that learn by trial and error for solving problems like the K-armed bandit. The setting we have here is also the topic of optimal control where there is a controller (agent) taking actions in a plant (environment) that minimize cost (maximize reward).

The earliest use of temporal difference method was in Samuel's checkers program written in 1959 (Sutton and Barto 1998). For every two successive positions in a game, the two board states are evaluated by the board evaluation function that then causes an update to decrease the difference. There has been much work on games because games are both easily defined and challenging. A game like chess can easily be simulated: The allowed moves are formal, and the goal is well defined. Despite the simplicity of defining the game, expert play is quite difficult.

TD-GAMMON

One of the most impressive application of reinforcement learning is the *TD-Gammon* program that learns to play backgammon by playing against itself (Tesauro 1995). This program is superior to the previous neurogammon program also developed by Tesauro, which was trained in a supervised manner based on plays by experts. Backgammon is a complex task with approximately 10^{20} states, and there is randomness due to the roll of dice. Using the TD(λ) algorithm, the program achieves master level play after playing 1,500,000 games against a copy of itself.

Another interesting application is in *job shop scheduling*, or finding a schedule of tasks satisfying temporal and resource constraints (Zhang and Dietterich 1996). Some tasks have to be finished before others can be started, and two tasks requiring the same resource cannot be done simultaneously. Zhang and Dietterich used reinforcement learning to quickly find schedules that satisfy the constraints and are short. Each state is one schedule, actions are schedule modifications, and the program finds not only one good schedule but a schedule for a class of related scheduling problems.

Recently hierarchical methods have also been proposed where the problem is decomposed into a set of subproblems. This has the advantage that policies learned for the subproblems can be shared for multiple problems, which accelerates learning a new problem (Dietterich 2000). Each subproblem is simpler and learning them separately is faster. The disadvantage is that when they are combined, the policy may be suboptimal.

Though reinforcement learning algorithms are slower than supervised learning algorithms, it is clear that they have a wider variety of application and have the potential to construct better learning machines (Ballard 1997). They do not need any supervision, and this may actually be better since then they are not biased by the teacher. For example, Tesauro's TD-Gammon program in certain circumstances came up with moves that turned out to be superior to those made by the best players. The field of reinforcement learning is developing rapidly, and we may expect to see other impressive results in the near future.

18.9 Exercises

1. Given the grid world in figure 18.12, if the reward on reaching on the goal is 100 and $\gamma = 0.9$, calculate manually $Q^*(s,a)$, $V^*(S)$, and the actions of optimal policy.
2. With the same configuration given in exercise 1, use Q learning to learn the optimal policy.
3. In exercise 1, how does the optimal policy change if another goal state is added to the lower-right corner? What happens if a state of reward -100 (a very bad state) is defined in the lower-right corner?
4. Instead of having $\gamma < 1$, we can have $\gamma = 1$ but with a negative reward of $-c$ for all intermediate (nongoal) states. What is the difference?
5. In exercise 1, assume that the reward on arrival to the goal state is normal distributed with mean 100 and variance 40. Assume also that the actions are

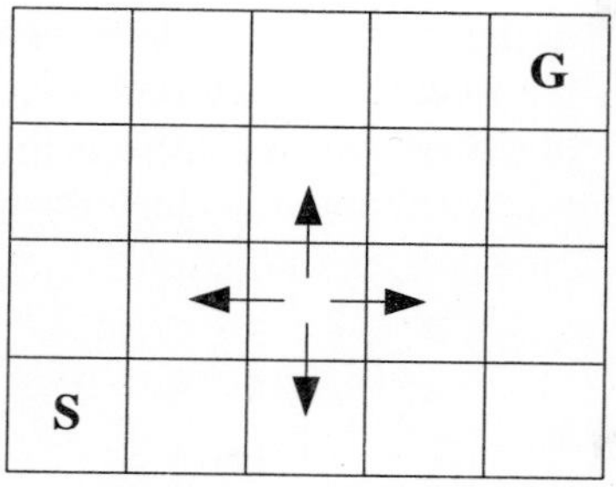

Figure 18.12 The grid world. The agent can move in the four compass directions starting from S. The goal state is G.

also stochastic in that when the robot advances in a direction, it moves in the intended direction with probability 0.5 and there is a 0.25 probability that it moves in one of the lateral directions. Learn $Q(s, a)$ in this case.

6. Assume we are estimating the value function for states $V(s)$ and that we want to use TD(λ) algorithm. Derive the tabular value iteration update.

SOLUTION: The temporal error at time t is

$$\delta_t = r_{t+1} + \gamma V(s_{t+1}) - V(s_t)$$

All state values are updated as

$$V(s) \leftarrow V(s) + \eta \delta_t e_t(s), \ \forall s$$

where the eligibility of states decay in time:

$$e_t(s) = \begin{cases} 1 & \text{if } s = s_t \\ \gamma\lambda e_{t-1}(s) & \text{otherwise} \end{cases}$$

7. Using equation 18.22, derive the weight update equations when a multilayer perceptron is used to estimate Q.

SOLUTION: Let us say for simplicity we have one-dimensional state value s_t and one-dimensional action value a_t, and let us assume a linear model:

$$Q(s, a) = w_1 s + w_2 a + w_3$$

We can update the three parameters w_1, w_2, w_3 using gradient descent (equation 16.21):

$$\begin{aligned} \Delta w_1 &= \eta \left[r_{t+1} + \gamma Q(s_{t+1}, a_{t+1}) - Q(s_t, a_t) \right] s_t \\ \Delta w_2 &= \eta \left[r_{t+1} + \gamma Q(s_{t+1}, a_{t+1}) - Q(s_t, a_t) \right] a_t \\ \Delta w_3 &= \eta \left[r_{t+1} + \gamma Q(s_{t+1}, a_{t+1}) - Q(s_t, a_t) \right] \end{aligned}$$

In the case of a multilayer perceptron, only the last term will differ to update the weights on all layers.

In the case of Sarsa(λ), $\boldsymbol{e}$ is three-dimensional: e^1 for w_1, e^2 for w_2, and e^3 for w_0. We update the eligibilities (equation 18.23):

$$\begin{aligned} e_t^1 &= \gamma\lambda e_{t-1}^1 + s_t \\ e_t^2 &= \gamma\lambda e_{t-1}^2 + a_t \\ e_t^3 &= \gamma\lambda e_{t-1}^3 \end{aligned}$$

and we update the weights using the eligibilities (equation 18.22):

$$\begin{aligned} \Delta w_1 &= \eta\left[r_{t+1} + \gamma Q(s_{t+1}, a_{t+1}) - Q(s_t, a_t)\right] e_t^1 \\ \Delta w_2 &= \eta\left[r_{t+1} + \gamma Q(s_{t+1}, a_{t+1}) - Q(s_t, a_t)\right] e_t^2 \\ \Delta w_3 &= \eta\left[r_{t+1} + \gamma Q(s_{t+1}, a_{t+1}) - Q(s_t, a_t)\right] e_t^3 \end{aligned}$$

8. Give an example of a reinforcement learning application that can be modeled by a POMDP. Define the states, actions, observations, and reward.
9. In the tiger example, show that as we get a more reliable sensor, the range where we need to sense once again decreases.
10. Rework the tiger example using the following reward matrix

$r(A, Z)$	Tiger left	Tiger right
Open left	−100	+10
Open right	20	−100

18.10 References

Ballard, D. H. 1997. *An Introduction to Natural Computation.* Cambridge, MA: MIT Press.

Bellman, R. E. 1957. *Dynamic Programming.* Princeton: Princeton University Press.

Bertsekas, D. P. 1987. *Dynamic Programming: Deterministic and Stochastic Models.* New York: Prentice Hall.

Bertsekas, D. P., and J. N. Tsitsiklis. 1996. *Neuro-Dynamic Programming.* Belmont, MA: Athena Scientific.

Dietterich, T. G. 2000. "Hierarchical Reinforcement Learning with the MAXQ Value Decomposition." *Journal of Artificial Intelligence Research* 13:227–303.

Hauskrecht, M. 2000. "Value-Function Approximations for Partially Observable Markov Decision Processes." *Journal of Artificial Intelligence Research* 13:33–94.

Jaakkola, T., M. I. Jordan, and S. P. Singh. 1994. "On the Convergence of Stochastic Iterative Dynamic Programming Algorithms." *Neural Computation* 6:1185–1201.

Kaelbling, L. P., M. L. Littman, and A. R. Cassandra. 1998. "Planning and Acting in Partially Observable Stochastic Domains." *Artificial Intelligence* 101:99–134.

Kaelbling, L. P., M. L. Littman, and A. W. Moore. 1996. "Reinforcement Learning: A Survey." *Journal of Artificial Intelligence Research* 4:237–285.

Narendra, K. S., and M. A. L. Thathachar. 1974. "Learning Automata—A Survey." *IEEE Transactions on Systems, Man, and Cybernetics* 4:323–334.

Sutton, R. S. 1988. "Learning to Predict by the Method of Temporal Differences." *Machine Learning* 3:9–44.

Sutton, R. S., and A. G. Barto. 1998. *Reinforcement Learning: An Introduction.* Cambridge, MA: MIT Press.

Tesauro, G. 1995. "Temporal Difference Learning and TD-Gammon." *Communications of the ACM* 38 (3): 58–68.

Thrun, S., W. Burgard, and D. Fox. 2005. *Probabilistic Robotics.* Cambridge, MA: MIT Press.

Watkins, C. J. C. H., and P. Dayan. 1992. "Q-learning." *Machine Learning* 8:279–292.

Zhang, W., and T. G. Dietterich. 1996. "High-Performance Job-Shop Scheduling with a Time-Delay TD(λ) Network." In *Advances in Neural Information Processing Systems 8*, ed. D. S. Touretzky, M. C. Mozer, and M. E. Hasselmo, 1024–1030. Cambridge, MA: The MIT Press.

19 *Design and Analysis of Machine Learning Experiments*

We discuss the design of machine learning experiments to assess and compare the performances of learning algorithms in practice and the statistical tests to analyze the results of these experiments.

19.1 Introduction

IN PREVIOUS chapters, we discussed several learning algorithms and saw that, given a certain application, more than one is applicable. Now, we are concerned with two questions:

1. How can we assess the expected error of a learning algorithm on a problem? That is, for example, having used a classification algorithm to train a classifier on a dataset drawn from some application, can we say with enough confidence that later on when it is used in real life, its expected error rate will be less than, for example, 2 percent?

2. Given two learning algorithms, how can we say one has less error than the other one, for a given application? The algorithms compared can be different, for example, parametric versus nonparametric, or they can use different hyperparameter settings. For example, given a multilayer perceptron (chapter 11) with four hidden units and another one with eight hidden units, we would like to be able to say which one has less expected error. Or with the k-nearest neighbor classifier (chapter 8), we would like to find the best value of k.

We cannot look at the training set errors and decide based on those. The error rate on the training set, by definition, is always smaller than the error rate on a test set containing instances unseen during training.

Similarly, training errors cannot be used to compare two algorithms. This is because over the training set, the more complex model having more parameters will almost always give fewer errors than the simple one.

So as we have repeatedly discussed, we need a validation set that is different from the training set. Even over a validation set though, just one run may not be enough. There are two reasons for this: First, the training and validation sets may be small and may contain exceptional instances, like noise and outliers, which may mislead us. Second, the learning method may depend on other random factors affecting generalization. For example, with a multilayer perceptron trained using backpropagation, because gradient descent converges to the nearest local minimum, the initial weights affect the final weights, and given the exact same architecture and training set, starting from different initial weights, there may be multiple possible final classifiers having different error rates on the same validation set. We thus would like to have several runs to average over such sources of randomness. If we train and validate only once, we cannot test for the effect of such factors; this is only admissible if the learning method is so costly that it can be trained and validated only once.

We use a *learning algorithm* on a dataset and generate a *learner*. If we do the training once, we have one learner and one validation error. To average over randomness (in training data, initial weights, etc.), we use the same algorithm and generate multiple learners. We test them on multiple validation sets and record a sample of validation errors. (Of course, all the training and validation sets should be drawn from the same application.) We base our evaluation of the learning algorithm on the *distribution* of these validation errors. We can use this distribution for assessing the *expected error* of the learning algorithm for that problem, or compare it with the error rate distribution of some other learning algorithm.

EXPECTED ERROR

Before proceeding to how this is done, it is important to stress a number of points:

1. We should keep in mind that whatever conclusion we draw from our analysis is conditioned on the dataset we are given. We are not comparing learning algorithms in a domain independent way but on some particular application. We are not saying anything about the expected error of a learning algorithm, or comparing one learning algorithm with another algorithm, in general. Any result we have is only true for the particular application, and only insofar as that application is rep-

NO FREE LUNCH THEOREM

resented in the sample we have. And anyway, as stated by the *No Free Lunch Theorem* (Wolpert 1995), there is no such thing as the "best" learning algorithm. For any learning algorithm, there is a dataset where it is very accurate and another dataset where it is very poor. When we say that a learning algorithm is good, we only quantify how well its inductive bias matches the properties of the data.

2. The division of a given dataset into a number of training and validation set pairs is only for testing purposes. Once all the tests are complete and we have made our decision as to the final method or hyperparameters, to train the final learner, we can use all the labeled data that we have previously used for training or validation.

3. Because we also use the validation set(s) for testing purposes, for example, for choosing the better of two learning algorithms, or to decide where to stop learning, it effectively becomes part of the data we use. When after all such tests, we decide on a particular algorithm and want to report its expected error, we should use a separate *test set* for this purpose, unused during training this final system. This data should have never been used before for training or validation and should be large for the error estimate to be meaningful. So, given a dataset, we should first leave some part of it aside as the test set and use the rest for training and validation. Typically, we can leave one-third of the sample as the test set, then use two-thirds for cross-validation to generate multiple training/validation set pairs, as we will see shortly. So, the training set is used to optimize the parameters, given a particular learning algorithm and model structure; the validation set is used to optimize the hyperparameters of the learning algorithm or the model structure; and the test set is used at the end, once both these have been optimized. For example, with an MLP, the training set is used to optimize the weights, the validation set is used to decide on the number of hidden units, how long to train, the learning rate, and so forth. Once the best MLP configuration is chosen, its final error is calculated on the test set. With k-NN, the training set is stored as the lookup table; we optimize the distance measure and k on the validation set and test finally on the test set.

4. In general, we compare learning algorithms by their error rates, but it should be kept in mind that in real life, error is only one of the criteria that affect our decision. Some other criteria are (Turney 2000):

- risks when errors are generalized using loss functions, instead of 0/1 loss (section 3.3),
- training time and space complexity,
- testing time and space complexity,
- interpretability, namely, whether the method allows knowledge extraction which can be checked and validated by experts, and
- easy programmability.

The relative importance of these factors changes depending on the application. For example, if the training is to be done once in the factory, then training time and space complexity are not important; if adaptability during use is required, then they do become important. Most of the learning algorithms use 0/1 loss and take error as the single criterion to be minimized; recently, *cost-sensitive learning* variants of these algorithms have also been proposed to take other cost criteria into account.

COST-SENSITIVE LEARNING

When we train a learner on a dataset using a training set and test its accuracy on some validation set and try to draw conclusions, what we are doing is experimentation. Statistics defines a methodology to design experiments correctly and analyze the collected data in a manner so as to be able to extract significant conclusions (Montgomery 2005). In this chapter, we will see how this methodology can be used in the context of machine learning.

19.2 Factors, Response, and Strategy of Experimentation

As in other branches of science and engineering, in machine learning too, we do experiments to get information about the process under scrutiny. In our case, this is a learner, which, having been trained on a dataset, generates an output for a given input. An *experiment* is a test or a series of tests where we play with the *factors* that affect the output. These factors may be the algorithm used, the training set, input features, and so on, and we observe the changes in the *response* to be able to extract information. The aim may be to identify the most important factors, screen the unimportant ones, or find the configuration of the factors that optimizes the response—for example, classification accuracy on a given test set.

EXPERIMENT

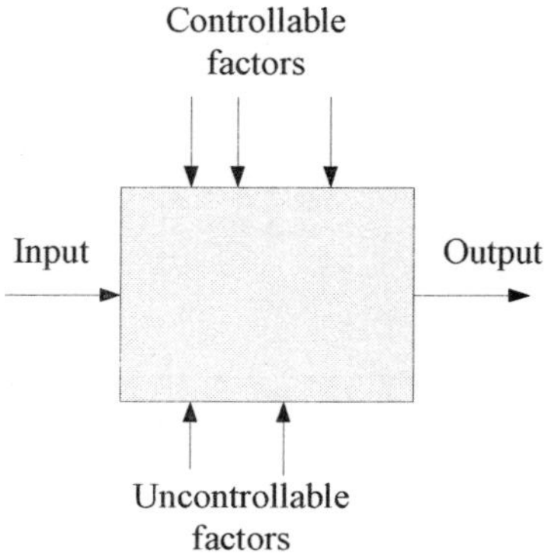

Figure 19.1 The process generates an output given an input and is affected by controllable and uncontrollable factors.

Our aim is to plan and conduct machine learning experiments and analyze the data resulting from the experiments, to be able to eliminate the effect of chance and obtain conclusions which we can consider *statistically significant*. In machine learning, we target a learner having the highest generalization accuracy and the minimal complexity (so that its implementation is cheap in time and space) and is robust, that is, minimally affected by external sources of variability.

A trained learner can be shown as in figure 19.1; it gives an output, for example, a class code for a test input, and this depends on two type of factors. The *controllable factors*, as the name suggests, are those we have control on. The most basic is the learning algorithm used. There are also the hyperparameters of the algorithm, for example, the number of hidden units for a multilayer perceptron, k for k-nearest neighbor, C for support vector machines, and so on. The dataset used and the input representation, that is, how the input is coded as a vector, are other controllable factors.

There are also *uncontrollable factors* over which we have no control, adding undesired variability to the process, which we do not want to affect our decisions. Among these are the noise in the data, the particular training subset if we are resampling from a large set, randomness in the optimization process, for example, the initial state in gradient descent with multilayer perceptrons, and so on.

We use the output to generate the *response* variable—for example, av-

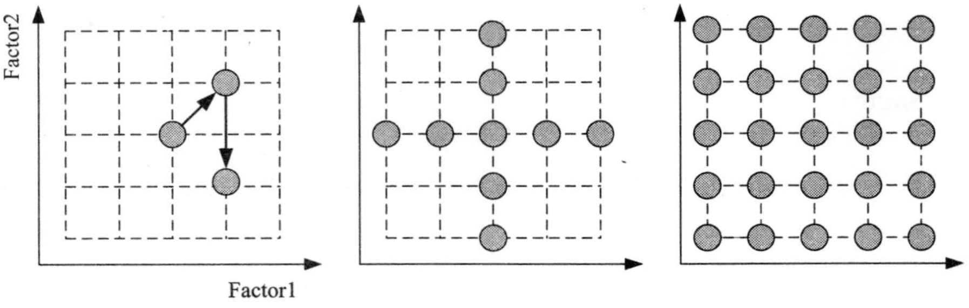

Figure 19.2 Different strategies of experimentation with two factors and five levels each.

erage classification error on a test set, or the expected risk using a loss function, or some other measure, such as precision and recall, as we will discuss shortly.

Given several factors, we need to find the best setting for best response, or in the general case, determine their effect on the response variable. For example, we may be using principal components analyzer (PCA) to reduce dimensionality to d before a k-nearest neighbor (k-NN) classifier. The two factors are d and k, and the question is to decide which combination of d and k leads to highest performance. Or, we may be using a support vector machine classifier with Gaussian kernel, and we have the regularization parameter C and the spread of the Gaussian s^2 to fine-tune together.

STRATEGIES OF EXPERIMENTATION

There are several *strategies of experimentation*, as shown in figure 19.2. In the *best guess* approach, we start at some setting of the factors that we believe is a good configuration. We test the response there and we fiddle with the factors one (or very few) at a time, testing each combination until we get to a state that we consider is good enough. If the experimenter has a good intuition of the process, this may work well; but note that there is no systematic approach to modify the factors and when we stop, we have no guarantee of finding the best configuration.

Another strategy is to modify *one factor at a time* where we decide on a baseline (default) value for all factors, and then we try different levels for one factor while keeping all other factors at their baseline. The major disadvantage of this is that it assumes that there is no *interaction* between the factors, which may not always be true. In the PCA/k-NN cascade we discussed earlier, each choice for d defines a different input space for k-NN where a different k value may be appropriate.

FACTORIAL DESIGN

The correct approach is to use a *factorial design* where factors are varied together, instead of one at a time; this is colloquially called *grid search*. With F factors at L levels each, searching one factor at a time takes $\mathcal{O}(L \cdot F)$ time, whereas a factorial experiment takes $\mathcal{O}(L^F)$ time.

19.3 Response Surface Design

To decrease the number of runs necessary, one possibility is to run a fractional factorial design where we run only a subset, another is to try to use knowledge gathered from previous runs to estimate configurations that seem likely to have high response. In searching one factor at a time, if we can assume that the response is typically quadratic (with a single maximum, assuming we are maximizing a response value, such as the test accuracy), then instead of trying all values, we can have an iterative procedure where starting from some initial runs, we fit a quadratic, find its maximum analytically, take that as the next estimate, run an experiment there, add the resulting data to the sample, and then continue fitting and sampling, until we get no further improvement.

RESPONSE SURFACE DESIGN

With many factors, this is generalized as the *response surface design* method where we try to fit a parametric response function to the factors as

$$r = g(f_1, f_2, \ldots, f_F | \phi)$$

where r is the response and $f_i, i = 1, \ldots, F$ are the factors. This fitted parametric function defined given the parameters ϕ is our empirical model estimating the response for a particular configuration of the (controllable) factors; the effect of uncontrollable factors is modeled as noise. $g(\cdot)$ is a (typically quadratic) regression model and after a small number of runs around some baseline (as defined by a so-called *design matrix*), one can have enough data to fit $g(\cdot)$ on. Then, we can analytically calculate the values of f_i where the fitted g is maximum, which we take as our next guess, run an experiment there, get a data instance, add it to the sample, fit g once more, and so on, until there is convergence. Whether this approach will work well or not depends on whether the response can indeed be written as a quadratic function of the factors with a single maximum.

19.4 Randomization, Replication, and Blocking

Let us now talk about the three basic principles of experimental design.

RANDOMIZATION

- *Randomization* requires that the order in which the runs are carried out should be randomly determined so that the results are independent. This is typically a problem in real-world experiments involving physical objects; for example, machines require some time to warm up until they operate in their normal range so tests should be done in random order for time not to bias the results. Ordering generally is not a problem in software experiments.

REPLICATION

- *Replication* implies that for the same configuration of (controllable) factors, the experiment should be run a number of times to average over the effect of uncontrollable factors. In machine learning, this is typically done by running the same algorithm on a number of resampled versions of the same dataset; this is known as *cross-validation*, which we will discuss in section 19.6. How the response varies on these different replications of the same experiment allows us to obtain an estimate of the experimental error (the effect of uncontrollable factors), which we can in turn use to determine how large differences should be to be deemed *statistically significant*.

BLOCKING

PAIRING

- *Blocking* is used to reduce or eliminate the variability due to *nuisance factors* that influence the response but in which we are not interested. For example, defects produced in a factory may also depend on the different batches of raw material, and this effect should be isolated from the controllable factors in the factory, such as the equipment, personnel, and so on. In machine learning experimentation, when we use resampling and use different subsets of the data for different replicates, we need to make sure that for example if we are comparing learning algorithms, they should all use the same set of resampled subsets, otherwise the differences in accuracies would depend not only on the algorithms but also on the different subsets—to be able to measure the difference due to algorithms only, the different training sets in replicated runs should be identical; this is what we mean by blocking. In statistics, if there are two populations, this is called *pairing* and is used in *paired testing*.

19.5 Guidelines for Machine Learning Experiments

Before we start experimentation, we need to have a good idea about what it is we are studying, how the data is to be collected, and how we are planning to analyze it. The steps in machine learning are the same as for any type of experimentation (Montgomery 2005). Note that at this point, it is not important whether the task is classification or regression, or whether it is an unsupervised or a reinforcement learning application. The same overall discussion applies; the difference is only in the sampling distribution of the response data that is collected.

A. Aim of the Study

We need to start by stating the problem clearly, defining what the objectives are. In machine learning, there may be several possibilities. As we discussed before, we may be interested in assessing the expected error (or some other response measure) of a learning algorithm on a particular problem and check that, for example, the error is lower than a certain acceptable level.

Given two learning algorithms and a particular problem as defined by a dataset, we may want to determine which one has less generalization error. These can be two different algorithms, or one can be a proposed improvement of the other, for example, by using a better feature extractor.

In the general case, we may have more than two learning algorithms, and we may want to choose the one with the least error, or order them in terms of error, for a given dataset.

In an even more general setting, instead of on a single dataset, we may want to compare two or more algorithms on two or more datasets.

B. Selection of the Response Variable

We need to decide on what we should use as the quality measure. Most frequently, error is used that is the misclassification error for classification and mean square error for regression. We may also use some variant; for example, generalizing from 0/1 to an arbitrary loss, we may use a risk measure. In information retrieval, we use measures such as precision and recall; we will discuss such measures in section 19.7. In a cost-sensitive setting, not only the output but also system parameters, for example, its complexity, are taken into account.

C. Choice of Factors and Levels

What the factors are depend on the aim of the study. If we fix an algorithm and want to find the best hyperparameters, then those are the factors. If we are comparing algorithms, the learning algorithm is a factor. If we have different datasets, they also become a factor.

The levels of a factor should be carefully chosen so as not to miss a good configuration and avoid doing unnecessary experimentation. It is always good to try to normalize factor levels. For example, in optimizing k of k-nearest neighbor, one can try values such as 1, 3, 5, and so on, but in optimizing the spread h of Parzen windows, we should not try absolute values such as 1.0, 2.0, and so on, because that depends on the scale of the input; it is better to find some statistic that is an indicator of scale—for example, the average distance between an instance and its nearest neighbor—and try h as different multiples of that statistic.

Though previous expertise is a plus in general, it is also important to investigate all factors and factor levels that may be of importance and not be overly influenced by past experience.

D. Choice of Experimental Design

It is always better to do a factorial design unless we are sure that the factors do not interact, because mostly they do. Replication number depends on the dataset size; it can be kept small when the dataset is large; we will discuss this in the next section when we talk about resampling. However, too few replicates generate few data and this will make comparing distributions difficult; in the particular case of parametric tests, the assumptions of Gaussianity may not be tenable.

Generally, given some dataset, we leave some part as the test set and use the rest for training and validation, probably many times by resampling. How this division is done is important. In practice, using small datasets leads to responses with high variance, and the differences will not be significant and results will not be conclusive.

It is also important to avoid as much as possible toy, synthetic data and use datasets that are collected from real-world under real-life circumstances. Didactic one- or two-dimensional datasets may help provide intuition, but the behavior of the algorithms may be completely different in high-dimensional spaces.

E. Performing the Experiment

Before running a large factorial experiment with many factors and levels, it is best if one does a few trial runs for some random settings to check that all is as expected. In a large experiment, it is always a good idea to save intermediate results (or seeds of the random number generator), so that a part of the whole experiment can be rerun when desired. All the results should be reproducable. In running a large experiment with many factors and factor levels, one should be aware of the possible negative effects of software aging.

It is important that an experimenter be unbiased during experimentation. In comparing one's favorite algorithm with a competitor, both should be investigated equally diligently. In large-scale studies, it may even be envisaged that testers be different from developers.

One should avoid the temptation to write one's own "library" and instead, as much as possible, use code from reliable sources; such code would have been better tested and optimized.

As in any software development study, the advantages of good documentation cannot be underestimated, especially when working in groups. All the methods developed for high-quality software engineering should also be used in machine learning experiments.

F. Statistical Analysis of the Data

This corresponds to analyzing data in a way so that whatever conclusion we get is not subjective or due to chance. We cast the questions that we want to answer in the framework of hypothesis testing and check whether the sample supports the hypothesis. For example, the question "Is A a more accurate algorithm than B?" becomes the hypothesis "Can we say that the average error of learners trained by A is significantly lower than the average error of learners trained by B?"

As always, visual analysis is helpful, and we can use histograms of error distributions, whisker-and-box plots, range plots, and so on.

G. Conclusions and Recommendations

Once all data is collected and analyzed, we can draw objective conclusions. One frequently encountered conclusion is the need for further experimentation. Most statistical, and hence machine learning or data mining, studies are iterative. It is for this reason that we never start with all the experimentation. It is suggested that no more than 25 percent of the available resources should be invested in the first experiment (Montgomery 2005). The first runs are for investigation only. That is also why it is a good idea not to start with high expectations, or promises to one's boss or thesis advisor.

We should always remember that statistical testing never tells us if the hypothesis is correct or false, but how much the sample seems to concur with the hypothesis. There is always a risk that we do not have a conclusive result or that our conclusions be wrong, especially if the data is small and noisy.

When our expectations are not met, it is most helpful to investigate why they are not. For example, in checking why our favorite algorithm A has worked awfully bad on some cases, we can get a splendid idea for some improved version of A. All improvements are due to the deficiencies of the previous version; finding a deficiency is but a helpful hint that there is an improvement we can make!

But we should not go to the next step of testing the improved version before we are sure that we have completely analyzed the current data and learned all we could learn from it. Ideas are cheap, and useless unless tested, which is costly.

19.6 Cross-Validation and Resampling Methods

For replication purposes, our first need is to get a number of training and validation set pairs from a dataset $\mathcal{X}$ (after having left out some part as the test set). To get them, if the sample $\mathcal{X}$ is large enough, we can randomly divide it into K parts, then randomly divide each part into two and use one half for training and the other half for validation. K is typically 10 or 30. Unfortunately, datasets are never large enough to do this. So we should do our best with small datasets. This is done by repeated use of the same data split differently; this is called *cross-validation*. The catch is that this makes the error percentages dependent as these different sets share data.

CROSS-VALIDATION

So, given a dataset $\mathcal{X}$, we would like to generate K training/validation set pairs, $\{\mathcal{T}_i, \mathcal{V}_i\}_{i=1}^K$, from this dataset. We would like to keep the training and validation sets as large as possible so that the error estimates are robust, and at the same time, we would like to keep the overlap between different sets as small as possible. We also need to make sure that classes are represented in the right proportions when subsets of data are held out, not to disturb the class prior probabilities; this is called *stratification*. If a class has 20 percent examples in the whole dataset, in all samples drawn from the dataset, it should also have approximately 20 percent examples.

STRATIFICATION

19.6.1 *K*-Fold Cross-Validation

K-FOLD CROSS-VALIDATION

In K-*fold cross-validation,* the dataset $\mathcal{X}$ is divided randomly into K equal-sized parts, $\mathcal{X}_i, i = 1, \ldots, K$. To generate each pair, we keep one of the K parts out as the validation set and combine the remaining $K - 1$ parts to form the training set. Doing this K times, each time leaving out another one of the K parts out, we get K pairs:

$$\begin{aligned}
\mathcal{V}_1 &= \mathcal{X}_1 & \mathcal{T}_1 &= \mathcal{X}_2 \cup \mathcal{X}_3 \cup \cdots \cup \mathcal{X}_K \\
\mathcal{V}_2 &= \mathcal{X}_2 & \mathcal{T}_2 &= \mathcal{X}_1 \cup \mathcal{X}_3 \cup \cdots \cup \mathcal{X}_K \\
&\vdots \\
\mathcal{V}_K &= \mathcal{X}_K & \mathcal{T}_K &= \mathcal{X}_1 \cup \mathcal{X}_2 \cup \cdots \cup \mathcal{X}_{K-1}
\end{aligned}$$

There are two problems with this. First, to keep the training set large, we allow validation sets that are small. Second, the training sets overlap considerably, namely, any two training sets share $K - 2$ parts.

K is typically 10 or 30. As K increases, the percentage of training instances increases and we get more robust estimators, but the validation set becomes smaller. Furthermore, there is the cost of training the classifier K times, which increases as K is increased. As N increases, K can be smaller; if N is small, K should be large to allow large enough training sets. One extreme case of K-fold cross-validation is *leave-one-out* where given a dataset of N instances, only one instance is left out as the validation set (instance) and training uses the $N - 1$ instances. We then get N separate pairs by leaving out a different instance at each iteration. This is typically used in applications such as medical diagnosis, where labeled data is hard to find. Leave-one-out does not permit stratification.

LEAVE-ONE-OUT

Recently, with computation getting cheaper, it has also become possible to have multiple runs of K-fold cross-validation, for example, 10×10-

fold, and use average over averages to get more reliable error estimates (Bouckaert 2003).

19.6.2 5 × 2 Cross-Validation

5 × 2 CROSS-VALIDATION

Dietterich (1998) proposed the *5 ×2 cross-validation*, which uses training and validation sets of equal size. We divide the dataset $\mathcal{X}$ randomly into two parts, $\mathcal{X}_1^{(1)}$ and $\mathcal{X}_1^{(2)}$, which gives our first pair of training and validation sets, $\mathcal{T}_1 = \mathcal{X}_1^{(1)}$ and $\mathcal{V}_1 = \mathcal{X}_1^{(2)}$. Then we swap the role of the two halves and get the second pair: $\mathcal{T}_2 = \mathcal{X}_1^{(2)}$ and $\mathcal{V}_2 = \mathcal{X}_1^{(1)}$. This is the first fold; $\mathcal{X}_i^{(j)}$ denotes half j of fold i.

To get the second fold, we shuffle $\mathcal{X}$ randomly and divide this new fold into two, $\mathcal{X}_2^{(1)}$ and $\mathcal{X}_2^{(2)}$. This can be implemented by drawing these from $\mathcal{X}$ randomly without replacement, namely, $\mathcal{X}_1^{(1)} \cup \mathcal{X}_1^{(2)} = \mathcal{X}_2^{(1)} \cup \mathcal{X}_2^{(2)} = \mathcal{X}$. We then swap these two halves to get another pair. We do this for three more folds and because from each fold, we get two pairs, doing five folds, we get ten training and validation sets:

$$
\begin{array}{ll}
\mathcal{T}_1 = \mathcal{X}_1^{(1)} & \mathcal{V}_1 = \mathcal{X}_1^{(2)} \\
\mathcal{T}_2 = \mathcal{X}_1^{(2)} & \mathcal{V}_2 = \mathcal{X}_1^{(1)} \\
\mathcal{T}_3 = \mathcal{X}_2^{(1)} & \mathcal{V}_3 = \mathcal{X}_2^{(2)} \\
\mathcal{T}_4 = \mathcal{X}_2^{(2)} & \mathcal{V}_4 = \mathcal{X}_2^{(1)} \\
\vdots & \\
\mathcal{T}_9 = \mathcal{X}_5^{(1)} & \mathcal{V}_9 = \mathcal{X}_5^{(2)} \\
\mathcal{T}_{10} = \mathcal{X}_5^{(2)} & \mathcal{V}_{10} = \mathcal{X}_5^{(1)}
\end{array}
$$

Of course, we can do this for more than five folds and get more training/validation sets, but Dietterich (1998) points out that after five folds, the sets share many instances and overlap so much that the statistics calculated from these sets, namely, validation error rates, become too dependent and do not add new information. Even with five folds, the sets overlap and the statistics are dependent, but we can get away with this until five folds. On the other hand, if we do have fewer than five folds, we get less data (fewer than ten sets) and will not have a large enough sample to fit a distribution to and test our hypothesis on.

Table 19.1 Confusion matrix for two classes

	Predicted class		
True class	Positive	Negative	Total
Positive	tp : true positive	fn : false negative	p
Negative	fp : false positive	tn : true negative	n
Total	p'	n'	N

19.6.3 Bootstrapping

BOOTSTRAP

To generate multiple samples from a single sample, an alternative to cross-validation is the *bootstrap* that generates new samples by drawing instances from the original sample *with* replacement. We saw the use of bootstrapping in section 17.6 to generate training sets for different learners in bagging. The bootstrap samples may overlap more than cross-validation samples and hence their estimates are more dependent; but is considered the best way to do resampling for very small datasets.

In the bootstrap, we sample N instances from a dataset of size N with replacement. The original dataset is used as the validation set. The probability that we pick an instance is $1/N$; the probability that we do not pick it is $1 - 1/N$. The probability that we do not pick it after N draws is

$$\left(1 - \frac{1}{N}\right)^N \approx e^{-1} = 0.368$$

This means that the training data contains approximately 63.2 percent of the instances; that is, the system will not have been trained on 36.8 percent of the data, and the error estimate will be pessimistic. The solution is replication, that is, to repeat the process many times and look at the average behavior.

19.7 Measuring Classifier Performance

For classification, especially for two-class problems, a variety of measures has been proposed. There are four possible cases, as shown in table 19.1. For a positive example, if the prediction is also positive, this is a *true positive*; if our prediction is negative for a positive example, this is a *false negative*. For a negative example, if the prediction is also negative, we

Table 19.2 Performance measures used in two-class problems

Name	Formula
error	$(fp + fn)/N$
accuracy	$(tp + tn)/N = 1-$error
tp-rate	tp/p
fp-rate	fp/n
precision	tp/p'
recall	$tp/p =$ tp-rate
sensitivity	$tp/p =$ tp-rate
specificity	$tn/n = 1-$ fp-rate

have a *true negative*, and we have a *false positive* if we predict a negative example as positive.

In some two-class problems, we make a distinction between the two classes and hence the two types of errors, false positives and false negatives. Different measures appropriate in different settings are given in table 19.2. Let us envisage an authentication application where, for example, users log on to their accounts by voice. A false positive is wrongly logging on an impostor and a false negative is refusing a valid user. It is clear that the two type of errors are not equally bad; the former is much worse. True positive rate, *tp-rate*, also known as *hit rate*, measures what proportion of valid users we authenticate and false positive rate, *fp-rate*, also known as *false alarm rate*, is the proportion of impostors we wrongly accept.

Let us say the system returns $\hat{P}(C_1|x)$, the probability of the positive class, and for the negative class, we have $\hat{P}(C_2|x) = 1 - \hat{P}(C_1|x)$, and we choose "positive" if $\hat{P}(C_1|x) > \theta$. If θ is close to 1, we hardly choose the positive class; that is, we will have no false positives but also few true positives. As we decrease θ to increase the number of true positives, we risk introducing false positives.

RECEIVER OPERATING CHARACTERISTICS

For different values of θ, we can get a number of pairs of (tp-rate, fp-rate) values and by connecting them we get the *receiver operating characteristics* (ROC) curve, as shown in figure 19.3a. Note that different values of θ correspond to different loss matrices for the two types of error and the ROC curve can also be seen as the behavior of a classifier

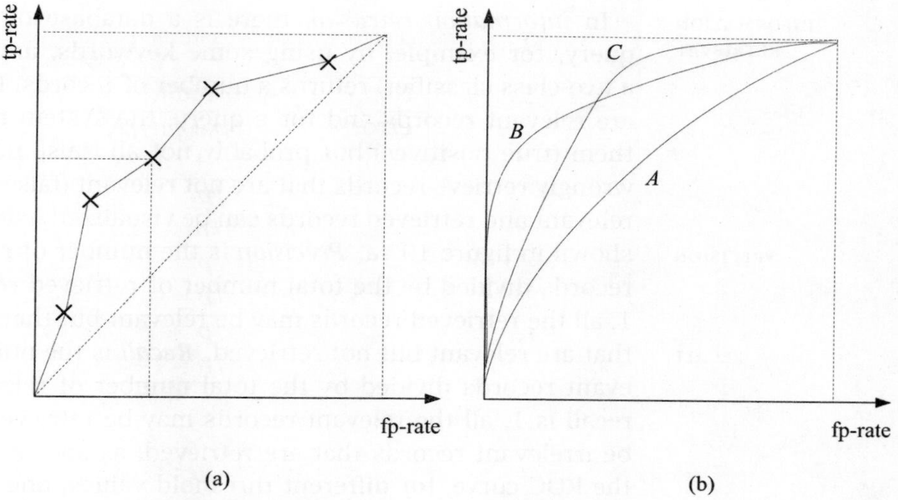

Figure 19.3 (a) Typical ROC curve. Each classifier has a threshold that allows us to move over this curve, and we decide on a point, based on the relative importance of hits versus false alarms, namely, true positives and false positives. The area below the ROC curve is called AUC. (b) A classifier is preferred if its ROC curve is closer to the upper-left corner (larger AUC). *B* and *C* are preferred over *A*; *B* and *C* are preferred under different loss matrices.

under different loss matrices (see exercise 1).

Ideally, a classifier has a tp-rate of 1 and an fp-rate of 0, and hence a classifier is better the more its ROC curve gets closer to the upper-left corner. On the diagonal, we make as many true decisions as false ones, and this is the worst one can do (any classifier that is below the diagonal can be improved by flipping its decision). Given two classifiers, we can say one is better than the other one if its ROC curve is above the ROC curve of the other one; if the two curves intersect, we can say that the two classifiers are better under different loss conditions, as seen in figure 19.3b.

AREA UNDER THE CURVE

ROC allows a visual analysis; if we want to reduce the curve to a single number we can do this by calculating the *area under the curve* (AUC) . A classifier ideally has an AUC of 1 and AUC values of different classifiers can be compared to give us a general performance averaged over different loss conditions.

INFORMATION RETRIEVAL

In *information retrieval*, there is a database of records; we make a query, for example, by using some keywords, and a system (basically a two-class classifier) returns a number of records. In the database, there are relevant records and for a query, the system may retrieve some of them (true positives) but probably not all (false negatives); it may also wrongly retrieve records that are not relevant (false positives). The set of relevant and retrieved records can be visualized using a Venn diagram, as shown in figure 19.4a. *Precision* is the number of retrieved and relevant records divided by the total number of retrieved records; if precision is 1, all the retrieved records may be relevant but there may still be records that are relevant but not retrieved. *Recall* is the number of retrieved relevant records divided by the total number of relevant records; even if recall is 1, all the relevant records may be retrieved but there may also be irrelevant records that are retrieved, as shown in figure19.4c. As in the ROC curve, for different threshold values, one can draw a curve for precision vs. recall.

PRECISION

RECALL

SENSITIVITY SPECIFICITY

From another perspective but with the same aim, there are the two measures of *sensitivity* and *specificity*. Sensitivity is the same as tp-rate and recall. Specificity is how well we detect the negatives, which is the number of true negatives divided by the total number of negatives; this is equal to 1 minus the false alarm rate. One can also draw a sensitivity vs. specificity curve using different thresholds.

CLASS CONFUSION MATRIX

In the case of $K > 2$ classes, if we are using 0/1 error, the *class confusion matrix* is a $K \times K$ matrix whose entry (i, j) contains the number of instances that belong to C_i but are assigned to C_j. Ideally, all off-diagonals should be 0, for no misclassification. The class confusion matrix allows us to pinpoint what types of misclassification occur, namely, if there are two classes that are frequently confused. Or, one can define K separate two-class problems, each one separating one class from the other $K - 1$.

19.8 Interval Estimation

INTERVAL ESTIMATION

Let us now do a quick review of *interval estimation* that we will use in hypothesis testing. A point estimator, for example, the maximum likelihood estimator, specifies a value for a parameter θ. In interval estimation, we specify an interval within which θ lies with a certain degree of confidence. To obtain such an interval estimator, we make use of the probability distribution of the point estimator.

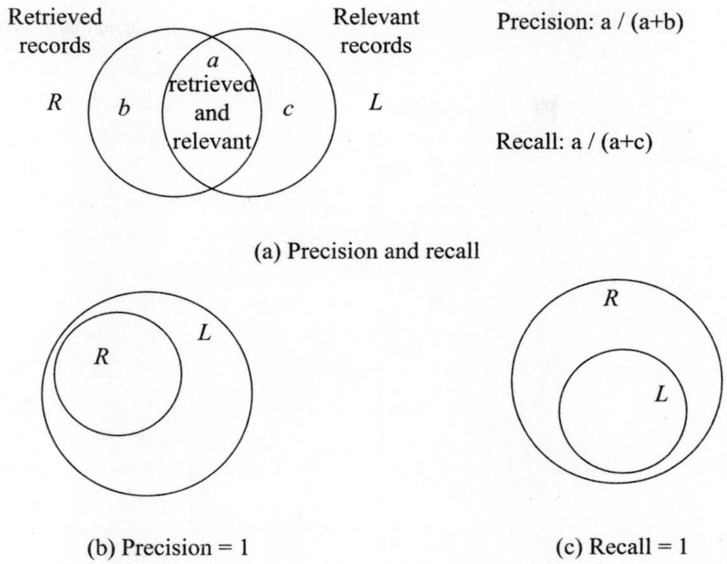

Figure 19.4 (a) Definition of precision and recall using Venn diagrams. (b) Precision is 1; all the retrieved records are relevant but there may be relevant ones not retrieved. (c) Recall is 1; all the relevant records are retrieved but there may also be irrelevant records that are retrieved.

For example, let us say we are trying to estimate the mean μ of a normal density from a sample $\mathcal{X} = \{x^t\}_{t=1}^N$. $m = \sum_t x^t/N$ is the sample average and is the point estimator to the mean. m is the sum of normals and therefore is also normal, $m \sim \mathcal{N}(\mu, \sigma^2/N)$. We define the statistic with a *unit normal distribution*:

UNIT NORMAL DISTRIBUTION

(19.1)
$$\frac{(m-\mu)}{\sigma/\sqrt{N}} \sim \mathcal{Z}$$

We know that 95 percent of $\mathcal{Z}$ lies in $(-1.96, 1.96)$, namely, $P\{-1.96 < \mathcal{Z} < 1.96\} = 0.95$, and we can write (see figure 19.5)

$$P\left\{-1.96 < \sqrt{N}\frac{(m-\mu)}{\sigma} < 1.96\right\} = 0.95$$

or equivalently

$$P\left\{m - 1.96\frac{\sigma}{\sqrt{N}} < \mu < m + 1.96\frac{\sigma}{\sqrt{N}}\right\} = 0.95$$

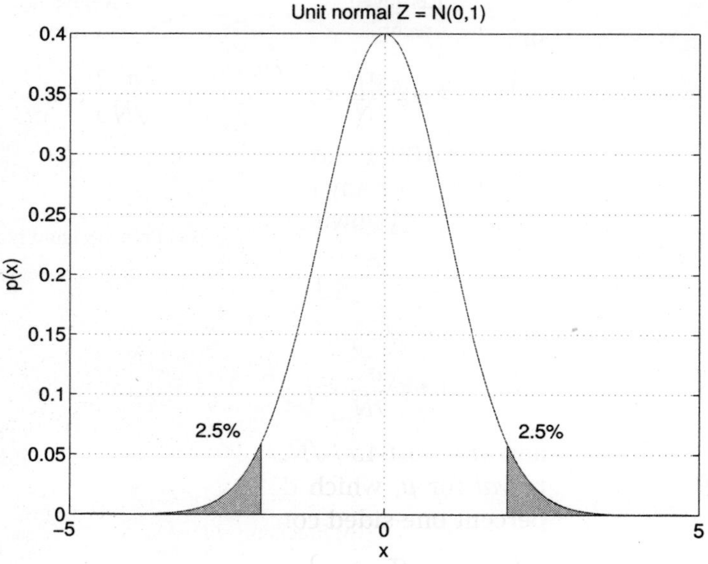

Figure 19.5 95 percent of the unit normal distribution lies between −1.96 and 1.96.

That is, "with 95 percent confidence," μ will lie within $1.96\sigma/\sqrt{N}$ units of the sample average. This is a *two-sided confidence interval*. With 99 percent confidence, μ will lie in $(m - 2.58\sigma/\sqrt{N}, m + 2.58\sigma/\sqrt{N})$; that is, if we want more confidence, the interval gets larger. The interval gets smaller as N, the sample size, increases.

TWO-SIDED CONFIDENCE INTERVAL

This can be generalized for any required confidence as follows. Let us denote z_α such that

$$P\{Z > z_\alpha\} = \alpha, \ 0 < \alpha < 1$$

Because Z is symmetric around the mean, $z_{1-\alpha/2} = -z_{\alpha/2}$, and $P\{X < -z_{\alpha/2}\} = P\{X > z_{\alpha/2}\} = \alpha/2$. Hence for any specified level of confidence $1 - \alpha$, we have

$$P\{-z_{\alpha/2} < Z < z_{\alpha/2}\} = 1 - \alpha$$

and

$$P\left\{-z_{\alpha/2} < \sqrt{N}\frac{(m-\mu)}{\sigma} < z_{\alpha/2}\right\} = 1 - \alpha$$

or

(19.2) $$P\left\{m - z_{\alpha/2}\frac{\sigma}{\sqrt{N}} < \mu < m + z_{\alpha/2}\frac{\sigma}{\sqrt{N}}\right\} = 1 - \alpha$$

Hence a $100(1 - \alpha)$ percent two-sided confidence interval for μ can be computed for any α.

Similarly, knowing that $P\{Z < 1.64\} = 0.95$, we have (see figure 19.6)

$$P\left\{\sqrt{N}\frac{(m-\mu)}{\sigma} < 1.64\right\} = 0.95$$

or

$$P\left\{m - 1.64\frac{\sigma}{\sqrt{N}} < \mu\right\} = 0.95$$

ONE-SIDED CONFIDENCE INTERVAL

and $(m - 1.64\sigma/\sqrt{N}, \infty)$ is a 95 percent *one-sided upper confidence interval* for μ, which defines a lower bound. Generalizing, a $100(1 - \alpha)$ percent one-sided confidence interval for μ can be computed from

(19.3) $$P\left\{m - z_{\alpha}\frac{\sigma}{\sqrt{N}} < \mu\right\} = 1 - \alpha$$

Similarly, the one-sided *lower* confidence interval that defines an upper bound can also be calculated.

In the previous intervals, we used σ; that is, we assumed that the variance is known. If it is not, one can plug the sample variance

$$S^2 = \sum_t (x^t - m)^2/(N-1)$$

instead of σ^2. We know that when $x^t \sim \mathcal{N}(\mu, \sigma^2)$, $(N-1)S^2/\sigma^2$ is chi-square with $N-1$ degrees of freedom. We also know that m and S^2 are independent. Then, $\sqrt{N}(m-\mu)/S$ is t-distributed with $N-1$ degrees of freedom (section A.3.7), denoted as

(19.4) $$\frac{\sqrt{N}(m-\mu)}{S} \sim t_{N-1}$$

t DISTRIBUTION

Hence for any $\alpha \in (0, 1/2)$, we can define an interval, using the values specified by the t *distribution*, instead of the unit normal Z

$$P\left\{t_{1-\alpha/2,N-1} < \sqrt{N}\frac{(m-\mu)}{S} < t_{\alpha/2,N-1}\right\} = 1 - \alpha$$

or using $t_{1-\alpha/2,N-1} = -t_{\alpha/2,N-1}$, we can write

$$P\left\{m - t_{\alpha/2,N-1}\frac{S}{\sqrt{N}} < \mu < m + t_{\alpha/2,N-1}\frac{S}{\sqrt{N}}\right\} = 1 - \alpha$$

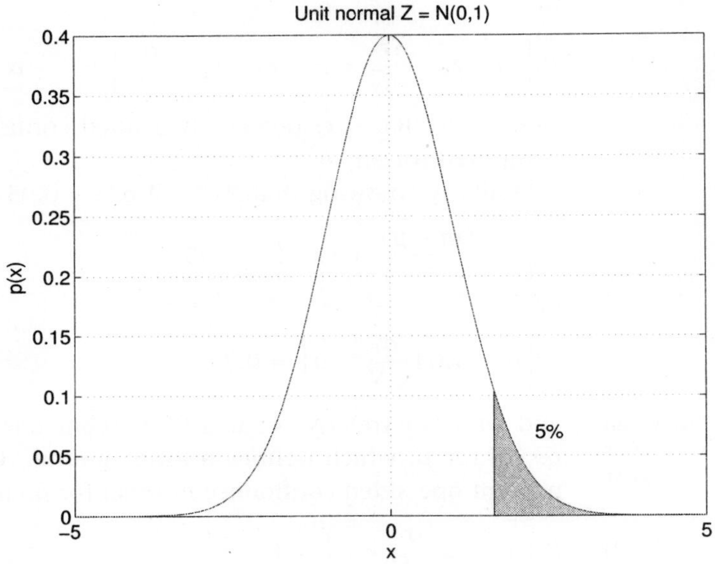

Figure 19.6 95 percent of the unit normal distribution lies before 1.64.

Similarly, one-sided confidence intervals can be defined. The t distribution has larger spread (longer tails) than the unit normal distribution, and generally the interval given by the t is larger; this should be expected since additional uncertainty exists due to the unknown variance.

19.9 Hypothesis Testing

Instead of explicitly estimating some parameters, in certain applications we may want to use the sample to test some particular hypothesis concerning the parameters. For example, instead of estimating the mean, we may want to test whether the mean is less than 0.02. If the random sample is consistent with the hypothesis under consideration, we "fail to reject" the hypothesis; otherwise, we say that it is "rejected." But when we make such a decision, we are not really saying that it is true or false but rather that the sample data appears to be consistent with it to a given degree of confidence or not.

HYPOTHESIS TESTING

In *hypothesis testing*, the approach is as follows. We define a statistic

Table 19.3 Type I error, type II error, and power of a test

	Decision	
Truth	Fail to reject	Reject
True	Correct	Type I error
False	Type II error	Correct (power)

that obeys a certain distribution if the hypothesis is correct. If the statistic calculated from the sample has very low probability of being drawn from this distribution, then we reject the hypothesis; otherwise, we fail to reject it.

Let us say we have a sample from a normal distribution with unknown mean μ and known variance σ^2, and we want to test a specific hypothesis about μ, for example, whether it is equal to a specified constant μ_0. It is denoted as H_0 and is called the *null hypothesis*

NULL HYPOTHESIS

$$H_0 : \mu = \mu_0$$

against the alternative hypothesis

$$H_1 : \mu \neq \mu_0$$

m is the point estimate of μ, and it is reasonable to reject H_0 if m is too far from μ_0. This is where the interval estimate is used. We fail to reject the hypothesis with *level of significance* α if μ_0 lies in the $100(1-\alpha)$ percent confidence interval, namely, if

LEVEL OF SIGNIFICANCE

$$\frac{\sqrt{N}(m-\mu_0)}{\sigma} \in (-z_{\alpha/2}, z_{\alpha/2}) \tag{19.5}$$

We reject the null hypothesis if it falls outside, on either side. This is a *two-sided test.*

TWO-SIDED TEST

If we reject when the hypothesis is correct, this is a *type I error* and thus α, set before the test, defines how much type I error we can tolerate, typical values being $\alpha = 0.1, 0.05, 0.01$ (see table 19.3). A *type II error* is if we fail to reject the null hypothesis when the true mean μ is unequal to μ_0. The probability that H_0 is not rejected when the true mean is μ is a function of μ and is given as

TYPE I ERROR

TYPE II ERROR

$$\beta(\mu) = P_\mu\left\{-z_{\alpha/2} \leq \frac{m-\mu_0}{\sigma/\sqrt{N}} \leq z_{\alpha/2}\right\} \tag{19.6}$$

POWER FUNCTION

$1 - \beta(\mu)$ is called the *power function* of the test and is equal to the probability of rejection when μ is the true value. Type II error probability increases as μ and μ_0 gets closer, and we can calculate how large a sample we need for us to be able to detect a difference $\delta = |\mu - \mu_0|$ with sufficient power.

ONE-SIDED TEST

One can also have a *one-sided test* of the form

$$H_0 : \mu \le \mu_0 \text{ vs } H_1 : \mu > \mu_0$$

as opposed to the two-sided test when the alternative hypothesis is $\mu \neq \mu_0$. The one-sided test with α level of significance defines the $100(1 - \alpha)$ confidence interval bounded on one side in which m should lie for the hypothesis not to be rejected. We fail to reject if

$$\frac{\sqrt{N}}{\sigma}(m - \mu_0) \in (-\infty, z_\alpha) \tag{19.7}$$

and reject outside. Note that the null hypothesis H_0 also allows equality, which means that we get ordering information only if the test rejects. This tells us which of the two one-sided tests we should use. Whatever claim we have should be in H_1 so that rejection of the test would support our claim.

If the variance is unknown, just as we did in the interval estimates, we use the sample variance instead of the population variance and the fact that

$$\frac{\sqrt{N}(m - \mu_0)}{S} \sim t_{N-1} \tag{19.8}$$

For example, for $H_0 : \mu = \mu_0$ vs $H_1 : \mu \neq \mu_0$, we fail to reject at significance level α if

$$\frac{\sqrt{N}(m - \mu_0)}{S} \in (-t_{\alpha/2,N-1}, t_{\alpha/2,N-1}) \tag{19.9}$$

t TEST

which is known as the *two-sided* t *test*. A one-sided t test can be defined similarly.

19.10 Assessing a Classification Algorithm's Performance

Now that we have reviewed hypothesis testing, we are ready to see how it is used in testing error rates. We will discuss the case of classification error, but the same methodology applies for squared error in regression, log likelihoods in unsupervised learning, expected reward in reinforcement learning, and so on, as long as we can write the appropriate parametric form for the sampling distribution. We will also discuss nonparametric tests when no such parametric form can be found.

We now start with error rate assessment, and, in the next section, we discuss error rate comparison.

19.10.1 Binomial Test

Let us start with the case where we have a single training set $\mathcal{T}$ and a single validation set $\mathcal{V}$. We train our classifier on $\mathcal{T}$ and test it on $\mathcal{V}$. We denote by p the probability that the classifier makes a misclassification error. We do not know p; it is what we would like to estimate or test a hypothesis about. On the instance with index t from the validation set $\mathcal{V}$, let us say x^t denotes the correctness of the classifier's decision: x^t is a 0/1 Bernoulli random variable that takes the value 1 when the classifier commits an error and 0 when the classifier is correct. The binomial random variable X denotes the total number of errors:

$$X = \sum_{t=1}^{N} x^t$$

We would like to test whether the error probability p is less than or equal to some value p_0 we specify:

$$H_0 : p \leq p_0 \text{ vs. } H_1 : p > p_0$$

If the probability of error is p, the probability that the classifier commits j errors out of N is

$$P\{X = j\} = \binom{N}{j} p^j (1-p)^{N-j}$$

It is reasonable to reject $p \leq p_0$ if in such a case, the probability that we see $X = e$ errors or more is very unlikely. That is, the *binomial test* rejects the hypothesis if

BINOMIAL TEST

$$P\{X \geq e\} = \sum_{x=e}^{N} \binom{N}{x} p_0{}^x (1-p_0)^{N-x} < \alpha \quad (19.10)$$

where α is the significance, for example, 0.05.

19.10.2 Approximate Normal Test

If p is the probability of error, our point estimate is $\hat{p} = X/N$. Then, it is reasonable to reject the null hypothesis if $\hat{p}$ is much larger than p_0. How large is large enough is given by the sampling distribution of $\hat{p}$ and the significance α.

Because X is the sum of independent random variables from the same distribution, the central limit theorem states that for large N, X/N is approximately normal with mean p_0 and variance $p_0(1-p_0)/N$. Then

$$\frac{X/N - p_0}{\sqrt{p_0(1-p_0)/N}} \dot{\sim} \mathcal{Z} \tag{19.11}$$

where $\dot{\sim}$ denotes "approximately distributed." Then, using equation 19.7, the *approximate normal test* rejects the null hypothesis if this value for $X = e$ is greater than z_α. $z_{0.05}$ is 1.64. This approximation will work well as long as N is not too small and p is not very close to 0 or 1; as a rule of thumb, we require $Np \geq 5$ and $N(1-p) \geq 5$.

APPROXIMATE NORMAL TEST

19.10.3 *t* Test

The two tests we discussed earlier use a single validation set. If we run the algorithm K times, on K training/validation set pairs, we get K error percentages, $p_i, i = 1, \ldots, K$ on the K validation sets. Let x_i^t be 1 if the classifier trained on $\mathcal{T}_i$ makes a misclassification error on instance t of $\mathcal{V}_i$; x_i^t is 0 otherwise. Then

$$p_i = \frac{\sum_{t=1}^N x_i^t}{N}$$

Given that

$$m = \frac{\sum_{i=1}^K p_i}{K}, \quad S^2 = \frac{\sum_{i=1}^K (p_i - m)^2}{K-1}$$

from equation 19.8, we know that we have

$$\frac{\sqrt{K}(m - p_0)}{S} \sim t_{K-1} \tag{19.12}$$

and the t test rejects the null hypothesis that the classification algorithm has p_0 or less error percentage at significance level α if this value is greater than $t_{\alpha,K-1}$. Typically, K is taken as 10 or 30. $t_{0.05,9} = 1.83$ and $t_{0.05,29} = 1.70$.

19.11 Comparing Two Classification Algorithms

Given two learning algorithms, we want to compare and test whether they construct classifiers that have the same expected error rate.

19.11.1 McNemar's Test

Given a training set and a validation set, we use two algorithms to train two classifiers on the training set and test them on the validation set and compute their errors. A *contingency table*, like the one shown here, is an array of natural numbers in matrix form representing counts, or frequencies:

CONTINGENCY TABLE

e_{00}: number of examples misclassified by both	e_{01}: number of examples misclassified by 1 but not 2
e_{10}: number of examples misclassified by 2 but not 1	e_{11}: number of examples correctly classified by both

Under the null hypothesis that the classification algorithms have the same error rate, we expect $e_{01} = e_{10}$ and these to be equal to $(e_{01}+e_{10})/2$. We have the chi-square statistic with one degree of freedom

$$\frac{(|e_{01} - e_{10}| - 1)^2}{e_{01} + e_{10}} \sim \mathcal{X}_1^2 \tag{19.13}$$

MCNEMAR'S TEST

and *McNemar's test* rejects the hypothesis that the two classification algorithms have the same error rate at significance level α if this value is greater than $\mathcal{X}^2_{\alpha,1}$. For $\alpha = 0.05$, $\mathcal{X}^2_{0.05,1} = 3.84$.

19.11.2 *K*-Fold Cross-Validated Paired *t* Test

This set uses K-fold cross-validation to get K training/validation set pairs. We use the two classification algorithms to train on the training sets $\mathcal{T}_i, i = 1, \ldots, K$, and test on the validation sets $\mathcal{V}_i$. The error percentages of the classifiers on the validation sets are recorded as p_i^1 and p_i^2.

If the two classification algorithms have the same error rate, then we expect them to have the same mean, or equivalently, that the difference of their means is 0. The difference in error rates on fold i is $p_i = p_i^1 - p_i^2$. This is a *paired test*; that is, for each i, both algorithms see the same training and validation sets. When this is done K times, we have a distribution of p_i containing K points. Given that p_i^1 and p_i^2 are both (approximately)

PAIRED TEST

normal, their difference p_i is also normal. The null hypothesis is that this distribution has 0 mean:

$$H_0 : \mu = 0 \text{ vs. } H_1 : \mu \neq 0$$

We define

$$m = \frac{\sum_{i=1}^{K} p_i}{K}, \quad S^2 = \frac{\sum_{i=1}^{K} (p_i - m)^2}{K-1}$$

Under the null hypothesis that $\mu = 0$, we have a statistic that is t-distributed with $K - 1$ degrees of freedom:

(19.14)
$$\frac{\sqrt{K}(m-0)}{S} = \frac{\sqrt{K} \cdot m}{S} \sim t_{K-1}$$

K-FOLD CV PAIRED t TEST

Thus the K-*fold cv paired* t *test* rejects the hypothesis that two classification algorithms have the same error rate at significance level α if this value is outside the interval $(-t_{\alpha/2,K-1}, t_{\alpha/2,K-1})$. $t_{0.025,9} = 2.26$ and $t_{0.025,29} = 2.05$.

If we want to test whether the first algorithm has less error than the second, we need a one-sided hypothesis and use a one-tailed test:

$$H_0 : \mu \geq 0 \text{ vs. } H_1 : \mu < 0$$

If the test rejects, our claim that the first one has significantly less error is supported.

19.11.3 5 × 2 cv Paired t Test

In the 5×2 cv t test, proposed by Dietterich (1998), we perform five replications of twofold cross-validation. In each replication, the dataset is divided into two equal-sized sets. $p_i^{(j)}$ is the difference between the error rates of the two classifiers on fold $j = 1, 2$ of replication $i = 1, \ldots, 5$. The average on replication i is $\overline{p}_i = (p_i^{(1)} + p_i^{(2)})/2$, and the estimated variance is $s_i^2 = (p_i^{(1)} - \overline{p}_i)^2 + (p_i^{(2)} - \overline{p}_i)^2$.

Under the null hypothesis that the two classification algorithms have the same error rate, $p_i^{(j)}$ is the difference of two identically distributed proportions, and ignoring the fact that these proportions are not independent, $p_i^{(j)}$ can be treated as approximately normal distributed with 0 mean and unknown variance σ^2. Then $p_i^{(j)}/\sigma$ is approximately unit normal. If we assume $p_i^{(1)}$ and $p_i^{(2)}$ are independent normals (which is not strictly true because their training and test sets are not drawn independently of each other), then s_i^2/σ^2 has a chi-square distribution with one degree of freedom. If each of the s_i^2 are assumed to be independent (which is not true because they are all computed from the same set of available data), then their sum is chi-square with five degrees of freedom:

$$M = \frac{\sum_{i=1}^{5} s_i^2}{\sigma^2} \sim \mathcal{X}_5^2$$

and

$$t = \frac{p_1^{(1)}/\sigma}{\sqrt{M/5}} = \frac{p_1^{(1)}}{\sqrt{\sum_{i=1}^{5} s_i^2/5}} \sim t_5 \tag{19.15}$$

5 × 2 CV PAIRED t TEST

giving us a t statistic with five degrees of freedom. The *5 × 2 cv paired* t *test* rejects the hypothesis that the two classification algorithms have the same error rate at significance level α if this value is outside the interval $(-t_{\alpha/2,5}, t_{\alpha/2,5})$. $t_{0.025,5} = 2.57$.

19.11.4 5 × 2 cv Paired F Test

We note that the numerator in equation 19.15, $p_1^{(1)}$, is arbitrary; actually, ten different values can be placed in the numerator, namely, $p_i^{(j)}, j = 1, 2, i = 1, \ldots, 5$, leading to ten possible statistics:

$$t_i^{(j)} = \frac{p_i^{(j)}}{\sqrt{\sum_{i=1}^{5} s_i^2/5}} \tag{19.16}$$

Alpaydın (1999) proposed an extension to the 5 × 2 cv t test that combines the results of the ten possible statistics. If $p_i^{(j)}/\sigma \sim \mathcal{Z}$, then $\left(p_i^{(j)}\right)^2/\sigma^2 \sim \mathcal{X}_1^2$ and their sum is chi-square with ten degrees of freedom:

$$N = \frac{\sum_{i=1}^{5}\sum_{j=1}^{2}\left(p_i^{(j)}\right)^2}{\sigma^2} \sim \mathcal{X}_{10}^2$$

Placing this in the numerator of equation 19.15, we get a statistic that is the ratio of two chi-square distributed random variables. Two such variables divided by their respective degrees of freedom is F-distributed with ten and five degrees of freedom (section A.3.8):

$$f = \frac{N/10}{M/5} = \frac{\sum_{i=1}^{5}\sum_{j=1}^{2}\left(p_i^{(j)}\right)^2}{2\sum_{i=1}^{5} s_i^2} \sim F_{10,5} \tag{19.17}$$

5 × 2 CV PAIRED F TEST

5 × 2 cv paired F *test* rejects the hypothesis that the classification algorithms have the same error rate at significance level α if this value is greater than $F_{\alpha,10,5}$. $F_{0.05,10,5} = 4.74$.

19.12 Comparing Multiple Algorithms: Analysis of Variance

In many cases, we have more than two algorithms, and we would like to compare their expected error. Given L algorithms, we train them on K training sets, induce K classifiers with each algorithm, and then test them on K validation sets and record their error rates. This gives us L groups of K values. The problem then is the comparison of these L samples for statistically significant difference. This is an experiment with a single factor with L levels, the learning algorithms, and there are K replications for each level.

ANALYSIS OF VARIANCE

In *analysis of variance* (ANOVA), we consider L independent samples, each of size K, composed of normal random variables of unknown mean μ_j and unknown common variance σ^2:

$$X_{ij} \sim \mathcal{N}(\mu_j, \sigma^2), j = 1, \ldots, L, \; i = 1, \ldots, K,$$

We are interested in testing the hypothesis H_0 that all means are equal:

$$H_0 : \mu_1 = \mu_2 = \cdots = \mu_L \text{ vs. } H_1 : \mu_r \neq \mu_s, \text{for at least one pair } (r, s)$$

The comparison of error rates of multiple classification algorithms fits this scheme. We have L classification algorithms, and we have their error rates on K validation folds. X_{ij} is the number of validation errors made by the classifier, which is trained by classification algorithm j on fold i. Each X_{ij} is binomial and approximately normal. If H_0 is not rejected, we fail to find a significant error difference among the error rates of the L classification algorithms. This is therefore a generalization of the tests we saw in section 19.11 that compared the error rates of two classification algorithms. The L classification algorithms may be different or may use different hyperparameters, for example, number of hidden units in a multilayer perceptron, number of neighbors in k-nn, and so forth.

The approach in ANOVA is to derive two estimators of σ^2. One estimator is designed such that it is true only when H_0 is true, and the second is always a valid estimator, regardless of whether H_0 is true or not. ANOVA then rejects H_0, namely, that the L samples are drawn from the same population, if the two estimators differ significantly.

Our first estimator to σ^2 is valid only if the hypothesis is true, namely, $\mu_j = \mu, j = 1, \ldots, L$. If $X_{ij} \sim \mathcal{N}(\mu, \sigma^2)$, then the group average

$$m_j = \sum_{i=1}^{K} \frac{X_{ij}}{K}$$

is also normal with mean μ and variance σ^2/K. If the hypothesis is true, then $m_j, j = 1, \ldots, L$ are L instances drawn from $\mathcal{N}(\mu, \sigma^2/K)$. Then *their* mean and variance are

$$m = \frac{\sum_{j=1}^{L} m_j}{L}, \quad S^2 = \frac{\sum_j (m_j - m)^2}{L-1}$$

Thus an estimator of σ^2 is $K \cdot S^2$, namely,

$$\hat{\sigma}_b^2 = K \sum_{j=1}^{L} \frac{(m_j - m)^2}{L-1} \tag{19.18}$$

Each of m_j is normal and $(L-1)S^2/(\sigma^2/K)$ is chi-square with $(L-1)$ degrees of freedom. Then, we have

$$\sum_j \frac{(m_j - m)^2}{\sigma^2/K} \sim \mathcal{X}_{L-1}^2 \tag{19.19}$$

We define SS_b, the between-group sum of squares, as

$$SS_b \equiv K \sum_j (m_j - m)^2$$

So, when H_0 is true, we have

$$\frac{SS_b}{\sigma^2} \sim \mathcal{X}_{L-1}^2 \tag{19.20}$$

Our second estimator of σ^2 is the average of group variances, S_j^2, defined as

$$S_j^2 = \frac{\sum_{i=1}^{K} (X_{ij} - m_j)^2}{K-1}$$

and their average is

$$\hat{\sigma}_w^2 = \sum_{j=1}^{L} \frac{S_j^2}{L} = \sum_j \sum_i \frac{(X_{ij} - m_j)^2}{L(K-1)} \tag{19.21}$$

We define SS_w, the within-group sum of squares:

$$SS_w \equiv \sum_j \sum_i (X_{ij} - m_j)^2$$

Remembering that for a normal sample, we have

$$(K-1)\frac{S_j^2}{\sigma^2} \sim \mathcal{X}_{K-1}^2$$

and that the sum of chi-squares is also a chi-square, we have

$$(K-1)\sum_{j=1}^{L}\frac{S_j^2}{\sigma^2} \sim \mathcal{X}^2_{L(K-1)}$$

So

$$\frac{SS_w}{\sigma^2} \sim \mathcal{X}^2_{L(K-1)} \tag{19.22}$$

Then we have the task of comparing two variances for equality, which we can do by checking whether their ratio is close to 1. The ratio of two independent chi-square random variables divided by their respective degrees of freedom is a random variable that is F-distributed, and hence when H_0 is true, we have

$$F_0 = \left(\frac{SS_b/\sigma^2}{L-1}\right) \bigg/ \left(\frac{SS_w/\sigma^2}{L(K-1)}\right) = \frac{SS_b/(L-1)}{SS_w/(L(K-1))} = \frac{\hat{\sigma}_b^2}{\hat{\sigma}_w^2} \sim F_{L-1,L(K-1)} \tag{19.23}$$

For any given significance value α, the hypothesis that the L classification algorithms have the same expected error rate is rejected if this statistic is greater than $F_{\alpha,L-1,L(K-1)}$.

Note that we are rejecting if the two estimators disagree significantly. If H_0 is not true, then the variance of m_j around m will be larger than what we would normally have if H_0 were true, and hence if H_0 is not true, the first estimator $\hat{\sigma}_b^2$ will overestimate σ^2, and the ratio will be greater than 1. For $\alpha = 0.05$, $L = 5$ and $K = 10$, $F_{0.05,4,45} = 2.6$. If X_{ij} vary around m with a variance of σ^2, then if H_0 is true, m_j vary around m by σ^2/K. If it seems as if they vary more, then H_0 should be rejected because the displacement of m_j around m is more than what can be explained by some constant added noise.

The name *analysis of variance* is derived from a partitioning of the total variability in the data into its components.

$$SS_T \equiv \sum_j \sum_i (X_{ij} - m)^2 \tag{19.24}$$

SS_T divided by its degree of freedom, namely, $K \cdot L - 1$ (there are $K \cdot L$ data points, and we lose one degree of freedom because m is fixed), gives us the sample variance of X_{ij}. It can be shown that (exercise 5) the total sum of squares can be split into between-group sum of squares and within-group sum of squares

$$SS_T = SS_b + SS_w \tag{19.25}$$

Table 19.4 The analysis of variance (ANOVA) table for a single factor model

Source of variation	Sum of squares	Degrees of freedom	Mean square	F_0
Between groups	$SS_b \equiv K \sum_j (m_j - m)^2$	$L - 1$	$MS_b = \frac{SS_b}{L-1}$	$\frac{MS_b}{MS_w}$
Within groups	$SS_w \equiv \sum_j \sum_i (X_{ij} - m_j)^2$	$L(K-1)$	$MS_w = \frac{SS_w}{L(K-1)}$	
Total	$SS_T \equiv \sum_j \sum_i (X_{ij} - m)^2$	$L \cdot K - 1$		

Results of ANOVA are reported in an ANOVA table as shown in table 19.4. This is the basic *one-way* analysis of variance where there is a single factor, for example, learning algorithm. We may consider experiments with multiple factors, for example, we can have one factor for classification algorithms and another factor for feature extraction algorithms used before, and this will be a *two-factor experiment with interaction.*

POST HOC TESTING

If the hypothesis is rejected, we only know that there is some difference between the L groups but we do not know where. For this, we do *post hoc testing,* that is, an additional set of tests involving subsets of groups, for example, pairs.

LEAST SQUARE DIFFERENCE TEST

Fisher's *least square difference test* compares groups in a pairwise manner. For each group, we have $m_i \sim \mathcal{N}(\mu_i, \sigma_w^2 = MS_w/K)$ and $m_i - m_j \sim \mathcal{N}(\mu_i - \mu_j, 2\sigma_w^2)$. Then, under the null hypothesis that $H_0 : \mu_i = \mu_j$, we have

$$t = \frac{m_i - m_j}{\sqrt{2}\sigma_w} \sim t_{L(K-1)}$$

We reject H_0 in favor of the alternative hypothesis $H_1 : \mu_1 \neq \mu_2$ if $|t| > t_{\alpha/2,L(K-1)}$. Similarly, one-sided tests can be defined to find pairwise orderings.

MULTIPLE COMPARISONS

When we do a number of tests to draw one conclusion, this is called *multiple comparisons,* and we need to keep in mind that if T hypotheses are to be tested, each at significance level α, then the probability that at least one hypothesis is incorrectly rejected is at most $T\alpha$. For example, the probability that six confidence intervals, each calculated at 95 percent individual confidence intervals, will simultaneously be correct is at least 70 percent. Thus to ensure that the overall confidence interval is at least $100(1 - \alpha)$, each confidence interval should be set at $100(1 - \alpha/T)$. This is called a *Bonferroni correction.*

BONFERRONI CORRECTION

Sometimes it may be the case that ANOVA rejects and none of the post hoc pairwise tests find a significant difference. In such a case, our conclusion is that there is a difference between the means but that we need more data to be able to pinpoint the source of the difference.

Note that the main cost is the training and testing of L classification algorithms on K training/validation sets. Once this is done and the values are stored in a $K \times L$ table, calculating the ANOVA or pairwise comparison test statistics from those is very cheap in comparison.

19.13 Comparison over Multiple Datasets

Let us say we want to compare two or more algorithms on several datasets and not one. What makes this different is that an algorithm depending on how well its inductive bias matches the problem will behave differently on different datasets, and these error values on different datasets cannot be said to be normally distributed around some mean accuracy. This implies that the parametric tests that we discussed in the previous sections based on binomials being approximately normal are no longer applicable and we need to resort to *nonparametric tests.* The advantage of having such tests is that we can also use them for comparing other statistics that are not normal, for example, training times, number of free parameters, and so on.

NONPARAMETRIC TESTS

Parametric tests are generally robust to slight departures from normality, especially if the sample is large. Nonparametric tests are distribution free but are less efficient; that is, if both are applicable, a parametric test should be preferred. The corresponding nonparametric test will require a larger sample to achieve the same power. Nonparametric tests assume no knowledge about the distribution of the underlying population but only that the values can be compared or ordered, and, as we will see, such tests make use of this order information.

When we have an algorithm trained on a number of different datasets, the average of its errors on these datasets is not a meaningful value, and, for example, we cannot use such averages to compare two algorithms A

and B. To compare two algorithms, the only piece of information we can use is if on any dataset, A is more accurate than B; we can then count the number of times A is more accurate than B and check whether this could have been by chance if they indeed were equally accurate. With more than two algorithms, we will look at the average *ranks* of the learners trained by different algorithms. Nonparametric tests basically use this rank data and not the absolute values.

Before proceeding with the details of these tests, it should be stressed that it does not make sense to compare error rates of algorithms on a whole variety of applications. Because there is no such thing as the "best learning algorithm," such tests would not be conclusive. However, we can compare algorithms on a number of datasets, or versions, of the same application. For example, we may have a number of different datasets for face recognition but with different properties (resolution, lighting, number of subjects, and so on), and we may use a nonparametric test to compare algorithms on those; different properties of the datasets would make it impossible for us to lump images from different datasets together in a single set, but we can train algorithms separately on different datasets, obtain ranks separately, and then combine these to get an overall decision.

19.13.1 Comparing Two Algorithms

Let us say we want to compare two algorithms. We both train and validate them on $i = 1, \ldots, N$ different datasets in a paired manner—that is, all the conditions except the different algorithms should be identical. We get results e_i^1 and e_i^2 and if we use K-fold cross-validation on each dataset, these are averages or medians of the K values. The *sign test* is based on the idea that if the two algorithms have equal error, on each dataset, there should be $1/2$ probability that the first has less error than the second, and thus we expect the first to win on $N/2$ datasets. Let us define

SIGN TEST

$$X_i = \begin{cases} 1 & \text{if } e_i^1 < e_i^2 \\ 0 & \text{otherwise} \end{cases} \quad \text{and } X = \sum_{i=1}^{N} X_i$$

Let us say we want to test

$$H_0 : \mu_1 \geq \mu_2 \text{ vs. } H_1 : \mu_1 < \mu_2$$

If the null hypothesis is correct, X is binomial in N trials with $p = 1/2$. Let us say that we saw that the first one wins on $X = e$ datasets. Then, the probability that we have e or less wins when indeed $p = 1/2$ is

$$P\{X \leq e\} = \sum_{x=0}^{e} \binom{N}{x} \left(\frac{1}{2}\right)^x \left(\frac{1}{2}\right)^{N-x}$$

and we reject the null hypothesis if this probability is too small, that is, less than α. If there are ties, we divide them equally to both sides; that is, if there are t ties, we add $t/2$ to e (if t is odd, we ignore the odd one and decrease N by 1).

In testing

$$H_0 : \mu_1 \leq \mu_2 \text{ vs. } H_1 : \mu_1 > \mu_2$$

we reject if $P\{X \geq e\} < \alpha$.

For the two-sided test

$$H_0 : \mu_1 = \mu_2 \text{ vs. } H_1 : \mu_1 \neq \mu_2$$

we reject the null hypothesis if e is too small or too large. If $e < N/2$, we reject if $2P\{X \leq e\} < \alpha$; if $e > N/2$, we reject if $2P\{X \geq e\} < \alpha$—we need to find the corresponding tail, and we multiply it by 2 because it is a two-tailed test.

As we discussed before, nonparametric tests can be used to compare any measurements, for example, training times. In such a case, we see the advantage of a nonparametric test that uses order rather than averages of absolute values. Let us say we compare two algorithms on ten datasets, nine of which are small and have training times for both algorithms on the order of minutes, and one that is very large and whose training time is on the order of a day. If we use a parametric test and take the average of training times, the single large dataset will dominate the decision, but when we use the nonparameric test and compare values separately on each dataset, using the order will have the effect of normalizing separately for each dataset and hence will help us make a robust decision.

We can also use the sign test as a one sample test, for example, to check if the average error on all datasets is less than two percent, by comparing μ_1 not by the mean of a second population but by a constant μ_0. We can do this simply by plugging the constant μ_0 in place of all observations from a second sample and using the procedure used earlier;

that is, we will count how many times we get more or less than 0.02 and check if this is too unlikely under the null hypothesis. For large N, normal approximation to the binomial can be used (exercise 6), but in practice, the number of datasets may be smaller than 20. Note that the sign test is a test on the median of a population, which is equal to the mean if the distribution is symmetric.

The sign test only uses the sign of the difference and not its magnitude, but we may envisage a case where the first algorithm, when it wins, always wins by a large margin whereas the second algorithm, when it wins, always wins barely. The *Wilcoxon signed rank test* uses both the sign and the magniture of differences, as follows.

WILCOXON SIGNED RANK TEST

Let us say, in addition to the sign of differences, we also calculate $m_i = |e_i^1 - e_i^2|$ and then we order them so that the smallest, $\min_i m_i$, is assigned rank 1, the next smallest is assigned rank 2, and so on. If there are ties, their ranks are given the average value that they would receive if they differed slightly. For example, if the magnitudes are $2, 1, 2, 4$, the ranks are $2.5, 1, 2.5, 4$. We then calculate w_+ as the sum of all ranks whose signs are positive and w_- as the sum of all ranks whose signs are negative.

The null hypothesis $\mu_1 \leq \mu_2$ can be rejected in favor of the alternative $\mu_1 > \mu_2$ only if w_+ is much smaller than w_-. Similarly, the two-sided hypothesis $\mu_1 = \mu_2$ can be rejected in favor of the alternative $\mu_1 \neq \mu_2$ only if either w_+ or w_-, that is, $w = \min(w_+, w_-)$, is very small. The critical values for the Wilcoxon signed rank test are tabulated and for $N > 20$, normal approximations can be used.

19.13.2 Multiple Algorithms

KRUSKAL-WALLIS TEST

The *Kruskal-Wallis test* is the nonparametric version of ANOVA and is a multiple sample generalization of a rank test. Given the $M = L \cdot N$ observations, for example, error rates, of L algorithms on N datasets, $X_{ij}, i = 1, \ldots, L, j = 1, \ldots, N$, we rank them from the smallest to the largest and assign them ranks, R_{ij}, between 1 and M, again taking averages in case of ties. If the null hypothesis

$$H_0 : \mu_1 = \mu_2 = \cdots = \mu_L$$

is true, then the average of ranks of algorithm i should be approximately halfway between 1 and M, that is, $(M + 1)/2$. We denote the sample average rank of algorithm i by $\overline{R}_{i\bullet}$ and we reject the hypothesis if the average ranks seem to differ from halfway. The test statistic

$$H = \frac{12}{(M+1)L} \sum_{i=1}^{L} \left(\overline{R}_{i\bullet} - \frac{M+1}{2} \right)$$

is approximately chi-square distributed with $L - 1$ degrees of freedom and we reject the null hypothesis if the statistic exceeds $\mathcal{X}_{\alpha,L-1}$.

Just like the parametric ANOVA, if the null hypothesis is rejected, we can do post hoc testing to check for pairwise comparison of ranks. One method for this is *Tukey's test*, which makes use of the *studentized range statistic*

TUKEY'S TEST

$$q = \frac{\overline{R}_{max} - \overline{R}_{min}}{\sigma_w}$$

where $\overline{R}_{max}$ and $\overline{R}_{min}$ are the largest and smallest means (of ranks), respectively, out of the L means, and σ_w^2 is the average variance of ranks around group rank averages. We reject the null hypothesis that groups i and j have the same ranks in favor of the alternative hypothesis that they are different if

$$|\overline{R}_{i\bullet} - \overline{R}_{j\bullet}| > q_\alpha(L, L(K-1))\sigma_w$$

where $q_\alpha(L, L(K-1))$ are tabulated. One-sided tests can also be defined to order algorithms in terms of average rank.

Demsar (2006) proposes to use CD (critical difference) diagrams for visualization. On a scale of 1 to L, we mark the averages, $\overline{R}_{i\bullet}$, and draw lines of length given by the critical difference, $q_\alpha(L, L(K-1))\sigma_w$, between groups, so that lines connect groups that are not statistically significantly different.

19.14 Multivariate Tests

All the tests we discussed earlier in this chapter are univariate; that is, they use a single performance measure, for example, error, precision, area under the curve, and so on. However we know that different measures make different behavior explicit; for example, misclassification error is the sum of false positives and false negatives and a test on error cannot make a distinction between these two types of error. Instead, one can use a bivariate test on these two that will be more powerful than a univariate test on error because it can also check for the type of misclassification. Similarly, we can define, for example, a bivariate test on [tp-rate, fp-rate] or [precision, recall] that checks for two measures together (Yıldız, Aslan, and Alpaydın 2011).

Let us say that we use p measures. If we compare in terms of (tp-rate, fp-rate) or (precision, recall), then $p = 2$. Actually, all of the performance measures shown in table 19.2, such as error, tp-rate, precision, and so on, are all calculated from the same four entries in table 19.1, and instead of using any predefined measure we can just go ahead and do a four-variate test on [tp, fp, fn, tn].

19.14.1 Comparing Two Algorithms

We assume that $\boldsymbol{x}_{ij}$ are p-variate normal distributions. We have $i = 1, \ldots, K$ folds and we start with the comparison of two algorithms, so $j = 1, 2$. We want to test whether the two populations have the same mean vector in the p-dimensional space:

$$H_0 : \boldsymbol{\mu}_1 = \boldsymbol{\mu}_2 \text{ vs. } H_1 : \boldsymbol{\mu}_1 \neq \boldsymbol{\mu}_2$$

For paired testing, we calculate the paired differences: $\boldsymbol{d}_i = \boldsymbol{x}_{1i} - \boldsymbol{x}_{2i}$, and we test whether these have zero mean:

$$H_0 : \boldsymbol{\mu}_d = \mathbf{0} \text{ vs. } H_1 : \boldsymbol{\mu}_d \neq \mathbf{0}$$

To test for this, we calculate the sample average and covariance matrix:

(19.26)
$$\boldsymbol{m} = \sum_{i=1}^{K} \boldsymbol{d}_i / K$$
$$\mathbf{S} = \frac{1}{K-1} \sum_i (\boldsymbol{d}_i - \boldsymbol{m})(\boldsymbol{d}_i - \boldsymbol{m})^T$$

HOTELLING'S MULTIVARIATE TEST

Under the null hypothesis, the *Hotelling's multivariate test* statistic

(19.27)
$$T'^2 = K\boldsymbol{m}^T\mathbf{S}^{-1}\boldsymbol{m}$$

is Hotelling's T^2 distributed with p and $K-1$ degrees of freedom (Rencher 1995). We reject the null hypothesis if $T'^2 > T^2_{\alpha,p,K-1}$.

When $p = 1$, this multivariate test reduces to the paired t test we discuss in section 19.11.2. In equation 19.14, $\sqrt{K}m/S$ measures the normalized distance to 0 in one dimension, whereas here, $K\boldsymbol{m}^T\mathbf{S}^{-1}\boldsymbol{m}$ measures the squared Mahalanobis distance to $\mathbf{0}$ in p dimensions. In both cases, we reject if the distance is so large that it can only occur at most $\alpha \cdot 100$ percent of the time.

If the multivariate test rejects the null hypothesis, we can do p separate post hoc univariate tests (using equation 19.14) to check which one(s) of the variates cause(s) rejection. For example, if a multivariate test on [fp, fn] rejects the null hypothesis, we can check whether the difference is due to a significant difference in false positives, false negatives, or both.

It may be the case that none of the univariate differences is significant whereas the multivariate one is; this is one of the advantages of multivariate testing. The linear combination of variates that causes the maximum difference can be calculated as

$$\boldsymbol{w} = \mathbf{S}^{-1}\boldsymbol{m} \tag{19.28}$$

We can then see the effect of the different univariate dimensions by looking at the corresponding elements of $\boldsymbol{w}$. Actually if $p = 4$, we can think of $\boldsymbol{w}$ as defining for us a new performance measure from the original four values in the confusion matrix. The fact that this is the Fisher's LDA direction (section 6.8) is not accidental—we are looking for the direction that maximizes the separation of two groups of data.

19.14.2 Comparing Multiple Algorithms

We can similarly get a multivariate test for comparing $L > 2$ algorithms by the multivariate version of ANOVA, namely, MANOVA. We test for

$$\begin{aligned} H_0 &: \boldsymbol{\mu}_1 = \boldsymbol{\mu}_2 = \cdots = \boldsymbol{\mu}_L \text{ vs.} \\ H_1 &: \boldsymbol{\mu}_r \neq \boldsymbol{\mu}_s \text{ for at least one pair } r, s \end{aligned}$$

Let us say that $\boldsymbol{x}_{ij}, i = 1, \ldots, K, j = 1, \ldots, L$ denotes the p-dimensional performance vector of algorithm j on validation fold i. The multivariate ANOVA (MANOVA) calculates the two matrices of between- and within-scatter:

$$\begin{aligned} \mathbf{H} &= K \sum_{j=1}^{L} (\boldsymbol{m}_j - \boldsymbol{m})(\boldsymbol{m}_j - \boldsymbol{m})^T \\ \mathbf{E} &= \sum_{j=1}^{L} \sum_{i=1}^{K} (\boldsymbol{x}_{ij} - \boldsymbol{m}_j)(\boldsymbol{x}_{ij} - \boldsymbol{m}_j)^T \end{aligned}$$

Then, the test statistic

$$\Lambda' = \frac{|\mathbf{E}|}{|\mathbf{E} + \mathbf{H}|} \tag{19.29}$$

is Wilks's Λ distributed with $p, L(K-1), L-1$ degrees of freedom (Rencher 1995). We reject the null hypothesis if $\Lambda' > \Lambda_{\alpha,p,L(K-1),L-1}$. Note that rejection is for small values of Λ': If the sample mean vectors are equal, we expect $\mathbf{H}$ to be 0 and Λ' to approach 1; as the sample means become more spread out, Λ' becomes "larger" than $\mathbf{E}$ and Λ' approaches 0.

If MANOVA rejects, we can do post hoc testing in a number of ways: We can do a set of pairwise multivariate tests as we discussed previously, to see which pairs are significantly different. Or, we can do p separate univariate ANOVA on each of the individual variates (section 19.12) to see which one(s) cause a reject.

If MANOVA rejects, the difference may be due to some linear combination of the variates: The mean vectors occupy a space whose dimensionality is given by $s = \min(p, L-1)$; its dimensions are the eigenvectors of $\mathbf{E}^{-1}\mathbf{H}$, and by looking at these eigenvectors, we can pinpoint the directions (new performance measures) that cause MANOVA to reject. For example, if $\lambda_i / \sum_{i=1}^{s} \lambda_i > 0.9$, we get roughly one direction, and plotting the projection of data along this direction allows for a univariate ordering of the algorithms.

19.15 Notes

The material related to experiment design follows the discussion from (Montgomery 2005), which here is adapted for machine learning. A more detailed discussion of interval estimation, hypothesis testing, and analysis of variance can be found in any introductory statistics book, for example, Ross 1987.

Dietterich (1998) discusses statistical tests and compares them on a number of applications using different classification algorithms. A review of ROC use and AUC calculation is given in Fawcett 2006. Demsar (2006) reviews statistical tests for comparing classifiers over multiple datasets.

When we compare two or more algorithms, if the null hypothesis that they have the same error rate is not rejected, we choose the simpler one, namely, the one with less space or time complexity. That is, we use our prior preference if the data does not prefer one in terms of error rate. For example, if we compare a linear model and a nonlinear model and if the test does not reject that they have the same expected error rate, we should go for the simpler linear model. Even if the test rejects, in choosing one algorithm over another, error rate is only one of the criteria.

Other criteria like training (space/time) complexity, testing complexity, and interpretability may override in practical applications.

This is how the post hoc test results are used in the MultiTest algorithm (Yıldız and Alpaydın 2006) to generate a full order. We do $L(L-1)/2$ one-sided pairwise tests to order the L algorithms, but it is very likely that the tests will not give a full order but only a partial order. The missing links are filled in using the prior complexity information to get a full order. A topological sort gives an ordering of algorithms using both types of information, error and complexity.

There are also tests to allow checking for *contrasts*. Let us say 1 and 2 are neural network methods and 3 and 4 are fuzzy logic methods. We can then test whether the average of 1 and 2 differs from the average of 3 and 4, thereby allowing us to compare methods in general.

Statistical comparison is needed not only to choose between learning algorithms but also for adjusting the hyperparameters of an algorithm, and the experimental design framework provides us with tools to do this efficiently; for example, response surface design can be used to learn weights in a multiple kernel learning scenario (Gönen and Alpaydın 2011).

Another important point to note is that if are comparing misclassification errors, this implies that from our point of view, all misclassifications have the same cost. When this is not the case, our tests should be based on risks taking a suitable loss function into account. Not much work has been done in this area. Similarly, these tests should be generalized from classification to regression, so as to be able to assess the mean square errors of regression algorithms, or to be able to compare the errors of two regression algorithms.

In comparing two classification algorithms, note that we are testing only whether they have the same expected error rate. If they do, this does not mean that they make the same errors. This is an idea that we used in chapter 17; we can combine multiple models to improve accuracy if different classifiers make different errors.

19.16 Exercises

1. In a two-class problem, let us say we have the loss matrix where $\lambda_{11} = \lambda_{22} = 0$, $\lambda_{21} = 1$ and $\lambda_{12} = \alpha$. Determine the threshold of decision as a function of α.

   SOLUTION: The risk of choosing the first class is $0 \cdot P(C_1|x) + \alpha \cdot P(C_2|x)$ and the risk of choosing the second class is $1 \cdot P(C_1|x) + 0 \cdot P(C_2|x)$ (section 3.3).

We choose C_1 if the former is less than the latter and given that $P(C_2|x) = 1 - P(C_1|x)$, we choose C_1 if

$$P(C_1|x) > \frac{\alpha}{1+\alpha}$$

That is, varying the threshold decision corresponds to varying the relative cost of false positives and false negatives.

2. We can simulate a classifier with error probability p by drawing samples from a Bernoulli distribution. Doing this, implement the binomial, approximate, and t tests for $p_0 \in (0, 1)$. Repeat these tests at least 1,000 times for several values of p and calculate the probability of rejecting the null hypothesis. What do you expect the probability of reject to be when $p_0 = p$?

3. Assume that $x^t \sim \mathcal{N}(\mu, \sigma^2)$ where σ^2 is known. How can we test for $H_0 : \mu \geq \mu_0$ vs. $H_1 : \mu < \mu_0$?

   SOLUTION: Under H_0, we have

$$z = \frac{\sqrt{N}(m - \mu_0)}{\sigma} \sim \mathcal{Z}$$

   We accept H_0 if $z \in (-z_\alpha, \infty)$.

4. The K-fold cross-validated t test only tests for the equality of error rates. If the test rejects, we do not know which classification algorithm has the lower error rate. How can we test whether the first classification algorithm does not have higher error rate than the second one? Hint: We have to test $H_0 : \mu \leq 0$ vs. $H_1 : \mu > 0$.

5. Show that the total sum of squares can be split into between-group sum of squares and within-group sum of squares as $SS_T = SS_b + SS_w$.

6. Use the normal approximation to the binomial for the sign test.

   SOLUTION: Under the null hypothesis that the two are equally good, we have $p = 1/2$ and over N datasets, we expect the number of wins X to be approximately Gaussian with $\mu = pN = N/2$ and $\sigma^2 = p(1-p)N = N/4$. If there are e wins, we reject if $P(X < e) > \alpha$, or if $P(Z < \frac{e-N/2}{\sqrt{N/4}}) > \alpha$.

7. Let us say we have three classification algorithms. How can we order these three from best to worst?

8. If we have two variants of algorithm A and three variants of algorithm B, how can we compare the overall accuracies of A and B taking all their variants into account?

   SOLUTION: We can use *contrasts* (Montgomery 2005). Basically, what we would be doing is comparing the average of the two variants of A with the average of the three variants of B.

9. Propose a suitable test to compare the errors of two regression algorithms.

   SOLUTION: In regression, we minimize the sum of squares that is a measure of variance, which we know is chi-squared distributed. Since we use the *F* test to compare variances (as we did in ANOVA), we can also use it to compare the squared errors of two regression algorithms.

10. Propose a suitable test to compare the expected rewards of two reinforcement learning algorithms.

19.17 References

Alpaydın, E. 1999. "Combined 5 × 2 cv *F* Test for Comparing Supervised Classification Learning Algorithms." *Neural Computation* 11:1885–1892.

Bouckaert, R. R. 2003. "Choosing between Two Learning Algorithms based on Calibrated Tests." In *Twentieth International Conference on Machine Learning*, ed. T. Fawcett and N. Mishra, 51–58. Menlo Park, CA: AAAI Press.

Demsar, J. 2006. "Statistical Comparison of Classifiers over Multiple Data Sets." *Journal of Machine Learning Research* 7:1–30.

Dietterich, T. G. 1998. "Approximate Statistical Tests for Comparing Supervised Classification Learning Algorithms." *Neural Computation* 10:1895–1923.

Fawcett, T. 2006. "An Introduction to ROC Analysis." *Pattern Recognition Letters* 27:861–874.

Gönen, M. and, E. Alpaydın. 2011. "Regularizing Multiple Kernel Learning using Response Surface Methodology." *Pattern Recognition* 44:159–171.

Montgomery, D. C. 2005. *Design and Analysis of Experiments*. 6th ed. New York: Wiley.

Rencher, A. C. 1995. *Methods of Multivariate Analysis*. New York: Wiley.

Ross, S. M. 1987. *Introduction to Probability and Statistics for Engineers and Scientists*. New York: Wiley.

Turney, P. 2000. "Types of Cost in Inductive Concept Learning." Paper presented at Workshop on Cost-Sensitive Learning at the Seventeenth International Conference on Machine Learning, Stanford University, Stanford, CA, July 2.

Wolpert, D. H. 1995. "The Relationship between PAC, the Statistical Physics Framework, the Bayesian Framework, and the VC Framework." In *The Mathematics of Generalization*, ed. D. H. Wolpert, 117–214. Reading, MA: Addison-Wesley.

Yıldız, O. T., and E. Alpaydın. 2006. "Ordering and Finding the Best of $K > 2$ Supervised Learning Algorithms." *IEEE Transactions on Pattern Analysis and Machine Intelligence* 28:392–402.

Yıldız, O. T., Ö. Aslan, and E. Alpaydın. 2011. "Multivariate Statistical Tests for Comparing Classification Algorithms," In *Learning and Intelligent Optimization (LION) Conference*, ed. C. A. Coello Coello, 1–15. Heidelberg: Springer.

A Probability

We review briefly the elements of probability, the concept of a random variable, and example distributions.

A.1 Elements of Probability

A RANDOM experiment is one whose outcome is not predictable with certainty in advance (Ross 1987; Casella and Berger 1990). The set of all possible outcomes is known as the *sample space* S. A sample space is *discrete* if it consists of a finite (or countably infinite) set of outcomes; otherwise it is *continuous*. Any subset E of S is an *event*. Events are sets, and we can talk about their complement, intersection, union, and so forth.

One interpretation of probability is as a *frequency*. When an experiment is continually repeated under the exact same conditions, for any event E, the proportion of time that the outcome is in E approaches some constant value. This constant limiting frequency is the probability of the event, and we denote it as $P(E)$.

Probability sometimes is interpreted as a *degree of belief*. For example, when we speak of Turkey's probability of winning the World Soccer Cup in 2018, we do not mean a frequency of occurrence, since the championship will happen only once and it has not yet occurred (at the time of the writing of this book). What we mean in such a case is a subjective degree of belief in the occurrence of the event. Because it is subjective, different individuals may assign different probabilities to the same event.

A.1.1 Axioms of Probability

Axioms ensure that the probabilities assigned in a random experiment can be interpreted as relative frequencies and that the assignments are consistent with our intuitive understanding of relationships among relative frequencies:

1. $0 \le P(E) \le 1$. If E_1 is an event that cannot possibly occur, then $P(E_1) = 0$. If E_2 is sure to occur, $P(E_2) = 1$.
2. S is the sample space containing all possible outcomes, $P(S) = 1$.
3. If $E_i, i = 1, \ldots, n$ are mutually exclusive (i.e., if they cannot occur at the same time, as in $E_i \cap E_j = \varnothing, j \neq i$, where $\varnothing$ is the *null event* that does not contain any possible outcomes), we have

$$P\left(\bigcup_{i=1}^{n} E_i\right) = \sum_{i=1}^{n} P(E_i) \tag{A.1}$$

For example, letting E^c denote the *complement* of E, consisting of all possible outcomes in S that are not in E, we have $E \cap E^C = \varnothing$ and

$$P(E \cup E^c) = P(E) + P(E^c) = 1$$

$$P(E^c) = 1 - P(E)$$

If the intersection of E and F is not empty, we have

$$P(E \cup F) = P(E) + P(F) - P(E \cap F) \tag{A.2}$$

A.1.2 Conditional Probability

$P(E|F)$ is the probability of the occurrence of event E given that F occurred and is given as

$$P(E|F) = \frac{P(E \cap F)}{P(F)} \tag{A.3}$$

Knowing that F occurred reduces the sample space to F, and the part of it where E also occurred is $E \cap F$. Note that equation A.3 is well-defined only if $P(F) > 0$. Because $\cap$ is commutative, we have

$$P(E \cap F) = P(E|F)P(F) = P(F|E)P(E)$$

which gives us *Bayes' formula*:

$$P(F|E) = \frac{P(E|F)P(F)}{P(E)} \tag{A.4}$$

When F_i are mutually exclusive and exhaustive, namely, $\bigcup_{i=1}^{n} F_i = S$

$$E = \bigcup_{i=1}^{n} E \cap F_i$$

$$P(E) = \sum_{i=1}^{n} P(E \cap F_i) = \sum_{i=1}^{n} P(E|F_i)P(F_i) \tag{A.5}$$

Bayes' formula allows us to write

$$P(F_i|E) = \frac{P(E \cap F_i)}{P(E)} = \frac{P(E|F_i)P(F_i)}{\sum_j P(E|F_j)P(F_j)} \tag{A.6}$$

If E and F are *independent*, we have $P(E|F) = P(E)$ and thus

$$P(E \cap F) = P(E)P(F) \tag{A.7}$$

That is, knowledge of whether F has occurred does not change the probability that E occurs.

A.2 Random Variables

A *random variable* is a function that assigns a number to each outcome in the sample space of a random experiment.

A.2.1 Probability Distribution and Density Functions

The *probability distribution function* $F(\cdot)$ of a random variable X for any real number a is

$$F(a) = P\{X \le a\} \tag{A.8}$$

and we have

$$P\{a < X \le b\} = F(b) - F(a) \tag{A.9}$$

If X is a discrete random variable

$$F(a) = \sum_{\forall x \le a} P(x) \tag{A.10}$$

where $P(\cdot)$ is the *probability mass function* defined as $P(a) = P\{X = a\}$. If X is a *continuous* random variable, $p(\cdot)$ is the *probability density function* such that

(A.11) $$F(a) = \int_{-\infty}^{a} p(x)dx$$

A.2.2 Joint Distribution and Density Functions

In certain experiments, we may be interested in the relationship between two or more random variables, and we use the *joint* probability distribution and density functions of X and Y satisfying

(A.12) $$F(x, y) = P\{X \le x, Y \le y\}$$

Individual *marginal* distributions and densities can be computed by marginalizing, namely, summing over the free variable:

(A.13) $$F_X(x) = P\{X \le x\} = P\{X \le x, Y \le \infty\} = F(x, \infty)$$

In the discrete case, we write

(A.14) $$P(X = x) = \sum_j P(x, y_j)$$

and in the continuous case, we have

(A.15) $$p_X(x) = \int_{-\infty}^{\infty} p(x, y)dy$$

If X and Y are *independent*, we have

(A.16) $$p(x, y) = p_X(x)p_Y(y)$$

These can be generalized in a straightforward manner to more than two random variables.

A.2.3 Conditional Distributions

When X and Y are random variables

(A.17) $$P_{X|Y}(x|y) = P\{X = x|Y = y\} = \frac{P\{X = x, Y = y\}}{P\{Y = y\}} = \frac{P(x, y)}{P_Y(y)}$$

A.2.4 Bayes' Rule

When two random variables are jointly distributed with the value of one known, the probability that the other takes a given value can be computed using *Bayes' rule*:

$$P(y|x) = \frac{P(x|y)P_Y(y)}{P_X(x)} = \frac{P(x|y)P_Y(y)}{\sum_y P(x|y)P_Y(y)} \tag{A.18}$$

Or, in words

$$\text{posterior} = \frac{\text{likelihood} \times \text{prior}}{\text{evidence}} \tag{A.19}$$

Note that the denominator is obtained by summing (or integrating if y is continuous) the numerator over all possible y values. The "shape" of $p(y|x)$ depends on the numerator with denominator as a normalizing factor to guarantee that $p(y|x)$ sum to 1. Bayes' rule allows us to modify a prior probability into a posterior probability by taking information provided by x into account.

Bayes' rule inverts dependencies, allowing us to compute $p(y|x)$ if $p(x|y)$ is known. Suppose that y is the "cause" of x, like y going on summer vacation and x having a suntan. Then $p(x|y)$ is the probability that someone who is known to have gone on summer vacation has a suntan. This is the *causal* (or predictive) way. Bayes' rule allows us a *diagnostic* approach by allowing us to compute $p(y|x)$: namely, the probability that someone who is known to have a suntan, has gone on summer vacation. Then $p(y)$ is the general probability of anyone's going on summer vacation and $p(x)$ is the probability that anyone has a suntan, including both those who have gone on summer vacation and those who have not.

A.2.5 Expectation

Expectation, *expected value*, or *mean* of a random variable X, denoted by $E[X]$, is the average value of X in a large number of experiments:

$$E[X] = \begin{cases} \sum_i x_i P(x_i) & \text{if } X \text{ is discrete} \\ \int x p(x) dx & \text{if } X \text{ is continuous} \end{cases} \tag{A.20}$$

It is a weighted average where each value is weighted by the probability that X takes that value. It has the following properties ($a, b \in \Re$):

$$\begin{aligned} E[aX + b] &= aE[X] + b \\ E[X + Y] &= E[X] + E[Y] \end{aligned} \tag{A.21}$$

For any real-valued function $g(\cdot)$, the expected value is

$$E[g(X)] = \begin{cases} \sum_i g(x_i)P(x_i) & \text{if } X \text{ is discrete} \\ \int g(x)p(x)dx & \text{if } X \text{ is continuous} \end{cases} \tag{A.22}$$

A special $g(x) = x^n$, called the nth moment of X, is defined as

$$E[X^n] = \begin{cases} \sum_i x_i^n P(x_i) & \text{if } X \text{ is discrete} \\ \int x^n p(x)dx & \text{if } X \text{ is continuous} \end{cases} \tag{A.23}$$

Mean is the first moment and is denoted by μ.

A.2.6 Variance

Variance measures how much X varies around the expected value. If $\mu \equiv E[X]$, the variance is defined as

$$\mathrm{Var}(X) = E[(X-\mu)^2] = E[X^2] - \mu^2 \tag{A.24}$$

Variance is the second moment minus the square of the first moment. Variance, denoted by σ^2, satisfies the following property ($a, b \in \Re$):

$$\mathrm{Var}(aX+b) = a^2\mathrm{Var}(X) \tag{A.25}$$

$\sqrt{\mathrm{Var}(X)}$ is called the *standard deviation* and is denoted by σ. Standard deviation has the same unit as X and is easier to interpret than variance.

Covariance indicates the relationship between two random variables. If the occurrence of X makes Y more likely to occur, then the covariance is positive; it is negative if X's occurrence makes Y less likely to happen and is 0 if there is no dependence.

$$\mathrm{Cov}(X,Y) = E[(X-\mu_X)(Y-\mu_Y)] = E[XY] - \mu_X\mu_Y \tag{A.26}$$

where $\mu_X \equiv E[X]$ and $\mu_Y \equiv E[Y]$. Some other properties are

$$\begin{aligned} \mathrm{Cov}(X,Y) &= \mathrm{Cov}(Y,X) \\ \mathrm{Cov}(X,X) &= \mathrm{Var}(X) \\ \mathrm{Cov}(X+Z,Y) &= \mathrm{Cov}(X,Y) + \mathrm{Cov}(Z,Y) \end{aligned}$$

$$\mathrm{Cov}\left(\sum_i X_i, Y\right) = \sum_i \mathrm{Cov}(X_i, Y) \tag{A.27}$$

$$\mathrm{Var}(X+Y) = \mathrm{Var}(X) + \mathrm{Var}(Y) + 2\mathrm{Cov}(X,Y) \tag{A.28}$$

$$\mathrm{Var}\left(\sum_i X_i\right) = \sum_i \mathrm{Var}(X_i) + \sum_i \sum_{j \neq i} \mathrm{Cov}(X_i, X_j) \tag{A.29}$$

If X and Y are independent, $E[XY] = E[X]E[Y] = \mu_X\mu_Y$ and $\mathrm{Cov}(X, Y) = 0$. Thus if X_i are independent

(A.30) $$\mathrm{Var}\left(\sum_i X_i\right) = \sum_i \mathrm{Var}(X_i)$$

Correlation is a normalized, dimensionless quantity that is always between -1 and 1:

(A.31) $$\mathrm{Corr}(X, Y) = \frac{\mathrm{Cov}(X, Y)}{\sqrt{\mathrm{Var}(X)\mathrm{Var}(Y)}}$$

A.2.7 Weak Law of Large Numbers

Let $\mathcal{X} = \{X^t\}_{t=1}^N$ be a set of independent and identically distributed (iid) random variables each having mean μ and a finite variance σ^2. Then for any $\epsilon > 0$,

(A.32) $$P\left\{\left|\frac{\sum_t X^t}{N} - \mu\right| > \epsilon\right\} \to 0 \text{ as } N \to \infty$$

That is, the average of N trials converges to the mean as N increases.

A.3 Special Random Variables

There are certain types of random variables that occur so frequently that names are given to them.

A.3.1 Bernoulli Distribution

A trial is performed whose outcome is either a "success" or a "failure." The random variable X is a 0/1 indicator variable and takes the value 1 for a success outcome and is 0 otherwise. p is the probability that the result of trial is a success. Then

(A.33) $$P\{X = 1\} = p \text{ and } P\{X = 0\} = 1 - p$$

which can equivalently be written as

(A.34) $$P\{X = i\} = p^i(1-p)^{1-i}, i = 0, 1$$

If X is Bernoulli, its expected value and variance are

(A.35) $$E[X] = p, \ \mathrm{Var}(X) = p(1-p)$$

A.3.2 Binomial Distribution

If N identical independent Bernoulli trials are made, the random variable X that represents the number of successes that occurs in N trials is binomial distributed. The probability that there are i successes is

$$P\{X = i\} = \binom{N}{i} p^i (1-p)^{N-i}, i = 0 \ldots N \tag{A.36}$$

If X is binomial, its expected value and variance are

$$E[X] = Np, \ \mathrm{Var}(X) = Np(1-p) \tag{A.37}$$

A.3.3 Multinomial Distribution

Consider a generalization of Bernoulli where instead of two states, the outcome of a random event is one of K mutually exclusive and exhaustive states, each of which has a probability of occurring p_i where $\sum_{i=1}^{K} p_i = 1$. Suppose that N such trials are made where outcome i occurred N_i times with $\sum_{i=1}^{k} N_i = N$. Then the joint distribution of $N_1, N_2, \ldots, N_K$ is multinomial:

$$P(N_1, N_2, \ldots, N_K) = N! \prod_{i=1}^{K} \frac{p_i^{N_i}}{N_i!} \tag{A.38}$$

A special case is when $N = 1$; only one trial is made. Then N_i are 0/1 indicator variables of which only one of them is 1 and all others are 0. Then equation A.38 reduces to

$$P(N_1, N_2, \ldots, N_K) = \prod_{i=1}^{K} p_i^{N_i} \tag{A.39}$$

A.3.4 Uniform Distribution

X is uniformly distributed over the interval $[a, b]$ if its density function is given by

$$p(x) = \begin{cases} \frac{1}{b-a} & \text{if } a \le x \le b \\ 0 & \text{otherwise} \end{cases} \tag{A.40}$$

If X is uniform, its expected value and variance are

$$E[X] = \frac{a+b}{2}, \ \mathrm{Var}(X) = \frac{(b-a)^2}{12} \tag{A.41}$$

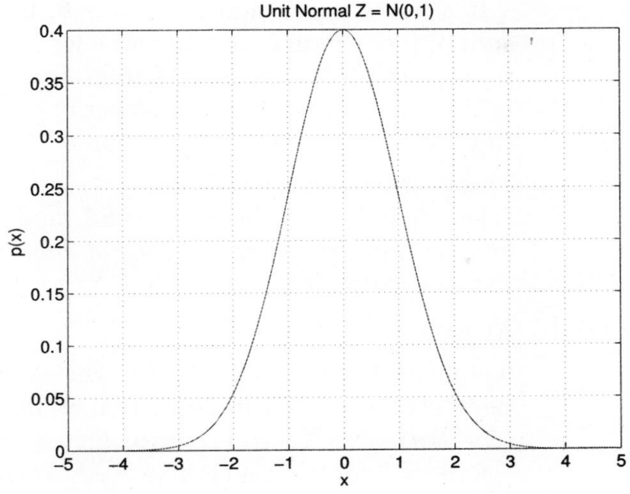

Figure A.1 Probability density function of $\mathcal{Z}$, the unit normal distribution.

A.3.5 Normal (Gaussian) Distribution

X is normal or Gaussian distributed with mean μ and variance σ^2, denoted as $\mathcal{N}(\mu, \sigma^2)$, if its density function is

$$p(x) = \frac{1}{\sqrt{2\pi}\sigma} \exp\left[-\frac{(x-\mu)^2}{2\sigma^2}\right], -\infty < x < \infty \tag{A.42}$$

Many random phenomena obey the bell-shaped normal distribution, at least approximately, and many observations from nature can be seen as a continuous, slightly different versions of a typical value—that is probably why it is called the *normal* distribution. In such a case, μ represents the typical value and σ defines how much instances vary around the prototypical value.

68.27 percent lie in $(\mu - \sigma, \mu + \sigma)$, 95.45 percent in $(\mu - 2\sigma, \mu + 2\sigma)$, and 99.73 percent in $(\mu - 3\sigma, \mu + 3\sigma)$. Thus $P\{|x - \mu| < 3\sigma\} \approx 0.99$. For practical purposes, $p(x) \approx 0$ if $x < \mu - 3\sigma$ or $x > \mu + 3\sigma$. $\mathcal{Z}$ is unit normal, namely, $\mathcal{N}(0, 1)$ (see figure A.1), and its density is written as

$$p_{\mathcal{Z}}(x) = \frac{1}{\sqrt{2\pi}} \exp\left[-\frac{x^2}{2}\right] \tag{A.43}$$

If $X \sim \mathcal{N}(\mu, \sigma^2)$ and $Y = aX + b$, then $Y \sim \mathcal{N}(a\mu + b, a^2\sigma^2)$. The sum of independent normal variables is also normal with $\mu = \sum_i \mu_i$ and $\sigma^2 = \sum_i \sigma_i^2$. If X is $\mathcal{N}(\mu, \sigma^2)$, then

(A.44) $$\frac{X - \mu}{\sigma} \sim Z$$

This is called z-normalization.

CENTRAL LIMIT THEOREM

Let $X_1, X_2, \ldots, X_N$ be a set of iid random variables all having mean μ and variance σ^2. Then the *central limit theorem* states that for large N, the distribution of

(A.45) $$X_1 + X_2 + \ldots + X_N$$

is approximately $\mathcal{N}(N\mu, N\sigma^2)$. For example, if X is binomial with parameters (N, p), X can be written as the sum of N Bernoulli trials and $(X - Np)/\sqrt{Np(1-p)}$ is approximately unit normal.

Central limit theorem is also used to generate normally distributed random variables on computers. Programming languages have subroutines that return uniformly distributed (pseudo-)random numbers in the range $[0, 1]$. When U_i are such random variables, $\sum_{i=1}^{12} U_i - 6$ is approximately Z.

Let us say $X^t \sim \mathcal{N}(\mu, \sigma^2)$. The estimated sample mean

(A.46) $$m = \frac{\sum_{t=1}^{N} X^t}{N}$$

is also normal with mean μ and variance σ^2/N.

A.3.6 Chi-Square Distribution

If Z_i are independent unit normal random variables, then

(A.47) $$X = Z_1^2 + Z_2^2 + \ldots + Z_n^2$$

is chi-square with n degrees of freedom, namely, $X \sim \mathcal{X}_n^2$, with

(A.48) $$E[X] = n, \ \mathrm{Var}(X) = 2n$$

When $X^t \sim \mathcal{N}(\mu, \sigma^2)$, the estimated sample variance is

(A.49) $$S^2 = \frac{\sum_t (X^t - m)^2}{N - 1}$$

and we have

(A.50) $$(N-1)\frac{S^2}{\sigma^2} \sim \mathcal{X}_{N-1}^2$$

It is also known that m and S^2 are independent.

A.3.7 *t* Distribution

If $Z \sim \mathcal{Z}$ and $X \sim \mathcal{X}_n^2$ are independent, then

$$T_n = \frac{Z}{\sqrt{X/n}} \tag{A.51}$$

is *t*-distributed with *n* degrees of freedom with

$$E[T_n] = 0, n > 1, \text{Var}(T_n) = \frac{n}{n-2}, n > 2 \tag{A.52}$$

Like the unit normal density, *t* is symmetric around 0. As *n* becomes larger, *t* density becomes more and more like the unit normal, the difference being that *t* has thicker tails, indicating greater variability than does normal.

A.3.8 *F* Distribution

If $X_1 \sim \mathcal{X}_n^2$ and $X_2 \sim \mathcal{X}_m^2$ are independent chi-square random variables with *n* and *m* degrees of freedom, respectively,

$$F_{n,m} = \frac{X_1/n}{X_2/m} \tag{A.53}$$

is *F*-distributed with *n* and *m* degrees of freedom with

$$E[F_{n,m}] = \frac{m}{m-2}, m > 2, \text{Var}(F_{n,m}) = \frac{m^2(2m+2n-4)}{n(m-2)^2(m-4)}, m > 4 \tag{A.54}$$

A.4 References

Casella, G., and R. L. Berger. 1990. *Statistical Inference.* Belmont, CA: Duxbury.

Ross, S. M. 1987. *Introduction to Probability and Statistics for Engineers and Scientists.* New York: Wiley.

Index

Adaptive Computation and Machine Learning

Thomas Dietterich, Editor

Christopher Bishop, David Heckerman, Michael Jordan, and Michael Kearns, Associate Editors

Bioinformatics: The Machine Learning Approach, Pierre Baldi and Søren Brunak

Reinforcement Learning: An Introduction, Richard S. Sutton and Andrew G. Barto

Graphical Models for Machine Learning and Digital Communication, Brendan J. Frey

Learning in Graphical Models, Michael I. Jordan

Causation, Prediction, and Search, second edition, Peter Spirtes, Clark Glymour, and Richard Scheines

Principles of Data Mining, David Hand, Heikki Mannila, and Padhraic Smyth

Bioinformatics: The Machine Learning Approach, second edition, Pierre Baldi and Søren Brunak

Learning Kernel Classifiers: Theory and Algorithms, Ralf Herbrich

Learning with Kernels: Support Vector Machines, Regularization, Optimization, and Beyond, Bernhard Schölkopf and Alexander J. Smola

Introduction to Machine Learning, Ethem Alpaydın

Gaussian Processes for Machine Learning, Carl Edward Rasmussen and Christopher K. I. Williams

Semi-Supervised Learning, Olivier Chapelle, Bernhard Schölkopf, and Alexander Zien, eds.

The Minimum Description Length Principle, Peter D. Grünwald

Introduction to Statistical Relational Learning, Lise Getoor and Ben Taskar, eds.

Probabilistic Graphical Models: Principles and Techniques, Daphne Koller and Nir Friedman

Introduction to Machine Learning, second edition, Ethem Alpaydın

Machine Learning in Non-Stationary Environments: Introduction to Covariate Shift Adaptation, Masashi Sugiyama and Motoaki Kawanabe

Boosting: Foundations and Algorithms, Robert E. Schapire and Yoav Freund

Machine Learning: A Probabilistic Perspective, Kevin P. Murphy

Foundations of Machine Learning, Mehryar Mohri, Afshin Rostami, and Ameet Talwalker

Introduction to Machine Learning, third edition, Ethem Alpaydın